D1691949

The cover design is inspired by two projects that won awards in this year's competition: the "Human Rights Tattoo" project, whose website – designed by the Dutch agency Freshheads – was this year awarded a Red Dot: Grand Prix, and the Söhne Collection font family for which Klim Type Foundry in New Zealand received a Red Dot: Best of the Best from the jury. The resulting design is a fusion of both award-winning projects. While the shape of the letters is based on the Söhne Mono typeface, the colours of the letters reflect the different skin colours of the people who, as part of the "Human Rights Tattoo" project, had themselves tattooed with one of the 6,773 letters contained in the Universal Declaration of Human Rights. The text reproduced on the cover is part of this declaration, published by the United Nations General Assembly in 1948. You can read more about both projects on pages 94–95 and 174–175 in Volume 2 of this yearbook.

INTERNATIONAL YEARBOOK BRANDS & COMMUNICATION DESIGN 2020/2021
[Edited by PETER ZEC]

reddot award
brands & communication design

VOL 1

Contents

- 4 **Preface**
- 6 **Red Dot: Agency of the Year**
  Interbrand
- 18 **Brands**
- 90 **Brand Design & Identity**
- 202 **Corporate Design & Identity**
- 260 **Annual Reports**
- 288 **Advertising**
- 318 **Packaging Design**
- 494 **Fair Stands**
- 516 **Retail Design**
- 544 **Red Dot: Junior Award Vol. 1**
- 614 **Designer Profiles Vol. 1**
- 674 **Index Vol. 1**

Find more in Volume 2
Publishing & Print Media – Posters – Typography – Illustrations
Sound Design – Film & Animation – Online – Apps
Interface & User Experience Design – Spatial Communication
Red Dot: Junior Award Vol. 2 – Designer Profiles Vol. 2
Jury Portraits

Preface	Red Dot: Agency of the Year	Brands	Brand Design & Identity	Corporate Design & Identity	Annual Reports
4	6	18	90	202	260

Advertising	Packaging Design	Fair Stands	Retail Design	Red Dot: Junior Award	Designer Profiles	Index
288	318	494	516	544	614	674

Dear Readers,

At the end of March, the United Nations (UN) launched an open call for help from the international design community. It was triggered by COVID-19, whose spread had by then reached its first global peak. The organisation's action highlighted the fact that the pandemic and its serious consequences for the international community also became a communication issue. The UN asked designers to come up with solutions that would make the messages about containment of the pandemic easy to understand for everyone – irrespective of language, origin, age or education. António Guterres emphasised the significance of this appeal, saying "the creativity of the responses must match the unique nature of this crisis – the magnitude of the responses must match its scale." The reaction was immense. Countless international designers volunteered exceptional ideas.

This successful initiative is proof of the design sector's tremendous commitment and illustrates the relevance of communication design, particularly in times of crisis. In this instance, the design industry was able to make an important contribution to ensuring greater clarity and transparency. Self-reflection and a constant change of perspective allow communication designers to keep reinventing their role and function in society. This ability is not only helpful in emergency situations, but also across the entire spectrum of designs and projects in a dynamic environment. Communication designers will therefore continue to excel in their traditional field of activity after the acute phase of the pandemic, while also making an important contribution to society in new areas and accompanying transformation processes.

What, however, are the likely repercussions of the current situation on brands? I am convinced that brands are key to the successful development of customer loyalty, particularly in unfamiliar situations. A strong brand, whose communication not only gives careful consideration to compelling features but also factors in new needs as well as the relevance of specific changes, is more important than ever before. That is why designers and agencies continue to explore new approaches and creative solutions. Companies are also required to do their part in actively monitoring changes in (consumer) culture and in questioning how their brand should position itself in the new context. A meaningful, emotional relationship between consumers and brands will continue to become more relevant. The benefit of relationships that transcend purely material aspects is that they are enduring.

New, emotional approaches were also sought-after at the Red Dot Award: Brands & Communication Design 2020. For the first time since the start of the competition, all submissions were evaluated solely online. The 24 international members of the jury professionally and meticulously assessed every brand and project individually over the course of several days. The large number of high-quality projects we received are proof of the strong reputation of our evaluation process – regardless of how it is carried out.

The International Yearbook Brands & Communication Design 2020/2021 documents the best brands and creative work of the year that are just waiting to be discovered by you. As the world has changed dramatically since the competition opened to submissions at the end of February 2020, this yearbook is also an extraordinary historic document. It continues to be a showpiece for a sector that knows how to meet every challenge methodically and strategically. I hope you will find it inspiring to read, and I would like to offer all award-winners my heartfelt congratulations on their success.

Yours sincerely,

Professor Dr. Peter Zec
Founder and CEO of Red Dot

Red Dot: Agency of the Year

Preface	Red Dot: Agency of the Year	Brands	Brand Design & Identity	Corporate Design & Identity	Annual Reports
4	6	18	90	202	260

Interbrand

- San Francisco
- New York
- Mexico City
- São Paulo
- Buenos Aires
- London
- Cologne
- Zürich
- Milan
- Madrid
- Mumbai
- Seoul
- Shanghai
- Tokyo
- Sydney

Red Dot: Agency of the Year 2020

The Red Dot: Agency of the Year 2020 title goes to Interbrand, a global brand consultancy. Originally founded under the name "Novamark" in London by John Murphy in 1974, Interbrand has been owned by Omnicom since 1993 and has 15 offices in 14 countries. The consultancy delivers international projects for leading global brands from New York, Brazil, South Korea, Japan, Great Britain and Germany. The focus is always on an evolving understanding of brand management – for customers including BMW, Deutsche Telekom, Juventus and Samsung Bioepis.

Interbrand takes an interdisciplinary approach that analyses business challenges from the perspective of the respective brand. This is a strategy whose success is reflected in the Red Dot Design Award. Interbrand has now managed to rack up 45 awards, including 42 Red Dot and three Red Dot: Best of the Best awards.

Interbrand also stands out thanks to its special corporate culture. Based on its values of "Lead with love", "Speak up", "Make it happen" and "Be brave", Interbrand has built a global community whose members are in constant dialogue with one another. There is a lively exchange of knowledge and projects on the platform the company set up specifically for this purpose. This has allowed Interbrand successfully to respond to regional as well as global questions and challenges over many decades. This achievement is being honoured this year with the special award "Red Dot: Agency of the Year".

Interbrand

Founded
1974

Founder
John Murphy

Headquarters
New York, USA

Number of locations
15 offices in 14 countries

Key people
Charles Trevail, Global Chief Executive Officer
Andy Payne, Global Chief Creative Officer
Gonzalo Brujó, Global Chief Growth Officer

Service
Brand consulting, Branding

Partner
Omnicom

Participant in the Red Dot Award: Brands & Communication Design
since 2002

Awards
42 Red Dots
3 Red Dot: Best of the Best

Website
www.interbrand.com

"If you are not pushing the boundaries in your category into a wider arena, then someone else will be."
Andy Payne

Andy Payne, Global Chief Creative Officer

Andy, you are Global Chief Creative Officer. Could you explain in one sentence what your primary role is as a global creative manager at Interbrand?

In essence, my role is to make sure that our methodology and knowledge is coherently applied and shared across all our practice leaders in all geographies, so that our expertise is current, and ready to solve our clients' needs both locally and globally. We want to guarantee a consistent level of excellence around the globe, and ensure we are at the forefront of the brand building category. That is critical because our clients need to have the confidence and assurance that we can maintain that level of knowledge and quality when they are working across global markets.

Could you explain how this knowledge and quality is related to creativity?

The knowledge is our creativity. It resides in the work we do across the network. Our knowledge allows us to solve different business issues through creativity, insights, ideation, design interaction, and it enables us to build new and evolved expressions and experiences. This creative agility and the ability to stay relevant during dynamic changes in markets (whilst meeting both customer and audience needs) is vital.

And how do you manage your creative teams? Do you use specific tools?

In recent times, we have been working a lot more on collaborative creative platforms which means we can sketch live across our teams and with our client partners. A key to global collaboration is that we all know each other, so we have a common bond built through past global and regional creative meetings. We feel like a team. People can reach out to each other for live support and advice without overprocessing everything. And the way in which we work depends on the nature of the remit. A creative team in Tokyo will have a brief specific to that market. That local team will then take the lead and call for global knowledge as needed. On the other hand, if it's a global project, we will have a number of teams working together to create the brand's ambition and platform ideas. This is what we call "Trajectories" – the driving force for the brand to realise its ambition. We focus on building new and evolved tangible interactions (what we call "Moves") where the brand connects to its audiences to deliver on the "Trajectories". Here, the orchestration of the team and the directions we are taking must ensure we are leveraging all of our expertise and knowledge to develop a range of approaches. From the clients' point of view, they will be able to see a global response to their problem or challenge.

Advertising	Packaging Design	Fair Stands	Retail Design	Red Dot: Junior Award	Designer Profiles	Index
288	318	494	516	544	614	674

Interbrand agency impressions

What do clients look for at Interbrand? Is it creativity, is it brand consulting or do they want to reach a new cultural level within their company?

They come to us to find a high level of professionalism in articulating the use of the brand in solving business challenges and realising business strategy. While the customisation depends on the client's specific business challenge, accessing the strategy and moves of the 100 Best Global Brands every year and finding out what makes them strong can produce great and tangible use cases that demonstrate the power of brand building as a business tool.

Is design a business transformation tool or a brand transformation tool?

For us, design is the most powerful tool to realise strategy. We see it both as a business tool and a brand building tool. Design is the realisation and clear expression of the core strategic platform idea. It's the "Trajectory", realised through activation, and the "Moves" – the physical and/or virtual connections between a brand and its audience.

It seems to me that many people, even business people, take design for granted nowadays. Is design underestimated as a tool for brand experience and brand value?

I think, overall, it is still undervalued. Not all organisations have a unified design philosophy. Some are making physical products which they can use as a foundation on which they build a wider design process and philosophy as part of the overall business strategy. But many others have less tangible manifestations and have yet to realise the power of design as a business tool. I believe awareness of design is growing. People are recognising the value of design itself. It allows freedom in terms of innovation and processes. The pandemic has put a focus on audiences, on their needs and what they see as essential. I think many organisations have become very close to their customers during this pandemic. That can only help us with design, because this relationship is really at the heart of solving the problems and needs we have in the world. The world is not fixed yet. There are things that we all still find frustrating. In my opinion, it is design's job to move our situation forward, to take us all forward so that we can improve things.

In the last decade, social media has become the tool par excellence for creating customer proximity. Could you describe the different stages when the relationship between brands and consumers changed significantly?

We are moving from the Age of Experience into the Age of the Customer – with experiences orchestrated around individuals. The two ages before the current ones were the Age of Identity, when brands focused on differentiation, followed by the Age of Value, during which brands took a seat at the boardroom table. Leaders understood that brands are valuable assets and became interested in finding ways to leverage those assets. The next step in the evolution of brands was to move beyond communication – "Saying" – into doing –

Preface	Red Dot: Agency of the Year	Brands	Brand Design & Identity	Corporate Design & Identity	Annual Reports
4	6	18	90	202	260

Yellow Balloon [Brand Design, Logo Design], Red Dot 2019

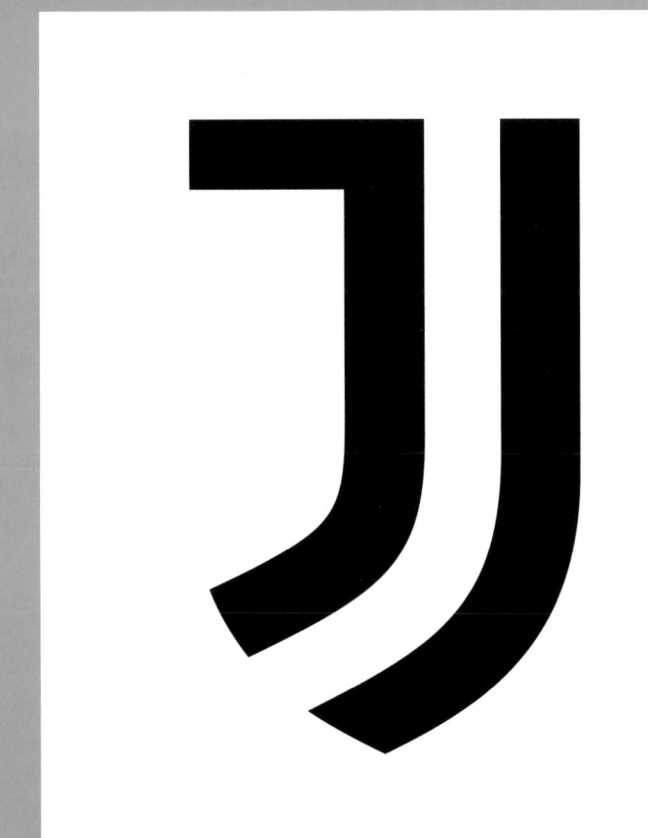

Advertising 288	Packaging Design 318	Fair Stands 494	Retail Design 516	Red Dot: Junior Award 544	Designer Profiles 614	Index 674

Life is a Matter of Black and White [Brand Design & Identity], Red Dot 2017 / **Juventus Fans – Black-and-White DNA** [Typography], Red Dot 2017

"Experiences". By that, I don't only mean experiences from a brand perspective, but from a shared perspective.

Now, in the Age of the Customer, we understand how to create interactions that meet the needs and aspirations of the individual – what we call the "Utility and Desire" of any "Move". This is the real content. The experiences and interactions that people feel are essential and meaningful in the context of what they are doing every day and aspiring to in the future.

All the eras I have mentioned coexist together. Ultimately though, the focal point is on the Age of the Customer. We are changing from a brand-centred world to a customer-centred world. We are going from brands that just say things to brands that "do" things. We need to see real tangible behaviour from brands that are authentic and true, on behalf of and in partnership with their customers. With what we are experiencing now, we are all looking for the essential and for greater meaning. When you have both, brands can be unstoppable.

Could you describe how social media in the Age of the Customer is changing brand management? Can you give an example?

Organisations like Netflix or Amazon are all customer-centric because they start from a need. They put the customer right at the centre and focus on understanding them. The challenge for a lot of legacy businesses that are built on legacy manufacturing platforms lies in changing quickly to become customer-centric. If you look at Tesla compared to the sector legacy giants, it is positioning itself as a force that is taking its customers to the low-carbon future. But the company is also extremely agile. Tesla doesn't have the legacy issues of the sector. It is aligning itself with the world we believe we need to create and is leaving behind the legacy of the past. That becomes very attractive to audiences because you are aligning with their desired future.

Isn't that not only important for companies like Netflix or Amazon but also for insurance companies and banks?

I think the challenge for many sectors is that customers don't see them as sectors, but more as interconnected arenas. So, the more these industry sectors such as banking and insurance begin to contextualise and humanise the service they are delivering, the greater the resilience and growth they will have. PayPal and Apple Pay (among others) all make things very simple and easy for us. The more customer-centric a company is, the more flexible the platform is being made and the more agile it is as a banking or payment system. The easier the system, the more it will drive customers and audiences to be part of it.

MINI interior concept

The fear of irrelevance is forcing legacy businesses and sectors towards putting customers first and that, in turn, pushes transformation forward.

The older legacy businesses in the sectors have the trust of customers, but they are wrestling with transformation and achieving that responsive agility that some of the newer platforms can offer. We have developed a living and evolving manifesto called "Brand Leadership for an Anxious World", where we have highlighted several insights, observations and actions for businesses and organisations during these times. If you are not pushing the boundaries in your category into a wider arena, then someone else will be.

And how does Interbrand create a creative and agile corporate culture to remain a leading agency?

The collaboration of the creative community across Interbrand is essential. We have the Interbrand Academy, which is our internal and external learning faculty, where we build and share work, and stories about that work. One week, Tokyo takes the platform stage about a particular use case. The next week, it will be New York's turn. This weekly sharing of practice and knowledge builds a creative dialogue and creative culture which is essential for us to keep as a regular behaviour. That culture is underpinned by our values, which we call "Behaviours". Of these we have four: "Lead with love", which is about respecting the individual; "Speak up", to ensure everyone has a voice; the idea of "Make it happen", which means we drive change and success; and to "Be brave" by taking on the challenges of the market and trying to push ourselves to do more transformational work.

Could you explain your approach, your way of thinking and its importance for the companies?

Our belief is that the fundamentals of brand building have not only changed but accelerated drastically in the last few years. Now, an always-on, dynamic and customer-centric approach is essential. Customers' expectations move faster than businesses, meaning that brands need to make bold moves in order to build trust, focus on what's essential and provide meaning for their customers. This is what shapes "Interbrand Thinking" – which has three components.

The first component is about gaining "Human Truths"– insights to understand the nature of audiences, the nature of customers and what their needs and desires are, what utility they want from things and what aspirations they have for themselves and the wider world. From here, we move into "Economics", which consists of understanding the potential of an opportunity that we see is not being met (which can be measured through financial metrics). The last is "Experiences" – which is how we can capitalise on the opportunity

MINI store concept

We Never Drop the Ball [Logo Design, Brand Identity], Red Dot: Best of the Best 2018

and its economic scope. Those three hemispheres, what we call our "Three Lenses", are then used as roadmaps for growth, including purpose, ambitions and "Trajectories" which is the prelude to making "Iconic Moves". These moves are the big changes that brands and businesses make to lead the markets or to alter the dynamics of the market. When a business makes an "Iconic Move", it alters the competitive landscape, capturing people's imagination. The move shifts customer expectations, creates a temporary monopoly, drives internal change – and delivers extraordinary business results.

Our behaviours and philosophy guide that culture. We use that way of thinking to evaluate our work, our talents and everything we do.

You previously mentioned the Interbrand Academy as an internal and external knowledge base. How does this platform work and does Interbrand offer such tools for clients?

The Interbrand Academy is both an online platform and a physical faculty that is based on modules of knowledge and experience in the field. It is our centre of excellence for brand intelligence and education, and a platform for collaboration, co-creation, innovation and inspiration.

As an "Interbrander", you can go on to the platform and do a module independently. We run an online academy every week in which we share knowledge and best practice. We call these our "On Air" sessions. They are for our teams, but of course, we also sometimes offer them for clients and tailor our academy to their needs, so they have individual training around their brand and what's relevant for them.

The other part of our academy is what we call the "Masterclass". This is more an event session where we bring clients, our people and challenges together. We run a week-long, residential session every year in order to accelerate our rising talent across the Interbrand Group and our global network. Our faculty comprises practice leaders and senior leaders from the Interbrand Group, alongside leaders from our partner brands. We use our "Interbrand Thinking" and our values to develop that event.

How do you find your creative talents and make sure they fit with Interbrand?

I work with the global HR director but also with the executive committee of each office not only to look for new talent but also to guide and mentor the development of the talent. We use "Interbrand Thinking" as a way of evaluating talent when they come to us, to see if they have the right fit or the right way of thinking and the right curiosity in their approach. This is how we grow and maintain talent.

And how do you evaluate these talents?

When we consider new candidates, we look at the way in which they have dealt with past projects. But when we get to a shortlist of candidates, we tend to use live briefs that we are working on at the moment in our evaluation process. We will ask the candidate to approach the problem as part of the interview process. It is actually about understanding how they tackle a problem, and how they think. Anyone can present a great piece of work, or tell a great story, but to test them on something new and live is the way to unpack how they think. We are looking not just for a star mindset, we are looking for an evaluative mindset that understands the dimensions of the market, the dimensions of audiences, the dimensions of maintaining relevance. We will be looking for these signals when candidates present the challenge we gave them back to us.

GA_P Fill in the gap [Corporate Design], Red Dot 2017

Once you have discovered creative talents and they have been working for Interbrand for many years, what role do competitions play for your work?

Our global awards programme – which we call the "Iconic Awards" – looks at the best awards for brand building, design and experiences, and, of course, Red Dot is one of those. We will expect each of our creative directors around the world to be developing award-worthy work.

We invite each office internally to enter for an award in several different categories. As with all award submissions, we invite them to interrogate the context and scope of the work and the impact it created for the client. But we also invite entrants to think of the awards through our "Three Lenses". They have to explain why it matters to customers (Human Truths), what the risks/opportunities were for the brand and the business (Economics) and how it was designed to deliver behavioural change (Experiences).

We want them to reach a benchmark in quality that means the project can be entered for global awards. The way we look at awards is through the lens of clarity. We use awards as a way of editing and keeping our thinking clear, because the work has to translate very quickly for a jury. For us, it's a good benchmark always to have global awards in mind because that helps us to keep our focus on the clarity of our work.

And what role does the Red Dot Award: Brands & Communication Design play?

I think, for us, Red Dot has always been a significant benchmark in terms of recognising all levels of design, from the product side and the brand building side. We have a similar belief in the power of design and the role it can play in solving problems, and creating to change the world for the better. Red Dot embodies that kind of design thinking, which is great.

One last question about Red Dot: What does the title "Red Dot: Agency of the Year 2020" mean to you?

From Interbrand's point of view and my point of view, the title has a significant meaning not just for the creative community at Interbrand, but for all our employees. From our client-facing teams, such as our consultants and strategists, to our internal teams such as HR and finance, this award highlights that every employee has played their part in delivering excellence. Being recognised as Red Dot: Agency of the Year 2020 showcases that Interbrand's work regularly delivers at a high-quality standard across the organisation. That level of consistency and attainment of a high-quality benchmark across the Interbrand network is what we aim to deliver. That is why clients have the confidence to come to an organisation like Interbrand. They know we drive quality across the global platform.

Brands

Preface	Red Dot: Agency of the Year	Brands	Brand Design & Identity	Corporate Design & Identity	Annual Reports
4	6	18	90	202	260

Polestar symbol

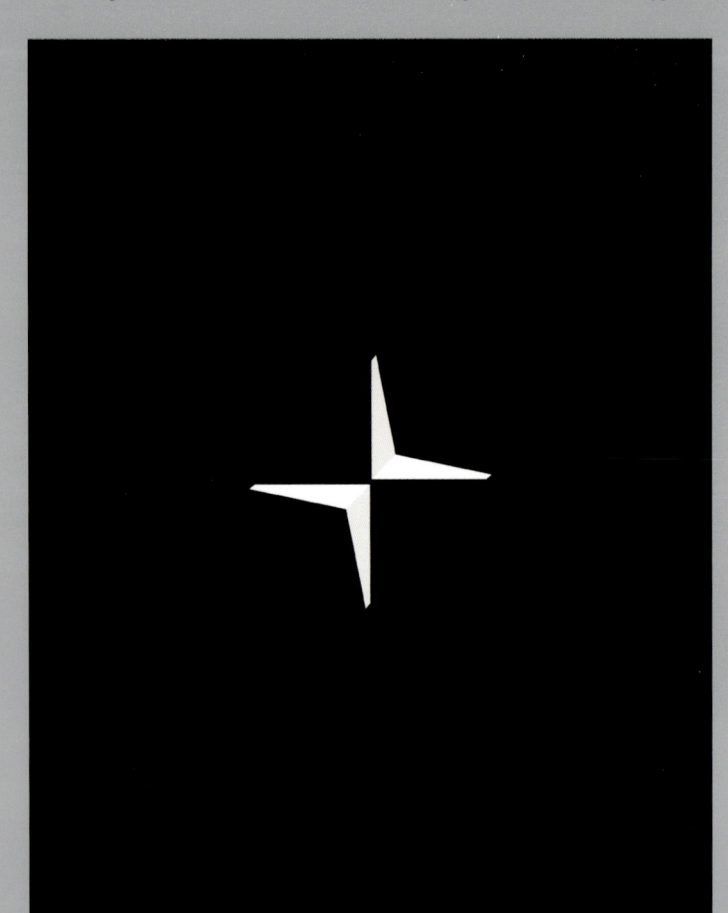

Polestar headquarters

Polestar
Red Dot: Brand of the Year

reddot winner 2020
automotive brand of the year

Polestar, long known primarily as a modification provider for Volvo, is an automotive brand jointly owned by Volvo and its Chinese parent company Geely. Since 2017, Polestar has positioned itself as an independent brand for electric cars under its own name and is recognisable by the stylised Polestar logo. The company entered the market with the aim of developing and building cars featuring high-end electric performance engines that push the boundaries of conventional automotive industry conventions. The focus in development and communication is on the performance of the cars, which is also clearly reflected in the overall design. The outstanding technological components and functions of the cars are highlighted in colour and attract a high level of attention. Everything else has been designed with an equally elegant and purist effect, with the designers paying a lot of attention to the smallest details in order to create a holistic high-tech user experience. As of today, the company has released two cars of its own: the Polestar 1 with an electric hybrid drivetrain in 2017 and the five-door all-electric fastback Polestar 2 in 2020. The simple numerical model designation can be stringently continued and thus epitomises the brand's future orientation.

As a new competitor in the fast-growing electric car segment, Polestar has opted right from the start for a holistic branding with high recognition value in order to optimally position itself as a visionary, design-oriented and technology-driven car manufacturer. A reduction to essentials, which clearly dominates the design of the cars, also characterises the entire brand identity – from the corporate design to the architecture of the headquarters in Gothenburg, Sweden, and that of the production sites in Chengdu and Lugiao,

Polestar 2

China, as well as the homepage design and all campaigns. Featuring a modular approach, the corporate design is based on clear grids and an equally clear corporate typography that make it work flexibly across a wide range of media and layouts. Last but not least, the Polestar Spaces have emerged as brand experience centres – minimalist monochrome spaces with a gallery-like character and product specialists standing ready to explain the car technology using wall-mounted glossy photographs of high-grade components, as well as monolithic battery exhibits or brakes in glass displays.

Statement by the jury
Launching a new brand in an overcrowded automotive market is not an easy task. Polestar has passed this test with flying colours. The holistic brand identity at the time of the launch illustrates how much energy is driving the conception and development of the brand. Polestar impresses with a cool, electrifying and stylistically durable brand appearance that perfectly befits a Nordic car manufacturer. The overall brand appearance is vigorous in its simplicity and at the same time rich in subtle detailing. Polestar combines a crystal-clear message with outstanding design purity.

Company
Polestar AB

Founding Year
2015

Headquarters
Gothenburg, Sweden

Lead Agency
Stockholm Design Lab
Stockholm, Sweden

Company Founder
Thomas Ingenlath

Number of Employees
300

Claim
Pure Progressive Performance

Website
www.polestar.com

Red Dot Awards
2020

→ Designer profile on page 661
→ You can also find this brand on the pages 206–207 in Volume 1 and 33 in Volume 2.

Preface	Red Dot: Agency of the Year	Brands	Brand Design & Identity	Corporate Design & Identity	Annual Reports
4	6	18	90	202	260

01

02

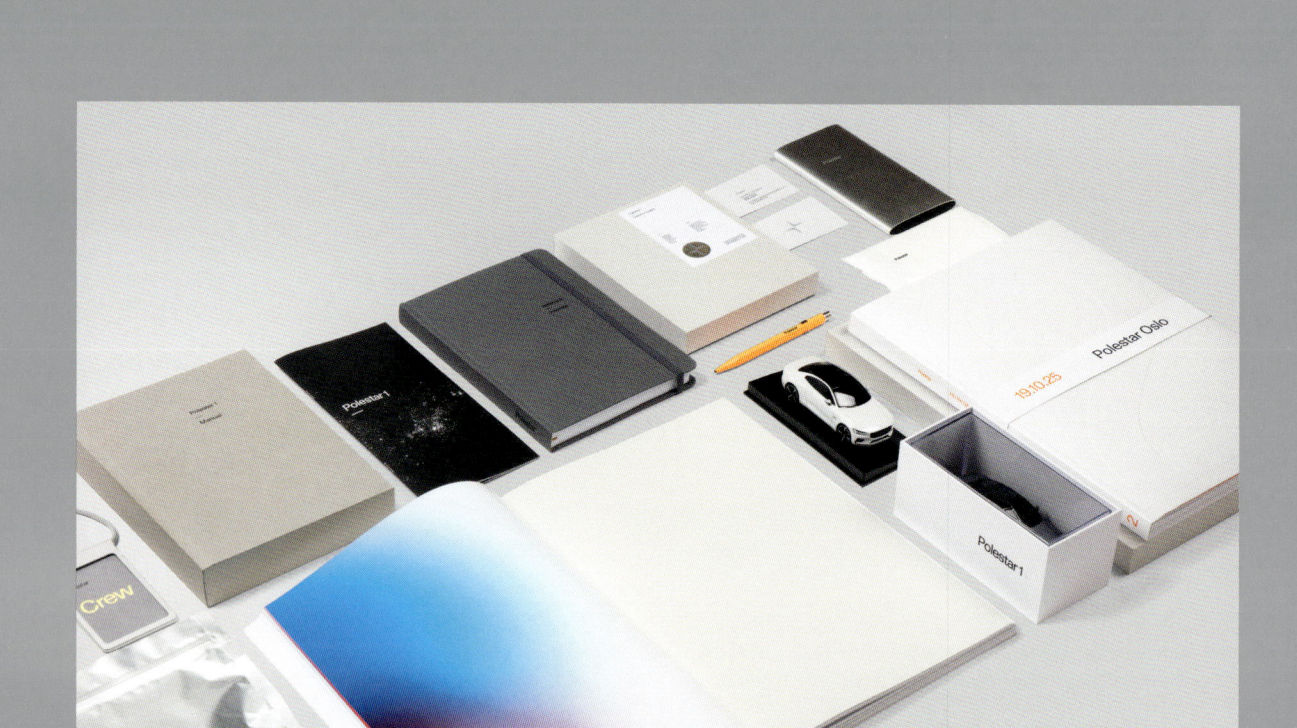

03

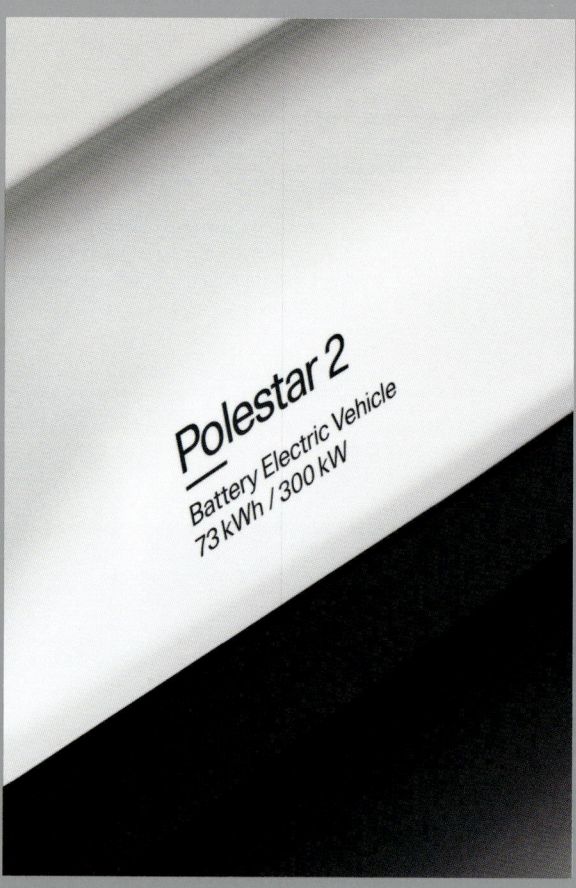

01 Business stationery and packaging

02 Retail space and display

03 Polestar marking

Advertising	Packaging Design	Fair Stands	Retail Design	Red Dot: Junior Award	Designer Profiles	Index
288	318	494	516	544	614	674

04

05

04 Event design

05 Website

GIRA

Gira logo

Gira
Red Dot:
Best Smart Building Brand

reddot winner 2020
best smart building brand

The German family-owned company Gira, founded in 1905, develops system solutions for electromechanical building control. Today, the company is one of the leading providers and one of the most distinctive, well-known brands in the industry. In the eyes of customers, the company has been predominantly associated with switches. However, in view of the trend towards smart homes and smart buildings, Gira recognised that this would not be enough to lead the Gira brand into the future. Therefore, the company decided to reposition the brand in 2020. In concrete terms, the task was to open the Gira brand towards the end customer on the one hand and to establish it in the smart home and smart building sector on the other. The brand was to find customer favour in the field of intelligent building control and be established as an integral part of architectural planning.

With its new brand identity, Gira is consciously focusing on different ways of addressing partners from the electronics trade and industry on the one hand and end customers on the other. While the focus in the B2B area is on technically sound, factual arguments and expressive product demonstrations, the B2C target group is addressed with emotional texts and human motifs, the skilful play of light and shadow and the selective application of spectral colours at an emotional level. Although technology plays a communicative role at Gira, the perspective clearly changes in that people should not have to understand technology, but instead technology should understand people.

Advertising	Packaging Design	Fair Stands	Retail Design	Red Dot: Junior Award	Designer Profiles	Index
288	318	494	516	544	614	674

GIRA

We are the ones with the switches. But we're so much more.

Image brochure

Gira Pushbutton Sensor 4 [Smart Home Automation], Red Dot: Best of the Best 2020

The new brand identity has been implemented in a two-phase campaign. In the first phase, the Gira employees were involved and actively contributed to answering surprising and courageous questions that encourage people to think or start a dialogue, questions such as "Will we still need switches tomorrow?" or "Isn't intuition the best control element?". This teaser campaign was intended to attract the attention of the trade audience and increase the level of commitment to the brand, especially among employees and specialist partners. In a second phase, the so-called "On/Off" campaign was launched across brochures, advertisements, on social media platforms and so forth in order to expand the target group address to include end customers. The campaign has culminated in the new claim: "We are the ones with the switches. But we're also so much more. Smart home pioneers, KNX partners and shapers of the future."

Statement by the jury
Repositioning a long-established brand is anything but easy. The Gira brand succeeds in doing this in an impressive manner by starting from its most famous product – the switch – and forging a link to everything that is locatable between "on" and "off", between "light" and "dark". In terms of both visuals and communication, the brand repositioning campaign opens up a "whole world of between" and combines this with notions of how new smart home technologies can improve our quality of life. Gira thus addresses its customers at an emotional level and positions itself credibly as a smart home provider.

Company
Gira Giersiepen GmbH & Co. KG

Founding Year
1905

Headquarters
Radevormwald, Germany

Lead Agency
thjnk Düsseldorf GmbH
Düsseldorf, Germany

Company Founder
Gustav Giersiepen, Richard Giersiepen

Number of Employees
1,200

Website
www.gira.com

Red Dot Awards
1999, 2001, 2003, 2004, 2007,
2009–2012, 2018–2020

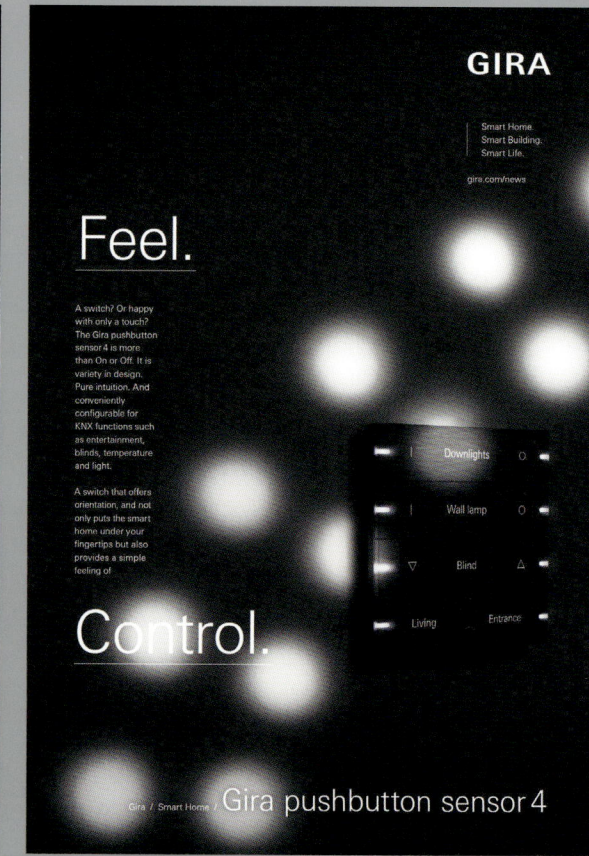

Preface	Red Dot: Agency of the Year	Brands	Brand Design & Identity	Corporate Design & Identity	Annual Reports
4	6	18	90	202	260

01 Fair stand

02 | 03 Advertising

01

02

03

Advertising	Packaging Design	Fair Stands	Retail Design	Red Dot: Junior Award	Designer Profiles	Index
288	318	494	516	544	614	674

04

05

06

04 Gira G1 [Intelligent Control Center]

05 | 06 Advertising

VO ÜS

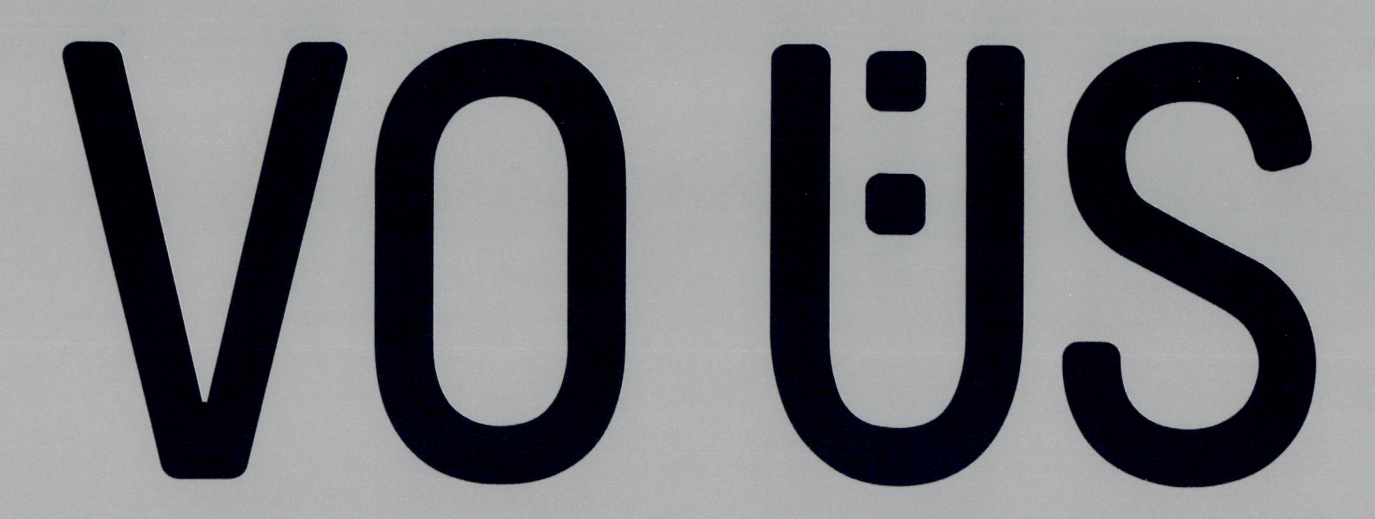

AUS VORARLBERG – NICHT VON IRGENDWO

VO ÜS logo

VO ÜS
Red Dot: Best Food & Beverage Brand

reddot winner 2020
best food & beverage brand

VO ÜS is a very young soft drinks brand launched on the market in May 2020. Behind the brand is the VO ÜS Vorarlberger Limo Werk GmbH, a joint venture between the two Vorarlberg breweries Frastanzer and Mohrenbräu. By founding this new company at the beginning of 2020, they entered the non-alcoholic beverage market for the first time, although they already had a wealth of market experience and could provide the distribution network needed. The home of the two breweries, the Austrian state of Vorarlberg, plays a key role in the positioning of the soft drinks brand: VO ÜS means something like "from us", "from here" or "our very own" in Vorarlberg dialect, a notion that is further underlined by extending the claim with "From Vorarlberg – not from just anywhere". Proudly displaying a strong connection to its homeland, the soft drinks brand thus clearly communicates right from the outset how it wants to be perceived – as a regional alternative to major international beverage brands. Thus, every time a customer asks for a VO ÜS cola or a VO ÜS soft drink, they are automatically asking for "our" cola and soft drinks.

True to the communicative regional positioning of the brand, the product itself is made with clear water from the mountain springs of Vorarlberg and contains fruits, stone pine, nettle, elderberry or other ingredients, all of which grow in or are associated with the small state. The product itself already has all the qualities to be credibly marketed through restaurants and food retail outlets in Vorarlberg. This is complemented by a sustainability approach comprising short supply chains and climate-neutral reusable bottles, which further contributes to the credibility of the brand as

Advertising	Packaging Design	Fair Stands	Retail Design	Red Dot: Junior Award	Designer Profiles	Index
288	318	494	516	544	614	674

VO ÜS product line

it epitomises the shared values of the people of Vorarlberg and their respect for the natural surroundings and resources. So far, around 20 different types of soft drinks and juices have been developed, most of which are already available on the market. The wide range of taste varieties is held together by a consistent corporate and packaging design, which through the stylised peaks of the Vorarlberg mountains – the shape and colour of which differs depending on the type of drink – not only emphasises the regional connection once again but also projects a high brand recognition value.

Statement by the jury
The VO ÜS soft drinks brand impresses with its clear positioning as a regional brand. This regional connection has been consistently imprinted in a charming and convincing manner across all areas of the brand identity – from the product itself to its name, the claim and the entire design appearance. Imbued with pride in the homeland of Vorarlberg, this lends the brand a strong and uncompromising charisma, which is further emphasised by its distinctive and clear look. In combination with the somewhat reduced, systematically structured brand design, the soft drinks have emerged with a homogeneous brand image that should get them a lot of customer attention on retail shelves.

Company
VO ÜS Vorarlberger Limo Werk GmbH

Founding Year
2019

Headquarters
Dornbirn, Austria

Lead Agency
zurgams Kommunikationsagentur GmbH
Dornbirn, Austria

Company Founder
Thomas Pachole, Kurt Michelini

Number of Employees
3

Claim
VO ÜS – Aus Vorarlberg. Nicht von irgendwo

Website
www.voues.at

Red Dot Awards
2020

Preface	Red Dot: Agency of the Year	Brands	Brand Design & Identity	Corporate Design & Identity	Annual Reports
4	6	18	90	202	260

01

02

03

01–03 Advertising

UNSEREN DIALEKT
VERSTEHT NICHT JEDER.
UNSEREN APFELSAFT SCHON.
APFELSAFT GESPRITZT
VO ÜS
NICHT VON IRGENDWO
I MAG AN
SAFT
VO ÜS
BODENSEE
APFELSAFT GESPRITZT
VO ÜS
AUS VORARLBERG – NICHT VON IRGENDWO

Red Dot: Automotive Brand

Volkswagen

For more than 70 years, Volkswagen has been manufacturing cars with innovative technologies and many award-winning designs, including iconic cars such as the Beetle or the Golf. Today, some 70 different models are produced worldwide and more than six million Volkswagen cars are delivered to customers around the world each year. As part of a fundamental reorientation towards electric drives, full networking and carbon neutrality, Volkswagen underwent a comprehensive rebranding in 2019 and proclaimed it the year of the "New Volkswagen". E-mobility has been identified as the most important future technology for the brand; and with the new ID. family of cars, Volkswagen aims to become the world's biggest electric automobile brand by 2025 and a provider of modern mobility services and smart devices.

In 2019, Volkswagen presented its new logo and brand identity for the first time at the International Automotive Exhibition (IAA) in Frankfurt, Germany – accompanied in the product side by the simultaneous launch of the fully electric ID.3 car. Form and visual language, corporate identity and communication style have all been completely revised for the new brand design. The logo of the brand has been further developed in that it is reduced to its essential components and now consistently digitally oriented as a 2D logo. The colour palette has been expanded to include another shade of blue and allow for additional colour logo variants – such as a VW logo in red for the GTI models. In addition, for the various product categories, distinct realms of images have been developed that differ in details. The new visual language has become more colourful and documentary in style than in the past. Thus, the way cars are visually promoted has also changed in that they are no longer shown in perfectly illuminated settings. Instead, the cars feature in more realistic situations that customers can more easily relate to. Other key changes include a new layout system and the elimination of the brand claim, which has been replaced by a sound logo and a female brand voice.

01

Advertising	Packaging Design	Fair Stands	Retail Design	Red Dot: Junior Award	Designer Profiles	Index
288	318	494	516	544	614	674

Company
Volkswagen AG

Founding Year
1937

Headquarters
Wolfsburg, Germany

Number of Employees
671,200

Website
www.volkswagen.com

Red Dot Awards
2004, 2005, 2007, 2009–2013, 2015, 2018, 2019

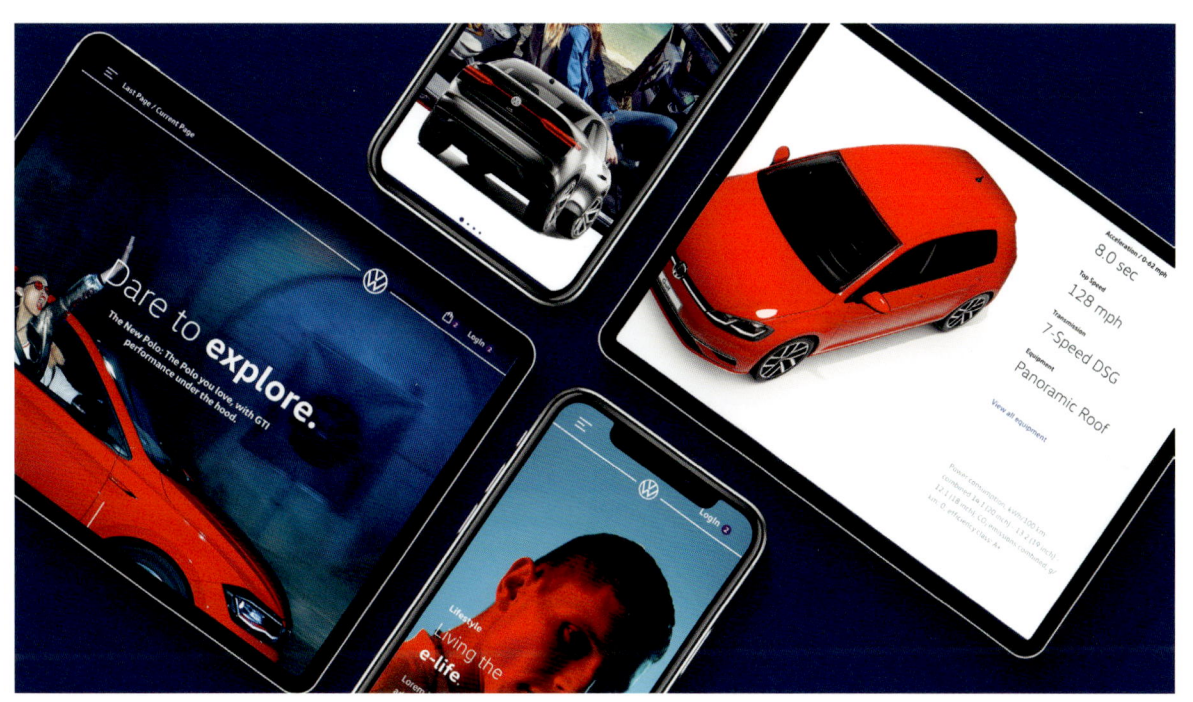

01 Volkswagen logo

02 VW ID.3 1st [Electric Vehicle]

03 | 04 Advertising

05 Digital platforms

Red Dot: Transportation Brand

bwegt

The German state of Baden-Württemberg started a local public transport initiative in 2017 with a campaign to improve its railway service quality and start the operation of more than 250 new trains. The aim of the initiative is to create a sustainable mobility culture and to double the local transport passenger figures by 2030. Since Baden-Württemberg's transport infrastructure is very heterogeneous and its services are provided by 22 associations and 50 transport companies, including 20 rail transport companies, a new public transport umbrella brand was to be developed to pool all services provided by the public authorities and all the transport companies in the region.

The key idea behind the umbrella brand bwegt is to offer people in Baden-Württemberg a new freedom of movement and thus to motivate more people to rely on local public transport. The word mark bwegt is made up of the acronym BW for Baden-Württemberg and the key term "bewegt" (moved, transported) as the guiding principle of a new mobility in the region. The logo mark consists of the brand name "bwegt", the heraldic animal of the state and the claim "Mobilität für Baden-Württemberg" (Mobility for Baden-Württemberg), while using the state's crest colours, black and yellow, as brand colours. Moreover, a corporate typography with a specially developed typeface was created as part of the new brand image. The so-called bwegt swoosh, which is reminiscent of the side view of a passing branded train, has emerged as another recurring design element. The corporate design is applicable in printed and digital media, as well as in the design of trains and ticket machines.

Movement both literally and in the figurative sense of touching is also placed centre stage in the campaign's motifs and moving images. Photos and videos were created in close cooperation with the company of choreographer Eric Gauthier in order to express the idea and vision of movement in dance and capture it in images. This lends the public transport brand an aesthetic and emotionality that is unusual and very unique for the industry, which in turn leads to a high level of recognition: within two years, public awareness of the brand rose from zero to 38 per cent, and the brand is being associated predominantly with the notions of "dynamism", "modernity" and "sustainability".

Advertising	Packaging Design	Fair Stands	Retail Design	Red Dot: Junior Award	Designer Profiles	Index
288	318	494	516	544	614	674

Company
Ministerium für Verkehr Baden-Württemberg

Founding Year
2017

Headquarters
Stuttgart, Germany

Lead Agency
Statement GmbH Agentur für Marketing- und Designlösungen
Saarbrücken, Germany
Beaufort 8 GmbH
Stuttgart, Germany

Claim
bwegt – Mobilität für Baden-Württemberg

Website
www.bwegt.de

Red Dot Awards
2020

01 bwegt logo

02 Advertising

03 Ticket machine

04 Advertising

Red Dot: Transportation Brand

Stromer

The Swiss e-bike manufacturer Stromer, based in Bern, was founded in 2010. Using new technologies and Swiss engineering, the company develops speed-pedelecs with integrated design and connectivity, which are generally targeted at both people with an active lifestyle who appreciate high quality and good design, as well as in particular at commuters who want to avoid rush hour traffic. The Stromer Campus in Oberwangen near Bern unites all production areas under one roof – from research and development, construction, customer service and management to the flagship store itself. Measuring 4,400 sqm, the campus enables a quick exchange of ideas between all areas, making it the centre for in-house technology and a catalyst for innovation. The e-bikes themselves are marked by their clear design, which skilfully merges aesthetics and technology. The cockpit is tidy and clear. The on-board computer is integrated into the top tube. The frame silhouette projects a purist appearance thanks to the internal cable routing and integrated battery, while the motor sits almost invisibly in the rear axle.

The brand identity features a design that is just as clear as the pedelecs themselves. The logo mark is made up of the brand name in capital letters, preceded by a plus sign and followed by a minus sign, as well as three rectangles placed below in light grey, dark grey and red, which are reminiscent of battery charge indicators. Depending on the application, the logo can be used set positively with black lettering on white or negatively inverted with white lettering on black. The black-and-white or light-versus-dark contrasts also define the rest of the brand's visual appearance and are flanked by clear structures and grids, dramatically illuminated product images and a dynamic visual language full of atmosphere. The result is a brand identity that works across both analogue and digital media and the conciseness of which makes the brand easy to recognise and remember after a single contact. Both the brand products and the brand communication thus contribute to the claim "Drive the difference" by filling it with life. Ten years after its foundation, Stromer has become the leader in eight markets and is represented in another eleven.

Advertising	Packaging Design	Fair Stands	Retail Design	Red Dot: Junior Award	Designer Profiles	Index
288	318	494	516	544	614	674

Company
myStromer AG

Founding Year
2010

Headquarters
Oberwangen, Switzerland

Company Founder
Thomas Binggeli

Number of Employees
70

Claim
Drive the difference

Website
www.stromerbike.com

Red Dot Awards
2014, 2020

01 Stromer logo

02 Stromer ST5 [S-Pedelec], Red Dot 2020

03 Business stationery and packaging

Red Dot: Technology Brand

WAVE SUMMIT 2020

WAVE SUMMIT 2020 is a summit on artificial intelligence (AI) that is organised in China by the National Engineering Laboratory for Deep Learning Technology and Application and in collaboration with the Chinese search engine operator Baidu. The motto in 2020 is "Deep Learning Developer Summit". The Wave Summit, which is being held online due to the COVID-19 pandemic, provides technical courses and conferences at which the latest scientific findings and technologies are presented and made available. In addition, the event also serves developers in the field of deep learning as an important communication and interaction platform and it displays the emerging geek culture in local science and technology enterprises. The event is targeted at everybody who is deeply involved with AI technology, from developers, scientists and companies to university lecturers, students and technophiles.

The brand name "Wave" identifies the wave of scientific and technological developments as the driving force for advancement today – it is assumed that artificial intelligence will develop in three waves, of which we are currently in the second. The visual identity of the brand is based on mathematics and aims to optimally represent the propagation of the wave for the respective medium. Since deep learning ultimately relies on high computing power, computer algorithms were used to generate these wave patterns. This innovative use of electronic data processing to generate a visual idiom thus reflects the technical way of thinking underlying the entire summit. Geometric patterns create an impression of movement, an appearance that is further reinforced by colour gradients in the brand colours of blue and green as well as pink. This design look is consistently applied to all media ranging from print materials, website and merchandising items to presentations as well as the animation and augmented reality design.

01

Advertising	Packaging Design	Fair Stands	Retail Design	Red Dot: Junior Award	Designer Profiles	Index
288	318	494	516	544	614	674

Company
Baidu Online Network Technology (Beijing) Co.,Ltd.

Founding Year
2000

Headquarters
Beijing, China

Company Founder
Robin Li

Number of Employees
45,887

Claim
Making the complicated world simpler through technology.

Website
www.wavesummit.com.cn

Red Dot Awards
2020

02

03

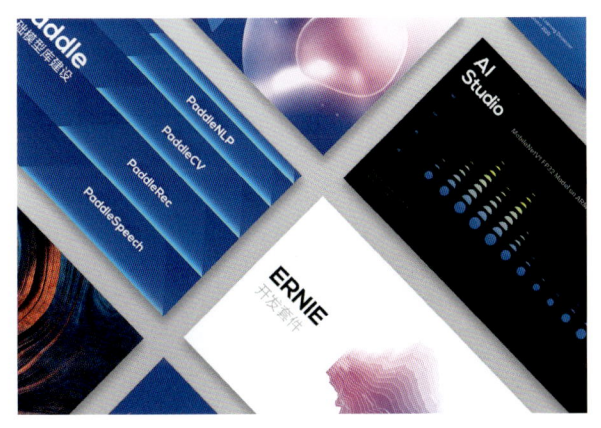

04 05

01 WAVE SUMMIT 2020 logo

02 Large-scale poster advertising

03–05 Business stationery and packaging

Red Dot: Online Services Brand

NAVER Cloud Platform Workplace & Workbox

NAVER is a South Korean internet company that was founded in 1999 and started with a web portal that offered a Korean-language search engine. The NAVER Business Platform (NBP) is a subsidiary of NAVER that supports the IT infrastructure of NAVER as well as its affiliated companies. The services the company offers also include the NAVER Cloud Platform (NCP), a work series which, consisting of a Workplace and a Workbox, provides business application services to SaaS (software as a service) with accumulated technology and know-how from various market experiences. In order to raise more public awareness of the Workplace and Workbox as global services and thus take a leap forward, the offer underwent a complete rebranding.

The new brand identity is based on the brand claim of "Simple, Share, and Solid". Following the idea of these concept keywords, the image of the NAVER Cloud Platform was formed as an easy-to-use and intuitive service for global companies and start-ups, as well as embodying an efficient tool for collaborations. The focus of the new brand identity is on the use of images, symbols and pictograms, aimed at easy-to-understand usability of the Workplace, a cloud-based integrated communication solution, as well as the Workbox, a file-sharing service. The logos of the two services are each based on a hexagonal grid that symbolises the cloud-based work environment. In the case of the Workplace, the grid features two opposing surfaces that stand for "Place" and "Connection". With the Workbox logo, a box that is open at the top and bottom is created within the grid, symbolising the "Box" as the cloud-based storage space, on the one hand, and the "Sync" as the real-time sharing of files, on the other. Various shades of blue, one green tone and white are used as the main brand colours. The combination of blue and green lends the logos a three-dimensional appeal, while the use of the colours across all media creates a homogeneous brand appearance with a high recognition value. The corporate typography of neo-grotesque sans-serif Calibre ensures that copy, digital and analogue, is easy to read even in small font sizes.

Advertising	Packaging Design	Fair Stands	Retail Design	Red Dot: Junior Award	Designer Profiles	Index
288	318	494	516	544	614	674

Company
NAVER BUSINESS PLATFORM Corp.

Founding Year
1999

Headquarters
Seongnam, South Korea

Lead Agency
newtype Imageworks
Seoul, South Korea

Company Founder
Weongi Park

Number of Employees
456

Website
www.ncloud.com

Red Dot Awards
2019, 2020

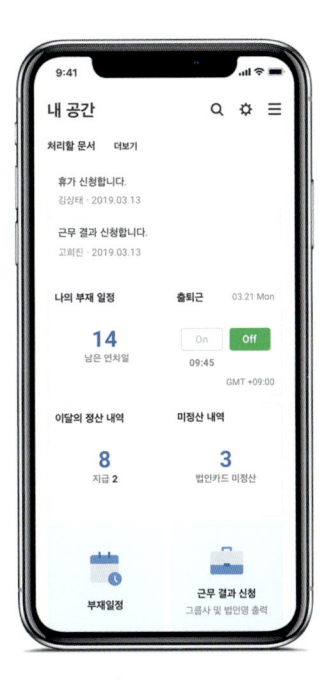

01 NAVER Cloud Platform
Workplace & Workbox logos

02 Icons

03 App

Red Dot: Software Brand

Kaspersky

Kaspersky is an international cybersecurity company founded in Russia in 1997 by Natalja Kasperskaya and Yevgeny Kaspersky. The company uses deep threat intelligence and security expertise to develop solutions that protect critical infrastructures of businesses and governments, as well as consumers around the globe. As of today, Kaspersky is more than an anti-virus laboratory. The business focus has moved towards a much broader concept – namely that of cyber immunity. This shift in focus made it necessary to redesign and reposition the entire brand, with "Building a safer world" aimed at epitomising the corporate goal. In future, security technology should also be associated with humanity, transparency, warmth and generosity.

The identity system was reformed to express this new focus by simultaneously steering the brand away from the dystopian imagery otherwise typical of the industry. This repositioning is reflected in the new core principle: "Engineered for immunity", with the word "engineered" referring to Kaspersky's high level of technical expertise in the field of cybersecurity. To reflect this deep knowledge and focus in the design, the typeface Kaspersky Sans was developed, a typeface that alternates open and closed characters in a geometric, mathematically exact format. A grid system creates highly structured layouts. Furthermore, the word "immunity" was sparked by the idea that, rather than dark and fearful, internet security should inspire a sense of freedom and safety. This aspect is visualised through the use of variable hexagonal surfaces, so-called safe spaces, which are shielded from the outside by bright colours. These elements are combined with an emotional imagery and slogans such as "Make friends safely". This new brand identity system, which has been revised down to the last detail, combines technical and human aspects and, in so doing, clearly communicates that the Kaspersky brand is not taking advantage of the fears of its customers, but instead wants to stand for security, as well as openness and trust.

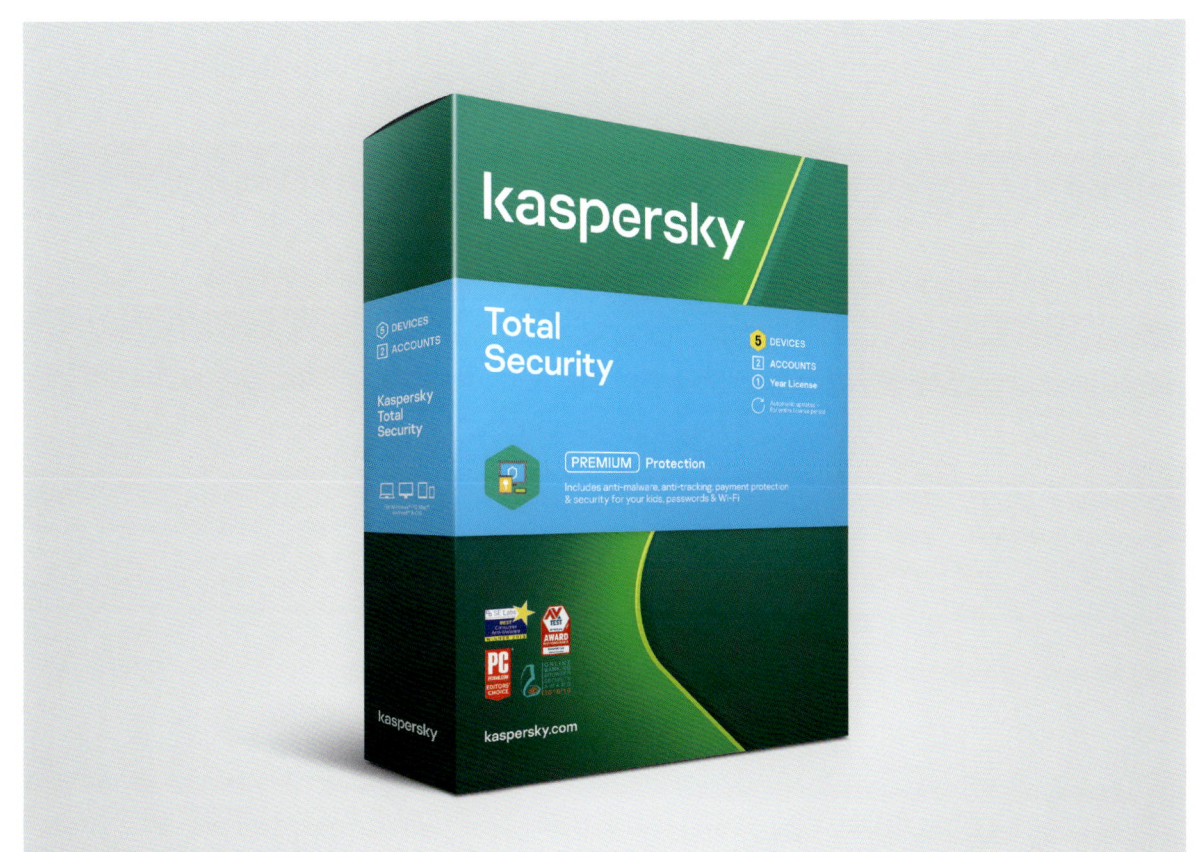

Advertising	Packaging Design	Fair Stands	Retail Design	Red Dot: Junior Award	Designer Profiles	Index
288	318	494	516	544	614	674

Company
AO Kaspersky Lab

Founding Year
1997

Headquarters
Moscow, Russia

Lead Agency
Moving Brands
London, United Kingdom

Company Founder
Eugene Kaspersky

Number of Employees
More than 4,000

Claim
Bring on the future

Website
www.kaspersky.com

Red Dot Awards
2015, 2017, 2020

02

03

01 Kaspersky logo

02 Software packaging

03 Advertising

Red Dot: Technology Brand

Finanz Informatik

Finanz Informatik, based in Frankfurt, Germany, is the IT service provider of the Sparkassen-Finanzgruppe (Savings Banks Finance Group). It was created in 2008 from a merger between FinanzIT (Hannover) and Sparkassen Informatik (Frankfurt). The new company thus became the joint IT service provider for all German savings banks and other companies in the Sparkassen-Finanzgruppe and the financial services sector. Finanz Informatik offers complete IT services – from application development, infrastructure and data centre operation to consulting, training and support. Today, with OSPlus, the company is one of the leading total banking systems in the German market.

The IT service provider's trademark clearly indicates that it is part of the savings banks group. The iconic "S" symbol of the Sparkasse and the strong red corporate colour of the banking group are taken up in the logo mark. At the same time, the brand name simply follows the "S" and is written in small letters, conveying seriousness and emphasising the focus of the company through the bold use of the term IT for informatics. A separate logo in the corporate red of the Sparkasse integrates the initial letters "f" and "i" in a square and serves as a memorable, space-saving identifier. A sound spectrum based on a triad in the key of F sharp serves as the corporate sound and varies depending on the area of application. The website of Finanz Informatik has been consistently optimised for display on smartphones. Image formats are defined following the 16:9 ratio principle. Since nowadays touch surfaces with icons for orientation often represent the first contact with the brand, a brand-typical icon language was developed that complements and stringently continues the basic elements of the corporate design.

The self-proclaimed Finanz Informatik mission is to accompany customers into the digital future. This is expressed in the slogan "Wir sichern den digitalen Vorsprung" (We care for digitisation) and is filled with life at live events, as well as in internal and external communication. Customer and employee magazines, commercials and image films aim to take away the fear of digitisation, to make people embrace change or to inspire reflection and thus establish an emotional level in brand loyalty.

Advertising	Packaging Design	Fair Stands	Retail Design	Red Dot: Junior Award	Designer Profiles	Index
288	318	494	516	544	614	674

Company
Finanz Informatik GmbH & Co. KG

Founding Year
2008

Headquarters
Frankfurt/Main, Germany

Lead Agency
beierarbeit GmbH
Bielefeld, Germany

Number of Employees
3,767

Claim
Wir sichern den digitalen Vorsprung

Website
www.f-i.de

Red Dot Awards
2003, 2004, 2009, 2011–2019

01 Finanz Informatik logo

02 Digital annual report

03 Boxes for FI-Connect, management digital conference

04 Advertising

Red Dot: Online Services Brand

hellonature

hellonature is a South Korean premium online foods store specialising in organically grown products. Founded in 2012, the company has been offering an early-morning delivery service for fresh food since 2017. In order to improve the public's awareness of the brand and its presence in the fast-growing food delivery market, and promote its "dawn delivery" service in particular, the company opted to renew their brand design.

The company sees itself as a pioneer in terms of internal quality standards, fair ways of operation with suppliers and the delivery of products for a healthy lifestyle. That is why hellonature initially expanded its product portfolio to include carefully selected seasonal foods. In addition, new product ranges have been introduced that support food-related lifestyles such as veganism or LCHF (low-carb, high-fat) and which are flanked by recipes from popular restaurants. Moreover, hellonature excludes disposable items and non-recyclable materials as much as possible.

In the rebranding, the brand name "hellonature" was scrutinised because of its apparent simplicity, but the name was ultimately retained. Instead, it was decided to use the positive and clear meaning of those two words and redesign the word mark accordingly, making it communicate the brand values and the early-morning delivery service in an intuitive-to-understand way. For the new logo, the word "hello" was converted into a curved handwritten script and the word "nature" was placed underneath, making the new logo reminiscent of a hand raised in greeting. The already established green brand colour was used in an adjusted form for the lettering and complemented by lemon yellow, which is aimed at evoking a feeling of welcome and an association with dawn. Considering the fact that the main interface used by the customer is an app, the logo was designed to fit in a shape that is suitable for a mobile app icon. The sweeping arcs of the "hello" lettering in the logo play an additional role in the brand design: slightly pulled apart, they form a curved line that seems to consistently tie in everything – from the app's various sub-pages and the products to the recipes and the packaging design. The new brand identity invites customers to become part of the hellonature world.

Advertising	Packaging Design	Fair Stands	Retail Design	Red Dot: Junior Award	Designer Profiles	Index
288	318	494	516	544	614	674

Company
hellonature

Founding Year
2012

Headquarters
Seoul, South Korea

Lead Agency
studio fnt (Brand Identity)
Seoul, South Korea

Company Founder
Byungyul Park

Number of Employees
122

Claim
Tasty Journey hellonature

Website
www.hellonature.co.kr

Red Dot Awards
2020

01 hellonature logo

02 Rice packaging

03 Grocery delivery bag

04 Snack jars

05 Voucher booklet

Red Dot: Technology Brand

Busch-Jaeger

Founded in 1879, Busch-Jaeger is one of the leading manufacturers of electrical installation technology today. The company belongs to the ABB Group and employs around 1,000 people in the German cities of Lüdenscheid and Aue and exports its products to more than 60 countries. The product portfolio ranges from complete electrical installation range switches, sockets, modular devices and motion detectors, to door communication systems and electronic high-end products for building automation in smart homes and smart buildings. In order to differentiate itself from the competition, especially in the area of smart building technology, Busch-Jaeger repositioned itself by turning "Smart Home" into "Smarter Home" and combining this with a corresponding overhaul of its brand identity. The aim of the rebranding was to sharpen the appearance of Busch-Jaeger and to adapt the corporate design to digital media requirements.

The new brand identity is marked by clarity, flexibility and a high level of visual impact working in both the analogue and the digital realm. Conceived for great optical flexibility, the design principle grants the freedom to use all individual elements as needed, whereby the corporate design allows catering for a high variety of different content. Averta, which is a contemporary, geometric, sans-serif font that can be used across all media, was selected as the corporate typography. The new imagery puts young protagonists at the centre of photos and videos, showing them in living spaces that are reduced, yet elegant in appearance and cleverly complemented by smart home solutions. This strategic sharpening of the profile is intended to help the brand reach a younger, lifestyle-oriented target group. The company's website has also been redesigned in order to make it appeal not only to installers and architects, but to end customers as well. The subject area of "Smarter Home" provides answers to all questions around smart home solutions and, supplemented by application videos highlighting the specific functions, explains the various systems for all target groups.

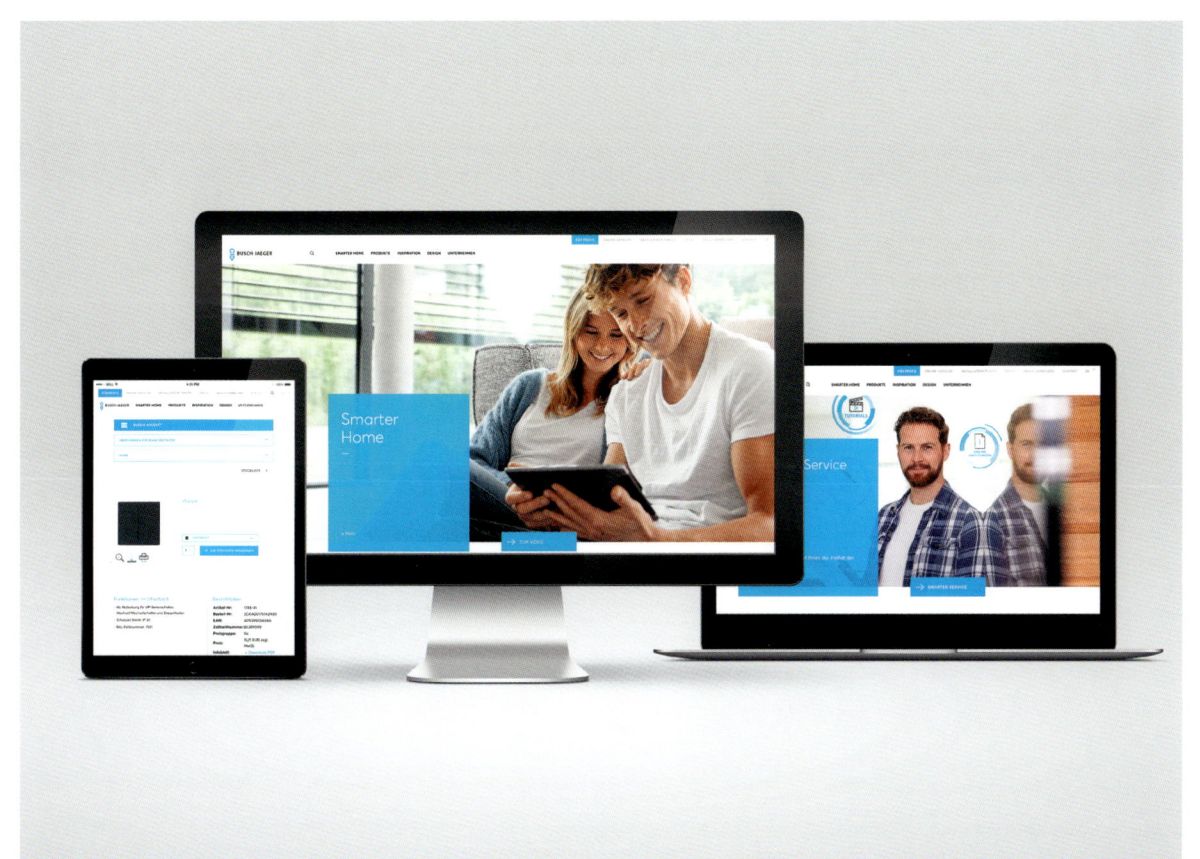

Advertising	Packaging Design	Fair Stands	Retail Design	Red Dot: Junior Award	Designer Profiles	Index
288	318	494	516	544	614	674

Company
Busch-Jaeger Elektro GmbH

Founding Year
1879

Headquarters
Lüdenscheid, Germany

Lead Agency
vistapark GmbH
Wuppertal, Germany

Company Founder
Hans-Curt Jaeger, Georg Jaeger

Number of Employees
1,000

Website
www.busch-jaeger.de

Red Dot Awards
2004, 2005, 2007, 2008,
2010–2015, 2017–2020

02

03

01 Busch-Jaeger logo

02 Digital platforms

03 Busch-Jaeger icon

04 Smarter Home news magazine

04

Red Dot: Construction Brand

OMA by the Sea

OMA by the Sea is a real estate project developed by Wing Tai Properties in Hong Kong's Tuen Mun District, which is a very green area located directly by the sea. The brand name OMA by the Sea is made up of the Hawaiian word "OMA" for green and the addition "by the Sea" – the latter clearly pointing to the geographic location of the project. The word mark OMA by the Sea, on the other hand, takes up the colours of green and blue, with the green dominating and being flanked by two blue squares. The real estate project is aimed primarily at the target group of newly married couples and first-time home buyers, people who are looking for something special that clearly stands out from traditional real estate.

Against this background, a brand identity was developed that fundamentally differs from projects that are primarily aimed at mature investors and therefore want to convey trustworthiness through photos showing attractive people in luxuriously furnished surroundings. Instead, the unique selling proposition of this project – the location surrounded by sea and greenery – is placed centre stage in the brand image. Powerful and colourful illustrations are thus used on billboards and buses, in advertisements and in print media, as well as on the internet, all showing people who do sports and animals such as seals, otters and dolphins in relaxed poses on the beach and in the midst of nature, set against a bright yellow background. Together with the slogan "Let's chill", this creates a strong contrast to the typical advertising of other Hong Kong residential properties, which are always located within the city and focus on luxury and a cosmopolitan lifestyle. Unusual for the industry, the imagery of OMA by the Sea thus attracts attention and piques curiosity. Buses were specifically chosen as advertising media, as they drive around Hong Kong's bustling Tsuen Wan and Tuen Mun Districts, as well as in the city centre where the young target group lives and works. The use of this playful illustration style in all marketing materials, including an animated short film, has resulted in a strong synergetic effect that strengthens the advertising message across the various touchpoints of the brand. Ultimately, 210 of the total of 268 units were sold on the first day the sales office opened. Most of the buyers are millennials, more than half of them between 26 and 35 years old.

01

Advertising	Packaging Design	Fair Stands	Retail Design	Red Dot: Junior Award	Designer Profiles	Index
288	318	494	516	544	614	674

Company
Wing Tai Properties Limited

Founding Year
1991

Headquarters
Hong Kong

Lead Agency
MRPAUL & PARTNERS
Hong Kong

Number of Employees
470

Claim
We don't just build, we craft

Website
www.omabythesea.com

Red Dot Awards
2020

01 OMA by the Sea logo

02 | 03 Print advertising

04 Penthouse rendering

Red Dot: Medical Brand

Tend

The US start-up company Tend was founded with the aim of reinventing the dental studio by providing dental treatments that are personalised, straightforward and fear-free. Tend was launched as a brand in October 2019. The idea grew from studies showing that very few patients in the US are satisfied with their experience at the dentist. This sets a vicious circle in motion that discourages people from visiting dentists, which in turn often results in overall poorer oral health and the need for more complicated and costly restorative services over time.

Tend focuses on a new dental experience. To this end, every step from making an appointment to leaving the dental studio was designed around the idea of a branded giveaway. The dentist studios were designed as bright spaces with a calm atmosphere, a dedicated room for brushing one's teeth or just freshening up ("The Brushery") and a welcoming reception area. Consistently matched architectural and interior design elements include round shapes, natural light, warming woods, cafe-style tables, green tiles with a winding floss-like pattern and white walls with a playful, toothpaste-like texture. The exam rooms feature headphones and ceiling-mounted TVs; a monitor greets patients by name when they enter. The dentists and dental hygienists wear uniforms in grey and white to project the notions of trustworthiness and expertise.

The visual brand identity reflects the company's mission statement of service orientation and patient-centred friendliness. The "e" in Tend's word mark is tilted to make it look like it is smiling, creating a sense of warmth. Nantes and Founders Grotesk were chosen as corporate typefaces. Linear key lines direct users through information and establish a clear division between pieces of content. The colour palette comprises warm, muted colours that create a sense of calm; at the centre, however, the green brand colour is featured to add authority, as green has been associated with medicine for more than a century. The visual language of Tend places mouths of all kinds at the centre of photographic materials, conveying that everyone is welcome.

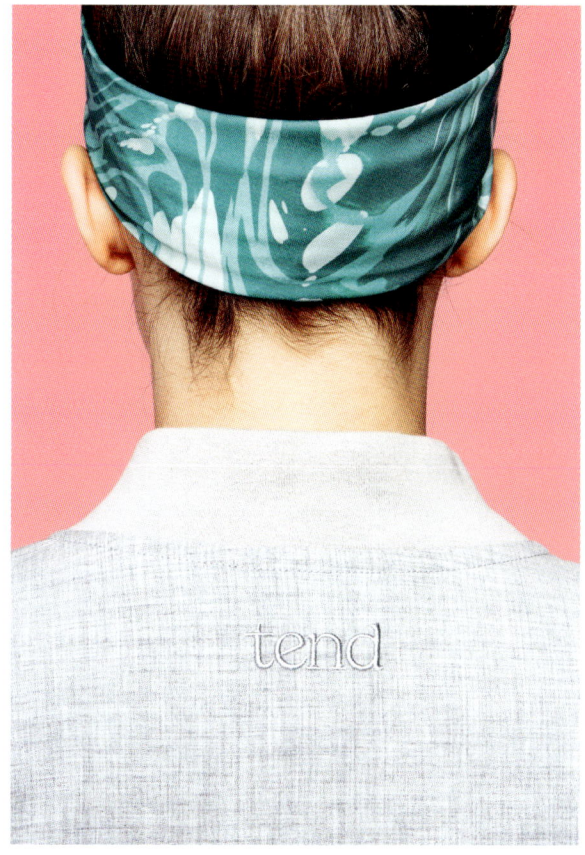

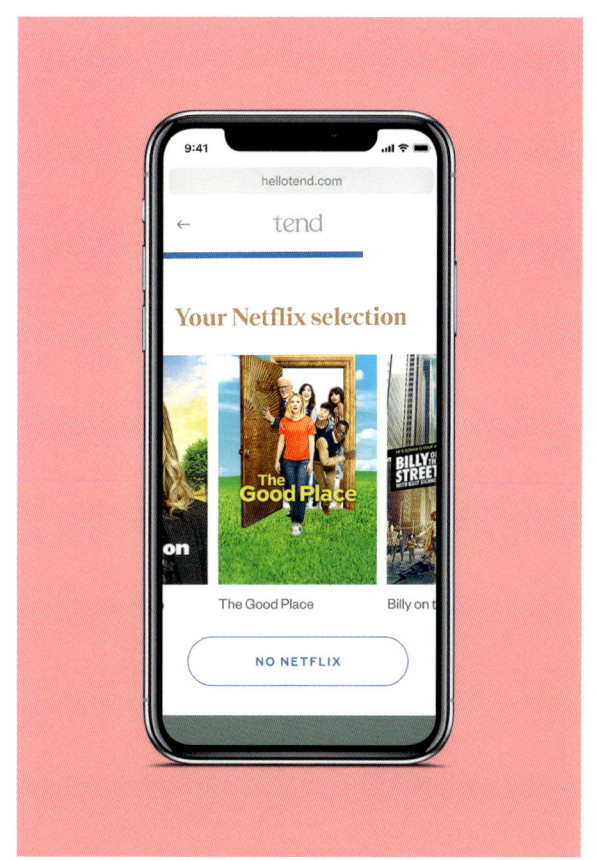

Advertising	Packaging Design	Fair Stands	Retail Design	Red Dot: Junior Award	Designer Profiles	Index
288	318	494	516	544	614	674

Company
Tend

Founding Year
2018

Headquarters
New York, Nashville, USA

Lead Agency
Mythology
New York, USA

Company Founder
Doug Hudson, Michael Stenclik, Andy Grover

Number of Employees
100

Claim
Look forward to the dentist

Website
www.hellotend.com

Red Dot Awards
2020

01 Tend logo

02 Work attire

03 Website with entertainment programme

04 Reception desk

05 Advertising

Red Dot: Medical Brand

Minuendo

Minuendo is a start-up company based in Oslo, Norway, that has developed an innovative hearing protection product. Minuendo was founded in 2018 with the aim of developing pioneering products that protect the sense of hearing, but without compromising on sound quality. Hearing damage will be one of the largest global health issues going forward. By 2050, an estimated 900 million people will suffer from disabling hearing loss due to noise exposure. Yet, most earplugs available on the market today are uncomfortable, hard to use and many do not even provide the necessary protection. Against this background, Minuendo combines advanced technology and sleek design to create individually adjustable, lossless hearing protection.

The brand is targeted in particular at professional musicians and music lovers who place great value on natural sound quality. The "no loss" or "lossless" property is consequently highlighted as a unique selling proposition in communication and in combination with other features, such as "lossless earplugs", "Every detail. No loss." and "Full protection. No loss.". These messages are incorporated into images showing emotional concert situations in which the volume can be literally felt. The advertisements and commercials directly address musicians in order to draw their attention to the dangers of being exposed to excessive volume and to offer a solution to the problem at the same time.

The logo mark consists of the Minuendo lettering and an M logo. It begins with a single point and then extends into a straight line reminiscent of a sound waveform. Pictograms are used to communicate the special product features in an easy-to-understand manner. The packaging of the earplugs, a cube made of cardboard, opens from above like a jewellery box and presents the elegantly designed products against a black background. Using these methods, Minuendo succeeds in visualising and conveying its brand promise and unique selling proposition in the best possible way and specifically tailored to the target group and at the same time in lending the brand high credibility.

Advertising	Packaging Design	Fair Stands	Retail Design	Red Dot: Junior Award	Designer Profiles	Index
288	318	494	516	544	614	674

Company
Minuendo AS

Founding Year
2018

Headquarters
Oslo, Norway

Lead Agency
Designit
Copenhagen, Denmark

Company Founder
Knut Håkon Breivik, Olav Kvaløy, Stian Aldrin, Tom Trones

Claim
Every detail. No loss.

Website
www.minuendo.com

Red Dot Awards
2020

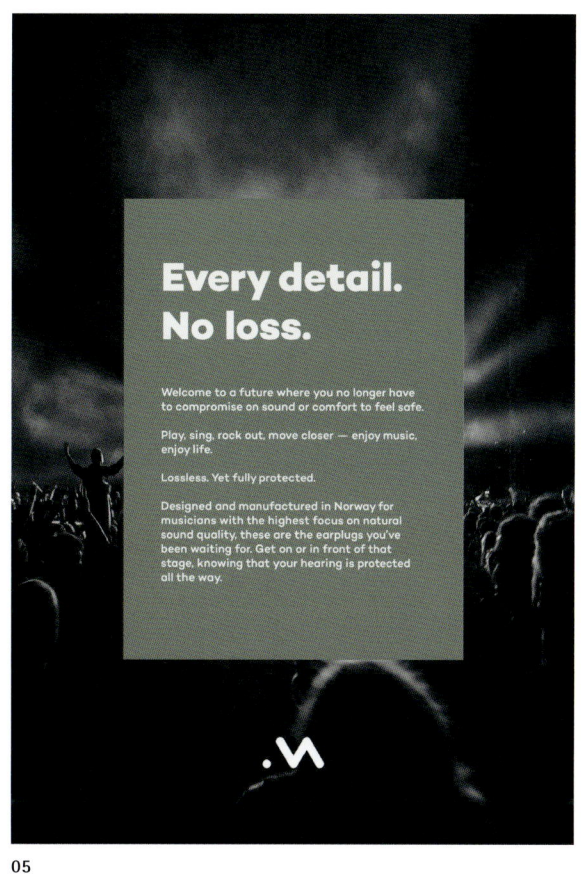

01 Minuendo logo

02 Advertising

03 Packaging

04 | 05 Large-scale poster advertising

Red Dot: Medical Brand

Drawbridge Health

The US healthcare technology company Drawbridge Health was founded in 2015 by GE Ventures and GE Healthcare. The company's goal is to advance blood sampling solutions so everyone everywhere can get insights into their personal health. Drawbridge Health launched the OneDraw Blood Collection Device as its first product in 2020. The small and innovative blood sample device was developed to make taking a blood sample easy and convenient and to stabilise the sample. Instead of a needle, it uses tiny lancets and vacuum technology to take blood from the upper arm and draw it into a removable cartridge. The blood is absorbed and stabilised, which means that the sample can be mailed without the need for it to be refrigerated.

The brand presence creates a close visual connection to the subject of blood sampling. The graphically designed red drop in the logo symbolises the convenient and comfortable blood sampling approach, which leads to optimised health via data and actionable insights. The simplicity of the logo thus reflects the ease of this process. The drop is placed in front of the brand name as part of the logo mark. At the same time, the drop represents the connecting element across all media in the entire visual brand identity. The clear, simple shape and surface of the drop can be used to display information and as an outline for numbering or pictograms; a multitude of small, colourful drops can serve as a decorative frieze or format-filling background of an advertisement. Matching individual health subjects, the outline of the drop can also be filled with suitable structures. The key visual element thus combines great creative freedom with an equally strong sense of identity. The brand design of Drawbridge Health is simple and memorable, enabling people to identify with the brand and recognise it at any time – regardless of whether they encounter the brand in a doctor's office, on billboards, in advertisements or on social media.

01

Advertising	Packaging Design	Fair Stands	Retail Design	Red Dot: Junior Award	Designer Profiles	Index
288	318	494	516	544	614	674

Company
Drawbridge Health, Inc.

Founding Year
2015

Headquarters
San Diego, USA

Lead Agency
Ruby Consulting Group
San Jose, USA

Number of Employees
15–20

Claim
Advancing blood sampling solutions to empower everyone everywhere with insights into their personal health, while preserving public health.

Website
www.drawbridgehealth.com

Red Dot Awards
2020

02

03

04

01 Drawbridge Health logo

02 OneDraw&Know advertising with award-winning OneDraw™ [Blood Collection Device]

03 Brand identity

04 Large-scale advertising

Red Dot: Energy Brand

Tibber

Tibber is a Norwegian digital energy company that was founded in 2016 with the aim of supplying households with 100 per cent renewable energy, while also offering end customers transparency and control over their electricity consumption and costs via a user-friendly smartphone app. With this idea, the start-up initially became popular mainly among early adopters who shared an affinity for technology. In the early stages, Tibber's brand communication was imbued more by the technological aspects – promoting the app and its high-tech features as key differentiators. Visually too the brand was at first associated more as a tech start-up than an established energy provider.

In order to reach end users worldwide, Tibber had to be redefined and repositioned. The challenge was to transform the brand in such a way that it would resonate with a broader audience and build trust, without losing its original identity, twist and appeal. The aim was to raise interest with a different, smart and playful approach in order to set itself apart as a young brand from the competition of established electricity providers.

The existing values of human centricity, sustainability, usability as well as curiosity were defined as a central starting point in the repositioning of the brand. The aim was to create a resonating identity for a broader audience, which would also shift the focus in communication towards comprehensible benefits instead of purely technical features. The core attributes of the brand were defined as the basis for the new brand identity – Tibber should be perceived as dynamic and smart, yet always humane and inclusive. Today, Tibber also uses word plays, but remains clear in the message and avoids technical jargon altogether. Meanwhile, the visual identity has also been sharpened: the concise logo in light blue combines a stylised lightning bolt with the brand name in small letters. The visual approach combines photographs of modern family lifestyles with quirky and disruptive details derived from pop culture. Visual and tonal elements complement each other by enriching the same message in order to ensure that the brand is uniformly recognised.

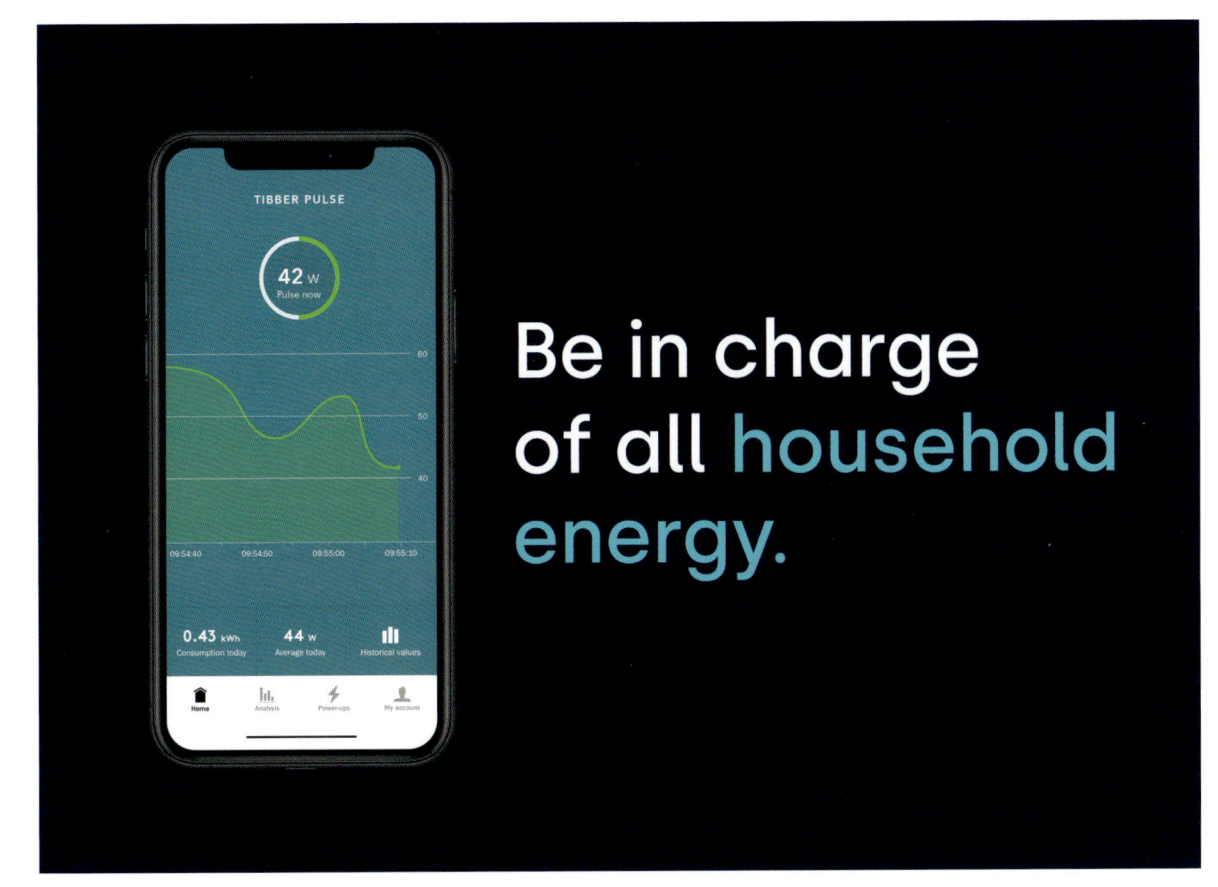

Advertising	Packaging Design	Fair Stands	Retail Design	Red Dot: Junior Award	Designer Profiles	Index
288	318	494	516	544	614	674

Company
Tibber AB

Founding Year
2016

Headquarters
Førde, Norway

Lead Agency
Wörks
Helsinki, Finland

Company Founder
Edgeir Vardal Aksnes, Daniel Lindén

Number of Employees
50

Claim
More power. Less electricity. /
Join the Electric Revolution

Website
www.tibber.com

Red Dot Awards
2020

02

03

01 Tibber logo

02 App advertising

03 Banner advertising

Red Dot: Household Brand

Mr. Eco

Mr. Eco is a sub-brand of the company MARTINI SPA, a leader in Italy in the field of home care and personal care accessories. MARTINI SPA has taken an environmentally friendly and more sustainable approach for many years. However, it is in 2020 that the brand Mr. Eco was presented as the company's response to the increasing demand for environmentally friendly products. Under the brand name Mr. Eco, a new collection of sponges and accessories for household cleaning are being launched, all made from organic, biodegradable raw materials. The product range comprises sponges made of vegetable cellulose, loofah and natural fibre scrubbers, antibacterial dish brushes made of copper and stainless steel, scouring sponges made of wood with sisal bristles and viscose cloths made of bamboo and cotton.

Constituting the key element of the visual brand identity, the logotype of the brand name reminds one of a face due to the lettering and two complementing leaves, which are positioned below the brand name and thus look like a moustache. The "Mr." stands in a smaller font above "Eco", drawing additional attention to the message that the products are environmentally friendly. The font Walsheim with its geometric sans-serif letters was chosen as it projects the notions of openness and friendliness. As for the visual language, the logo is placed on a green sponge turning it into the charming brand ambassador Mr. Eco, who even has grown arms and legs in order to come to life in both print media and short films to provide consumers with tips on recycling and environmental protection.

The packaging, in which all Mr. Eco products present themselves in retail, consists exclusively of FSC-certified paper. The packaging design too is dominated by the dark green logo on a white background. It is complemented by product information placed prominently below it in different font sizes, yet in the same typography and colour. The MARTINI SPA lettering forms the footer, which is also featured here in the same colour, so that a harmonious overall appearance is created despite the co-branding.

Advertising	Packaging Design	Fair Stands	Retail Design	Red Dot: Junior Award	Designer Profiles	Index
288	318	494	516	544	614	674

Company
MARTINI SPA

Founding Year
1969

Headquarters
Coenzo di Sorbolo Mezzani, Italy

Lead Agency
AD STORE ITALIA
Parma, Italy

Company Founder
Fulvio Martini

Number of Employees
53

Claim
#SOFTENYOURLIFE

Website
www.martinispa.com

Red Dot Awards
2020

01 Mr. Eco logo

02 Sponges with printing

03 Booth

Red Dot: Tableware Brand

Luzerne

Luzerne draws on over 70 years of tableware manufacturing expertise from its parent company Hiap Huat Holdings headquartered in Singapore. Since 2004, Luzerne has been designing and producing premium-quality tableware for renowned restaurants, hotels and chefs around the world, as well as for Singapore Airlines. Among other things, Luzerne pioneered the creation of fine china without animal bone ash. Today, Luzerne produces up to 28 million pieces of ceramic and stone tableware annually at their fully-automated factory in Dehua, China, a city that is also known as the World Ceramics Capital. Every piece is refined and perfected by hand at the end of the production process – it is painted or glazed by hand according to the design specifications. Luzerne also produces series that are created in cooperation with artists, architects and external designers.

The Luzerne word mark consists of a characteristically curved custom script "L" and the rest of the company name, which appears in Times Regular. The brand's primary colour palette comprises a turquoise blue (Pantone 3115 C) and a grey tone (Pantone 877 C), as well as black and white. The brand vision of Luzerne is "Everyday Best", which expresses the claim that it offers tableware of high quality in terms of design, craftsmanship and manufacturing for use in everyday life as well as for special occasions. This claim is further underlined by an image style that stages the tableware as part of stylishly laid tables and artfully arranged dishes – in many cases photographed frontally from above, resulting in an appearance of strong geometric structures.

In order to bring the brand to life, "The Luzerne" was opened in Dehua in 2019, a hybrid of hotel, museum and factory, in which guests are invited to learn about the rich tradition and present of the porcelain craft. Ceramic culture is omnipresent there: in the rooms, while dining in the teahouse or on the rooftop terrace, as works of art in the hallways, in the shop, in the museum and in the artist workshops, where guests are welcomed to lend a hand themselves. In addition, Luzerne also acts as a sponsor of events such as the World Gourmet Summit, which ensures a high level of brand recognition in the hotel and catering industry.

01

Advertising	Packaging Design	Fair Stands	Retail Design	Red Dot: Junior Award	Designer Profiles	Index
288	318	494	516	544	614	674

02

03

Company
Luzerne Pte Ltd

Founding Year
1947

Headquarters
Singapore

Lead Agency
The Secret Little Agency
Singapore

Company Founder
Lek Song Cheng

Number of Employees
700

Claim
Everyday Best

Website
www.luzerne.com

Red Dot Awards
2020

04

05

01 Luzerne logo

02 | 03 Tableware set-up

04 Interior of The Luzerne

05 Fair stand

Red Dot: Sanitary Brand

Geberit

Geberit is a global, stock-listed company that produces sanitaryware, and was originally founded in 1874 by Caspar Melchior Albert Gebert in Rapperswil-Jona, Switzerland. For a long time the company focused on the B2B market and targeted wholesalers, installers and planners with the claim "Know-How Installed". In 2015, however, Geberit acquired the Finnish Sanitec Group with its many different ceramic brands that were all primarily focused on B2C. This made it necessary to reposition Geberit as a B2B2C brand, as end consumers were also to be reached directly in the future.

The old brand claim "Know-How Installed" clearly referred to Geberit's competencies behind the wall, a B2B positioning that has remained unchanged in the newly developed brand identity. For the B2C area, however, the focus was placed on the combination of design and functionality in order to differentiate Geberit from the competition that primarily focuses on the connection between bathroom and wellness. The new claim for the target group of interior architects and end consumer reads "Design Meets Function".

In 2019 and 2020, some local ceramic brands were integrated into the Geberit brand with a uniform new design defined by a new, consolidated visual corporate identity. Apart from the well-established square of the Geberit brand, the letter "G" serves as a key visual element. The new corporate design uses the same fonts and grids in both the B2B and the B2C communications. Differences are allowed, however, in the picture styles and the colour spectrum, which provides warm natural tones for the B2C area. The brand concepts and their attributes were also translated into a sound DNA, on the basis of which the new Geberit brand sound identity was developed.

The new B2B2C brand identity is to be further developed in 2020 and 2021 and to be implemented in marketing campaigns, showrooms, POS concepts, as well as events and trade fairs, which will ensure a consistent and strong identity across all elements.

Advertising	Packaging Design	Fair Stands	Retail Design	Red Dot: Junior Award	Designer Profiles	Index
288	318	494	516	544	614	674

Company
Geberit AG

Founding Year
1874

Headquarters
Rapperswil-Jona, Switzerland

Lead Agency
Kunde & Co.
Copenhagen, Denmark

Company Founder
Caspar Melchior Albert Gebert

Number of Employees
12,000

Claim
Design meets Function,
Know-How Installed

Website
www.geberit.com

Red Dot Awards
2012, 2015, 2016, 2018–2020

01 Geberit logo

02 Corporate design guidebook

03 | 04 Advertising

Red Dot: Sanitary Brand

INAX

INAX is a Japanese manufacturer of sanitaryware and bathroom fittings that can look back on a long tradition. The company's origins go back to 1915 when architect Frank Lloyd Wright was commissioned to design a new building for the Imperial Hotel in Tokyo. As the terracotta tiles for the walls required special firing techniques, a dedicated factory was established back then in Tokoname, Aichi Prefecture. Hatsunojo Ina and his son Chozaburo Ina were invited to become technical advisors for this project. Upon the completion of the hotel, they took on the workers and the equipment of that factory, creating Ina Seito Co., Ltd. in 1924, which later became INAX Corporation. INAX has made a name for itself over the years by developing innovations such as the first made-in-Japan shower toilet with hot water and an air dryer function in 1967 and later with automatic and contactless fittings.

In 2019, INAX presented its new brand identity at the Milan Design Week. At the heart of the new brand identity is the "INAX Blue" brand colour that is used in different gradients depending on the medium and which creates a consistent brand experience across all media from advertising and packaging to communication media such as catalogues, trade fair and showroom designs, as well as the products themselves. While the colour is used offensively in communication design to ensure concision and a high level of visibility for the brand, its use on products is kept very subtle. For example, if operating parts such as buttons and levers are operated on the products, they appear in the INAX brand colour, which makes the status and operation of the product intuitive to understand for users. However, the colour remains invisible when the product is not in use, preventing it from interfering with the bathroom environment.

In addition to the colour details and in order to create a signature look, INAX uses easy-to-recognise design elements such as the so-called "squoval" shapes. Defined as a hybrid that is part square and part oval, this shape incorporates strictly geometric and organic elements and thus epitomises the connection between people and architecture, a connection that INAX aims to strengthen and harmoniously enhance with the design of its products.

INAX

01

Advertising	Packaging Design	Fair Stands	Retail Design	Red Dot: Junior Award	Designer Profiles	Index
288	318	494	516	544	614	674

Company
LIXIL Corporation

Founding Year
1924 (Ina Seito Co., Ltd.)

Headquarters
Tokyo, Japan

Company Founder
Chozaburo Ina

Claim
THE RITUALS OF WATER
TRANSFORM EVERYDAY LIFE

Website
www.inax.com

Red Dot Awards
2020

→ You can also find this brand on the pages 187 and 499.

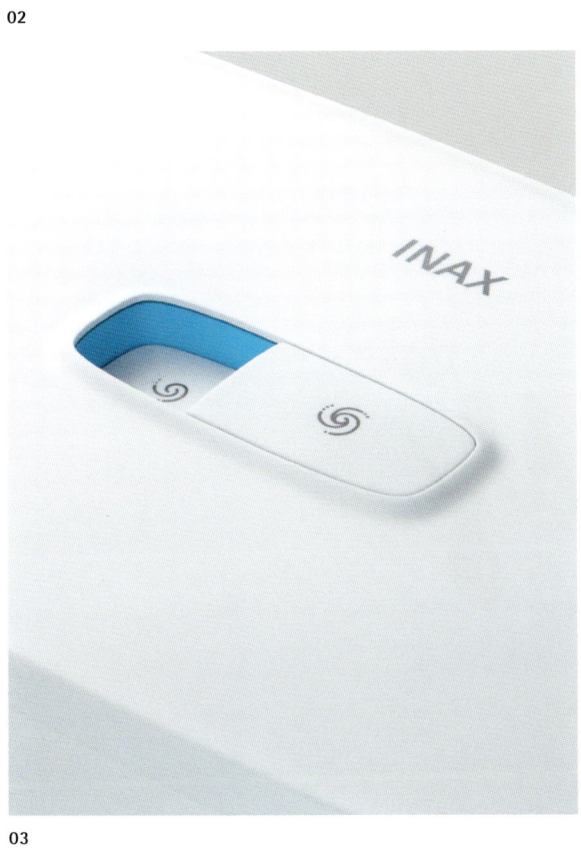

02

03

04

01 INAX logo

02 Packaging

03 | 04 Brand identity

Red Dot: Sanitary Brand

Callaly

Callaly is a British start-up company that develops and sells period products under the motto "Reinventing Period Care". It was founded by gynaecologist Alex Hooi who teamed up with garment technologist Ewa Radziwon to design a new product that – more than 80 years after the first tampon was launched on the market – brings innovation to the industry. The result is the tampliner, a hybrid two-in-one combination of tampon and mini panty liner. The Callaly brand was created based on this product innovation. In addition to tampliners, the company also produces pads and liners made of organic cotton and sells the products directly to customers.

Following the guiding principle "Reinventing Period Care", the brand and the products sold under the brand name should also visually stand out from other period products previously available on the market. The brand's visual identity also pushes the boundaries of the industry standard packaging, which otherwise looks either neutral and clinical or pretty and feminine. Instead, Callaly uses bold colours in combination with a contemporary-looking graphic style. This makes for attractively packaged products that can easily lie around visibly instead of being hidden deep down inside a bag or the bathroom cabinet. Also specially designed for the brand was a distinctive font, which is based on handwriting and is therefore marked by rounded shapes and soft lines that are also inspired by feminine curves. For direct sales, a delivery box system has been developed that can be flexibly packed according to customer needs. The boxes feature a discreet outer layer for mailing. They unfold when opened and reveal a colourful interior featuring appealingly designed information about the brand and the products, complemented by a reminder to recycle the packaging after use. Inside the boxes, every single product comes in its own compostable or biodegradable packaging, which is produced using a variable printing technique so that no two packs are exactly alike.

In combination with a clear visual language and the direct appeal to end customers, this brand has emerged with an image appeal that is self-confident, engaging and open.

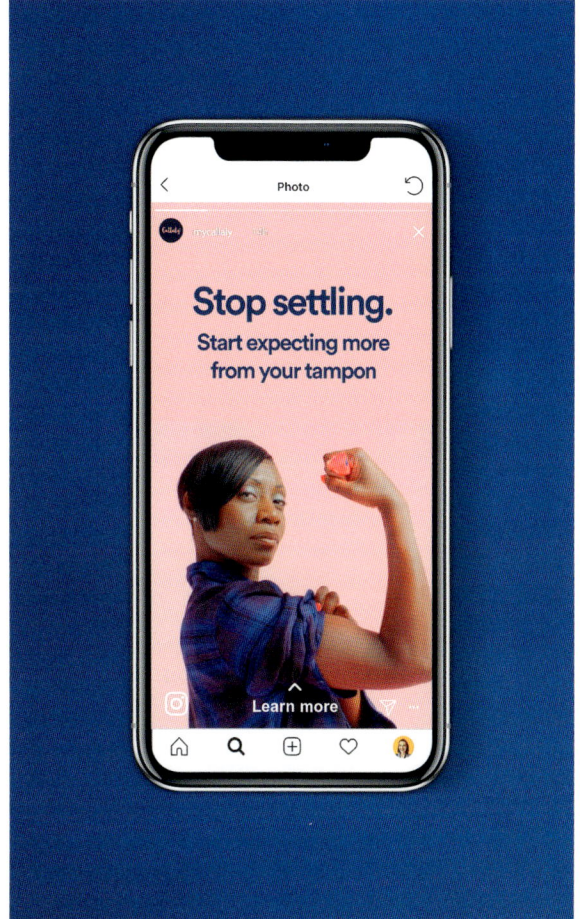

Advertising	Packaging Design	Fair Stands	Retail Design	Red Dot: Junior Award	Designer Profiles	Index
288	318	494	516	544	614	674

Company
Calla Lily Personal Care Ltd

Founding Year
2014

Headquarters
London, United Kingdom

Lead Agency
Design Bridge London
London, United Kingdom

Company Founder
Dr. Alex Hooi, Thang Vo-Ta, Ewa Radziwon

Number of Employees
22

Website
www.calla.ly

Red Dot Awards
2020

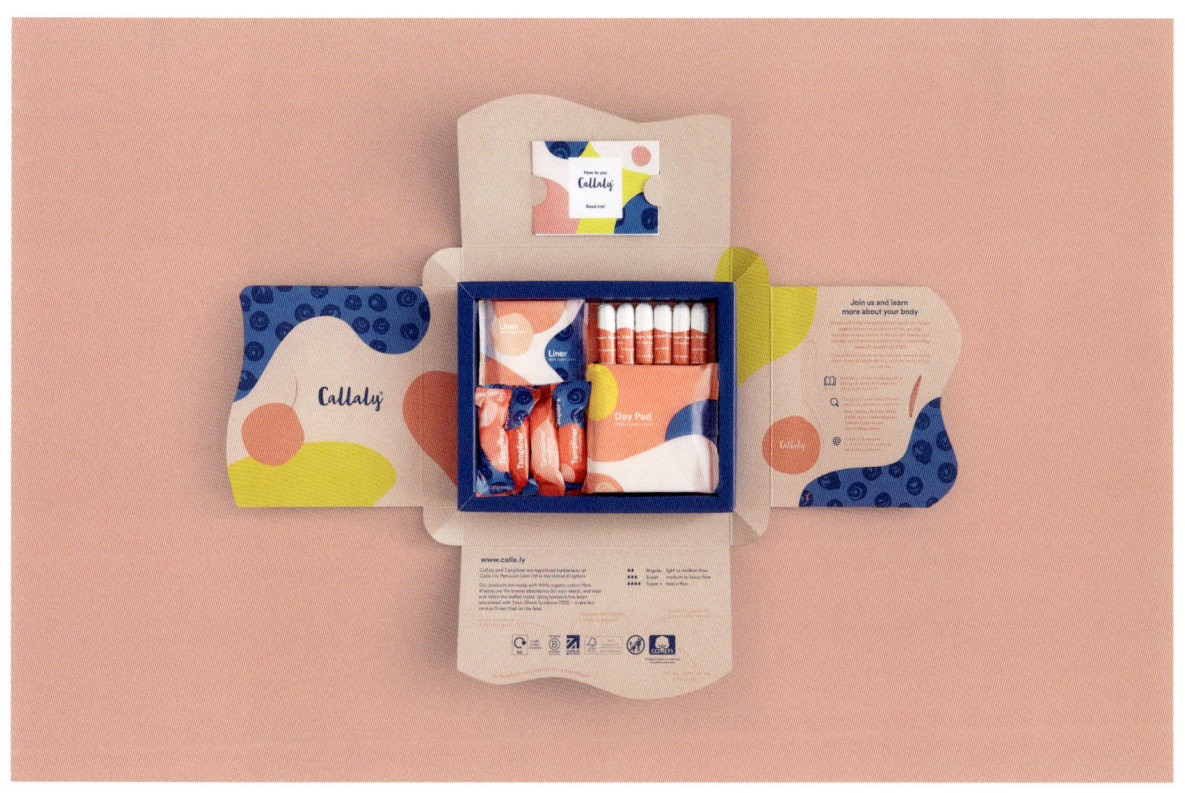

01 Callaly logo

02 Product line

03 Tampliner

04 Social media

05 Packaging

Red Dot: Beauty & Care Brand

YUNOS

Founded in Berlin in 2019, YUNOS produces and sells skincare products and dietary supplements for men. The brand name YUNOS is an amalgamation of different notions. The Y illustrates the various decisions one has to make at the forks in life. The letter U stands for the English "you", while NOS is derived from the Spanish word for "us". These letters aim at expressing the deep and trusting connection between consumers and the brand. In addition, the letter Y also serves as a concise trademark. The products of the brand are all developed and manufactured in Germany and are free of any potentially harmful ingredients. This uncompromising philosophy is vividly expressed by the claim "Clean Performance for Men".

All products, their packaging and communication media are crafted in-house. The design language combines classic design elements with contemporary qualities to form a minimal and focused brand appearance that projects vibrancy and self-confidence. The black colour embodies the aspect of "Performance", while white is intuitively associated to symbolise "Clean" in terms of purity. The expressive packaging design successfully visualises the brand's character flexibly across various shapes and materials, thereby creating a uniform brand appearance with a high level of brand recognition.

The products are only distributed online. This makes the YUNOS online shop the major consumer touchpoint with the brand. The shop was designed using a mobile-first approach to cater to the fact that most purchases are today made from mobile devices. Large product and lifestyle images mirror the brand's core elements of self-confidence and sophistication. Social media channels in particular are mainly used to attract the attention of customers, to engage them in a meaningful dialogue and thus to achieve lasting customer loyalty.

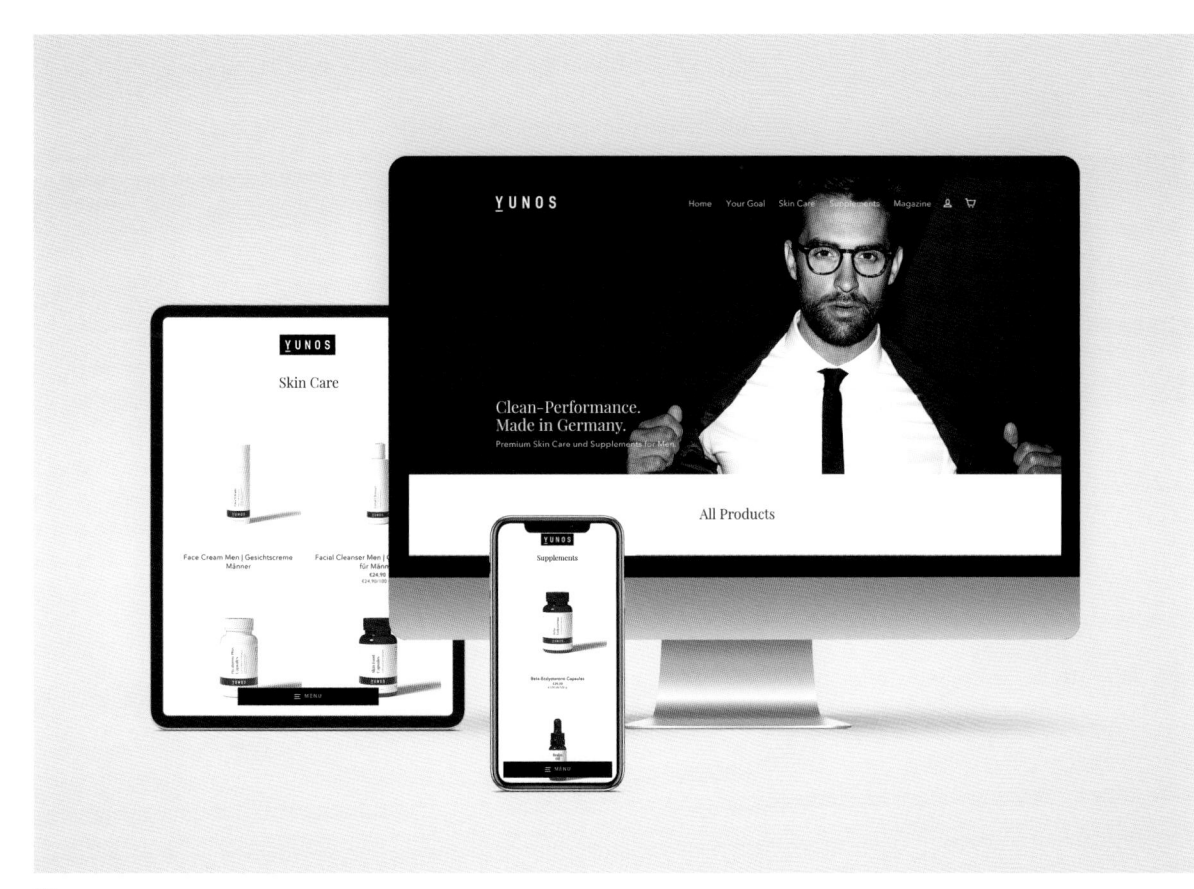

Advertising	Packaging Design	Fair Stands	Retail Design	Red Dot: Junior Award	Designer Profiles	Index
288	318	494	516	544	614	674

Company
Yunos GmbH

Founding Year
2019

Headquarters
Berlin, Germany

Lead Agency
New Fuel
Berlin, Germany

Company Founder
Mischa Rugolo, Moritz Hellwig

Number of Employees
5

Claim
Clean Performance for Men

Website
www.yunos.de

Red Dot Awards
2020

02

01 YUNOS logo

02 Digital platforms

03 Product line

03

Red Dot: Personal Care Brand

Satisfyer

Satisfyer is a brand that belongs to the Triple A Internetshops GmbH based in Bielefeld, Germany, and which provides sexual wellness products and devices. Since it was founded in 2016, the Satisfyer brand has relied on a diversified portfolio that is targeted at women, men and couples. Steadily growing since then, the brand today is one of the leading international providers in the category of sexual wellness with more than 200 love toy products that combine technical innovations with ergonomics and design. In 2019, it was decided to reposition the brand with the aim of getting the products out of the rather perceived sleazy market image and offering people worldwide equal access to products for sexual well-being – regardless of gender, sexual orientation or socio-economic background. The branding and the products thus were to pique curiosity about the diverse and colourful world of sexuality.

The new appearance clearly communicates the new positioning of Satisfyer. Thus, the brand design, for example, offers the possibility of combining an infinite number of colours with one another. In this way, the Satisfyer word mark can appear against plain backgrounds in continually different colours. The logo is made up of the abstracted letters S and F, which feature two dots as heads to make them reminiscent of playing figures. Galano Grotesque, a font that is geometric, easy-to-read and expressive, was selected as the corporate typography. The packaging design is marked by filigree illustrations that identify the products as belonging to specific categories. In addition, a pictogram system also based on illustrations consisting of 60 symbols was developed that highlight the most important product features; a further 80 pictograms communicate the various product benefits on the back of the packaging. The points of contact between brand and consumer – such as the website, advertising, app and the products themselves – have been designed to project a modern, playful and courageous appeal and at the same time express diversity, individuality and sexual self-confidence as part of a contemporary lifestyle. The imagery is colourful and visualises a wide variety of different people to promote the diversity of sexual wellness.

01

Advertising	Packaging Design	Fair Stands	Retail Design	Red Dot: Junior Award	Designer Profiles	Index
288	318	494	516	544	614	674

Company
Triple A Internetshops GmbH

Founding Year
2016

Headquarters
Bielefeld, Germany

Company Founder
André Geske

Number of Employees
200

Claim
Join the App RLOVEution

Website
www.satisfyer.com

Red Dot Awards
2017, 2018, 2020

→ You can also find this brand on page 445.

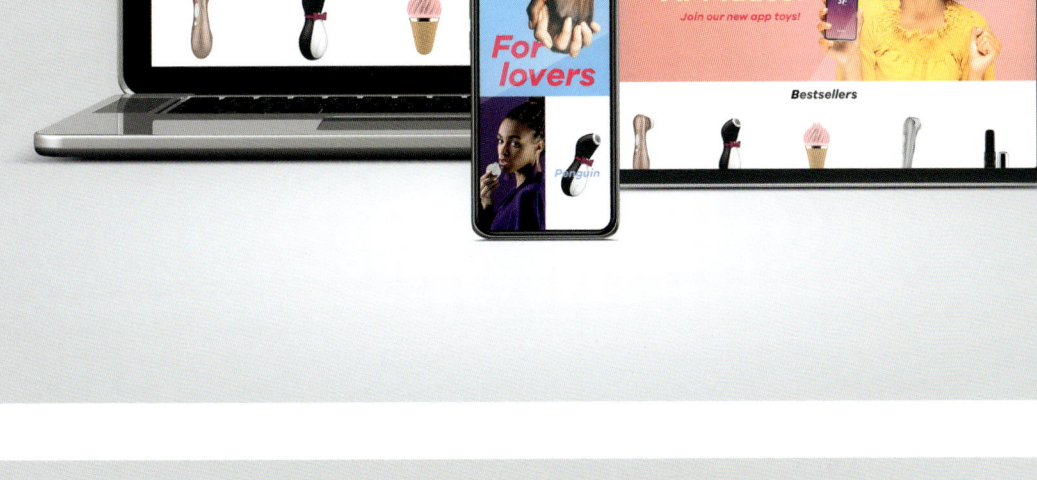

02

03

01 Satisfyer logo

02 Digital platforms

03 Product line, packaging design

Red Dot: Sports Brand

UYN

UYN is a high-tech functional apparel brand launched in 2018 by Trerè Innovation, a leading Italian company in the development, production and distribution of high-tech clothing, with more than 60 years of experience in the segment. Sportswear is developed under the UYN brand that combines purely natural raw materials with high-tech innovations, guaranteeing functionality and comfort. The brand thus appeals to both recreational sports enthusiasts and Olympic champions across many disciplines. A multidisciplinary in-house creative team was entrusted with the development of the new brand and the expanded brand communication.

The brand name UYN, which has been transferred to a distinctive word mark, is an acronym for the brand slogan "Unleash Your Nature". The slogan also includes an invitation to buyers to do their best, as well as the company's promise to support any type of athlete with products and help athletes to get the best performance out of themselves. The communication strategy aims to focus the promotion on innovation and the resulting product performance. The imagery in advertisements, presentations, lookbooks and so forth harmoniously locates the brand between cutting-edge technology and high design demands, successfully appealing to a young, style-conscious target group with great sporting ambitions. The short films showcase the products in use from partially unusual and surprising angles. Sometimes technical features are highlighted, while at other times well-known professional athletes have their say as brand ambassadors.

The packaging of the products is made of environmentally friendly FSC-certified materials and has been designed to clearly communicate the special product characteristics through text and icons. The technical-stylish brand appearance consistently extends into the look of exhibition stands and pop-up stores: architecture and interior design come together to attract attention and create a three-dimensional brand experience.

Advertising	Packaging Design	Fair Stands	Retail Design	Red Dot: Junior Award	Designer Profiles	Index
288	318	494	516	544	614	674

Company
Trerè Innovation S.r.l

Founding Year
1992

Headquarters
Asola, Mantua Province, Italy

Company Founder
Luigi Redini

Number of Employees
800

Claim
Unleash your nature

Website
www.uynsports.com

Red Dot Awards
2020

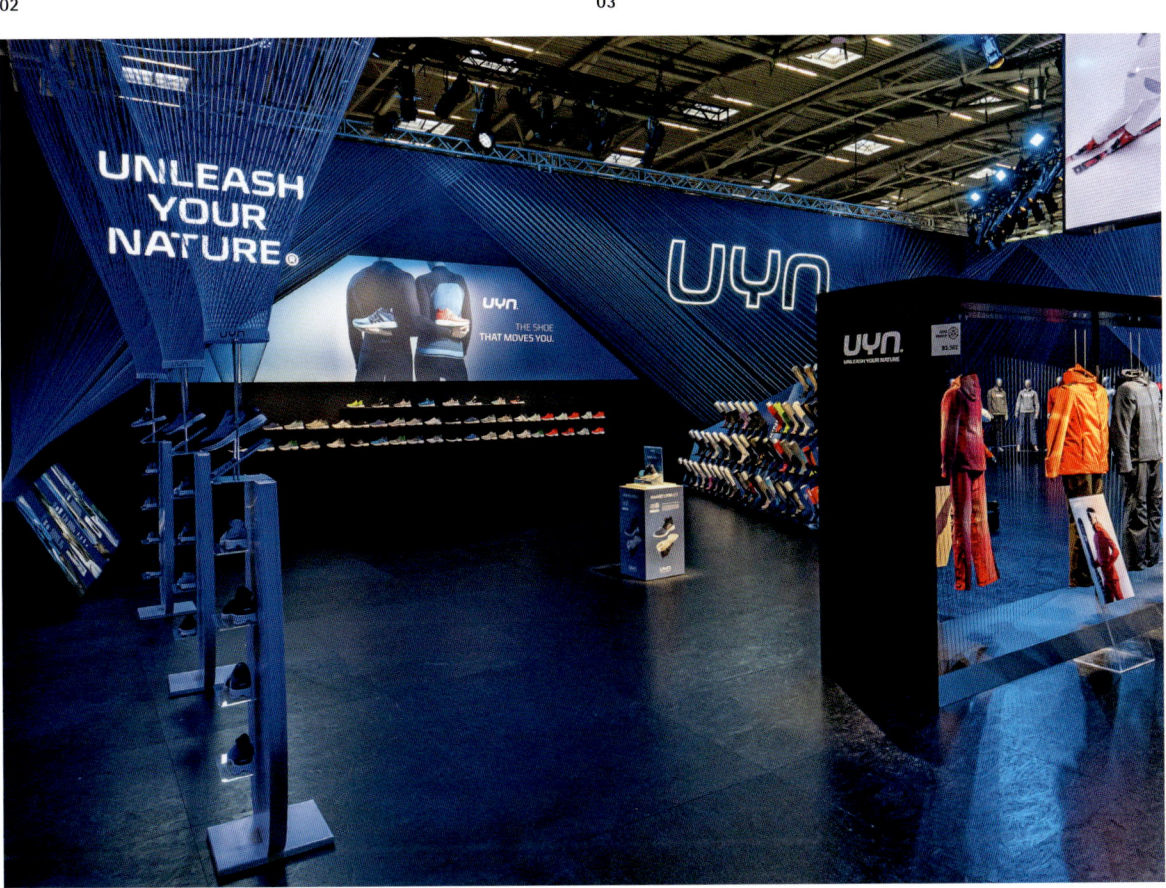

01 UYN logo

02 | 03 Advertising

04 Fair stand at ISPO, Munich, Germany

Red Dot: Outdoor Brand

ULAC

ULAC's beginnings go back to 1982, when ULAC started off as an original equipment manufacturer in Taiwan working with international brands including Master Lock, Panasonic, Giant Bicycles and Assa Abloy. After accumulating experience with locks for over 25 years, the company launched its in-house brand in 2015 under which the silicone locks of the Si Works collection were brought onto the market. The second step was the development of a fingerprint lock release, which brought the brand to the next level. Today, new product concepts are created in-house in the U-Lab in close cooperation with designers and engineers and are produced in the company's own factory so that they can be tested directly. ULAC has made a name for itself in the cycling industry with the introduction of new technologies such as fingerprint release locks, alarm systems or RFID in bicycle locks, as well as with the award-winning designs of the locks themselves. With the presentation of the IRON fingerprint padlock at the Taipei Cycle Show 2019, the brand achieved international reach for the first time. The distinctive word mark with the two dots above the letter A features on all products and in all cross-media communication.

The brand identity of ULAC is based on the idea of experimenting with the latest technologies when developing the locks, while at the same time playing with colours and shapes. The message behind this is that ULAC's locks offer more than just functionality – they are also a way of expressing one's own individuality. Driven by the guiding principle "A bike lock is not just a bike lock", the brand positions itself as a lifestyle brand for urban cyclists. Accordingly, the advertising campaigns illustrate how the locks are used by trend-conscious young people in everyday life. This approach is reinforced by the Lonely Riders Cult, a cycling community set up by ULAC under its own logo and which invites cycling enthusiasts to exchange ideas. In addition, the brand also has a strong social media presence and it partners with many international influencers, artists, local bike shops and cycling events to further strengthen the brand's image in the cycling community.

01

Advertising	Packaging Design	Fair Stands	Retail Design	Red Dot: Junior Award	Designer Profiles	Index
288	318	494	516	544	614	674

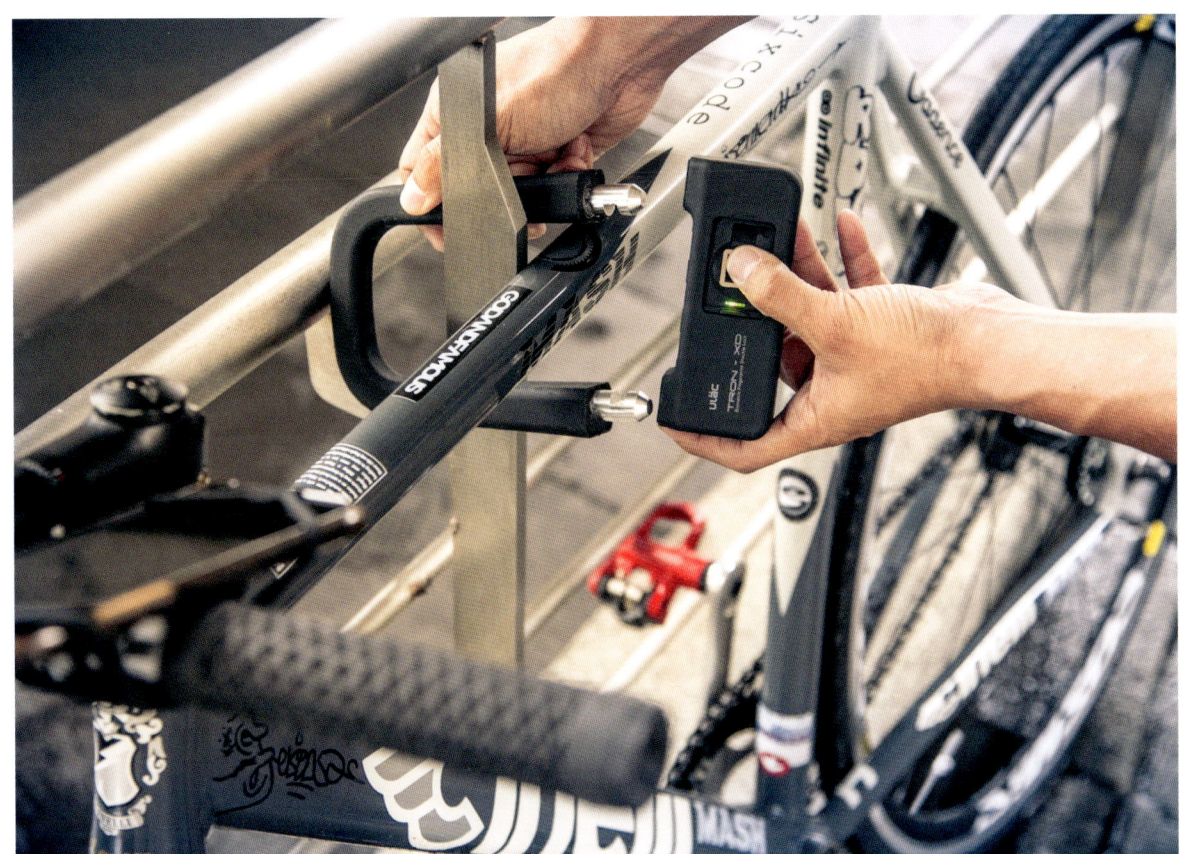

Company
ULAC Corporation

Founding Year
1982

Headquarters
Taipei, Taiwan

Company Founder
KC Shen

Number of Employees
30

Website
www.ulaclock.com

Red Dot Awards
2020

02

03

01 ULAC logo

02 TRON – XD [Fingerprint Shackle Lock]

03 Share your stories campaign

Red Dot: Tourism Brand

Sojeho Project

The Sojeho Project is a local district development project in South Korea that aims to save the village of Soje-dong, located in Daejeon, from extinction and demolition. The old railroad village was built during the Japanese colonial era as a quarter for the workers along the then new railway line between Seoul and Busan. Located in the area of Lake Soje (Sojeho), the lake itself was filled back then for this very purpose. In total, there used to be over 100 residences in the area, of which only about 40 are left. Although some people still live in those residences, they are in danger of demolition due to rapid redevelopment. In 2017, urban developers recognised the potential of the district with its geographical location, as well as its architecture and history. Taking its name from the former lake, the Sojeho Project aims to preserve the historic structures of the railway villages and to fill them with new life in order to inform the public about local history.

The lake also plays a key role in the project's brand identity. It serves as a symbol connecting past and present. The motto of the project reads "Back to Lake" and the logo is made up of the defining elements of the quarter – the houses and the lake, symbolised by a triangle and horizontal lines that represent stylised waves. The "Sojeho Blue", which represents the lake and can also be used in combination with light reflections, as well as various hues of grey reflecting the epochs were conceived of as brand colours.

The old houses have been repaired and revitalised according to the guidelines of the project, which envisions the settlement of businesses with a local reference, a history and following sustainable approaches. Today, displays highlighting the corporate design of the project and discreet glass plates installed at each location guide visitors through the quarter and provide information about the original function and history of the buildings, thus making the present and the past converge. Moreover, the function or value embodied by the local cafe, boutique, atelier or craft studio, for instance, is communicated through a sophisticated system of abbreviations: Local Resource (Lo), Farm to Table (Fa), Curation (Cu), Eco Friendly (Ec), Craftsmanship (Cr). All of these measures not only brought new life to the neighbourhood, but also received a lot of media and public attention, turning Daejeon into an attractive tourist destination.

01

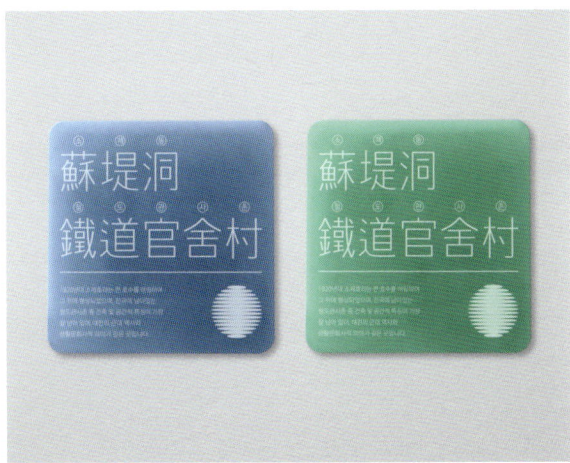

Advertising	Packaging Design	Fair Stands	Retail Design	Red Dot: Junior Award	Designer Profiles	Index
288	318	494	516	544	614	674

Company
Iksundada Studio

Founding Year
2014

Headquarters
Seoul, South Korea

Company Founder
Hanah Park, Jihyun Park

Number of Employees
25

Claim
The More, The Better.

Website
http://sojeho.kr

Red Dot Awards
2020

01 Sojeho Project logo

02 Nameplate

03 Coaster

04 Tea room

05 Information signboard in Daejeon, South Korea

06 Brochure with map

Red Dot: Fashion Brand

NEIXIU

The Chinese eyewear brand NEIXIU was founded in 2014 by Tong Xu, a professor at the China Central Academy of Fine Arts, and Minghong Shi, a PhD candidate at the National Taiwan University of Arts. The unique selling proposition of the NEIXIU Silverwork Glasses brand consists of a combination of the traditional Chinese handicraft of silversmithing with a contemporary, international eyewear design appearance. The brand logo is composed of the calligraphic Chinese characters for "nei" (inside, included) and "xiu" (fabulous, exhibit). The appearance of the two characters is reminiscent of the carillon from the Warring States period (around 475–221 BC). This logo, which can also combine with the NEIXIU lettering depending on its use, characterises the entire brand identity. Executed in silver, the two characters dominate the design of the otherwise minimalist, white packaging and the eyewear boxes, lending them an elegant and high-quality appeal. With their concise appearance, these characters clearly communicate the brand behind the eyewear on advertisements and at the point of sale.

The eyewear itself is characterised by sophisticatedly handcrafted silver elements on the temples, bridge and nose pads, which lend the simple and contemporary glasses a stylish look like jewellery. The ornaments vary depending on the series and are inspired by traditional Chinese motifs, which always project a deeper meaning. Since the exclusivity of the eyewear rests in the silversmith work, these are also brought into focus through detailed shots in advertisements. Also featured in advertisements are photographs showing self-reliant and modern-looking people using the eyewear. In addition to the calligraphic logo, often used in communication is a square with rounded corners, which frames the statement "NEIXIU Sterling Silver Accessories" in a clear, sans serif font and serves as a kind of seal to visualise and communicate the most important features of the eyewear using a few words.

Since its foundation in 2014, the NEIXIU brand has positioned itself on the Asian market as a high-quality eyewear brand thanks to its clear and consistent appearance.

Advertising	Packaging Design	Fair Stands	Retail Design	Red Dot: Junior Award	Designer Profiles	Index
288	318	494	516	544	614	674

Company
BJ GuanXiu International Trade Co., Ltd

Founding Year
2013

Headquarters
Beijing, China

Company Founder
Tong Xu, Minghong Shi

Number of Employees
20

Claim
Soft as water, Modest in soul.

Red Dot Awards
2020

01 NEIXIU logo

02 | 03 | 04 Advertising

Red Dot: Baby & Children Brand

Mokki Click & Change

Mokki is an Oslo-based Norwegian manufacturer of sunglasses. The company was founded over 31 years ago by Moshe Ohana, who had been backpacking in Norway at that time and decided to settle there to create sunglasses that are inspired by the Norwegian lifestyle and combine contemporary Nordic design with top-notch eye protection and non-compromising quality. The brand rapidly won local recognition that allowed it to expand into new markets. One of these expansions included launching the Mokki Click & Change sub-brand in 2019, a name under which special sunglasses for children are developed and sold.

The Click & Change eyewear models were developed together with children and are marked by a particularly flexible, child-friendly design. Targeted at different age groups, each model is sold in colour-coordinated packs of two – that is, one pair of sunglasses for protecting against normal sunlight and a second pair for protecting against the strong reflected UV light common in a Nordic winter. They are complemented by extra temples, as well as head and neck straps that can be flexibly clicked onto the glasses' rims and thus interchanged easily. The accessories can also be combined in various colours so that the sunglasses can be customised individually. Every package includes a glasses cleaning cloth featuring an animal head, with the aim of making cleaning the glasses fun for children.

Addressing a new and younger target group required adjusting the brand identity, including the expansion of the brand's colour palette – the predominantly black and white appearance was therefore supplemented with cheerful colours. The word mark consists of the established but now more closely spaced Mokki lettering with the two interlaced Ks, enhanced by the "Click & Change" subline. The double K also acts as a brand identifier on the children's glasses products. The entire brand identity of Mokki Click & Change is characterised by a combination of playful elements on the one hand and a purist aesthetic on the other. Many of their advertisements, for instance, focus on children wearing sunglasses, all set against a brightly coloured background, while the product films make use of stop-motion technology, which is as playful as it is simple. This results in a coherent appearance across all media, conveying the pure joy of living and appealing to both parents and children alike.

01

Advertising	Packaging Design	Fair Stands	Retail Design	Red Dot: Junior Award	Designer Profiles	Index
288	318	494	516	544	614	674

Company
MOKKI AS

Founding Year
2003

Headquarters
Oslo, Norway

Company Founder
Moshe Ohana

Number of Employees
6

Claim
We help parents make healthy choices

Website
https://mokki.com

Red Dot Awards
2020

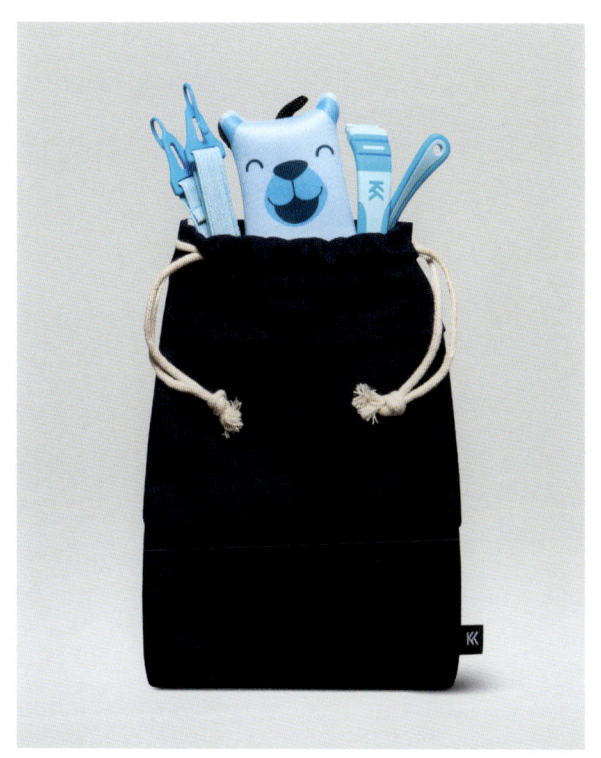

01 Mokki Click & Change logo

02 Packaging of glasses and accessory kit

03 | 04 Click & Change system to go

Red Dot: Baby & Children Brand

Konny by Erin

Konny by Erin is a manufacturer of baby carriers. The South Korea-based company was founded in 2017 by Erin Lim and her husband, Donghyun Kim, who just previously had had their first child. Due to a health problem, Erin developed severe back pain when trying to carry her child in one of the existing baby carrier systems on the market. She thus decided to design her own. The result is a product that has redeveloped baby carriers from scratch and which would meet the young mother's own high demands on safety, comfort, wearability and durability. A fundamental difference to competing products is that Konny is worn like a fitted T-shirt. The timeless, minimalist design and the careful selection of fabrics and colours also contribute to the fact that mothers feel "attached" to the system in a literal sense.

The baby carrier is designed, produced and sold under the brand name Konny by Erin. The brand name was inspired by the nickname of the couple's first child and means clean and pure. The addition "by Erin" makes it clear that the founder personally guarantees the quality of the brand. The penguin as part of the logo was inspired by a documentary on emperor penguins who watch over their offspring with utmost care and affection.

The entire communication is dominated by lovingly crafted elements (such as in the packaging design) and a personal voice in addressing customers. Conveying a high level of trustworthiness, the website and social media activities feature the company founder repeatedly reporting on her experiences as well as customer ratings, which both play a major role. The quality of the products is to speak for itself and parents all over the world are invited to share their experiences with the products at customer evaluation events and give tips to other parents.

The trustworthiness of the brand is further underlined by the fact that the company, which has seen sales of 14 million dollars already in its second full year, is highly family-friendly. Of the 16 full-time employees, a total of 14 are women and 12 of them are mothers who work from home.

Advertising	Packaging Design	Fair Stands	Retail Design	Red Dot: Junior Award	Designer Profiles	Index
288	318	494	516	544	614	674

Company
Konny by Erin Inc.

Founding Year
2017

Headquarters
Seoul, South Korea

Company Founder
Erang Lim, Donghyun Kim

Number of Employees
16

Website
https://konnybaby.com

Red Dot Awards
2020

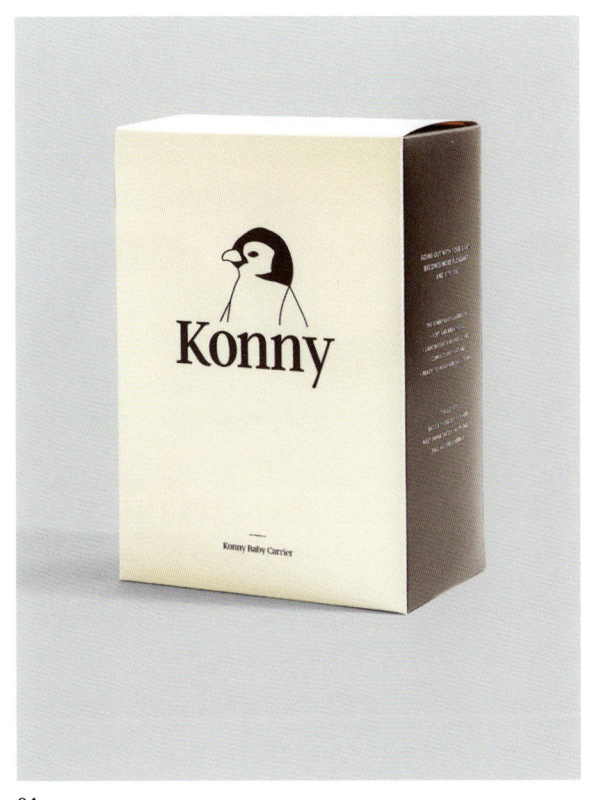

01 Konny by Erin logo

02 Konny Baby Carrier SUMMER

03 | 04 Packaging of Konny Baby Carrier

Red Dot: Baby & Children Brand

NUNA

Nuna is a brand of the Taiwanese company Wonderland Nurserygoods. Since its launch in 2007, Nuna has been positioned as a design brand for baby and toddler products to attract attention in the highly competitive baby products market. The first product ever to be launched under the Nuna brand name was the ZAAZ high chair, which was designed in Amsterdam. Its development was triggered by the question of what suitable seating for babies and toddlers at a family table could look like. The result was a high chair of comparatively simple design which, thanks to featuring a pneumatic system, was easy to adjust in height and, thanks to its compact dimensions, could be pushed right up to the table. It is products like this that fill the brand's mission statement of "Designed around your life" with energy and credibility.

Nuna has repeatedly proven its consistent design standing in various competitions, including the Red Dot Award in which numerous Nuna products have already been assessed and awarded. These design prizes are also used aggressively in communications, for example in the form of advertisements or billboard campaigns to further underline the design claim. Over the years, Nuna has thus managed to establish itself as a premium baby gear brand on a global level. Today, the brand with its organically soft lettering is an epitome of simple, functionally sophisticated and above all well-designed high-quality products.

Social media also plays a key role in increasing brand awareness, especially through influencers with whom Nuna works at a regional level in order to achieve particularly credible communication of product features. Since baby gear is still a product range that customers want to see, touch and try in a store before buying, Nuna places high importance on achieving a strong presence at the POS – with lovingly crafted shop-in-shop systems and individual products. The company's visual communication is dominated by an imagery that visualises the products in use, complemented by a distinctive typography and pastel-coloured surfaces. The resulting overall appearance projects the Nuna brand as innovative, modern, functional and likeable.

01

Advertising	Packaging Design	Fair Stands	Retail Design	Red Dot: Junior Award	Designer Profiles	Index
288	318	494	516	544	614	674

Company
Nuna International BV

Founding Year
2007

Headquarters
Leiderdorp, Netherlands

Company Founder
Kenny Cheng

Number of Employees
150–200

Claim
Nuna – Designed around your life

Red Dot Awards
2010, 2012, 2014, 2015, 2017–2020

02

03

01 NUNA logo

02 Flagship store in Taipei, Taiwan

03 Advertising

Red Dot: Food & Beverage Brand

FACT.COFFEE

FACT.COFFEE is a Shanghai-based start-up company that was founded in 2018 and aims to establish premium coffee and coffee culture in China. With an annual per capita consumption of only four cups of coffee, China's coffee market has a lot of potential for growth. In addition, thanks to China's pronounced tea culture, there is already a deep understanding of the various levels of quality for hot tea drinks, so that a premium product in the coffee sector should also generate interest. The premium strategy also offered the opportunity to support coffee farmers who, instead of growing and selling widely available low-price commercial grade coffee, can earn up to ten times the amount for specialty coffee. These background conditions led to the decision to bring specialty coffee to China under the brand name FACT.COFFEE and thereby support a sustainable coffee production. The brand name is composed of the first letters of the words Farmers, Associated, Coffee and Traders, which expresses the closeness and fair trade relations between the company and the coffee producers. At the same time, the resulting English word, "fact", also stands for something that is known or proven to be true.

Following a premium approach, the coffee is launched onto the market in limited editions. Specially designed aluminium cans in three sizes and colours – black, silver and white – have been chosen to serve as packaging. The Black Edition is the brand's most exclusive series in terms of quality and price and is limited to 50 cans. Limited to 500 cans, the Silver Edition is launched with a new variety every month, each with its own story about the featured beans, the region and the farmers. Meanwhile the White Edition series is aimed at a broader target group.

In order to position FACT.COFFEE as a premium lifestyle product in the market, the brand relies not only on limited product editions but also on an elegant and consistently purist appearance. Awareness of the brand is created through partnerships with premium brands in other industries – for instance, with the car brand McLaren – and social media campaigns that show how easily the products fit into the existing everyday life of trend- and style-conscious young people.

FACT.COFFEE

01

Advertising	Packaging Design	Fair Stands	Retail Design	Red Dot: Junior Award	Designer Profiles	Index
288	318	494	516	544	614	674

Company
FACT.COFFEE

Founding Year
2018

Headquarters
Shanghai, China

Company Founder
Patrick Pesch

Number of Employees
6

Website
www.fact.coffee

Red Dot Awards
2020

01 FACT.COFFEE logo

02 | 03 Product line

Brand Design & Identity

Red Dot: Best of the Best

BASECOFFEE®
[Brand Design]

Founded in Bamberg, Germany, in 2019 under the motto "Feel the Base", BASECOFFEE is a sustainably managed cafe with tasty soul food creations and high-quality coffee specialties. The concept is to support the fitness and well-being of its guests with healthy and lovingly prepared organic products and, with its club atmosphere and cosy furniture, to do something good for body and soul in an urban environment. Clear and minimalist, the visual appearance therefore features the basic colour of mint green complemented by additional pastel colours, which are intended to lend the notion of quality to the brand, as well as a certain lightness, independence and freshness. The new appearance is linked to hand-painted drawings that give the brand identity its own individuality and assigns different characteristics in the form of bizarre and exotic figures to the various types of coffee, which can also be ordered via the online shop. With these figures, the packaging is a real eye-catcher.

Statement by the jury
The visual identity for the sustainability-based concept of BASECOFFEE fascinates with a consistent approach that merges colours, illustrations and typography to form a coherent unit. The inviting and humorous aesthetic of the branding for a cafe, including its own coffee brand, has been well conceived and convincingly promotes the brand's contemporary urban and ecological claim.

Client
basecoffee GmbH
Bamberg, Germany

Design
rozanka GmbH
Dortmund, Germany

→ Designer profile on page 663

Red Dot: Best of the Best

Into The Great Wide Open

[Festival Campaign, Visual Identity]

The music festival "Into The Great Wide Open" on the island of Vlieland, the Netherlands, is heavily dependent on the weather conditions. Rain can cause people to stay away, whereas when the sun shines everyone is relaxed. The weather and all the data and numbers that are constantly being collected serve as the basis for the design of this campaign. In order to capture the rich ambience of the festival, a special visual language was to be developed that harmonises an artistic feel with a data-driven experiment. A poster generator was created based on the weather data of Vlieland, in that the data determined the composition of the posters and the individual elements on them. The large number of compositions showing simple geometric shapes in a friendly colour spectrum – especially light green and red tones – was used for the entire brand appearance across analogue and digital media. Over time, the generator produced a variety of compositions, giving insights into the dramatic weather changes surrounding the island in a playful manner.

Statement by the jury
The branding campaign for this festival not only fascinates with the outstanding idea of feeding the weather data surrounding the island into a generator and thus generating a high variety of compositions. The campaign also creates an aesthetic and exciting identity that takes on again and again new and different appearances, yet remains easily recognisable. This has resulted in an overall great project.

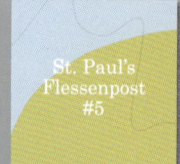

Advertising	Packaging Design	Fair Stands	Retail Design	Red Dot: Junior Award	Designer Profiles	Index
288	318	494	516	544	614	674

Client
Into The Great Wide Open
Amsterdam, Netherlands

Design
CLEVER°FRANKE
Utrecht, Netherlands
Studio Bas Koopmans
Amsterdam, Netherlands

Project Team
Studio Bas Koopmans:
Bas Koopmans (Creative Direction)

CLEVER°FRANKE:
Gert Franke (Art Direction)
Thomas Clever (Art Direction)
Roel de Jonge (Visual Design)
Jonas Groot Kormelink (Creative Coder)

→ Designer profile on page 629

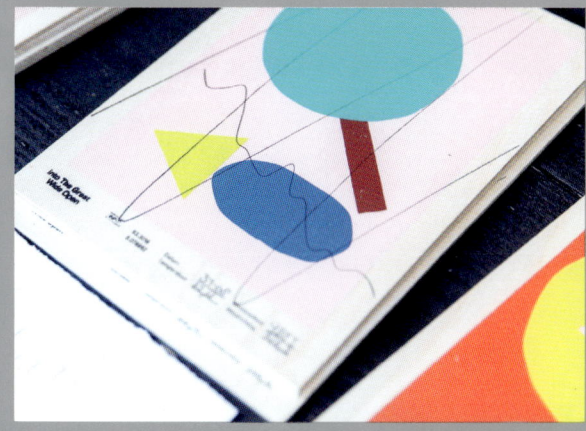

cafe noote

[Brand Design]

Client
cafe noote
New Taipei City, Taiwan

Design
think brand consultancy
Taipei City, Taiwan

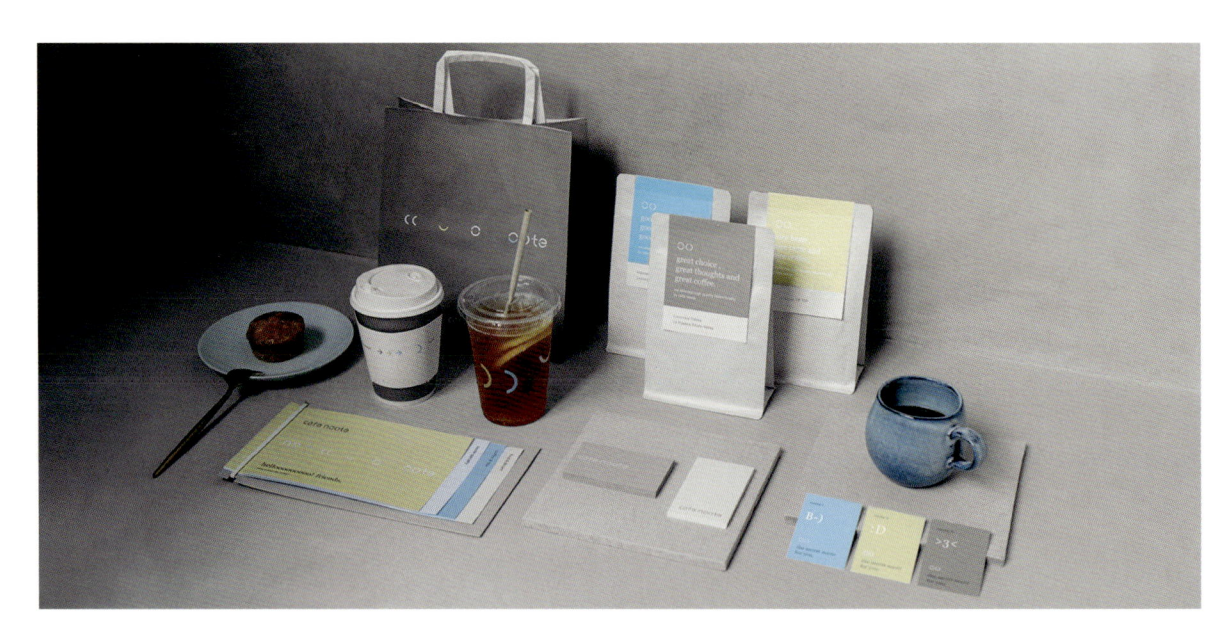

cafe noote is an indie coffee shop with a brand design that blends the minimalist character of its interior design with the emotional quality of encounters between people. Drawing upon the idea of a handwritten note, the development of the logo started with the letter "O" split into two halves to symbolise interaction and conversation. Grey is used as the main colour to create a contemporary urban look, while the bright sky blue and beige yellow add bright colour accents. In addition, handwritten messages and half circles serve as eye-catchers both in the interior design and on printed items.

ERBEN
[Brand Design Relaunch]

Client
Franz Wilhelm Langguth
Erben GmbH & Co. KG
Traben-Trarbach, Germany

Design
Pentagram
New York, USA

Project Team
Pentagram:
Paula Scher (Creative Direction)

Franz Wilhelm Langguth Erben:
Patrick F.W. Langguth (CEO)
Tajana Köhler (Design Implementation)

Advertising	Packaging Design	Fair Stands	Retail Design	Red Dot: Junior Award	Designer Profiles	Index
288	318	494	516	544	614	674

The ERBEN brand is part of a German family-owned winery established in 1789 and based in Traben-Trarbach on the Moselle River. Its relaunch is characterised by a brand design that has been pared down to the essentials. The design combines tradition with the spirit of the contemporary era, exudes poise and underlines the vision of the company to offer a wine for every taste and every occasion. The logo has been given a contemporary makeover to achieve a high level of brand recognition. It aims to appeal to young and uncomplicated wine drinkers. The logo is derived from the historical coat of arms of the company's location.

AT BEER

[Brand Design]

In order to stand out from countless other beer brands on the international market, the brand design of AT BEER focuses on the colour and texture of various beer types and has an unusually purist look. From the brand stationery to the packaging design, it showcases a contemporary design language that is characterised by colour contrasts and a distinctive logo. The claim "Delight with your color" expresses the diversity of products and underlines a joyful brand experience. Geometric ornaments on the bottleneck and can rim represent the colour and texture of foam heads.

Client
AT BEER
Seoul, South Korea

Design
Seungkwan Kang, SK Telecom
Seoul, South Korea
Yona Kang, FLAG Studio
Seoul, South Korea
Won Lim, hebe the youth
Seoul, South Korea

Mriya

[Brand Design Relaunch]

Mriya is a well-known spice brand in Ukraine. As part of its relaunch, the brand was split into two sub-brands. The brand design for the confectionery sector aims to successfully address both new, younger buyers and already existing customers. Thus, the Baby Mia character was created – a cute cupcake acting as granddaughter to her grandmother, who represents the Mriya brand itself. In addition, storytelling was used as a device to attract consumers' attention. The final step was the digital implementation, including social media and the creation of a sticker pack for messenger apps.

Client
TM Mriya
Chernihiv, Ukraine

Design
iden.team branding agency
Kyiv, Ukraine

Project Team
Maria Sencha (Creative Direction)
Kate Lebid (Art Direction)
Inna Malysh (Graphic Design)
Alexandra Shvetsova (Graphic Design)
Alice Shein (Digital Concept)
Greg Rudenko (Programming)

Wagyu Star

[Brand Design, Logo Design]

Wagyu Star is a new brand supplying Wagyu, the beef of a Japanese cattle breed that is popular with gourmets. In accordance with the name, the logo shows the graphical symbiosis of a cow's head and a star. The shiny, gold-coloured circle lends the symbol a luxurious look and feel. The overall design of the logo is based on a traditional Japanese layout style. The distinctive overall appearance is intended to give the brand an unmistakable image that expresses both trust in tradition and a first-class feel for superior meat quality.

Client
Yu-Ho Food Co., Ltd.
New Taipei City, Taiwan

Design
TU DESIGN OFFICE
Taipei City, Taiwan

Project Team
Tu Ming-Shiang (Art Director)
Tseng Yu-Wen (Graphic Design)
Lin Yi (Design Assistent)
Jane Chang (Photography)

Advertising	Packaging Design	Fair Stands	Retail Design	Red Dot: Junior Award	Designer Profiles	Index
288	318	494	516	544	614	674

Eatrix
[Brand Design]

Eatrix is a pioneering Ukrainian delivery service for dark kitchens whose key feature is a 30-minute delivery time. The brand design was entirely launched with the objective to convey a new, futuristic and bold brand experience. The brand design focuses primarily on the impact of the two major colours to deliver its futuristic brand message. Inspired by space, black was chosen as the main colour, while the bright green colour accents are intended to evoke the image of humanoid aliens. The logo picks up on the topic of food delivery and, at the same time, hints at the speed of the service as a unique selling proposition.

Client
Eatrix
Kyiv, Ukraine

Design
Madcats Agency
Kyiv, Ukraine

City Deli – Meals Made for City Life

[Brand Design]

Located in Seoul, City Deli combines the advantages of casual restaurants and convenience stores. Various deli selections are offered as takeaway meals to meet the demands of today's working adults in particular. In line with this concept, a brand design with an urban look was developed to complement the brand name. The high-rising typography of the word mark creates a visual reference to the city's skyline, while the neon green brand colour represents the freshness of the food and ingredients. A series of illustrations of snacks and the landmarks of metropolises round off the brand image in an appealing manner.

Client
SPC Samlip
Seoul, South Korea

Design
SPC Samlip Design Team
Seoul, South Korea
Charlie Smith Design
London, United Kingdom

Project Team
SPC Samlip Design Team:
Seo Yoon Yang (Creative Direction)
Ja Young Kim (Graphic Design)
Kang Yeon Lee (Graphic Design)
Ga Yean Suh (Structural Design)
So Yeon Jang (Visual Merchandising)
Hyun Wuk Jung (Visual Merchandising)

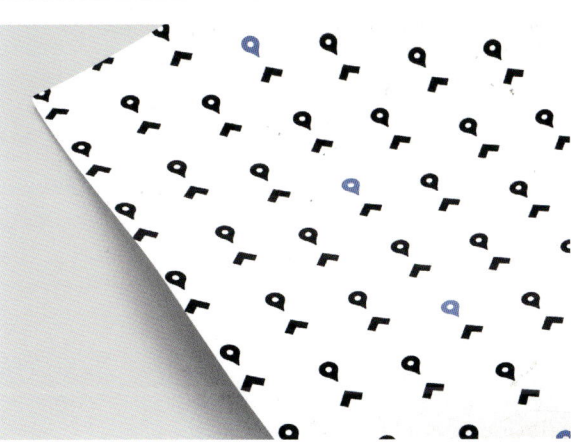

Advertising	Packaging Design	Fair Stands	Retail Design	Red Dot: Junior Award	Designer Profiles	Index
288	318	494	516	544	614	674

Find your freshness over here, FRESH AVENUE

[Brand Design]

Guided by the ambition to offer reliable product freshness, a South Korean supermarket chain developed the retail brand FRESH AVENUE to be perceived as a trustworthy brand. The brand logo was designed to express the formative beauty of the Korean alphabet, Hangeul. In addition, a visual and spatial image was incorporated to express the brand concept intuitively, using pin and focus symbols to pinpoint the location of "a place with fresh products" and set the "focus on fresh products". This resulted in unified design characteristics being applied to all elements of the brand design, including the logo, packaging and shops.

Client
GS Retail Co., Ltd.
Seoul, South Korea

Design
GS Retail Co., Ltd.
Seoul, South Korea

Project Team
GS Retail:
Chang Yoon Yang (Creative Direction)
Young Seok Han (Creative Direction)
Jae Woong Bae (Graphic Design)
Kang Hee Chung (Graphic Design)
Eun Hye Park (Graphic Design)
Jung Sonu (Copywriter)

Jae Min Park (Artwork), 2b

LOTTE Duty Free – 40th Anniversary

[Brand Promotion]

Client
LOTTE Duty Free
Seoul, South Korea

Design
ASCENDER BRANDING
Seoul, South Korea
Steven Wilson Studio
London, United Kingdom

Project Team
ASCENDER BRANDING:
Jei Jae-Kook Chagh (Creative Direction)
Yuna Moon (Creative Direction)
Eryn Ye-Rim Lee (Graphic Design)

Steven Wilson Studio:
Steven Wilson (Creative Direction)
Ji-Su Park (Art Direction)

Daehong Communication:
Yumi Jung (Project Management)

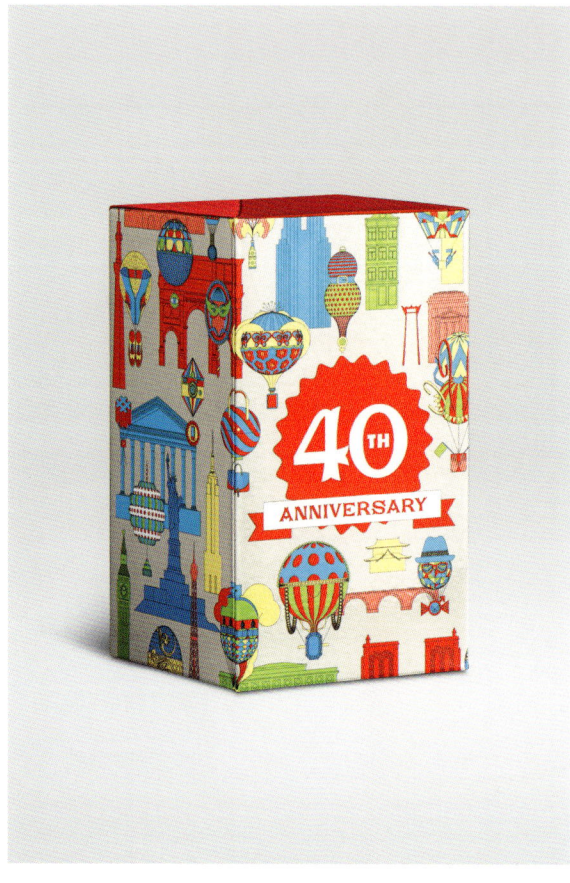

Advertising	Packaging Design	Fair Stands	Retail Design	Red Dot: Junior Award	Designer Profiles	Index
288	318	494	516	544	614	674

This brand promotion was developed for the 40th anniversary of LOTTE Duty Free, a large duty-free retailer on the Asian Pacific market. A range of colourful key visuals feature across the entire campaign, including printed and digital communications. They all share the same association with a rising hot-air balloon, used as a symbol of future projects. The motifs are also used throughout in-store graphics and on the product range. The vivid design language represents the celebration of 40 years of history and aims to appeal to a wide target group.

Garo Golmok

[Brand Design]

Client
IGIS Asset Management
Seoul, South Korea

Design
SPEN Design Agency
Seoul, South Korea

Project Team
Yeonggil Yoon (Art Direction)
Yeonkyung Son (Art Direction)
Hyunsoo Joo (Graphic Design)
Hyeyeong Kong (Graphic Design)
Seongwook Heo (Graphic Design)

Advertising	Packaging Design	Fair Stands	Retail Design	Red Dot: Junior Award	Designer Profiles	Index
288	318	494	516	544	614	674

작지만
멋진 것들을 위한
커뮤니티 공간

**COMMUNITY MALL
GARO GOLMOK**

GRAND OPEN

—

8.30. Fri

OPERATING HOURS
11:00 ~ 21:00
DAILY OPEN

@garogolmok

Hello! 골목

Garo Golmok is a new type of shopping mall located in Seoul, South Korea. It is derived from the concept of alley markets and aims at establishing a community culture. A systematic brand design, which can be flexibly expanded, brings this concept to life with a lifestyle feel. The word mark consists of the Korean characters for "alley", geometrically arranged in a square. A vertical and horizontal axis emerge between these four characters and are reminiscent of the straight streets of a big city. The bright brand colours evoke the image of a bright and pleasant scene.

Lamoda

[Brand Design Relaunch]

Client
Lamoda Group
Moscow, Russia

Design
Shuka Design
Moscow, Russia

Project Team
Lamoda:
Olga Shapoval (Brand Director)
Yuliya Nikitina (Chief Digital Officer)
Vladimir Bolshakov (Art Direction)
Maria Efremova (Lead of Fashion &
Creative Department)

Shuka Design:
Ivan Vasin (Creative Director)
Ivan Velichko (Creative Director)
Alexander Koltsov (Art Director)
Marina Gaiman (Lead Designer)
Valentina Lazareva (Designer)
Konstantin Frolov (Designer)
Dmitry Okulich-Kazarin
(Motion Designer)

Ivan Knyazev (Contributing Creative
Director of Photo Production)

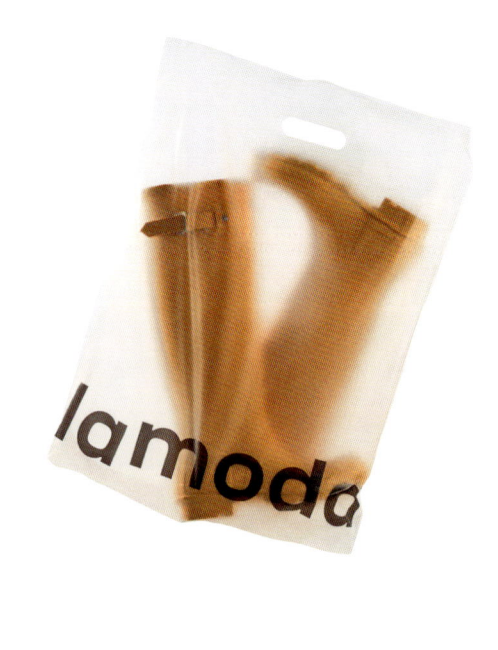

Advertising	Packaging Design	Fair Stands	Retail Design	Red Dot: Junior Award	Designer Profiles	Index
288	318	494	516	544	614	674

Although this online fashion retailer is well known in Russia, the overly technological feel of its previous brand image had grown outdated. Therefore, a brand design relaunch was implemented to establish Lamoda as a design-oriented fashion specialist. The goal was to develop a consistent visual system for both online and offline communication that can effectively appeal to millennials. The word "moda" (fashion) proclaimed in the name appears like a label that evokes the legacy of the textile industry, while the tilted "la" of the word mark is used separately as a signet. The brand design showcases lively colours and lends the appearance an emotional appeal.

Preface	Red Dot: Agency of the Year	Brands	Brand Design & Identity	Corporate Design & Identity	Annual Reports
4	6	18	90	202	260

F — I — L

[Brand Design, Logo Design]

F — I — L is a new buyers' shop of designer collections, offering a variety of interesting design items. Based on the fact that "fil" in French means line, the brand design takes up the simple geometry of lines. In the logo, the three letters of the brand name are connected by lines. The length of the lines varies depending on the media and is thus reminiscent of a progress bar or regulator. In addition, the yellow lines stand out prominently from the typography on white or black backgrounds. Despite the flexible application, with different lengths and positioning, the result is a unified brand image.

Client
FIL Gallery
Fuzhou, China

Design
Fuzhou BY-ENJOY Brand Design Co., Ltd.
Fuzhou, China

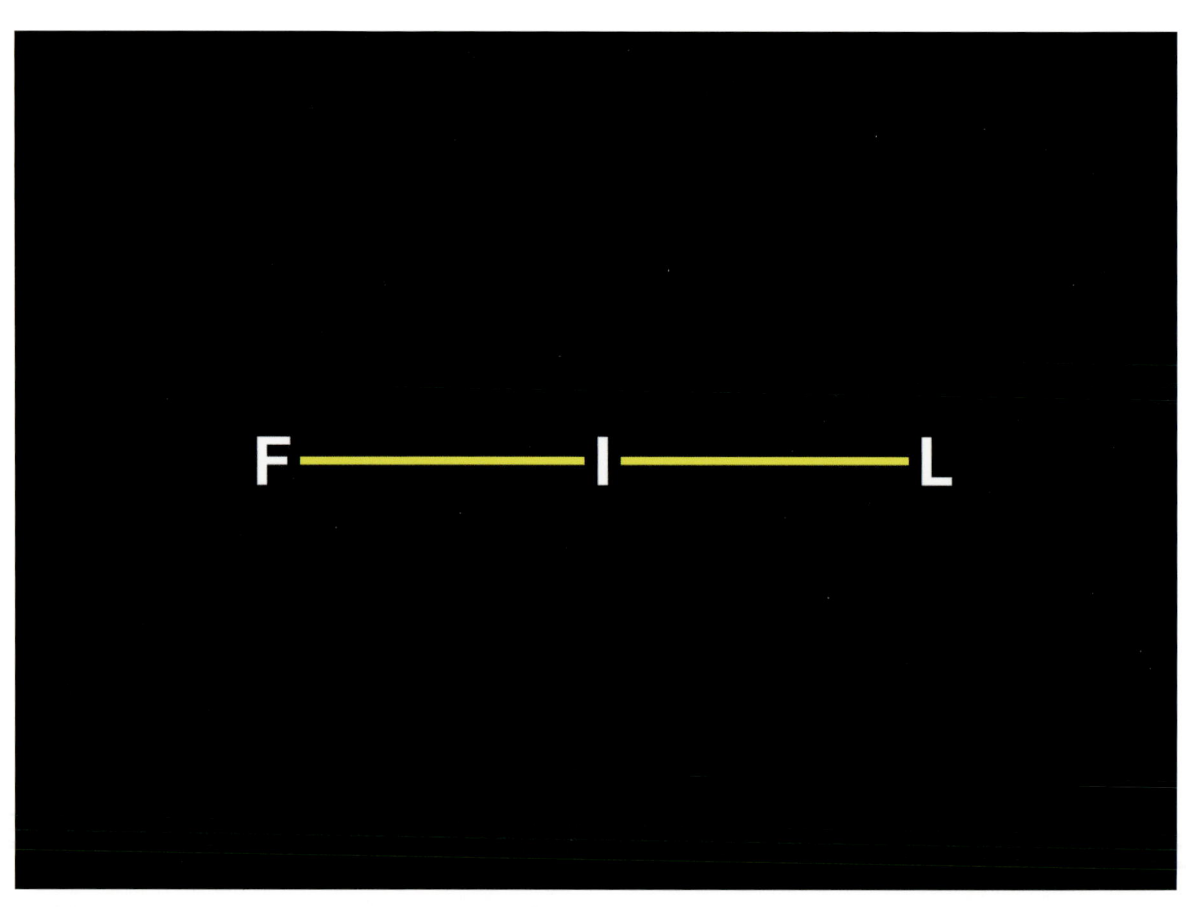

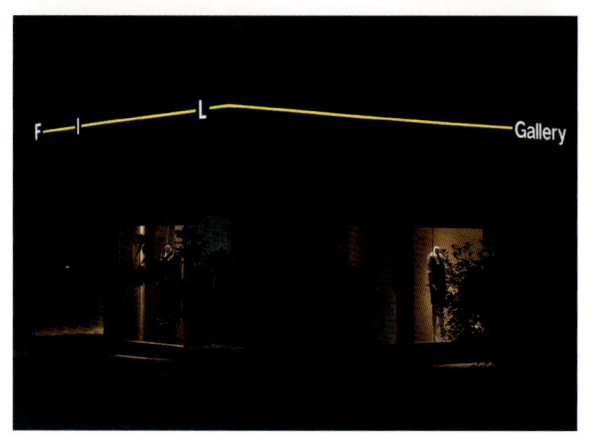

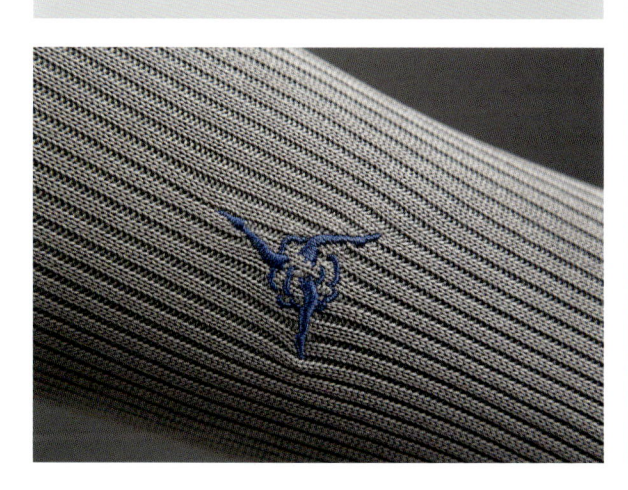

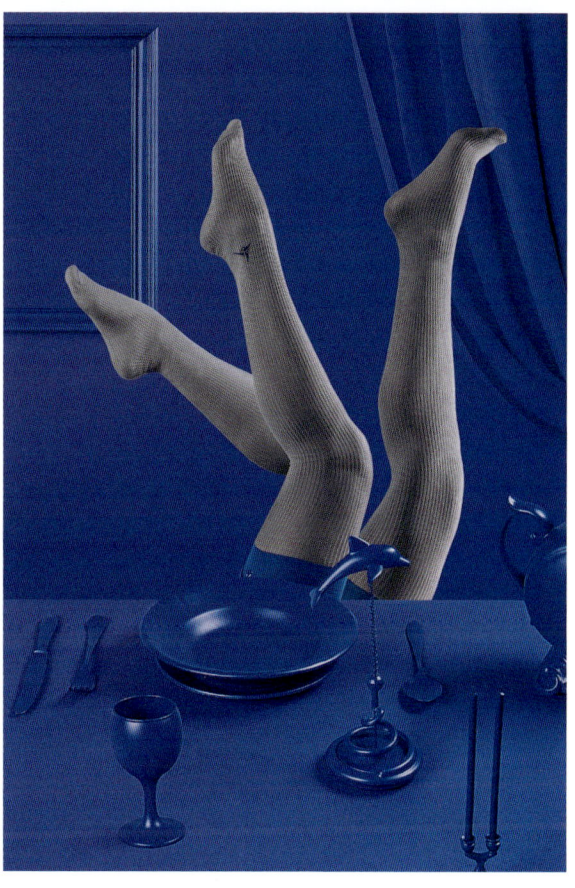

Advertising	Packaging Design	Fair Stands	Retail Design	Red Dot: Junior Award	Designer Profiles	Index
288	318	494	516	544	614	674

Shur Shur

[Brand Design]

Shur Shur is a brand that offers stockings, garter belts and knee socks with an unusual character. The name refers to the specific sound made by legs rubbing against stockings. This association has also influenced the logo design. The structure of the brand logo is based on the triskeles symbol; however, the logo is not illustrated in the style of traditional heraldic triskeles, but instead picks up on the spirit of cabaret to convey the joy of life. The two corporate colours of pink and night blue underline the elegant look, which is consistently maintained throughout – from product branding to packaging design.

Client
Shur Shur
Kyiv, Ukraine

Design
CREVV
Kyiv, Ukraine

Project Team
Natalia Ivanova (Design Concept)
Anton Ivanov (Design Concept)
Eugene Sulimenko (Photography)

Preface	Red Dot: Agency of the Year	Brands	Brand Design & Identity	Corporate Design & Identity	Annual Reports
4	6	18	90	202	260

Munchkin

[Brand Design Relaunch]

Client
Munchkin Inc.
Los Angeles, USA

Design
Munchkin Inc.
Los Angeles, USA

→ Designer profile on page 650
→ Clip online

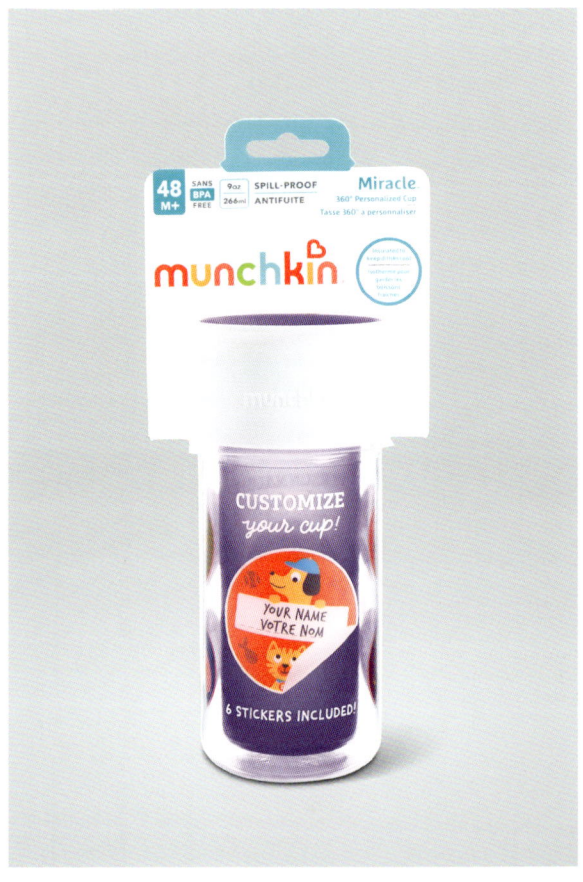

Advertising	Packaging Design	Fair Stands	Retail Design	Red Dot: Junior Award	Designer Profiles	Index
288	318	494	516	544	614	674

Munchkin is a manufacturer of products for babies and small children. The company decided to undergo a relaunch in view of its 30-year brand history. The task was to create a brand design that is inviting to customers. The contours of the previous logo type were first rounded off so that the lettering now shows a harmonious geometry. In the next step, the colours of the logo were updated, creating an appealing, child-friendly colour scheme that runs through the entire product range. The red heart as the dot on the "i" in the brand name is also used separately as a graphic element.

Yummy

[Brand Identity]

Yummy bear is the brand mascot of Chinese kitchen manufacturer TOKIT, which aims to emotionally appeal to the young generation. It communicates the joy of cooking and shapes the brand identity as well. The graphic design of the mascot captures individual aspects of the "TK family" brand logo; for example, the eye-catching nose of the mascot is based on the design language of the signet. The illustration style is characterised by contrasting colour areas and reduced lines, while the rich orange symbolises energy and warmth. Comic-style key visuals show Yummy preparing delicious dishes.

Client
Shanghai Chunmi Electronic
Technology Co., Ltd.
Shanghai, China

Design
Shanghai Chunmi Electronic
Technology Co., Ltd.
Shanghai, China

Project Team
Liyuanxun Chen (Concept)
Xulei Peng (Graphic Design)

Advertising	Packaging Design	Fair Stands	Retail Design	Red Dot: Junior Award	Designer Profiles	Index
288	318	494	516	544	614	674

Mitka

[Brand Design]

Mitka is a new spray-paint brand from Ukraine. The brand name is the Ukrainian word for "spot" and can be interpreted as meaning that buyers can use the brand's products to mark things with their colour design. In order to attract as much attention as possible at the point of sale, the word mark was designed to feature as large as possible on a spray can. Thus, the distinctive capital letters fill the entire height and width of the spray can. Furthermore, the logo is also printed in the respective paint colour to facilitate product selection. The reduced brand design yields a contemporary, purist appearance.

Client
GPL
Poltava, Ukraine

Design
Madcats Agency
Kyiv, Ukraine

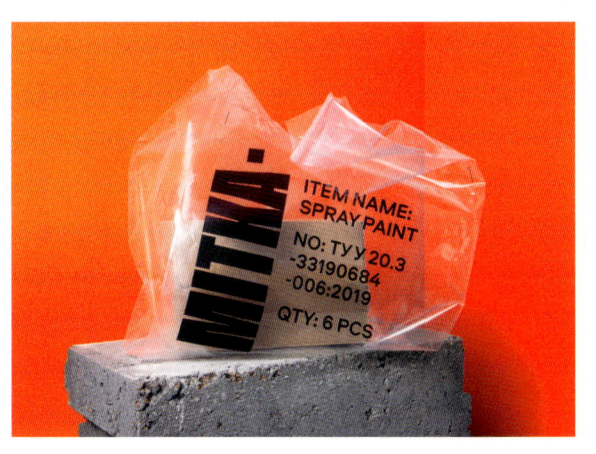

OM

[Brand Identity]

OM is a German skincare brand offering hyaluronic acid products for men and women. To support its launch in Germany, Austria and Switzerland, a complete brand identity was developed, including packaging design and product photography. The logo's typeface, Monument Grotesk, was created in Berlin and gives the brand a minimalist style. The result is an elegant appearance, which is reinforced by the contrast of black typography on a white background. It is critical for skincare brands to be transparent about their formulations, so the typeface is compact enough to accommodate all of the ingredients on the packaging.

Client
Point Rouge GmbH
Grünwald, Germany

Design
Navarra.is
Berlin, Germany

EASY PEASY
[Brand Design]

EASY PEASY is a beauty brand that specialises in stick-type cosmetics. The brand name conveys the products' great ease of use and represents the key concept of the brand. Targeting millennials, the colourful brand design creates a youthful, cheerful and freedom-loving vibe. The word mark acquires a lively quality through playful variations of character length and height. The uppercase E and P in the heart-shaped signet reference to the brand name, while the arrangement of the letters resembles a smiling face, aimed at appealing to the target group emotionally.

Client
Amorepacific
Seoul, South Korea

Design
Amorepacific
Seoul, South Korea

Project Team
Amorepacific:
Ohkyung Lee (Designer)
Hyejin Lee (Designer)
Damee Hong (Designer)
Hyuna Kwon (Visual Direction)
Sangwoo Shin (Photographer)
Juwon Oh (Technical Direction)

cfc:
Charry Jeon (Creative Direction)

2020RE:CALENDAR

[Branding Product]

Client
ALINE STUDIO
Beijing, China

Design
ALINE STUDIO
Beijing, China

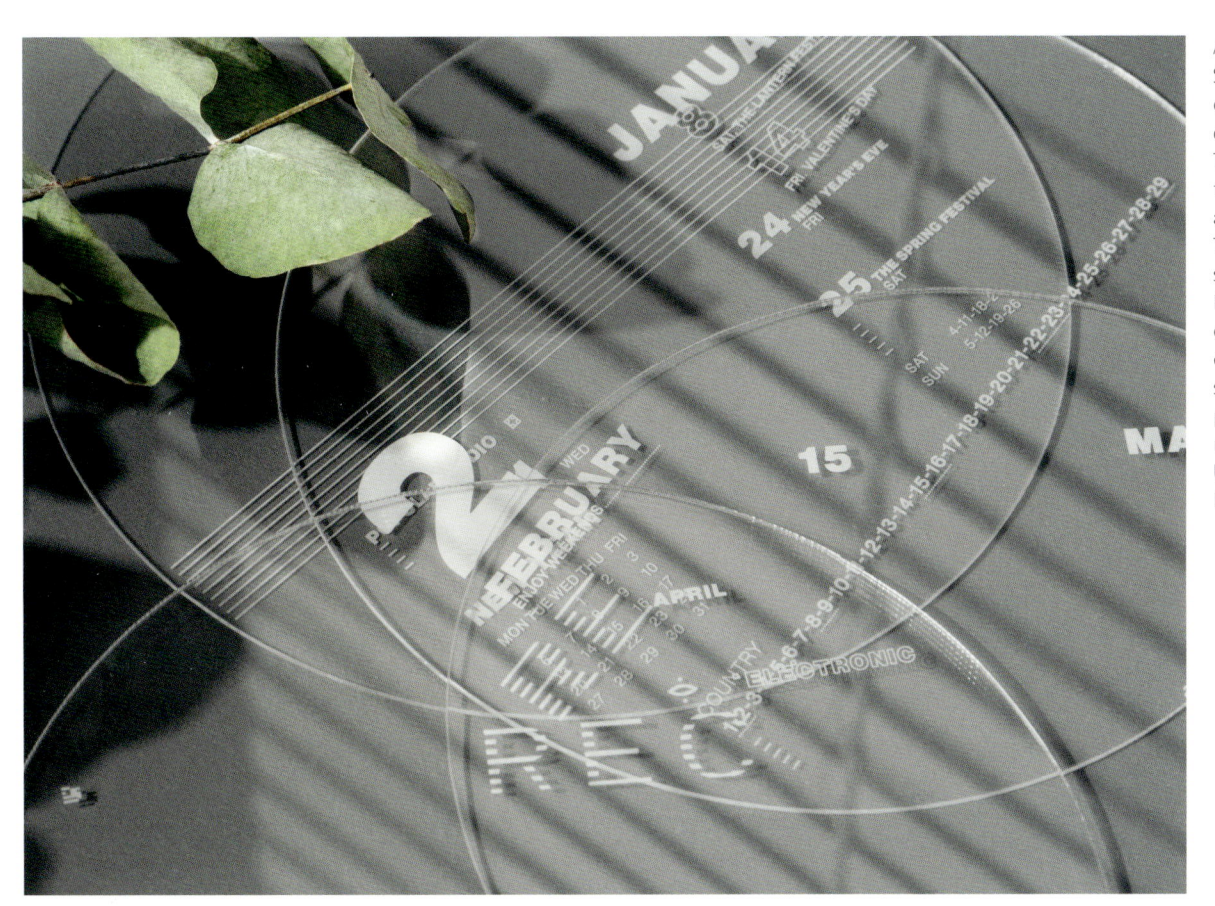

Advertising	Packaging Design	Fair Stands	Retail Design	Red Dot: Junior Award	Designer Profiles	Index
288	318	494	516	544	614	674

As an ambitious design studio, ALINE STUDIO strengthens its brand image by creating and releasing an independently designed branding product each year. The 2020RE:CALENDAR was designed for their brand promotion in 2020 and is available via a Chinese online platform. The design of the calendar box is inspired by the repeated numbers in 2020. Furthermore, it borrows the aesthetic of compact discs to express the concept of making, recording and playing back sound. The box comprises twelve transparent discs, each representing one month of the year and featuring an album cover that captures the specific look and feel of the month.

Happygo

[Brand Identity]

Happygo is a membership-based e-commerce platform mainly targeted at younger consumers. By purchasing a membership card, a person can share the benefits of membership with their entire family. The brand identity aims to portray the emotional benefits of shopping together and to connect the brand with love, happiness, sharing and fun. Thus, an emotionally appealing logo was created based on the gesture for ILY (I love you), which is well-known even among people who do not use sign language. The signal red signet also catches attention through the comic-style illustration of the eyes.

Client
Happygo Network Technology Co., Ltd.
Shanghai, China

Design
Dongdao Creative Branding Group
Beijing, China

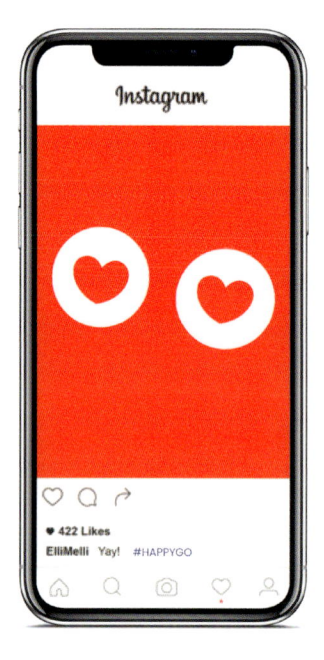

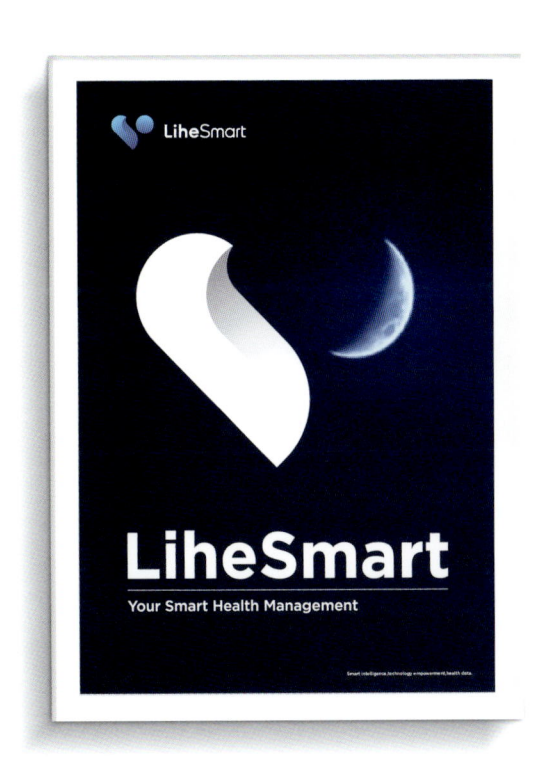

LiheSmart

[Brand Identity]

LiheSmart is a one-stop platform, integrating departments such as a pharmacy, a convenience store, a cosmetics section and a beauty clinic. The multi-functional service concept differs from traditional chain pharmacies by offering a more comprehensive shopping experience. To convey these values, the brand design comprises a striking symbol and a visual system that is flexible and easily adaptable. The creative work focused on establishing an emotional brand identity, with a woodpecker serving as inspiration. The three-dimensional logo featuring an abstract contour of this intelligent bird conveys a sense of friendliness.

Client
Beijing Lihe Pharmaceutical Co., Ltd.
Beijing, China

Design
Dongdao Creative Branding Group
Beijing, China

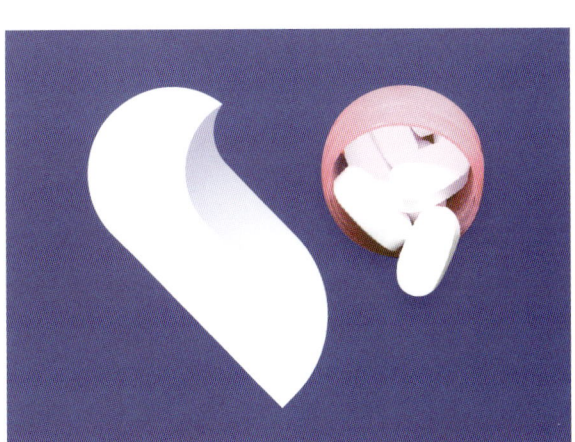

D.TAILS

[Brand Design]

D.TAILS is a Danish e-commerce consulting agency specialised in providing solutions for a popular e-commerce platform. Their visual identity is defined by a brand design that illustrates their expertise. The design concept is based on the binary code – a fundamental element of the digital world. A monospaced-inspired typeface was created to establish a direct visual link to the look of actual code. This approach is also visible in the logo design, which focuses on glyphs often seen in coding languages. The result is a uniquely fitting visual identity, logo, typeface, stationery and website design.

Client
D.TAILS
Copenhagen, Denmark

Design
Lazy snail Design
Copenhagen, Denmark

Project Team
Lazy snail Design:
Ioanna Drakaki (Head of Design)
Eleni Pavlaki (Creative Director)
Serafim Stroubis (Senior Art Director)

Trine Rask (Type Designer)
Jeshua Martina (Copywriter)

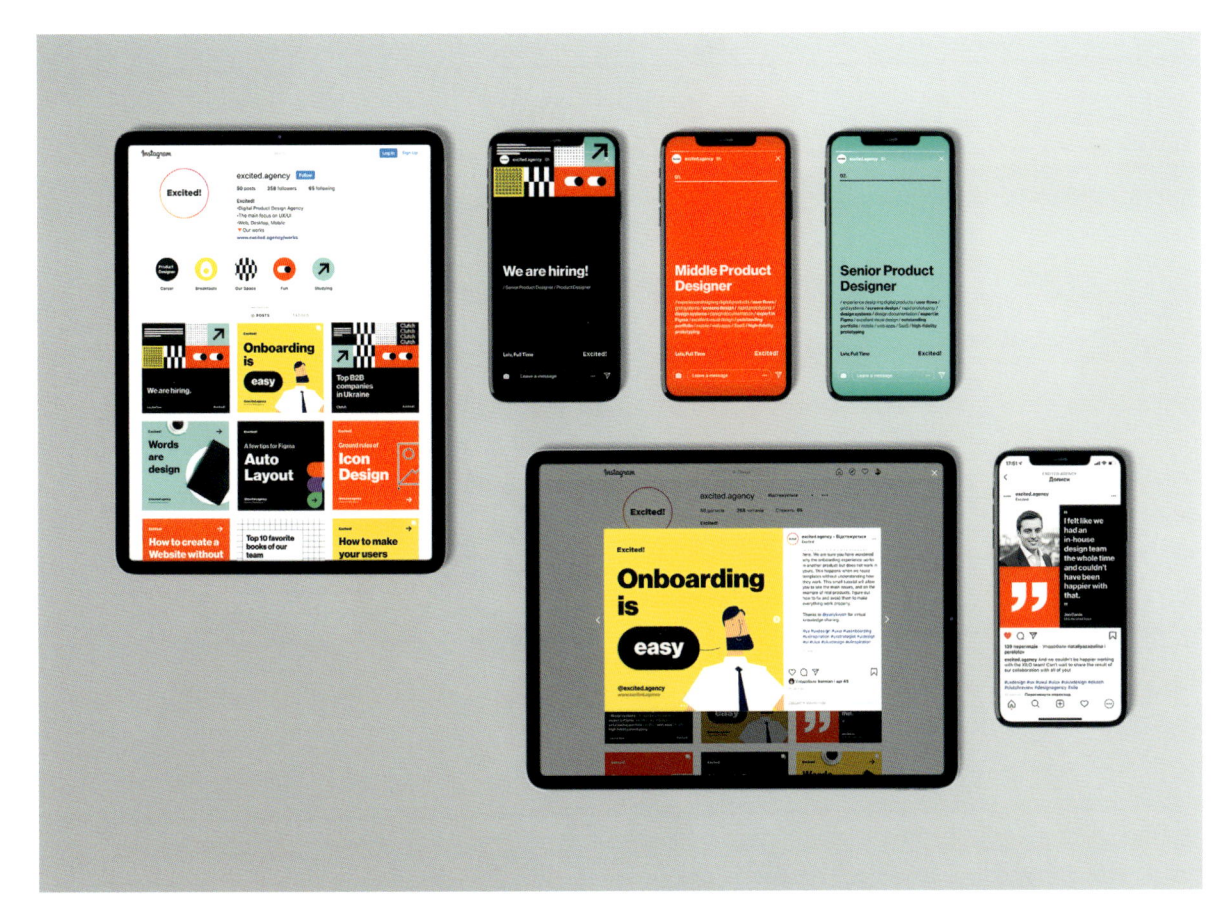

Excited

[Brand Design]

Excited is an agency that helps businesses and start-ups to create a digital design for their products and solve critical business challenges through innovation workshops. The primary purpose of this brand design was to establish a unique identity that catches the eye. The varied visuals convey creativity and fill the overall appearance with life and emotions. Interface elements, such as identity building blocks used by the staff in their everyday work, were used and mixed with bright colours to achieve an expressive look. As a result, awareness of the brand has been strengthened both internally and externally.

Client
Excited
Lviv, Ukraine

Design
Excited
Lviv, Ukraine

Project Team
Oleksandr Perelotov (Creative Direction)
Aneliia Zazulina (Creative Direction)
Yuliia Yatseniuk (Designer)
Mark Altytsia (Motion Design)

LINX

[Brand Identity]

LINX is focused on improving people's daily lives and paying close attention to the relationship between individuals and groups. To enhance the brand, its visual symbols were redesigned, highlighting the company's emphasis on individuals. The new design uses rectangular elements shaped like the letter "I" as a key visual, each element representing a different individual. At the same time, the elements are grouped into blocks to convey the strength and illustrate the visual impact of group cohesion. As a whole, this constitutes a contemporary visual identity system that is both purist and clear.

Client
Beijing Xin You Lingxi
Technology Co., Ltd.
Beijing, China

Design
XIVO Design
Shenzhen, China

Project Team
Yinan Lyu (Designer)
Tianguang Zhong (Designer)
Min Wei (Designer)

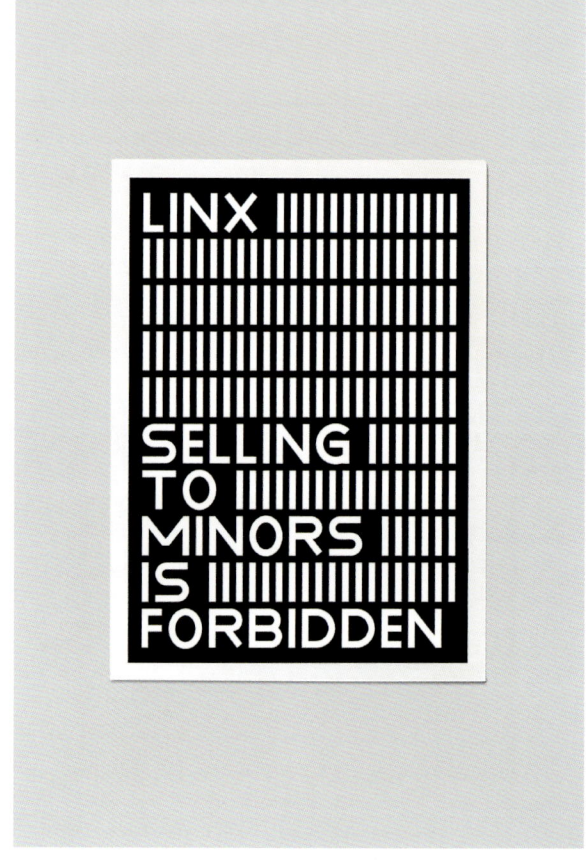

DonHa

[Brand Identity]

DonHa is a technology-based enterprise that mainly focuses on smart wearable devices. The full name of the brand and its main letters are used as the key elements of the brand design. Thus, the signet features the letters "DH" in contemporary lines. The broad application of black and white, complemented with yellow to highlight more detailed information, not only increases its visibility, but also fulfils the company's goal to differentiate itself from the conservative impression of the industry through direct and contemporary brand communications.

Client
Shenzhen Do Intelligent
Technology Co., Ltd.
Shenzhen, China

Design
XIVO Design
Shenzhen, China

Project Team
Xicheng Yin (Designer)
Yinan Lyu (Designer)
Ruiyi Chen (Designer)
Min Wei (Designer)
Tianguang Zhong (Designer)

whowho

[Brand Identity]

Client
whowho&company
Seoul, South Korea

Design
LAY:D, Brand and Design Studio
Seoul, South Korea

Project Team
Kim Seungheon (Creative Direction)
Heo Taebum (Creative Direction)
Jeon Chaeun (Graphic Design)
Kim Minchae (Graphic Design)
Yoo Songhee (Graphic Design)
Moon Chanwoo (Graphic Design)
Hwang Injung (Graphic Design)
Kang Sangman (Graphic Design)

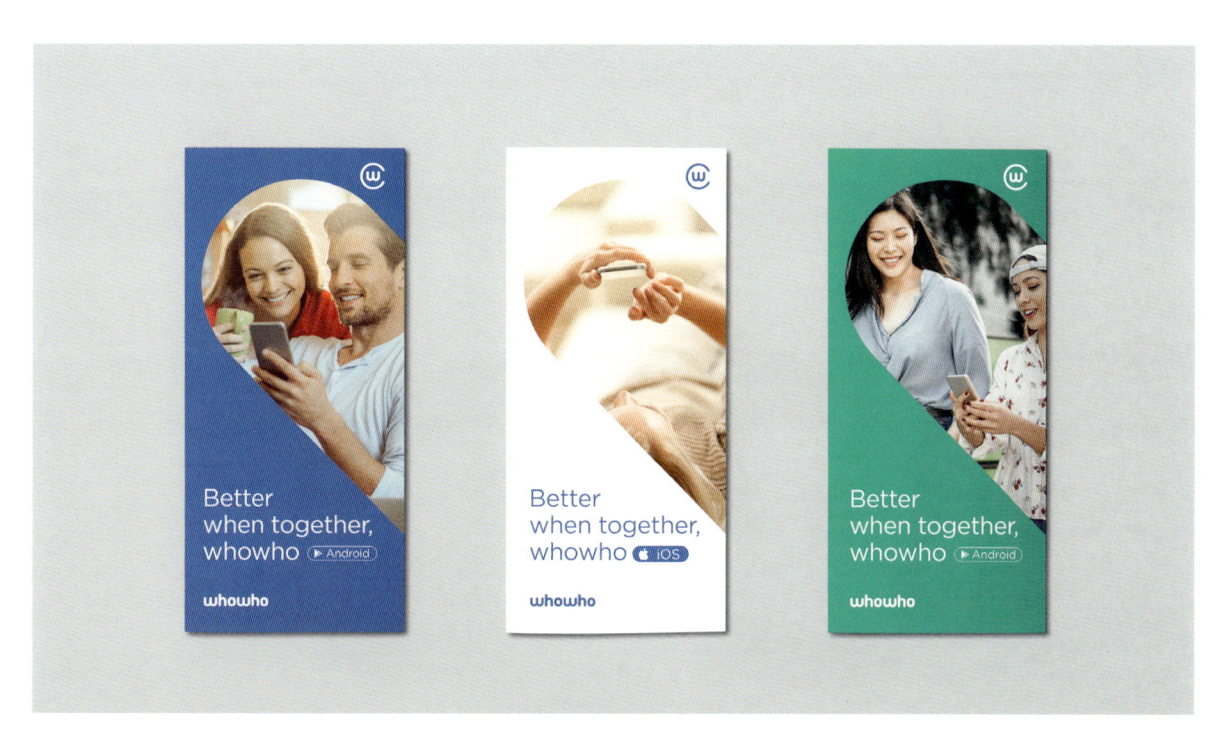

whowho is a Korean mobile service brand that offers convenient products and services. The development of the visual brand identity was inspired by the slogan "Better when together, whowho", which aims to reflect the brand value. The word mark and graphic element in the form of a blue heart are emphasised by the monochrome colour palette, while the rich, vibrant blue embodies the brand's technological nature. The word mark and graphic element are also consistently implemented throughout the various online and offline channels, including merchandise und stationery, to enhance the brand experience.

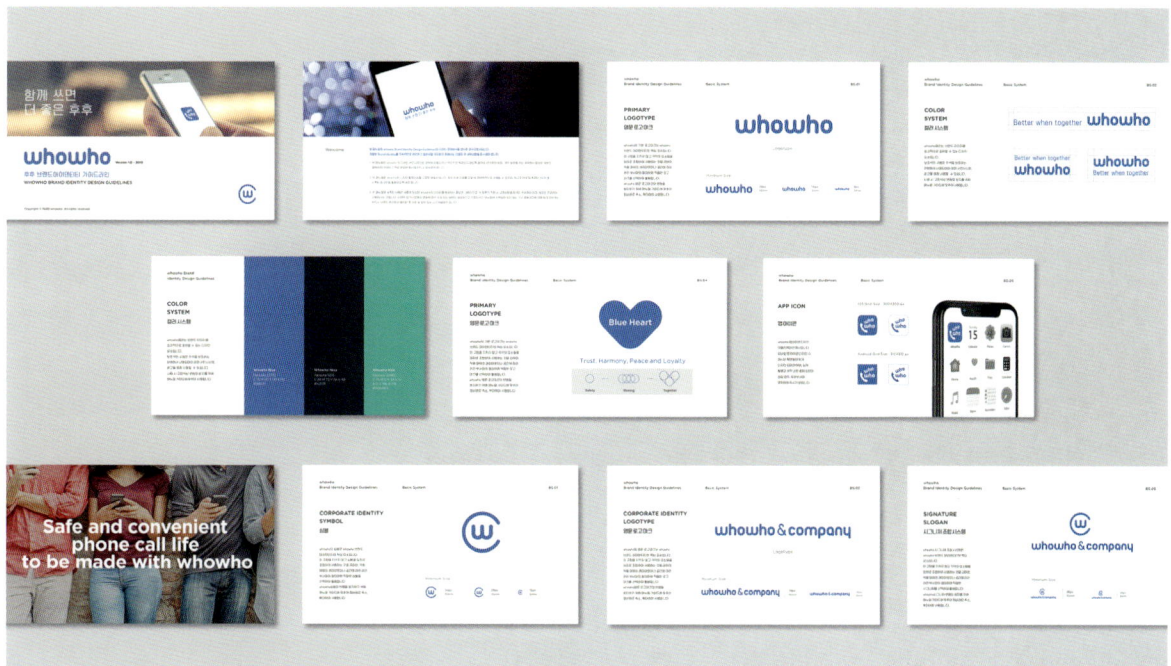

ZEM

[Brand Design, Brand Identity]

SK Telecom, a large mobile carrier in South Korea, launched the brand ZEM to initiate a new mobile culture for digital natives. Geared mainly towards primary school pupils, the service concept is designed to protect children from harmful mobile exposure by offering parental control functions. The playful typography of the brand name is enhanced by a vibrant colour palette. A flexible design system enables broad application to all aspects of the marketing. In addition, an exclusive mobile device offering a variety of content was designed to enhance the brand experience.

Client
SK Telecom
Seoul, South Korea

Design
SK Telecom
Seoul, South Korea

Project Team
Jongwhi Cha (Creative Direction)
Sangeun Lee (Project Lead)
Sejin Noh (Brand Design)
Jongwon Won (Brand Design)
Jungin Kim (Product Design)
Bumhee Han (Product Design)
Junghan Doh (Brand Naming)
Junhyung Park (Brand Naming)
Choonghyeon Hwang (Brand Naming)

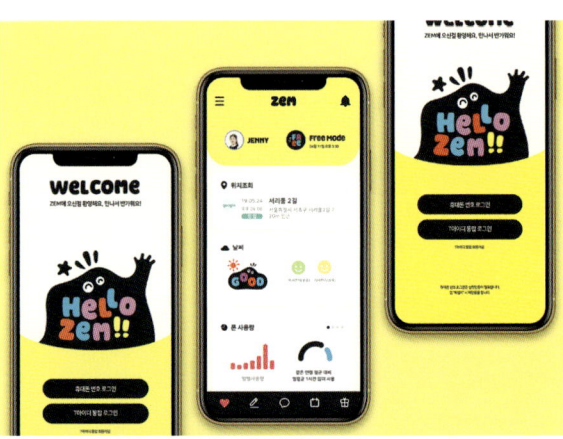

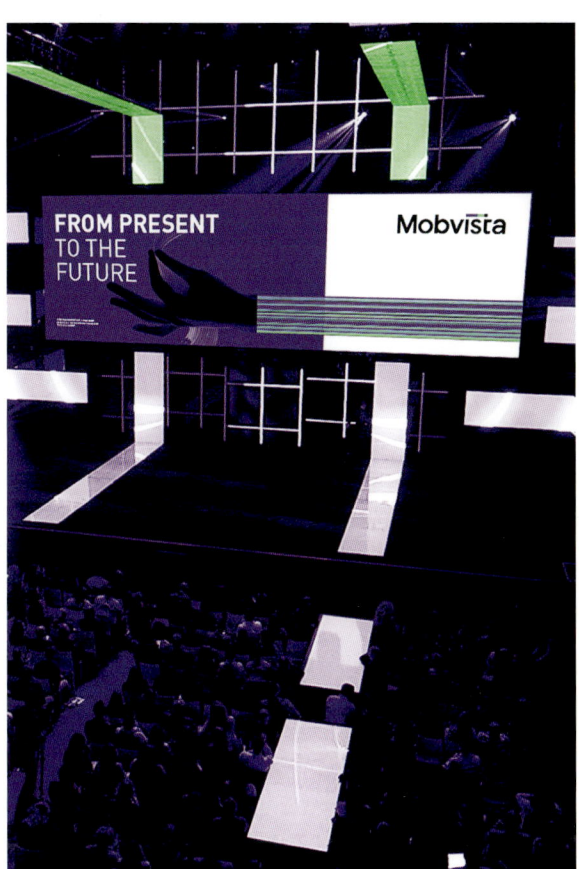

Mobvista

[Brand Design Relaunch, Logo Design]

Mobvista, which started as a mobile advertising platform in 2013, has grown into a corporate group comprising a variety of brands. Therefore, a unified and flexible brand design was developed with the aim to redefine the Mobvista group's brand strategy and brand architecture. The relaunch uses a visual language that conveys the image of a leading people-oriented technology platform that connects the world and drives global business growth. A contemporary brand logo in combination with a flexible design system highlights the core competencies and brand association to strengthen the market presence of the corporate group.

Client
Mobvista
Guangzhou, China

Design
FutureBrand China
Shanghai, China

Project Team
Sam Yang (Creative Direction)
Feifei Jiang (Graphic Design Lead)
Zhe Li (Graphic Design)
Sijia Zhang (Graphic Design)
Sophie Cheng (Project Management)
Cary Liu (Account Management)

→ Designer profile on page 638

1theK

[Brand Design]

1theK (pronounced as WonderK) is the brand name of a K-pop distribution channel that connects South Korean pop stars with their fans by providing highly popular music contents. The brand name calls to mind a music wonderland where all music wishes can come true. Reminiscent of a dynamically flying flag, the logo is a symbiosis of the number "1" and the letter "K". In combination with a variety of contrasting colours, the logo defines the entire brand world which, depending on the channel, is complemented by sub-brands such as Official and Originals. Each channel is characterised by various visual elements that appeal to its target audience.

Client
Kakao M
Seoul, South Korea

Design
HuskyFox
Seoul, South Korea

Project Team
Doohee Lee (Creative Direction)
Kiyoung Jung (Creative Direction)
Taehee Lee (Strategic Planning)
Yonghyeok Shin (Graphic Design)
Heewon Kim (Graphic Design)
Dahye Moon (Graphic Design)

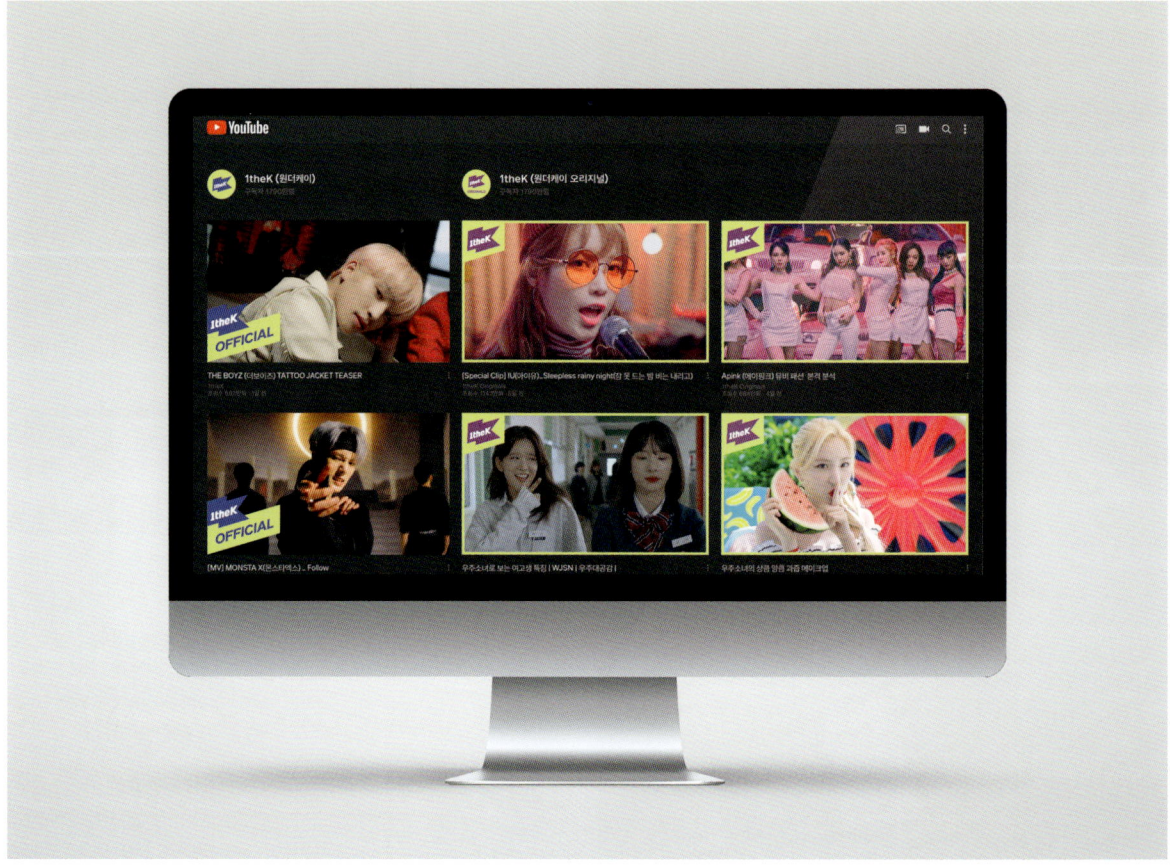

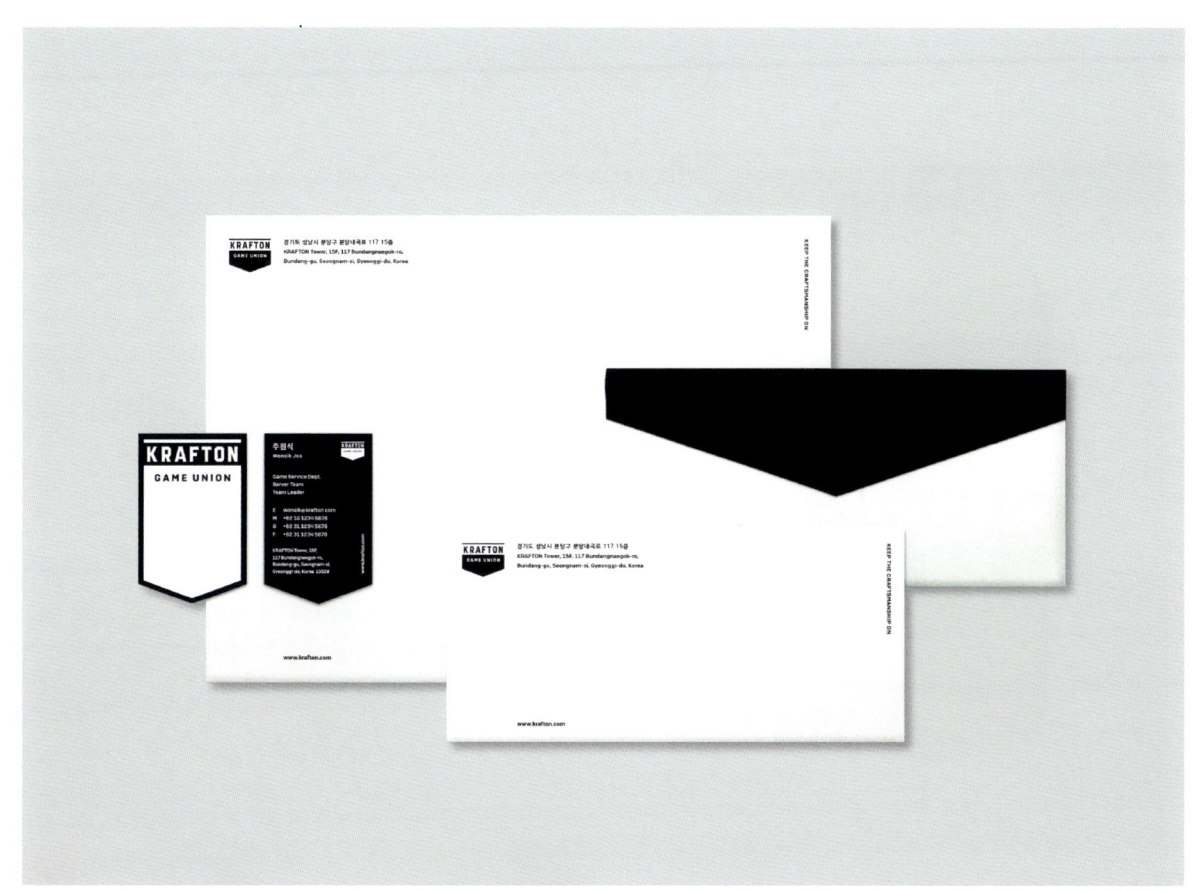

KRAFTON Game Union
[Brand Design Relaunch]

KRAFTON is the brand name of a game union that aims to establish itself as a master of game creation on the market. Therefore, the group looks for organisations with strong development capabilities and invests in them, providing an environment in which members can seamlessly develop their games. As each member operates independently, it was necessary to create a central brand design that integrates them all. By building a logo design system that can accommodate both the uniqueness of each member brand and the consistency of the group brand, the new brand design has been given a harmonious overall image with different identification colours and graphical symbols.

Client
KRAFTON
Seongnam, South Korea

Design
PlusX
Seoul, South Korea

Project Team
KRAFTON BX Department:
Minhyung Jo
Taegu Yoon
Kyungwoo Kim
Kyosun Koo

PlusX:
Myungsup Shin (Creative Direction)
Sabum Byun (Creative Direction)
Jangsoon Choe (Creative Direction)
Jisu Kim (Strategic Planning)
Bohyun Kook (Strategic Planning)
Minho Jang (Strategic Planning)
Wonsik Joo (Graphic Design)
Suji Choi (Graphic Design)
Jihoon Noh (Graphic Design)
Hyunmin Han (Graphic Design)
Kwangmyung Lim (Motion Design)
Yoojin Jeon (Web Design)
Dongbeen Choi (Web Design)
Kiwon Jang (Web Design)
Chulhee Kim (Web Design)
Hyungyu Lee (Web Design)
Gmo Song (Technical Direction)
Jeonghyuck Won (Technical Direction)
Mira Jung (Technical Direction)
Minju Kim (Technical Direction)

Vira

[Brand Design Relaunch]

Vira is a Ukrainian brand that manufactures engine oils and lubricants for cars. The company's product strategy is to offer good value for money. It realigned its brand strategy in order to more clearly convey the pure quality of its engine oils without additives. The brand comprises two product lines: Vira Oil lubricants and Vira Cool liquids. Therefore, the original brand name was shortened to Vira and a new logo was created. The two product lines are now marked with different symbols: a drop for oil and a snowflake for antifreeze.

Client
GPL
Poltava, Ukraine

Design
Madcats Agency
Kyiv, Ukraine

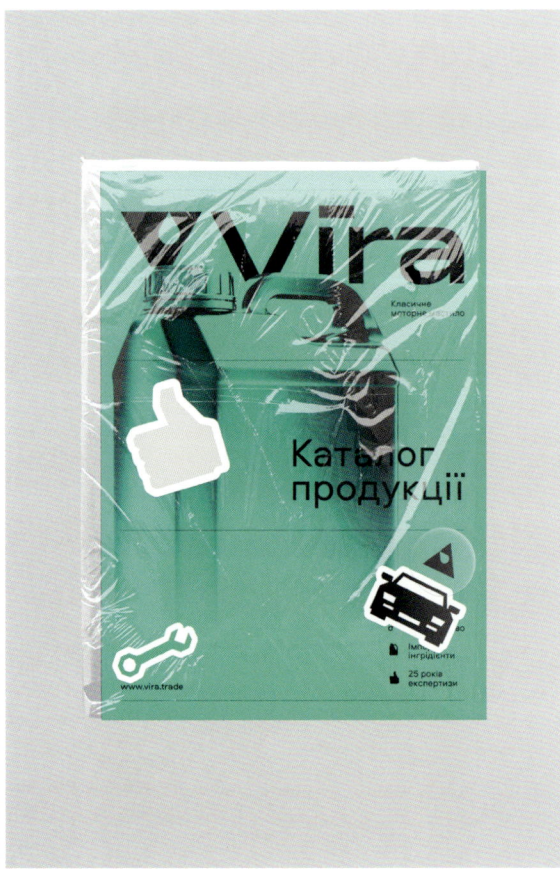

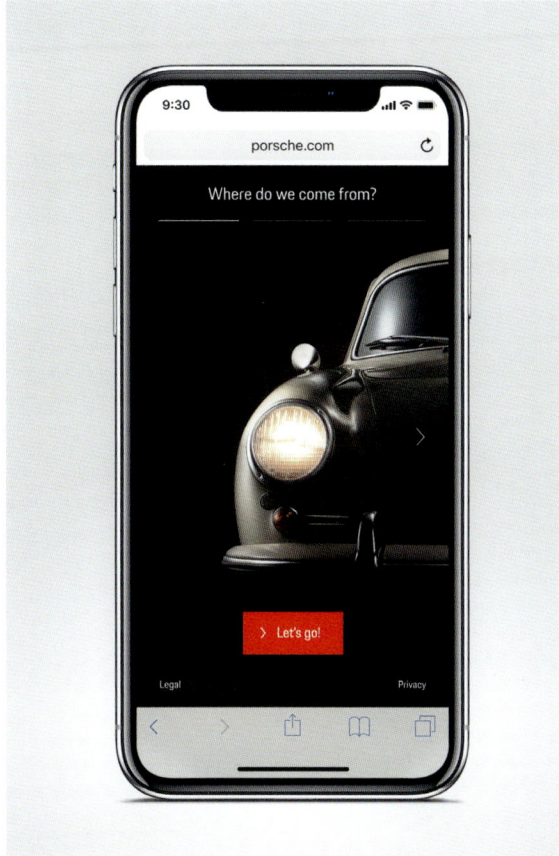

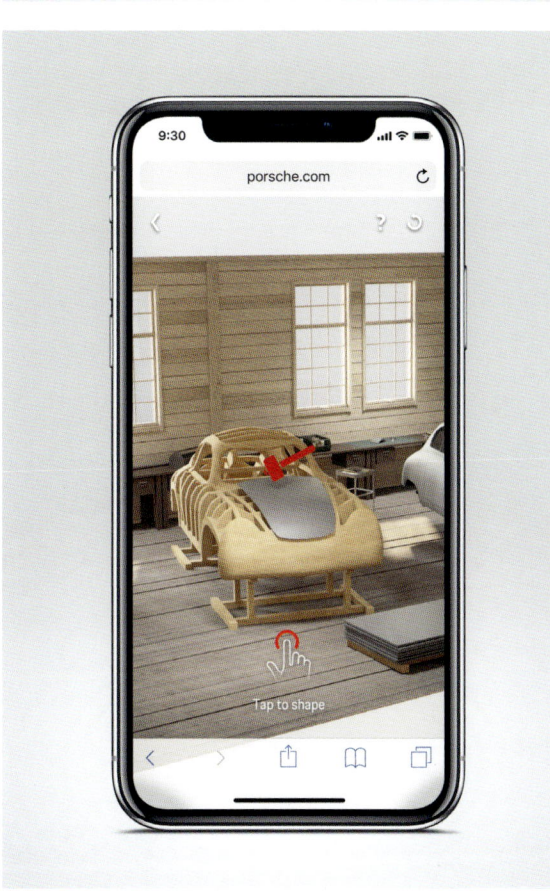

Advertising	Packaging Design	Fair Stands	Retail Design	Red Dot: Junior Award	Designer Profiles	Index
288	318	494	516	544	614	674

Porsche Digital Brand Academy – The state-of-the-art WebAR Training

[Brand Promotion]

To reach both new and established employees, as well as dealers and partners worldwide, a first-to-market educational app was developed for brand promotion and training. The Porsche Digital Brand Academy conveys brand values in an interactive and appealing way. Users can immerse themselves in an augmented reality scene at the location of their choice simply by using their smartphones. A Porsche worker guides them through the web-based app as an avatar providing information, encouraging interaction with their surroundings and rewarding users with emotional content. This new form of presentation evokes positive emotions in users as they discover the characteristics of the Porsche brand.

Client
Dr. Ing. h.c. F. Porsche AG
Stuttgart, Germany

Design
innovation.rocks consulting gmbh
Vienna, Austria
Keko GmbH
Berlin, Germany

Project Team
innovation.rocks consulting
(Concept, Design, UX/UI):
Deniz Örs (Head of Design)
Sophia Luftensteiner
(User Interface Design)
Alexander Kvasnicka (3D Artist)
Ilker Cirakoglu (Junior Art Director)

Keko (Video & Audio):
Tobias Schwaiger (Creative Director)
Daniel Knisatschek (Senior Copywriter)
Swenja Krosien (Head of Digital Content)

→ Clip online

Arlanda Express

[Visual Identity Relaunch]

The 20th anniversary visual identity relaunch shows Stockholm's local airport train, the Arlanda Express, in a contemporary look. In preparation for future endeavours, the brand logo has been reduced to two letters, complementing the product name that carries a well-known heritage and awareness. The hand-cut, vibrating font Transfer Sans is central and defines the brand identity in contrast to the summery yellow colouring. The design concept also uses large wedge-shaped rooms, waves and surfaces. English-language slogans, a new system for finding your way, pictograms and even more attractive trains round off the brand experience in an appealing manner.

Client
A-Train AB, Arlanda Express
Stockholm, Sweden

Design
itch
Stockholm, Sweden

Project Team
Joakim Holmqvist (Creative Direction)
Hanna Rosenblom (Concept)

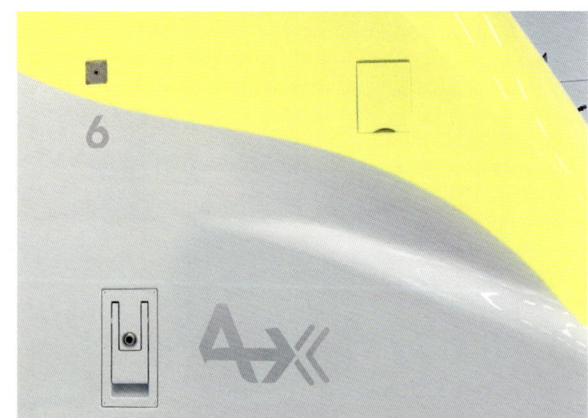

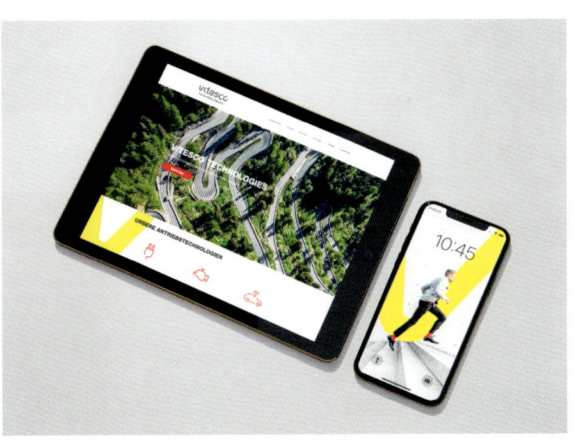

Electric Future

[Brand Design]

The topic of sustainability and climate protection calls for new concepts. With the launch of a new independent brand, Continental AG is reacting to the rapidly changing demands for vehicle drives. The company's powertrain division has been spun off into a new brand under the name Vitesco Technologies to establish itself as a developer and manufacturer of drive technologies for electric vehicles. The goal of the brand design is to contribute to the visibility of the new brand in the international B2B sector. The naming is derived from the Latin word vita (life) to represent liveliness. With its flowing forms, the word mark conveys dynamism and movement.

Client
Vitesco Technologies GmbH
Regensburg, Germany

Design
loved GmbH
Hamburg, Germany

Project Team
Vitesco Technologies:
Thomas Hackl (Brand Management)
Birgit Mehlhorn (Brand Management)

loved:
Maik Beimdieck
(Executive Creative Director)
Sebastian Körner (Senior Art Director)
Jonathan Amelung
(Client Service Director)
Carsten Eggers (Account Director)
Frauke Stürmer (Senior Account Manager)
Sarah Güstrau (Senior Account Manager)

Preface	Red Dot: Agency of the Year	Brands	Brand Design & Identity	Corporate Design & Identity	Annual Reports
4	6	18	90	202	260

Gearbox by Gamesa

[Brand Identity]

Client
Gamesa Gearbox
Zamudio, Spain

Design
Bronce Estudio
Pamplona, Spain

Advertising	Packaging Design	Fair Stands	Retail Design	Red Dot: Junior Award	Designer Profiles	Index
288	318	494	516	544	614	674

As an industrial unit within Siemens Gamesa, Gearbox produces gear solutions for wind turbines. The aim was to re-imagine the brand concept in a way that was true to its industrial heritage, while renewing the company's positioning as a manufacturer of clean energy. The challenge was to translate the positioning into a visual identity and to build a wider set of elements – a design system that was overall simpler to work with. Taking the world of gears and their function within drives as a reference point, a simple yet powerful design concept was developed. The choice of contrasting colours increases the brand identity's recognition value.

Dynamo Fencing Center

[Brand Identity]

Dynamo Fencing Center is a professional fencing club in Boston, USA. The successful school has already turned out several generations of world champions. The name Dynamo is widely used and has strong associations. Therefore, it was important to create a brand identity that would establish a new connotation that would work for the fencing club. The brand logo itself is constructed around the illustration of a line, which represents the movement of the sabre tip during an attack. The dark blue colour symbolises the opponent's shadow, while the golden yellow glow reflects the sabre's movement.

Client
Dynamo Fencing Center Inc.
Newton, MA, USA

Design
iden.team branding agency
Kyiv, Ukraine

Project Team
Maria Sencha (Creative Direction)
Kate Lebid (Art Direction)
Inna Malysh (Graphic Design)
Alexandra Shvetsova (Graphic Design)
Nika Kosmina (Graphic Design)
Alice Shein (Artwork)

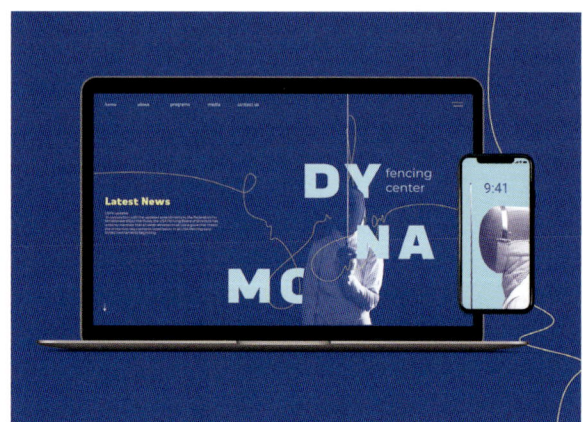

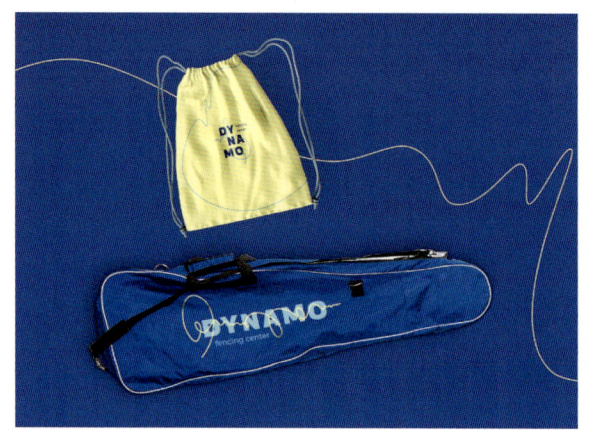

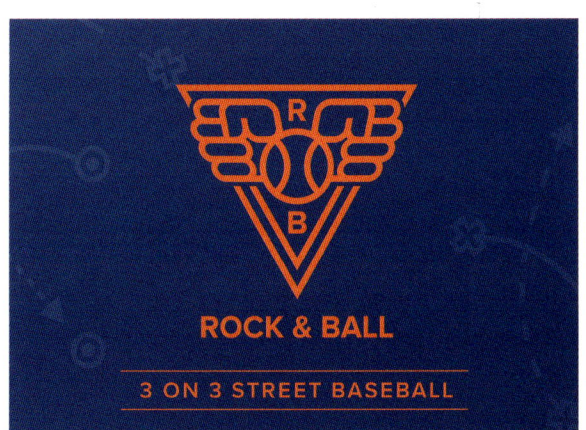

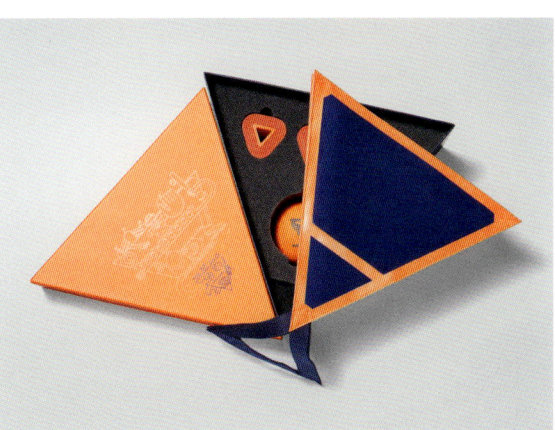

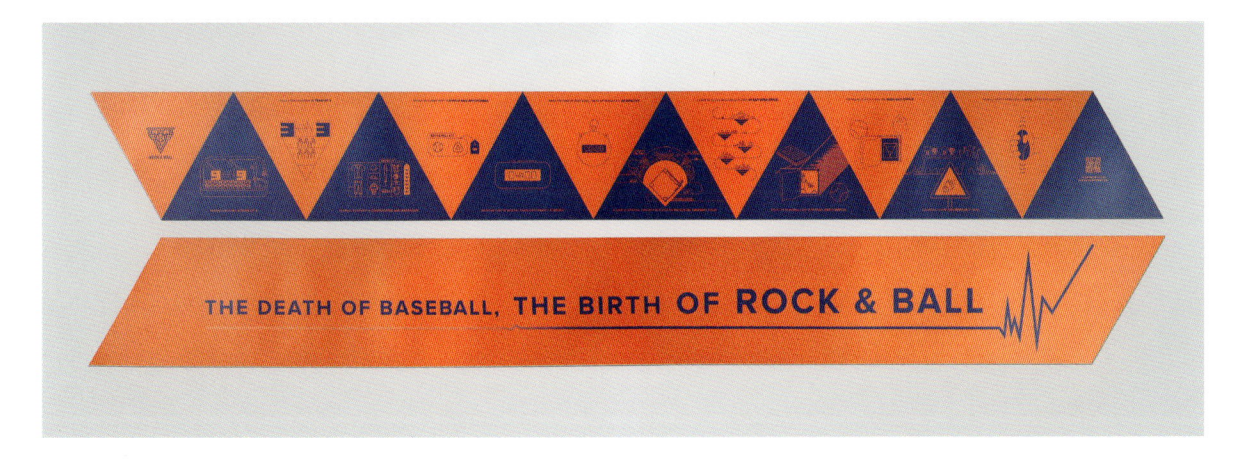

3 on 3 Street Baseball – Rock & Ball

[Brand Design, Brand Promotion]

Inspired by baseball, a sport that requires a proper playing field, this three-on-three street baseball game called Rock & Ball was created. It is a new kind of game that can be played on a much smaller scale. The brand design provides a clear reference to baseball through the choice of colours, with the signal colour orange ensuring good visibility both indoors and outdoors. The triangular graphic element of the logo was derived from the number of players on a team and places the ball in the centre of attention. The implementation of the design includes a play kit which, like the logo, features a triangular shape and contains detailed instructions on how to play the game.

Client
Hanwha Eagles
Daejeon, South Korea

Design
TIVE
Seoul, South Korea

Project Team
Yong Dong Kim (Head of Marketing)
Hee Sook Yu (Marketing Planner)
Hae Chan Ahn (Project Management)
Ian Tae Woong Jeon (Creative Direction)
Ilchan Chun (Art Direction)
Hyo In Chung (Graphic Design)
Kidon Bae (Symbol Design)
Jin Ho Park (Strategic Planning)

Hardio

[Brand Design]

Hardio is a cycling club in Kyiv that organises group races in different parts of the world. In addition, it offers a functional training gym with cycling simulators. The main idea behind the development of the logo was to visually represent movement. The symbol, which is in the shape of an arrow, is reminiscent of a cyclist's movement and also captures the contour of the letter "H". In advertising media, the blue line complements the brand design as a graphic element and a metaphor for the finishing line of cycle races. The branded jersey and helmet feature black speckles that symbolise water and mud splashes from the bike, expressing the feeling of freedom.

Client
Hardio
Kyiv, Ukraine

Design
CREVV
Kyiv, Ukraine

Project Team
Anton Ivanov (Design Concept)
Natalia Ivanova (Design Concept)
Serhii Irkhin (Motion Design)

BlackYak

[Brand Design Relaunch]

BlackYak is an outdoor brand currently undergoing various changes. The mission and values of the brand were analysed in order to meet challenges such as the main target group getting older and the need to open up new markets. Three aspects that epitomise the brand were identified: authenticity as symbolised by the mountain panorama, the tough nature of the yak, and a technology-oriented corporate culture. Based on this, a new brand design was developed that reinforced the core values of the brand and, in combination with high-contrast colours, successfully revitalised the company's image.

Client
BlackYak
Seoul, South Korea

Design
PlusX
Seoul, South Korea

Project Team
BlackYak:
Taesun Kang
Junsuk Kang
Ilchan Hwang
Jaemin Yoon

PlusX:
Myungsup Shin (Creative Direction)
Jangsoon Choe (Creative Direction)
Bohyun Kook (Strategic Planning)
Jeonga Kim (Graphic Design)
Hyunwoo Kim (Graphic Design)
Sunghwan Im (Graphic Design)
Heejae Jang (Graphic Design)

Sikinnis

[Brand Design]

Client
Sikinnis
Heraklion, Greece

Design
Lazy snail Design
Copenhagen, Denmark

Project Team
Lazy snail Design:
Ioanna Drakaki (Head of Design)
Eleni Pavlaki (Creative Director)
Serafim Stroubis (Senior Art Director)
Carolina Salassa (Art Director)
Kostas Kiriakakis (Illustrator)

Nikolas Leventakis (Photographer)

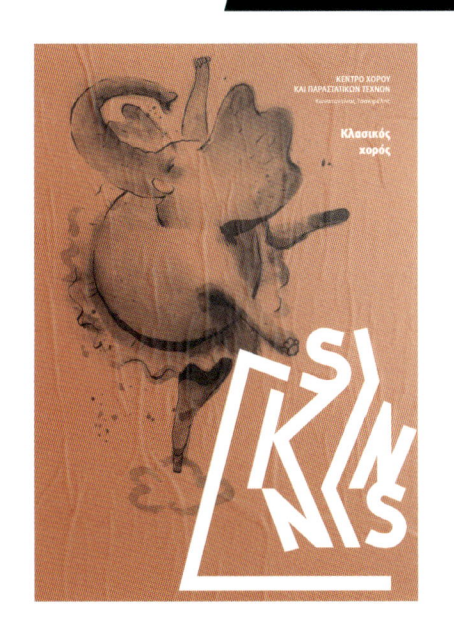

Sikinnis is a newly founded dance and performing arts centre whose name refers to the dance of the chorus in ancient Greek satyric drama. This contemporary establishment warranted a boldly designed logo that expresses both movement and the solid structure of the building. The logo was created by transforming every turn in the heavy font into a pivot point, giving the final structure a sense of movement captured in a snapshot rather than an overly static look. Complementing this structural design with gestural illustrations that present, among other things, characters from past performances, the brand design exudes a personal touch.

TAQA Theater de Vest/Grote Kerk Alkmaar

[Brand Identity]

TAQA Theater de Vest and Grote Kerk Alkmaar, a theatre and a church in the Netherlands, form a remarkable cultural cooperation. A flexible design system was created to visually connect the two and help promote their programmes and festivals. The new brand design is based on geometric forms that create attention-grabbing patterns and interact with photographs. Even though the combination of forms and colours is always different, the overall image is cohesive. The vibrant colour scheme and typefaces lend the brand a welcoming character and pique interest, from billboards to business cards to programme brochures.

Client
TAQA Theater de Vest/Grote Kerk Alkmaar
Alkmaar, Netherlands

Design
Vruchtvlees
Den Haag, Netherlands

Advertising	Packaging Design	Fair Stands	Retail Design	Red Dot: Junior Award	Designer Profiles	Index
288	318	494	516	544	614	674

Shenzhen Symphony Children's Choir

[Brand Design]

The brand design of the Shenzhen Symphony Children's Choir combines concise graphics with colourful effects to create a visual identity that the target group can easily relate to. The logo comprises six symbols, which allude to singing children as well as musical notes. The position of the mouths represents the three different vocal registers in the choir: high, middle and low. The supporting graphic system is derived from sound waves, while the rich colours express the children's lively temperament. Sound waves in six different sizes and in different colours are superimposed on each other, symbolising the intertwined beauty of different voices singing together.

Client
Shenzhen Symphony Children's Choir
Shenzhen, China

Design
Shenzhen Zdesign Co., Ltd.
Shenzhen, China

Project Team
Jiong Li (Art Direction)
Ali Wang (Graphic Design)
Mingjie Chen (Graphic Design)
E Lin (Music Design)

147

Jetlag Books

[Brand Identity]

Jetlag books is a bookstore in Beijing that focuses on lifestyle, travel, art and design. The word mark features a combination of letters, extending longitudinally up and down to symbolise different time zones. Furthermore, the circles on the letters "e", "a" and "g" indicate the altitude of the sun in different time zones. This dynamic design principle was also applied to other keywords of the brand communication. Grey as the basic colour provides a neutral frame for the accent colours of sky blue, sun yellow and evening red, which symbolise the lighting moods at different times of the day and as such characterise the brand identity.

Client
Jetlag Books
Beijing, China

Design
L3 Branding Experience Design
Beijing, China

Project Team
Guanru Li (Creative Direction)
Zhenxing Shi (Artwork)

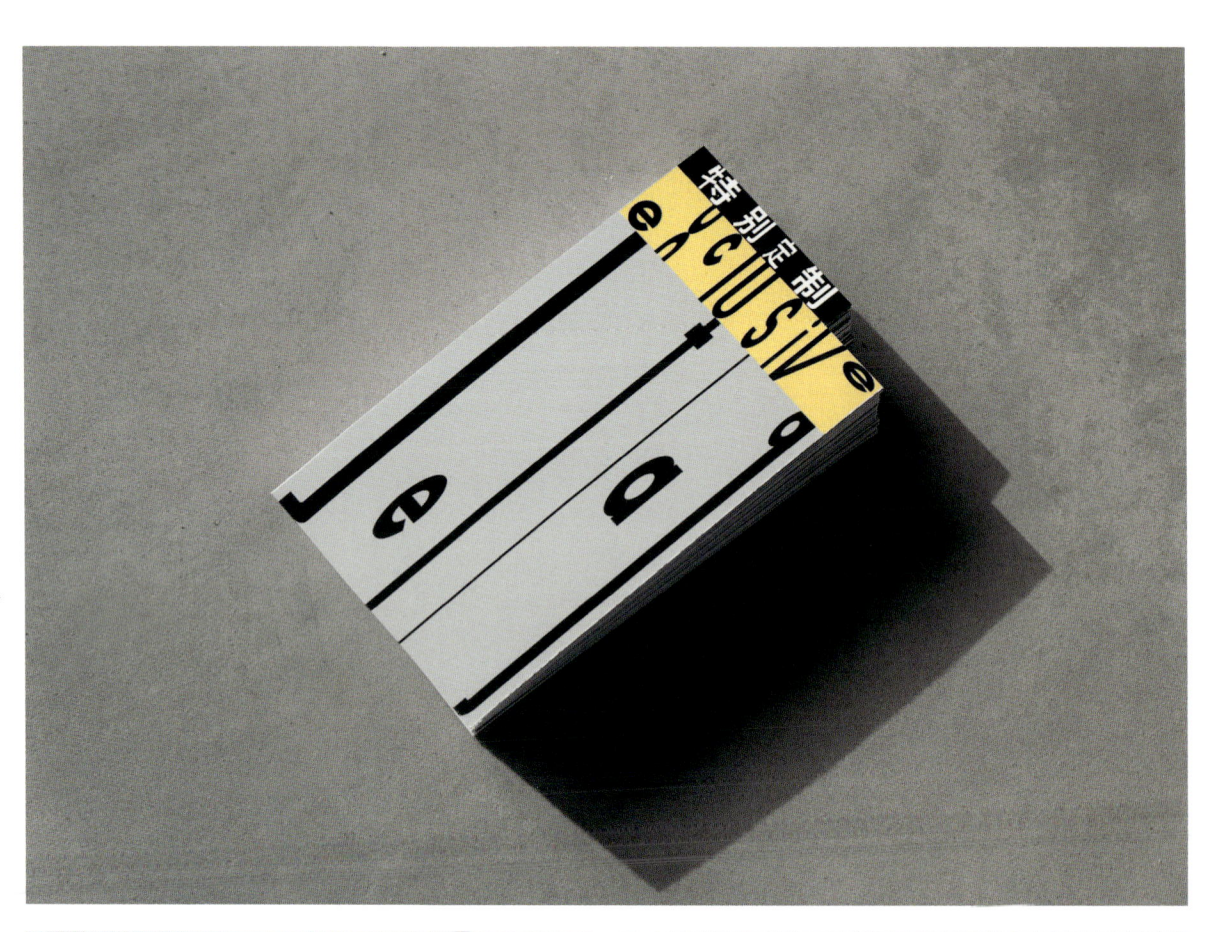

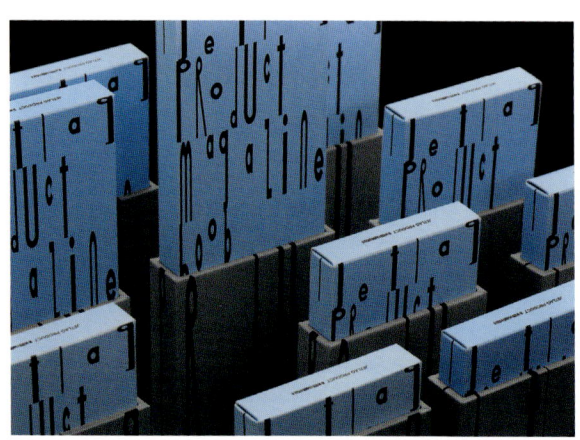

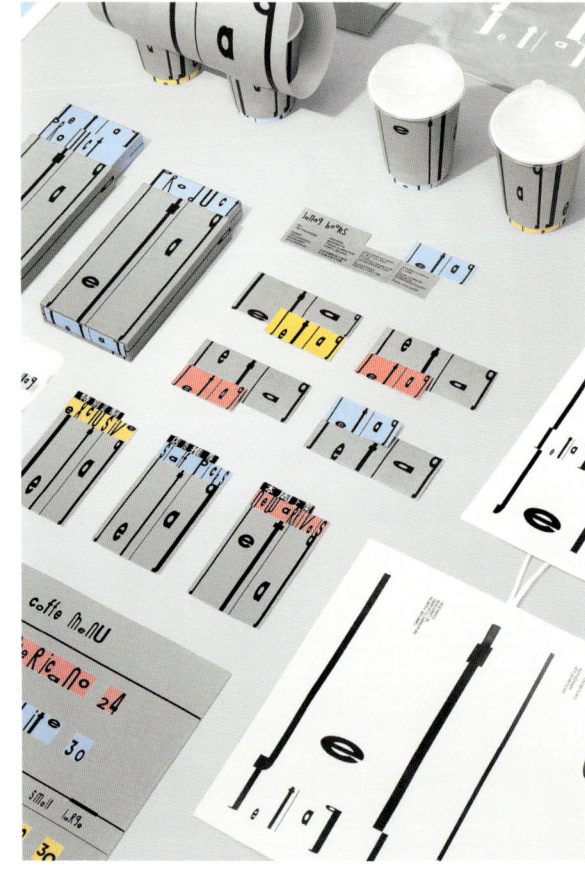

Grand Park Hotel Rovinj
[Brand Design]

Guests of the Grand Park Hotel Rovinj are given a travelogue and an instant Polaroid camera as a branded welcome gift to encourage them to record their personal experience in Rovinj. With appealing stories and legends, it motivates guests to go on a discovery tour through the city. In order to promote the attractive location of the hotel as a unique selling proposition and to build a distinctive brand identity, the branding extends discreetly to the hotel premises, such as on window stickers that invite guests to "remember" particularly impressive views from the windows.

Client
Maistra
Rovinj, Croatia

Design
Bruketa&Zinic&Grey
Zagreb, Croatia

Project Team
Davor Bruketa (Creative Director)
Mirna Pticek (Art Director)
Masa Ivanov (Client Service Director)
Zrinka Pozar (Account Manager)
Eman Ahel (Designer)
Dora Kasun (Designer)
Mia Maric (Designer)
Vesna Durasin (Production Manager)
Hana Tintor (Illustrator)
Danijel Srdarev (Illustrator)
Klara Rusan (Illustrator)
Marko Tadic (Illustrator)

Preface	Red Dot: Agency of the Year	Brands	Brand Design & Identity	Corporate Design & Identity	Annual Reports
4	6	18	90	202	260

pêt à porter
[Brand Design, Brand Identity]

The Korean brand pêt à porter sells a range of fashionable pet items with a brand design that focuses on the emotional relationship between people and their pets. Inspired by the French fashion term prêt-à-porter, the logo conveys the premium quality of the products. Combining the shapes of a dog and a cat, it portrays these pets in the spotlight on a catwalk, an image that is enhanced by the colour scheme. In addition, the claim "ready to walk" refers to the catwalk and offers fashion-conscious animal owners an appealing brand experience.

Client
Leferi
Seoul, South Korea

Design
B:SCOPE STUDIO
Seoul, South Korea

Advertising	Packaging Design	Fair Stands	Retail Design	Red Dot: Junior Award	Designer Profiles	Index
288	318	494	516	544	614	674

Wedding Book
[Brand Design]

Wedding Book is the name of a smart wedding planner, an online platform that assists couples in every step of their wedding planning process. The brand logo picks up on the emotionality of the target group and shows two hearts that become one. Three additional graphic motifs are derived from the contours of the symbol: a door, curtains and a heart. These illustrations guide users through various intuitive apps that can deliver personalised user experience. A harmonious colour palette rounds off the brand design, lending the brand identity a high recognition value.

Client
Wedding Book
Seoul, South Korea

Design
HuskyFox
Seoul, South Korea

Project Team
Doohee Lee (Creative Direction)
Kiyoung Jung (Creative Direction)
Taehee Lee (Strategic Planning)
Hyuncheol Ahn (Graphic Design)

The Dark Sky Project

[Brand Design]

In 2012, the Aoraki Mackenzie International Dark Sky Reserve was launched and light pollution became strictly controlled within the area covered by the reserve. Part of the project involved branding this new tourist attraction in New Zealand. The name "The Dark Sky Project" epitomised the ongoing pursuit and cause-driven aspect of the entity. The brand design centred on a core mark that represented the Southern Cross, the most dominant constellation in the southern sky, along with a word grid that enabled the assembly of word-based constellations to create messaging, statements and names that could be used across all visitor touchpoints.

Client
Ngai Tahu Tourism
Christchurch, New Zealand

Design
ThoughtFull
Auckland, New Zealand

Project Team
Geoff Suvalko (Creative Director)
Aaron Richardson (Design Director)
Andrea Fouhey (Design Manager)

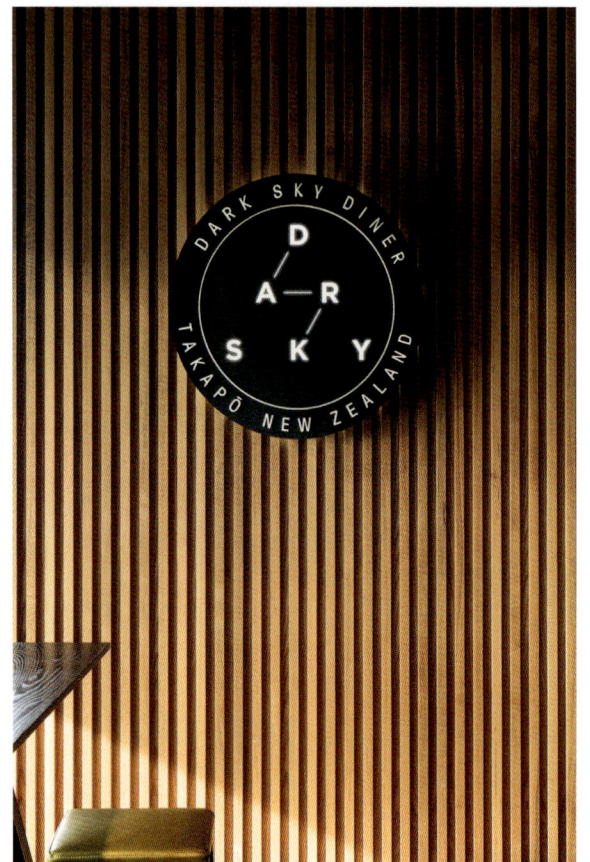

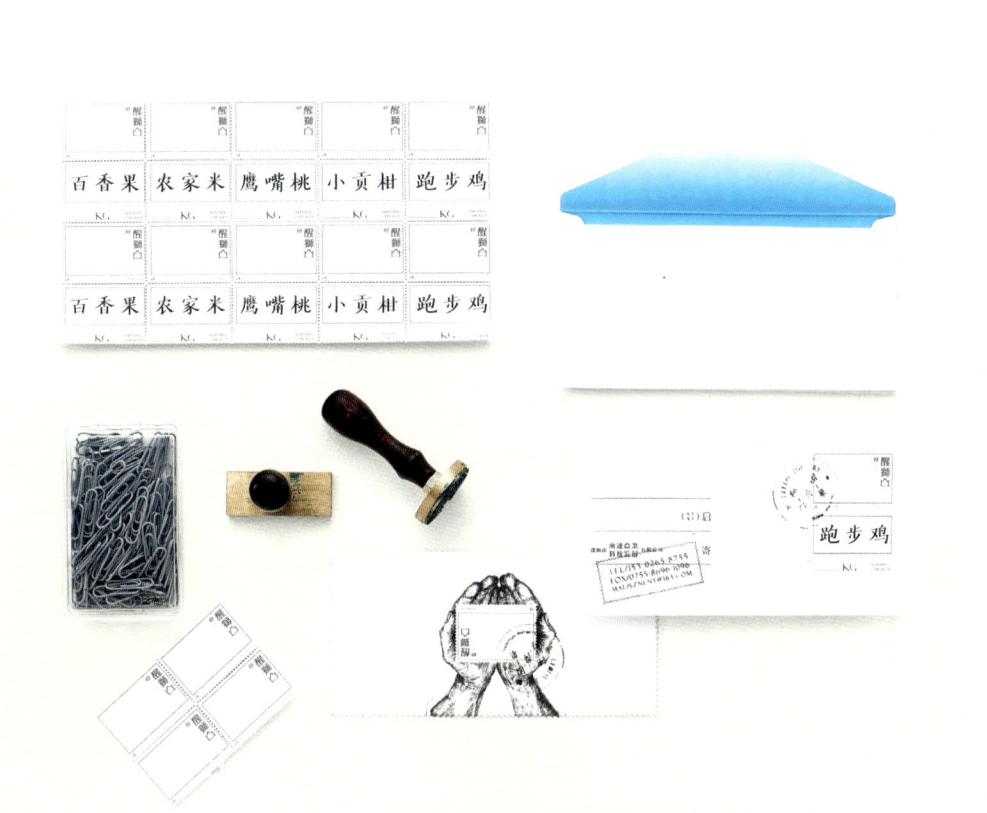

Advertising	Packaging Design	Fair Stands	Retail Design	Red Dot: Junior Award	Designer Profiles	Index
288	318	494	516	544	614	674

Xing Shi Shan

[Brand Design]

The Poverty Alleviation Project aims to use branding to increase the sales of agricultural products from unprofitable farms and thus end the poverty of the farmers. The focus of the brand strategy is lasting customer loyalty. The design was developed on the premise of minimising production costs, yet achieving a strong visual effect. All materials are environmentally friendly and handmade by farmers, lending the brand a personal feel. Exploring new ideas in the design of packaging for express deliveries, the brand communication aims to convey a sense of warmth in the form of traditional handwritten letters, motivating customers to purchase again.

Client
Nanlian Agricultural
Shenzhen, China

Design
Shenzhen One More Culture
Communication Co., Ltd.
Shenzhen, China

Project Team
Xia Jiangnan (Project Management)
Zhang Haiqiang (Project Management)
Meng Shenhui (Project Management)
Huang Fupeng (Project Management)
Mao Jian (Project Management)
Qiu Yang (Project Management)

→ Designer profile on page 658

Preface	Red Dot: Agency of the Year	Brands	Brand Design & Identity	Corporate Design & Identity	Annual Reports
4	6	18	90	202	260

Jin Hui Organic Farm

[Brand Design]

Jin Hui Organic Farm was established in 2012 as a company that integrates vegetable production and organic field agriculture. An eye-catching brand design was developed to increase brand awareness. A new set of graphic symbols reflect the product diversity. The illustrations are characterised by bright yellow and green hues, as well as geometric figures inspired by the abstract form of fruits and vegetables. The logo is designed in a handwritten style to lend the two complicated Chinese characters of Jin Hui a more graphic appeal and enhance the recognisability of the brand.

Client
Jin Hui Organic Farm
Beijing, China

Design
San Yang Studio
Beijing, China

Project Team
Yuening Bai (Art Direction)
Zihan Meng (Graphic Design)
Jin Bai (Graphic Design)
Yiyao Zhao (Graphic Design)

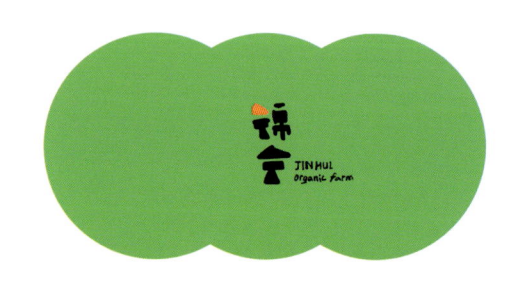

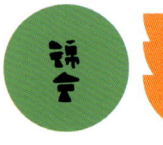

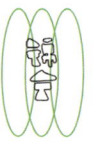

Advertising	Packaging Design	Fair Stands	Retail Design	Red Dot: Junior Award	Designer Profiles	Index
288	318	494	516	544	614	674

Food & Beyond
[Brand Design]

Climate change and ever-growing consumer expectations place food at the intersection of trends shaping our world. The Technical Research Centre of Finland (VTT) initiated the development of a platform for a future-oriented ecosystem built around food, encompassing innovative food products, technologies and services. The platform was named "Food & Beyond" to communicate its collaborative and inclusive nature. The development of the brand design set out to go beyond the brand foundation, visual identity and a website. One of the key drivers was the consideration of how to scale the brand to other ecosystems by embracing system thinking.

Client
VTT Technical Research Centre of Finland Ltd.
Espoo, Finland

Design
Fjord
Helsinki, Finland

Project Team
VTT:
Mirva Lampinen
Tatu Vienamo
Niall Shakeshaft

Fjord:
Stéphanie Del Rey (Design Director)
Ville Kovanen (Visual Design Lead)
Sunwha Park (Visual Designer)
Konstantin Berger (Design Lead)

Revert
[Brand Design]

Client
BGF ecobio
Seoul, South Korea

Design
PROJECT EDDY
Seoul, South Korea

Project Team
BGF ecobio:
Junghyuk Hong (Project Direction)
Junghoo Oh (Project Direction)
Byunghak Kang (Creative Direction)
Minji Kim (Creative Direction)

PROJECT EDDY:
Yeda Cho (Creative Direction)
Dayeon Park (Creative Direction)
Minjin Lee (Graphic Design)
Hyerin Kang (Graphic Design)

→ Clip online

Advertising	Packaging Design	Fair Stands	Retail Design	Red Dot: Junior Award	Designer Profiles	Index
288	318	494	516	544	614	674

Revert is a new brand of eco-friendly biodegradable plastic materials that will naturally decompose within six months. Based on the company's sustainable technology, a new visual identity has been designed to underline the message of "return the Earth to a clean and healthy state of nature". The symbol used in the figurative mark consistently conveys the brand identity with diagonal and arrow graphics. Complementary icons in the style of the logo visually represent nature, such as trees or water drops. The result is a coherent design language combined with a clear colour code that defines the overall appearance – from the logo to its various applications.

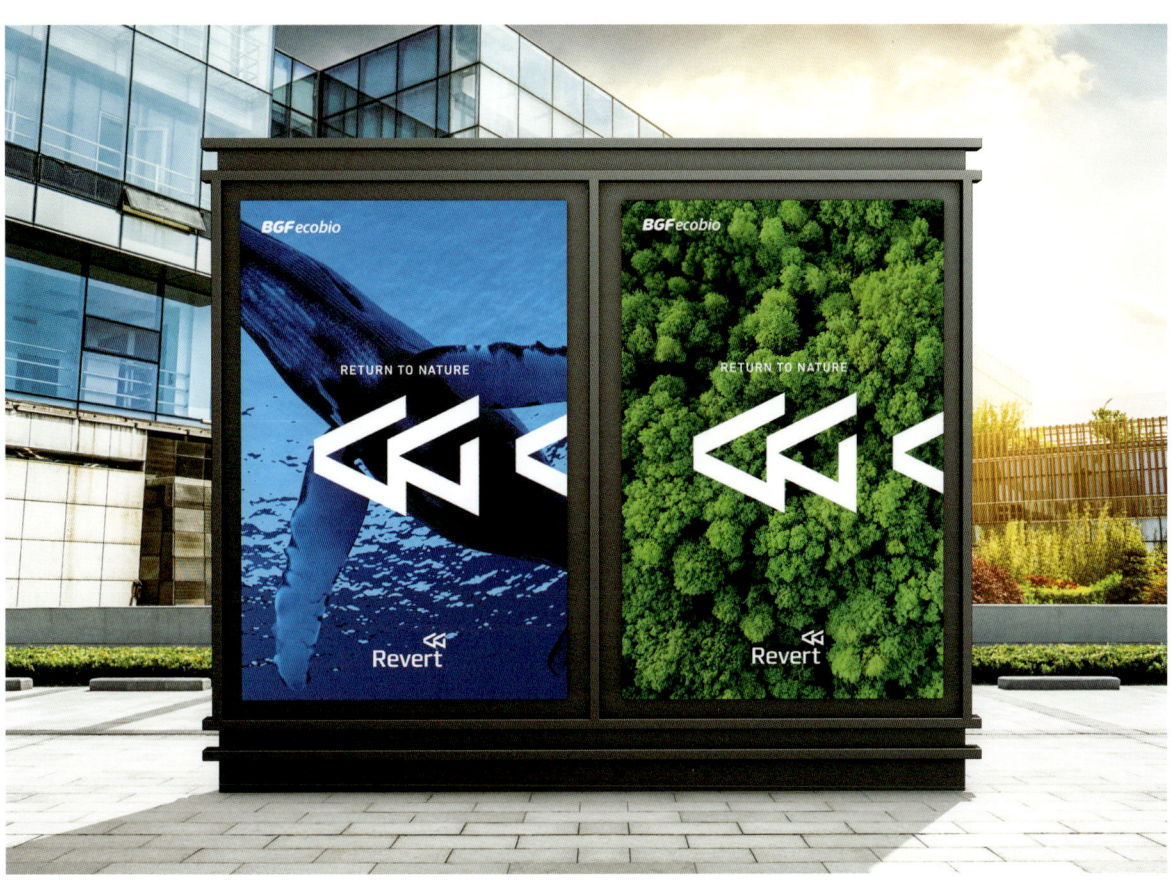

Between Contrasts

[Brand Design, Visual Identity]

The Entre Contrastes (Between Contrasts) exhibition featured handicrafts made of waste from the textile and paper industry in Brazil. The logo played on the contrasts between the different exhibits, the words being formed through an effect of presence and absence of letters. Black and white stand in contrast to the abundance of colours visible in the handicrafts. The chosen brand design solutions reduced waste at the end of the event. By bringing up concepts such as creative reuse, the exhibition appealed to visitors to reflect on consumption and its consequences for the environment and future generations.

Client
Sebrae/SC
Florianópolis, Brazil

Design
Yepá Estúdio
Florianópolis, Brazil

Project Team
Carolina Dentice (Creative Direction)
Luana Dentice (Creative Direction)
Cristiane Amaral (Graphic Design)
Priscyla Falkenburger (Graphic Design)

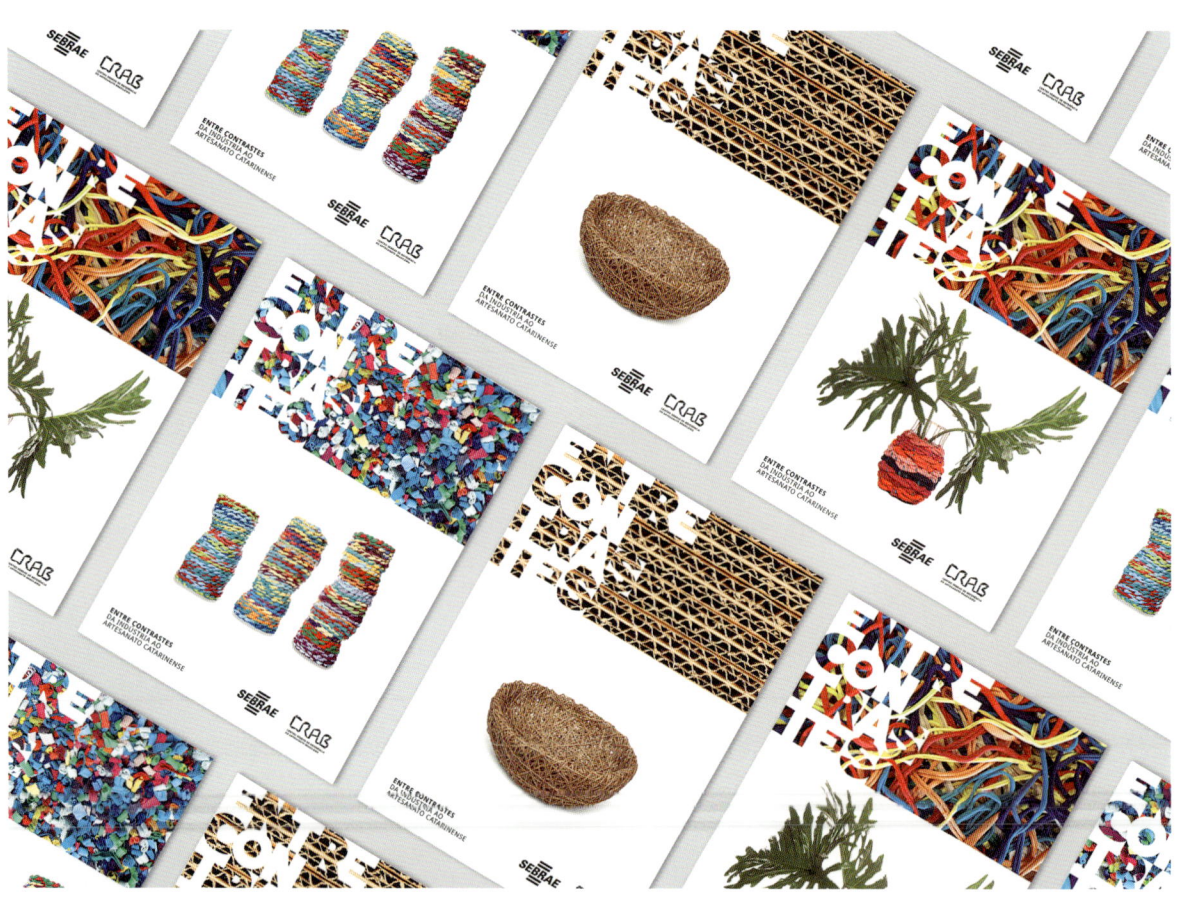

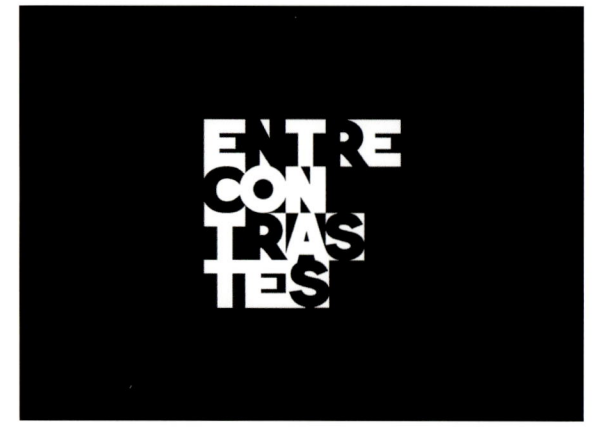

PLUS 1
[Brand Identity]

PLUS 1 is the brand name of a street-based photography exhibition organised with the intention to support the families of fallen servicemen and create memorials out of their stories. In addition, the objective of the brand identity is to build a new socio-cultural image of Ukrainians as defenders of the values of democracy and freedom. The language of the imagery is based on the fact that plus and minus are inseparable concepts: where there is a minus, there is always a plus, and vice versa. Based on this, 28 graphic symbols were created to be added to a modular grid. Each grid has one blank section, but the viewer will find the missing symbol in the photo motif.

Client
Public Organization
"Euro-Atlantic Course"
Kyiv, Ukraine

Design
VANDOG agency
Kyiv, Ukraine

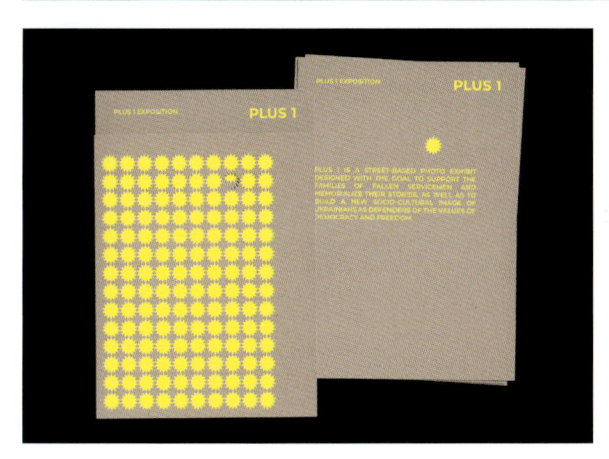

Preface	Red Dot: Agency of the Year	Brands	**Brand Design & Identity**	Corporate Design & Identity	Annual Reports
4	6	18	90	202	260

FRESH BLOOD
DG YOUTH

[Brand Design, Exhibition Design]

Client
FRESH BLOOD DG YOUTH
Dongguan, China

Design
xiexie design
Dongguan, China

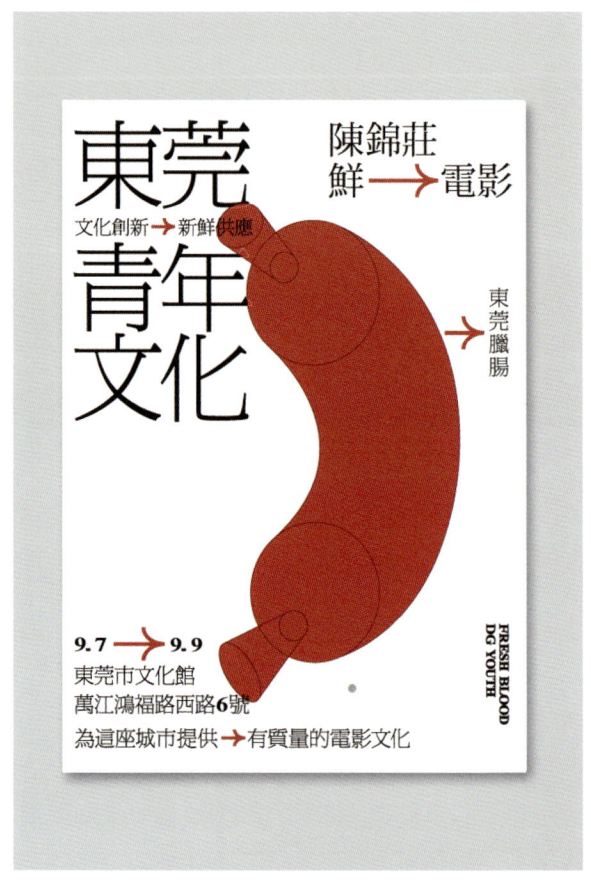

Advertising	Packaging Design	Fair Stands	Retail Design	Red Dot: Junior Award	Designer Profiles	Index
288	318	494	516	544	614	674

In 2019, FRESH BLOOD DG YOUTH was invited to participate in a special exhibition organised by the Public Cultural Products Purchasing Association, bringing together six young people who have had achievements in various cultural fields to form a travelling exhibition. The visuals of the exhibition design were inspired by the food industry and took the form of six motifs, each showing a typical food from the artists' home towns. Reminiscent of paper cutting, the key visuals are reduced to their contours and implemented in different colours, which results in a diverse yet consistent overall image.

Eurovision Song Contest 2020

[Visual Identity]

The Eurovision Song Contest is a world-famous TV music show. The 2020 edition was supposed to take place in the Netherlands but had to be cancelled due to the COVID-19 pandemic. The task was to create a range of key visuals that complement the generic Eurovision brand logo. An iconic data-driven identity was developed using special software to honour the long history of the contest in a contemporary manner. The visual identity conveys international openness by connecting the flag colours of the participating countries and creating a unified, yet diverse feel.

Client
NPO/NOS/AVROTROS
in collaboration with EBU
Hilversum, Netherlands

Design
CLEVER°FRANKE
Utrecht, Netherlands

Project Team
Thomas Clever (Creative Direction)
Gert Franke (Creative Direction)
Roel de Jonge (Graphic Design)
Bas van der Burgh (Graphic Design)
Jonas Groot Kormelink (Programming)
Wilco Tomassen (Programming)

Ben Prins (Graphic Design)

→ Designer profile on page 629

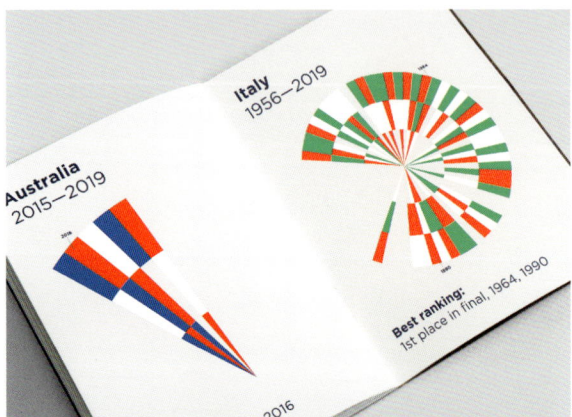

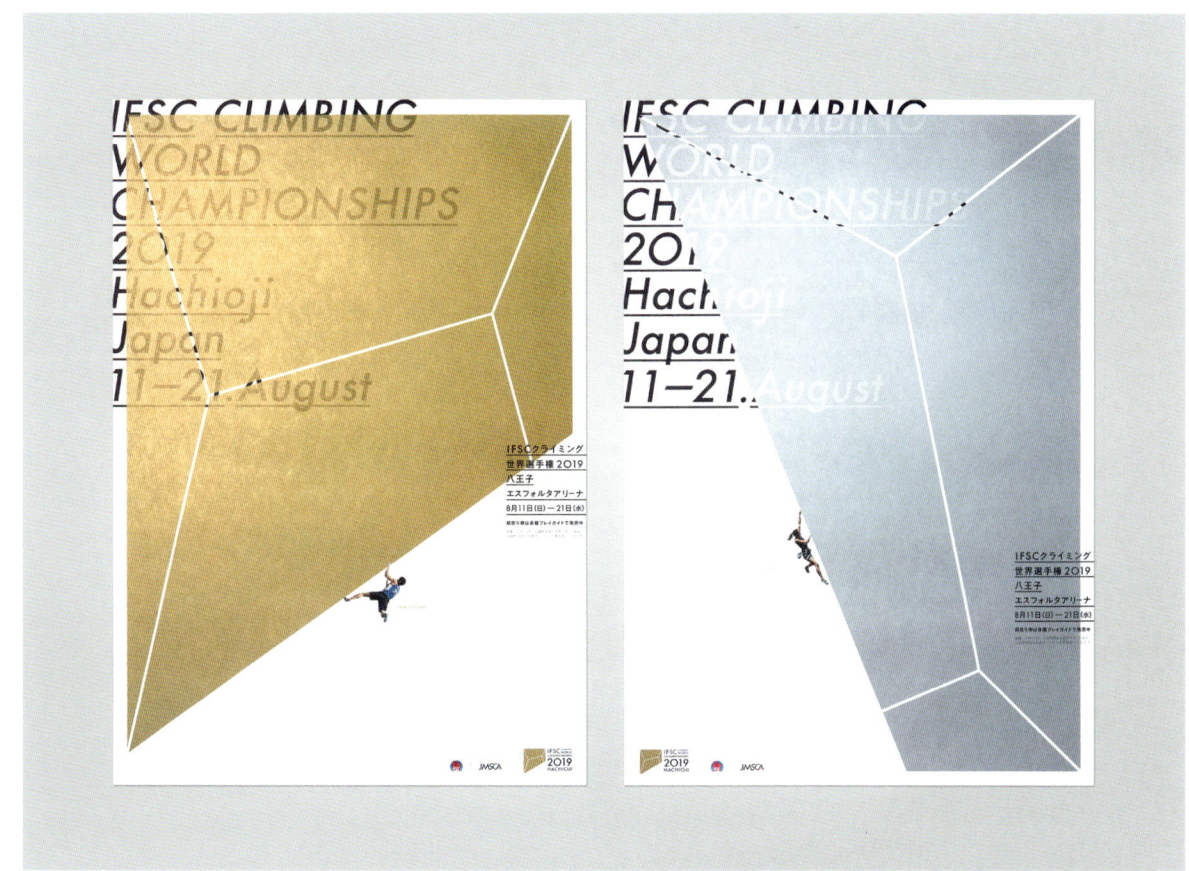

The Huge Wall – IFSC Climbing World Championships 2019

[Brand Design]

Sport climbing was approved for the 2020 Olympics, raising the profile of this minor sport in Japan. An eye-catching brand design was developed to emphasise the significance of the IFSC Climbing World Championships 2019, which was held in Hachioji, Tokyo. Representing the name of the city, the letter "H" was integrated into an abstract image of a climbing wall to form the brand's symbol. On key visual aids such as posters, this symbol was printed so that it overlaps the event information. Overprinting the typography with gold and silver ink resulted in a fascinating visual effect that causes the text to fade and the wall to appear more clearly when viewed under a spotlight.

Client
International Federation of Sport Climbing
Turin, Italy

Design
PEN.Inc.
Tokyo, Japan
Japan Mountaineering & Sport Climbing Association
Tokyo, Japan

Project Team
Japan Mountaineering & Sport Climbing Association:
Ryusuke Fujieda (Creative Direction)

PEN.Inc.:
Taiji Kimura (Art Direction)

Dentsu On Demand Graphic Inc.:
Shinya Tamura (Printing)

2019 GLOBAL WOW PROJECT AWARD

[Brand Design, Brand Identity]

LINE supports global business development in cooperation with programmers, designers, marketers, sales personnel and PR managers. As part of the annual GLOBAL WOW PROJECT AWARDS, members around the world tuned in to a global live stream to vote for their favourite among the nominated projects. The logo borrows the lines from the event organiser's brand design in order to illustrate their close connection. The WOW=NO.1 graphic motif was used as a visual element for the award ceremony as well as on posters, videos and various items, including trophies and t-shirts, to encourage participation in the next award.

Client
LINE Plus Corporation
Seongnam, South Korea

Design
LINE Plus Corporation
Seongnam, South Korea

Advertising	Packaging Design	Fair Stands	Retail Design	Red Dot: Junior Award	Designer Profiles	Index
288	318	494	516	544	614	674

2019 World Manufacturing Convention

[Brand Design]

The brand design of this conference aims to highlight a "new era in the manufacturing industry" by focusing on the creative aspects of craftsmanship and placing the brand in an international context. The overall visual image is a combination of Chinese and foreign styles. Its universal design language expresses both openness and trend awareness. Complementary colours underline a distinctive collage of geometric forms. Contemporary western design techniques were used to construct the Chinese character Zao (meaning to manufacture), integrating both cultures into the conference's image for its external communication.

Client
World Manufacturing Convention
Bureau of Expo
Hefei, China

Design
Hefei Designdo Industrial Design Co., Ltd.
Hefei, China
Shenzhen Zdesign Co., Ltd.
Shenzhen, China

Project Team
Jiong Li (Art Direction)
Mingjie Chen (Graphic Design)
Fajin Yi (Graphic Design)

Keep Running – 2019 The 9th China International Poster Biennial

[Brand Design]

A particularly eye-catching brand design was developed for the 9th China International Poster Biennial in 2019. A series of key visuals illustrates the motto "Keep Running" with layers of poster paper accumulating to form the contours of a human body. These unusual motifs are made up of three different combinations of yellow, red and pink paper. Relentlessly pushing forward, the key visuals illustrate the diversity of the international participants and their shared interest in the dynamic progress of poster design.

Client
China Academy of Art
Hangzhou, China

Design
Weichen Wu
Hangzhou, China

Advertising	Packaging Design	Fair Stands	Retail Design	Red Dot: Junior Award	Designer Profiles	Index
288	318	494	516	544	614	674

2019 Haiyan County Cultural Creative Design Competition

[Key Visuals]

The 2019 Haiyan County Creative Design Competition was aimed at encouraging college students to collect and develop innovative product concepts that reflect the characteristics of Haiyan County. The visual identity conveys a young and colourful image and showcases iconic symbols of Haiyan County, such as buildings and cultural relics, drawn in a uniform, abstract style. The resulting key visuals were combined into high-contrast collages to make a strong visual impact on the target group and were featured on items including outdoor posters, badges, invitations and tickets.

Client
Haiyan County People's Government
Haiyan, China

Design
Zhejiang Gongshang University
Hangzhou, China

Project Team
Ying Gao (Graphic Design)
Kan Zhao (Graphic Design)
Ping Yang (Graphic Design)

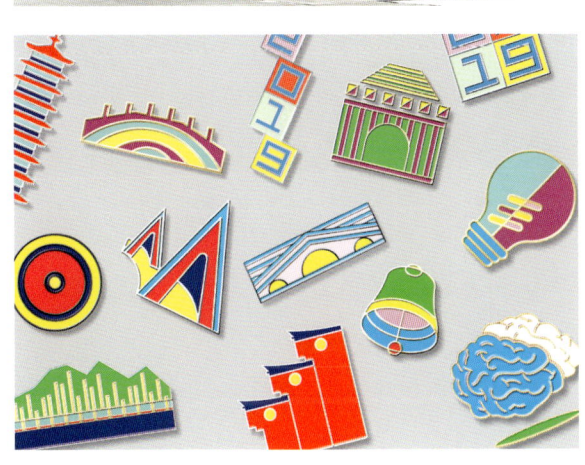

4th International Industrial Design Innovations Forum PUSHKA

[Brand Design]

PUSHKA is an international industrial design innovations forum, where design students can establish contacts with manufacturers and get an opportunity to realise their projects. Its brand design is built on the product portfolio of its sponsors and showcases three-dimensional figures of kitchen sinks, taps, hoods and blenders, turning everyday kitchen items into art objects. Furthermore, modern dynamic font compositions represent the creative approach of the students. Thus, the brand design's visual elements are characterised by a wide variety of shapes, allowing it to be flexibly applied on posters and other media.

Client
Omoikiri Rus
Saint Petersburg, Russia

Design
Omoikiri Rus
Saint Petersburg, Russia

Project Team
Pavel Keiv (CEO)
Natalia Makarova (Art Direction)
Alina Matasova (Main Graphic Design)
Natalia Belozerova (Graphic Design)
Denis Borisov (3D Design)
Anna Korovkina (Web Design)
Anna Ovsiannikova (Industrial Design)
Vladislav Krivorot
(Front-End Web Development)

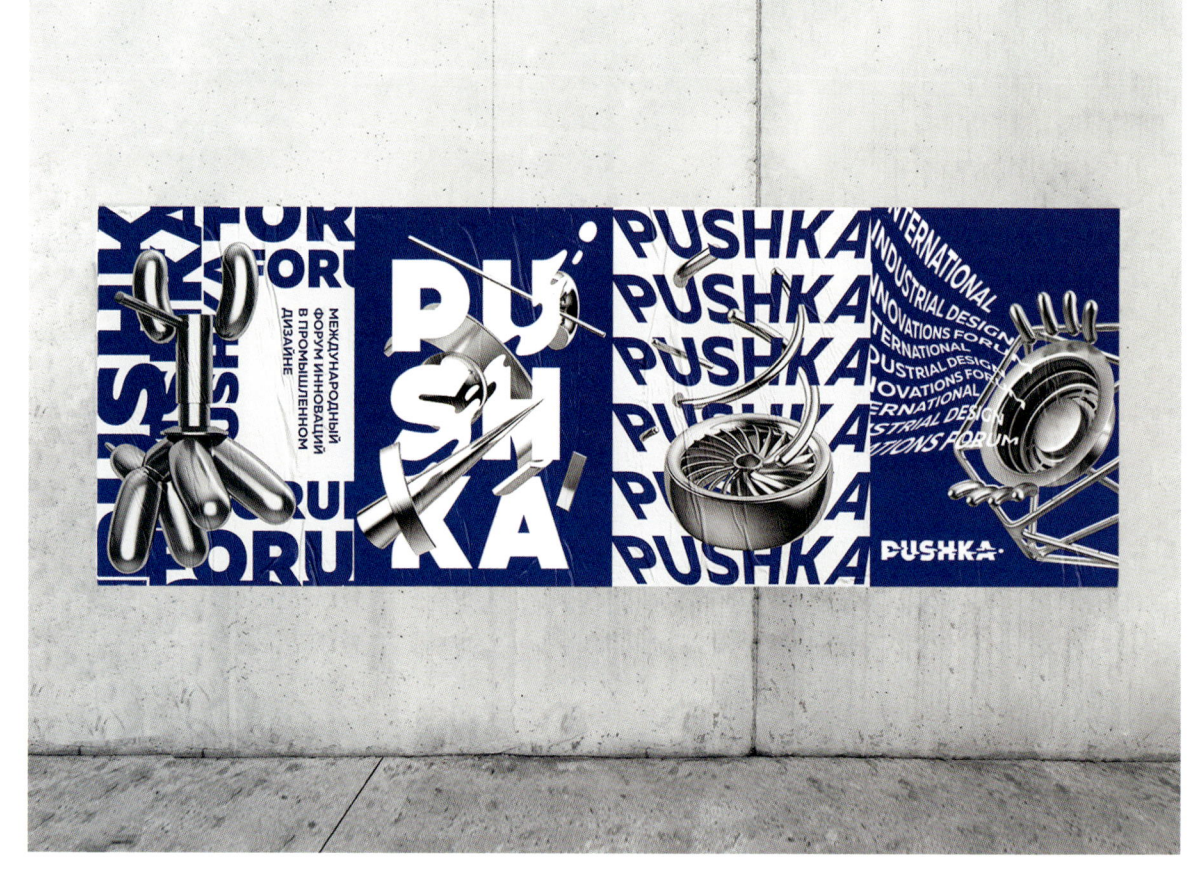

Advertising	Packaging Design	Fair Stands	Retail Design	Red Dot: Junior Award	Designer Profiles	Index
288	318	494	516	544	614	674

Bauhaus 100 – Manifest of Practice in Taiwan

[Visual Identity]

To celebrate the centenary of Bauhaus design, Taiwan Tech University and Weimar Bauhaus University cooperated on a series of workshops and exhibitions to show current design education methods that are influenced by Bauhaus design education from a century ago. The events took place at Taiwan Tech and aimed not only to promote the universities' programmes but also to illustrate the ideas of the Bauhaus. The spirit of Bauhaus design was condensed into a background motif composed of straight horizontal lines. A variety of key visuals were created and integrated into the grid through the participation of the visitors.

Client
National Taiwan University of Science and Technology
Taipei City, Taiwan
Weimar Bauhaus University
Weimar, Germany

Design
Ken-Tsai Lee Design Lab/Taiwan Tech
Taipei City, Taiwan

Project Team
Ken-Tsai Lee (Creative Director)
Po-En Wang
Pei-Rong Chen
Ruo-Jieh Chen
Ming-Huei Lyu
Zong-Yi Xie
Brynn Wang
Chang Chiao
Chan-Ming Hsu
Han Hang
Jhih-Sing Yang
I-Hao Liao
Adrian Palko

Digital Civilization Conference

[Brand Identity]

The brand design for the Digital Civilization Conference visually represents the topic of the symposium in a fascinating manner. The logo is at the centre of the brand identity. The circles and squares of the graphical element represent the digits 0 and 1 used in the binary system. The specific arrangement of the circles and squares corresponds to binary codes that translate to the acronym for the conference: the binary code 01000100 stands for the letter D and 01000011 for C. The brand image, consistently implemented in black and white plus different shades of grey, is complemented by a colour symbol reminiscent of a globe.

Client
Oxford (Hainan) Blockchain Research Institute Co., Ltd.
Hainan, China

Design
Dongdao Creative Branding Group
Beijing, China

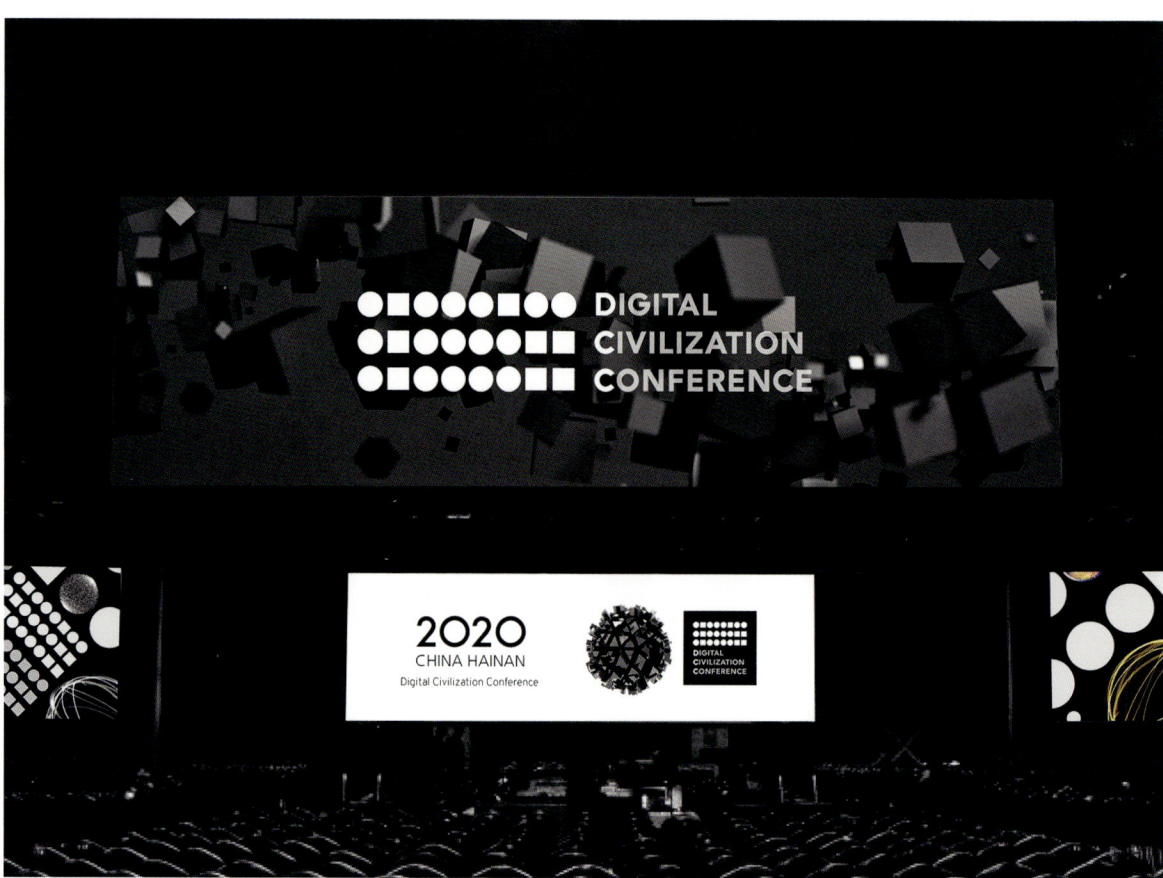

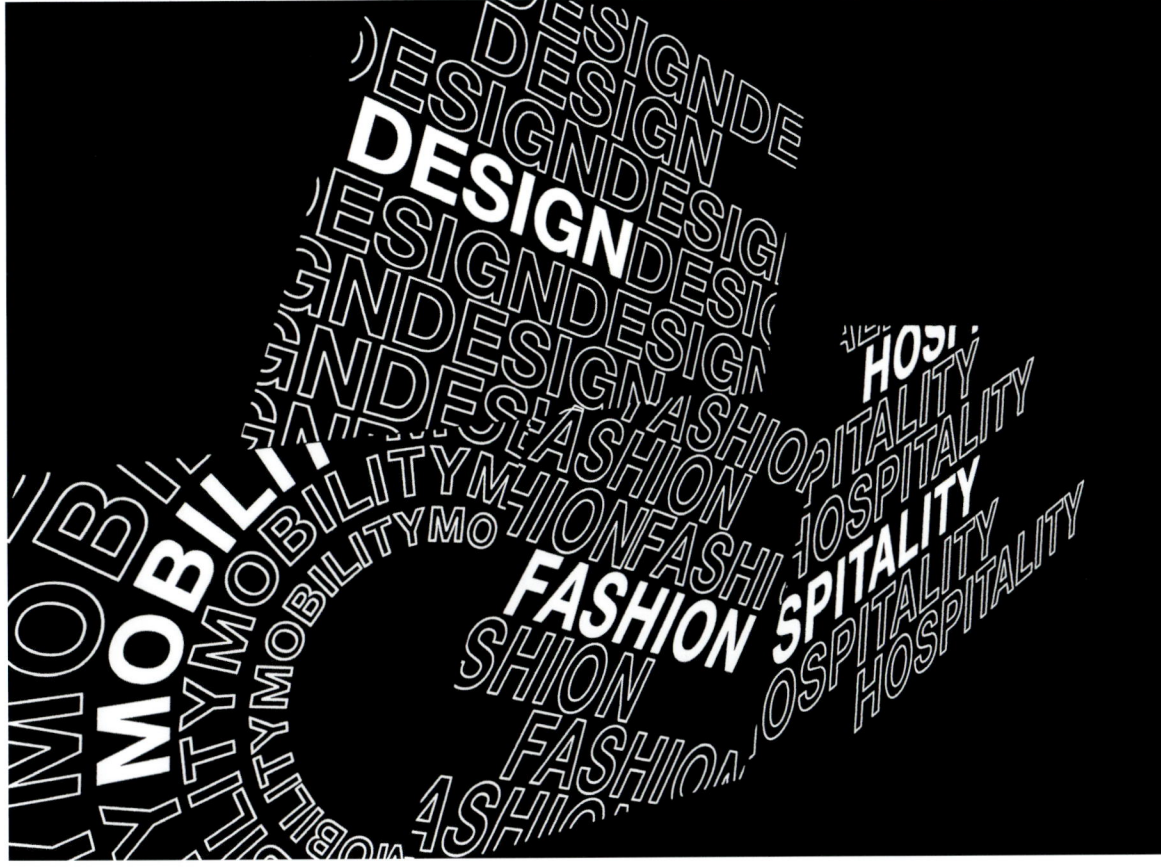

Next Design Perspectives 2019

[Brand Identity,
Integrated Communication]

Next Design Perspectives is an annual conference in Italy that discusses the impact of social and technological changes through the lens of design and creativity. It brought together an international line-up of designers, entrepreneurs and researchers for the second time in 2019. With regard to a broad cultural identity, a timeless brand design was created based on a distinctive black-and-white word mark. The stringent implementation achieved a distinctive overall image, including across digital and social media platforms, specific communication materials as well as promotional items for the participants.

Client
Fondazione Altagamma
Milan, Italy

Design
Nascent Design
Milan, Italy

Project Team
Max Bosio (Creative Direction)
Paloma Valls (Graphic Design)
Gabriele Gastaldin (Graphic Design)
Gabriele Calvi (Motion Design)
Eleonora Molin (Project Management)
Francesca Conte (Project Management)

→ Designer profile on page 651

SKVOT

[Brand Design]

Client
SKVOT
Kyiv, Ukraine

Design
CREVV
Kyiv, Ukraine

Project Team
Anton Ivanov (Design Concept)
Natalia Ivanova (Design Concept)
Serhii Irkhin (Animation)

→ Clip online

SKVOT is a Ukrainian online school for creative people. The school aims at positioning itself as an "onoffline school", a term that conveys the concept of combining online courses and self-organised learning. The logo features a graphic element derived from the squatter symbol. The arrow has been turned upside down to make the symbol appear like an "S", referring to the first capital letter of the brand name. The typographical design of the lettering also captures the on/offline concept by combining the two fonts Helvetica and New Pixel Grotesk. In addition, the brand design is enhanced by different identification colours for the courses and stylish portraits of the lecturers.

Samsung KX

[Visual Identity]

The Samsung KX in London offers a contemporary space free of merchandising to inspire digital culture. The venue is astounding, from its heritage-focused design to thoughtful furnishings to creative programming. During the creation of its visual identity, the challenge was to find a solution that would make the location stand out as a one-of-a-kind cultural destination while working within the brand identity system of Samsung. Matching the location at King's Cross, the logo features a combination of the letters "K" and "X". The monogram is designed to adapt and evolve. It acts as a graphic container for graphic elements that make the overall experience vibrant.

Client
Samsung Electronics Co., Ltd.
Suwon, South Korea

Design
Cheil Worldwide
Seoul, South Korea

Design Team
Simon Hong (Executive Creative Director)
Jaehun Heo (Creative Director)
Heeyoung Lee (Senior Designer)
Soyeon Yoo (Senior Designer)
Seungtae Kim (Designer)

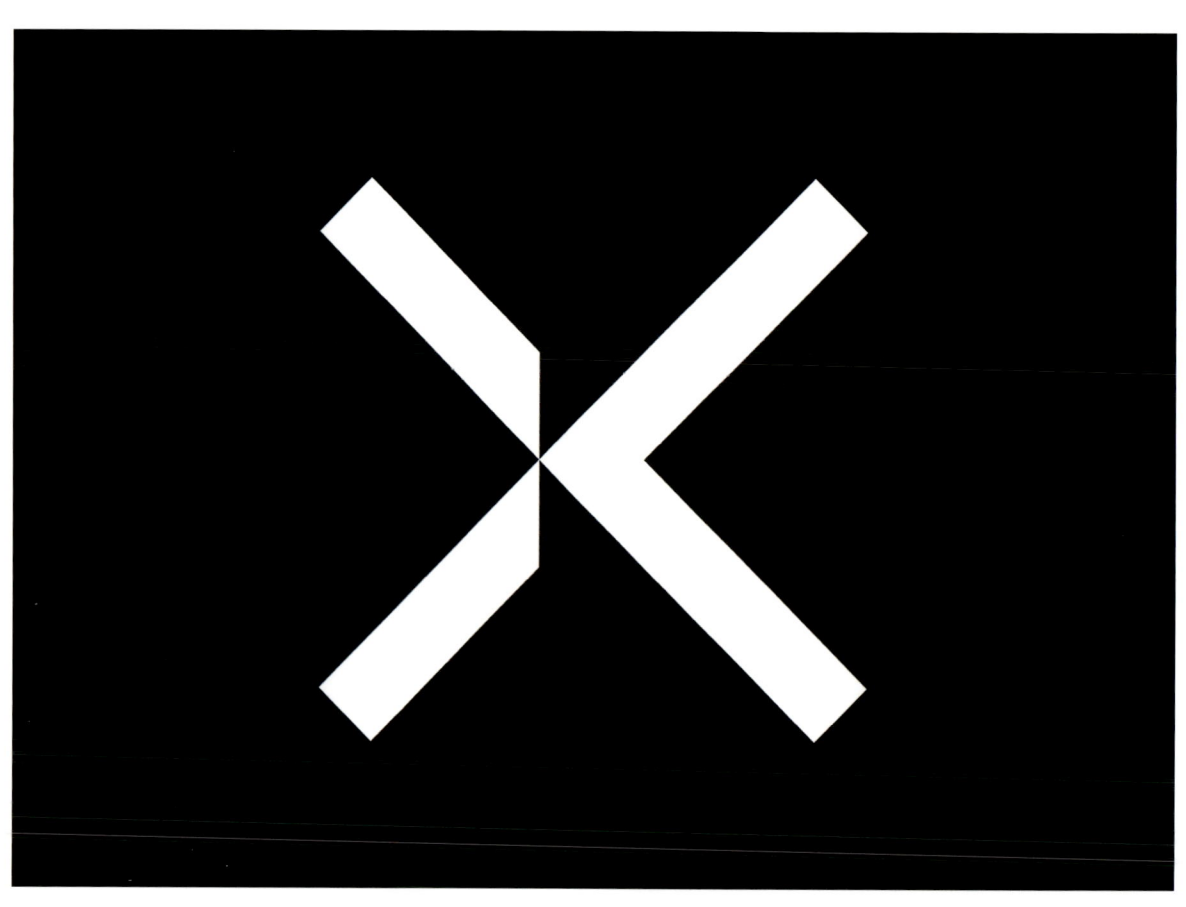

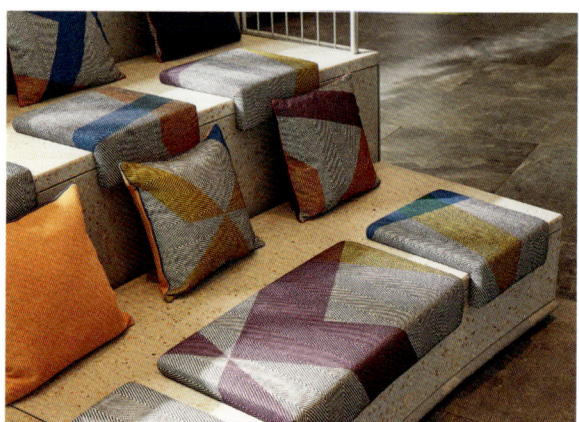

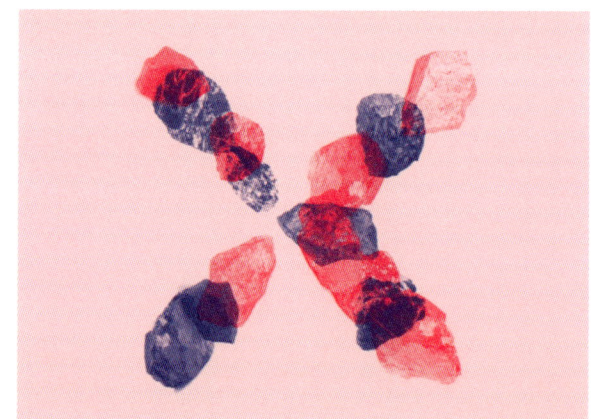

Advertising	Packaging Design	Fair Stands	Retail Design	Red Dot: Junior Award	Designer Profiles	Index
288	318	494	516	544	614	674

cociety
[Brand Design, Brand Identity]

cociety is a platform for creators to support their business and design projects. The brand name stands for "co-society" and communicates the idea of a community of like-minded designers who grow through mutual exchange. Based on this concept, the brand identity is revealed by the distinctive word mark in a lowercase serif typeface with delicate details. Representing inspiration and ambition, the bold orange colour creates a strong contrast to the typography and key visuals. The brand design has been consistently implemented, from brand stationery to the welcome kit for new members.

Client
cociety
Seoul, South Korea

Design
UMP
Seoul, South Korea

Project Team
Taeyang Wui (Creative Direction)
Hyuna Lee (Graphic Design)
Siuk Kang (Graphic Design)
Arang Lee (Graphic Design)

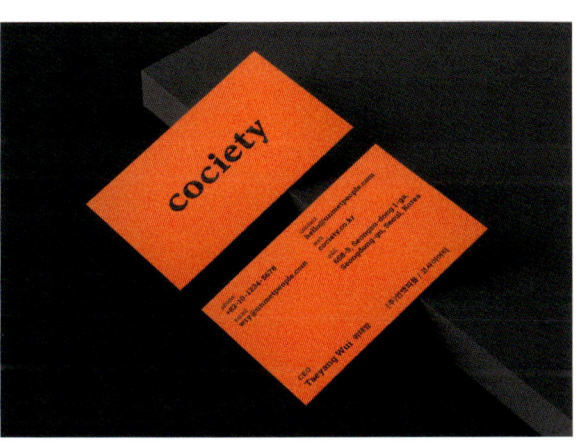

theDesk

[Brand Identity]

Client
theDesk
Hong Kong

Design
Toby Ng Design
Hong Kong

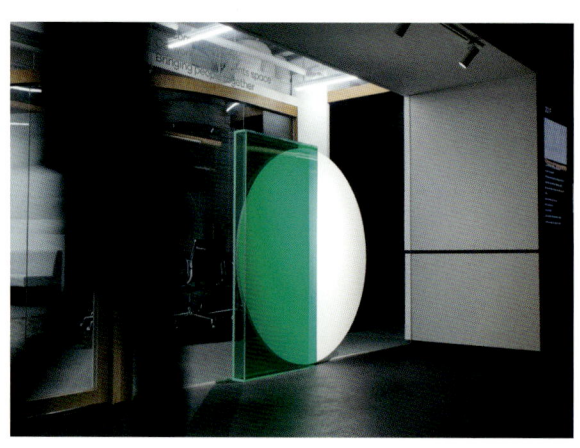

Advertising	Packaging Design	Fair Stands	Retail Design	Red Dot: Junior Award	Designer Profiles	Index
288	318	494	516	544	614	674

theDesk is a co-working space founded in Hong Kong with the ambition to build communities, enabling business growth for both its members and the surrounding neighbourhood. The goal was to establish a brand identity as a market differentiator by emphasising the company's focus on community and connection. The graphic element of the logo consists of a circle and a rectangle, representing tables joined together to form a "D", an abbreviation of the brand name. Inspired by a modernist approach, the geometric simplicity of this graphic element aims to reflect the space's minimal architecture. The branding also extends to a set of stationery and print applications.

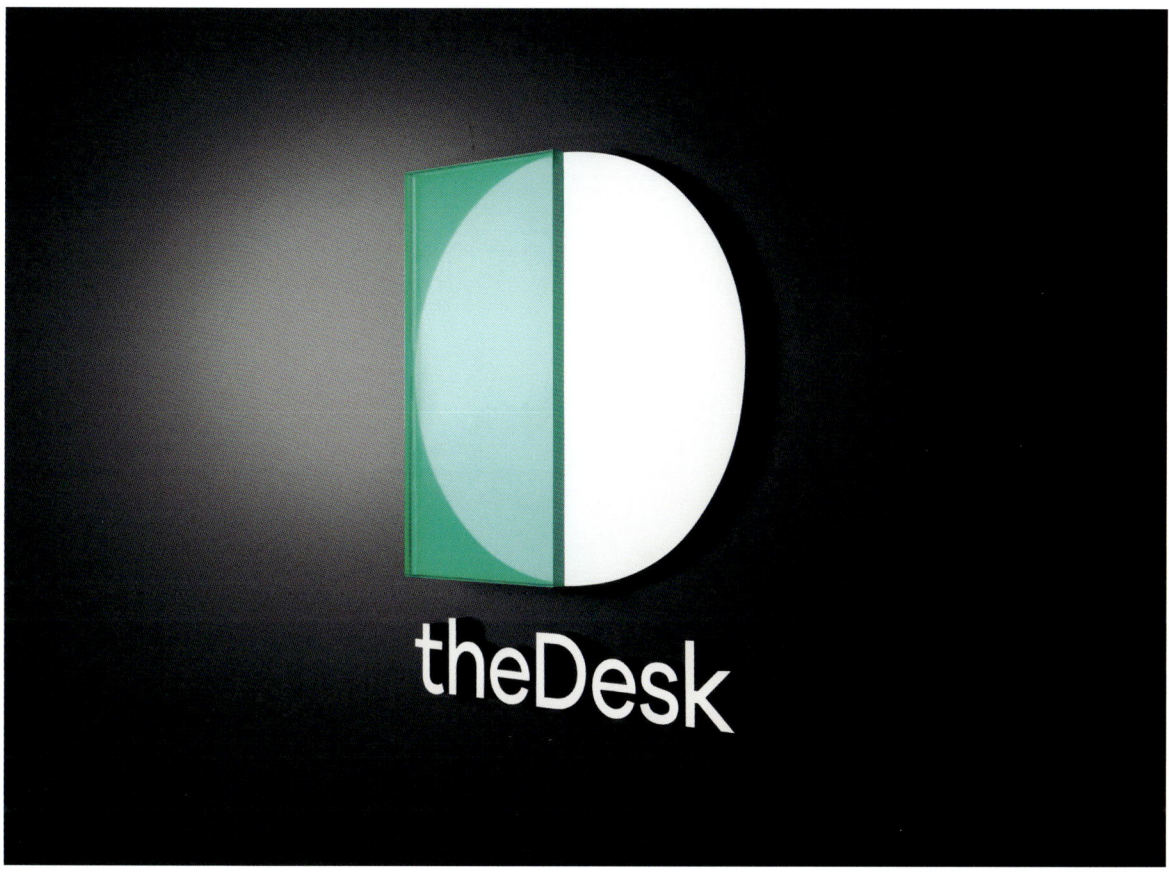

DREAMPLUS
[Brand Design]

Client
Hanwha Life Insurance
Seoul, South Korea

Design
Hanwha Life Insurance
Brand Strategy Team
Seoul, South Korea
Hara Design Institute,
Nippon Design Center
Tokyo, Japan

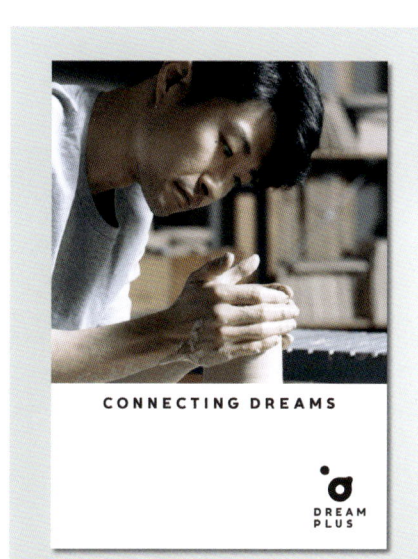

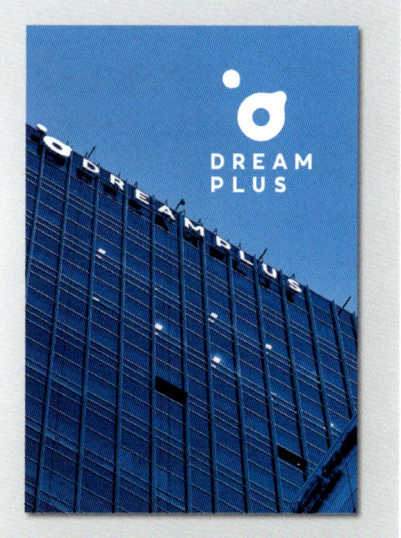

DREAMPLUS is a new brand initiative of Hanwha Insurance Open Innovation that seeks to create an open space where start-ups, corporations and investors can realise their visions and establish a sustainable environment of sharing, new business opportunities and discoveries. The logo represents constant, infinite movement and fluid relationships: a single circle produces a new one; new circles separate from their original, become independent and then multiply on their own. Furthermore, the logo refers to the cycle of life: visions connecting to other ideas, alliances and innovations supported by the company.

Cola Neko
[Brand Design Relaunch]

Cola Neko is a well-known Japanese learning platform. The purpose of its relaunch was to modernise the brand identity and reinforce the brand values. The new brand design conveys the joy and simplicity of the learning system as its core message. The logo incorporates the neko (cat) brand mascot, books and a smile, resulting in a brand look that is both professional and friendly. Complementary visuals include patterns and cat characters that are funny and fresh. The redesign has been applied to the textbooks as well as the website, featuring new imagery to illustrate the learning experience.

Client
Cola Neko Japanese Learning
Yunlin County, Taiwan

Design
think brand consultancy
Taipei City, Taiwan

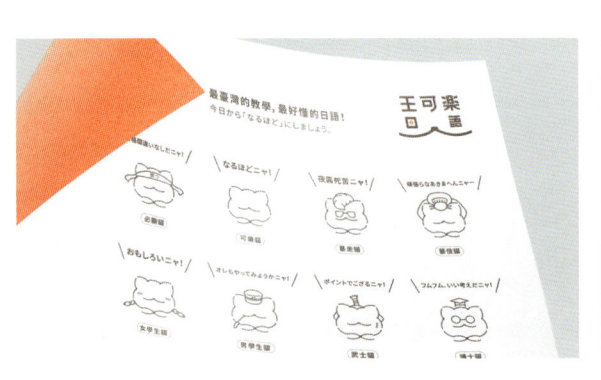

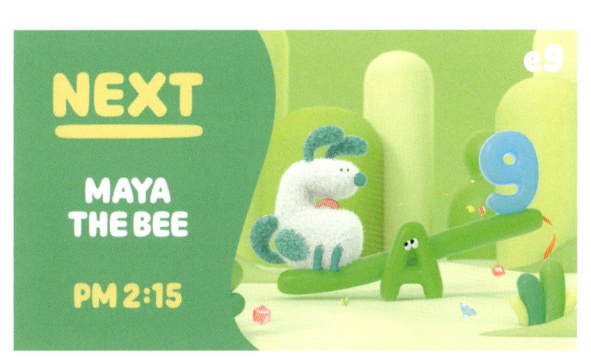

English Gem

[Brand Design]

English Gem is a paid children's channel in South Korea that broadcasts educational English content with the goal of making learning English fun. The design of the word mark is reminiscent of a malleable playdough or clay creation to illustrate how educational content can shape a child. In addition, the gently rounded letters evoke sympathy and blend harmoniously into the cheerful colour palette of the brand. The signet takes the "e" and "g" of the brand name and places them facing each other, making them look like a mother and her child.

Client
CJ ENM
Seoul, South Korea

Design
HuskyFox
Seoul, South Korea

Project Team
CJ ENM:
Jungah Kwon
Yuhye Kang
Seunghee Chae
Kangseok Kim
Daejung Kim
Najin Kim
Jungmin Lee

HuskyFox:
Kiyoung Jung (Creative Direction)
Doohee Lee (Creative Direction)
Taehee Lee (Strategic Planning)
Hyuncheol Ahn (Graphic Design)

Preface	Red Dot: Agency of the Year	Brands	Brand Design & Identity	Corporate Design & Identity	Annual Reports
4	6	18	90	202	260

Peng Stars
[Brand Design]

The Peng Stars swimming school was founded by former world champion swimmer Wu Peng. His educational concept involves getting parents to accompany their small children during swimming lessons. Thus, the playful brand design is inspired by the close bond between parents and children. The logo shows two overlapping whales that emphasise the close parent-child relationship. The dark blue represents professionalism, while the light blue stands for water and freedom. The combination of the two brand colours signifies the harmonious co-existence of these two aspects. Additional design elements further underline the child-friendly brand image.

Client
Hangzhou Pengstars
Sport Culture Pty. Ltd.
Hangzhou, China

Design
Inbetween Creative Pty. Ltd.
Hangzhou, China

Advertising	Packaging Design	Fair Stands	Retail Design	Red Dot: Junior Award	Designer Profiles	Index
288	318	494	516	544	614	674

JAMJAMBOX
[Brand Design]

JAMJAMBOX is a project to help malnourished children from low-income families. It encourages people to pay attention not only to children's need for food but also to their hopes and dreams by organising birthday parties. The brand name is a combination of "JAM", a phonetic abbreviation of the word fun in Korean, and "BOX", which symbolises the packaging of a birthday present. A pattern reminiscent of a party's fireworks and confetti was designed to provide an emotionally appealing brand experience. With regards to sustainability, the boxes can also be repurposed into frames to display pictures or messages.

Client
MYM Co., Ltd.
Seoul, South Korea

Design
MYM Co., Ltd.
Seoul, South Korea

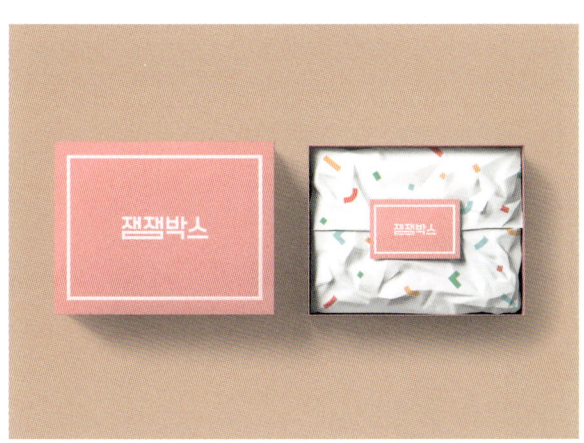

Preface	Red Dot: Agency of the Year	Brands	Brand Design & Identity	Corporate Design & Identity	Annual Reports
4	6	18	90	202	260

Land of Hope

[Brand Identity Relaunch]

Client
Land of Hope
Aarhus, Denmark

Design
Creuna Denmark A/S
Aarhus, Denmark

Project Team
Sara Marie Alvad (Creative Direction)
Julie Renee Jensen (Art Direction)
Stine Skovgaard (Copywriting)

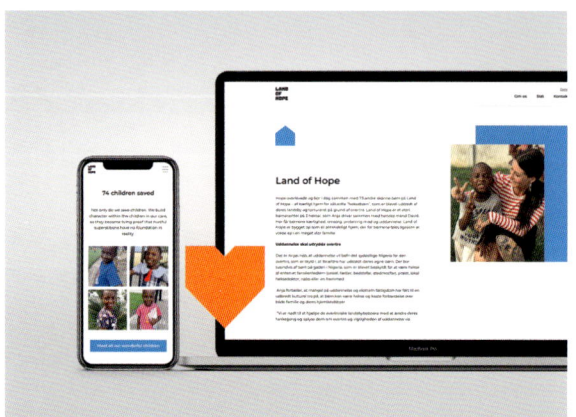

→ Clip online

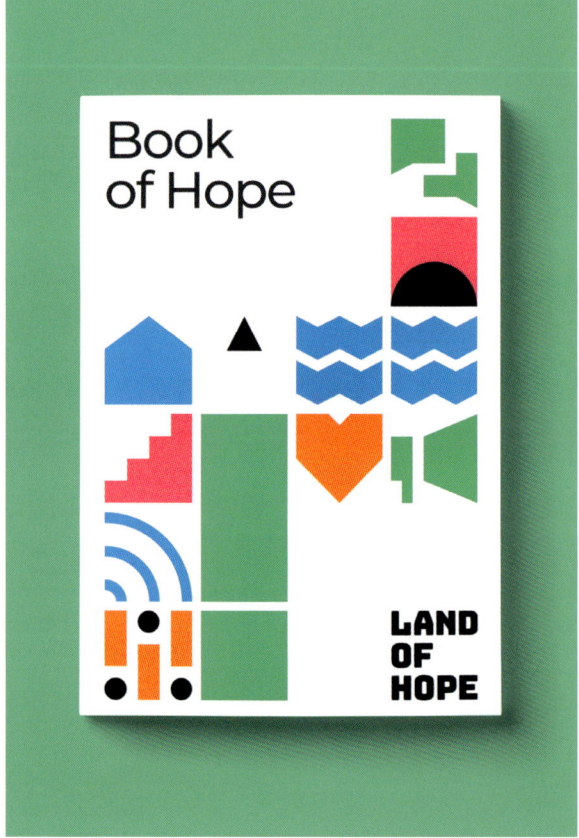

"Land of Hope" is a Danish charity that has fought to protect marginalised children in Nigeria since 2012 and has established a large children's centre there. A new brand design was developed to give the organisation a strong, international identity. The interplay of the word mark "Land of Hope" with diverse symbols in cheerful colours attracts a high level of attention. A brand book tells fundamental stories of the organisation's core values: humanity, empathy and strength. In addition, the message "United against Superstition" is also clearly communicated in online media.

International Water & Wellness

[Visual Identity]

International Water & Wellness Ltd. is a bathroom and plumbing fixture manufacturer with corporate offices in London and facilities in Spain. The brand stands for premium, design-oriented quality, and aims to appeal to architects and interior designers. The letter-mark reflects a balanced movement reminiscent of the slight movement of waves. The typography's body in a deep blue colour is bold, with soft finishes reinforcing its brief presence. Complimenting its identity, clean and elegant symbols were created to represent different product families with light, minimalistic strokes to obtain a sleek design that floats on the white background.

Client
International Water & Wellness Ltd.
Buckinghamshire, United Kingdom

Design
Boro Serra
Valencia, Spain

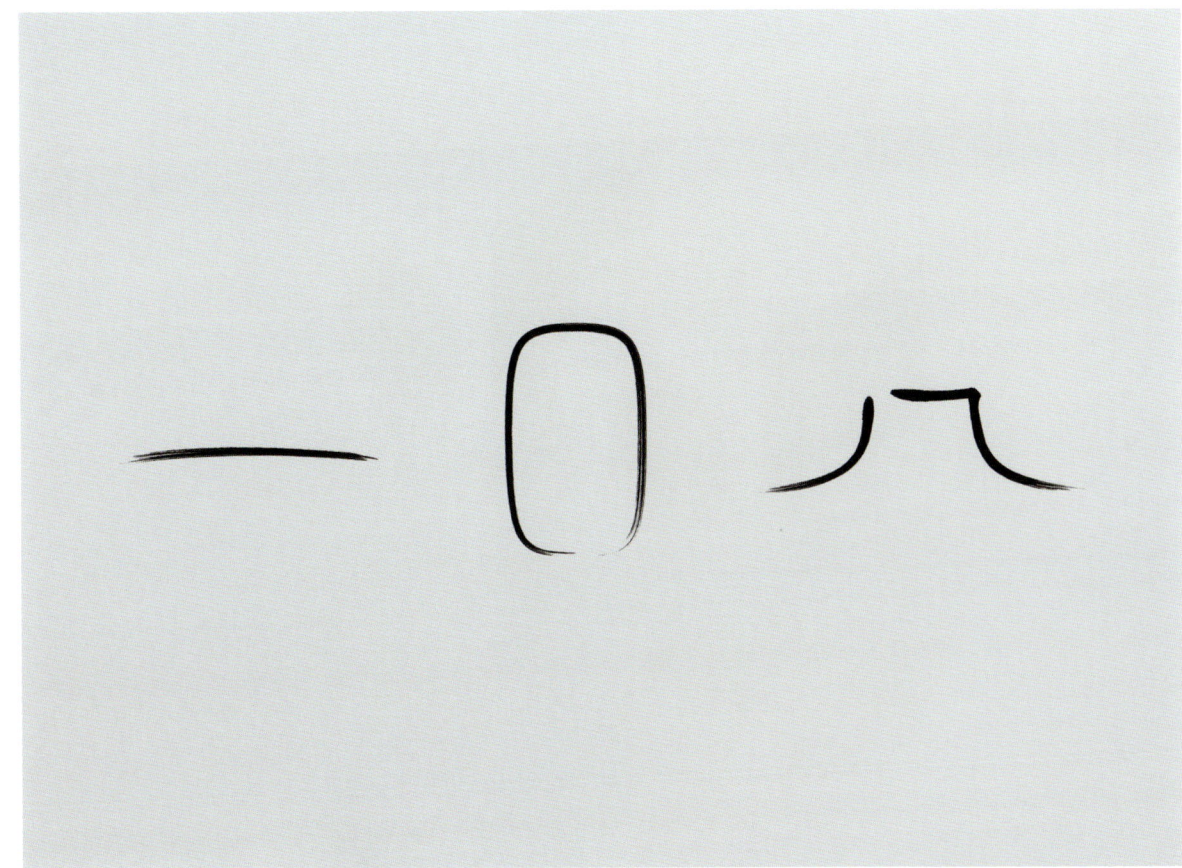

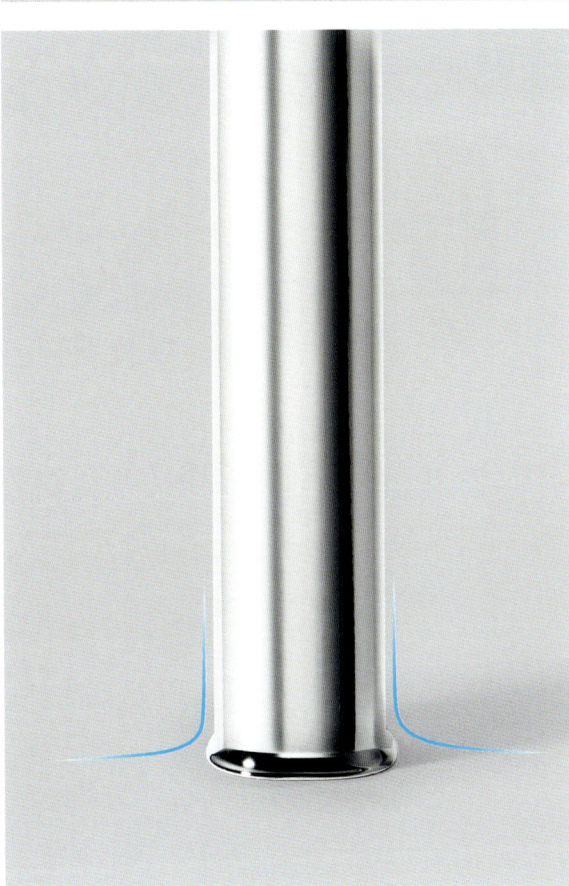

INAX
Signature Elements
[Brand Key Elements, Brand Design]

INAX is a Japanese sanitaryware manufacturer whose brand design features three key elements that are all derived from the silhouette of selected products and reminiscent of calligraphic brushstrokes, thus creating a recognisable brand aesthetic. The subtle and elegant lines achieve a high level of abstraction that piques interest. Together, they visually define the product portfolio and enable consumers to identify the brand from a distance. In line with the company's overarching philosophy of "humanitecture", the brand signature balances human and architectural aspects.

Client
LIXIL Corporation
Tokyo, Japan

Design
LIXIL Corporation
Tokyo, Japan

AIRMATE

[Brand Design Relaunch]

Client
AIRMATE
Shenzhen, China

Design
ALINE STUDIO
Beijing, China

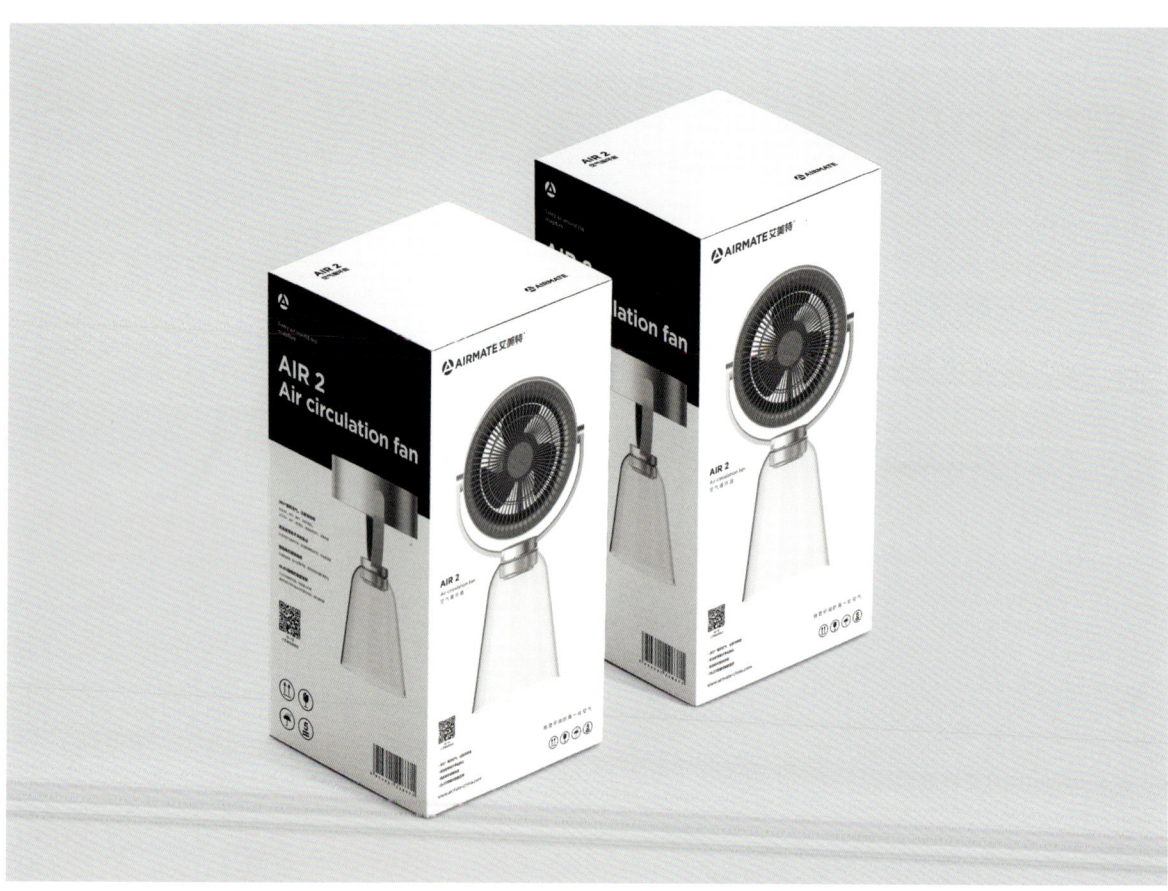

AIRMATE is a household appliance manufacturer with a history of nearly 50 years that specialises in electric fans. Its former brand logo had not been updated for 20 years and no longer reflected the company's current market positioning. The new brand design keeps the brand name, but introduces typographic modifications and is complemented by a new logo. The new logo's shape is derived from an electric fan. Three fan blades are arranged in a circle to form the letter "A", representing the three aspects of the company's quality standards: air temperature, air humidity and air cleanliness.

Preface	Red Dot: Agency of the Year	Brands	**Brand Design & Identity**	Corporate Design & Identity	Annual Reports
4	6	18	90	202	260

ACRO
[Brand Design]

Client
DAELIM Industrial Co., Ltd.
Seoul, South Korea

Design
DAELIM Industrial Co., Ltd.
Seoul, South Korea

Project Team
Victoria Kim (Creative Direction)
Contents Planning Team
(Brand Experience Strategy)
Hyemi Moon (Brand Experience Design)
Jungeol Bae (Brand Experience Design)
Yongha Jeong (Brand Experience Design)

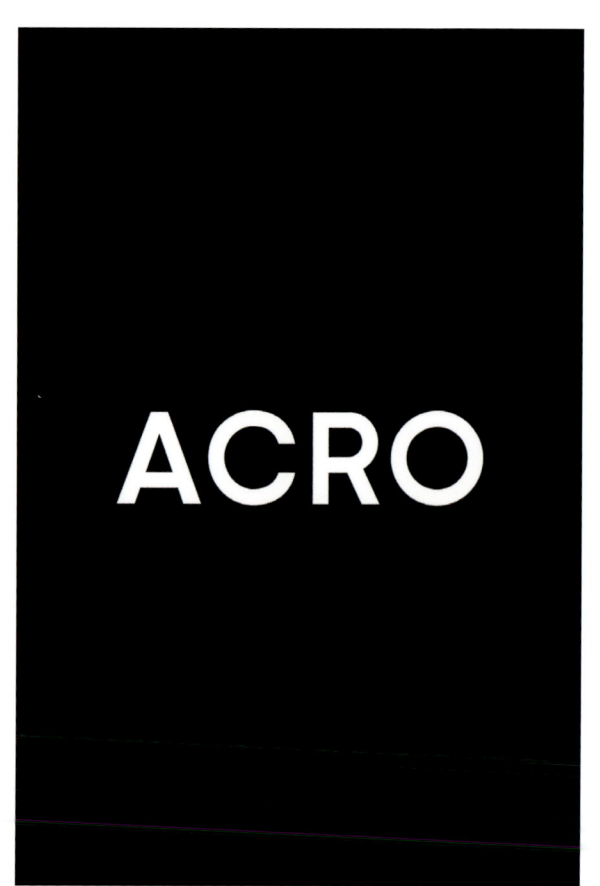

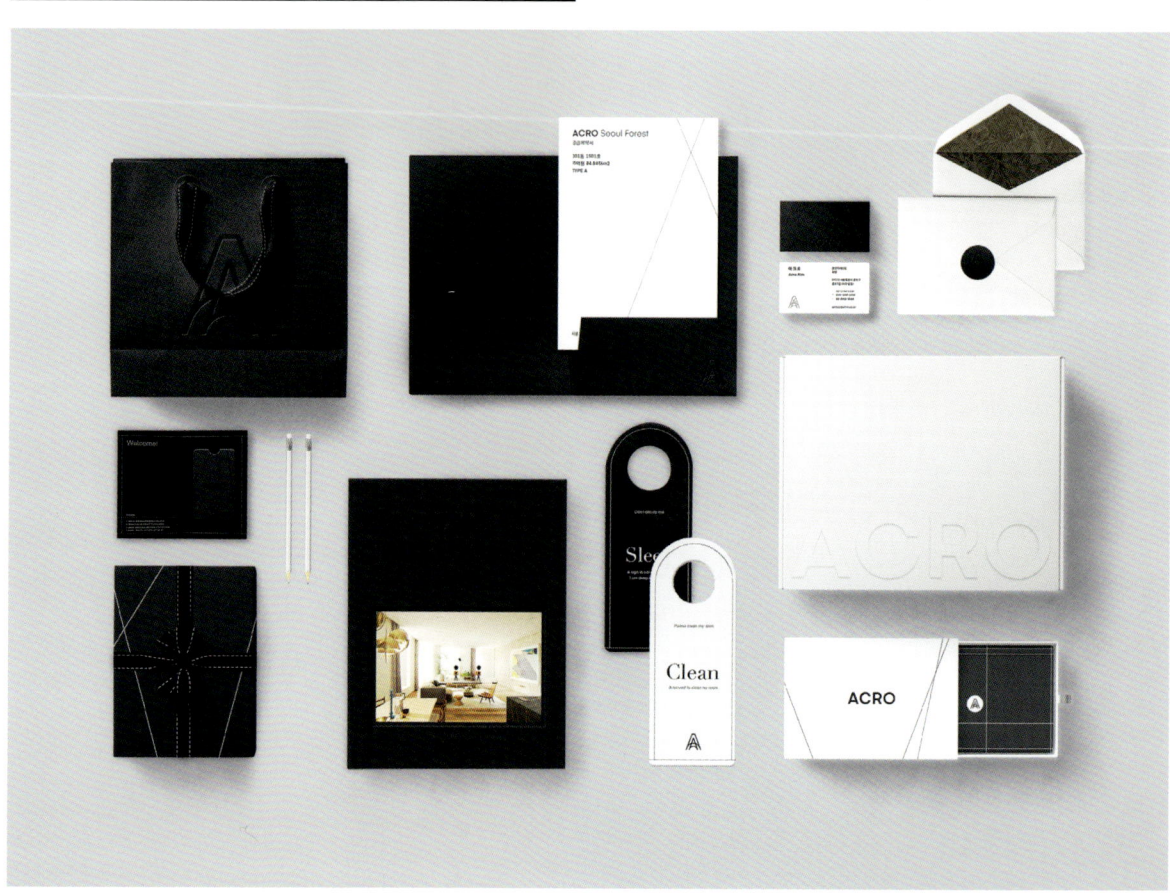

Advertising	Packaging Design	Fair Stands	Retail Design	Red Dot: Junior Award	Designer Profiles	Index
288	318	494	516	544	614	674

As a leading construction company for exclusive high-rise buildings in South Korea, ACRO launched a flexible brand identity that underlines the concept of contemporary minimalism. The solid black brand logo was made even bolder to represent the brand's high-end nature, while its symbolism was strengthened by resetting the proportions. The straightforward colour palette uses a deep black to express the essential aspects of the brand and leaves a lot of white space when shaping customer experiences. The monogram underlines the brand's prestigious aspirations and showcases appealingly stylish lines.

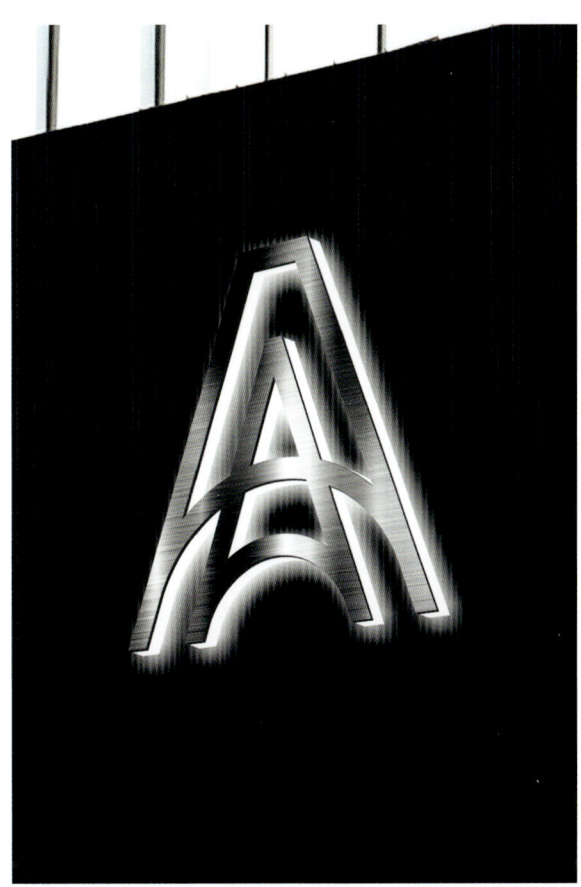

Sodexo Peru Offices

[Brand Design, Environmental Branding]

The aim of this environmental branding project was to transform the former brand identity into a more dynamic one that reflects the spirit of the Sodexo Group in every part of the office. The new branding should not only resonate with employees and create a motivating work environment that encourages creativity and teamwork, but also retain the original brand logo and its basic guidelines. With a focus on the company's motto of "making people happier in their workplace", a playful graphic system was created. Contemporary graphics and icons, including emoji-inspired ones, were used to highlight the value of teamwork and happiness as the key focus of the company services.

Client
Sodexo Peru
Lima, Peru

Design
Amigo Invisible Studio
Lima, Peru

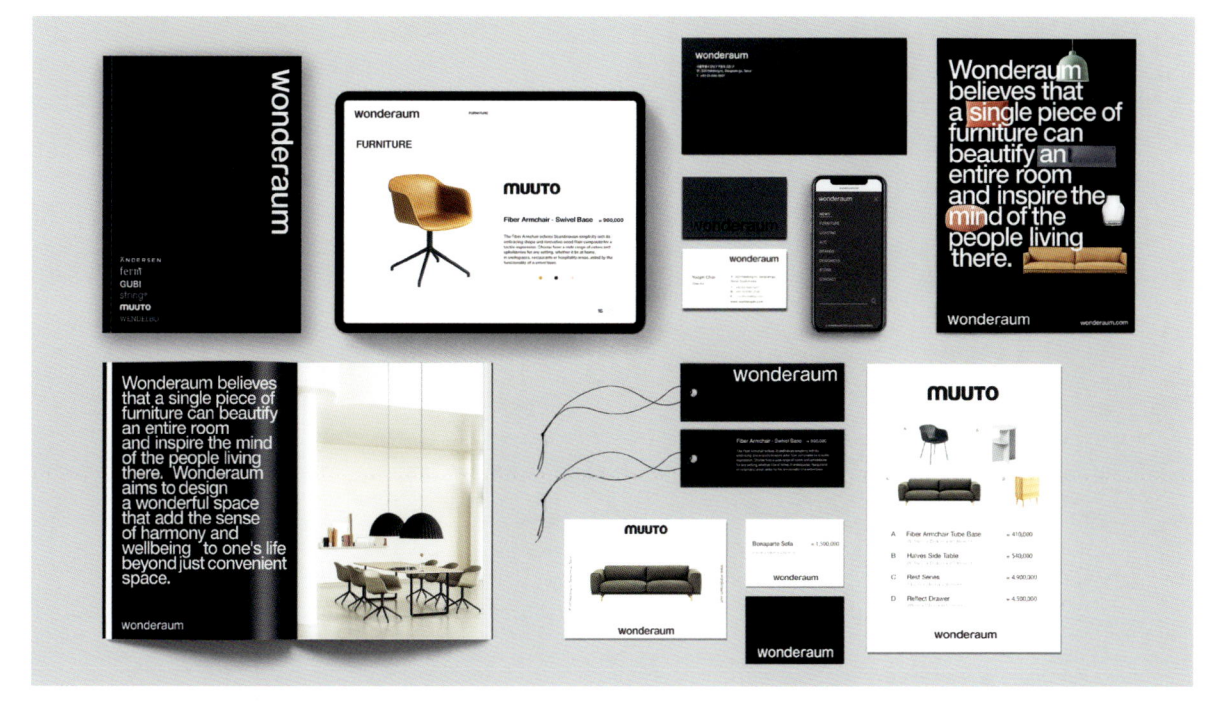

Wonderaum

[Brand Identity]

The Korean furniture store Wonderaum presents furniture collections with a high standard of design and quality. Following the design philosophy of the Bauhaus, the brand identity conveys the image of a professional business partner and seeks to create harmony between various furniture brands. Inspired in style by the smooth curves of a piece of furniture, a simple, contemporary design concept was developed. The word mark was created by customising the Helvetica typeface, softening its contours and adjusting each thickness and space to harmonise the characters. The monochrome colour palette serves as a neutral background for presenting the diverse furniture.

Client
Wonderaum
Seoul, South Korea

Design
YNL Design
Seoul, South Korea

Project Team
Yoona Lee (Creative Director)
Kwangsu Shin (Brand Designer)

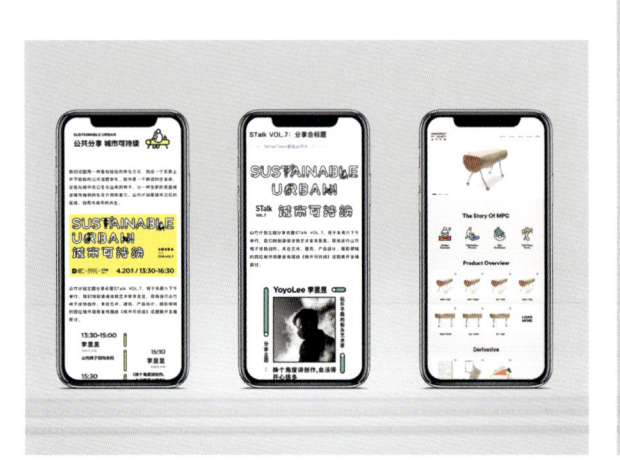

Mangkhut Project

[Brand Design, Brand Identity]

In September 2018, parts of South East Asia were hit by typhoon Mangostan, which left in its wake a huge mess, including mountains of broken tree branches. The Mangkhut project seeks to commemorate this natural disaster in the megacity of Shenzhen and at the same time appeal to people's environmental awareness. Some of the scrap wood from these branches was used to create attractive benches to form new seating areas in public places and encourage conversation and reflection. The brand design reflects the subject matter of the project by integrating an illustrated tree trunk into the lettering. Key visuals explain the project in the same graphical style.

Client
SenseTeam
Shenzhen, China

Design
SenseTeam
Shenzhen, China

València World Design Capital 2022

[Brand Design, Brand Identity]

The World Design Organization designates and promotes a host city as the "World Design Capital" every two years. For their application, cities are required to create a special brand design that will be used if they succeed in their bid. València will take over the mantle in 2022. The visual identity created by the city is based on a simple and modular solution with great flexibility that is built upon the geometric simplification of the initials VWDC. Geometry was used as a universal and timeless design language. The result is a strong, recognisable and memorable brand image. The brand identity has been widely promoted by both general and specialist media.

Client
Associació València Capital del Disseny
Valencia, Spain

Design
Ibán Ramon – Design Studio
Valencia, Spain

25th Anniversary Independence Day of Republic of Palau

[Brand Identity]

A distinctive brand identity was created to celebrate the 25th anniversary of Palau's independence. The design for the event was based on the archipelago's cultural and historical background: in the Republic of Palau, the mythical bird Delerrok represents good luck, pride and prosperity, while Chedechuul is the god of construction and repels evil spirits. The logo depicts these mythical creatures in an illustrative style typical of Palau. In addition, the design concept uses tribal totems, symbols of nature and famous sights, a maritime image language, as well as the national colours of blue and yellow, which represent the ocean and sunlight.

Client
P.I.E. Printing
Koror, Palau

Design
Triangler Co., Ltd.
Taipei City, Taiwan

Project Team
Chun-Yao Huang (Art Direction)
Chi-Yao Tang (Graphic Design)
Jian-He Lin (Graphic Design)

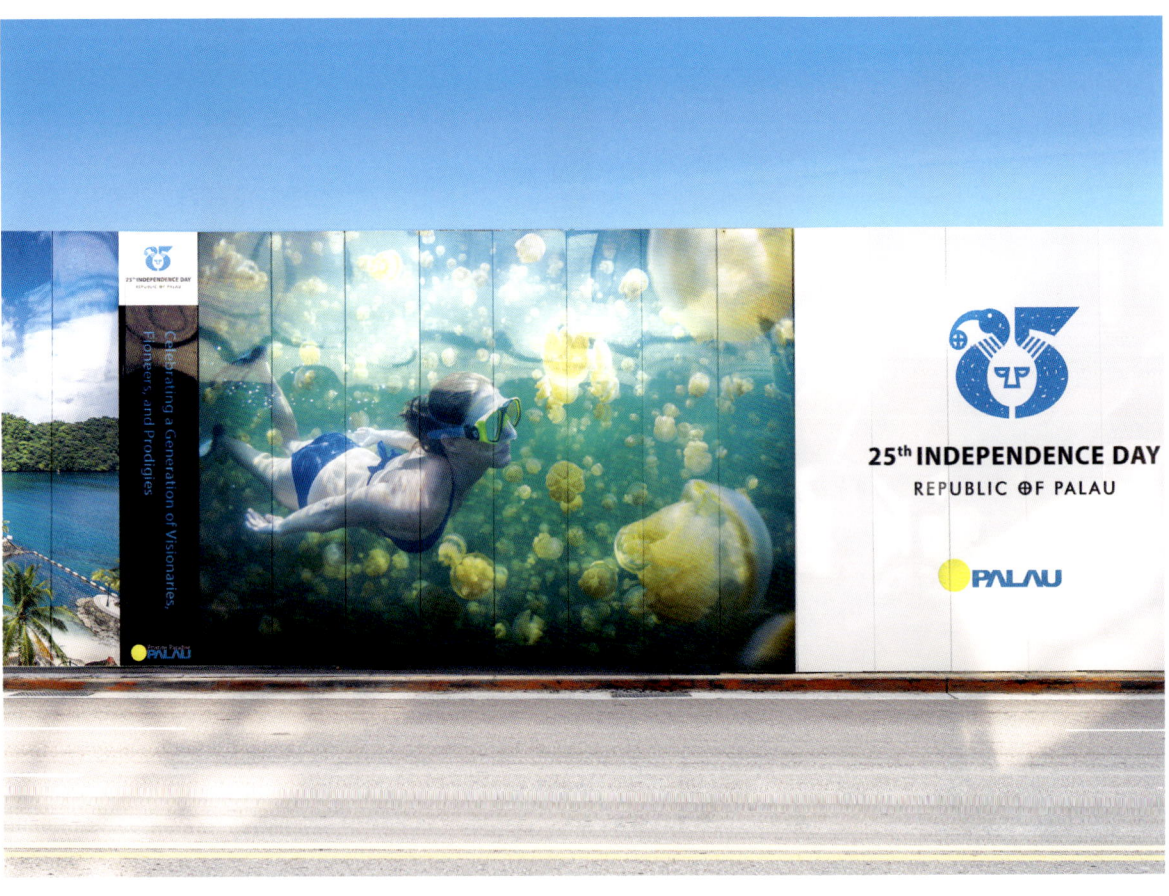

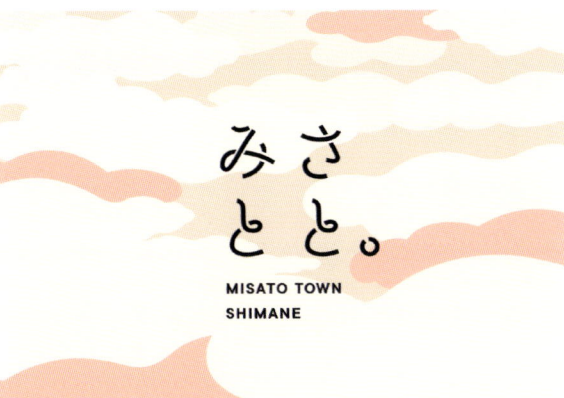

Advertising	Packaging Design	Fair Stands	Retail Design	Red Dot: Junior Award	Designer Profiles	Index
288	318	494	516	544	614	674

Misato Town
[Brand Design Relaunch]

The objective of the relaunch project for the town of Misato was to communicate the benefits of this Japanese small town to its citizens and visitors in a creative manner. After looking around the town for motifs, the designers created illustrations of unusual sights. The colourful key visuals characterise a brand design that draws the attention of non-residents to the town and also makes locals proud. The pictures presented on the website and in the photo exhibition are freely available. In addition to the website and new business cards for employees of the town hall, several town newspapers and a town guide have been published.

Client
Misato Town
Shimane, Japan

Design
SHIFTBRAIN
Tokyo, Japan

Project Team
Masaya Yamamoto (Creative Direction)
Masashi Fujiyoshi (Art Direction)
Junichi Nishiyama (Motion Design)
Yuhei Yasuda (Programming)
Hiroaki Yasutomo (Programming)
Masakazu Tsuru (Production)

Daming Palace

[Brand Design, Visual Identity]

Client
Daming Palace
Xian, China

Design
WWS (Beijing) Cultural
Propagation Co., Ltd.
Tianjin, China

Project Team
Daming Palace:
Junang Shi (Account Management)
Yifei Li (Account Management)

WWS:
Chengfu Wang (Art Direction)
Peng Chen (Graphic Design)
Junjie Zhao (Graphic Design)

Yindi:
Yifei Zhu (Account Management)
Shiyu Wang (Account Management)

→ Designer profile on page 673

Advertising	Packaging Design	Fair Stands	Retail Design	Red Dot: Junior Award	Designer Profiles	Index
288	318	494	516	544	614	674

Daming Palace, the former political centre and the national symbol of the Tang Dynasty, is located in Xi'an, the oldest city in China. The architecture of this magnificent building complex influenced the construction of palaces throughout East Asia at that time. This brand design was developed to represent the grand scenes of ancient Chinese palaces. A luxurious colour palette underlines a unique visual identity that appeals to people's growing interest in historical monuments. In addition to the brand logo, a series of key visuals were designed featuring delicate lines that resemble the silhouettes of the individual buildings.

Raon Women's Clinic

[Brand Identity]

The brand design for Raon Women's Clinic aims to build an emotionally appealing image that is consistent with the clinic's brand identity, reflecting its core values such as a trusting doctor-patient relationship. An elegant design language characterises the overall image, while the use of print finishing techniques enhances the exclusive appearance. The homogeneous colour palette was selected to achieve the desired light effects, giving rise to a shiny logo with a copper-coloured sheen. In addition, the artistically designed signet conveys a sense of security and confidence.

Client
Raon Women's Clinic
Seoul, South Korea

Design
YNL Design
Seoul, South Korea

Project Team
Yoona Lee (Creative Director)
Yena Park (Brand Designer)
Kwangsu Shin (Brand Designer)

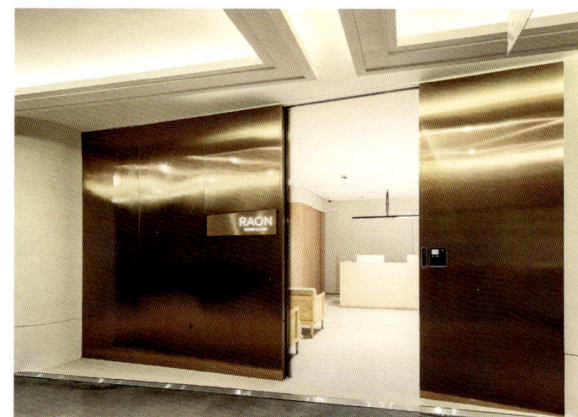

Passion for Health: Pure Joy in Life

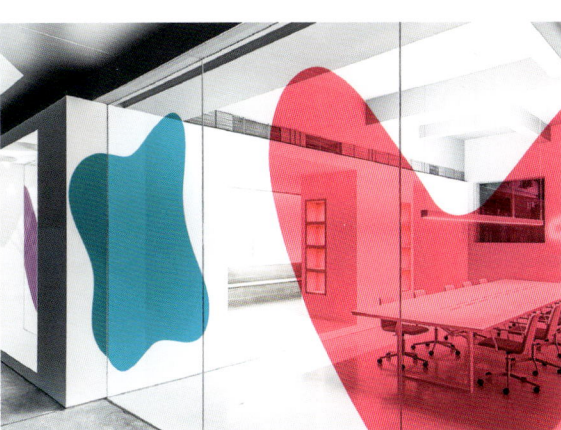

[Brand Design, Key Visuals]

The brand identity of Samsung Bioepis is influenced by the aspiration to provide patients with a positive product experience and thereby improve their quality of life. Based on this, a brand design was developed with colourful key visuals that has a positive impact on viewers' state of mind. Taking inspiration from the moments of joy that nature brings, the brand design concept of "Passion for Health: Pure Joy in Life" came to life. Organic shapes were used to evoke feelings of peace often felt in nature, while the colour coding facilitates product differentiation.

Client
Samsung Bioepis
Incheon, South Korea

Design
Interbrand Seoul
Seoul, South Korea
Samsung Bioepis
Incheon, South Korea

Project Team
Interbrand Seoul:
Uzin Hwang (Creative Director)
Hajin Jung (Design Director)
Namgyu Kim (Designer)
Jackie Lim (Designer)
Jiwon Lee (Designer)
Juyoung Kim (Designer)
Yeeun Kim (Designer)
Jeongmin Lee (Designer)

Samsung Bioepis:
Nayoung Kim (Designer)
Jiwon Lee (Designer)
Uisin Kim (Designer)

Corporate Design & Identity

Red Dot: Best of the Best

mmcité+

[Corporate Design]

The company mmcité+ is active in public space and transport infrastructure projects by contributing city furniture designs including park benches, bike racks, waiting halls and information systems. The overall concept of its visual identity is inspired by the mission statement that the company's products and projects should not attract attention primarily through their design, but rather through their guarantee of functionality and appropriate placement in the environment. The result is a typographic logotype supplemented by an encircled "+" symbol aimed at visualising the main features of the companies belonging to the group: bold visions, interconnections and closeness. The newly designed Cité Grotesk font contains rounded, vertical and horizontal shapes originating in the graphic symbol of the logotype. The three font styles ensure a consistent visual language across digital presentations, invoices and other documents. For short claims and posters, a graphic system connecting key words can be used, such as "DESIGN + CONSTRUCTION" or "FORM + FUNCTION".

Statement by the jury
The corporate design for mmcité+ as a visual identity in public spaces projects a highly consistent appearance. The Cité Grotesk typeface matches the simple, clear lines of the graphic symbol and can be combined with trendy yellow – or with black/white or grey – and thus conveys the message of timelessness and quality just like the company's products. In addition, the logo allows for flexible use with key terms both vertically and horizontally.

Client
mmcité+ a.s.
Bílovice, Czech Republic

Design
Jan Novák, Marek Nedelka
Prague, Czech Republic

→ Designer profile on page 655

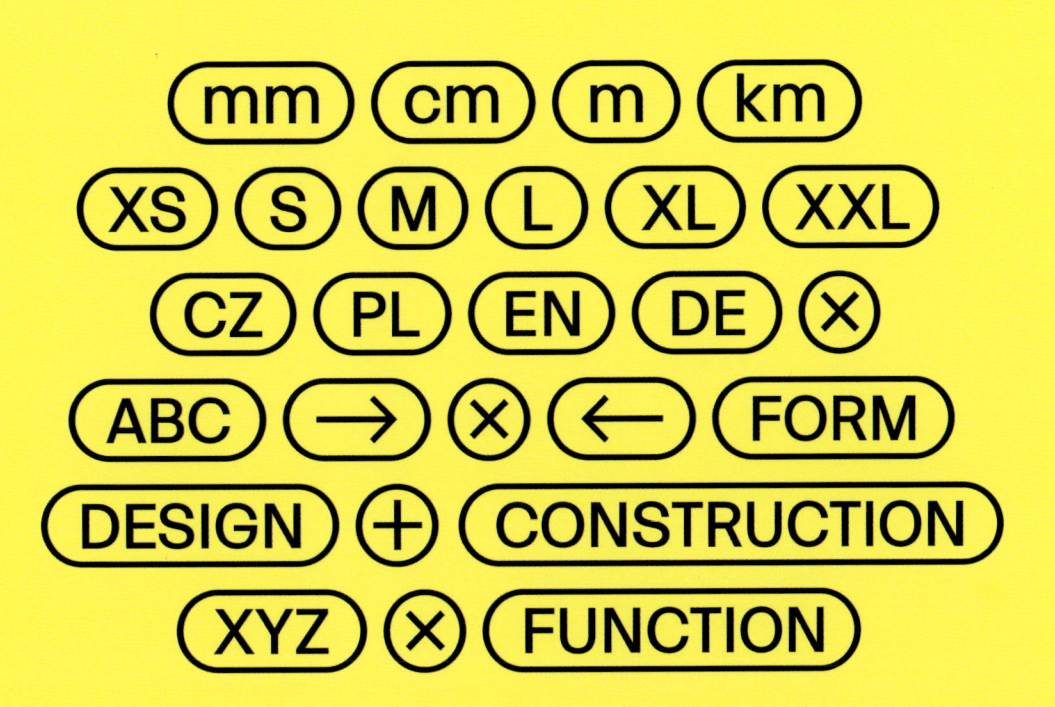

Red Dot: Best of the Best

Polestar
[Corporate Identity]

The electric car brand Polestar breaks with established conventions in the car industry. While many companies use chrome and flashes to mark their presence, Polestar highlights technological advancement and makes its products appear as works of art. With a focus on eliminating abundance even in the smallest of details, these works thus manage to deliver an unparalleled, holistic brand experience. Alongside a toolbox, the development of the corporate identity also comprised implementations for all brand touchpoints, including retail, digital, communication and printed matters. The symbol is an interpretation of the name, Polestar, the guiding northern star, which has been developed seamlessly with the cars and is intended for iconic application throughout the brand universe. The typographic marking system of reduced design serves as the backbone to highlight the performance features and information throughout the brand and its products. The monochrome approach to colour creates a touch of timeless elegance and sophistication.

Statement by the jury
In an era in which sustainability is a strategic priority for manufacturers, the Polestar automotive brand and its corporate design truly stand out. Down to the last detail, the design follows the principle of reduction to the essentials. The result is an aesthetic that impresses with minimalism and elegance. The unobtrusive typeface and the logo, which is visualised as an abstract star in the sky, merge to create an expression of high quality.

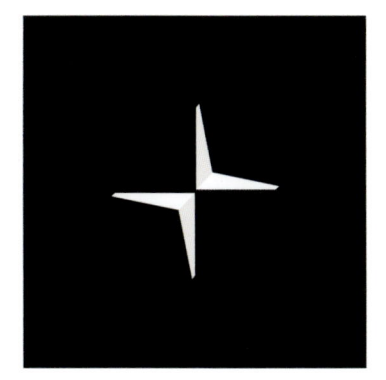

Advertising	Packaging Design	Fair Stands	Retail Design	Red Dot: Junior Award	Designer Profiles	Index
288	318	494	516	544	614	674

Client
Polestar
Gothenburg, Sweden

Design
Stockholm Design Lab
Stockholm, Sweden
Polestar
Gothenburg, Sweden

→ Designer profile on page 661
→ Clip online

City of Chuncheon

[Corporate Identity]

Client
City of Chuncheon
Chuncheon, South Korea

Design
CDR associates
Seoul, South Korea

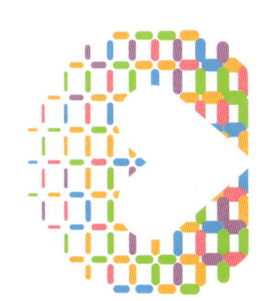

Advertising	Packaging Design	Fair Stands	Retail Design	Red Dot: Junior Award	Designer Profiles	Index
288	318	494	516	544	614	674

Chuncheon, a city located in Gangwon Province, South Korea, is a tourist destination well known for its beautiful lakes and mountains. In order to reflect its improved urban environment, a new corporate design was developed. The word mark is combined with a key visual that merges the letter "C", which stands for Chuncheon, city and citizen, with a heart motif. The symbol not only highlights the city's motto of "Citizens are the owners of the city" but also signifies happiness. The blue colour represents the lakes that serve as landmarks of the region. As a key colour for identification, it can be alternated with various other colours and graphic motifs to represent landscape, architecture and other highlights of the city.

Tashkent

[Identity Design]

Tashkent is the capital of Uzbekistan, a state that once isolated itself from global integration. In recent years, due to political changes, the country has shown signs of becoming more open to the world. Therefore, its capital needed a distinctive corporate design to unite a wide range of services and events in the city. The logo features not only the initial "T", but also a stylised gate that suggests openness to visitors and references the many historic city gates of Tashkent. The design language can be flexibly adapted through the use of different identification colours and illustrations. Diverse patterns and symbols reflect the architecture and motifs of a mixed culture.

Client
Public Council of Tashkent City
Tashkent, Uzbekistan

Design
MA'NO Branding
Tashkent, Uzbekistan

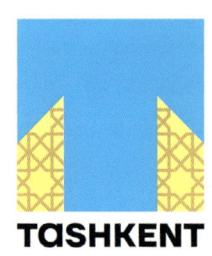

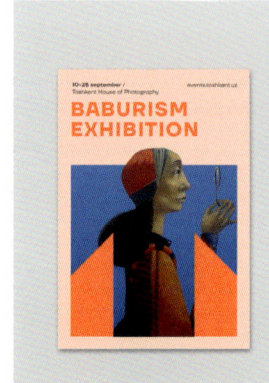

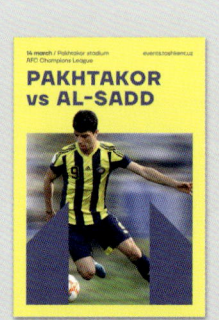

Advertising	Packaging Design	Fair Stands	Retail Design	Red Dot: Junior Award	Designer Profiles	Index
288	318	494	516	544	614	674

Zhejiang Think Tank

[Corporate Design]

Zhejiang Think Tank is a professional institution established in 2019 to provide policy advice and research for the development of China and the province of Zhejiang. The logo is reminiscent of traditional jade carvings and symbolises an open gate with the Chinese character for wisdom integrated in it. The overall effect is that the logo yields the appearance of a seal that reflects think tank's attributes of calmness and industry leadership. In the graphical implementation of the logo, its fragments are combined with corresponding elements to create new forms symbolising multi-faceted thinking.

Client
Zhejiang Federation of Humanities and Social Sciences Circles
Hangzhou, China

Design
Zhejiang Gongshang University
Hangzhou, China

Project Team
Kan Zhao (Design)
Ying Gao (Design)
Wenjun Xu (Design)

Pingtung Martial Arts Hall

[Corporate Design, Logo Design]

The corporate design for this contemporary museum was developed to create an easily recognisable identity for targeting a huge audience in Asia. The logo comprises both the Mandarin character for martial arts and an abstract illustration of the museum's distinctively curved roof. In addition, a flexible system of patterns was developed using the building's architectural details as inspiration. The design focuses on appreciating the architectural appearance and showing how it holds the essence of artmaking. This approach allowed the design to be applied broadly across other media for the purpose attracting more online followers and museum visitors.

Client
Pingtung County Government
Pingtung, Taiwan

Design
Mengdom Design Lab
Taipei City, Taiwan

Project Team
Mengdom Design Lab:
Meng Chih Chiang (Creative Direction)
Pei Rong Lu (Account Management)

James Lin (Photography)

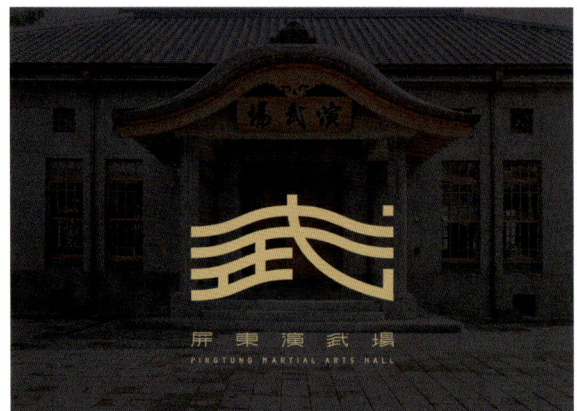

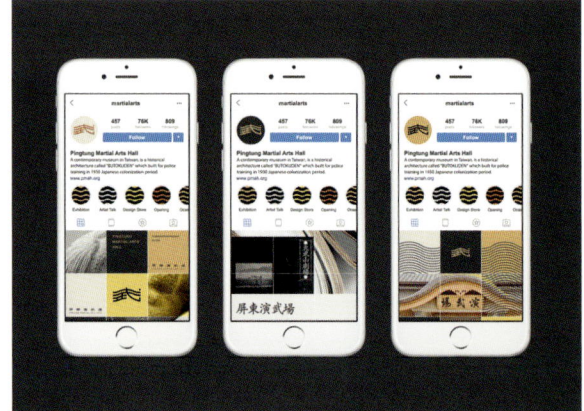

Advertising	Packaging Design	Fair Stands	Retail Design	Red Dot: Junior Award	Designer Profiles	Index
288	318	494	516	544	614	674

Forum Groningen

[Corporate Identity]

Forum Groningen is a vibrant cultural centre that opened in Groningen, Netherlands, on 29 November 2019. The 11-storey landmark building offers an attractive variety of facilities and cultural programmes aimed at a wide audience. The central idea and key identifier of the corporate identity mirror both the iconic shape of the building and the programmatic idea of the centre: a dynamic frame to host different kinds of content. Based on this idea, a design system was created that can take many shapes, is easily recognisable, flexible to use and able to present all sorts of topics in a dynamic and energetic manner.

Client
Forum Groningen
Groningen, Netherlands

Design
G2K Creative Agency
Groningen, Netherlands

Project Team
Frank Baas (Creative Direction)
Hans Geluk (Creative Direction)
Rudmer van Hulzen (Lead Design)
Yuri Nauta (Digital Concept)
Tobias van der Valk (Motion Design)
Inge Wolthuis (Project Management)

Future Exhibition

[Corporate Design]

Future Exhibition is an art salon with an exhibition of the same name showcasing contemporary works by artists from different fields to explain the connection between works of art in relation to future art. The corporate design sets up a seemingly clear visual network for the exhibition and mixes it with illustrations of the Chinese characters for future. In this way, a logo and a series of key visuals were created, all of which form a closed unit in their lines, while the characters interrupt the neatly arranged image in a surprising manner to catch the viewer's attention.

Client
Calx Station
Beijing, China

Design
Yinan Lyu
Shenzhen, China

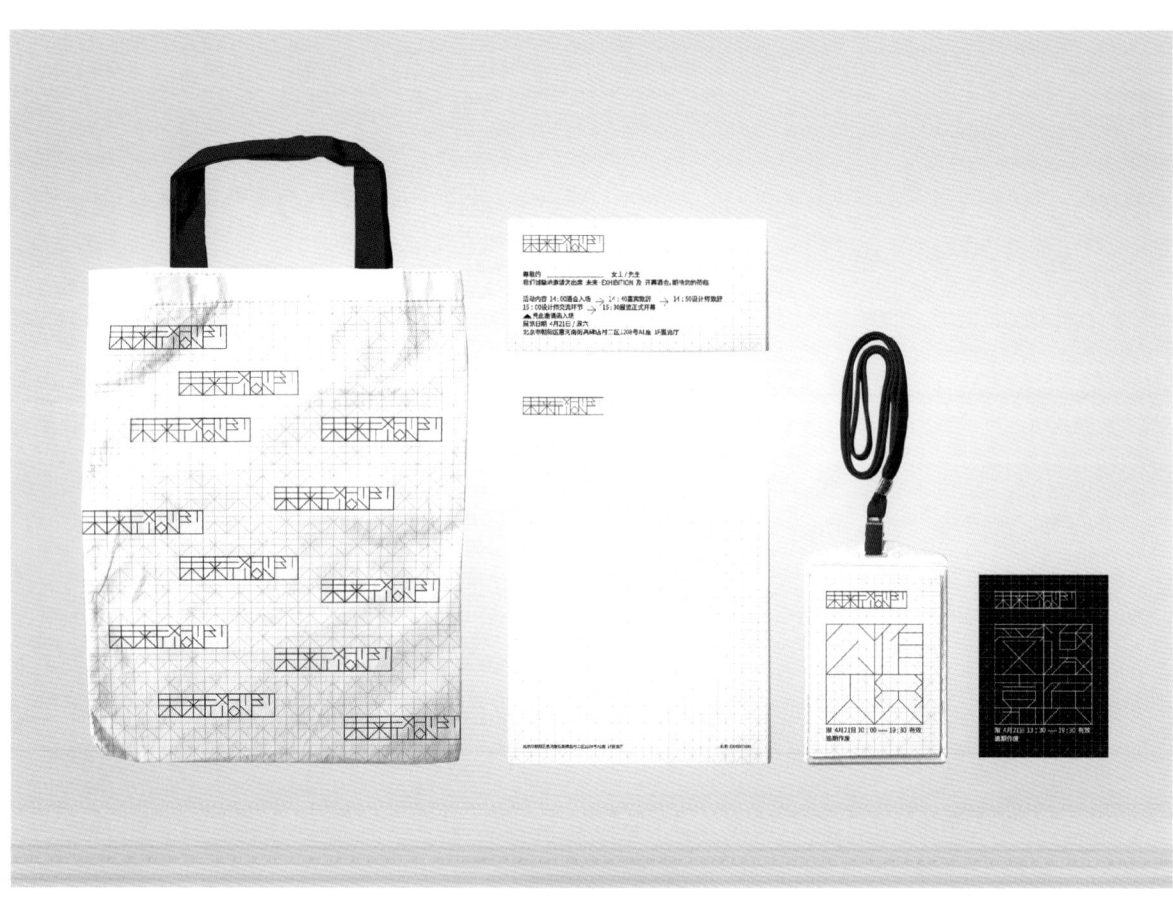

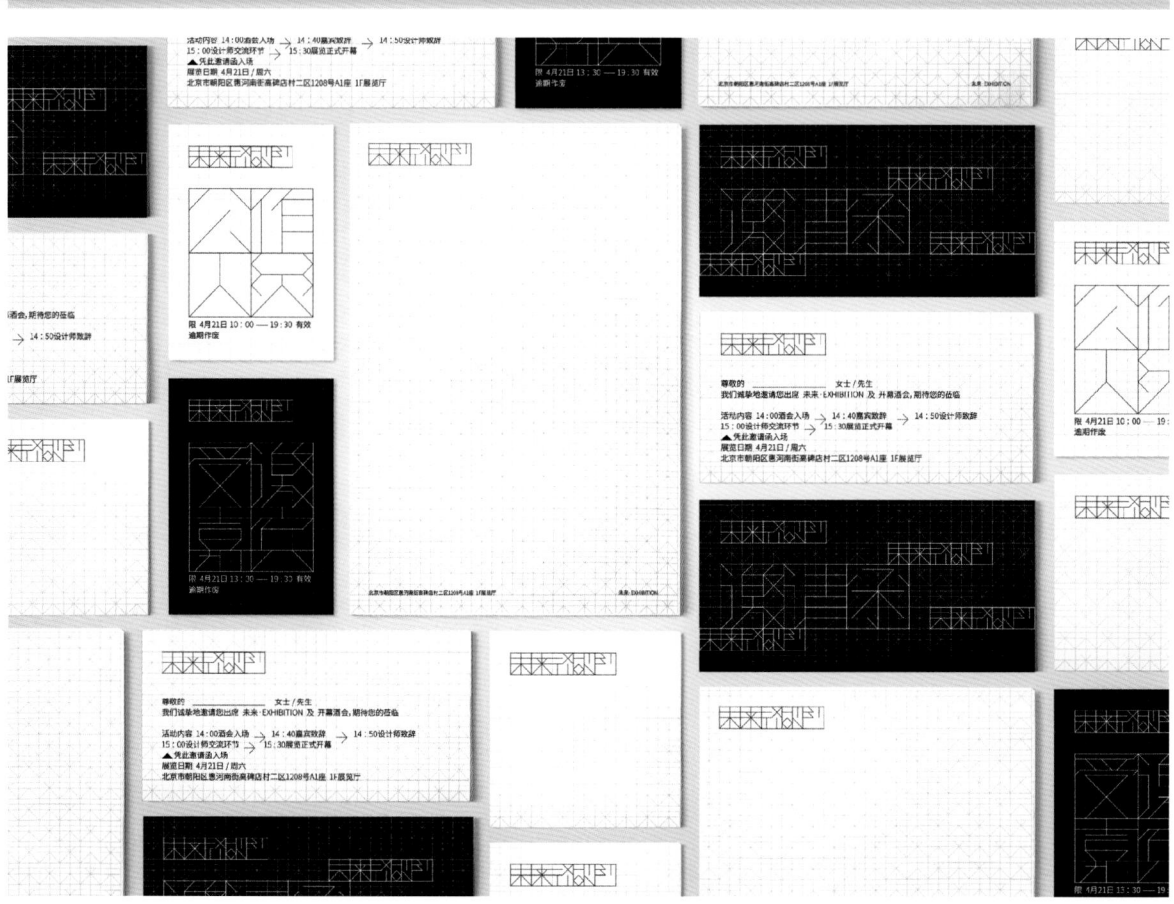

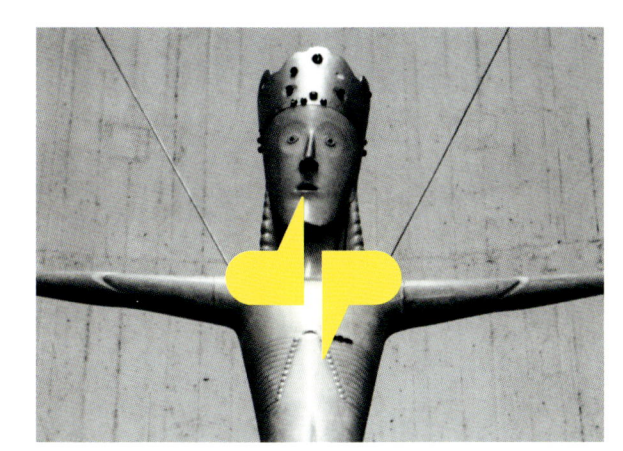

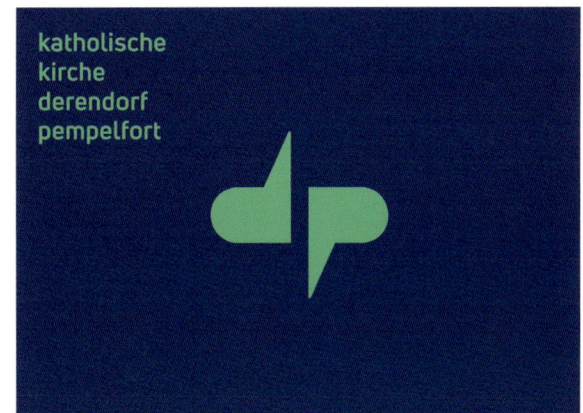

Katholische Kirche Derendorf Pempelfort

[Corporate Design Relaunch]

The Derendorf Pempelfort Catholic Church is an open-minded parish in Düsseldorf, Germany. The new logo features an abstract cross composed of the initials of the neighbouring urban districts: a lowercase "d" and a lowercase "p" representing Derendorf and Pempelfort respectively. The cross also forms two speech bubbles and thus symbolises the church's openness to dialogue. It reflects how the church wants to communicate, namely approachable and direct in their conversation with people and, of course, with God. The corporate design relaunch ensures that both their internal and external communication are memorable and consistent when used in analogue and digital media.

Client
Katholische Kirchengemeinde
Heilige Dreifaltigkeit
Düsseldorf, Germany

Design
die Gutgestalten GbR
Düsseldorf, Germany

Land of Hope

[Corporate Identity Relaunch]

Client
Land of Hope
Aarhus, Denmark

Design
Creuna Denmark A/S
Aarhus, Denmark

Project Team
Sara Marie Alvad (Creative Direction)
Julie Renee Jensen (Art Direction)
Stine Skovgaard (Copywriting)

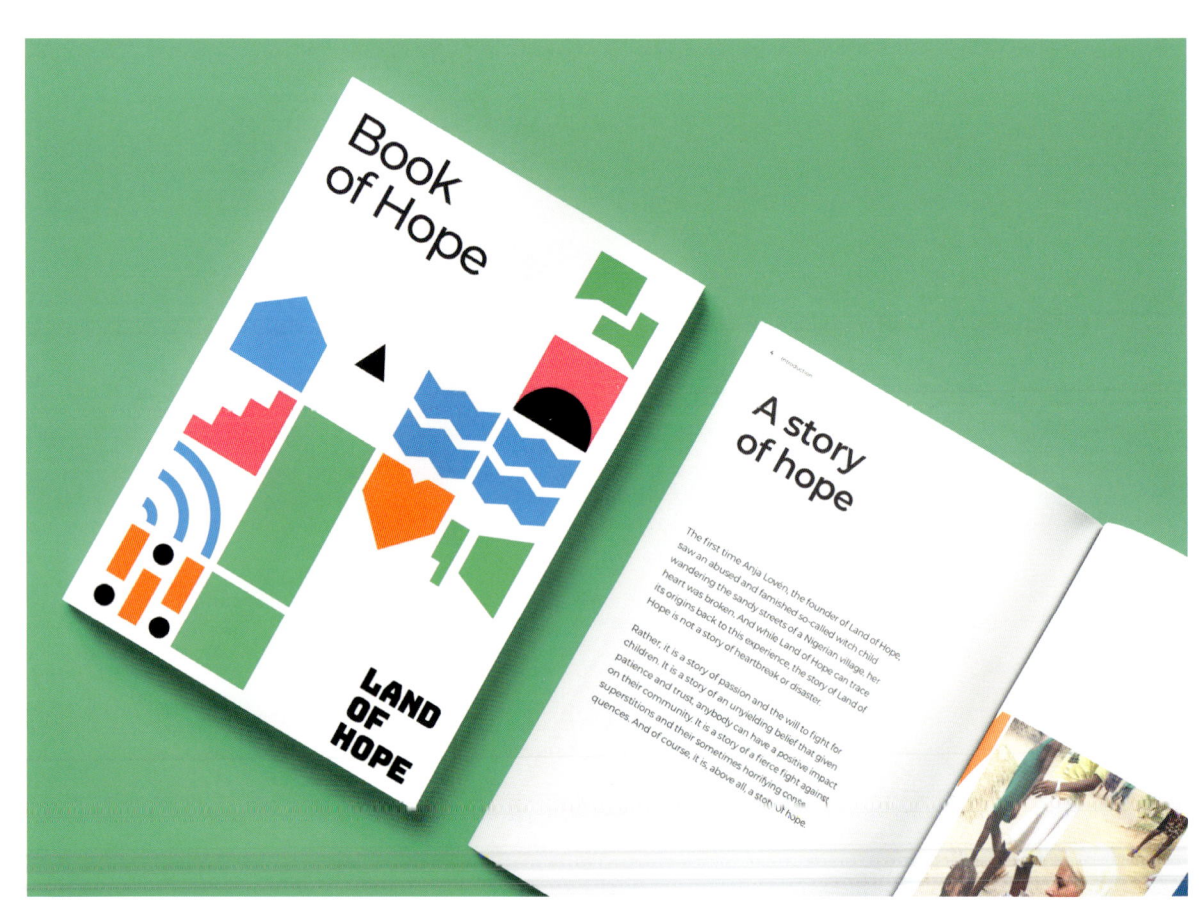

→ Clip online

Advertising	Packaging Design	Fair Stands	Retail Design	Red Dot: Junior Award	Designer Profiles	Index
288	318	494	516	544	614	674

Since 2012, Danish charity organisation DINNødhjælp has been fighting to protect marginalised children in Nigeria against the harmful superstitions of adults. They have helped more than one thousand children who have been wrongfully accused of witchcraft and established a large children's centre in West Africa. Based on their revamped corporate identity, a strong, international profile has been created under the new name "Land of Hope". The overhaul includes giving the brand a new logo, new colours and ten symbols as key cross-media design elements for use on the website, in the brand book called "Book of Hope" as well as on various kinds of merchandise.

Life of the Children
[Corporate Design Relaunch]

Life of the Children is a private aid organisation that supports children in developing countries. As part of the corporate design relaunch, a geometric graphic language was developed that aims to portray a hug. While the individual circles stand for neglected children, the connecting lines symbolise the NGO, which provides support for children in need. Furthermore, the hollow circle is a visual representation of transparency as the core value of the organisation. The strong contrast of complementary colours emphasises the visual conciseness of the graphic elements, while a bold yellow is chosen as the main colour to convey a positive impression.

Client
Life of the Children
Seoul, South Korea

Design
Slowalk
Seoul, South Korea

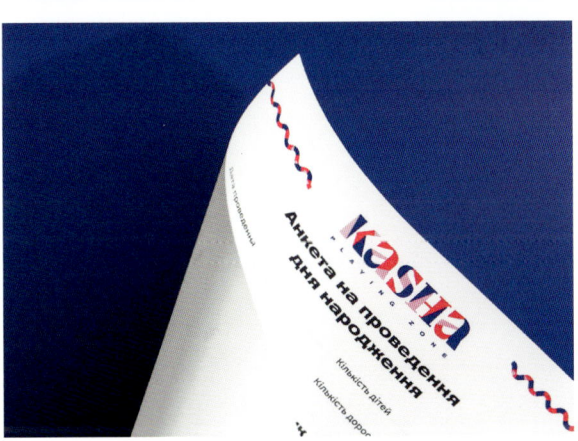

KASHA playing zone
[Corporate Identity]

Kasha is a playing zone for kids, equipped with interesting and trendy toys. It is a space for children to romp around, make up new games and enjoy childhood. The name Kasha, which literally means cereals, is also a synonym for jumble in the Ukrainian language. In order to underline the creativity of children, the logo features an abstract collage of differently coloured areas. Every single letter captures attention and is based on a creative collection of various graphic elements. Their deliberately chaotic arrangement characterises the overall dynamic appearance – down to the interior design.

Client
KASHA playing zone
Kyiv, Ukraine

Design
LLIWELL branding agency
Kyiv, Ukraine

Project Team
Glib Kaporikov (Creative Direction)
Nonna Starushchenko (Art Direction)
Dima Muzychenko (Head of Design)
Daria Sukhova (Graphic Design)
Arina Lukovina (Image Editing)

Bukak-Maeul

[Corporate Design]

Client
Bukak-Maeul
Gwangju, South Korea

Design
Coreintive
Gwangju, South Korea

Advertising	Packaging Design	Fair Stands	Retail Design	Red Dot: Junior Award	Designer Profiles	Index
288	318	494	516	544	614	674

Bukak-Maeul is a company that makes and sells Kimbukak, a traditional Korean seaweed snack. A natural-looking corporate design was created to convey one of their USPs – their manual manufacturing process that takes place in cooperation with local villagers. From product packaging to stationery, the design features a coherent colour palette with delicate patterns. These patterns were inspired by the structure of seaweed, whose growth rings are similar in cross-section to those of trees. In addition to the rings, the logo shows the wavy silhouette of heartwood, whose stability symbolises the company's core values.

UTB

[Corporate Design Relaunch]

With over 10 years of experience, Urban Taste & Beyond (UTB) is one of the leading coffee manufacturers in Korea. As part of a relaunch, a new visual identity was created to capture the core values of the company, using a flexible design and dynamic comprehensive branding. As a key visual, the first letter of the word mark showcases an abstract smiling face. The expression of a contemporary vision has been symbolically incorporated into the design to convey a modern image, and yet loosely coupled with elements of authenticity and tradition to help the brand stand out.

Client
UTB
Seoul, South Korea

Design
eyeteeth design
Seoul, South Korea
Wallstreetdocs
London, United Kingdom
Covenant
Seoul, South Korea

Project Team
Yunyoung Lee (Art Direction)

Dongho Kim (Art Direction)

Naehee Kim (Art Direction)

→ Designer profile on page 637

Advertising	Packaging Design	Fair Stands	Retail Design	Red Dot: Junior Award	Designer Profiles	Index
288	318	494	516	544	614	674

Chunmi

[Corporate Design]

As a kitchen appliance manufacturer, Chunmi aims to address a young, lifestyle-oriented target group and to position its products in the context of consumption upgrade. The entire corporate design centres on a round, orange logo, whose warm colour symbolises the warmth felt when cooking, while the signal effect allows for far-reaching visibility. In addition, the initial "C" is a versatile design element that stands for the innovative potential of the company. The claim is underlined by the homogeneous colour palette, which achieves a high level of recognition both in the interior design and in external communication.

Client
Shanghai Chunmi
Electronic Technology Co., Ltd.
Shanghai, China

Design
Shanghai Chunmi
Electronic Technology Co., Ltd.
Shanghai, China

Project Team
Liyuanxun Chen (Creative Direction)
Xulei Peng (Motion Design)
Huixin Ding (Web Design)

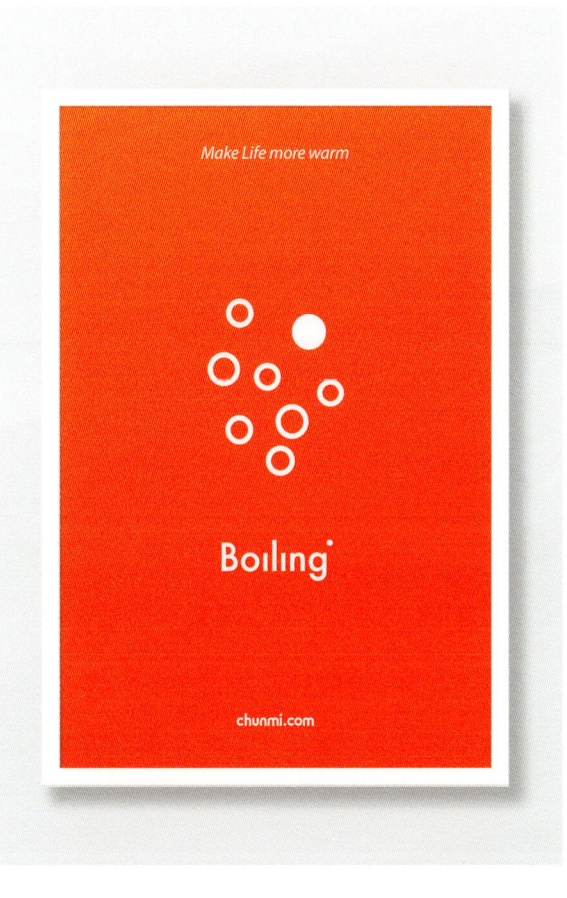

Aeris

[Corporate Design Relaunch]

Client
Aeris GmbH
Haar, Germany

Design
Mortar Pestle Studio
London, United Kingdom

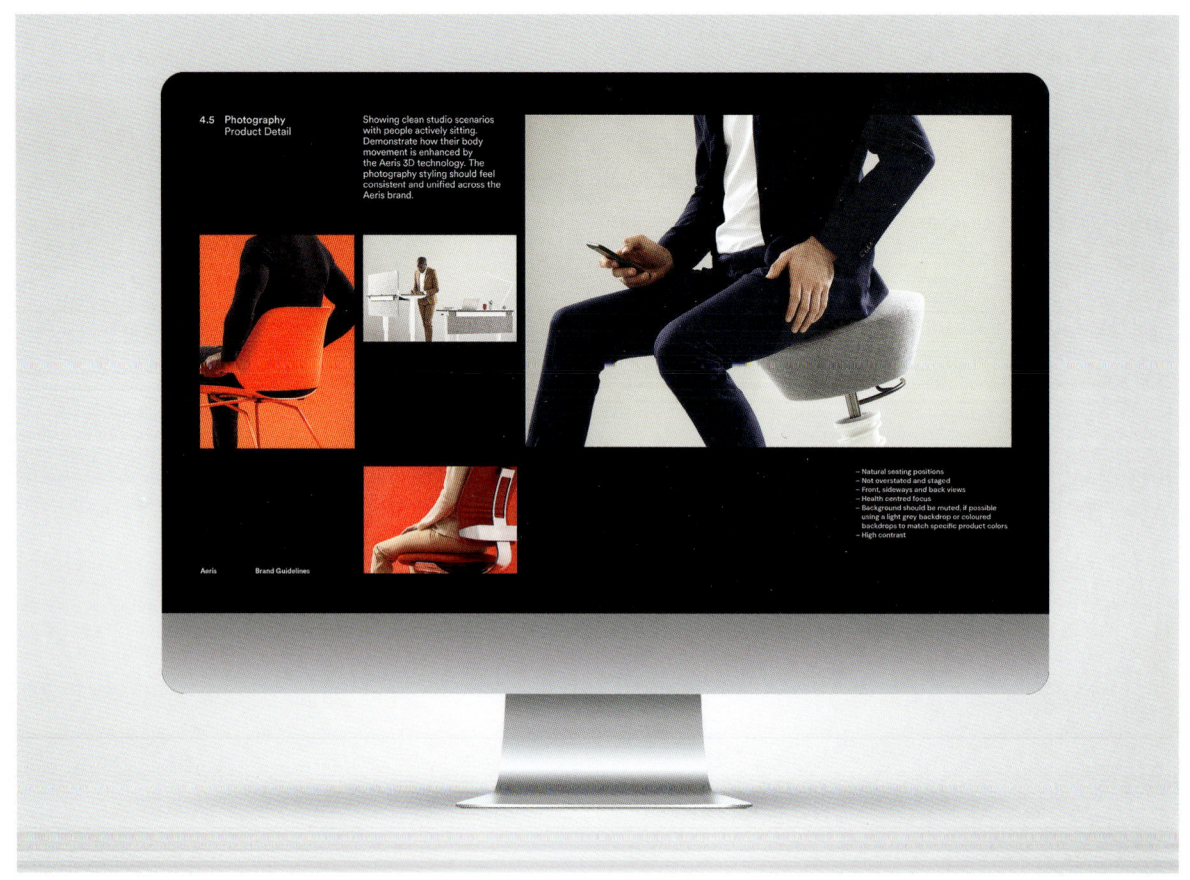

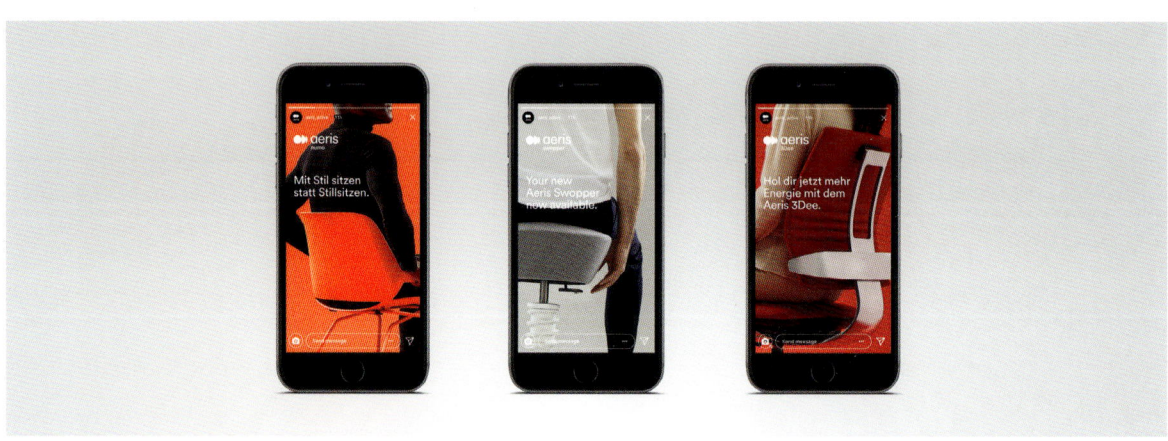

Over the past 25 years, Aeris has become a well-known manufacturer of ergonomic office furniture, even though the success of the Aeris Swopper has somewhat overshadowed the corporate image. Based on the newly developed brand slogan "Never Just Sit.", the relaunched corporate design appears strikingly dynamic, featuring a logo with high visual flexibility. The new tone of voice is emotional, connecting and authentic, with a slightly cheeky sense of humour. The clearly defined colour palette yields a contemporary appeal, functioning as a subtle yet emotive call to action. The result is a consistent, recognisable and engaging visual identity.

Biberkopf
[Logo Design]

Client
Arlberg Biberkopf Tourismus GmbH
Feldkirch, Austria

Design
pfeifer marketing
Memmingen, Germany

Project Team
Hans-Martin Pfeifer (Concept)
Elena Bopp (Concept)
Jamela Maria Goulebe (Concept)

→ Clip online

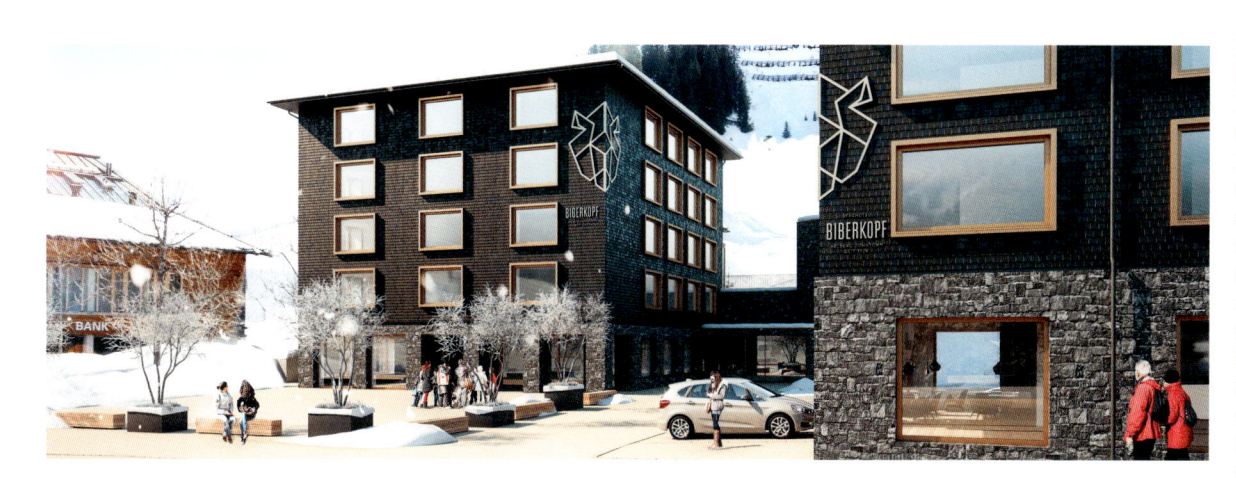

Berghotel Biberkopf is an adults-only hotel in Warth am Arlberg, Austria. Based on the hotel's name, a logo was developed that incorporated both the historical and regional connection of the hotel. The logo combines the silhouette of Biberkopf (beaver head) mountain with the shape of a beaver's head in a timeless style. The logo can be used in different colours and applications. A special variant of the beaver head logo features a texture filling and is suitable for embroidery. Furthermore, it can be used as an ornament or pattern and thus is also featured in the interior design of the hotel.

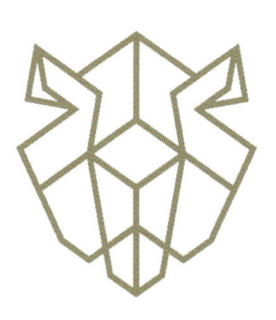

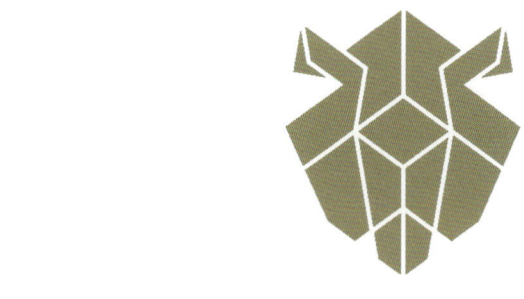

BERGHOTEL
BIBERKOPF
ARLBERG DOWNTOWN
SEIT 1928

ELA Container

[Corporate Identity Relaunch]

ELA Container, one of the leading international producers and service providers of mobile space solutions in container construction, decided to relaunch its corporate image. The new corporate identity includes a logotype, a consistent icon system, as well as the photographic representation of products and services. The distinctive word mark uses a clear typography with square brackets alluding to the structure of containers. Furthermore, these brackets serve as icons. The corporate identity has been consistently realised across campaigns, product catalogues, customer magazines and the new website.

Client
ELA Container GmbH
Haren (Ems), Germany

Design
schmitz Visuelle Kommunikation
Wuppertal, Germany

Project Team
Hans Günter Schmitz
(Creative Direction)
Marcus Sonntag (Art Direction)
Arne Sänger (Design)

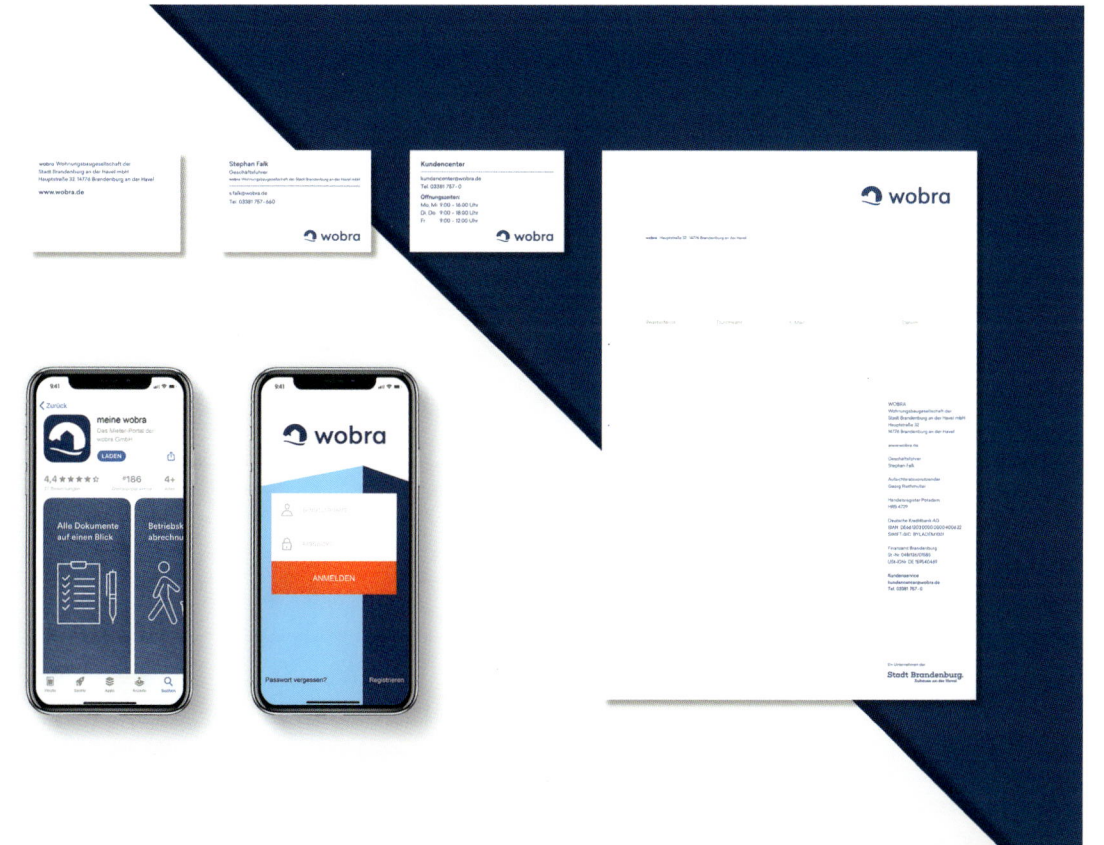

wobra Wohnungsbaugesellschaft der Stadt Brandenburg

[Corporate Design Relaunch]

wobra is a municipal housing association offering modern and affordable housing in the city of Brandenburg an der Havel, Germany. Objective of the redesign was to showcase the company as a reliable partner across all communication channels. The city's urban and natural character is visualised by silhouettes of buildings and a lively range of colours, dominated by shades of blue – representing the city's most attractive feature: its closeness to water. A waved line completes the logo – reminiscent of the Havel river flowing through the city. In addition, a geometric typography lends the logo a timeless character.

Client
wobra Wohnungsbaugesellschaft der Stadt Brandenburg an der Havel mbH
Brandenburg an der Havel, Germany

Design
Bureau Steffi Holz
Brandenburg an der Havel, Germany

Project Team
Steffi Holz (Art Direction)
Susanne Uhlmann (Graphic Design)
Linda Haseloff (Graphic Design)

Keys
Asset Management

[Corporate Design Relaunch]

Since 2011, Keys Asset Management has specialised in the development and management of alternative real estate investment funds for professional investors. Their design relaunch is driven by a new slogan, "Et votre patrimoine prend un temps d'avance" (your assets take a step ahead) and is accompanied by a new visual identity, in the form of an unstructured system of layered images that expresses the company's creative approach and joins the highly structured geometric shapes that reflect its expertise. The precise word mark reveals itself inside an invisible frame, playing with the basic idea of the tangible versus the intangible.

Client
Keys Asset Management
Paris, France

Design
Pixelis
Paris, France

Project Team
Mathilde Theve (Creative Director)
Valentine Proust (Art Director)
Virginie Lucas (Art Director)
Audrey Camara (Art Director)
Christine Yau (Account Management)
Fruzsina Piukovics
(Account Management)
Laurence Leguay (Account Management)
Nathalie Guerin (Graphic Design)
Laurence Aziza (Graphic Design)

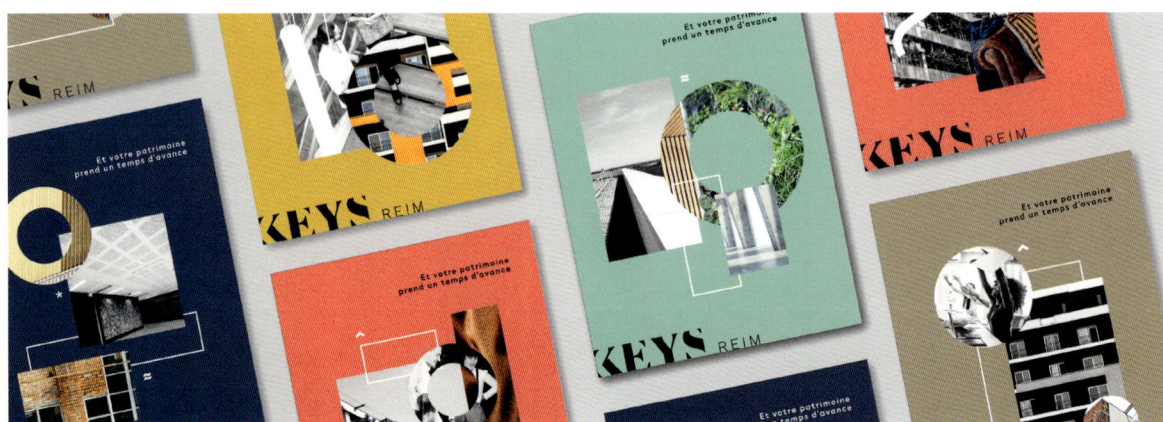

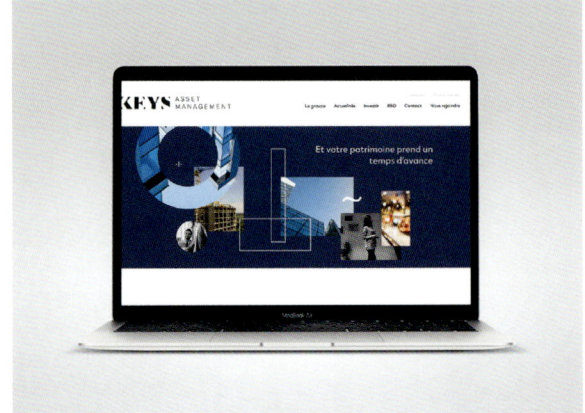

OCC Assekuradeur
[Corporate Design Relaunch]

As part of a company-wide digitalisation project, the provider of insurances for vintage cars aimed at a full relaunch. The new corporate design is based on typical elements from the classic car scene, such as iconic automotive paint shades and rally-themed buttons. The emotionally appealing buttons are used as information carriers and appear across all online and print media. The playful icon concept combines clear lines with a bold typography to produce a distinctive appearance, while the new claim "Wir versichern Klassiker." (We insure classic cars) underlines the USP of the insurance company.

Client
OCC Assekuradeur GmbH
Lübeck, Germany

Design
SUAN Conceptual Design GmbH
Basel, Switzerland

Project Team
OCC Assekuradeur:
Désirée Mettraux (CEO)
Magdalena Behr (Marketing Specialist)
Jessica Dobrig (Marketing Specialist)
Lisa Hofmann
(Team Lead Events & Sponsoring)

SUAN Conceptual Design:
Susanne Hartmann (Creative Direction)
André Konrad (Creative Direction)
Déborah Mayer (Art Direction)

Stefan Weber (Web Design),
Kontour Design Studio
Marc Baur (Programming),
youEngineering AG

→ Designer profile on page 668

Carrot Direct Insurance

[Corporate Identity]

In order to effectively appeal to a young target group, the corporate design of the South Korean insurance company exudes a great sense of style. In keeping with the company name, the key visual shows a carrot as a distinctive element of the overall appearance. The colour scheme juxtaposes a vibrant orange with a strong blue, creating a high degree of brand recognition. A friendly visual language explaining the different insurance products with distinctive illustrations helps users select and conveniently take out the right insurance online.

Client
Carrot General Insurance
Seoul, South Korea

Design
Interbrand Seoul
Seoul, South Korea

Project Team
Uzin Hwang (Creative Director)
Hajin Jung (Design Director)
Namgyu Kim (Brand Designer)
Hyo Jung Lim (Brand Designer)
Juyoung Kim (Brand Designer)
Yeeun Kim (Brand Designer)
Jeongmin Lee (Brand Designer)

City Clinical Hospital No. 40

[Logo Redesign]

This hospital in Moscow, which opened at the end of the 19th century, has developed into a modern clinic over time. Its new logo features a rendering of the cross – a well-known icon for medicine – and merges it with the number 40. The lines are reminiscent of the white stripes of bandages and the cancer support ribbon, while the circular shape evokes the association with pills. The transparent shades of blue have a calming effect on patients; blue is also considered the colour of technology. In addition to stationery, the logo also features on both the building's facade and the staff's workwear.

Client
City Clinical Hospital No. 40
Moscow, Russia

Design
Art. Lebedev Studio
Moscow, Russia

Project Team
Artemy Lebedev (Artistic Director)
Erken Kagarov (Artistic Director)
Anton Zhukov (Graphic Design)
Dmitry Mikhailov (Graphic Design)
Valeriya Komleva (Project Management)
Irina Aron (Project Management)

uncorporate.design

[Corporate Design]

Client
uncorporate.design, Institute for Project and Discourse Design
Krefeld, Germany

Design
eskalade werbeagentur GmbH
Krefeld, Germany

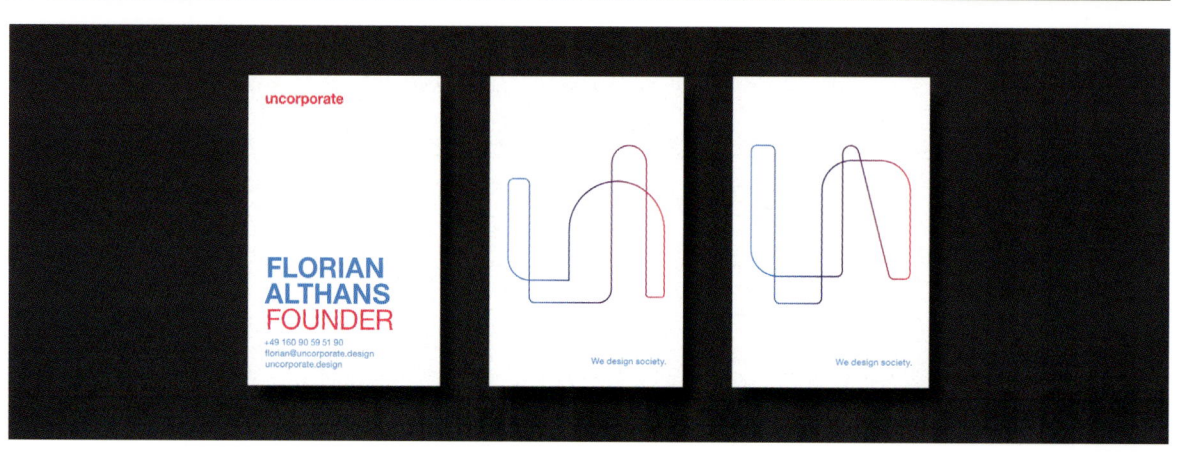

Advertising	Packaging Design	Fair Stands	Retail Design	Red Dot: Junior Award	Designer Profiles	Index
288	318	494	516	544	614	674

uncorporate.design focuses on human-centred design and researches design processes that address not only users and stakeholders, but also critics of the objects to be designed. Against this background, the term uncorporate – more precisely the prefix "un-" – is paramount to the company's image. From this prefix, a set of amorphous pictograms were developed in the form of lines for structuring areas or frames for displaying photographs and illustrations. Cyan and magenta were selected as primary colours to not only provide a strong visual presence but also symbolise clarity and simplicity.

Preface	Red Dot: Agency of the Year	Brands	Brand Design & Identity	Corporate Design & Identity	Annual Reports
4	6	18	90	202	260

Nacht der jungen Leaders

[Corporate Design]

The "Nacht der jungen Leaders" (night of the young leaders) is an annual event for young entrepreneurs, managers and leaders under the age of 40 who work in the field of economics or politics and are based in Northwestern Switzerland or beyond. The corporate design is intended to be provocative towards the event's assertive target group. It deliberately polarises by incorporating the age limit of 40 years and combining it with cheeky headlines in an expressive typeface. In turn, the graphic design is reduced and serves to emphasise the typography with striking colour contrasts.

Client
Junior Chamber International Basel
Handelskammer beider Basel
Basel, Switzerland

Design
SUAN Conceptual Design GmbH
Basel, Switzerland

Project Team
SUAN Conceptual Design:
André Konrad (Creative Direction)
Susanne Hartmann (Creative Direction)

Markus Stauffiger (Programming),
4eyes GmbH

→ Designer profile on page 668

Fincap Law
[Corporate Design Relaunch]

Fincap Law LLP is a law firm that utilises automation as part of its service provision. The relaunch aimed to update the former logo and give it a stylised, contemporary look. Another goal was to develop a benchmark design for the legal and financial sectors. The distinguishing features of the new corporate design are meant to represent the firm's core values of continuous improvement, legal protection and networking. These values have been meticulously integrated into the visual identity, with connecting lines and contact points forming flexible patterns embedded in a monochrome colour scheme.

Client
Fincap Law
London, United Kingdom

Design
Wallstreetdocs
London, United Kingdom
eyeteeth design
Seoul, South Korea

Project Team
Dongho Kim (Art Direction)

Yunyoung Lee (Art Direction)

→ Designer profile on page 637

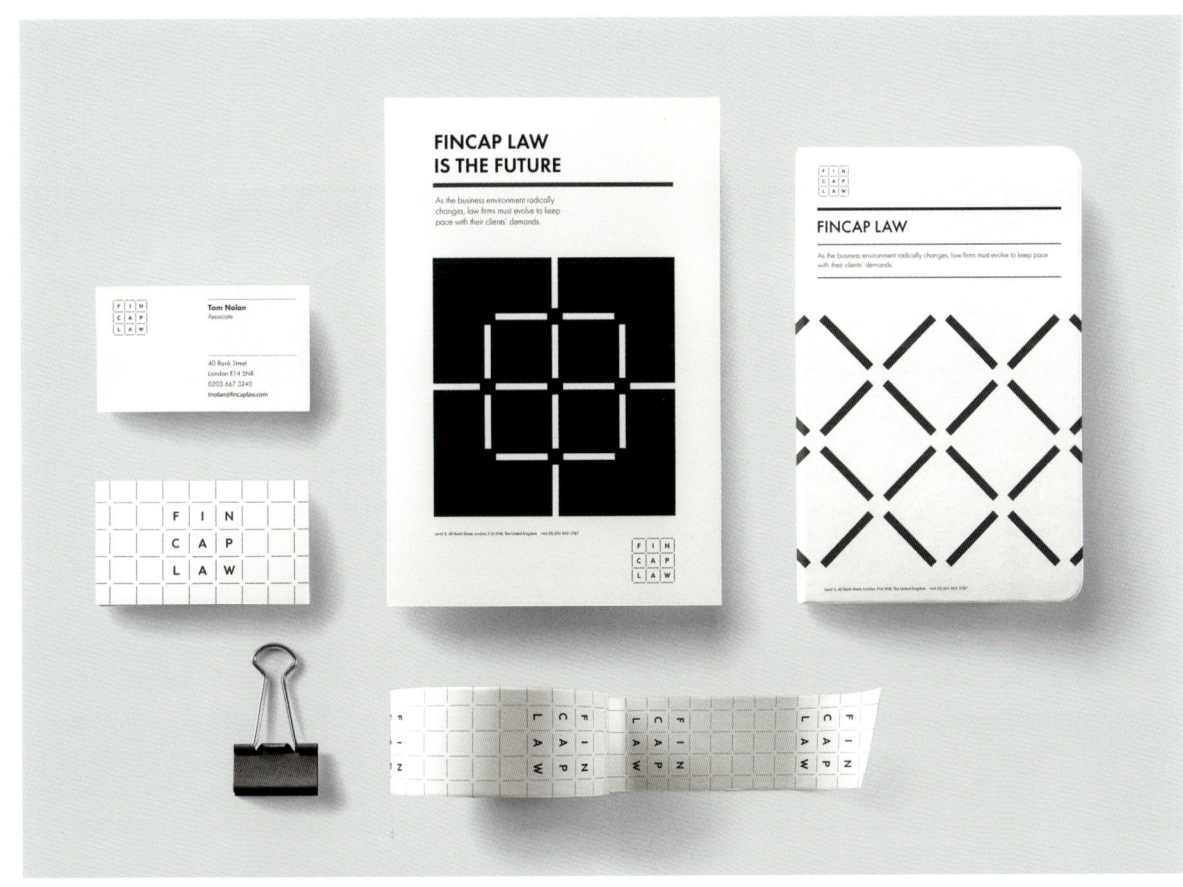

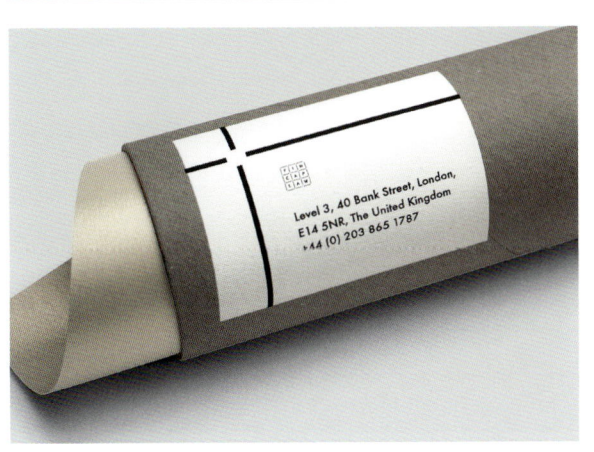

VECO

[Corporate Design Relaunch]

Client
VECO Group SA
Lugano, Switzerland

Design
Autentic Consulting Sagl
Lugano, Switzerland

→ Designer profile on page 623

Advertising	Packaging Design	Fair Stands	Retail Design	Red Dot: Junior Award	Designer Profiles	Index
288	318	494	516	544	614	674

We look at the future through your eyes.
Today. Tomorrow. Always.

Lugano London Dubai Hong Kong Malta   vecogroup.ch

VECO is an independent private group based in Lugano, Switzerland, with offices in London, Dubai, Hong Kong and Malta. Since 1973, they have specialised in helping their clients succeed in the private and commercial sectors. The purpose of the relaunch was to transform an almost 25-year-old visual identity into a timeless, more digital-oriented corporate design. During the process, they decided to remove the word "group" and put the company name VECO in a more prominent position. The corporate colours of red and black were kept for recognition. Black-and-white photography was chosen to lend the identity a more refined appearance.

about:communication

[Corporate Design Relaunch]

The Cologne-based agency has made a name for itself as a PR specialist for the automotive, industrial and technology sectors. Having expanded its range of services in recent years, the agency now offers complete packages that cover not only PR but also social media, events and marketing consulting. The new corporate design aims to reflect this development both visually and with a new agency name, with communication taking centre stage: a stylised speech bubble carries the word mark and can be used flexibly as a design element. The company's acronym serves as a signet. In addition, bold colours and a distinctive typography ensure a striking appearance.

Client
ac about communication GmbH & Co. KG
Cologne, Germany

Design
31M Agentur für Kommunikation GmbH
Essen, Germany

Project Team
Daniel Bürger (Creative Direction)
Dieter Rehmann (Text)

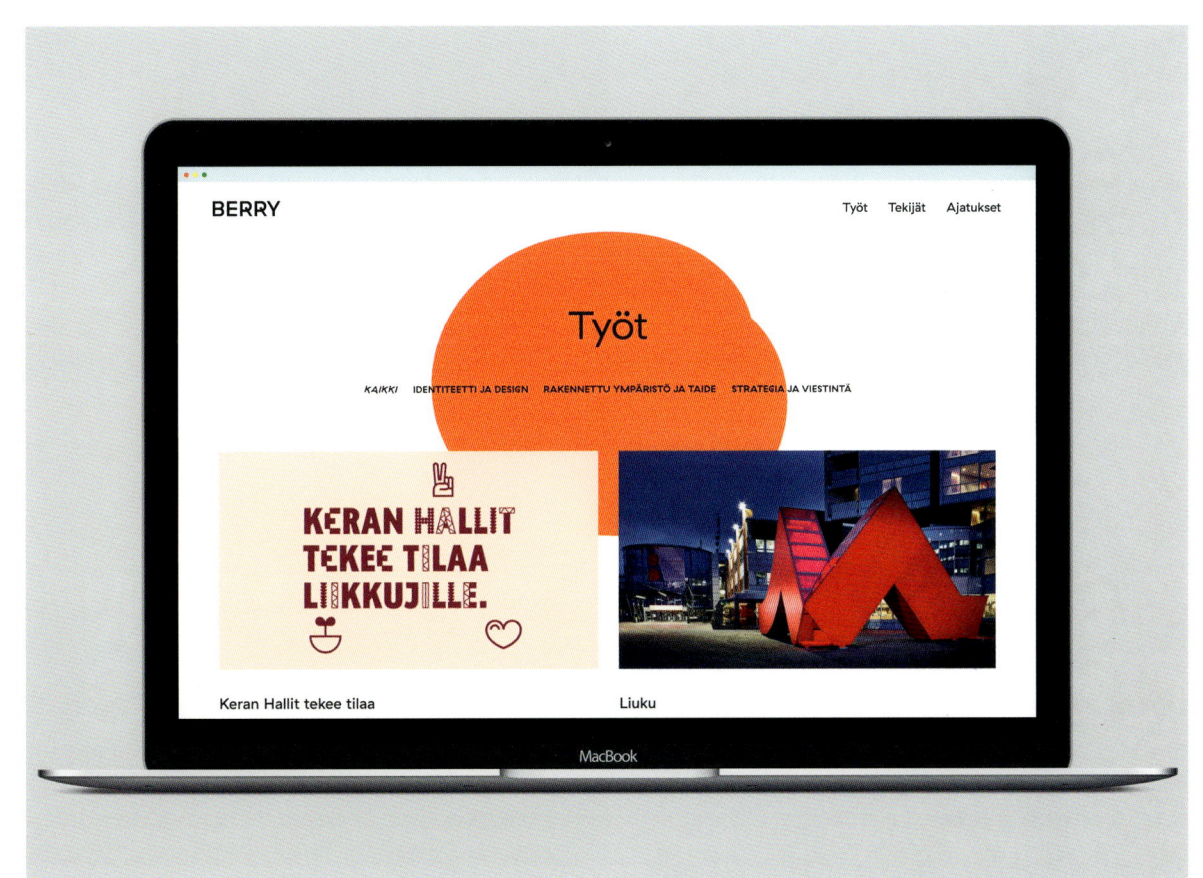

Berry Creative

[Visual Identity]

Berry Creative is a creative agency aiming to stand out from their competitors and highlight their strengths through a design relaunch. With the goal to surprise and distinguish themselves from others, the new visual identity combines a minimal design language, colourful shapes and rotating letters in unusual ways. This allows the agency to underscore their USP: a joyful approach to design challenges and an inspirational presence when working face to face with clients. The overall imagery is characterised by versatile, emotionally appealing illustrations conveying a gentle and creative atmosphere.

Client
Berry Creative
Helsinki, Finland

Design
Berry Creative
Helsinki, Finland

Project Team
Berry Creative:
Julia Nyyssölä (Art Direction)
Petteri Tuukkanen (Graphic Design)
Vilma Tuominen (Artwork)
Mirka Larjomaa (Artwork)

Paavo Lehtonen (Photography)
Johannes Neumeier – Underscore (Logotype)
Joni Kaunismäki – Mediaani (Web Development)

→ Designer profile on page 625

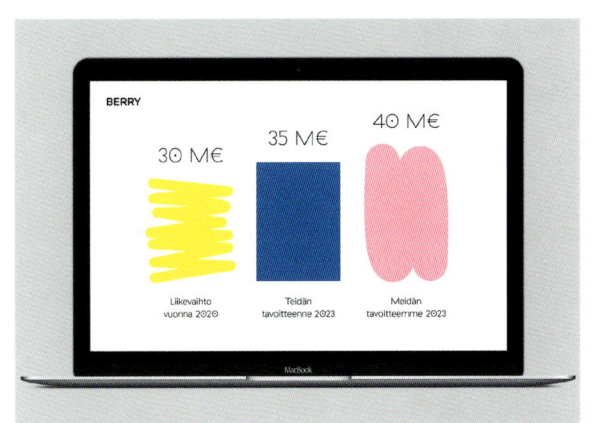

Berlin Decks

[Corporate Design, Logo Design]

Client
CONVALOR Projektpartner GmbH
Cologne, Germany
BEOS AG
Berlin, Germany
neos GP GmbH
Berlin, Germany

Design
Cee Cee Creative
Berlin, Germany

Project Team
BEOS AG:
Tony Paumer (Project Lead)
Nina Krasemann (Head of Marketing)
Holger Matheis (Board Member)

→ Designer profile on page 628

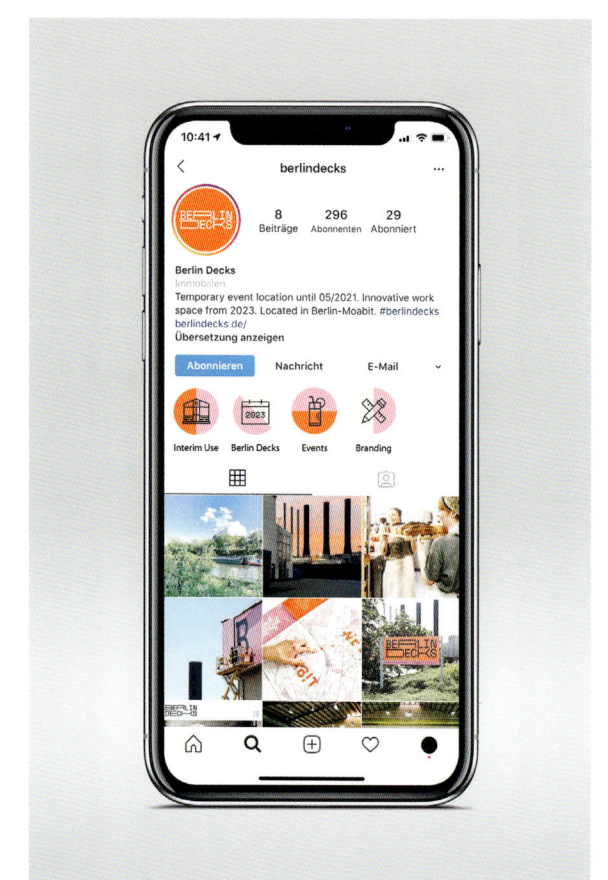

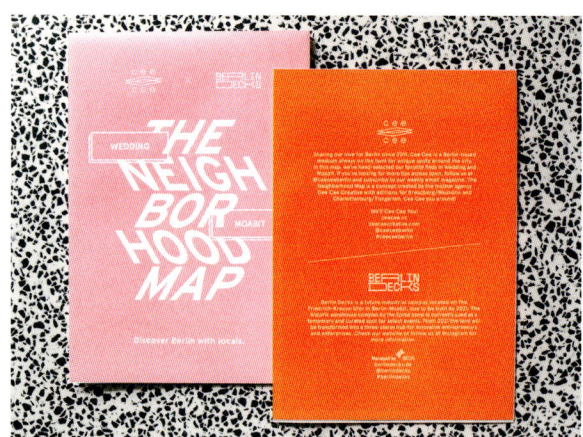

Advertising	Packaging Design	Fair Stands	Retail Design	Red Dot: Junior Award	Designer Profiles	Index
288	318	494	516	544	614	674

Berlin Decks is an innovative campus for entrepreneurs and creative people that is being developed in an urban neighbourhood with an industrial past. The naming was inspired by the waterside location near Berlin's docklands, while the dynamic corporate design was influenced by the building's modularity. In digital form, the logo changes shape, with its letterforms extending to resemble ship decks. The simple typography is a reference to the bold lettering on shipping containers. The two corporate colours were chosen to form a strong contrast: while the vivid orange, which is often seen on industrial machinery, signifies the location's industrial past, the light pink is used to project a contemporary, digital-hub vibe.

Preface	Red Dot: Agency of the Year	Brands	Brand Design & Identity	Corporate Design & Identity	Annual Reports
4	6	18	90	202	260

Excited Agency
[Corporate Design Relaunch]

Digital design agency Excited specialises in helping businesses and start-ups create a digital design for their products, including by offering innovation workshops. The primary goal of their new corporate design is to create a visual identity that is eye-catching, showcases creativity and imbues the agency's image with life and emotions. Therefore, the new design concept uses the very same interface elements that the agency staff use in their work every day, such as identity building blocks, and mixes these blocks with bright colours to achieve an expressive overall impression.

Client
Excited
Lviv, Ukraine

Design
Excited
Lviv, Ukraine

Project Team
Oleksandr Perelotov (Creative Direction)
Aneliia Zazulina (Creative Direction)
Yuliia Yatseniuk (Designer)
Mark Altytsia (Motion Design)

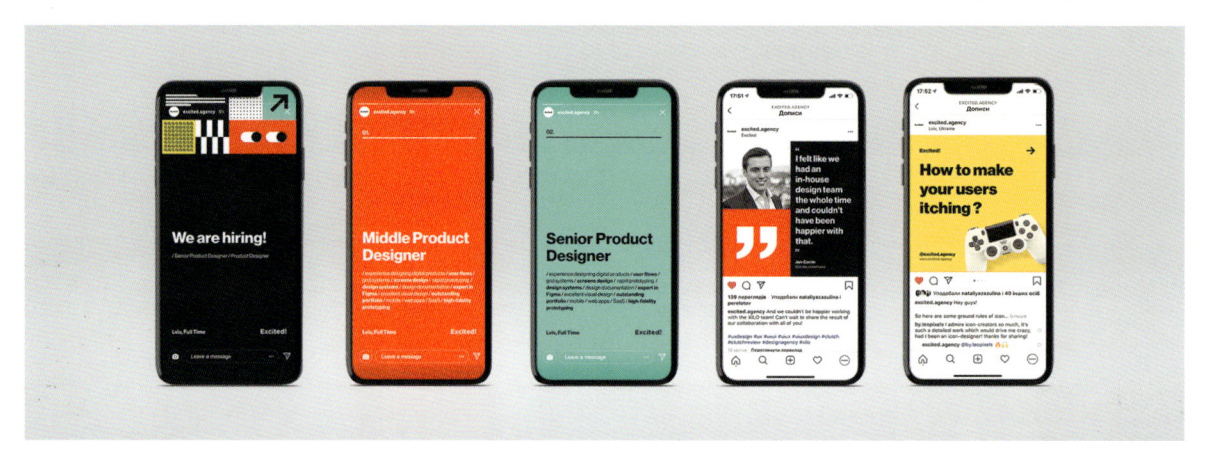

244

Red Dog Culture House

[Corporate Identity Relaunch]

With this relaunch, the South Korean animation studio Red Dog Culture House aims to establish itself on the market as a leading subculture company with new core values. The intuitive word mark, which is combined with various illustrations of a red dog, expresses the company's character and cohesion. The corporate identity was created with flexibility in mind, allowing the studio's artists to personalise their business cards, badges and other company-related items with their own version of the red dog. This results in a creative overall image and enhances the sense of community among staff.

Client
Red Dog Culture House
Bucheon, South Korea

Design
Studio H.I.M.
Seoul, South Korea

Project Team
Byungwook Kang (Creative Direction)
Hyungkun Kim (Graphic Design)

VERGISSMEINNICHT

[Corporate Design]

This "film agency for memories" produces biographical films for people who want to tell their story and preserve it for themselves or others, for instance because they are facing senility or imminent death. The challenge was to develop a corporate design that clearly conveys seriousness, professionalism and value, as well as to appeal to people of different age groups. The result is a solution whose guiding creative principle reflects the flexibility of memories. Thus, the dynamic logo on the website takes on over 50 different forms while maintaining its recognisability. Different versions of the logo can also be seen on printed materials.

Client
VERGISSMEINNICHT –
filmagentur für erinnern
Cologne, Germany

Design
thjnk Düsseldorf
Düsseldorf, Germany

Project Team
Kai Röffen (Managing Director Creation)
Patrick Reichert-Young
(Creative Director Design)
Till Köster (Creative Director Copy)
Janik Bienemann (Junior Designer)

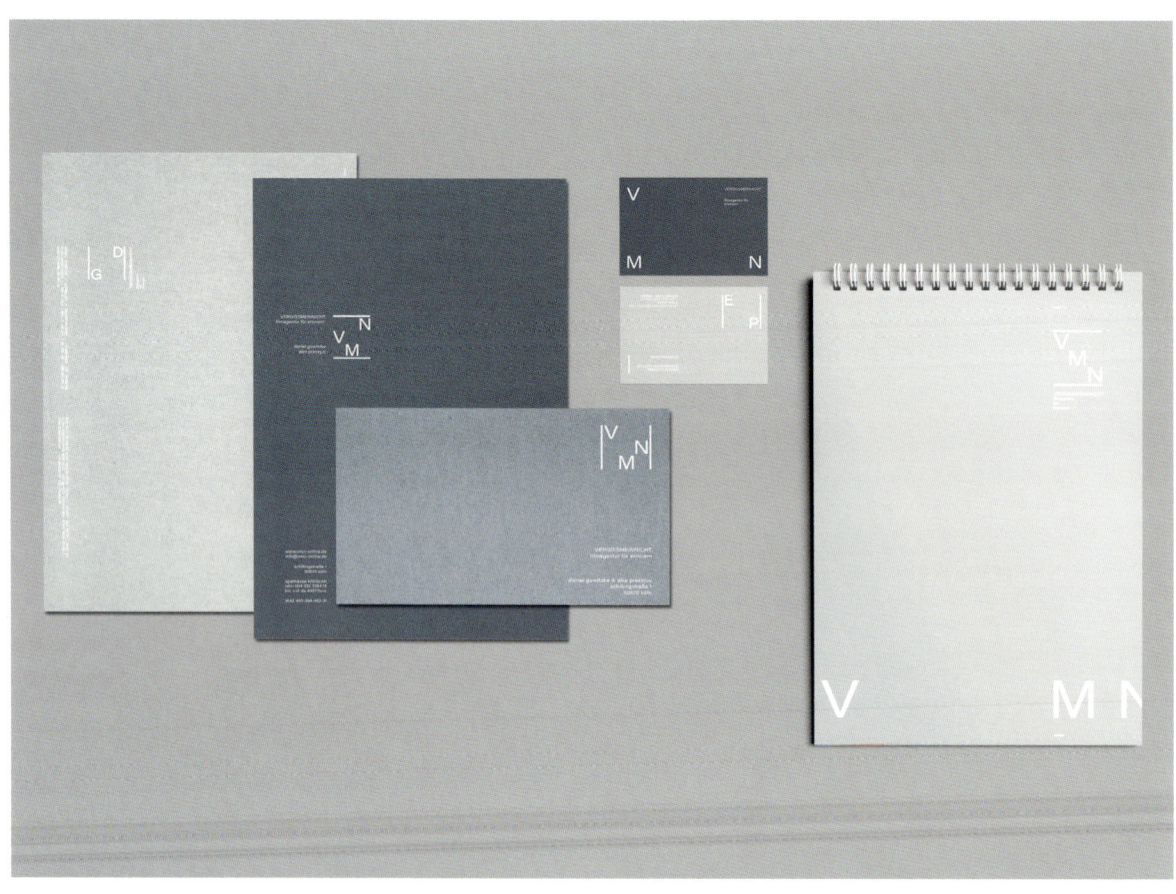

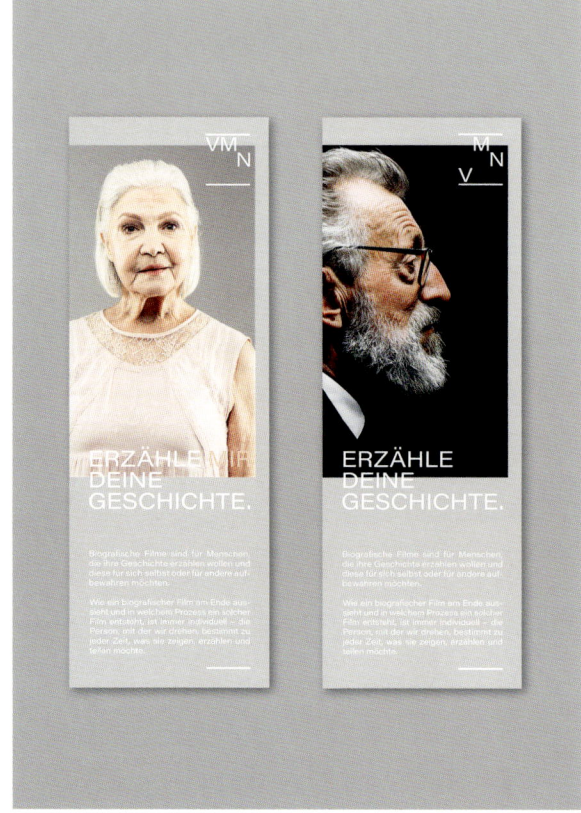

Eigenland
[Corporate Design]

The German company Eigenland develops online tools that support organisations in the implementation of Multi-sense workshops. With the objective of a memorable positioning on the market, a dynamic corporate design was created that reflects the versatility and modernity of Eigenland. The new corporate design includes a word mark, an eye-catching colour spectrum and an emotionally appealing typography. The dynamic design language has been consistently carried over to the corporate website, the mobile app and print media, such as posters, business cards and stationery.

Client
eigenland
Haltern am See, Germany

Design
cyclos design GmbH
Münster, Germany

Project Team
Jutta Schnieders (Creative Direction)
Youngju Köhler (Creative Direction)

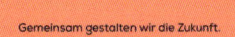

calligraphy cut®

[Corporate Design Relaunch]

The calligraph blade is a scientifically tested and patented hairdressing tool that cuts at a 21-degree angle to give the hair more volume. The new corporate design translates the exclusive product experience into a visual language that meets the needs of the globally recognised brand. Therefore, the company values were translated into a targeted and unique appearance. The logo, featuring the letter "C", embodies the product's characteristics by incorporating the advantages of the 21-degree cutting angle. Together with a new, modern corporate typeface, the homogenous colour palette underlines the brand's elegant look and feel.

Client
The Calligraphy Cut Company GmbH
Oelde, Germany

Design
UNGESTRICHEN
Strategisches Kommunikationsdesign
Krefeld, Germany

Project Team
Jens Könen (Creative Direction)
Lars Mewes (Graphic Design)

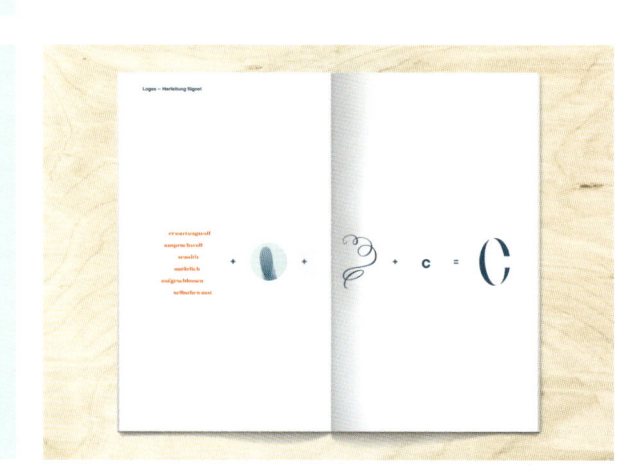

Backstage, Beauty Salons Chain

[Logo Redesign]

Backstage is a large chain of beauty salons in Kyiv, Ukraine, that allows its customers to retreat from everyday stress in a relaxing atmosphere. The existing logo was redesigned based on the chain's new positioning statement in the context of "urban stress relief". The new logo design delivers a relaxed vibe, which expresses a sense of exclusivity by borrowing from the world of show business. The playful use of reflection and symmetry, which are the main features of beauty, defines the wavelike arrangement of the letters. Featuring the company's initials, the BS lettermark complements the corporate identity.

Client
Backstage
Kyiv, Ukraine

Design
Madcats Agency
Kyiv, Ukraine

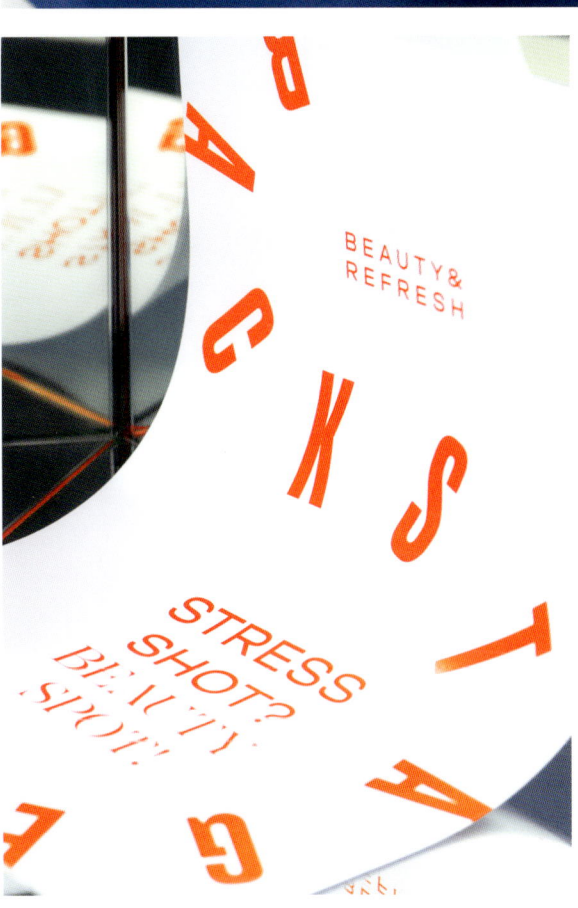

Preface	Red Dot: Agency of the Year	Brands	Brand Design & Identity	**Corporate Design & Identity**	Annual Reports
4	6	18	90	202	260

CHANNEL A

[Visual Branding, Corporate Identity]

The popular Korean television network CHANNEL A was facing the challenge of conveying a consistent image with a flexible visual branding. Building on their previous brand identity of "open & creative canvas", the company expanded their corporate design concept into an "infinite canvas" that can accommodate more diverse contents. This concept portrays the enlargement, change and movement of a canvas as an extension to graphic elements. Canvases transformed into abstract colour fields are key visuals, which are implemented in many different ways to create a dynamic overall image of unmistakable individuality.

Client
CHANNEL A
Seoul, South Korea

Design
CHANNEL A B&C
Seoul, South Korea
mmpx
Seoul, South Korea
NF
Seoul, South Korea

Project Team
CHANNEL A B&C:
Jisang Yu (Creative Direction)
Jongbeom Choi (Creative Direction)

mmpx:
Hojong Chun (Graphic Design)
Cheolhee Hwang (Graphic Design)

NF:
Horyong Jeong (Motion Design)
Kyungjin Moon (Motion Design)

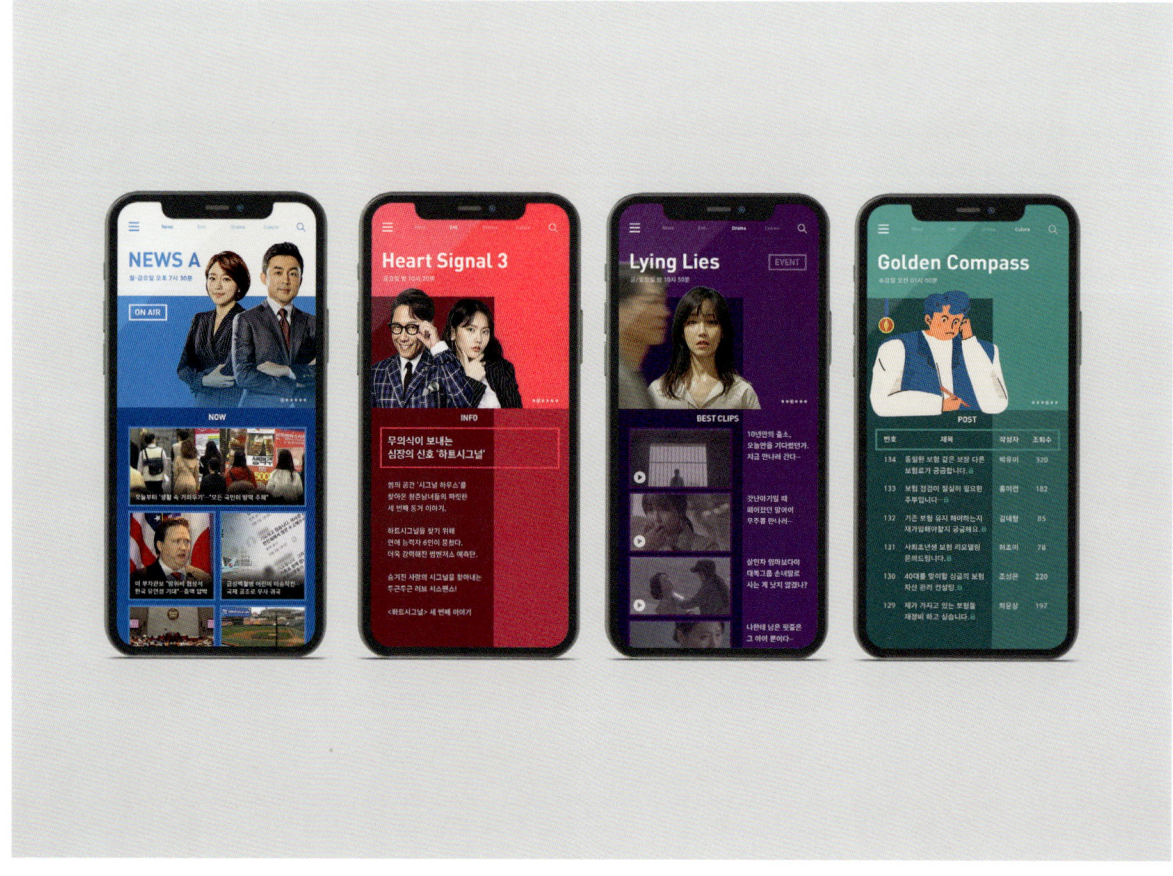

250

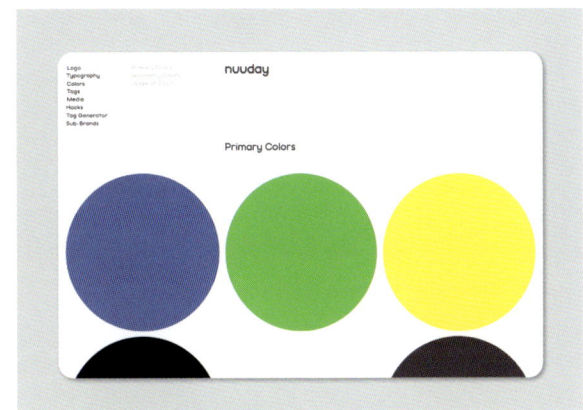

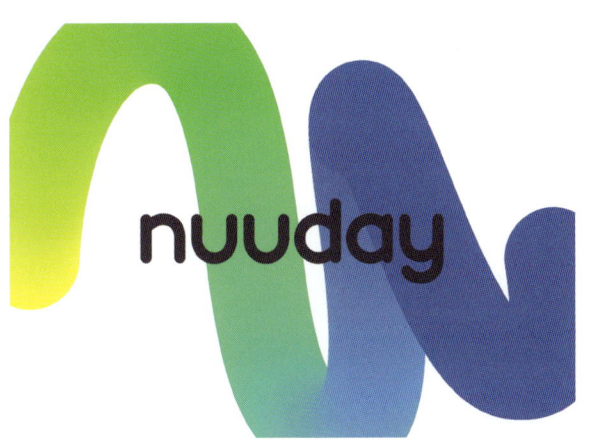

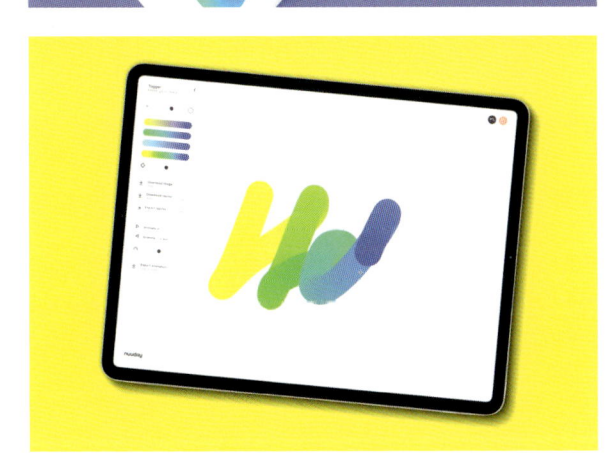

Nuuday

[Corporate Identity]

Nuuday is a new family of strong brands providing TV, broadband, network and telecommunication services to the majority of Denmark. It strives to be perceived as a company run by a close-knit team of good rebels who understand technology. The design concept was in particular inspired by the name Nuuday, which means "new day" in Danish. Therefore, the corporate design aims to convey the positive feeling of waking up to an exciting day. The bright, cheerful colour palette of the flexible key visual allows for a friendly and open-minded brand expression that clearly stands out from competitors.

Client
Nuuday
Copenhagen, Denmark

Design
1508
Copenhagen, Denmark

Project Team
Tore Rosbo (Design Lead)
Susanne Mouritsen (Designer)
Emilie Fafner (Designer)
Christoffer Birkkjær (Developer/Animator)
Per C. Jackson (Front-End Developer)
Morten Øhlenschlæger Andersen
(Client Lead)

Mobvista

[Visual Identity, Logo Design]

Client
Mobvista
Guangzhou, China

Design
FutureBrand China
Shanghai, China

Project Team
Sam Yang (Creative Direction)
Feifei Jiang (Graphic Design Lead)
Zhe Li (Graphic Design)
Sijia Zhang (Graphic Design)
Sophie Cheng (Project Management)
Cary Liu (Account Management)

→ Designer profile on page 638
→ Clip online

Advertising	Packaging Design	Fair Stands	Retail Design	Red Dot: Junior Award	Designer Profiles	Index
288	318	494	516	544	614	674

Launched in 2013 as a mobile advertising platform, Mobvista has become a leading technology platform today. A consistent and flexible visual identity was developed in the course of a redefinition of the brand strategy. The contemporary, science-inspired logo is used in both monochrome and colour; the coloured version features accents in the striking corporate colours. The claim "From Present to the Future" in combination with a distinctive visual system helps Mobvista to highlight its core competencies and brand association in a dynamic-looking manner.

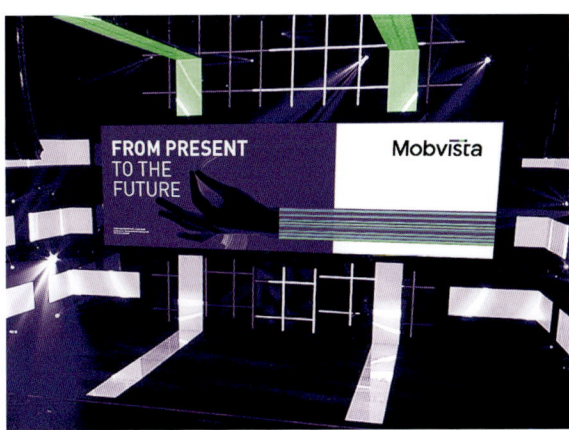

SK Telecom

[Onboarding Kit]

SK Telecom is a leading information and communications technology conglomerate in South Korea. On their first day of work, new employees receive an onboarding kit containing relevant information and heartfelt welcome messages from the company. Resembling a parcel branded with the corporate design, the kit includes a handbook plus six must-haves in the office. Its design features colours, shapes and lines that signify the company's core industries. The main messages are teamwork and growth. Thus, the on-boarding kit helps motivate and ease new employees into their work environment.

Client
SK Telecom
Seoul, South Korea

Design
HuskyFox
Seoul, South Korea

Project Team
SK Telecom:
Jongwhi Cha
Sangeun Lee
Seungjun Rhee
Sejin Noh
Jongwon Won

HuskyFox:
Doohee Lee (Creative Direction)
Kiyoung Jung (Creative Direction)
Taehee Lee (Strategic Planning)
Seongmin Park (Graphic Design)
Dahye Moon (Graphic Design)

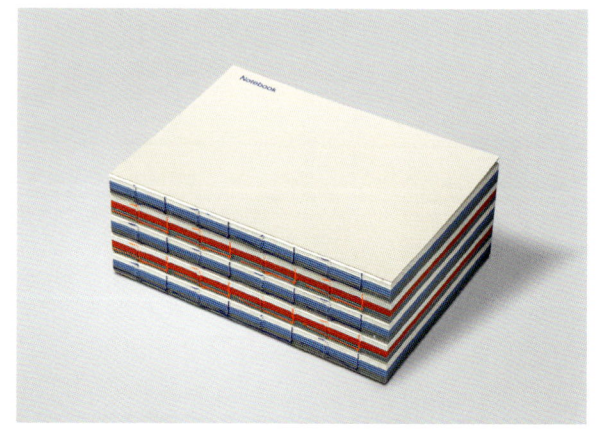

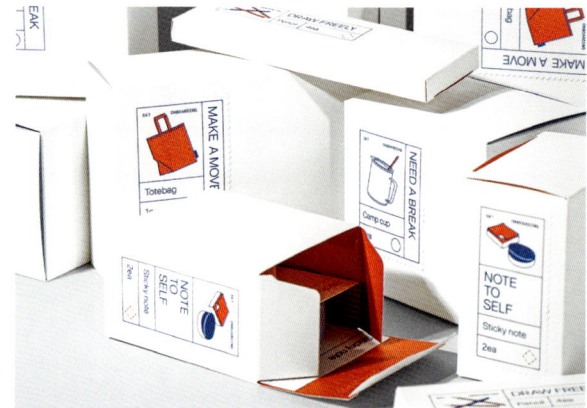

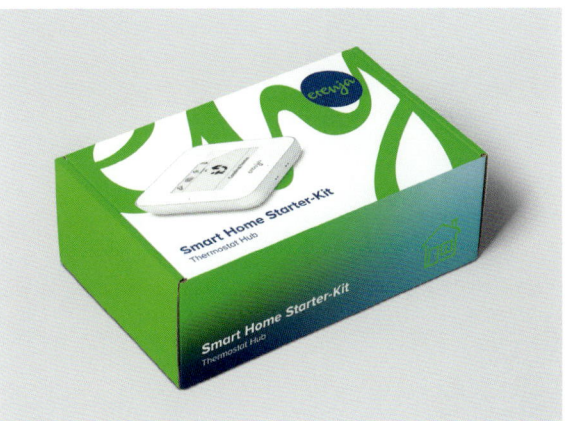

erenja

[Corporate Design]

Newly launched by GELSENWASSER AG, erenja is a brand that provides green electricity, natural gas and district heating. With the syllable "Ja" (yes) in its name, erenja positions itself as an optimistic brand that exemplifies the transition to eco-friendly consumption. The joyful affirmation of new energy solutions is expressed by the stimulating colour palette featuring neon green as the key colour. The handwriting-like typography gives the logo a personal touch. The corporate design stands out positively from the competition and attracts attention through the bright green used on the brand's stationery and advertising materials.

Client
Gelsenwasser AG
Gelsenkirchen, Germany

Design
31M Agentur für Kommunikation GmbH
Essen, Germany

Project Team
Daniel Bürger (Creative Direction)
Timo Leßmöllmann (Art Direction)
Dieter Rehmann (Project Management)

PBST

[Corporate Identity]

Client
MAN Energy Solutions SE
Augsburg, Germany

Design
LIQUID | Agentur für Gestaltung
Augsburg, Germany

Project Team
LIQUID | Agentur für Gestaltung:
Ilja Sallacz (Creative Direction)
Stefani Wiatowski (Art Direction)
Sönke Uden (Film Production)
Pauline Kühner (Graphic Design)

Peter Lemke (Animation),
Gosetti Dokumentation & Grafik GmbH
Maximilian Nieberle
(Music/Sound Design)

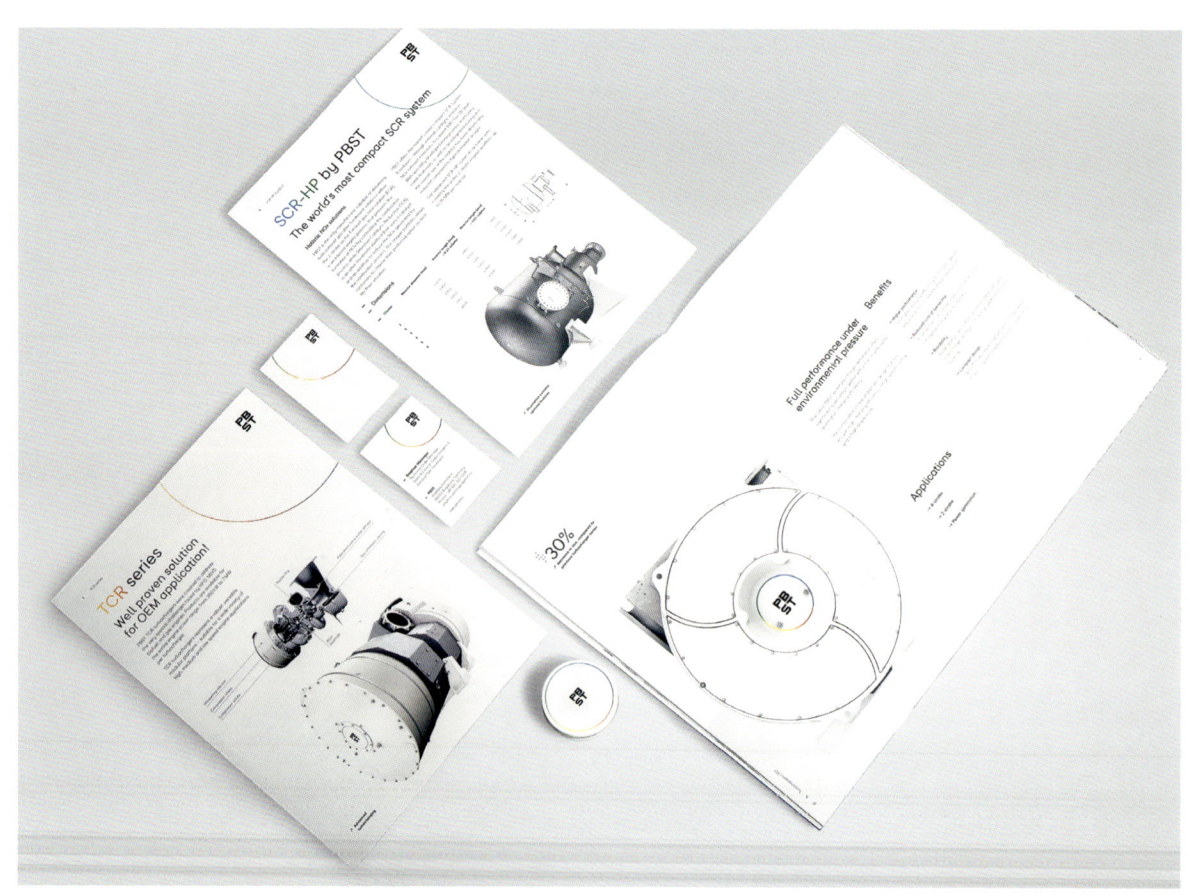

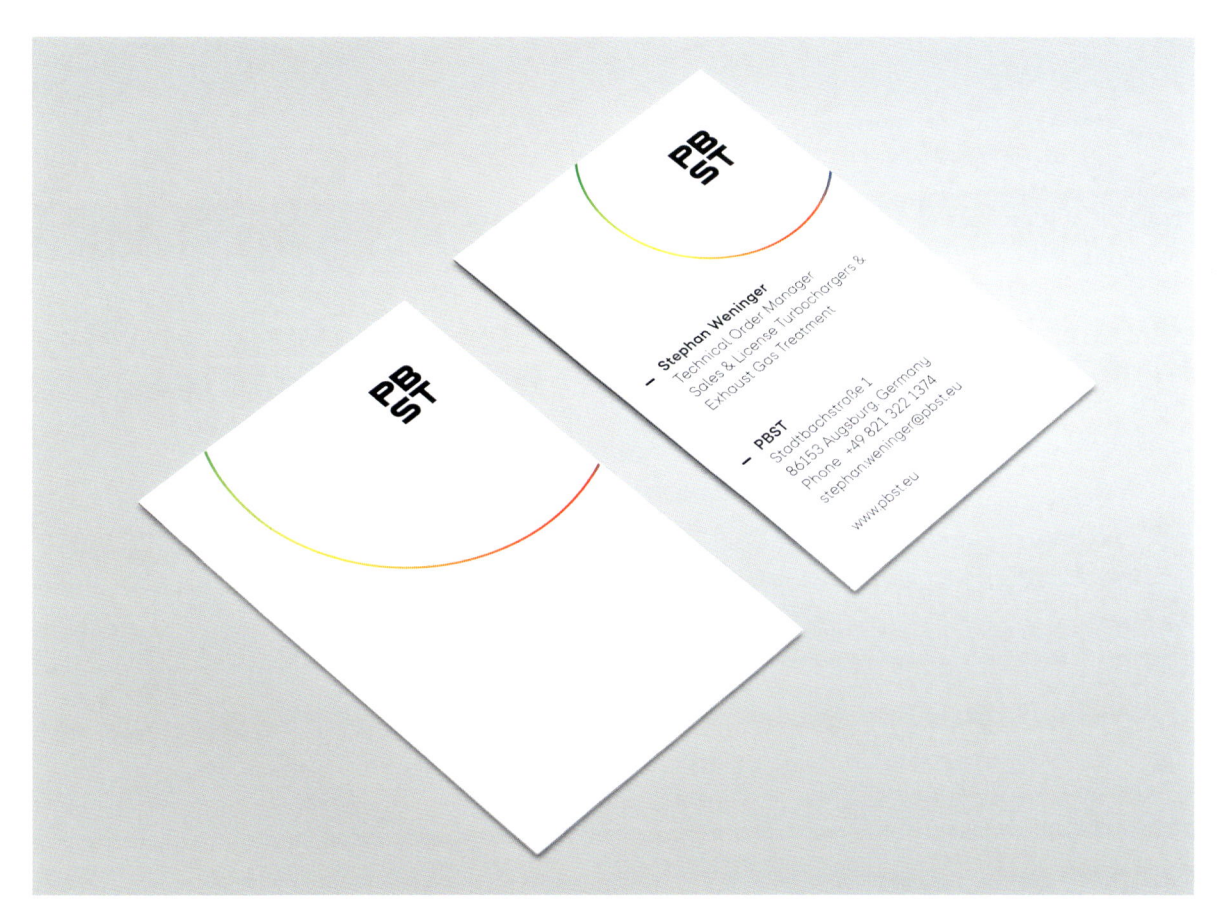

Advertising	Packaging Design	Fair Stands	Retail Design	Red Dot: Junior Award	Designer Profiles	Index
288	318	494	516	544	614	674

The new corporate design of PBST, a manufacturer of turbochargers, is based on the features of the company's core products and services. Thus, as an inherent characteristic, the company logo features a rotating movement around a centre: the distinctive word mark in the centre forms a solid constant, while the circle enclosing it is applied in different radii. Another striking element is the use of a wide colour spectrum to illustrate the diversity in products and services. The geometric formal language exudes a homogenous appeal with texts, product images and colour accents standing out distinctively against the generous white spaces.

Livet AG

[Corporate Design]

Livet develops fast and reliable molecular point-of-care tests for infectious diseases in animals. The medical technology start-up from Switzerland needed a corporate design that embodies and expresses the core attributes of the company: fast, uncomplicated, reliable, young and dynamic. The design concept comprises a word mark combined with a fresh colour scheme and a clear design language for all design elements. Similar to an instant messenger, an abstract speech bubble represents the uncomplicated and fast communication of medical results. The speech bubble is used as a graphic element across all media.

Client
Livet AG
Bern, Switzerland

Design
Visuelle Fabrik
Basel, Switzerland

Project Team
Roman Albertini (Creative Director)
Linda Albertini (Art Director)
Martina Doležalová (Graphic Design)

→ Designer profile on page 672

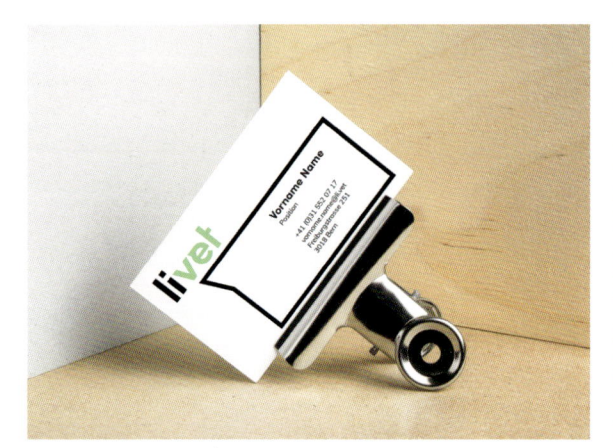

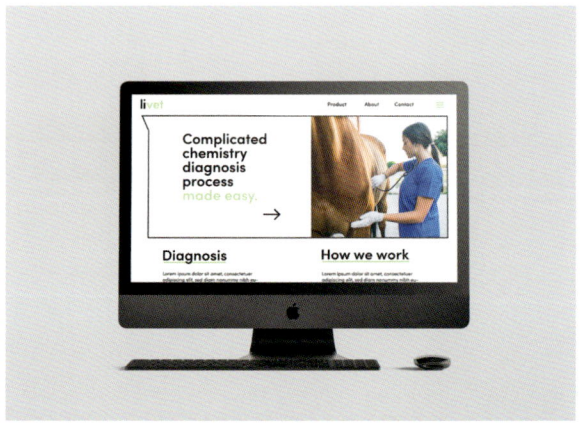

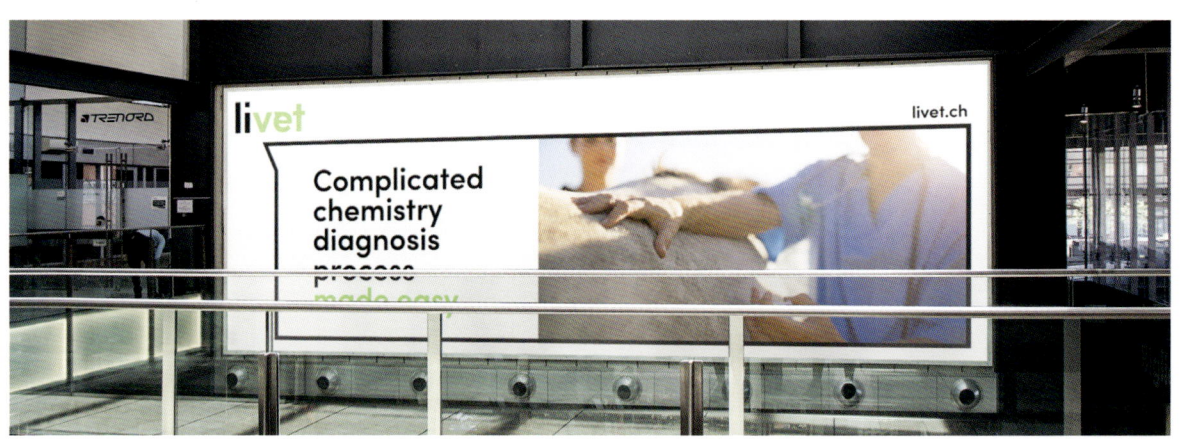

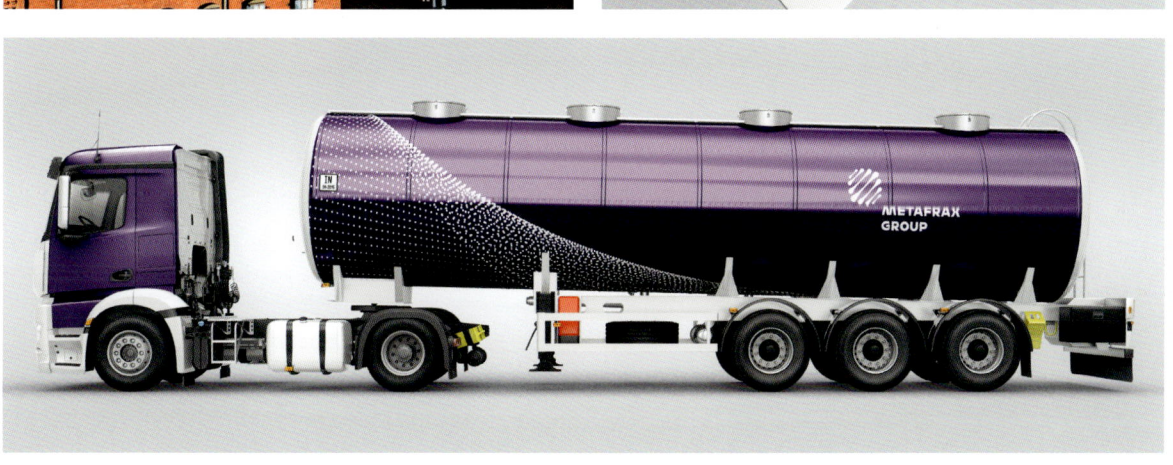

Metafrax Group
[Corporate Design Relaunch]

The Metafrax Group is a methanol producer in Europe, exporting globally to 75 countries. The corporate group comprises over 12 different brands that had no obvious visual connection to one another. The new corporate design aims to unite the entire group under one branding. Symbolising unity and integrity, dots are used as the central element of the logo. The connections between the dots represent the combination of resilience and movement. The corporate colour, deep purple, not only stands for wisdom and science, but also emphasises the dynamic pattern, which is both stable and flexible, conveying the idea of sustainability. The custom-made font represents the integration of technology and industry.

Client
Metafrax Group
Perm, Russia

Design
Electric Brand Consultants,
Electric Creative LLC
Moscow, Russia

Project Team
Beso Turazashvili (CEO)
Irina Skabelkina (Creative Director)
Dmitry Tretyakov (Commercial Director)
Daria Vorobyova
(Head of Account Management)
Mikhail Bobylev (Head of Brand Strategy)
Dimitrina Mitakova (Brand Strategist)

→ Clip online

Annual Reports

Red Dot: Grand Prix

PUMA Online Annual Report 2019

The Puma brand stands for people and their peak performances: for the fastest runners, the longest jumps and the best products. The imperative slogan "Prepare to Perform!" opens the sporting goods manufacturer's online annual report, which itself carries the analogy between high-performance sports and corporate performance. In the report, world-class athletes such as the two-time world champion in the 400-metre hurdle race, Karsten Warholm, or pole-vaulter Yaroslava Mahuchikh provide insights into how they prepare for top performances, while small animations make their achievements visible. And the fastest man in the world, Usain Bolt, reveals in video statements and short texts how to become better every day. A strong colour system of red and blue tones on a black background provides the content with the intensity it needs to highlight the emotional context of the brand and its faces. The subpages of the management report, in turn, present data and facts on a white background and thus convey a strong sense of clarity and overview.

Statement by the jury
This online annual report is a highly remarkable example of how an annual report can follow a fresh, convincing approach. Readers immerse themselves directly in the Puma brand, the company and the athletes, and receive fascinating insights through the athletes and their stories, as well as insights into the brand's powerful strategy. The clear, emotional design creates an engaging and lasting experience.

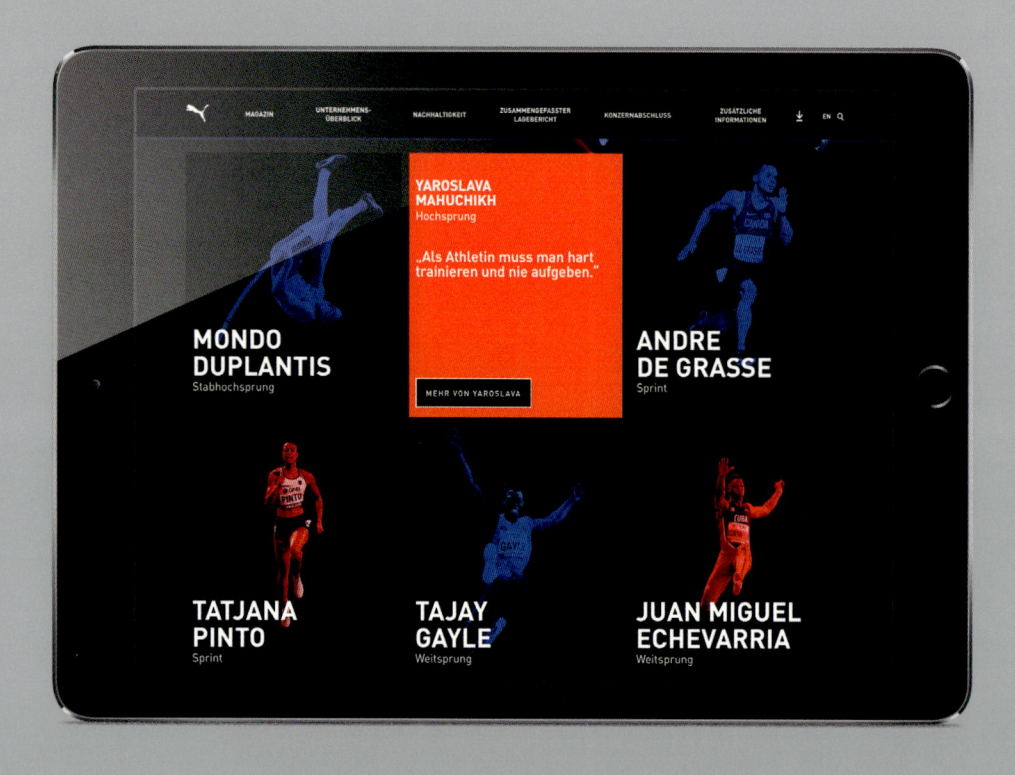

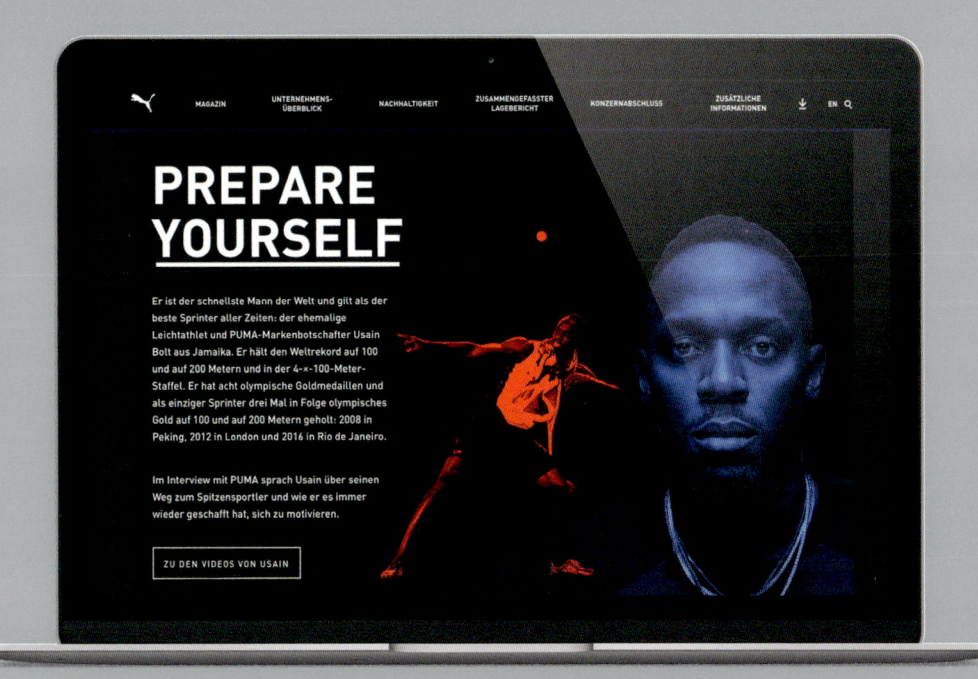

Advertising	Packaging Design	Fair Stands	Retail Design	Red Dot: Junior Award	Designer Profiles	Index
288	318	494	516	544	614	674

reddot winner 2020
grand prix

Client
PUMA SE
Herzogenaurach, Germany

Design
3st kommunikation GmbH
Mainz, Germany

Project Team
Marcel Teine (Creative Direction)
Thilo Breider (Conception)
Sarah Pilgrim (Art Direction)
Kai Stabel (Programming)

→ Designer profile on page 617

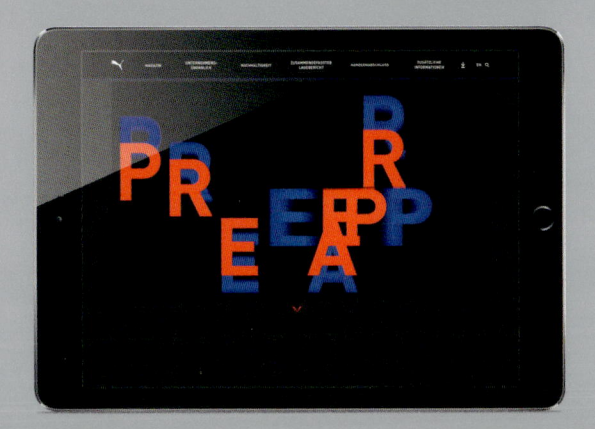

Red Dot: Best of the Best

Porsche AG Annual and Sustainability Report 2019

Sustainability is a central pillar of Porsche's corporate strategy and implemented comprehensively at the economic, ecological and social levels, as documented in the annual and sustainability report entitled "Pioneering Spirit". A large number of information graphics, illustrating measures and results with regard to sustainable corporate management, contribute to the publication's clear presentation. The topics are complemented by exciting photo series that visualise the claim of this premium-quality car manufacturer. A special shade of blue was used as a design element, based on the launch campaign for the Taycan electric sports car, whereas the materials were consistently selected with sustainability in mind. Thus, all papers are fully recyclable, with the financial section being printed on a pale grey, ecological uncoated paper, which is made from 100 per cent waste paper, while the content section is produced in a climate-neutral way and is FSC-certified. Moreover, to avoid microplastics, Porsche also relied entirely on deinkable printing inks.

Statement by the jury
The annual and sustainability report of Porsche AG convinces with a high congruence of form and content. While the imagery communicates the excellence of the car manufacturer in a powerful and expressive manner, the layout and typeface also follow the concept of sustainability in that they link rigour and clarity with just one colour, a clean blue. Ecological materials and processes round off this harmoniously designed publication.

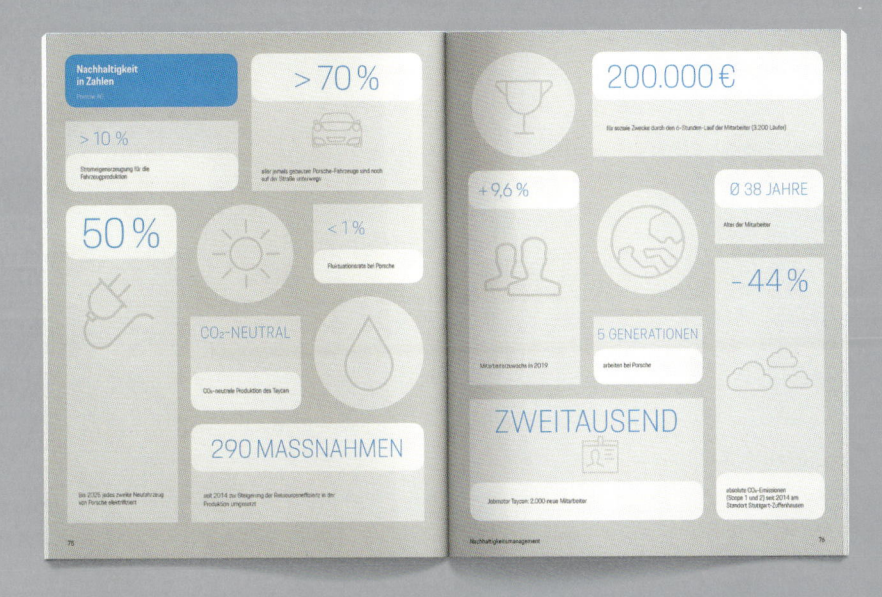

Advertising	Packaging Design	Fair Stands	Retail Design	Red Dot: Junior Award	Designer Profiles	Index
288	318	494	516	544	614	674

Client
Dr. Ing. h.c. F. Porsche AG
Stuttgart, Germany

Design
Meiré und Meiré GmbH & Co. KG
Cologne, Germany

Project Team
Ralf Vogl (Printing)

→ Designer profile on page 648

Red Dot: Best of the Best

Baden-Württemberg Stiftung Annual Report 2018

The annual report of the Baden-Württemberg Stiftung, a state-funded foundation, explores the microcosm of coexistence as exemplified by a street neighbourhood in the west of Stuttgart. The neighbourhood there is experiencing ruptures due to a process of rapid gentrification. Starting with the question of what unites society, the annual report focuses foremost on people. A teaser campaign was launched in the shops and cafes of the quarter, which involved all people across the street in the topic via beer coasters, postcards, pins and friendship ribbons and thus made the Schwabstraße in Stuttgart turn into a laboratory of society. In numerous videos and interviews, the local people talk about their lives, their street and their quarter in the west of Stuttgart, a neighbourhood in which diverse lifestyles, different cultures and subcultures collide and live together. As a vivid collage of pictures, portraits and interviews, the annual report thus mirrors both the diversity and ruptures at the same time. In an authentic approach, it conveys what most moves the foundation and which programmes and projects it offers.

Statement by the jury
The idea of depicting the work of the Baden-Württemberg Stiftung through the neighbourhood of a street is marvellous. The generous layout provides ample space for presenting the topic and creates exciting tension using typefaces and documentary-style photographs. Just like life on that street, the design exudes vividness and authenticity, while also implementing the essential facts and figures in a high-quality style.

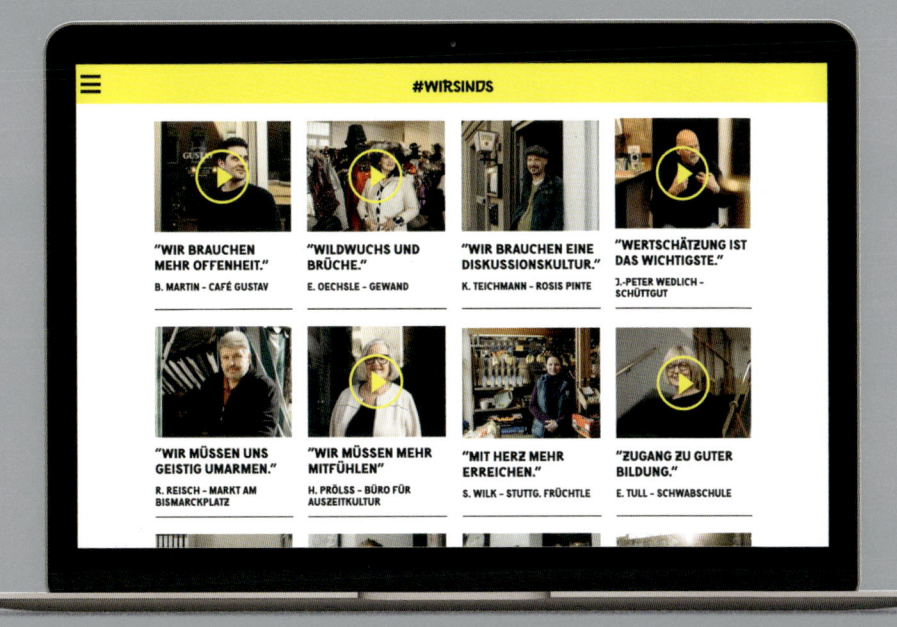

Advertising	Packaging Design	Fair Stands	Retail Design	Red Dot: Junior Award	Designer Profiles	Index
288	318	494	516	544	614	674

Client
Baden-Württemberg Stiftung gGmbH
Stuttgart, Germany

Design
STRICHPUNKT
Stuttgart/Berlin, Germany

→ Designer profile on page 667

enercity
Annual Report 2019

The annual report of the enercity AG presents its positive business results for 2019 in a way that reflects the company's strategic positioning as a driving force towards a more digital world based on sustainable energies. The digital report was designed as a stand-alone microsite, which provides a compact overview of the company's profile, strategy and service portfolio, as well as success stories. The content includes an introductory video interview with the management board and 14 dynamically designed sections focusing on corporate activities. Moreover, an exclusive notebook was produced to accompany the digital report, representing the most impressive facts and inviting readers to experience the full report online.

Client
enercity AG
Hannover, Germany

Design
C3 Creative Code and Content GmbH
Hamburg, Germany

Project Team
enercity:
Dirk P. Lindgens
(Head of Corporate Communications)
Lea Weitekamp (Project Lead)
Tanja Requardt (Editorial Manager)
Marcella Klaas (Project Assistant)

C3 Creative Code and Content:
Benjamin Schnitzer (Business Director)
Kaye Gummlich (Project Manager)
Erik Bloch (Senior Art Director)
Elena Rudolph (Senior Editor)
Ric Eickholt (Senior Content Creative)
Jessica Winter (Senior Art Director)
Annegret Strauss (Senior Photo Editor)

F7 Media GmbH:
Björn Crüger (Front-End Developer)

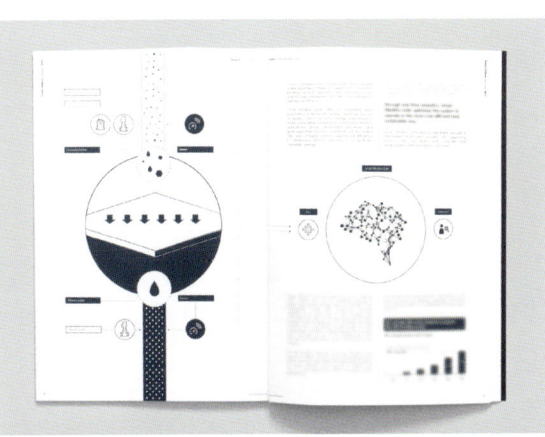

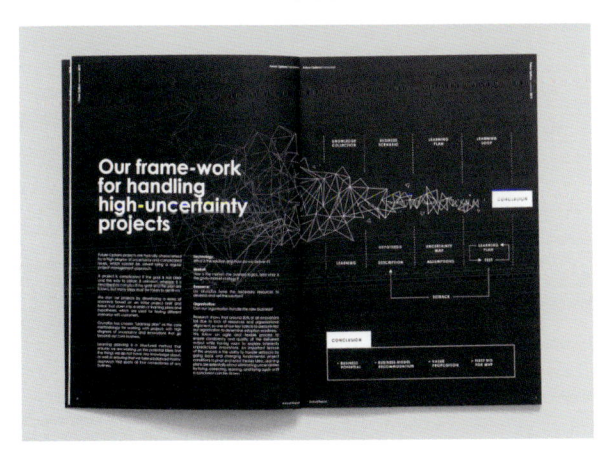

Advertising	Packaging Design	Fair Stands	Retail Design	Red Dot: Junior Award	Designer Profiles	Index
288	318	494	516	544	614	674

Grundfos Future Options Innovation Report 2019

The purpose of Future Options is to ensure the constant availability of long-term, impactful, customer-validated business opportunities for Grundfos. The design of the innovation report follows the theme of looking to the future, grasping and shaping ideas and concepts. A triangular shape represents both mystery and precision, and serves as a base for the entire layout. Multiple triangles in more or less abstract forms illustrate each project and follow the ideas of transformation, changeability, and parts that create a whole. A clean monochrome illustration style based on a triangular isometric grid is used to achieve uniformity across the projects.

Client
Grundfos Holding A/S
Bjerringbro, Denmark

Design
Made by Makers
Højbjerg, Denmark

Project Team
Grundfos:
Mathis Dahlqvist (Strategic Direction)
Helle K. Rehmeier (Copywriting)
Søren Vigsø (Copywriting)
Rune Højsholt (Copywriting)
Eva Kühne (Copywriting)
Mads Salling-Mortensen (Copywriting)
Jeanette D. Svenningsen (Copywriting)

Made by Makers:
Carsten Petersen (Creative Direction)
Anne Krogh Jessen (Design)
Charlotte Bech Juel (Design)

Max-Planck-Gesellschaft zur Förderung der Wissenschaften e.V. (MPG) Annual Report and Highlights 2018

Client
Max-Planck-Gesellschaft zur Förderung der Wissenschaften e.V. (MPG)
Munich, Germany

Design
mattweis
Munich, Germany

Project Team
mattweis:
Matthias Meier-Stuckenberger (Creative Direction)
Gunther Weis (Creative Direction)
Sabine Thernes (Senior Design)

Janina Lermer (Graphic Design)
Veronika Schmidt (Graphic Design)

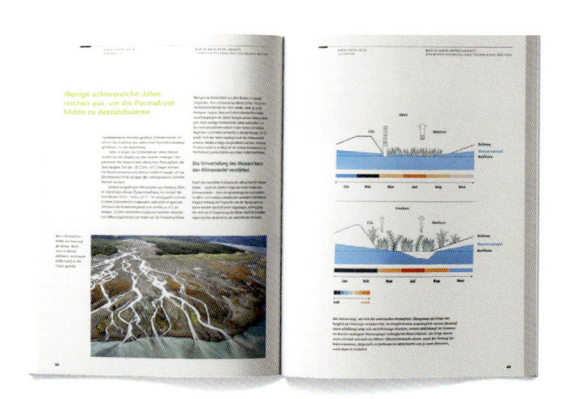

Advertising	Packaging Design	Fair Stands	Retail Design	Red Dot: Junior Award	Designer Profiles	Index
288	318	494	516	544	614	674

The non-profit association Max-Planck-Gesellschaft zur Förderung der Wissenschaften e.V. (MPG) is one of the leading German institutions in the field of basic scientific research. The challenge for its communication design is to make complex scientific facts and sometimes boring data easily accessible to readers. For this annual report, an easy-to-consume layout grid and accessible illustrative style were developed that interpret the scientific topics in an emotional way. Vivid illustrations accompany the texts rather playfully, accentuating them in a striking manner, while attractive infographics were designed in close cooperation with the scientific authors.

IW: Logbuch
Annual Report
2018/2019

Client
Institut der deutschen Wirtschaft e.V.
Cologne, Germany

Design
Institut der deutschen Wirtschaft
Köln Medien GmbH
Cologne, Germany

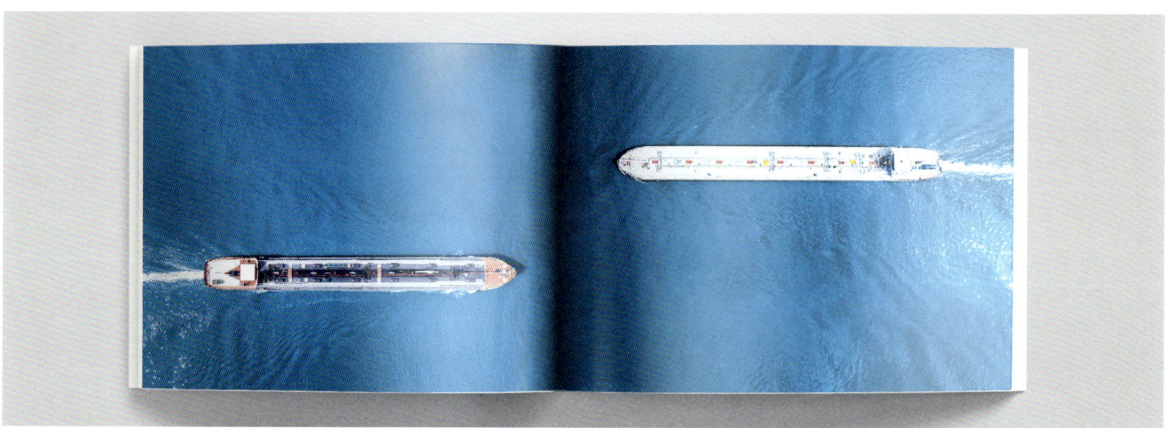

Advertising	Packaging Design	Fair Stands	Retail Design	Red Dot: Junior Award	Designer Profiles	Index
288	318	494	516	544	614	674

Reflecting its title, the German Economic Institute's 2018/2019 Annual Report is designed as a logbook. The language of the main texts makes liberal use of maritime metaphors. The layout and structure of the pages incorporate special margins, which accompany the wide columns of the main texts, to provide information such as on the "crews" or "geographical coordinates" of each chapter, just like the facts and figures in real logbooks. Additional inserts in handwritten typography round off the overall image. Shades of grey and blue derived from the institute's corporate colours dominate the inner pages, while the cover – a strong grey-blue uncoated paper – was inspired by the Atlantic Ocean.

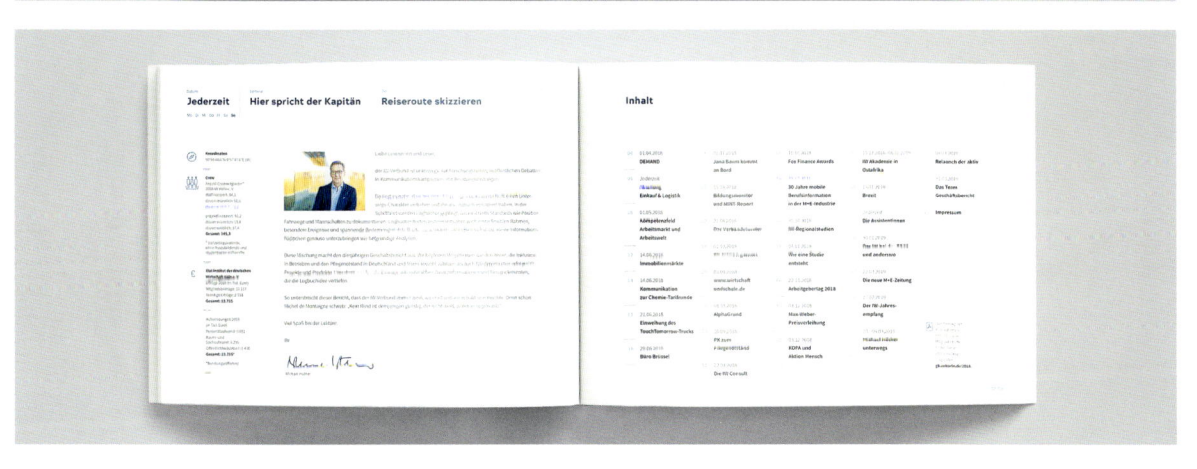

Arup
Annual Report 2019

Client
Arup
London, United Kingdom

Design
OPX
London, United Kingdom

Project Team
Arup:
Karim Klaus Emara
(Chief Marketing Officer)
Macdara Ferris (Editor)

OPX:
David Bennett (Creative Director)
Adam Quilliam (Design)
Larraine Datta (Account Management)
Frances Jackson (Project Lead)

Advertising	Packaging Design	Fair Stands	Retail Design	Red Dot: Junior Award	Designer Profiles	Index
288	318	494	516	544	614	674

Arup is an engineering firm headquartered in London and with international offices worldwide, providing versatile services in the building and construction industry. For their 2019 annual report, they wanted to showcase how their work benefits people and pay special attention to their engineers. Reflecting this core idea, the report is divided into two distinct sections: the people section explores Arup's employees working at all levels within the organisation, while the projects section introduces the buildings. The inclusion of real imagery taken from Instagram illustrates how the wider community interacts with and benefits from the company's designs.

Bechtle AG
Annual Report 2019

The Bechtle Annual Report 2019 was published with the inclusion of the magazine ZUKUNFTSSTARK ("Future-oriented"), which for the fourth year in a row supplements the annual balance sheet with 70 pages on the main topic of security. At Bechtle, the customer promise of IT security is paired with an attractive equity investment, which is why the annual report is entitled GE-SICHERT WACHSEN ("Secured Growth"). The motto is also taken up by the visual design, which is featured on all 240 pages of the report. As a connecting element, the corporate colours of green and yellow define the full-page key visuals, complemented by alternating illustrations and dynamic photos.

Client
Bechtle AG
Neckarsulm, Germany

Design
waf.berlin GmbH
Berlin, Germany

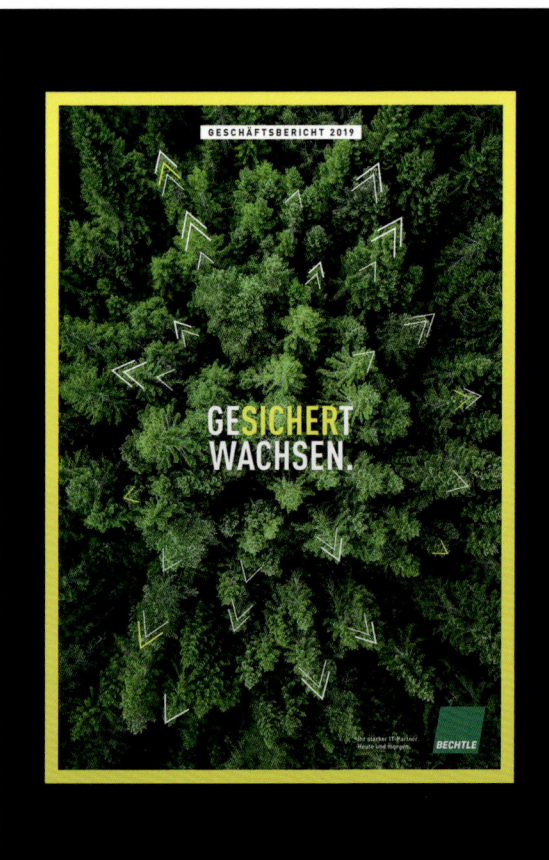

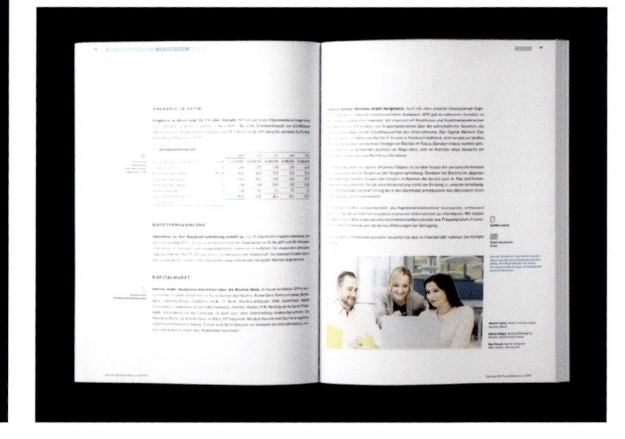

Clariant Integrated Report 2019

For the Clariant Integrated Report 2019, the theme of progress was the guiding principle for the concept. In a complex world in which much is known but little is certain, true progress requires orientation. Based on this consideration, the design concept is inspired by the visual and symbolic world of a radar. Thus, a radar-like look was implemented into the layout using a distinctive neon colour and the radar cross, as well as influencing the design of infographics and text highlights. Future-oriented stories were also told in various editorial formats, accompanied by black-and-white photography and a bold typeface.

Client
Clariant International AG
Muttenz, Switzerland

Design
MUTABOR Design GmbH
Hamburg, Germany

Project Team
MUTABOR:
Sven Ritterhoff (Creative Direction)
Martin Skoeries (Concept)
Lara Resch (Design)
Dominic Meißner
(Client Service Management)

Bernd Kasemir (Consulting),
Sustainserv GmbH
Arne Büdts (Head of Design),
Kammann Rossi GmbH
Martin Sagmüller (Web Design),
Nexxar GmbH

We connect – VP Bank Annual Report 2019

This annual report focuses on the topic of connectivity as a corporate megatrend. Starting with a multi-faceted understanding of change, VP Bank provides an overview of the connection process. Selected specialists serve as the bank's messengers to describe the areas and topics where VP Bank is forging new conceptual connections. Seven central themes, including client experience, corporate responsibility, investment solutions, fund expertise and financial strength, are presented through a series of striking illustrations and in the style of a teaser campaign. More in-depth interviews can be read in the online annual report.

Client
VP Bank AG
Vaduz, Liechtenstein

Design
Stephan Schmitz
Zurich, Switzerland

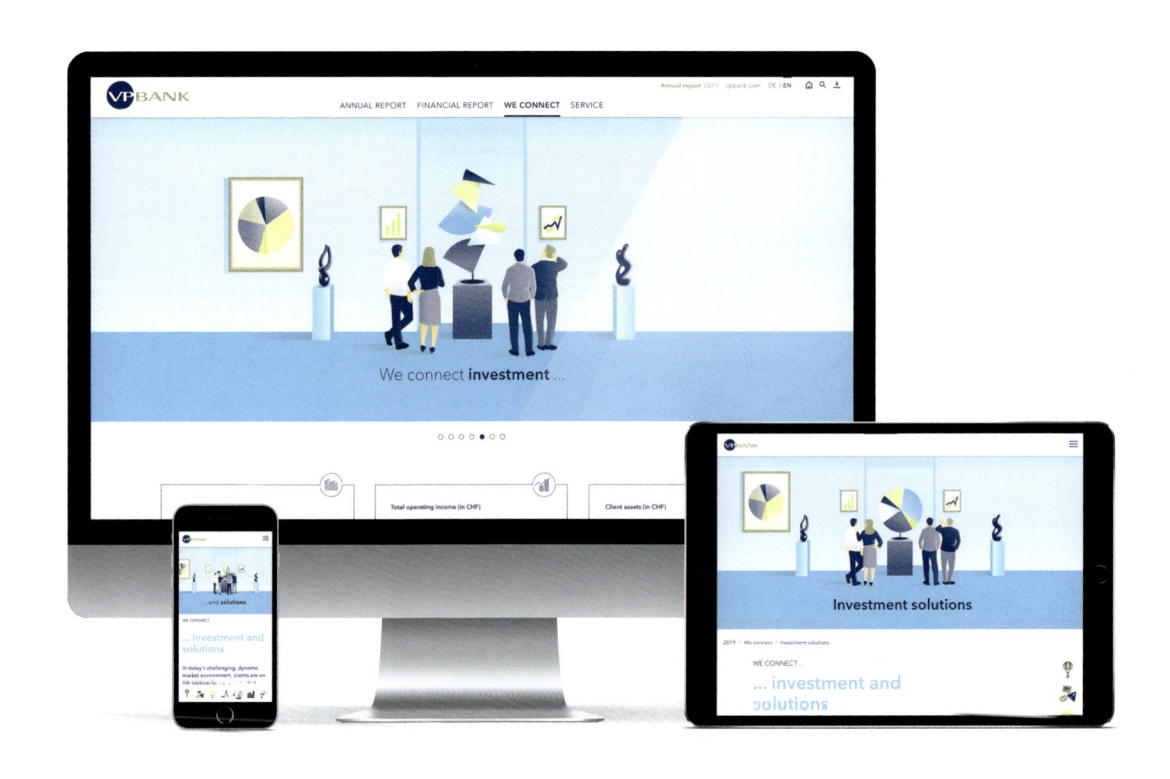

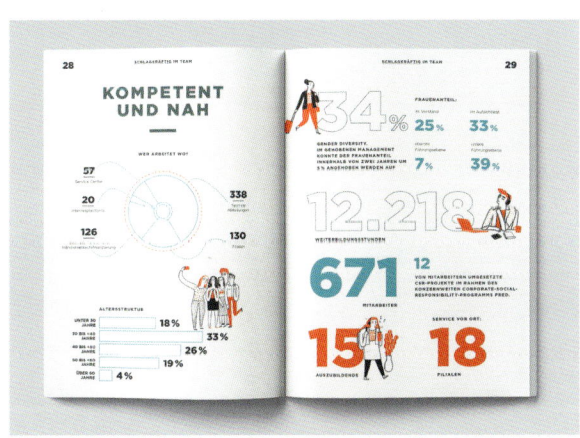

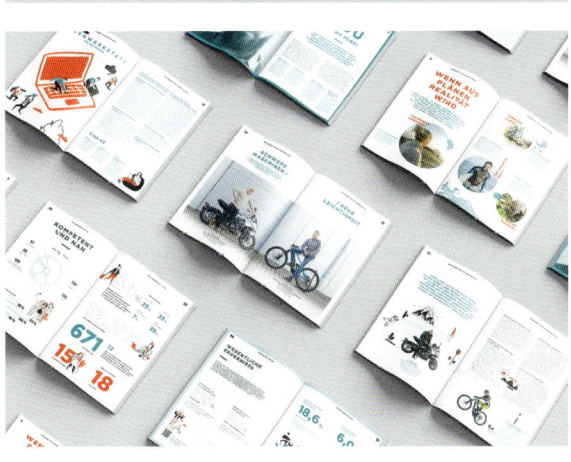

Jeden Tag ein bisschen smarter
Corporate Magazine
2019

As alternative to a printed annual report, Creditplus Bank publishes a corporate magazine in a handy format. Its first part deals with company-relevant topics, while the second part gives a brief summary of the annual report with key statements on strategy and the economic situation. The complete financial report is published online. Readers can sense the message of the bank's claim "Jeden Tag ein bisschen smarter" (Every day a little smarter) reflected in all of the chapters of the magazine, which combines authentic images with fine illustrations. The tongue-in-cheek style of the illustrations forms the framework for the versatile layout.

Client
Creditplus Bank AG
Stuttgart, Germany

Design
HGB Hamburger
Geschäftsberichte GmbH & Co. KG
Hamburg, Germany

Project Team
Creditplus Bank:
Daniel Knellesen (Publisher)

HGB:
Christa Eickmeyer (Concept)
Katharina Marx (Creative Direction)

PeopleFund
Annual Report 2019

Client
PeopleFund
Seoul, South Korea

Design
PeopleFund
Seoul, South Korea

Project Team
Changhyun Kim (Creative Direction)
Jisoo Kwon (Design)
Gihwan Jegal (Design)
Euna Cook (Editorial Work)
Sunggu Kim (Photography)

Advertising	Packaging Design	Fair Stands	Retail Design	Red Dot: Junior Award	Designer Profiles	Index
288	318	494	516	544	614	674

PeopleFund is a fintech marketplace lending platform that aims to provide financial freedom to more individuals. Before showcasing its strong business results and corporate reporting, the 2019 annual report provides a visualisation of the financial problems experienced by people in South Korea as a result of the strict credit conditions set by conventional banks. Using tiered pages with cut-out images that lead from one page to the next, it depicts examples of solutions. This introduction sets the tone for the rest of the report and gives readers a better understanding of the platform's motto "Extraordinary finance, for the ordinary".

Preface	Red Dot: Agency of the Year	Brands	Brand Design & Identity	Corporate Design & Identity	Annual Reports
4	6	18	90	202	260

Stadtreinigung Hamburg
Company and Sustainability Report 2018/Sustainability Magazine LOOP

Client
Stadtreinigung Hamburg,
Anstalt des öffentlichen Rechts
Hamburg, Germany

Design
:response – Inh. Arved Lüth
Frankfurt/Main, Germany
SHE – Kommunikationsagentur GmbH
Frankfurt/Main, Germany

Project Team
:response:
Arved Lüth (Creative Direction)
Marten Deuter (Concept)
Isabell Lenz (Editorial Work)

SHE:
Beate Scheufele (Art Direction)
Paulina Olejniczak (Graphic Design)

Oliver Schwarzwald (Photography)

→ Designer profile on page 616
→ Clip online

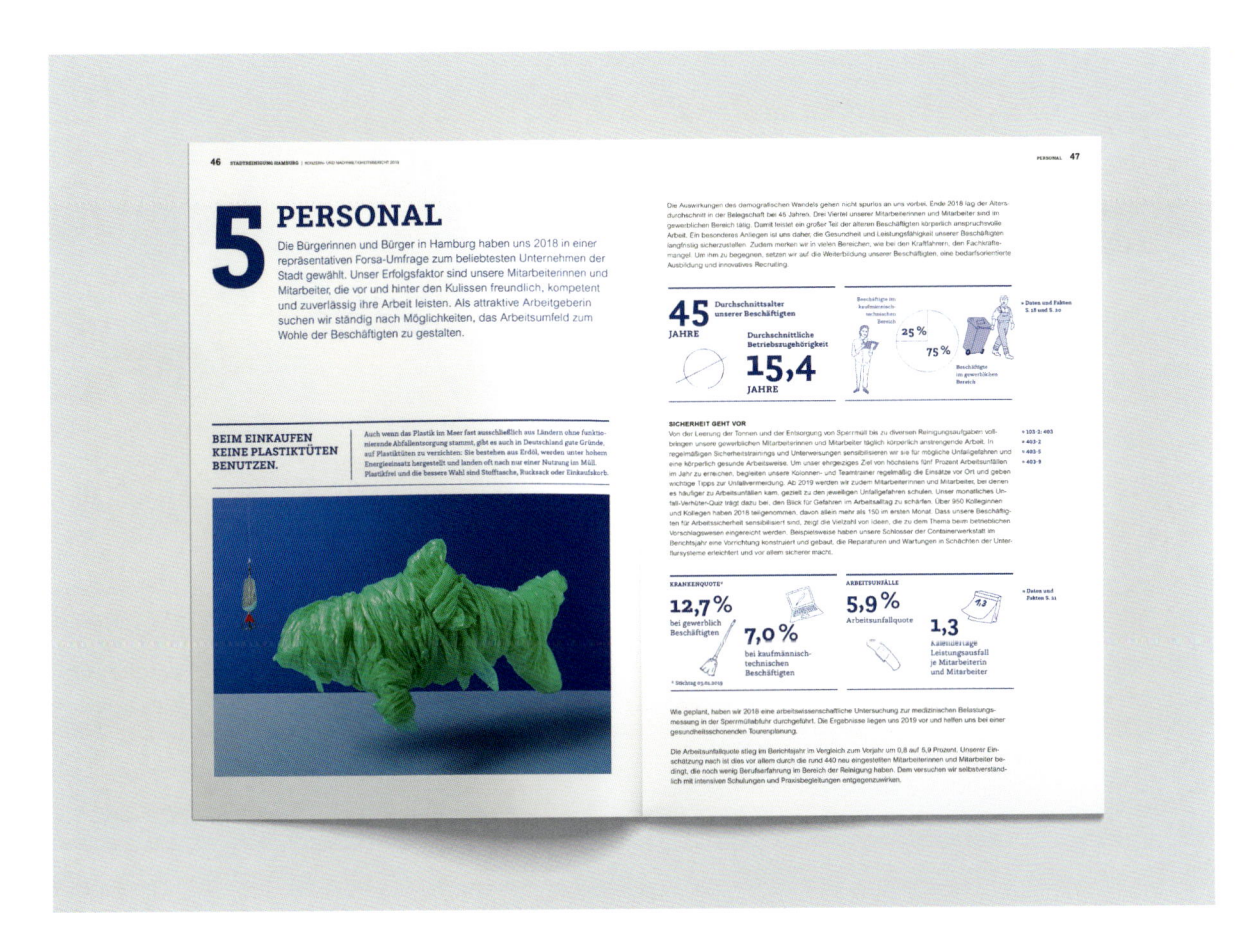

Advertising	Packaging Design	Fair Stands	Retail Design	Red Dot: Junior Award	Designer Profiles	Index
288	318	494	516	544	614	674

With its core business of resource and waste management, Stadtreinigung Hamburg is one of the pioneers of the circular economy in Germany. Its company and sustainability report uses simple language, informative and concise content, as well as infographics that represent more complex relationships and the most important facts and figures, making the publication interesting for both experts and citizens. The sustainability magazine LOOP, published together with the report, presents the focal topic of plastic for a large target group from many angles, with interviews, infographics and articles. An eye-catching feature is the photo gallery, which contains tips for avoiding plastic.

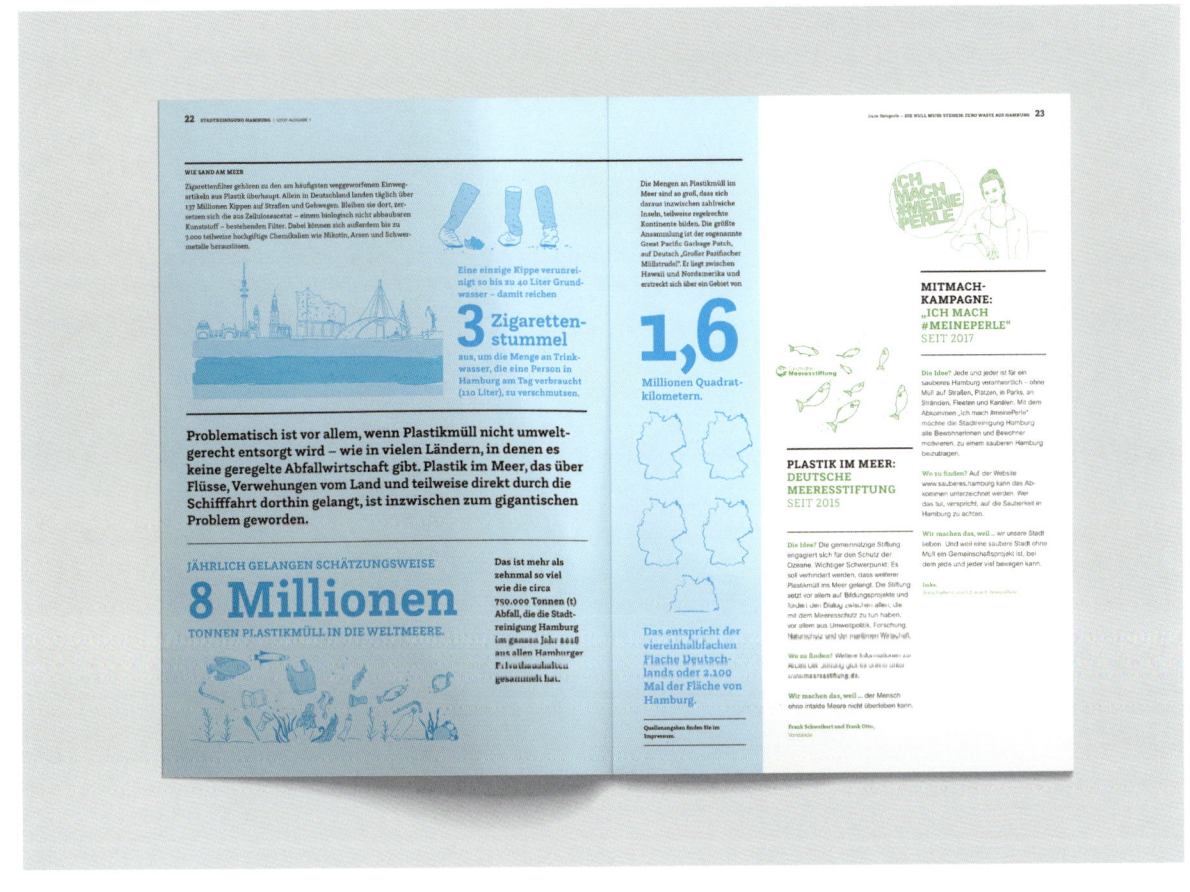

REWE Group Online Annual Report 2018

Client
REWE Group
Cologne, Germany

Design
KD1 Designagentur
Cologne, Germany

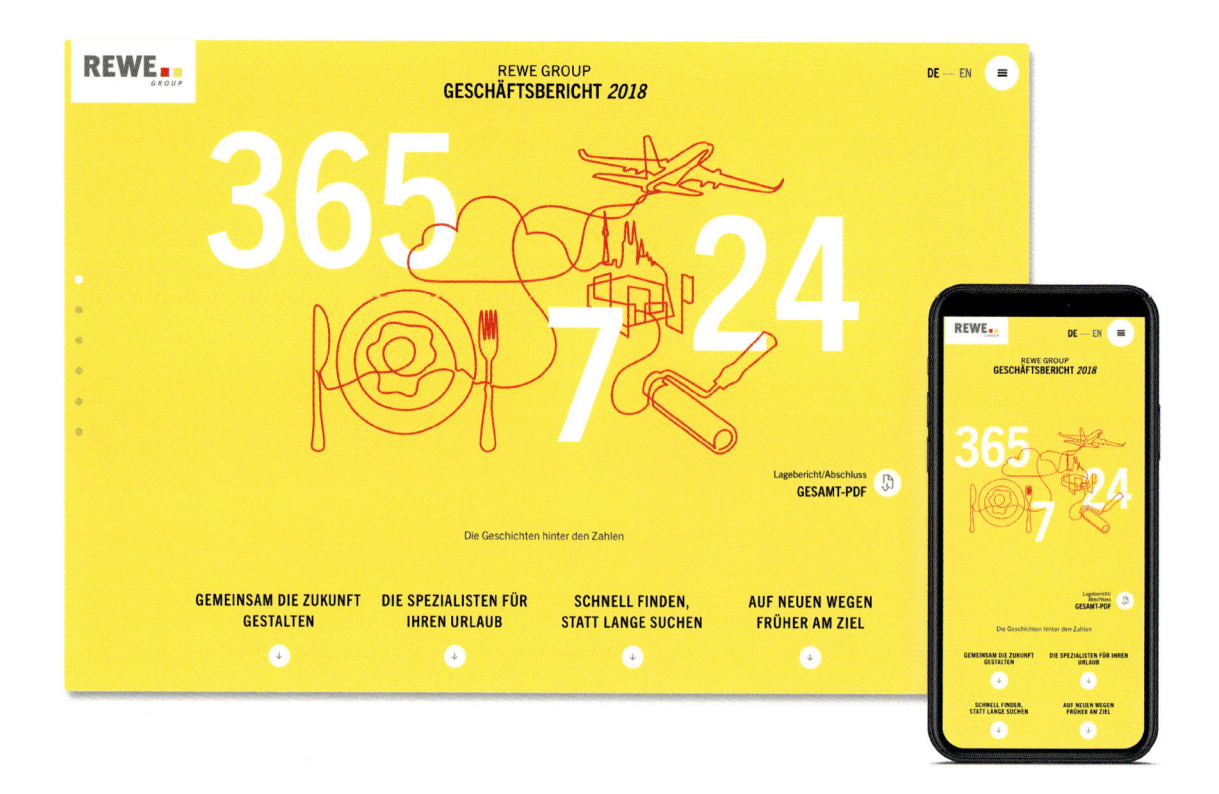

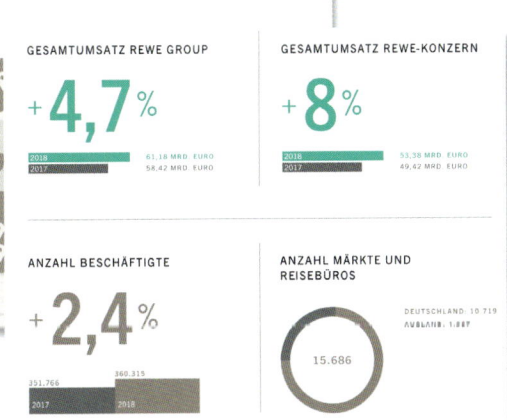

REWE Group's online annual report for 2018, entitled "365-7-24", contains key economic figures, the milestones of the year and general information about the company, as well as an entertaining magazine that includes a few stories behind the numbers. They show both the customer focus and the high service demands of the retail group in an exemplary manner, while the image language piques the reader's curiosity. Animated elements and a parallax effect on the report's website support the visual storytelling. Bold key figures and video contributions in the exclusively digital annual report provide additional information.

GEWOBA
Activity Report 2019

As a large property company in the German state of Bremen, GEWOBA shapes the cityscape with its innovative building projects. Designed as a packing case, the activity report illustrates this. The title "Gesagt. Getan." (Said and done) underlines the energy and vigour of the company. Corrugated cardboard, graphics and typographical ideas reinforce the message in a friendly tone. Illustrations and image compositions make complex concepts easy to understand. The consistent use of white ink subtly highlights in-depth marginalia. Hand-painted drawings create both contrast and a connection to the striking diagrams and tables.

Client
GEWOBA,
Aktiengesellschaft Wohnen und Bauen
Bremen, Germany

Design
POLARWERK GmbH
Bremen, Germany

Project Team
Thomas Theßeling (Creative Direction)
Meike Adler (Art Direction/Illustration)
Sebastian Kühnel (Art Direction)
Jennifer Pankratz (Design)
Marcel Koch (Final Artwork)
Melanie Borrs (Project Management)

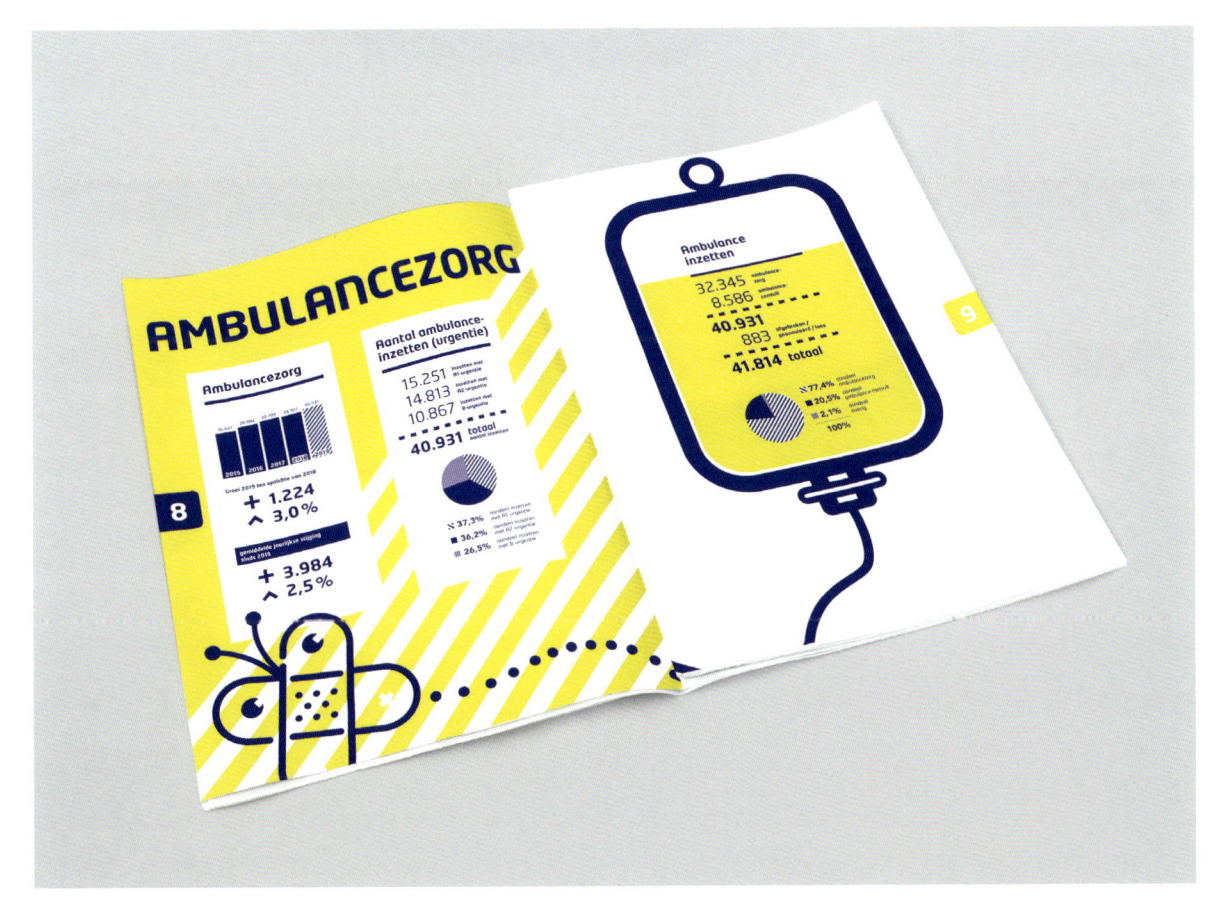

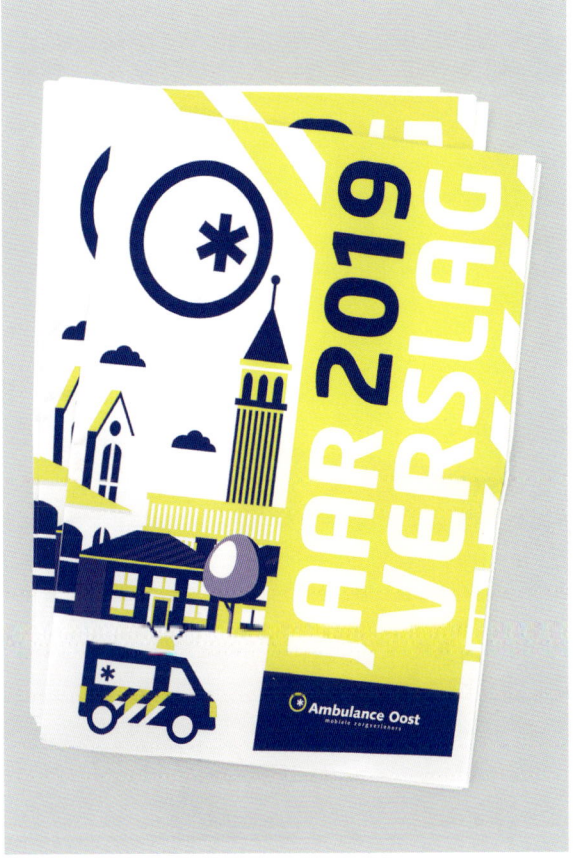

Ambulance Oost Annual Report 2019

Ambulance Oost is a non-profit care organisation that has been providing ambulance-based care for over 20 years in Twente, a region in the Netherlands. The tabloid newspaper format lends the annual report a distinct and striking look and feel. In addition, the use of a banderol with address information makes it easy to send the newspaper by post. Printed in just two Pantone colours on eco-friendly paper, the publication exudes a vivacious overall feel. The illustrations provide insights into the daily activities of the ambulance service in a cheerful and fresh manner. All information is presented in a way that is easy to understand and emotionally appealing.

Client
Ambulance Oost
Hengelo, Netherlands

Design
Keijzer Marketing Communicatie
Utrecht, Netherlands

Project Team
Bas Mulder (Creative Direction)
Charlotte van der Wiele (Account Management)
Sifra van Dalen (Graphic Design)
Eva Stijnman (Graphic Design)

Advertising

Red Dot: Grand Prix

BMW Concept i4
[Animated Social Media Campaign]

The launch of the BMW Concept i4 electric car, which was shifted to online due to the COVID-19 pandemic, was accompanied by a few short, looping animations. The animations were used on social media to engage the young, progressive target group. In an attempt to steer away from classical launch campaign, the idea was to create something unique for a unique car. The aim was to generate a buzz on social media – not only by using modern visuals and concepts, but also by integrating various ideas that the product carries in a stylised way. The Concept i4 is a concept car, but it is one that is close to a production vehicle. Therefore, the manufacturing process of a car was playfully visualised in the abstract setting of a bakery and animated with humorous ideas, such as a baking mould being filled with various needed ingredients including standard batteries or a finished shiny, bronze-coloured car coming out of the baking mould ready for action.

Statement by the jury
The animations for the BMW Concept i4 have succeeded in a highly innovative manner in reflecting the values of purity in design, sustainability and smart technology and implementing them with entertaining ideas. These values run consistently through all the animations, which were realised for the digital launch, and stand for the excellent design quality and implementation of the campaign.

Advertising	Packaging Design	Fair Stands	Retail Design	Red Dot: Junior Award	Designer Profiles	Index
288	318	494	516	544	614	674

reddot winner 2020
grand prix

Client
BMW Group
Munich, Germany

Design
Aixsponza GmbH
Munich, Germany

Project Team
BMW Group:
Fabio Olivotti
(Head of Design Identity BMW Group)
Uta Bodenstein (Creative Direction)
Florian Ströhlein (Project Lead)

Aixsponza:
Christian Tyroller (Creative Director)
Julian Fischer (Producer)
Christian Scheck (3D Artist)
Matthias Zabiegly (3D Artist)

Michael Fakesch (Music/SFX),
designingsounds

→ Designer profile on page 621
→ Clip online

Red Dot: Best of the Best

Second First Steps
[Integrated Campaign]

The "Second First Steps" project was inspired by a letter received from Jun-Beom Park, a para-archer of the Korean National Team. Ten years earlier he had lost the ability to walk in a car accident and has been in a wheelchair ever since. Hyundai Motor Group Robotics, which is specialising in wearable robotics (H-MEX) and focusing on "Technology for Humans", had the idea to give back the quality time he missed the most by using their research and development of intelligent technologies. Thus, Jun-Beom Park's second first step became the "first" first step for Hyundai. The company had managed to support the athlete so that he could stand up and walk again supported by technology. To redefine disabilities and help people rise up to the impossible – this mission by Hyundai is emphatically visualised in the campaign. After an overwhelming global response to Jun-Beom Park's filmed story, which touched people and the media around the world, the company is already working on the next steps and launched the project internationally.

Statement by the jury
The philosophy of automotive and technology company Hyundai of devoting its research and development entirely to the wellbeing of people is very well expressed in the emotionally convincing and authentically told film of this brand campaign. The metaphorical idea of "Second First Steps", which opened up an entirely new perspective for the protagonist, is presented in a vivid and inspiring manner.

Advertising	Packaging Design	Fair Stands	Retail Design	Red Dot: Junior Award	Designer Profiles	Index
288	318	494	516	544	614	674

Client
Hyundai Motor Company
Seoul, South Korea

Design
Innocean Worldwide
Seoul, South Korea

Project Team
Kiyoung Kim
(Executive Creative Director)
Hyunsuk Lee (Manager)
Saemi Shin (Senior Manager)
Daeyoung Eum (Copywriter)
Hyunchul Lim (Copywriter)
Moonhwi Lee (Copywriter)
Gahee Park (Creative Coordinator)
Gye Eun Chang (Account Management)
Bo Kyung Kim (Account Management)

→ Designer profile on page 645
→ Clip online

Red Dot: Best of the Best

Get Back, Tohoku.
[Image Campaign]

In 2011, Japan's Tohoku region was devastated by one of the most destructive earthquakes in recorded history. The "Get Back, Tohoku." campaign was launched a little later that same year and has continued for nine years since. The goal in creating the campaign was to revitalise the local tourism industry and help local residents "get back" the life they once knew. Focusing on the region's railways and artistically depicting trains and local scenery in a single moment of time, the campaign aims to evoke the sense of wonder of travel. The communication design of this nine-year campaign in the once devastated region took an analogue approach to graphic design and created posters featuring strictly graphic photos of trains, tracks, bridges, tunnels and natural scenery that capture the joy of travelling with a documentary touch. Each photo shoot was carefully choreographed to capture the perfect composition and moment, transforming ordinary commuter trains into heroic art.

Statement by the jury
The campaign to revitalise tourism in the Tohoku region after the 2011 earthquake is particularly striking as it adopts the viewing angle of potential customers and piques their interest through a series of pointedly composed shots of trains as well as architecturally enticing bridges and pillars. The overall design goal has been excellently realised in precisely composed photographs that turn each of the shots into a work of art.

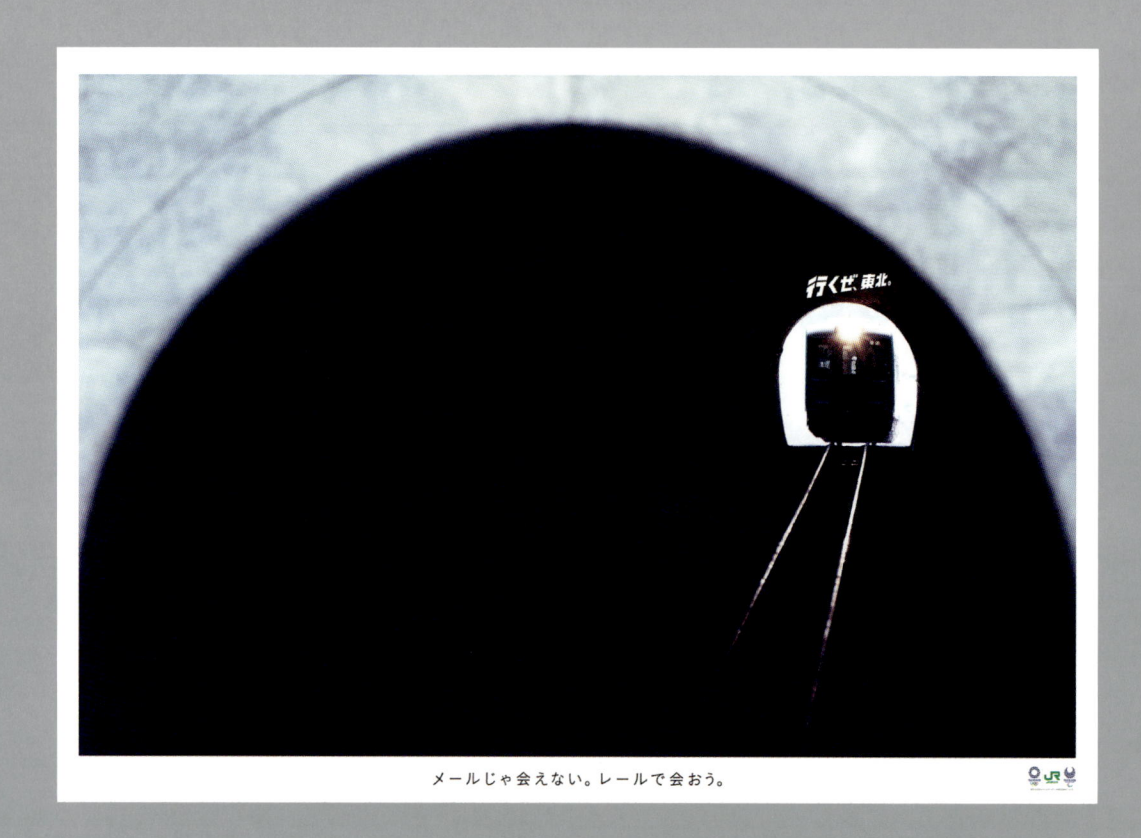

Client
East Japan Railway Company
Tokyo, Japan

Design
Dentsu Inc.
Tokyo, Japan

Project Team
Takuma Takasaki (Creative Direction)
Yoshihiro Yagi (Art Direction)
Hiroshi Ichikura (Copywriting)
Waca Sakamoto (Copywriting)
Daisuke Hatakeyama (Graphic Design)
Masashi Fujita (Graphic Design)
Fumihito Katamura (Photography)

→ Designer profiles on pages 630, 631
→ Clip online

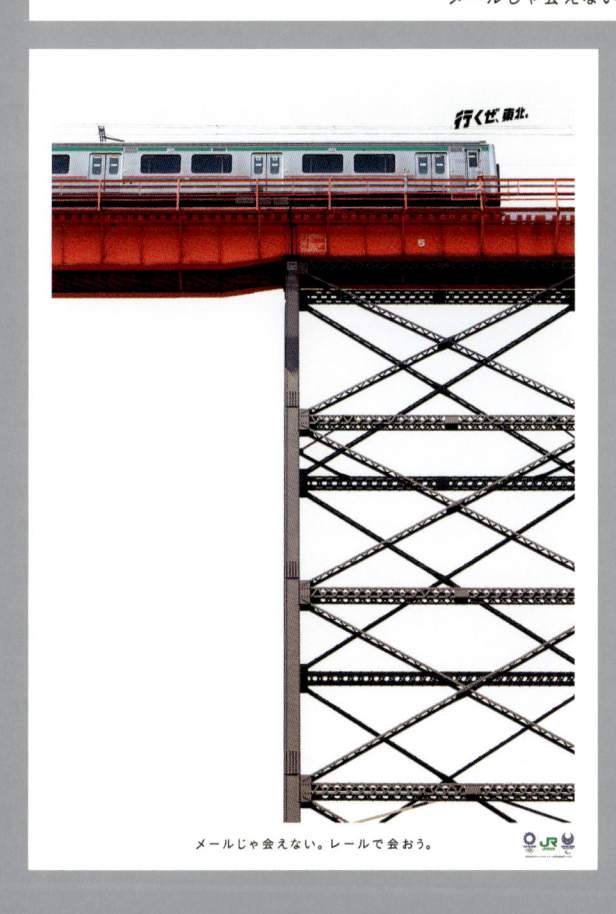

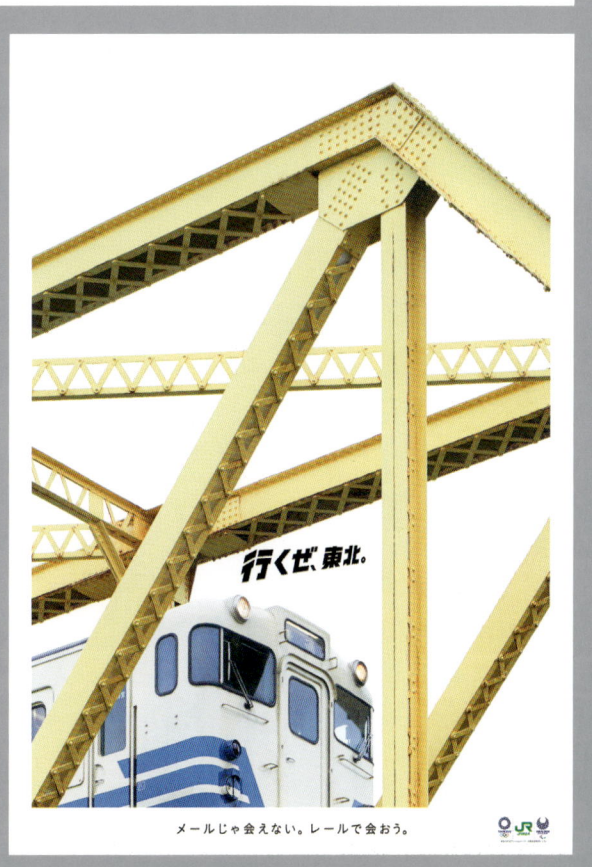

Red Dot: Best of the Best

Grace of Waste

[Direct Marketing]

Around 40 per cent of the plastic produced worldwide is used for packaging and most of this plastic is used only once before all too often ending up as plastic waste in the world's oceans. "Grace of Waste" was developed just in time for Christmas, a festival where presents often come in elaborate wrappings. The product wants to raise awareness for the issue of packaging waste and help alleviate this situation by reducing waste. It is inspired by the Japanese tradition of wrapping and handing over gifts in a furoshiki – a cloth that can be continuously reused and thus makes disposable packaging unnecessary. However, this furoshiki even helps reduce waste twice over, as it is made of recycled ocean plastic and contains a coded message. On closer inspection, its printed pattern illustrates the locations of the garbage patches in the world's oceans. Each time the gift-wrapping cloth is reused, this information is also passed on to a new recipient.

Statement by the jury
The "Grace of Waste" campaign is convincing in several ways. Its honest design is expressed in the simple aesthetics also of all the lovingly crafted details as well as in the double reduction of waste, because the cloth is not only made from recycled material itself, it also avoids ending up as waste itself as it can be reused again and again. To encourage recipients to cherish sustainability in this manner rounds off this outstanding concept.

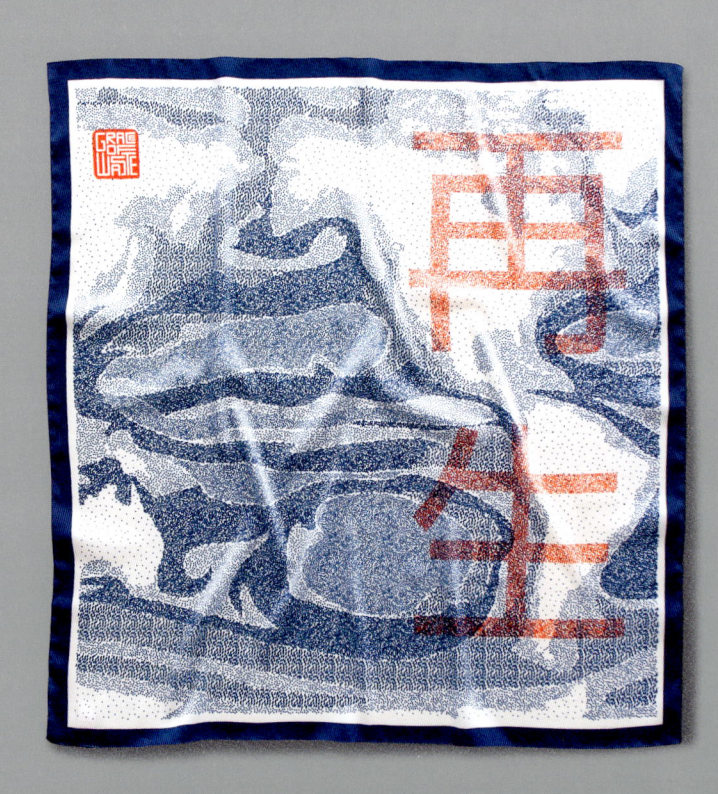

Client
Peter Schmidt Group
Hamburg, Germany

Design
Peter Schmidt Group
Munich, Germany

Project Team
Norbert Möller
(Executive Creative Director)
Ulrich Aldinger (Creative Director)
Sven Rieckmann (Creative Director)

→ Designer profile on page 665

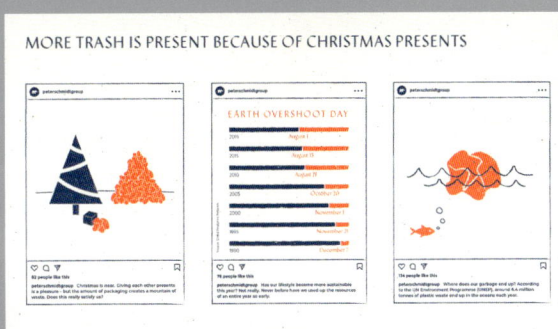

Red Dot: Best of the Best

Deutsche Oper Berlin
[Image Campaign]

The Deutsche Oper Berlin is the German capital city's largest opera house and highly regarded for outstanding productions and inviting world-famous artists. The task of the poster campaign was to communicate this profile and the promise of supplying "grand opera" to the public and develop new target groups. Therefore, moments of grand opera that are easily accessible to everyone were brought together on a graphic layer and complemented by photographs of places and details typical of the city, which in turn create a connection to the opera. The illustrator Christoph Niemann used a playful approach to details and situations to tell stories, some of which as grand as the opera. They all have one thing in common: they surprise and immediately entice beholders, opening their hearts. Graphically only hinted at, the anecdotes leave leeway for the punchline that emerges only in the mind of the beholder. The poetic content of the motifs is revealed only when combining and interpreting the apparently disparate elements as a coherent idea. The results are moments of great opera.

Statement by the jury
The image campaign for the Deutsche Oper Berlin impresses with a strong visual signature, with which it not only translates music into images but also manages to create a distinctive and highly self-sufficient appearance. Based on ingenuity, humour and creativity, these detailed posters remain highly recognisable despite their versatility and in a light-footed manner communicate the mission statement of evoking great opera moments.

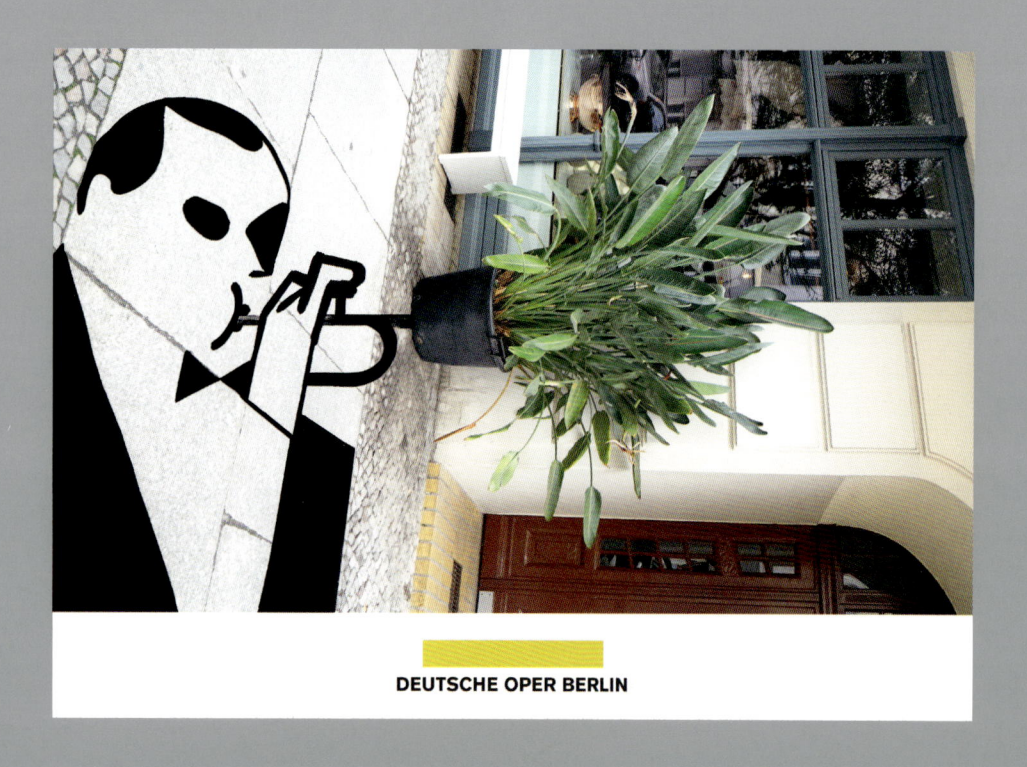

Advertising	Packaging Design	Fair Stands	Retail Design	Red Dot: Junior Award	Designer Profiles	Index
288	318	494	516	544	614	674

Client
Deutsche Oper Berlin
Berlin, Germany

Design
Realgestalt GmbH
Berlin, Germany
Studio Christoph Niemann
Berlin, Germany

Project Team
Anne Kohlermann (Creative Direction)
Jürgen Michalski (Strategic Planning)

→ Designer profile on page 662

TO MILAN
[Content Marketing]

The film "TO MILAN" is part of the online edition of the Audi magazine and focuses on the theme of transformation. The goal was to find additional examples of the same transformative spirit that drives development at Audi. The storyline connects a fashion-focused film aesthetic with a creative-looking brand world. It shows two young Italian entrepreneurs from the fashion industry driving through Milan in a bright green Audi, letting the audience experience surprisingly new facets of a fashion metropolis that shows a lot of potential and creativity – qualities that Audi should be associated with.

Client
AUDI AG
Ingolstadt, Germany

Design
loved GmbH
Hamburg, Germany

Project Team
loved:
Mieke Haase (Chief Creative Officer)
Julia Kerschbaum (Art Direction)
Alexander Müsgens (Art Direction)
Nadine Kaminski (Text)
Peggy Wellerdt (Head of Photography)

Mirko Borsche (Creative Director),
Bureau Borsche

T-Roc Bob

[Content Marketing]

This film aims to illustrate the driving characteristics of the VW T-Roc R, presenting it as a powerful, agile, dynamic car. It makes a cinematic allusion to bobsledding – a sport that requires power, focus and grip. The attributes of the car and the sport are juxtaposed in high-impact sequences: acceleration at the start, then focusing on the track, and showing the grip at every corner. The promotional film was distributed online through various social media channels, YouTube and via the website of the Volkswagen customer magazine.

Client
Volkswagen AG
Wolfsburg, Germany

Design
loved GmbH
Hamburg, Germany

Project Team
loved:
Mieke Haase (Chief Creative Officer)
Sabine Cole (Editor-in-Chief)
Alexander Müsgens (Creative Director)
Nadine Kaminski (Text)

Marc Schölermann (Director/DOP)
Simon Roloff (Camera)
Sören Görth (Film Editing)
Boris Salchow (Music/Sound Design)

NIKKEI BLEND

[Direct Marketing]

As one of the leading financial newspapers in Japan, Nikkei launched a direct marketing campaign to face the challenge of stimulating people's interest, especially that of young people, in the economy. The publishing house's promotion focused on the fluctuations in the stock market and associated them with a taste experience. The NIKKEI BLEND branded coffee changed its taste according to the Nikkei Stock Average and literally gave people a taste of the economic situation. In addition, the different labels on the cups served as a stock market barometer, as well as directing them to the publisher's website.

Client
Nikkei Inc.
Tokyo, Japan

Design
Dentsu Inc.
Tokyo, Japan

Project Team
Kazuhiro Shimura (Creative Director)
Yusuke Imai (Art Director)
Ryo Seki (Planner)
Junta Yoshikawa (Planner)
Ryo Sasaki (Copywriter)
Miki Kikuchi (Account Manager)
Togo Fujii (Account Manager)

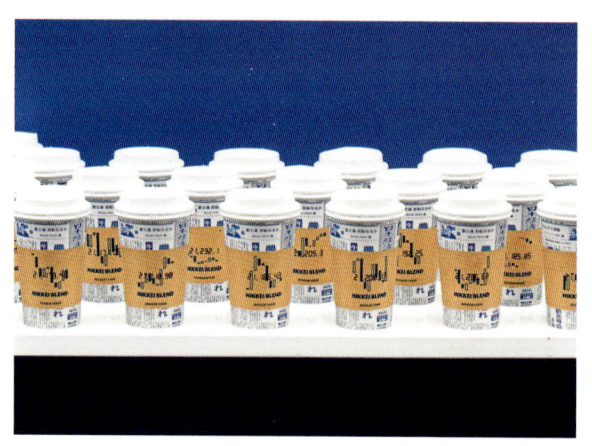

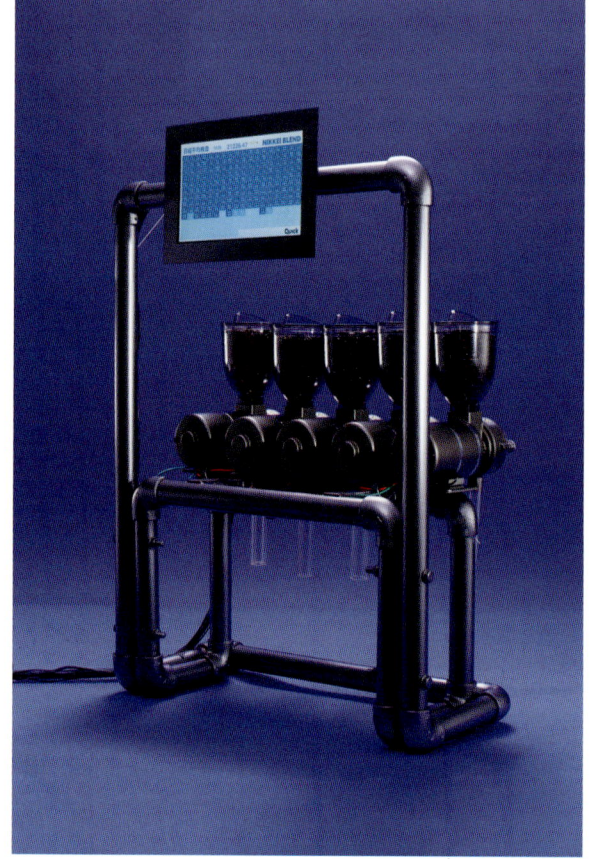

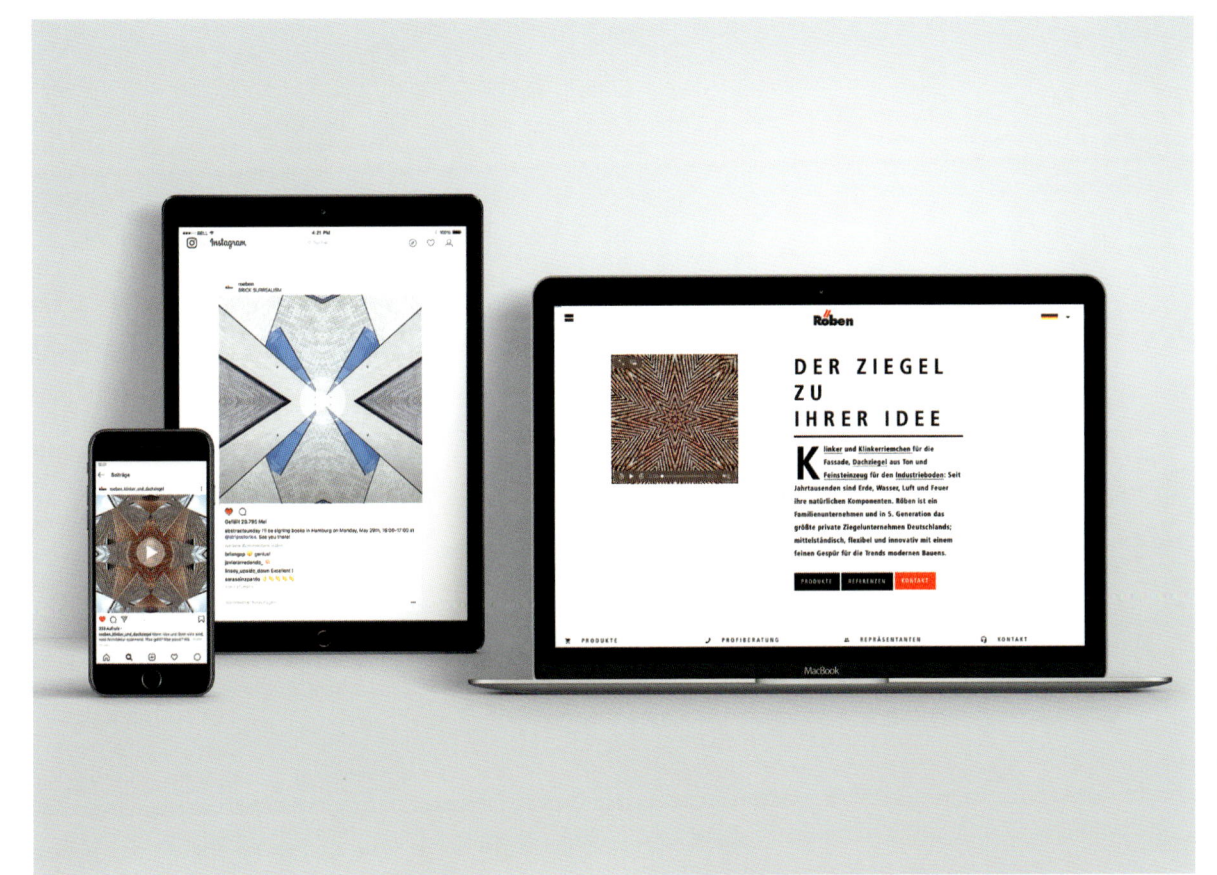

Röben Kaleidoscope

[Integrated Campaign]

With this campaign, the German clinker manufacturer Röben made a statement in support of creativity in the construction industry. Specifically addressing architects, it features the motto "Sie haben die Idee. Wir den Stein dazu." (You've got the idea. We've got the brick.) – a promise that the campaign reflects in a visually appealing manner. In the midst of complex, kaleidoscope-like architectural images, it shows clinker bricks as a building material that can be used creatively. Published both online and in print, visually stunning motifs and videos aim to encourage architects to hold onto their original ideas and implement them together with Röben.

Client
Röben Tonbaustoffe GmbH
Zetel, Germany

Design
Kopfkunst, Agentur für
Kommunikation GmbH
Münster, Germany

Project Team
Simon Hattrup (Creative Direction)
Florian Zimmermann
(Senior Art Direction)
Jens Kallfelz (Strategic Planning)
Dirk Knepper (Production)
Christoph Lojak (Web Design)
Dennis Harwardt (Animation Design)
Marc Fielers (Text)

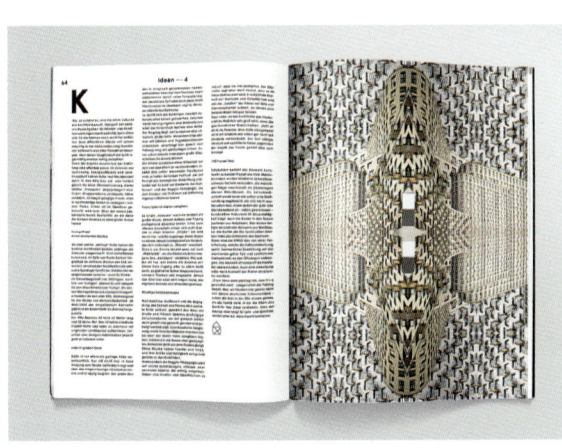

Preface	Red Dot: Agency of the Year	Brands	Brand Design & Identity	Corporate Design & Identity	Annual Reports
4	6	18	90	202	260

Welcome to Samsung Town

[Digital Campaign]

During the IFA 2019 trade fair in Berlin, this digital campaign attracted visitors' attention by offering them various interactive experiences. Under the banner "Welcome to Samsung Town", visitors were invited to use an app of the same name to become members of this event. They could take selfies and choose their own avatars, which were relayed in real time to the huge interactive media wall at the Samsung stand. Furthermore, participants could view the entire stand using the AR Observatory, which provided the products' locations and information through augmented reality.

Client
Samsung Electronics Co., Ltd.
Global Marketing Center
Suwon, South Korea

Design
Cheil Worldwide
Seoul, South Korea

Advertising	Packaging Design	Fair Stands	Retail Design	Red Dot: Junior Award	Designer Profiles	Index
288	318	494	516	544	614	674

Broken Display Maps
[Out-of-Home & Ambient]

Since the beginning of 2020, Samsung has been offering a drop-off repair service. Available in major cities throughout Germany and offering repairs by Samsung technicians on the spot, the task was to make the service widely known and to inform people about where to find local repair shops. The out-of-home poster placement in cities where the service was newly available showed illustrations of broken displays that upon closer inspection turned out to be maps of the respective city – including the local Smart Repair Service Point. Each visual is an interpretation of the city's layout and was meticulously drawn by hand to resemble the unique look of real shards of glass.

Client
Samsung Electronics Germany GmbH
Schwalbach am Taunus, Germany

Design
Cheil Germany GmbH
Schwalbach am Taunus, Germany

Project Team
Jörn Welle (Creative Direction)
Harald Linsenmeier (Creative Direction)
Thomas Schröder (Creative Direction)
Michael Fluhr (Designer)
Chris Drücks (Text)
Janine Krämer (Account Management)
Stefan Prilipp (Account Management)

Preface	Red Dot: Agency of the Year	Brands	Brand Design & Identity	Corporate Design & Identity	Annual Reports
4	6	18	90	202	260

Admind Employer Branding Campaign

[Recruitment Campaign]

Client
Admind Branding & Communications
Kraków, Poland

Design
Admind Branding & Communications
Kraków, Poland

Project Team
Karolina Pospischil (Creative Director)
Grzegorz Pach (Project Manager)
Magdalena Gawlik-Łęcka (Illustrator)
Małgorzata Macuda (Illustrator)
Marek Brol (Illustrator)
Dominika Konieczkowska-Kracik (Illustrator)

→ Designer profile on page 620
→ Clip online

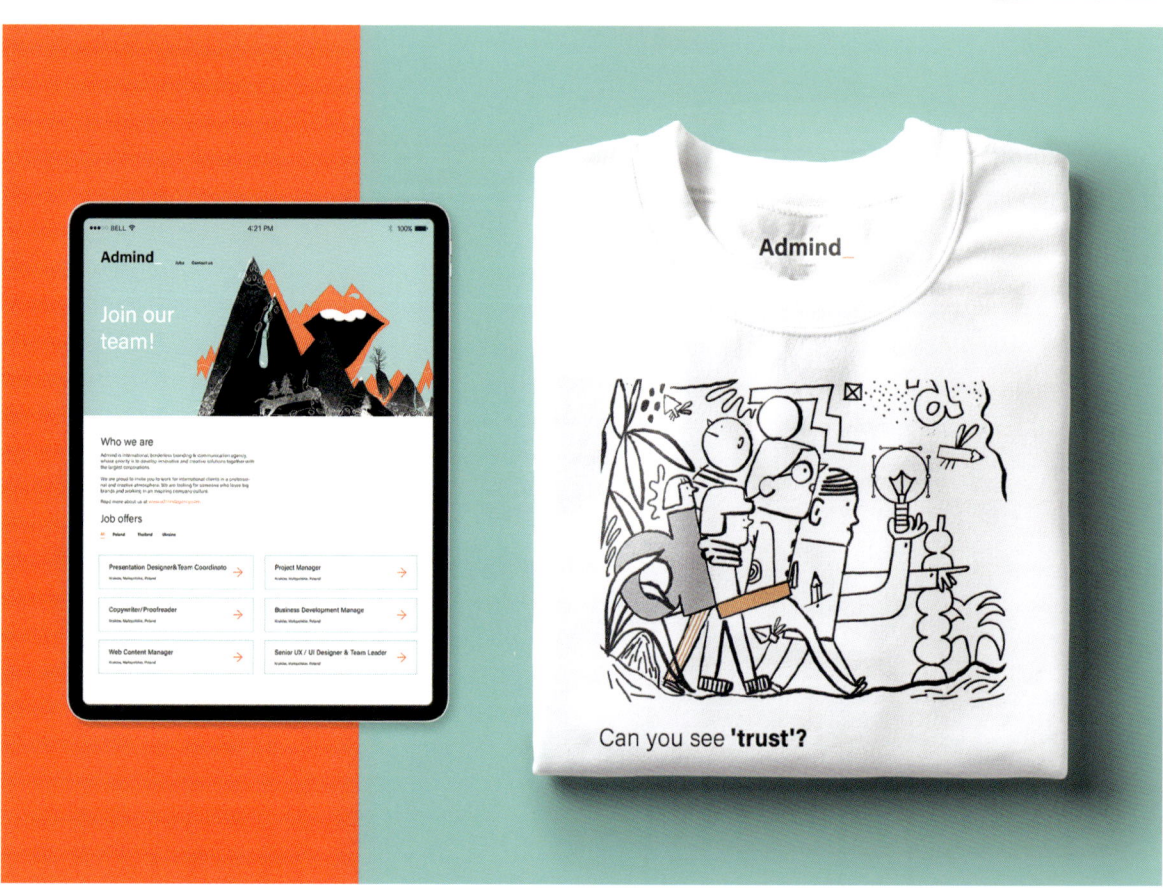

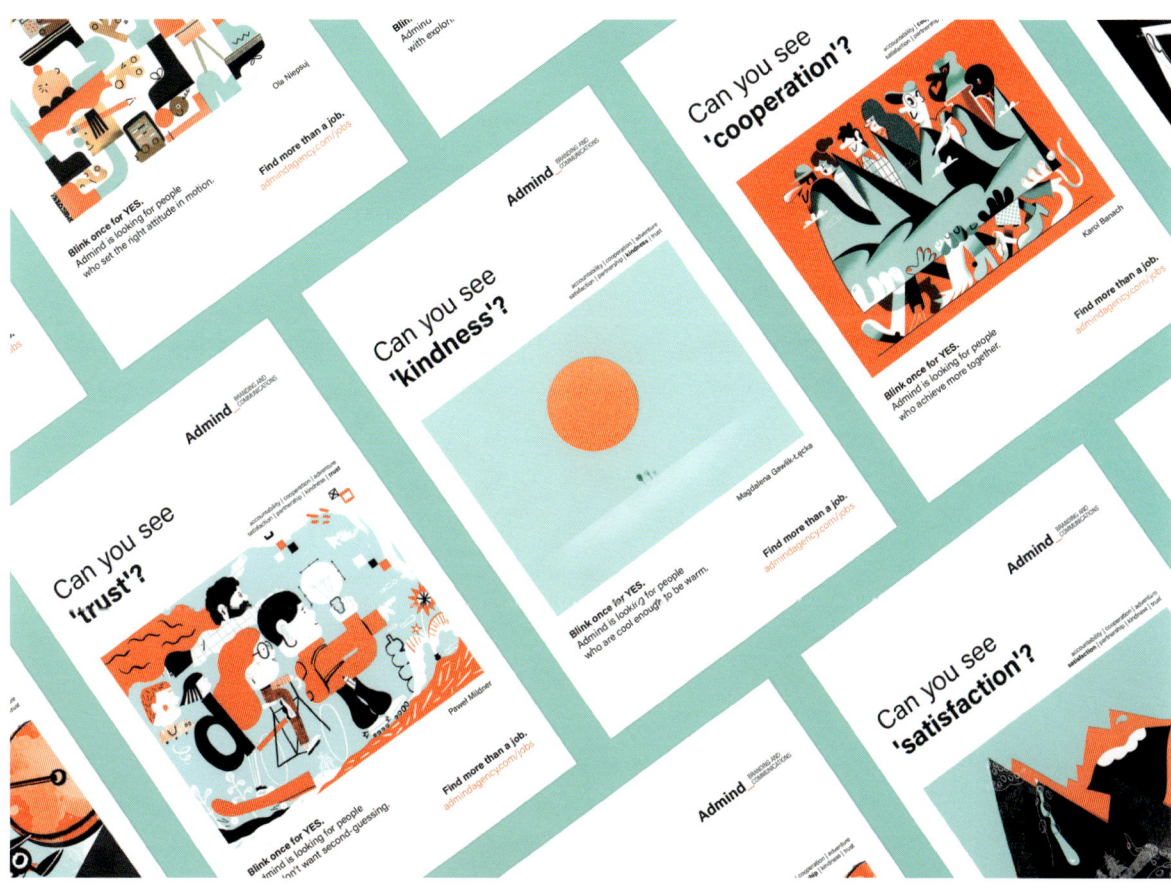

To make their recruitment campaign unique and versatile, advertising agency Admind asked well-known Polish illustrators to create a range of key visuals for posters in collaboration with their in-house designers. All of the motifs refer to the agency's values: trust, cooperation, responsibility, adventure, partnership, satisfaction and kindness. Another element shared by all of the posters is the brand colouring. The posters constitute an invitation to dialogue, with all of them featuring the same headline. The campaign not only led to new recruitments, but also more visitors to the agency's website.

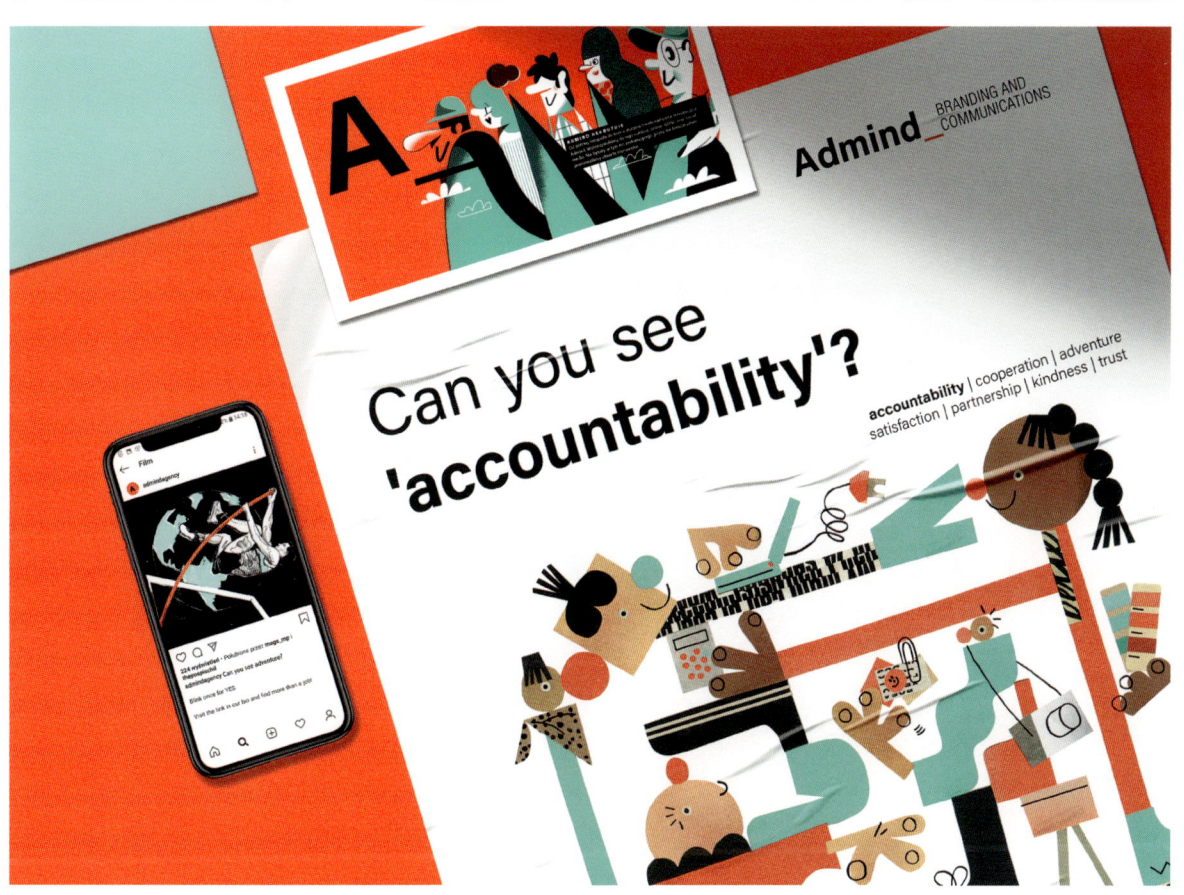

Hyundai x BTS NEXO Campaign

[Image Campaign]

Client
Hyundai Motor Company
Seoul, South Korea

Design
Hyundai Motor Company, Creative Works
Seoul, South Korea
Cueclyp
Seoul, South Korea

Project Team
Hyundai Motor Company:
Sungwon Jee (Creative Direction)
Young Jang (Design Management)
Kyra Cha (Designer)
Ji Soo Hwang (Designer)
Natalie Smith (Designer)
Seo Hee Park (Designer)

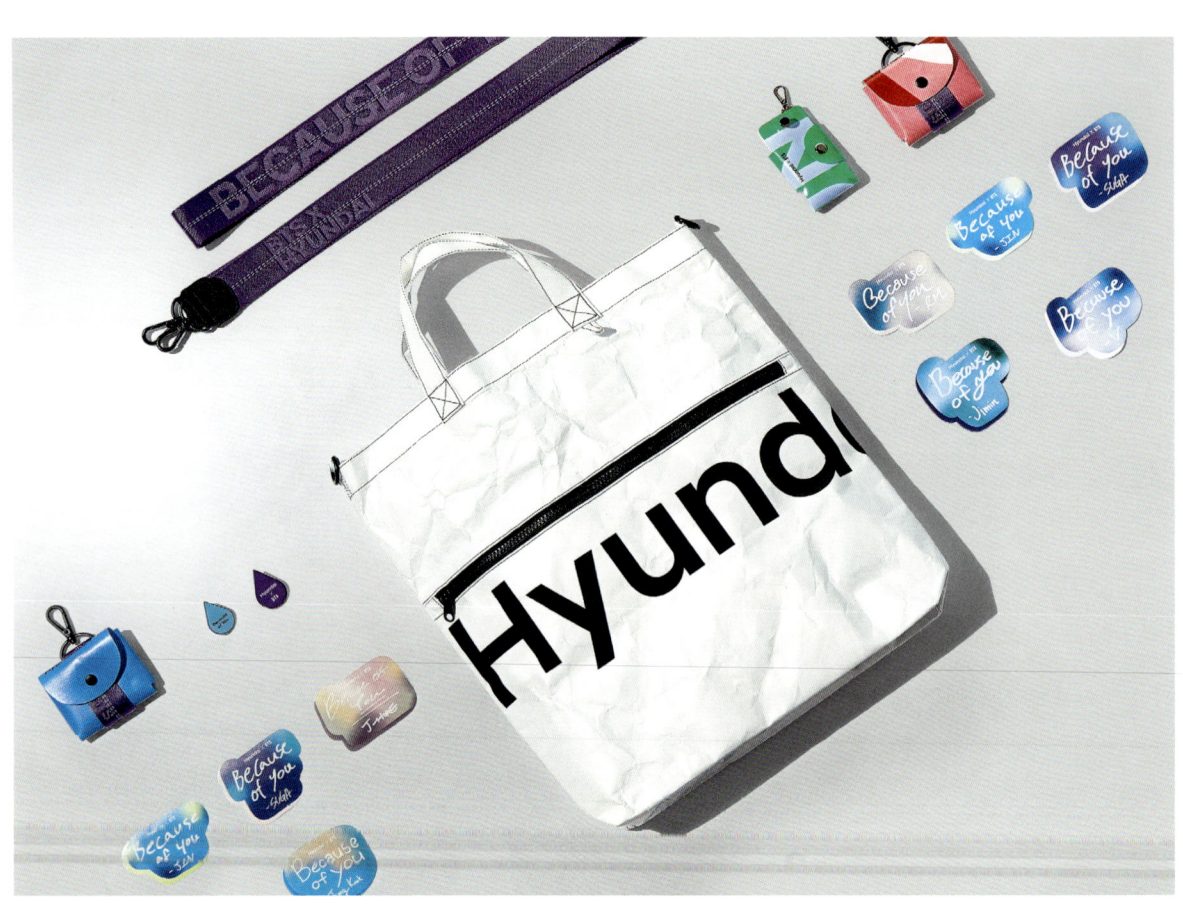

Advertising	Packaging Design	Fair Stands	Retail Design	Red Dot: Junior Award	Designer Profiles	Index
288	318	494	516	544	614	674

As part of its "Because of you" campaign, Hyundai partnered with South Korean boy band BTS to introduce their climate-friendly hydrogen technology. On World Environment Day, they launched a music video and soundtrack, presenting the hydrogen fuel cell powered car, NEXO. The campaign targets a young audience and aims to raise their environmental awareness while encouraging them to actively contribute to positive change for the future. An exclusively launched product line was made available to those who actively participated in social media events. The merchandise collection was produced by reusing, repurposing and recycling other materials.

A recipe for awareness – emergency food supplies

[Content Marketing]

In the aim of encouraging city-dwellers to stock up on emergency food supplies, this multi-channel campaign took advantage of the target group's media consumption habits. Without conjuring up alarming scenarios, the campaign organised by the State Ministry of the Environment and Agriculture in Saxony, Germany, talked about the daily usage of food supplies in an entertaining manner. Four local bloggers – who regularly write about cooking – were invited to take part in a competition. Their recipes, using typical store-cupboard ingredients, were then published in a weekly YouTube series and viewers were invited to vote for them.

Client
Sächsisches Staatsministerium für Energie, Klimaschutz, Umwelt und Landwirtschaft
Dresden, Germany

Design
Genese Werbeagentur GmbH
Magdeburg, Germany

Project Team
Andreas Georgi (Concept)
Sebastian Kahl (Concept)
Marc Uhlenhaut (Creative Direction)
Carola Sels (Project Management)

Advertising	Packaging Design	Fair Stands	Retail Design	Red Dot: Junior Award	Designer Profiles	Index
288	318	494	516	544	614	674

The first sunglasses made from 100% rePET – by Vöslauer Balance

[Integrated Campaign]

The Austrian beverage manufacturer Vöslauer produces all of its PET bottles from 100 per cent rePET – i.e. recycled bottles. To enable people to experience this sustainable claim and connect it with the brand, this integrated campaign for Vöslauer Balance offered sunglasses made from 100 per cent rePET as goodies. The sunglasses were given away in limited numbers via social media competitions. The winners received their sunglasses in packaging that, again, was part of the circular economy. In addition, the sunglasses came in colours reflecting the flavours of Vöslauer Balance.

Client
Vöslauer Mineralwasser GmbH
Bad Vöslau, Austria

Design
Die Goldkinder GmbH
Vienna, Austria

Project Team
Vöslauer Mineralwasser:
Yvonne Haider-Lenz (Marketing)
Thomas Reisner (Marketing)

Die Goldkinder:
Katja Claus (Creative Direction)
Michael Stebegg (Creative Direction)
Catherine Thaler (Account Management)
Annett Ackermann
(Account Management)
Nina Havlicek (Concept)
Silke Rössel (Copywriting)
Clemens Marischen (Social Media)
Alena Spitzer (Social Media)
Elisabeth Knauft (Social Media)
Theresa Markl (Motion Design)

Paul Asmuß (Design)
Manfred Haiberger (Manufacturer), Haratech
Philipp Schönauer (Photography)

→ Clip online

Tune-in: galvanizing storytelling

[Content Marketing]

The Mecklenburg-Vorpommern public transport company promoted their special summer holiday tickets aimed at students of all ages with content marketing. Using captivating storytelling, an episodic podcast told the adventures of the three main protagonists representing the different target groups. As they went on a mad dash treasure hunt across their home region, the summer holiday ticket was a means to an end, an entryway into that adventure. Five weekly episodes of ten to twelve minutes were published on Spotify. Each episode ended with riddles about regional sagas and myths, which could be solved on social media channels for a chance to win weekly prizes.

Client
Verkehrsgesellschaft
Mecklenburg-Vorpommern mbH
Schwerin, Germany

Design
Genese Werbeagentur GmbH
Magdeburg, Germany

Project Team
Andreas Georgi (Concept)
Sebastian Kahl (Concept)
Marc Uhlenhaut (Creative Direction)
Nina Hamel (Graphic Design)

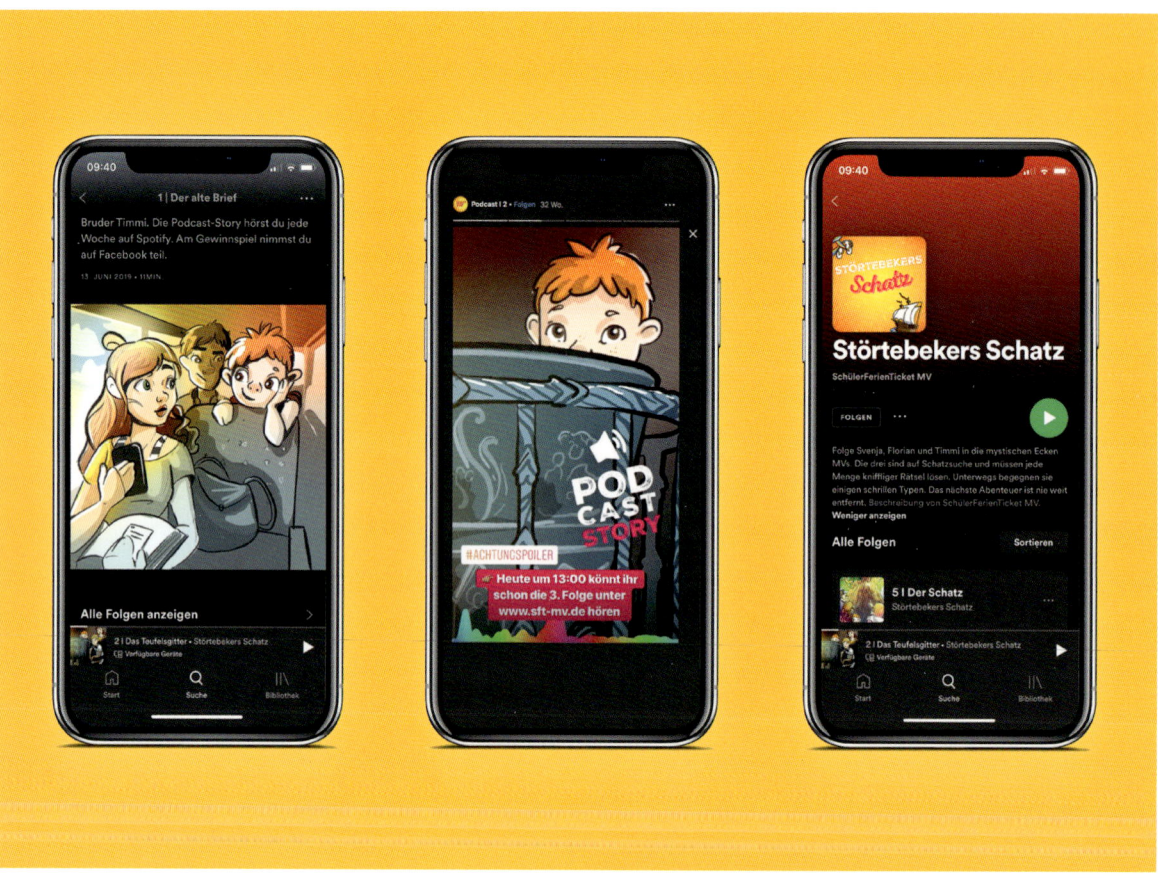

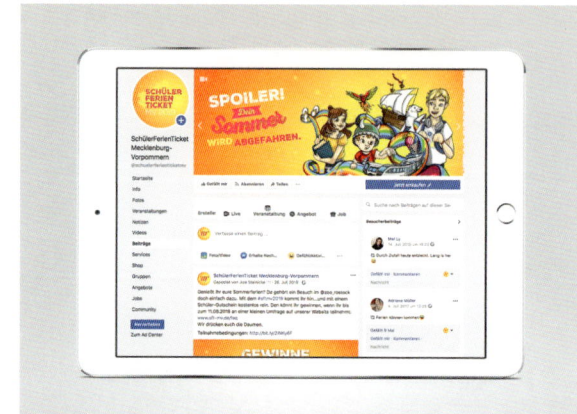

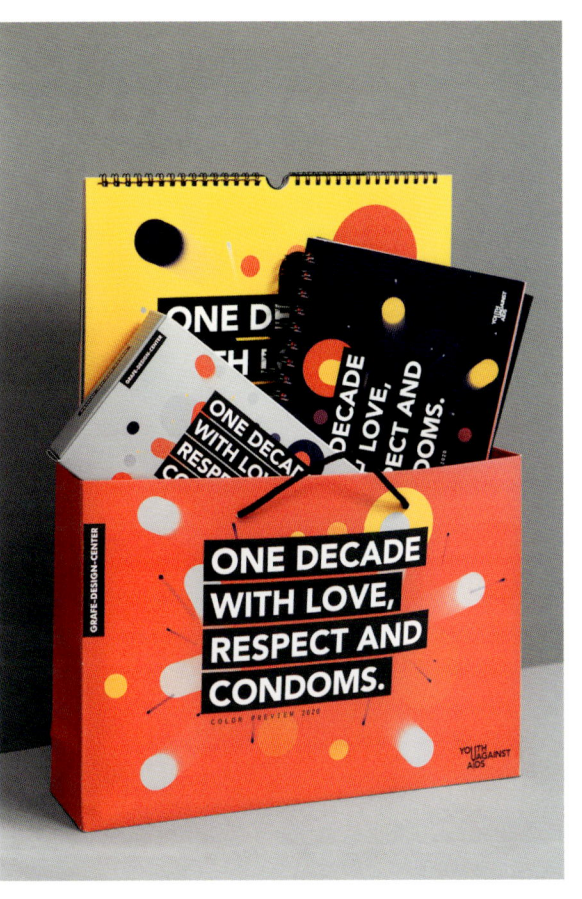

Looks good, feels bad.
[Content Marketing]

As sexually transmitted diseases are still widespread, "Jugend gegen AIDS" (Youth against AIDS) wants to educate young people about effective protection against them. With the slogan "One decade with love, respect and condoms", this content marketing refers to the 10th anniversary of the NGO, which was founded by young people. At the heart of the promotional materials is a calendar that reminds users every month to use condoms. The colourful motifs feature abstract illustrations of pathogens on the front, while the back gives facts about gonorrhoea, genital herpes and, of course, AIDS.

Client
Youth against AIDS
Hamburg, Germany

Design
loved GmbH
Hamburg, Germany

Project Team
Mieke Haase (Chief Creative Officer)
Alexander Müsgens (Creative Director)
Sabine Cole (Editor-in-Chief)
Valerie Bachert (Editor-in-Chief)
Jana Maria Herrmann (Art Direction)
Yannic Hefermann (Art Direction)
Susanne Sauer (Designer)
Isabella Bigler (Text)

FAQ YOU

[Content Marketing]

The NGO "Jugend gegen AIDS" (Youth against AIDS) focuses on a peer-to-peer concept in its communication strategy and trains young people to lead educational workshops in their schools. For their 10th anniversary, they published a sex education book available through book shops. This choice of medium was to protect the privacy of the target group, as a book does not leave any data traces. The editorial design is colourful and tailored to the target group, without being gaudy. The NGO's visual identity is reflected in the headline design, the use of colour and the abstract typographical elements used throughout the publication.

Client
Youth against AIDS
Hamburg, Germany

Design
loved GmbH
Hamburg, Germany

Project Team
Mieke Haase (Chief Creative Officer)
Alexander Müsgens (Creative Director)
Sabine Cole (Editor-in-Chief)
Valerie Bachert (Editor-in-Chief)
Jana Maria Herrmann (Art Direction)
Yannic Hefermann (Art Direction)
Susanne Sauer (Designer)
Isabella Bigler (Text)

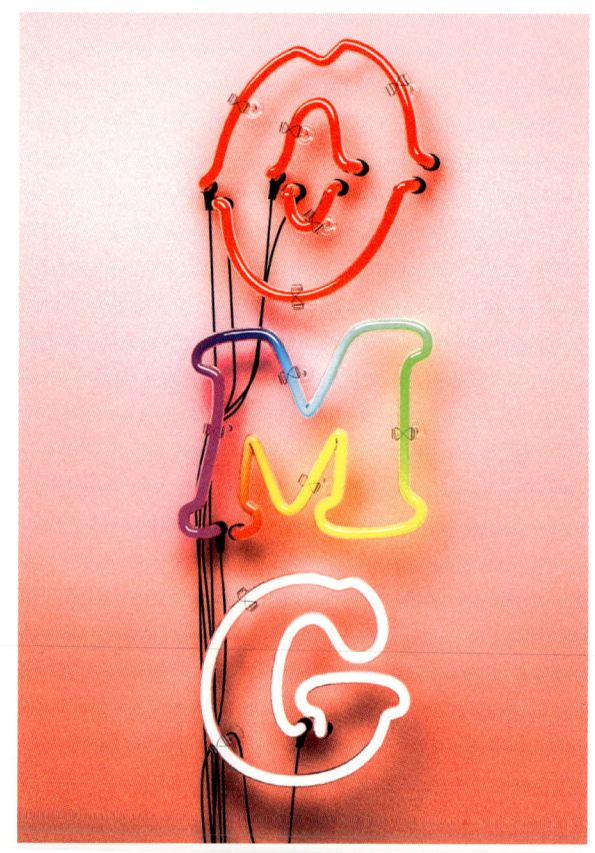

Don't forget !)

[Poster Campaign]

This poster campaign by the NGO "Jugend gegen AIDS" (Youth against AIDS) aims to make young people aware of the importance of safe sex and to remind them about the use of condoms. Six motifs were created, showing a knot adopting a phallic shape, which much like a knot in a handkerchief serves as a reminder. The attention-grabbing illustration style is targeted at young adults and is mixed with existing elements of the visual identity. As a result, the campaign was able to successfully convey the seriousness of the topic through an implementation that is both specific to the target group and playful.

Client
Youth against AIDS
Hamburg, Germany

Design
loved GmbH
Hamburg, Germany

Project Team
Alexander Müsgens (Creative Director)
Lukas Weber (Copywriting)
Marc Huth (Art Buying)
Lilli Oldag (Account Management)

JICA

[Promotion]

Client
JICA
Tokyo, Japan

Design
Grand Design Inc.
Tokyo, Japan

Project Team
Grand Design Inc.:
Katsunori Nishi
(Executive Creative Director)
Jun Fujiwara (Creative Director)
Tetsuya Utsumi (Art Director)
Kelvin Chen (Designer)

GEEK PICTURE Inc.:
Teruki Murakami (Producer)
Kenichi Sumide (Film Director)
Yuki Odaka (Planner)

Kaori Ishimatsu (Writer)

otoco inc.:
Shotaro Tsurumaru (Music Producer)

ADK Marketing Solutions Inc.:
Takehiro Nakano (Account Director)

→ Designer profile on page 639
→ Clip online

Advertising	Packaging Design	Fair Stands	Retail Design	Red Dot: Junior Award	Designer Profiles	Index
288	318	494	516	544	614	674

The Japanese aid organisation JICA carries out humanitarian work, provides technical assistance and develops funding programmes for developing countries. To address a young target audience, this image-based film presents individual aid projects and proves their success through numbers. The filmic implementation uses animated illustrations, initially showing the issue or problem in black and white. As the description of the relief operations unfolds, the scenery changes from monochrome to colour. The promotion film was published on social networks to generate interest in volunteering.

Packaging Design

Red Dot: Best of the Best

Judith Beck Wines – GRAPES.TALK
[Beverage Packaging]

The Austrian winemaker Judith Beck is known for wines that are described as unconventional, mysterious or dynamic and that "speak for themselves" in terms of taste. In order to not only make these wines clearly visible on the wine market, but also to make them being "heard", the vines in this set were given a "voice" in the form of an audible identification mark. First, the labels of the three bottles were designed. Featuring the same plain black-and-white scheme as the cardboard, the labels show artistic yet strongly distorted illustrations. The main idea, however, is the integrated barcodes that lead to a dedicated website when being scanned with a smartphone. Each of the three label illustrations thus allows listening to special stories behind the wine. For example, the head shown in profile on the label triggers the story of Judith who had nothing to call her own until she started making her own wines, while the woman in traditional costume leads to an explanation of how the new "Koreaa" came about in the middle of Austria. The wines thus literally start talking.

Statement by the jury
This work represents a truly self-reliant packaging design for a wine that has a special reputation already. And the title lives up to its promise, as the smart labels with barcode lead to audio files of these "talking wines". Moreover, the labels are beautifully illustrated, so that this brilliant idea has resulted in a design concept that is as surprising as it is convincing.

Advertising	Packaging Design	Fair Stands	Retail Design	Red Dot: Junior Award	Designer Profiles	Index
288	318	494	516	544	614	674

Client
Judith Beck GmbH
Gols, Austria

Design
Heimat Wien
Vienna, Austria

Project Team
Simon Pointner (Creative Direction)
Philip Krautsack (Creative Direction)
Robin Kappacher (Text)
Katharina Handlos (Graphic Design)
Markus Wieser (Head of Advertising)
Stefan Schäffer (Digital Concept)
Andreas Leitner (Illustration)

→ Designer profile on page 642

Red Dot: Best of the Best

LIDL Retsina Wine
[Beverage Packaging]

Retsina wine has more than 2,000 years of history. Already a folk's favourite in ancient Greece, it continues to be one of the most popular wines in the country, although it seems to lose connection with the younger generations who view it as old-fashioned. For the reintroduction, the design of the wine labels and illustrations takes up the almost euphoric union between people and nature at traditional festivals, which every Greek can relate to, no matter their age. The imagery showcases a timelessly naive style that bridges the long history of Retsina from antiquity to the present by drawing on imagery from ancient Greek festivities for Dionysus and modern painters who have made Greek culture famous around the world. Showing abstract vines and grapes, as well as typical lute players and dances, the motifs evoke a strong sense of Greek festivals, which are always outdoor celebrations and where people drink and dance traditional dances while holding hands.

Statement by the jury
To make the labels for a Greek wine feature a design with a kind of frieze above and below the information is a great idea. Inspired in terms of colour by the country's sun and in terms of content by the notion of the traditional Greek way of life with music, wine and dance, the illustrations visualise the image of the well-known Retsina in a harmonious manner to authentically promote it as a wine that is both classic and modern.

Advertising	Packaging Design	Fair Stands	Retail Design	Red Dot: Junior Award	Designer Profiles	Index
288	318	494	516	544	614	674

Client
LIDL HELLAS
Thessaloniki, Greece

Design
Caparo
Athens, Greece

→ Designer profile on page 627

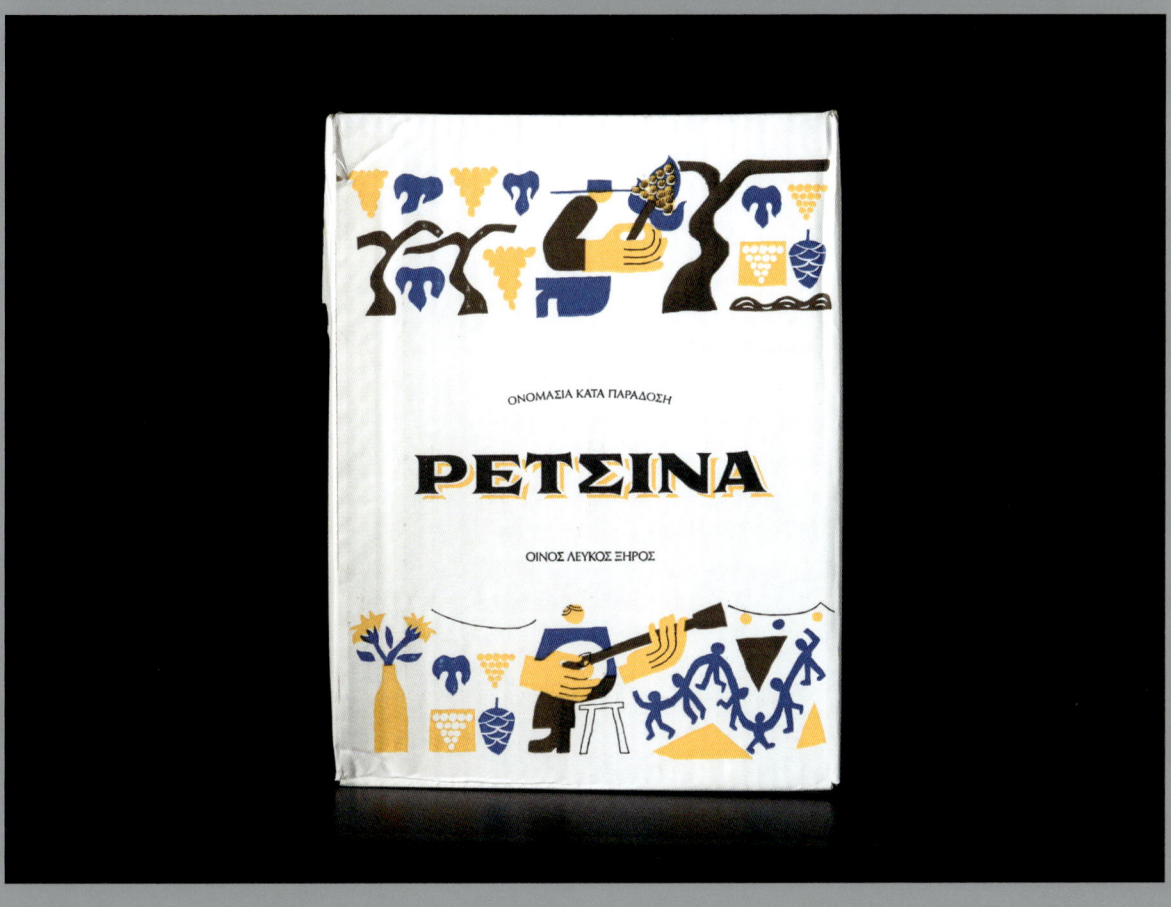

Red Dot: Best of the Best

Pocky THE GIFT
[Food Packaging]

Pocky sticks have been Japan's top-selling chocolate snack for decades. It is kids and teenagers in particular who love them because the chocolate sticks are easy to handle and share with friends. In order to appeal more to the target group of young adults and to give them a way to enjoy Pocky sticks, a stylish new packaging was created – for use exclusively at upscale shops and sales outlets. The result is an overall simple, rectangular packaging in various colours and sizes with an equally reduced printing, which allows the product to be presented and prepared in a variety of ways in the shops. With their simple and colourful appearance, they immediately catch the eye almost everywhere and encourage consumers to celebrate small and large moments with them or to give them to friends as a fashionable gift. The inside of the product boxes also features graphics to heighten the sense of surprise when opening the package.

Statement by the jury
The redesign of the legendary Pocky chocolate sticks packaging is a great example of the effect that target group-specific design and appeal can have. The new identity is marked by a bold, minimalist aesthetic that is sustainable and at the same time makes customers want the product – an overall very well-thought-out branding with a playful touch.

Advertising	Packaging Design	Fair Stands	Retail Design	Red Dot: Junior Award	Designer Profiles	Index
288	318	494	516	544	614	674

Client
Ezaki Glico Co., Ltd.
Osaka, Japan

Design
Dentsu Inc.
Tokyo, Japan

Project Team
Yoshihiro Yagi (Creative Direction)
Haruko Tsutsui (Copywriting)
Satomi Okubo (Graphic Design)
Taiji Kimura (Graphic Design)
Haruko Nakatani (Graphic Design)

→ Designer profiles on pages 630, 631
→ Clip online

Red Dot: Best of the Best

Brooklyn Soap's Advent Calendars 2020

[Packaging]

Brooklyn Soap Company is a grooming product range for men that was devised in Brooklyn and is made in Germany. It captivates with attention to detail and the use of natural ingredients that do not require microplastics, parabens or testing on animals. This is also reflected in the two advent calendars, which take up the German tradition of having a little mystery gift for every day of December until Christmas Eve. Inspired by the New York districts of Manhattan and Brooklyn, both designs incorporate not only characteristic landmarks of the metropolis but also classic barbershop tools such as brushes and razors, as well as typical Christmas elements. The motifs on the box are inspired by American billboards from the 1950s, illustrated in a neo-traditionalist style and coloured by hand. Complemented by suitable typographic elements, each of the 24 boxes contains a product from the segments of beard care, shaving and body care.

Statement by the jury
The packaging design of these two advent calendars gives the barber's craft a striking appearance in suitably subdued colour combinations. Moreover, it embodies the quality of this grooming product range for men in a credible manner as the products are based on natural ingredients. The handcrafted illustrations in their emphatically virile, powerful style further support this image.

Advertising	Packaging Design	Fair Stands	Retail Design	Red Dot: Junior Award	Designer Profiles	Index
288	318	494	516	544	614	674

Client
Brooklyn Soap Company
Hamburg, Germany

Design
Brooklyn Soap Company
Hamburg, Germany
Atelier Tietchen
Hamburg, Germany

Project Team
Brooklyn Soap:
Nico Liebetanz (Creative Direction)
Viktor Dik (Head of Marketing)
Michael Rademacher (Photography)
Felix Ermer (Strategic Planning)
Lukas Görlitz (Editorial Work)

Tobias Tietchen (Illustration),
Atelier Tietchen

→ Designer profile on page 670

Preface	Red Dot: Agency of the Year	Brands	Brand Design & Identity	Corporate Design & Identity	Annual Reports
4	6	18	90	202	260

Markgraf von Baden

[Beverage Packaging]

The design of these wine bottles shifted the focus on the nine-centuries-long tradition of the family of the Markgraf von Baden and their role as pioneers of wine culture in Baden. The "message in a bottle" concept dedicates each bottle to a personality within the family, with specially designed labels in the style of postal stamps. In this way, a unique and distinctive brand presence is created which aims to help position the vineyard among the top five of the region. The exclusive design is primarily geared towards male wine connoisseurs who are middle aged or older, and are demanding in terms of quality.

Client
Rotkäppchen-Mumm
Sektkellereien GmbH
Eltville, Germany

Design
Ruska, Martin, Associates GmbH
Berlin, Germany

Project Team
Francisca Martín (Creative Direction)
Roman Ruska (Creative Direction)
Andrea Tolosano (Design)

Das Markgräflich Badische Weinhaus

[Beverage Packaging]

These three Weinhaus wine series represent a modern and experimental wine culture. They are aimed at a younger target group who like to cook and are willing to try out new things. The design of the bottles reflects both creativity and high quality standards. The modern 360-degree layout of the labels combines heraldry, portraits, drawings and stories from the winemaker into expressive visual storytelling. It uses perforation as a central design element, thus staging the newly developed, combined wine names with a high impact.

Client
Rotkäppchen-Mumm
Sektkellereien GmbH
Eltville, Germany

Design
Ruska, Martin, Associates GmbH
Berlin, Germany

Project Team
Francisca Martín (Creative Direction)
Roman Ruska (Creative Direction)
Andrea Tolosano (Design)
João Colaço (Design)

Blandy's – The Winemaker's Selection

[Beverage Packaging]

Client
Madeira Wine Company
Funchal, Portugal

Design
Omdesign
Matosinhos, Portugal

→ Designer profile on page 656

To commemorate the discovery of the island of Madeira in 1419, the wine brand Blandy's launched a limited edition of Madeira wine, a mix of historical grape varieties of the region. The wine's valuable nature is highlighted by a luxurious packaging. The silver reliefs on the bottle associate the product with the exceptional bravery of the Portuguese navigators. The wooden crate in which the bottle is presented is just as sophisticated. With crafted inlays, it is likewise inspired by Portuguese culture, which is traditionally associated with wicker, silver and embroidery.

Album di Famiglia

[Beverage Packaging]

The label design of these three genuine, organic wines from Apulia is reminiscent of the lasting and unbreakable connection each individual has with their own roots. It creates an association with a family photo album, called "Album di Famiglia" in Italian, which tells the stories of different individuals and their special moments. Each label shows the bottom half of an authentic portrait photograph like those taken by the early 20th-century pioneers with a wooden view camera on a tripod. The photo is completed with the illustration of a plant which grows out of the portrait as if it grew out of a root.

Client
Brand Breeder S.r.l.s.
Pescara, Italy

Design
Spazio Di Paolo S.r.l.
Spoltore (Pescara), Italy

Il Segno

[Beverage Packaging]

The design of this bottle combines the Italian traditions of wine-making and ceramics. The idea is to leave behind a "mark" – "Il Segno" in Italian. The label is made from an ultra-thin ceramic material adapted to the shape of the bottle and produced entirely by hand with platinum and gold decoration. It is attached to the bottle with great precision and supplemented by a gilded banderole displaying the company name. The front of the bottle has the name and designation of the wine imprinted in gold using screen printing. A paper tag explaining the idea behind the wine rounds off the design.

Client
Cinquesegni S.r.l.
Salerno, Italy

Design
Cinquesegni S.r.l.
Salerno, Italy

Project Team
Osvaldo Camarin (CEO),
Vetri Speciali S.p.A.

Flavia Simone (Graphic Design),
Gieffe S.a.s.

Rocco Menna
(Product Development Manager),
Farnese Vini S.r.l.

Onofrio Acone (Ceramic Art Director),
Cinquesegni S.r.l.

Flower Pot

[Beverage Packaging]

The most interesting aspects of the Flower Pot brand are that its wines are strictly organic and come in light glass bottles weighing no more than 360 grams. Furthermore, the labels are made from eco-friendly seed paper. The latter can be removed under running water and planted in a pot to grow fresh flowers, which offer a biosphere for insects. This is where the product name comes from. The instructions are communicated clearly on the label, the design of which, with life sprouting out of the Flower Pot name, shows the special nature of the concept.

Client
F.W. Langguth Erben GmbH & Co. KG
Traben-Trarbach, Germany

Design
Agentur Jung GmbH
Kiel, Germany

Nachtlese

[Beverage Packaging]

The cool temperatures at night make it the perfect time to harvest grapes. The motto for this label design, "Nachtlese. Die Sterne standen günstig!" (Night harvest. The stars were aligned!), focuses on precisely this aspect. The label shows the exact starry sky on the very night which was chosen to harvest the grapes for this wine. It is a representation of the sky over the vineyards in the Hainfeld wine-growing area of the Palatinate region on 3 October 2018, which was provided by NASA, who supported the project by granting access to their comprehensive database.

Client
Weingut Lergenmüller
Hainfeld, Germany

Design
Agentur Jung GmbH
Kiel, Germany

LUXORO – Nozze D'Oro

[Beverage Packaging]

Client
LUXORO S.r.l.
Parona (Pavia), Italy

Design
Spazio Di Paolo S.r.l.
Spoltore (Pescara), Italy

Advertising	**Packaging Design**	Fair Stands	Retail Design	Red Dot: Junior Award	Designer Profiles	Index
288	318	494	516	544	614	674

This wine bottle brings together design, history, nature, passion and emotion. It echoes, for example, the feelings of those arriving at the winery for the first time and their first view of the vineyards, which reach as far as the eye can see. The three-dimensional design is also geared to a high level of interaction with the consumers. They have to open a blue banderole which resembles window shutters in order to catch a glimpse of the label. In fact, the colour is the same as the shade typically used to paint the window shutters and doors of the region where this wine comes from.

Twenty Stories

[Beverage Packaging]

Discount supermarket chain LIDL is commemorating its 20th year in Greece by introducing an exclusive and limited edition of a locally produced Syrah-Merlot premium wine. The design came about against the backdrop that wine is part of many people's lives, for example to celebrate a major event. Entitled "Twenty Stories", 20 unique labels tell 20 unique stories. To achieve that, each label has a free-hand illustration created in black and red. The illustrative intention is to pair everyday moments with their symbolic significance to a person's life.

Client
LIDL HELLAS
Thessaloniki, Greece

Design
Caparo
Athens, Greece

→ Designer profile on page 627

Untouched by Light
[Beverage Packaging]

Untouched by Light is a sparkling wine which is produced in complete darkness, as it is assumed that the exposure of wine to daylight decreases the quality of aromas. In a consistent move, the product is bottled in black glass. A vacuum-sealed, fully recyclable bag additionally blocks any light or air contact. The black packaging with just a few shimmering elements is immediately noticeable and stands out due to its simple elegance. While the colour black references the manufacturing process, associations with the darkness of the night lend the product a sensuous and mysterious air.

Client
Radgonske Gorice
Gornja Radgona, Slovenia

Design
Bruketa&Zinic&Grey
Zagreb, Croatia

Project Team
Bruketa&Zinic&Grey:
Tea Silvia Vlahovic
(Strategic Planning Director)
Mirna Pticek (Art Director)
Davor Bruketa (Creative Director)
Masa Ivanov (Account Director)
Vesna Durasin (Production Manager)
Ante Kantor (Account Executive)
Marko Zabrdac (Account Executive)
Ivan Tanic (Strategic Planning Director)
Josip Buzov (Strategic Planner)

Kaligraf:
Miho Karolyi (Packaging Consultant)

→ Clip online

Zui Jin Jiu

[Beverage Packaging]

Client
Shenzhen Excel Package Design Co., Ltd.
Shenzhen, China

Design
Shenzhen Excel
Brand Design Consultant Co., Ltd.
Shenzhen, China

Advertising	Packaging Design	Fair Stands	Retail Design	Red Dot: Junior Award	Designer Profiles	Index
288	318	494	516	544	614	674

This design concept breaks with the notion of what traditional Chinese rice wine bottles are supposed to look like and, instead, conveys a strong feeling of modernity. Thanks to a minimalist concept, Zui Jin Jiu is presented in a fresh and contemporary yet stylish look. The bottle features a vocabulary of round shapes, and half of it is designed in one of four pastel shades. The cap echoes the respective colour used, creating a harmonious impression. The upper half of the bottle is transparent, allowing the consumer to see the content.

No Man's Space – Capricorn

[Beverage Packaging]

The label of this dry vermouth represents the constellation of Capricorn. Innovative printing and cutting techniques and the overlapping of different materials give it a three-dimensional nature which encourages the consumer to interact with the design. Its minimalist character is underscored through the use of black as the main colour. This is contrasted by gold-coloured stars. Two of them are even embellished with gold leaf, enhancing their glow. The iconic design reflects the fact that No Man's Space is the result of a collaboration and mutual inspiration between design and aromatic chords.

Client
Brand Breeder S.r.l.s.
Pescara, Italy

Design
Spazio Di Paolo S.r.l.
Spoltore (Pescara), Italy

No Man's Space – Eclipse

[Beverage Packaging]

No Man's Space is the name of a line of alcoholic beverages which ably marry design and aromatic chords in an impressive manner. The packaging design for this gin uses the image of a lunar eclipse. The eclipse is shown on the three-dimensional label, which is bursting with vibrancy and invites consumers to engage with the product. A play of light and shade, suggested in a yellow hue, gives a refined feel to the product description "Gin". The bottle shows a distinct black-and-white design which exudes an extreme elegance.

Client
Brand Breeder S.r.l.s.
Pescara, Italy

Design
Spazio Di Paolo S.r.l.
Spoltore (Pescara), Italy

Preface	Red Dot: Agency of the Year	Brands	Brand Design & Identity	Corporate Design & Identity	Annual Reports
4	6	18	90	202	260

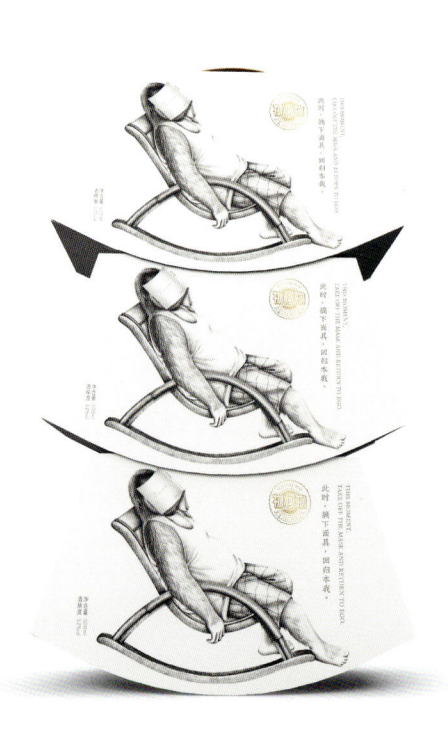

WU GUI WU

[Beverage Packaging]

The idea for the packaging design for this distilled wine is based in the slogan "At this time, take off the mask, return to oneself". Many people feel insecure as a result of the pressure created by the hectic pace of life as well as by family and work responsibilities. In response, they hide behind a mask. The label on the bottle visualises this scene with a black-and-white drawing of an ape in a suit, holding a clown's mask to its face. In contrast, the outer packaging provides a brief respite. It features a refined design with a rounded base, imitating the shape of a rocking chair in which the ape is sitting.

Client
Harbin Guangwei
Marketing Planning Co., Ltd.
Harbin, China

Design
Harbin Guangwei
Marketing Planning Co., Ltd.
Harbin, China

→ Clip online

Advertising	Packaging Design	Fair Stands	Retail Design	Red Dot: Junior Award	Designer Profiles	Index
288	318	494	516	544	614	674

Together We Create Absolut

[Beverage Packaging]

This limited edition of Absolut Vodka is sold at selected airports exclusively to travellers. Based on the motto "Together we create Absolut", the strong yet friendly design communicates the message that people can bring about change when they work together, regardless of where they come from. A powerful yet playful and accessible image of a fist, interpreted in a contemporary way, is placed at the heart of the design. Numerous additional details show diversity and personality. In order to underscore the positive nature of the message, the design uses neon colours which even light up in the dark.

Client
The Absolut Company
Stockholm, Sweden

Design
Kate Prior
London, United Kingdom
Happytear AB
Stockholm, Sweden

Project Team
Happytear:
Magnus Skogsberg Tear
(Creative Direction)
Martin Stolpe Margenberg (Art Direction)
Sanna Heyman (Account Management)

MMINNI X-LAB

[Beverage Packaging]

The "X" in the name of this brandy developed especially for young people is representative of their fearless spirit of discovery. The concept is to offer a wine mix as a base and then to provide wine blending additionally to allow consumers to mix different aromas which suit their individual taste. In order to break with the traditional image of a brandy and to attract attention, the packaging design is focused on the aspect of the unknown. On the other hand, it focuses on the use of strong, bright colours which are not only used in the alcohol itself but also on the outer packaging.

Client
Changyu Pioneer Wine Company Limited
Yantai, China

Design
Shenzhen Oracle Creative Design Co., Ltd.
Shenzhen, China

Project Team
Wen Liu (Creative Direction)
Weijie Kang (Creative Direction)
Qiumin Chen (Creative Direction)

Dong You Ji Baijiu

[Beverage Packaging]

The Guangxi region is known for its sugar cane production. It is this plant, rather than wheat or rice, which is used as a raw material in this baijiu, a type of Chinese liquor. It gives the drink a sweetness popular with younger consumers in particular. The design of the bottle uses the colours blue and white to echo the natural environment in Guangxi. Its label shows graphical elements inspired by the well-known legend "The Eight Immortals Cross the Sea". The easy-to-carry outer packaging is made from pressed bagasse, which decomposes naturally and is thus friendly to the environment.

Client
China Shaoxing
Yellow Rice Wine Group Co., Ltd.
Shenzhen, China

Design
Shenzhen Oracle Creative Design Co., Ltd.
Shenzhen, China

Project Team
Wen Liu (Creative Direction)
Bo Zheng (Creative Direction)
Weijie Kang (Creative Direction)

She De – Da Cheng

[Beverage Packaging]

The name of this liquor refers to a person or a thing that excels in a certain area. Therefore, the packaging design features illustrations of great Chinese philosophers such as Confucius and Mencius. Detailed depictions cover the bottle as a graceful pattern, conveying an impression of tradition and craftsmanship. The outer packaging showcases the bottle by allowing it to shine through the glass in a mysterious way. The transparent container resembles an ancient bamboo slip so that consumers can feel the charm of Eastern culture from the very first glance.

Client
Shenzhen Lingyun
Creative Packaging Design Co., Ltd.
Shenzhen, China

Design
Shenzhen Lingyun
Creative Packaging Design Co., Ltd.
Shenzhen, China

Project Team
Xiongbo Deng (Creative Direction)
Xing Liu (Illustration)
Hui Li (Illustration)

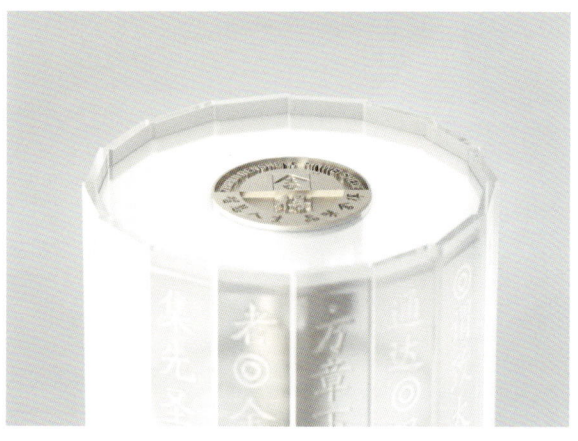

WuDu Black Porcelain

[Beverage Packaging]

The alcoholic beverage inside this packaging contains five herbal remedies. In classical Chinese medicine, the ingredients help to expel excess humidity, which accumulates in the human body due to external factors. Five creatures are regarded as symbols of these pathological factors: the snake, scorpion, centipede, gecko and toad. Therefore, they are depicted on the outer packaging and on the bottle itself. Artfully interwoven with patterns, the images lend the packaging a mysterious touch. The gift box can be pulled out and resembles a drawer where traditional Chinese medicines are placed.

Client
Shenzhen Lingyun
Creative Packaging Design Co., Ltd.
Shenzhen, China

Design
Shenzhen Lingyun
Creative Packaging Design Co., Ltd.
Shenzhen, China

Project Team
Xiongbo Deng (Creative Direction)

Preface	Red Dot: Agency of the Year	Brands	Brand Design & Identity	Corporate Design & Identity	Annual Reports
4	6	18	90	202	260

Sizhuang

[Beverage Packaging]

The design of these bottles, which are also offered in boxes of four, responds to the habit of many Chinese consumers to buy alcoholic beverages in sets. The main design element is water, which is also the main ingredient in this liquor. The streamlined body of the bottle features irregularly placed blue graphical elements. Each bottle has its own pattern, reflecting Oriental beauty among other things. In order to further emphasise the theme of "water", each bottle has a fish-shaped tag. The minimalist outer packaging communicates the concept of the brand, setting itself apart from garishly designed goods.

Client
Shenzhen Lingyun
Creative Packaging Design Co., Ltd.
Shenzhen, China

Design
Shenzhen Lingyun
Creative Packaging Design Co., Ltd.
Shenzhen, China

Project Team
Xiongbo Deng (Creative Direction)
Min Lin (Illustration)

Lovibond 30

[Beverage Packaging]

The name of the dark beer "Lovibond 30" refers to the British brewer Joseph Williams Lovibond. He is the inventor of the colorimeter, used to determine the quality of a beer. The number 30 denotes the colour value of the product. The design of the packaging is geared primarily towards younger consumers. The neck of the bottle is composed of 16 curved surfaces and tapers upwards, true to the slogan "Take your time". One box contains 12 bottles, each designed with different labels. They all feature the number "30" in order to draw attention to the brand name.

Client
Shenzhen Lingyun
Creative Packaging Design Co., Ltd.
Shenzhen, China

Design
Shenzhen Lingyun
Creative Packaging Design Co., Ltd.
Shenzhen, China

Project Team
Xiongbo Deng (Creative Direction)
Xing Liu (Illustration)
Min Lin (Illustration)
Shengxing Tang (Illustration)

Tsingtao White Beer

[Beverage Packaging]

Tsingtao White Beer is sold in bottles and in cans. Their design centres around the manufacturer's traditional coat of arms, with a new typeface to upgrade the appearance. An image of an ancient goddess adorns each side of the coat of arms, alongside references to brewing, such as hops, wheat or a master brewer. The imagery creates associations with freshness, aroma and the authentic taste of beer. The design combines the main colours of white and blue with a little red and gold. The bottle has a label around its neck, while the can features a blue pattern at its top end.

Client
Tsingtao Brewery Co., Ltd.
Qingdao, China

Design
Shenzhen Tigerpan
Packaging Design Co., Ltd.
Shenzhen, China

Project Team
Tiger Pan (Art Direction)
Qian Chi (Graphic Design)
Ping Yi (Illustration)
Juanjuan Wu (Image Editing)
Zhangkun Xie (Technical Direction)
Krystal You (Project Management)

→ Designer profile on page 671

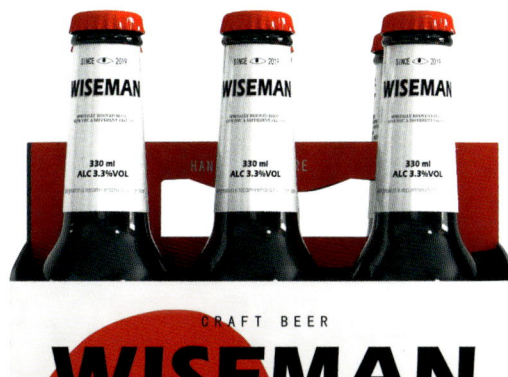

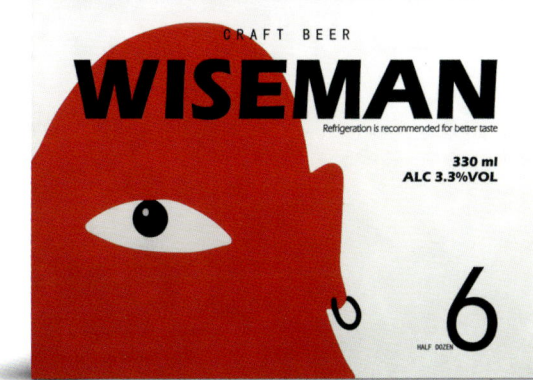

WISEMAN BEER

[Beverage Packaging]

Pictures of aliens and myths served as a source of inspiration for this bottle design, which is dominated by a one-eyed figure. In line with the name of the beer brand, the figure is interpreted as a wise man who keeps an eye on things like poetry and the aesthetics of life. This figure, who exudes wisdom, appeals to young people. In order to enhance its visual character even further, it is designed as a three-dimensional relief. The outer packaging, which holds six bottles, also features the image of the one-eyed figure, thus rounding off the concept.

Client
Shenzhen Chengzui
Cultural Communication Co., Ltd.
Shenzhen, China

Design
Shenzhen Oracle
Creative Design Co., Ltd.
Shenzhen, China

Project Team
Wen Liu (Creative Direction)
Henghong Yang (Creative Direction)
Weijie Kang (Creative Direction)

→ Clip online

Preface	Red Dot: Agency of the Year	Brands	Brand Design & Identity	Corporate Design & Identity	Annual Reports
4	6	18	90	202	260

Budweiser Chinese New Year 2020 | Budweiser Red

[Beverage Packaging]

Red is the colour of the traditional celebration of the Chinese New Year. In order to distinguish itself from other brands which also link their communication to this colour during that period, the design of the limited edition of Budweiser beer uses a new red sign. It is based on the famous brand logo, in the form of a bow tie, and is used together with Chinese New Year greetings which contain the word "red". The festive packaging design also shows a modern version of traditional icons, accentuated with the blue colour typically used by the brand. This creates a vibrant and unmistakeable look.

Client
Anheuser-Busch InBev (China) Sales Company Limited
Wuhan, China

Design
Jones Knowles Ritchie
Shanghai, China

Project Team
René Chen (Managing Director Creation)
Yolanda Tang
(Managing Director Creation)
Woei Yang Fang (Creative Direction)
Vivian Xie (Graphic Design)
Wendy Yang (Graphic Design)
Theresa Wu (Account Management)
Hermia Fung (Account Management)
Angel Tang (Account Management)

Advertising	Packaging Design	Fair Stands	Retail Design	Red Dot: Junior Award	Designer Profiles	Index
288	318	494	516	544	614	674

Beck's Ice | Breaking the Rules

[Beverage Packaging]

With the rebranding for the Vietnamese market, the Beck's Ice brand is targeting young people in particular. To do this, the design breaks with the conventional appearance of a beer steeped in tradition. It takes the original logo, a key in a coat of arms, and uses just the key in a much larger size and bright red colour. It cuts through the brand name, denoting a passion for breaking with convention and opening up new possibilities. Instead of silver as a symbol of freshness, the colour black is used to give the brand a distinctive and progressive personality.

Client
Anheuser-Busch InBev Vietnam Brewery Company Limited
Ho Chi Minh City, Vietnam

Design
Jones Knowles Ritchie
Shanghai, China

Project Team
René Chen (Managing Director Creation)
Yolanda Tang
(Managing Director Creation)
Woei Yang Fang (Creative Direction)
Sky Chen (Graphic Design)
Theresa Wu (Account Management)
Hermia Fung (Account Management)
Connie Chen (Account Management)

MTN DEW – A Can Has No Name

[Beverage Packaging]

There are many fans who love MTN DEW as well as the drama series Game of Thrones. Ahead of the last series, programme provider HBO challenged fans and brands alike with the question of what they would do for the throne. One outcome of this challenge is this limited edition of 9,000 cans which do not name the manufacturer or feature a visual identity. Instead of the iconic logo, the neon-green colour and the distinctive shards and splints, the can is designed just in white with the names of some of the characters from the series.

Client
PepsiCo
New York, USA

Design
PepsiCo Design & Innovation
New York, USA

MTN DEW AMP GAME FUEL – Team OpTic Champions
[Beverage Packaging]

This limited edition of MTN DEW AMP GAME FUEL was developed as a sign of commitment to the gaming community, especially to commemorate the last tournament of the OpTic Gaming team, one of the most popular e-sport teams for Call of Duty. To communicate key aspects of this team, the traditional appearance of the drinks cans was changed. At its core, the modern design features an illustration of each of the five team members. The colour white also plays a major role as the team is known to wear Championship white on the Sundays when tournaments were played. The colour concept is rounded off with hues of green.

Client
PepsiCo
New York, USA

Design
PepsiCo Design & Innovation
New York, USA

Preface	Red Dot: Agency of the Year	Brands	Brand Design & Identity	Corporate Design & Identity	Annual Reports
4	6	18	90	202	260

Pepsi x MOMHANDWORKS (China)

[Beverage Packaging]

The relationship between drinks manufacturer PepsiCo and the not-for-profit collaborative programme "MOMHANDWORKS" by China Women's Development Foundation, which supports traditional handicrafts, started on the occasion of the Bring Happiness Home Chinese New Year Campaign 2019. The collaboration culminated in the unfurling of a ten-metre-long roll of embroidery showing many of the customs of the Chinese New Year festival in traditional and modern designs. The three drinks cans from this limited edition celebrate this cultural heritage and show examples of three different regional embroidery styles set against a blue background.

Client
PepsiCo
New York, USA

Design
PepsiCo Design & Innovation
New York, USA

Pepsi x EXPO 2020

[Beverage Packaging]

The special edition "Pepsi x EXPO 2020" shows in three different variations how the themes of opportunity, mobility and sustainability come together. Each topic is allocated a vibrant colour. The abstract design centres around a stylised figure which has deliberately been kept flat in order to encourage open-ended thought and imagination. The design reflects how the future can look very different from one person to another. Each of the three themes also tells a unique story based on different cultures, experiences and backgrounds.

Client
PepsiCo
New York, USA

Design
PepsiCo Design & Innovation
New York, USA

Pepsi x CNY
Year of the Rat (China)

[Beverage Packaging]

The Lunar New Year is the most significant festival for many Chinese people, as it is a synonym for togetherness and going home to be with family. This limited edition can collection commemorates the New Year and the upcoming zodiac sign. 2020 is the Year of the Rat, a symbol of wealth and abundance. With cultural relevance in mind, three distinct and youthful rat characters have been developed. The characters are adorned with different auspicious Chinese symbols. One of the rats is dressed as a dragon, another as a fish and one is a lion, all signifying traditional New Year wishes.

Client
PepsiCo
New York, USA

Design
PepsiCo Design & Innovation
New York, USA

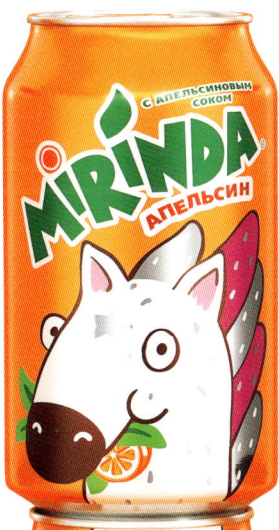

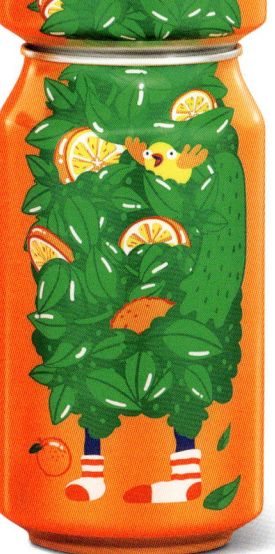

Advertising	Packaging Design	Fair Stands	Retail Design	Red Dot: Junior Award	Designer Profiles	Index
288	318	494	516	544	614	674

Mirinda Unexpected Combo Summer (Russia)

[Beverage Packaging]

The design of the Mirinda Unexpected Combo limited edition evokes a playful, vibrant and spontaneous mood. Six unique characters, whose upper or lower body are portrayed on different cans, invite consumers to create their own unexpected combinations. The edition encourages to collect the cans, rotate them, stack them up or play with them in many different ways. The cheerful, hashtag-worthy design reflects the character of the brand and makes sure the cans stand out on supermarket shelves. The concept was used to develop two collections, one for the Russian and one for the Polish market.

Client
PepsiCo
New York, USA

Design
PepsiCo Design & Innovation
New York, USA

Psiloreitis

[Beverage Packaging]

Client
Psiloreitis
Crete, Greece

Design
A.S. Advertising
Athens, Greece

Project Team
Antonia Skaraki (Art Direction)
Evri Makridis (Graphic Design)
Andreas Deskas (Graphic Design)
Valia Alousi (Web Design)
Sotiria Theodorou (Text)

→ Designer profile on page 618

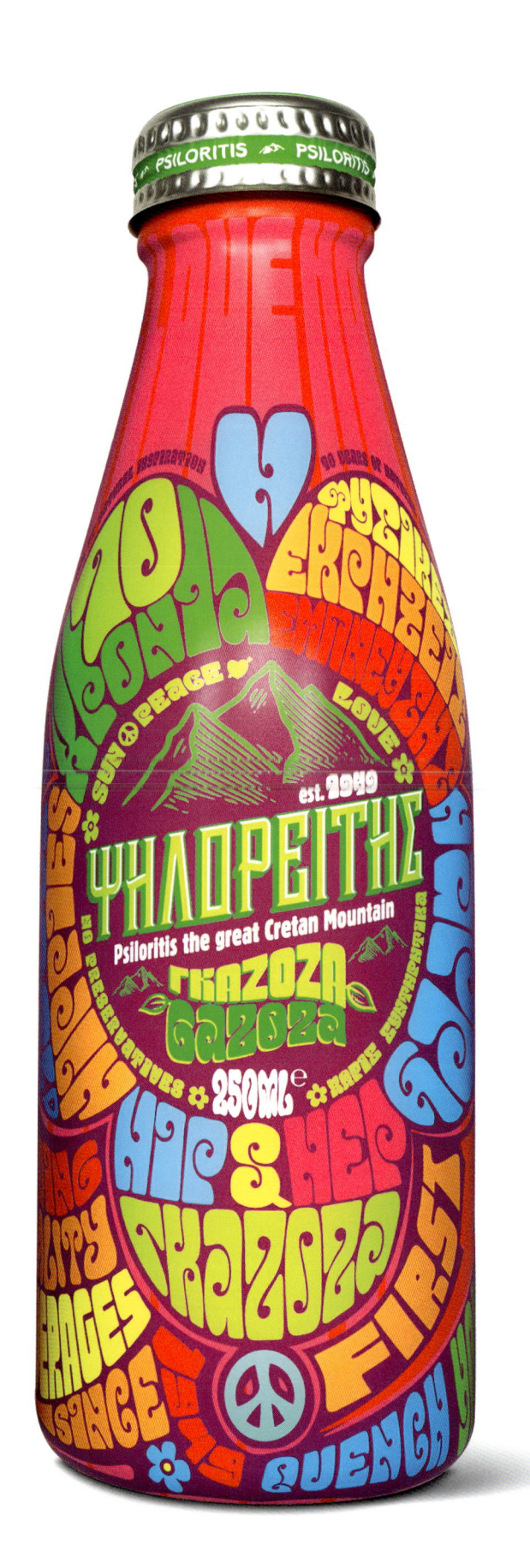

Advertising	**Packaging Design**	Fair Stands	Retail Design	Red Dot: Junior Award	Designer Profiles	Index
288	318	494	516	544	614	674

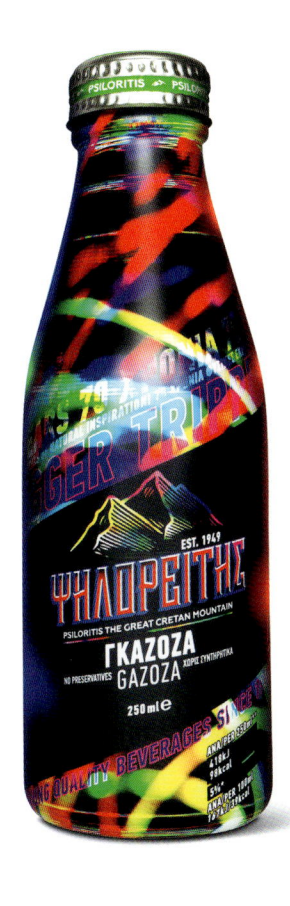

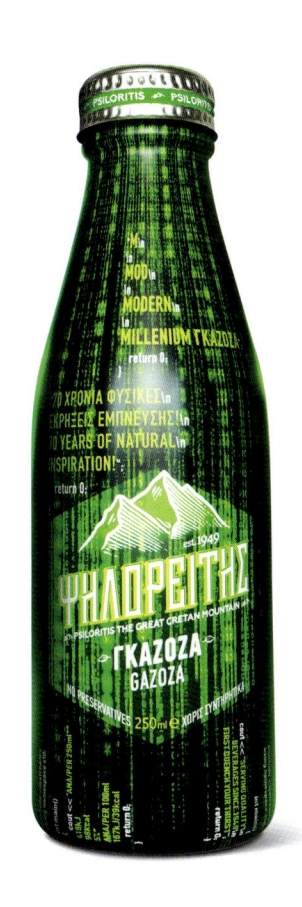

On the occasion of the 70th anniversary of the beverage Psiloreitis, this limited edition of bottles invites on a journey into the past. The bottles feature distinctive patchwork-style patterns. Inspired by seven decades, they reflect and distinguish different fashions: "Jeans & Jeanius" icons for the 1950s, Hippies & Positive Vibes for the 1960s, Disco Mood for the 1970s, Bright & Playful Colours for the 1980s, Fab Fashion for the 1990s, Tech for the 2000s and Trends for the 2010s. This kind of retrospective design demonstrates a level of quality which has remained unchanged since the product was first launched.

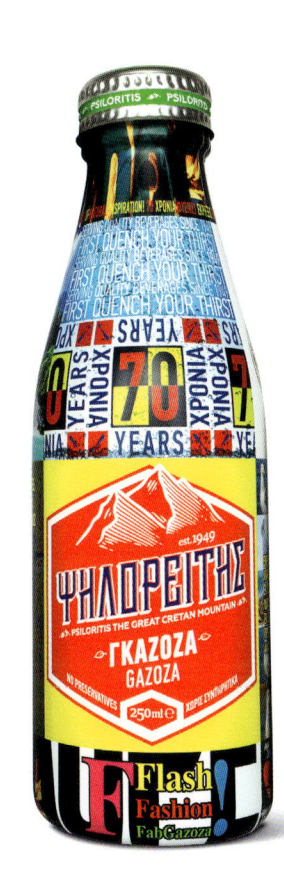

STUBBORN SODA

[Beverage Packaging]

Bold typography and striking colours were used for this brand refresh, which was developed to be applied in the concept for the packaging, the online presence and at the point of sale. A letterpress-like type gives the design a modern editorial aesthetic. The three flavours – Black Cherry Tarragon, Agave Vanilla Cream Soda and Classic Root Beer – are represented by non-primary, complementary colour blocks which reflect the unexpected combinations of ingredients. The alignment of the name intentionally mismatches the horizon line on the can as a subtle nod to the brand's stubborn ethos.

Client
PepsiCo
New York, USA

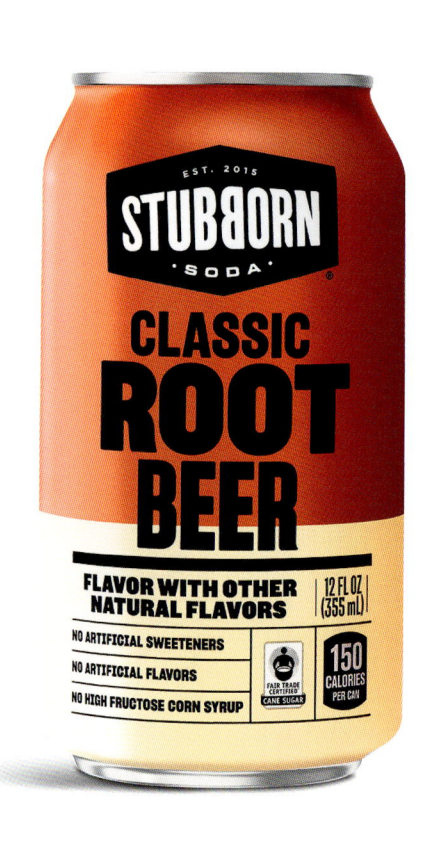

Design
PepsiCo Design & Innovation
New York, USA

Advertising	Packaging Design	Fair Stands	Retail Design	Red Dot: Junior Award	Designer Profiles	Index
288	318	494	516	544	614	674

Cold.t

[Beverage Packaging]

Iced tea brand Cold.t wants to raise its profile with a new and fresh design. The word mark with the memorable and independent name is presented in the typical Racing Green colour used by the manufacturer and in the modified typeface Bw Gradual. The ingredients for the three different iced tea blends are shown on the packaging using modern illustrations. Their fresh colours are reminiscent of aromatic herbs, young vegetables, sweet berries and juicy fruit. The beverage cartons are friendly to the environment and resealable what makes them ideal for being used on the go.

Client
J.J.Darboven GmbH & Co. KG
Hamburg, Germany

Design
Peter Schmidt Group
Hamburg, Germany

Project Team
Robert Bork (Design Director)
Katharina Geyer (Senior Designer)
Patrick Bädje (Junior Designer)
Laura Saramok (Junior Designer)

→ Designer profile on page 665

H2Om

[Sustainable Packaging]

Client
Omdesign
Matosinhos, Portugal

Design
Omdesign
Matosinhos, Portugal

→ Designer profile on page 656

Advertising	Packaging Design	Fair Stands	Retail Design	Red Dot: Junior Award	Designer Profiles	Index
288	318	494	516	544	614	674

A Portuguese design studio has created this gift package for toasting to 2020 with clients and partners. The recycled cardboard box originally contains a bottle of brandy (aguardente). However, as the designers are committed to sustainability, recipients are invited to reuse the elegant glass container for water (água). An hourglass in the cork is used as a reminder that water is a finite resource. When the bottle is pulled out, the cut-outs in the outer packaging provide aesthetic views, which give an impressive taste of the agency's creativity.

Preface	Red Dot: Agency of the Year	Brands	Brand Design & Identity	Corporate Design & Identity	Annual Reports
4	6	18	90	202	260

iRoman

[Beverage Packaging]

Client
iRoman (Shenzhen) Co., Ltd.
Shenzhen, China

Design
KL&K Design
Shenzhen, China

Project Team
Hong Ko (Creative Director)
Dayong Zhang (Designer)
Chengxi Hu (Designer)
Jie Zhang (Designer)
Peifang Li (Designer)
Guibin Zhuang (Illustrator)

368

Advertising	**Packaging Design**	Fair Stands	Retail Design	Red Dot: Junior Award	Designer Profiles	Index
288	318	494	516	544	614	674

iRoman is a mineral water and the design of its bottles is targeted at the youth of Generation Z. The 350 ml bottle is on the theme of love. It is decorated with half of a heart in different patterns – two halves together make up a whole. The patterns can be combined at will and animated messages can be initiated by using an AR scan. The large 520 ml bottles are designed around the motto of sport. They feature numbers to avoid the risk of mixing up bottles. In addition, several numbers can be combined to create digital Chinese words. For example, "520" means "I Love U".

Kuanzhai Mineral Water

[Beverage Packaging]

This mineral water comes from the Chengdu Plain. It is sourced from a very deep spring and is rich in strontium, on account of its rareness also described as "Giant Panda in Water", an animal which symbolises something quite rare itself. The design of the bottle is reflective of this analogy. On the front, there is a label with brand and product information while the back bears the image of a panda. The image can vary depending on the refraction of the light or the magnification. The result is a differing appearance which expresses fun and creativity.

Client
Chengdu Kuanzhai
Food Investment Co., Ltd.
Chengdu, China

Design
Chengdu Kuanzhai
Food Investment Co., Ltd.
Chengdu, China

Project Team
Longjun Yuan (Creative Director)
Lei Zhao (Designer)
Ming He (Graphic Designer)
Bei Zhang (Photography)

LIFEWTR Series 7: Art through Technology

[Beverage Packaging]

LIFEWTR is a premium mineral water brand committed to advancing and showcasing sources of creativity. Every few months, a new series of bottles is launched which focuses on a unique aspect in art. This seventh series is dedicated to the interaction between art and technology. The assumption is that technology broadens the boundaries of possibilities within art and design, making art a more participatory experience. The series shines a spotlight on this cultural tension and on three emerging artists who are practising within this discipline.

Client
PepsiCo
New York, USA

Design
PepsiCo Design & Innovation
New York, USA

4Life Mineral Water
[Beverage Packaging]

Client
DOI CHAANG Coffee Original Co., Ltd.
Bangkok, Thailand

Design
Prompt Design
Bangkok, Thailand

Project Team
Somchana Kangwarnjit
(Head of Advertising)
Nuttawuth Luengwatthanakul
(Graphic Design)

| Advertising | **Packaging Design** | Fair Stands | Retail Design | Red Dot: Junior Award | Designer Profiles | Index |
| 288 | 318 | 494 | 516 | 544 | 614 | 674 |

The design of these water bottles shows colourful illustrations of creatures that live in or near the water, which is depicted using blue and white stripes. It plays with the beauty of the movements of waves, which exude a certain degree of fascination. For example, the flamingo flies over the water and casts a shadow. The tiger swims and the crocodile crawls through the water, with the different movements reflected by differing wavy lines. The images are a reminder that water serves to preserve all life and therefore needs to be protected – just like the source from which the water for this beverage brand comes.

Kiyotomo

[Packaging]

The key visual of this tea packaging combines a window motif with a Chinese character. The latter merges the signs for "sun" and "moon", and stands for "brightness". By integrating the logogram into a filigree, flower-shaped form, the packaging design conveys a homely atmosphere, or more precisely the notion of having a decent cup of tea by the window. Debossing, silver stamping and laser cutting is used to visualise light that shines through the tracery. The main colours indigo blue and silver grey exude calmness and serenity, while the colours of the sealing stickers reflect the different shades of the teas.

Client
Kiyotomo
New Taipei City, Taiwan

Design
Triangler Co., Ltd.
Taipei City, Taiwan

Project Team
Chun-Yao Huang (Art Direction)
Chi-Yao Tang (Art Direction)
Yi Wang (Graphic Design)
Hsin-Hui Chen (Graphic Design)
Hsiang-Chia Wu (Account Management)

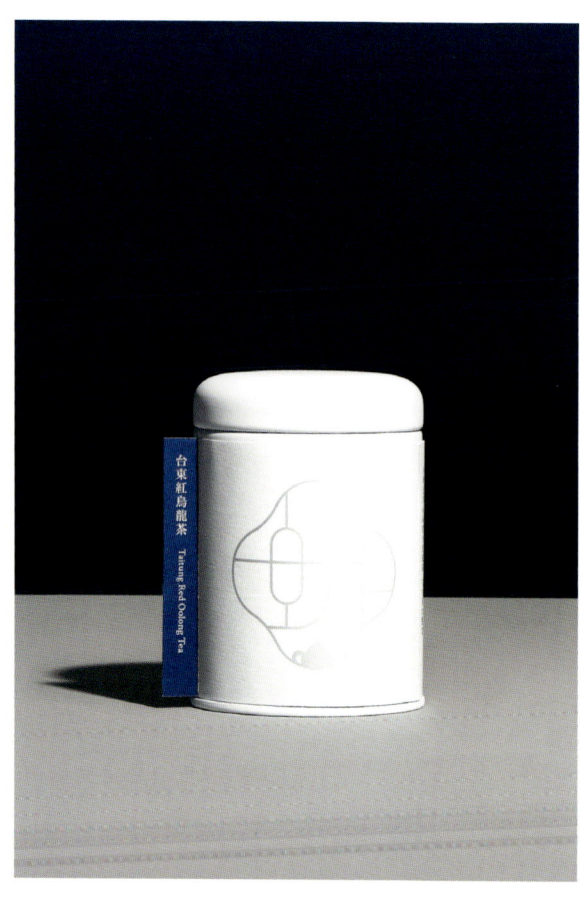

Jardin Class

[Packaging]

The motto for the design of these coffee bags is "Strange Garden", which is realised using illustrations of animals and plants, while photographs are deliberately not used. Instead, the animals are transformed and anthropomorphised in various forms to express surreal and mysterious images. The packaging in the form of a four-sided bag contains an illustration on the front and on the back, while the side parts are designed using the representative colours and patterns of the respective country of origin of the coffee beans. This allows consumers to distinguish between the different varieties very easily.

Client
Jardin
Seoul, South Korea

Design
Jardin
Seoul, South Korea

Project Team
Hayeon Jang (Graphic Design)
Sukyeong Choi (Graphic Design)

A TWOSOME PLACE

[Packaging]

Client
A TWOSOME PLACE
Seoul, South Korea

Design
A TWOSOME PLACE Design Team
Seoul, South Korea
CFC
Seoul, South Korea

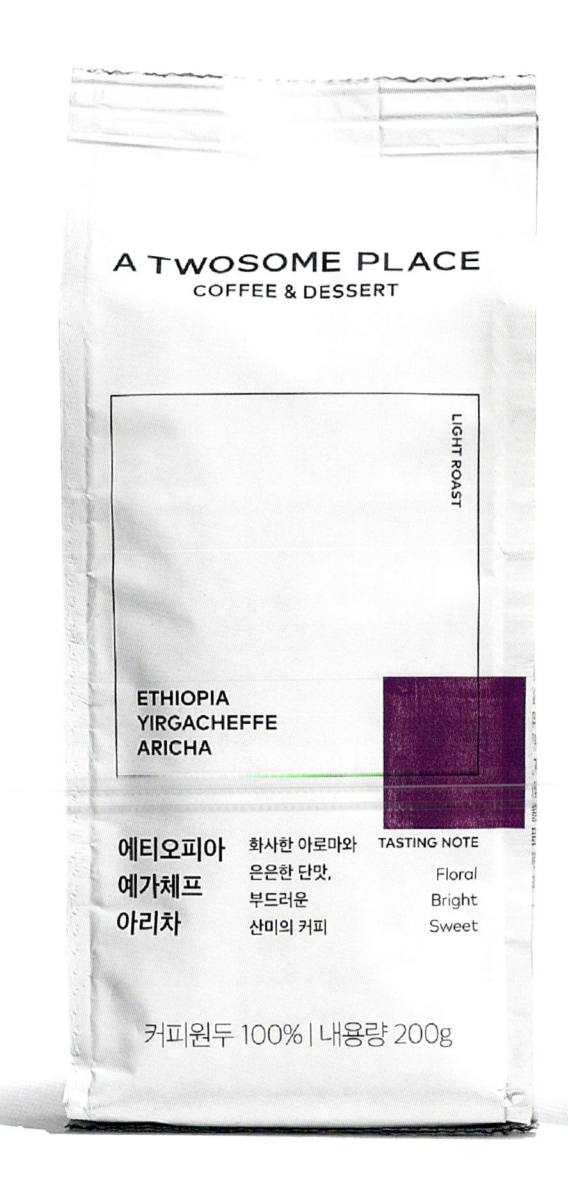

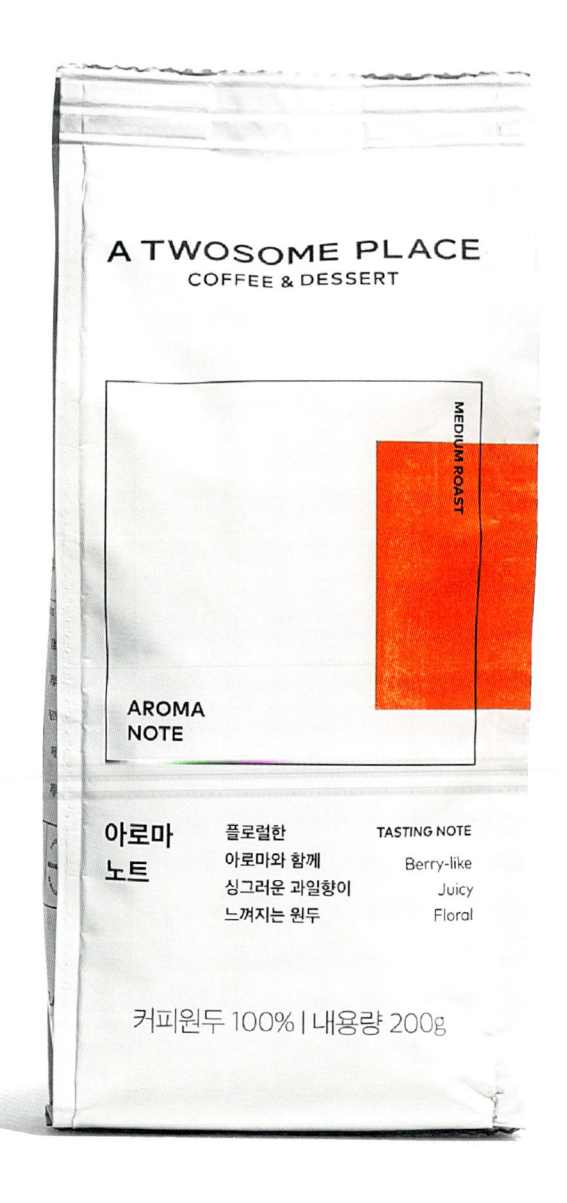

This coffee bean packaging has been created with the aim of meeting the principles of distinctiveness and consistency. Starting from a square at the centre of the bag, the graphics are based on an imaginary coordinate system. The horizontal axis shows the acidity of the coffee inside, while the vertical axis presents the degree of roasting. A striking colourblock square denotes the flavour. Thus, the geometrical design language characterises the brand, communicates the product's features in a transparent way and provides a variable packaging layout for the coffee range.

SOLVE Coffee – Coffee by Women

[Packaging]

SOLVE Coffee – Coffee by Women is a fair trade line distributed by a Korean non-profit foundation. The coffee packaging is eye-catching in a bid to raise awareness of the fact that women do most of the work in coffee production. Bold lettering, which takes up a third of the front, highlights the brand name. A brightly coloured section stands out from the black-and-white part of the packaging. With the stylised image of an African woman, it draws consumers' attention, giving the appearance a warm expression to make people empathise with the women involved.

Client
Beautiful Coffee
Seoul, South Korea

Design
Interbrand Seoul
Seoul, South Korea

Project Team
Uzin Hwang (Chief Creative Officer)
Claudia Yeong-Mi Kwon (Senior Designer)
Jackie Lim (Brand Designer)
Claire Choi (Brand Designer)
Huikyeong Yu (Motion Graphic Designer)

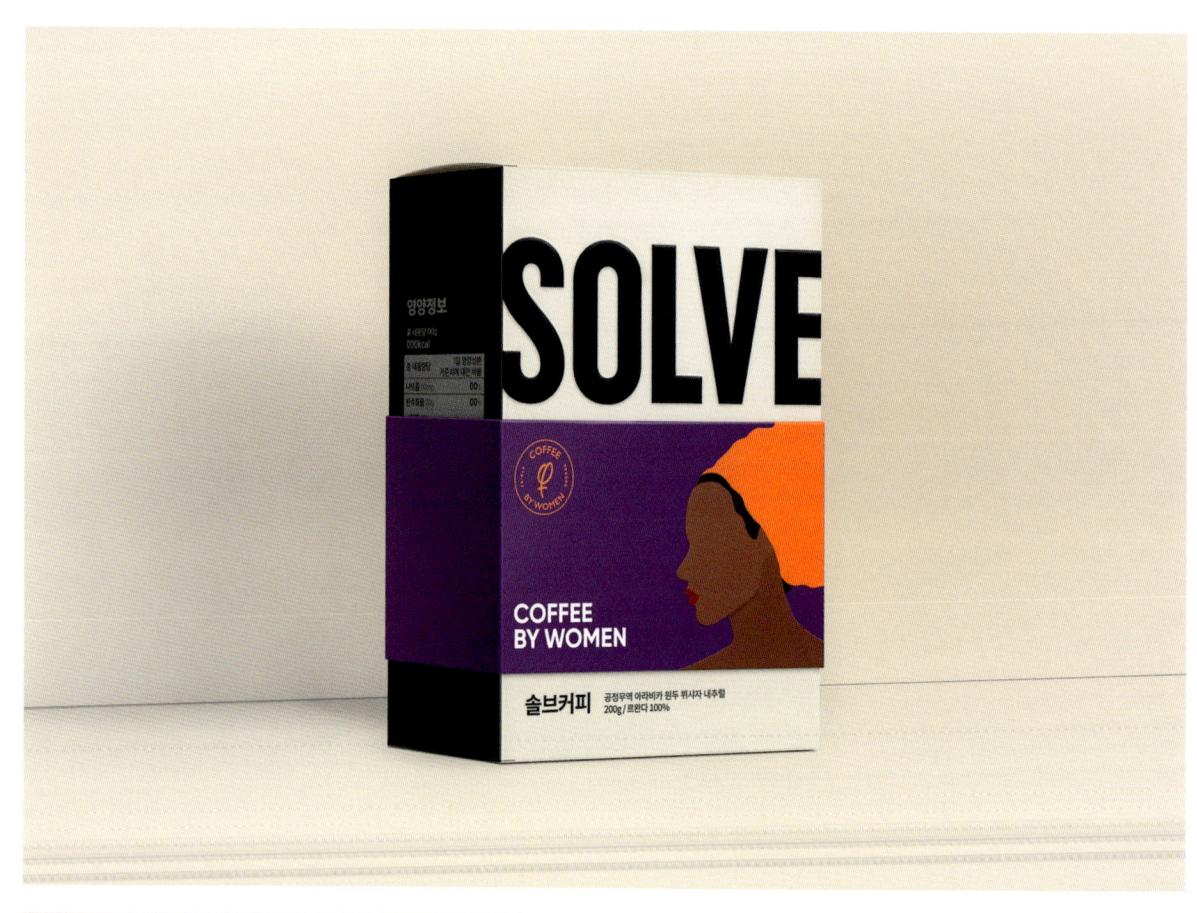

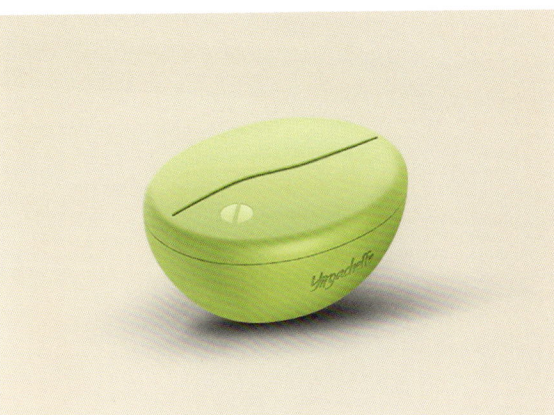

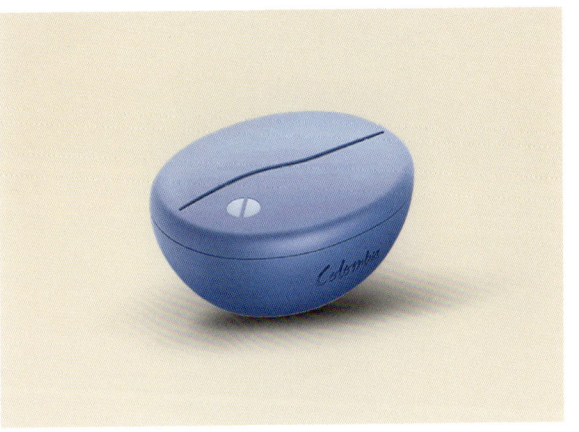

Advertising	Packaging Design	Fair Stands	Retail Design	Red Dot: Junior Award	Designer Profiles	Index
288	318	494	516	544	614	674

Coffee Beans

[Packaging]

In accordance with the "seed power" product concept, this packaging design, developed for the Chinese coffee brand metopia, draws attention to the single origin of the coffee beans as a special quality and product feature. The individual pods, made of food-grade plastic and shaped like a single coffee bean, come in different colours to indicate the country of origin of the beans inside. The 16-gram quantity per pack ensures the greatest possible freshness, ease of transport and allows users to make coffee without having to first weigh the beans.

Client
Shanghai Qiongqi
Enterprise Management Co., Ltd.
Shanghai, China

Design
Shanghai Mengji
Design Consulting Co., Ltd.
Shanghai, China

Project Team
Xia Xu (Creative Direction)
Lian Ning (Project Management)
Chen Jing (Designer)
Chen Yiwen (Designer)

Saturnbird Instant Coffee

[Packaging]

The handy packaging for Saturnbird Instant Coffee, an innovative brand which offers specialty coffee in powder form, is shaped like a mini takeaway cup. The small size is intended to appeal to consumers and to encourage them to imagine a wide range of scenarios in which they might enjoy the beverage on the move or at home. The different colours and numbers of the cups represent different flavours and product ranges. The brand has also launched a long-term recycling project which led to the return of more than one million mini cups at the end of the recent campaign.

Client
Changsha Saturnbird Coffee Co., Ltd.
Changsha, China

Design
Changsha Saturnbird Coffee Co., Ltd.
Changsha, China

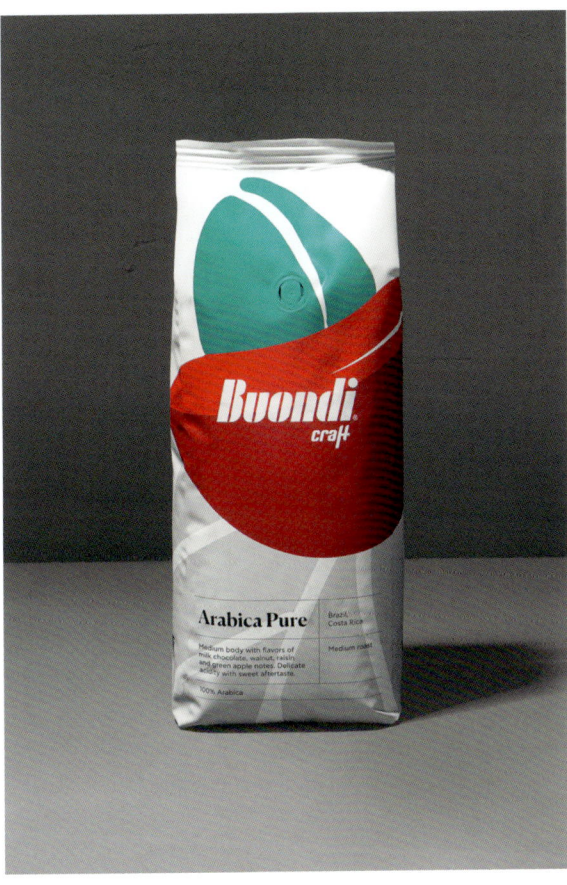

Buondi Craft

[Packaging]

The new brand strategy for Buondi Craft moves away from typical Italian coffee culture to an artisanal approach. The redesigned front of the packaging for the roasted, whole-bean coffees communicates the brand's dedication to quality, craftsmanship and origin through a visual journey that unfolds across the entire product series. The narrative follows the journey of the coffee bean from the flower on the coffee plant, to the cherry and finally the roasted coffee bean. A colourful pattern was used for the two single-origin coffee products in the series, inspired by the respective country of origin.

Client
Nestlé Hellas
Athens, Greece

Design
busybuilding
Athens, Greece

Project Team
Dimitris Gkazis (Creative Direction)
Vicky Nitsopoulou (Art Direction)
Effie Komninou (Strategic Planning)
Gina Mavrommati
(Account Management)
Sissy Karavia (Editorial Work)

Paris Baguette – Pocket Sand

[Food Packaging]

Client
SPC Group, Paris Croissant
Seoul, South Korea

Design
SPC Design Center
Seoul, South Korea

Project Team
Junnie Park (Creative Direction)
Inseong Song (Art Direction)
Daewook Do (Graphic Design)

Advertising	Packaging Design	Fair Stands	Retail Design	Red Dot: Junior Award	Designer Profiles	Index
288	318	494	516	544	614	674

The name of this product is an abbreviation of "pocket sandwich" and refers to a small white-bread sandwich with a jam filling. The packaging design focuses on the flavours of the filling. A transparent window in the shape of a fruit or a nut gives a tantalising glance of the product. It is decorated with images showing the respective ingredient and framed by jam which seems to flow through the window. The signature font underlines the affiliation with the brand. To create a visual link, the ivory-coloured bag is tuned to the colour of the sandwich.

Banbou Patisserie & Coffee Moon Cake

[Food Packaging]

Moon cake is a present given on different occasions in China. The packaging set for this speciality comprises a paper carrier bag as well as a square box containing four small individual boxes. A range of elaborate embossing and punching techniques are employed during production. The blue-and-white colour concept is supplemented, among other things, with gold-coloured stars adding an air of sophistication. They are in reference to the well-known lullaby "Twinkle, twinkle, little star", which parents sing to their children to forge a strong bond. In this way, the design shows that the moon cake is a gift for someone you love.

Client
Banbou Patisserie & Coffee
Dongguan, China

Design
Y.STUDIO
Shenzhen, China

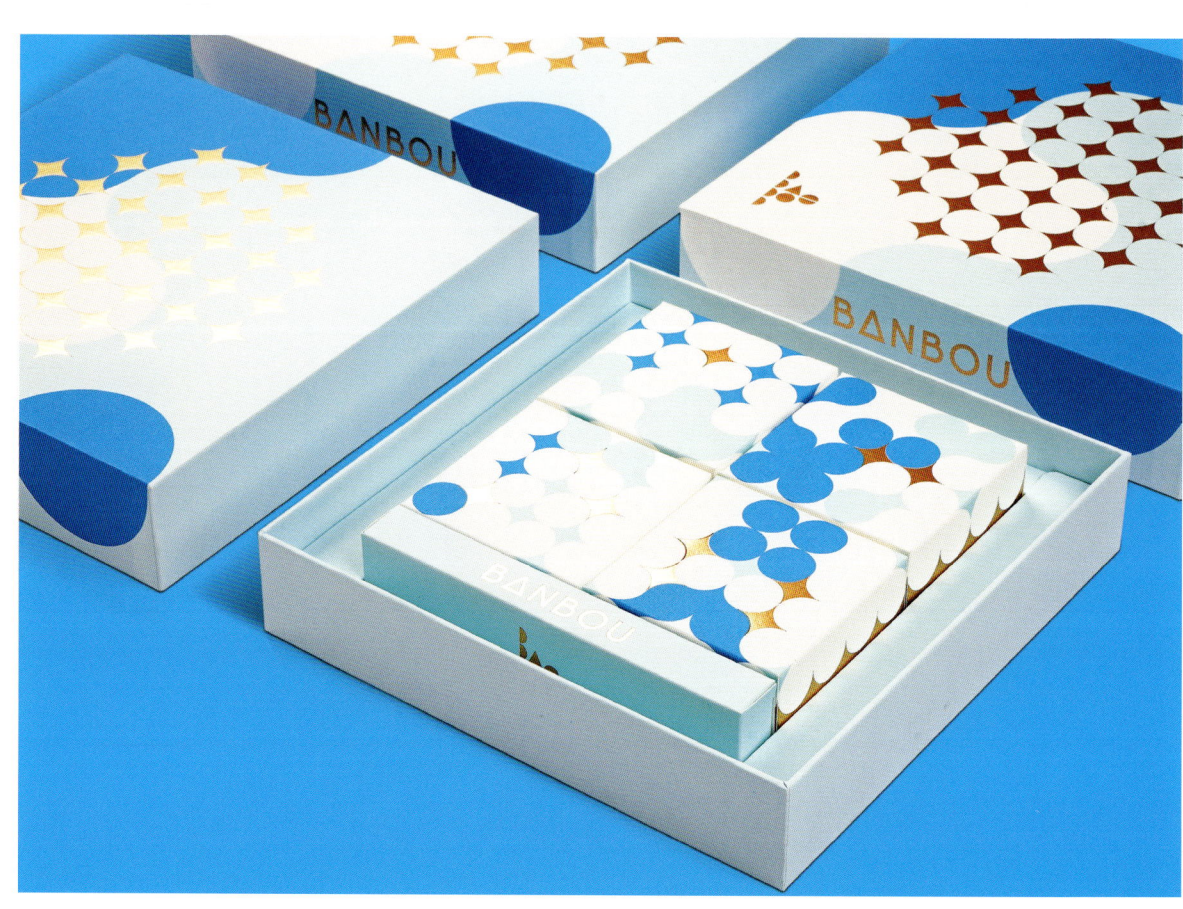

BIZEUN
Pure White Gift Set

[Food Packaging]

The colour white has played an important role in Korean culture since the Joseon dynasty. Pure white food with no particularly strong flavour is traditionally seen as a blessing, and having a breakfast of white rice cake at New Year is considered to bring well-being and a long life. This gift set reinterprets the local culture in an up-to-date manner. Rice cakes wrapped gracefully with a ribbon and seal exude a festive atmosphere, while the purist style of the boxes bridges the gap to contemporary taste. The recyclable material used as a wrapped fabric also adds a modern touch to the packaging.

Client
SPC Samlip
Seoul, South Korea

Design
SPC Samlip Design Team
Seoul, South Korea

Project Team
Seo Yoon Yang (Art Direction)
Yu Jeong Kim (Graphic Design)
Su Hee Lim (Graphic Design)

Preface	Red Dot: Agency of the Year	Brands	Brand Design & Identity	Corporate Design & Identity	Annual Reports
4	6	18	90	202	260

Paris Baguette – Traditional Dessert Series

[Food Packaging]

Client
SPC Group, Paris Croissant
Seoul, South Korea

Design
SPC Design Center
Seoul, South Korea

Project Team
Junnie Park (Creative Direction)
Inseong Song (Art Direction)
Semi Yoon (Graphic Design)
Jiin Bae (Graphic Design)
Taewoo Kim (Production)
Juhyeon Lee (Production)

Advertising	**Packaging Design**	Fair Stands	Retail Design	Red Dot: Junior Award	Designer Profiles	Index
288	318	494	516	544	614	674

In order to draw attention to a product line of pastries, this packaging features a new take on tradition. Using a gentle colour palette, lavish decoration and highlights with shiny gold, the design is a modern interpretation of French "savoir-vivre". Realistic pictures of the specialities inside are staged against a nostalgic backdrop, thus appealing to consumer desires. At the same time, the refined shape of the packaging emphasises the special care that has been taken in the preparation of the products.

Meegak Bakery

[Food Packaging]

Meegak Bakery sells mass-produced baked goods with high demands on quality. With transparent surfaces, the packaging design emphasises the image of the pastry itself while reducing graphic elements. The packaging thus establishes a link to key values like honesty and trustworthiness. In order to remind customers that the products originate from nature and have healthy ingredients, the packs also feature wheat ears in a decorative, minimalistic style. The product name adopts an appealing style by rounded angles added to the brand frame.

Client
SPC Samlip
Seoul, South Korea

Design
SPC Samlip Design Team
Seoul, South Korea

Project Team
SPC Samlip Design Team:
Seoyoon Yang (Graphic Design)
Yujeong Kim (Graphic Design)
Soyeong Kim (Graphic Design)
Kyungeun Seo (Graphic Design)

Studio Kinjo:
Inhyuk Jo (Graphic Design)

Anjuna Ice Pops

[Food Packaging]

Anjuna Ice Pops are available in six different flavours and the desire to spread the main message that "Summer is a lifestyle". The packaging is decorated with colour illustrations centred around the theme of summer: there are people at the beach, cycling in the park or taking a relaxing break in a hammock. It features also characters enjoying an ice pop without any feelings of remorse or guilt, since the popsicles are vegan and some varieties are even sugar free. The packaging is made from bio-degradable materials to promote sustainability.

Client
Anjuna Ice Pops
Budapest, Hungary

Design
DekoRatio Branding & Design Studio
Budapest, Hungary

Project Team
Szandra Mészáros (Graphic Design)
Dóra Novotny (Graphic Design)
Kevin Harald Campean (Photography)

Preface	Red Dot: Agency of the Year	Brands	Brand Design & Identity	Corporate Design & Identity	Annual Reports
4	6	18	90	202	260

00:00

[Food Packaging]

With the appearance of a pill, an iceberg and a flame, these unusual ice cream varieties confront consumers with current challenges posed by germs, glacial melting and forest fires. The message is emphasised by short texts printed on the wooden sticks. The product name "00:00" references a stopwatch. Since the digits indicate both the beginning and the end of a time period, they can be interpreted in two different ways: as a warning that the countdown for planet Earth has already ended or as a reminder that change is needed now to protect the environment.

Client
inDare Design Strategy Limited
Shenzhen, China

Design
inDare Design Strategy Limited
Shenzhen, China

Project Team
Jiarong Zeng
Fengming Chen
Yujie Chen
Junlong Yang
Yanhui Yan
Yichao Fan
Qingwei Li
Haiyong Wang
Qing Yu

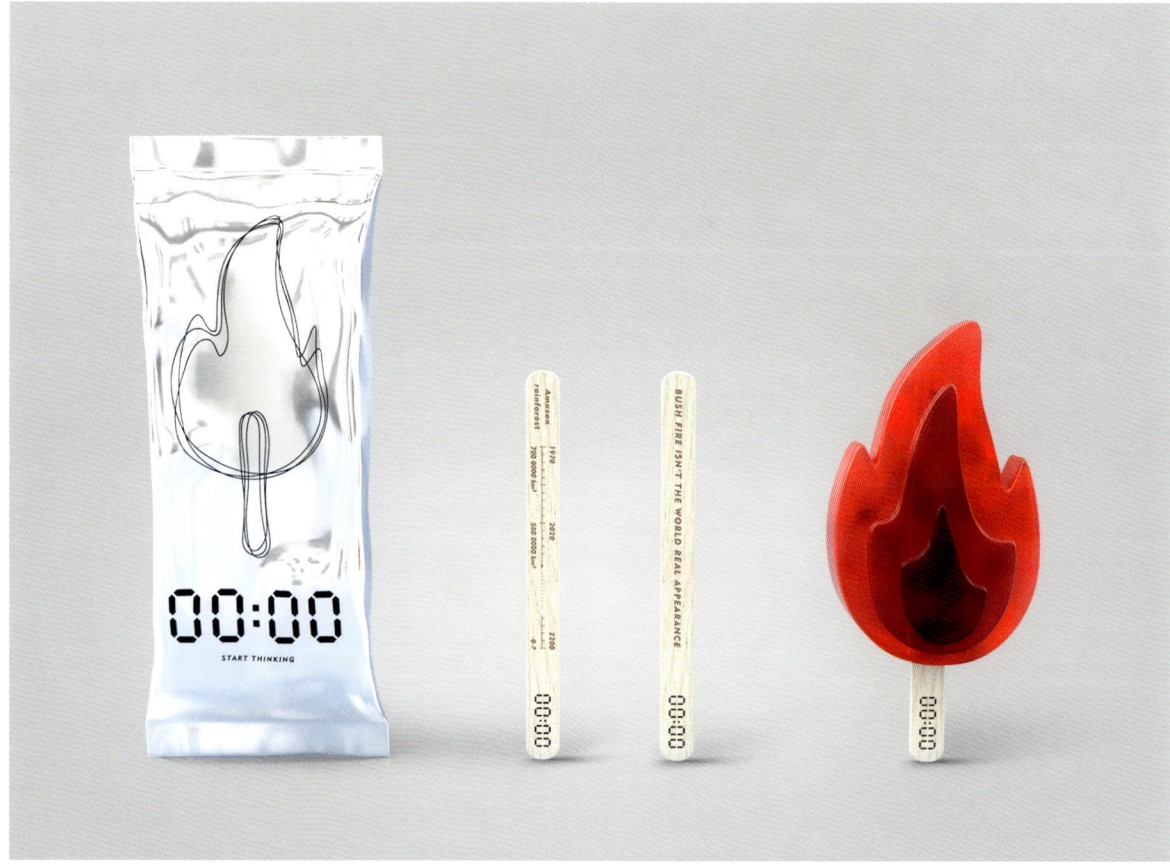

Megastar

[Food Packaging]

This concept enhances the packaging for a special product line of the Swiss ice-cream brand. Bright colours set against a dark background steer the consumer's attention to three original flavours. Simplicity on the left side of the packaging is combined with an appealing, more elaborate product shot to create a sense of harmony. By keeping the ice-cream at the centre of the composition and arranging magnified ingredients carefully around it, the already well-known brand is given a modern and sophisticated touch.

Client
Midor AG
Meilen, Switzerland

Design
ARD Design Switzerland
Vevey, Switzerland

Project Team
Alexandre Guignard (Art Direction)
Micael Rochat (Graphic Design)
Dylan Abt (Graphic Design)
Evelyne Koelbl Urano
(Project Coordination)

→ Designer profile on page 622

IDÜLL Ice Cream

[Food Packaging]

IDÜLL (idyll) is an ice cream brand produced for the Estonian market. Its packaging design is informed by Scandinavian restraint and makes reference to the art movements of suprematism and constructivism, which were popular in the 1920s when the first independent Estonian Republic was founded. The design also aims to communicate traditional values of Estonians and the beauty of their country by using photographs of Estonian houses and scenery. The matt white background gives the packaging a modern premium touch. Using materials which are as light and recyclable as possible, the goal is still to ensure the product is stored safely.

Client
Unilever
Tallinn, Estonia

Design
DPJN, Diena Pirms Janu Nakts
Riga, Latvia

Advertising	Packaging Design	Fair Stands	Retail Design	Red Dot: Junior Award	Designer Profiles	Index
288	318	494	516	544	614	674

Protami

[Food Packaging]

The protein ice cream Protami is a sweet snack for athletes as well as for all those who are interested in a calorie-conscious or gluten-free diet. On the packaging, bold numbers have been placed next to stacked ingredients to highlight the low count of calories. Small pieces of chocolate, nuts or slices of fruit appear to float above the ice cream scoop, creating an impression of lightness. The concept of the colour scheme combines the text and the images into a harmonious whole. Moreover, a colour-matched flash points out unmistakably that the product does not contain any added sugar.

Client
Promayro Food GmbH
Munich, Germany

Design
WIN CREATING IMAGES
Berlin, Cologne, Aachen, Germany
Zug, Switzerland

Das Gute Eis

[Food Packaging]

This design concept for a new ice cream with two varieties, vanilla and chocolate, primarily made from regional quality ingredients focuses the brand on global responsibility. The slogan "Ein Löffelchen für Dich. Ein Löffel für die Welt." (A small spoon for you, a spoon for the world.) and the design of the globe-shaped ice cream scoop communicates pleasure on the one hand, and social and ecological responsibility on the other. In adherence with the slogan, a share of the proceeds from the brand will be made available to support training projects, giving farmers the opportunity to gain further qualifications.

Client
MOS GmbH
Nürtingen, Germany

Design
in medias rees
Stuttgart, Germany

Project Team
Simone Rees (Creative Design)

→ Designer profile on page 644

King

[Food Packaging]

The King brand has been sold on the South East European market as an ice cream bar for many years. Now it is also available as an ice cream dessert in a cup which comes in four different flavours: pistachio, caramel, vanilla and chocolate. The brand is no longer restricted to retail; it is now also offered for sale as a Horeca product. The packaging features a noticeable, playful yet modern design. A stylised shape of a crown is placed underneath the name "King". This expresses that consuming the ice cream turns the moment into a "regal experience".

Client
LEDO plus
Zagreb, Croatia

Design
Studio Sonda
Vizinada, Croatia

Project Team
Jelena Fiskus (Creative Direction)
Sean Poropat (Creative Direction)
Aleksandar Zivanov (Graphic Design)
Mladen Gvozden (Account Management)

Preface	Red Dot: Agency of the Year	Brands	Brand Design & Identity	Corporate Design & Identity	Annual Reports
4	6	18	90	202	260

beleaf
[Food Packaging]

Under the brand name beleaf, a Swiss dairy company sells a range of almond and oat-based milk substitutes. The packaging uses a vibrant and adventurous imagery to capture the spirit of a health-conscious, vegan attitude. The colourful illustrations visualise the ingredients embedded in the midst of a green jungle. By striving to bring some exoticism to supermarket shelves, the packaging appeals to the consumers' sense of discovery. The brand appearance is rounded off by a succinct name and a carefully crafted logo which highlights the plant-based nature of the products.

Client
Emmi Management AG
Lucerne, Switzerland

Design
WIN CREATING IMAGES
Berlin, Cologne, Aachen, Germany
Zug, Switzerland

Like a bird

[Food Packaging]

This packaging design for cereal grains, such as special kind of rice or quinoa, focuses on a health-conscious group of consumers who watch their figure and eat "like a bird". Interpreting this turn of phrase literally, the packaging provides the relevant look with a graphic bird motif in bright colours. The spout of the cardboard box also opens like a bird's beak. By consistently exploiting similarities, a convenient packaging solution is created which stands out on the supermarket shelf with a good pinch of humour.

Client
LLC Polezzno
Moscow, Russia

Design
OTVETDESIGN
Saint Petersburg, Russia

Project Team
Vladimir Fedoseev (Creative Director)
Arina Yushkevich (Art Director)

SO NUTS

[Food Packaging]

SO NUTS is an on-the-go snack launched with the support of two popular chocolate brands. The new product is staged in a contemporary style. Matching the brand's positioning, the packaging displays a balanced ratio of chocolate and nuts. Appetising pictures emphasise the quality of the ingredients, while the wordplay in the brand name is highlighted through white spot colour. Warm colours help to convey a positive mood. By means of a clear hierarchy of information, product information is effectively combined with an incentive to buy.

Client
Chocolats Camille Bloch S.A.
Courtelary, Switzerland

Design
ARD Design Switzerland
Vevey, Switzerland

Project Team
Stève Pierrehumbert (Art Direction)
Annick Baehler (Graphic Design)
Esther Colin-Benz (Project Coordination)

→ Designer profile on page 622

hilo Life

[Food Packaging]

This trendy snack line has been specially created for the growing number of carb-counting consumers. The products were only introduced to retail after they had been launched digitally. In order to celebrate the fun of snacking and associate the brand with joy and ease, the packaging design uses cheerful colours, comic elements and pop art imagery. A distinctive mix of different typefaces also helps to create a youthful aesthetic. The nutritional information, which is crucial for the consumer, is cleverly integrated into the layout without being obtrusive.

Client
PepsiCo
New York, USA

Design
PepsiCo Design & Innovation
New York, USA

El Origen

[Food Packaging]

El Origen vegan chips are made from manioc or plantains and are produced in Ecuador under fair conditions. They are also organic, gluten-free and made without palm oil. The brand's main sales arguments are staged by an innovative packaging design, which appeals to the consumers' desire to discover new things when shopping. Papercut icons and keywords are designed in a deliberately imperfect manner and presented with bright colour contrasts. This results in a special mix of modern and ethnic styles which clearly aims for a powerful and lasting shelf impact.

Client
el origen food GmbH
Hamburg, Germany

Design
Peter Schmidt Group
Hamburg, Germany

Project Team
Robert Bork (Design Director)
Nicole Wenneborg (Designer)
Lisa Stehle (Senior Designer)
Nina Whitley-Jones (Designer)

→ Designer profile on page 665

Advertising	Packaging Design	Fair Stands	Retail Design	Red Dot: Junior Award	Designer Profiles	Index
288	318	494	516	544	614	674

Off the Eaten Path

[Food Packaging]

The design strategy for Off the Eaten Path is to satisfy an aspirational consumer group on the lookout for new culinary experiences. The brand offers plant-based snacks with unexpected blends of real vegetables like chickpeas, black beans and peas. The packaging brings to life the motto "Snacks for the curious" by combining close-ups of fresh ingredients with a photo of the finished product. Harmonising different typefaces, the graphic design remains true to the approach of surprising customers in a positive way. A striking colour, which stands for the flavour, rounds out the visual identity.

Client
PepsiCo
New York, USA

Design
PepsiCo Design & Innovation
New York, USA

Ricond Dried Fruits

[Food Packaging]

Ricond sweets with whole dried fruit and nuts come in a box with two pull-out compartments, storing the candies on different layers and giving the consumer a special unboxing experience. In line with the fancy box, the layout has been worked out in detail. Lovingly drawn illustrations are combined with water-colour shades that visualise the flavour of dried fruit. In order to further enhance the product, the packaging uses a relief stamping with gold foil. Bright corners in different colours make the item easy to identify.

Client
CJSC Ecotechnics
Kyiv, Ukraine

Design
iden.team branding agency
Kyiv, Ukraine

Project Team
Maria Sencha (Creative Direction)
Kate Lebid (Art Direction)
Inna Malysh (Graphic Design)
Alexandra Shvetsova (Graphic Design)
Alice Shein (Artwork)
Maria Chinkina (Project Management)

Advertising	Packaging Design	Fair Stands	Retail Design	Red Dot: Junior Award	Designer Profiles	Index
288	318	494	516	544	614	674

Jeju Premium Tarts
[Food Packaging]

Jeju Island is a popular holiday destination in Korea on account of its natural beauty and its tourist attractions. Local impressions mark the packs of Jeju Premium Tarts, pastries in a range of five different flavours, which are sold as a souvenir. The outer box stages the ingredient that gives taste to the tarts against the background of the island landscape. By linking charming views to the brand's image, the packaging concept reflects the need felt by many travellers to share holiday memories with others in an original and memorable way.

Client
SPC Samlip
Seoul, South Korea

Design
SPC Samlip Design Team
Seoul, South Korea

Project Team
Seoyoon Yang (Art Direction)
Hyeyoung Choi (Artwork)

Preface	Red Dot: Agency of the Year	Brands	Brand Design & Identity	Corporate Design & Identity	Annual Reports
4	6	18	90	202	260

Greens&Yellows

[Food Packaging]

Greens&Yellows is a range of handmade frozen vegan meals made following Cretan recipes. Inspired by the natural ingredients, the design concept conveys a sense of nature, innocence and honesty. It creates associations with typical Cretan experiences in a bid to raise the profile of the brand. The design combines a photo realistic illustration which depicts the product with an abstract environment comprising clear shapes and colours. This combination achieves a visual balance. The logo, like the meals, is handmade and shows the brand name in a contemporary style.

Client
Kiriakaki Antonia SA
Heraklion, Greece

Design
Lazy snail Design
Copenhagen, Denmark

Project Team
Ioanna Drakaki (Head of Design)
Eleni Pavlaki (Creative Director)
Serafim Stroubis (Senior Art Director)
Kostas Kiriakakis (Illustrator)
Christina Apostolidi (Brand Strategist)
Maro Tsagkaraki (Copywriter)

Advertising	Packaging Design	Fair Stands	Retail Design	Red Dot: Junior Award	Designer Profiles	Index
288	318	494	516	544	614	674

Supha Bee Farm Honey
[Food Packaging]

In view of the competitive Thai market for honey, the Supha Bee Farm brand introduces an unusual gift box. The outer packaging is inspired by a beehive frame. Appropriately, it is equipped with a paper honeycomb to protect the honey bottle inside. The reduced and aesthetically refined style of the packaging focuses on the key product values: natural, simple and beautiful. Furthermore, the elaborate design emphasises the quality of the content. A logo that plays with the brand initials "S" and "B" to create a bee-like shape rounds off the visual identity.

Client
Prompt Design
Bangkok, Thailand

Design
Prompt Design
Bangkok, Thailand

Aranya Jinshanling Honey

[Food Packaging]

Client
Chengde Aranya Real Estate
Development Co., Ltd.
Chengde, China

Design
Minuage Design
Qinhuangdao, China

Project Team
Chang Shi (Graphic Design)

→ Designer profile on page 649

Advertising	Packaging Design	Fair Stands	Retail Design	Red Dot: Junior Award	Designer Profiles	Index
288	318	494	516	544	614	674

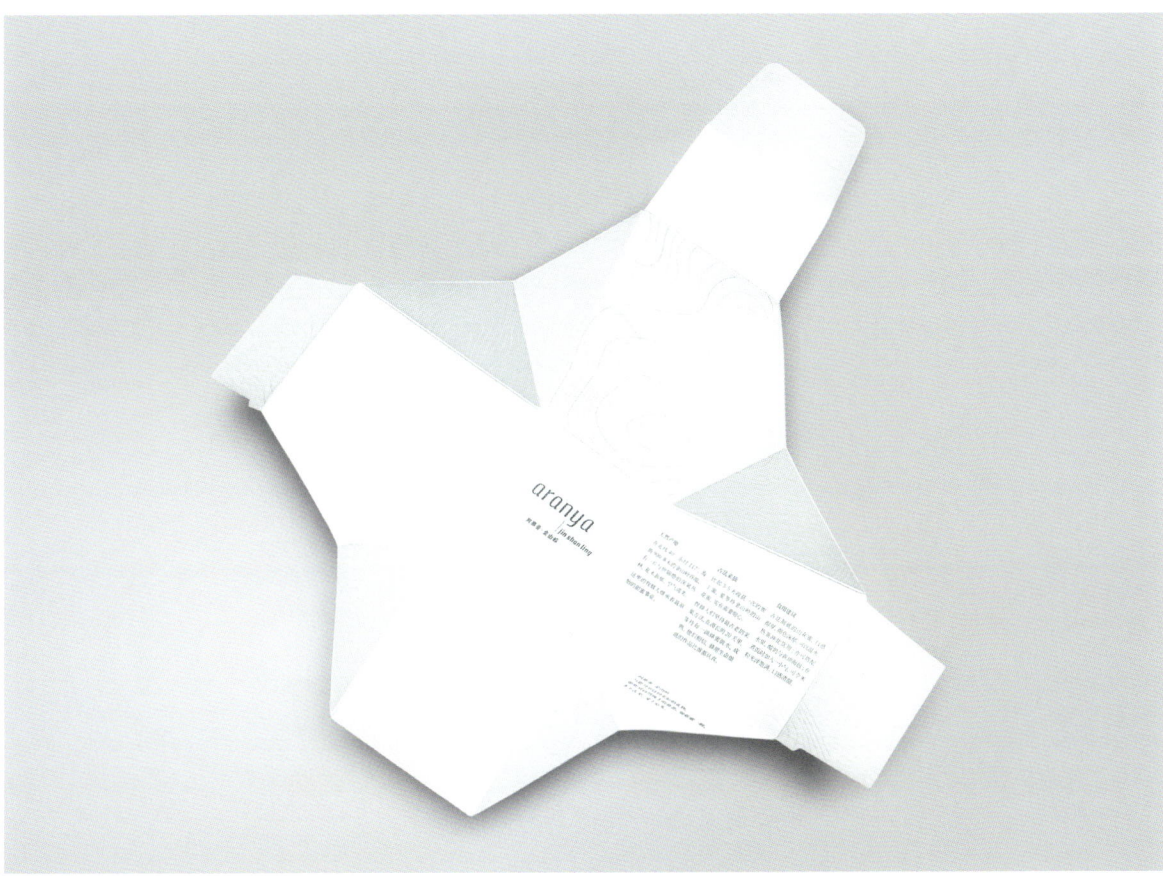

These two honey products come from the Jinshanling mountain area, where the client's exclusive and environmentally friendly estate is located. The name is written in italics and serves as a source of inspiration for the oblique shape of the white outer packaging. Made applying an adhesive-free folding technique, it conveys the eco-friendly brand value. An embossed pattern on the outer packaging resembles the region's mountain ranges in shape. This shape is repeated on the labels of the honey jars, giving consumers the feeling of being surrounded by nature.

Logothetis

[Food Packaging, Beverage Packaging]

The image of Mother Nature as the source of the Creation dates back to the culture of ancient Greece. The packaging concept takes up this image to portray the food and beverages from Logothetis Farm in Greece as unique gifts from Mother Nature. Its classic design is not only characterised by a strong identity but also has a playful side to it. Cute illustrations and soft pastel colours make sure the products are easily recognisable and exude an atmosphere of warmth, which serves as a welcoming message for the potential customer.

Client
Logothetis Farm
Zakynthos, Greece

Design
A.S. Advertising
Athens, Greece

Project Team
Antonia Skaraki (Art Direction)
Andreas Deskas (Graphic Design)
Valia Alousi (Graphic Design)
Evri Makridis (Graphic Design)
Sotiria Theodorou (Text)

→ Designer profile on page 618

Chaozhou Sanbao

[Food Packaging]

Chaozhou Sanbao is a group of three products from the Chaozhou region which are extracted from plants in that area, for example kumquat. These plants are known to have beneficial and protective effects on the human organism. Inspired by local crafts, the packaging evokes natural simplicity. The illustrations which portray the respective main ingredient and the typography are created using manual woodcut engraving. Both the illustrations and the typography are then applied to handmade paper applying manual screen printing. The paper is used for the labels as well as for the cover of the outer packaging.

Client
Shenzhen Yiyitong Trading Co., Ltd.
Shenzhen, China

Design
Shenzhen Fire Wolf
Graphic Design Co., Ltd.
Shenzhen, China

Project Team
Yang Zhen (Design Director)
Hu Yubin (Designer)
Lin Yiqing (Designer)
Li Feng (Designer)
Su Xiyu (Designer)

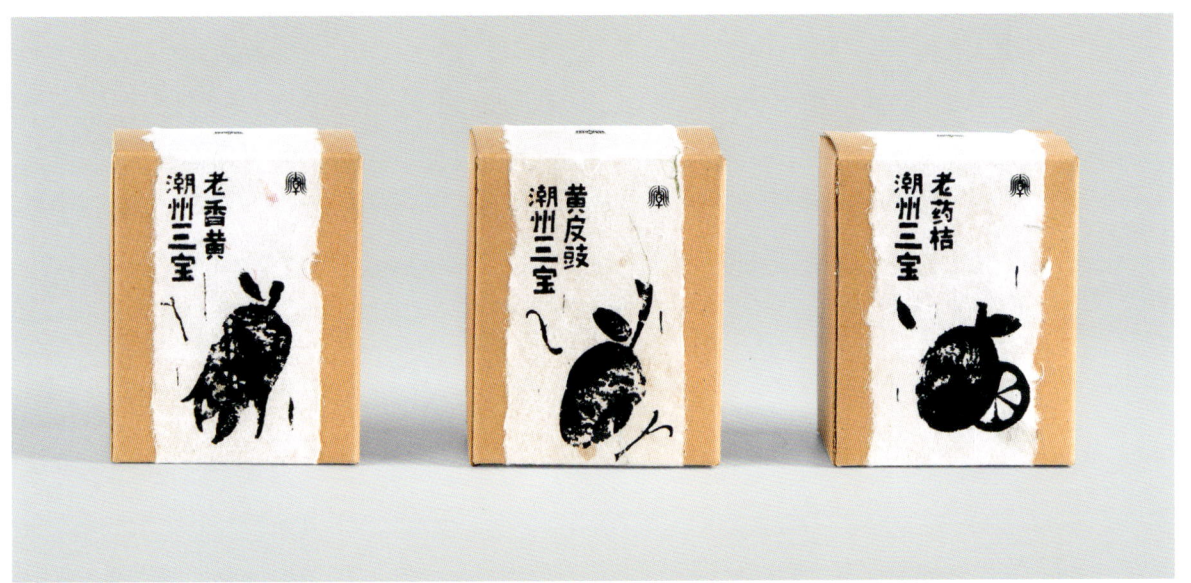

Smart Time – Premium

[Food Packaging]

The link to nature is a key element of this packaging concept for premium snacks. In tune with the brand's nature-oriented approach, plant shapes and light-coloured wood in the outer packaging reference the natural source of the dried fruit and nuts. The bright shade of orange used in the carrier handle on the box is an eye-catcher, while the cut-out shapes give an enticing glimpse of the snack tins inside. Featuring an animal motif with an elaborate graphic design, each tin reflects the value of the product and offers the possibility of immediate emotional attachment.

Client
COFCO
Beijing, China

Design
Beijing Perfect Point Design
Beijing, China

Project Team
Jeff Wu (Creative Direction)
Yao Li (Graphic Design)
Juanying Zheng (Graphic Design)

→ Designer profile on page 659

Oranginal

[Food Packaging]

Storytelling is at the heart of the visual concept for the Oranqinal packaging. Selected navel oranges from western Hubei are presented in woven bamboo baskets featuring a nostalgic design. Like the containers, the wood-cut style graphics on the labelling are inspired by Chinese handicraft. They show the process of traditional fruit-farming in artful detail. The ends of the removable banderole are shaped like fingers in reference to the farmers' hands holding oranges. Through its handmade charm and elaborate design, the packaging pays special tribute to the natural product inside.

Client
inDare Design Strategy Limited
Shenzhen, China

Design
inDare Design Strategy Limited
Shenzhen, China

Project Team
Jiarong Zeng
Fengming Chen
Yujie Chen
Junlong Yang
Yanhui Yan
Shuzhuan Huang
Haiyong Wang
Guoxiang Zheng
Qing Yu
Mengxuan Cai

Golden Pinghu

[Food Packaging]

Fresh, pure and ecological are the keywords characterising the agricultural products from the Golden Pinghu brand, which include asparagus, watermelon and mushrooms. For the design concept, this results in the following features: refreshing, beautiful and exquisite. Special product requirements are also taken into account. For example, the packaging design for asparagus uses a staggered, large opening design in fresh white and green colours. This ensures the ventilation and freshness of the asparagus, has an intuitive display effect and is also inexpensive.

Client
Pinghu Farmer Cooperative Economic Organization Union
Jiaxing, China

Design
Zhejiang Gongshang University
Hangzhou, China

Project Team
Ying Gao (Designer)
Kan Zhao (Designer)
Kaihao Zhu (Designer)

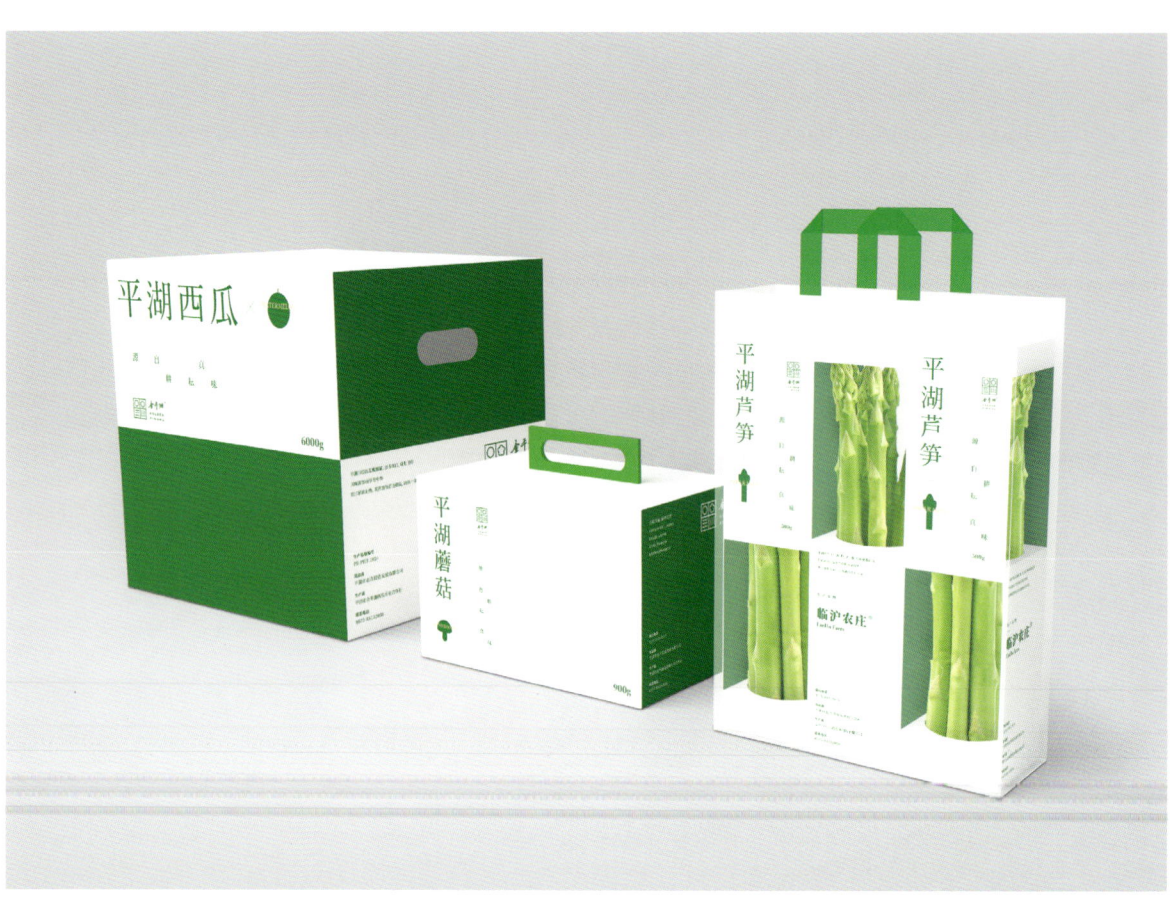

Huaxishangpin – Chilli

[Food Packaging]

The zany packaging design for this chilli sauce from Guizhou is marked by an exaggerated style. The jars and jute bags for the sauce feature a single red motif composed from simple geometric forms and meshed together using a white background. In the eyes of the consumer, the image quickly assimilates to show a chilli-shaped face with eyes wide open, mouth agape and dishevelled hair. This striking image succinctly conveys the fiery spice of the chilli peppers. The bold presentation of the brand prevents any confusion with similar products, even from a distance.

Client
Shenzhen Qansfough
Package Design Co., Ltd.
Shenzhen, China

Design
Shenzhen Qansfough
Package Design Co., Ltd.
Shenzhen, China

Project Team
Jun Li (Creative Direction)

Preface	Red Dot: Agency of the Year	Brands	Brand Design & Identity	Corporate Design & Identity	Annual Reports
4	6	18	90	202	260

Hokkaido Mackerel
[Food Packaging]

In Japan, it is customary to give gifts to close friends when the season changes. This design for tinned mackerels turns what is normally a cheap, commonplace product into a luxury gift item. The product's image is transformed by using, for example, "washi", a high-quality Japanese paper, for the label of the tin. Japanese gold foil embossing is used for the typography, developed in consideration of production lines and costs. It gives the containers a sophisticated, premium appearance in analogy to the claim to design a mackerel tin which looks like a piece of jewellery.

Client
Norfre Foods Co., Ltd.
Hokkaido, Japan

Design
omdr Co., Ltd.
Tokyo, Japan

→ Designer profile on page 657

Avgoulakia

[Food Packaging]

The design of these egg boxes revolves around the colourful and vivid illustrations of three chicken characters. They are portrayed as heroines, with Captain Mahe representing free-range eggs, Madame Coco synonymous with organic eggs and Miss Nelly with barn-laid eggs. Their names and clothes were chosen specially for the Greek market. For example, the word "mahe" means "fight" or "battle" in Greek. Captain Mahe wears denim overalls and a red bandana, has tattoos on her left arm and epitomises the image of a rebel. The inside of the egg boxes includes games such as word-search puzzles.

Client
Avgoulakia
Athens, Greece

Design
A.S. Advertising
Athens, Greece

Project Team
Antonia Skaraki (Art Direction)
Andreas Deskas (Graphic Design)
Evri Makridis (Graphic Design)
Valia Alousi (Web Design)
Sotiria Theodorou (Text)

→ Designer profile on page 618

Plant Meat

[Food Packaging]

This stylish packaging design was created for artificial meat. To indicate that the package does not contain a real animal product, the illustration features only half of an animal, accompanied by the overlapping words of "plant" and "meat". Rich colours distinguish the different flavours. For example, yellow set against blue signifies chicken flavour, while red set against green denotes beef. The basic colour black, which is commonly associated with the opulence of a premium brand, further enhances the appearance.

Client
MYS Group Co., Ltd.
Dongguang, China

Design
MYS Group Co., Ltd.
Shenzhen, China

Slices of flesh

[Food Packaging]

As part of a rebranding process, these hearty meat snacks are presented in a rough and dazzling way. Many consumers who like to have this product with a beer do not like its looks. In this context, the packaging design tackles potential disgust head-on rather than to shy away from it. While the exaggerated style hints at posters for horror films, the product name stands out due to disarming honesty. By highlighting the essence of the product in an almost provocative way, the packaging challenges consumers and openly declares its intention to outdo competitors.

Client
LLC AMZ
Barnaul, Russia

Design
OTVETDESIGN
Saint Petersburg, Russia

Thai Wisdom Rice

[Food Packaging]

This packaging design pays tribute to the traditional rice growing in Thailand. In order to convey the high quality of jasmine rice to the customer, the image of a hand-carved sculpture, which illustrates the laborious steps in the cultivation process, has been integrated into a close-up view of a grain of rice. The large oval shape is easily recognisable and invites the beholder to explore the microcosm on the packaging in more depth. In an artful way, the motif suggests that the organic rice in the packaging has been produced with just as much attention to detail.

Client
Prompt Design
Bangkok, Thailand

Design
Prompt Design
Bangkok, Thailand

Srisangdao

[Food Packaging]

This organically produced rice draws attention to itself through packaging that specifically focuses on recycling. The die-formed carton is made from chaff, a natural by-product in rice production. The embossed shape, which looks like a grain of rice, the graphic lines and burnt-on labelling have both a visual and a tactile appeal for customers. With a mixture of rustic and refined elements, the earth-coloured box underlines the value of the local product. A small rice sack inside features matching printed lettering. Once the sack is empty, the package can be reused as a tissue box.

Client
Srisangdow Rice Mill Co., Ltd.
Roi Et, Thailand

Design
Prompt Design
Bangkok, Thailand

Project Team
Somchana Kangwarnjit
(Creative Direction)
Rutthawitch Akkachairin
(Graphic Design)

Big City Pizza

[Food Packaging]

Client
Nestlé Wagner GmbH
Nonnweiler-Otzenhausen, Germany

Design
Berndt+Partner Creality GmbH
Berlin, Germany

Project Team
Marketing Team Wagner:
Verena Hensel (Head of Marketing)
Susanne Knabe (Senior Brand Manager)
Bob Stigter (Brand Manager)

Design & Branding Team B+P:
Laura Schmale (Creative Director)
Alexandra Kalkowski (Art Director)
Marisa Francisco (Graphic Designer)
Viola Schindler (Graphic Designer)

Advertising	Packaging Design	Fair Stands	Retail Design	Red Dot: Junior Award	Designer Profiles	Index
288	318	494	516	544	614	674

With this packaging relaunch, the brand makes the transition from a large American-style pizza to a product inspired by all of the world's big cities. The innovative design responds to the expectations of a young target group which, above all else, likes to have fun, appreciates variety and wants to experience something exciting. The front of the pack represents a natural looking corrugated cardboard box, just like the ones used by pizza delivery services, which is torn open and offers a view of the appetisingly arranged content. The torn lid stands for urbanity and the lifestyle associated with it.

POWERBROT
Backmischung –
Für richtig gutes Brot!

[Food Packaging]

The packaging design for this baking mix communicates a unique taste and quality experience as well as the aim of contributing to healthy nutrition. Among other things, this is achieved through the name "Powerbrot" (power bread) and supported with easy-to-understand illustrations. The packaging shows a photograph of a baked bread with the addition of two drawn-on strong arms. The design is characterised by handcrafted elements such as scratched typography or freely drawn illustrations, which emphasise the theme of "baking bread yourself". To protect the environment, the material used is fully compostable.

Client
Biovegan GmbH
Bonefeld, Germany

Design
Susanne Schneider
Gieleroth, Germany

Advertising	Packaging Design	Fair Stands	Retail Design	Red Dot: Junior Award	Designer Profiles	Index
288	318	494	516	544	614	674

bakin'mix

[Food Packaging]

bakin'mix is a series of seven baking mixes for bread, cake and biscuits. The name is a combination of English and Croatian and means "baking mix" and "Grandma's mix", since the Croatian word for "Grandma" is "baka". This appealing name is complemented with the warm and hearty key visual, which shows the stylised image of the head of a grandmother formed out of the baking mix contained in the package. The name and the key visual create associations with a taste which only granny can provide. Vibrant colours are used in the packaging design in order to gain the best visibility on supermarket shelves.

Client
A1 d.o.o.
Rijeka, Croatia

Design
Reedesign Studio
Rijeka, Croatia

Project Team
Veronika Uravic Colak (Art Direction)

Bibigo Kimchi Pot

[Food Packaging]

With its contemporary packaging design, Bibigo Kimchi, which is available in four flavours, is targeting the younger generation in particular. In order to achieve this, vibrant colours are used and the labels on the pots are decorated with illustrations which inform consumers of the respective flavour while also adding an air of modernity. The concept takes account of the fact that the number of single-person households in Korea is increasing. The product is therefore available in smaller, compact pots rather than the customary large containers.

Client
CJ Cheiljedang
Seoul, South Korea

Design
CJ Cheiljedang
Seoul, South Korea

Project Team
Kangkook Lee
(Executive Creative Director)
Yuljoong Kim (Design)
Hyungkyung Choi (Design)

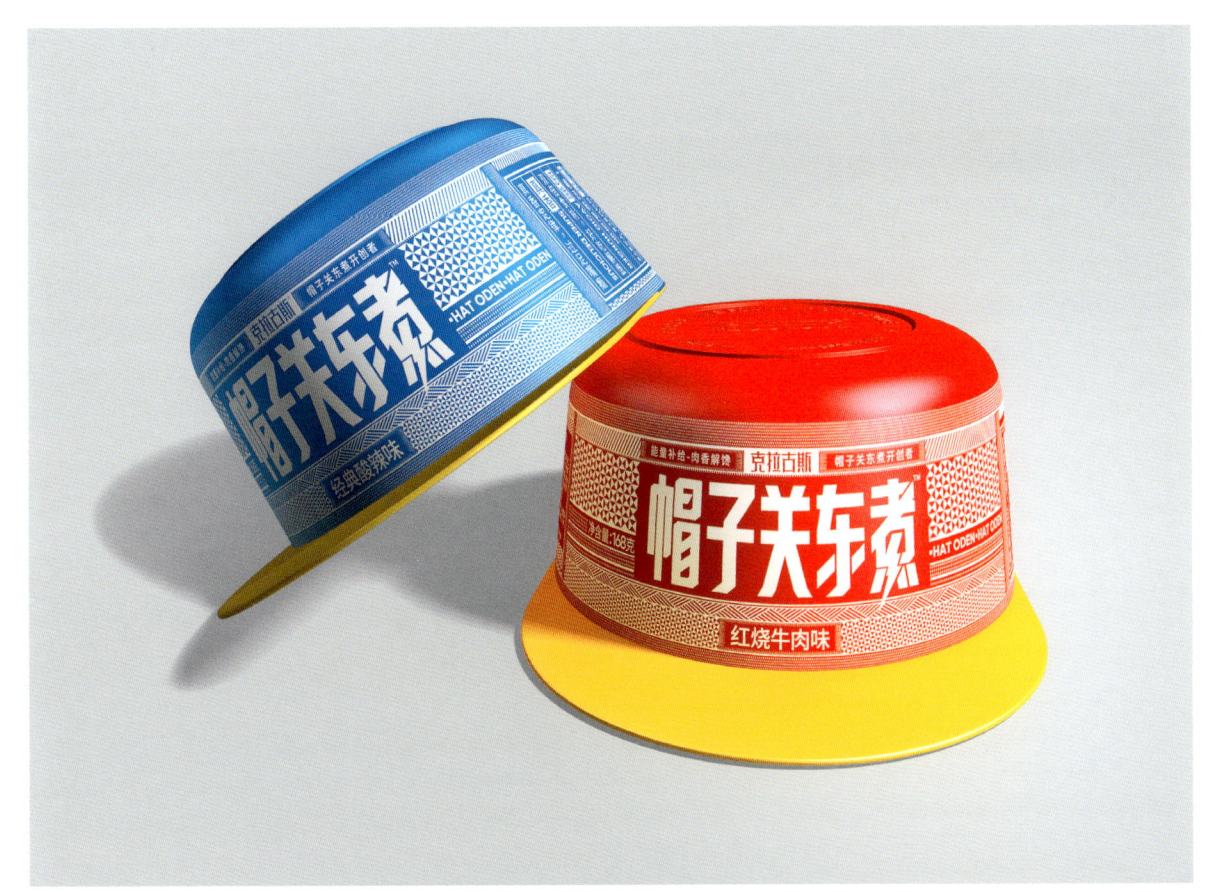

Kelagusi Oden Hat

[Food Packaging]

This new instant food brand is geared primarily towards young consumers. In order to target this group specifically, the concept of the design chooses not to use the bowl or cylinder-shaped packaging normally used in this segment. It consciously rebels against the uniformity in the sector and packages the convenience meals in containers which resemble baseball caps instead. This gives the consumer a sensually and visually attractive experience. The intense colour tones of the design emphasise the brand's vibrant personality and draw attention to the products.

Client
Shenyang Kelagusi Food Co., Ltd.
Shenyang, China

Design
Shandong Veikao Advertising Co., Ltd.
Shandong, China

Project Team
Gaowei Xin (Creative Direction)
Yuerong Liu (Packaging Design)
Cuipeng (Packaging Design)

Huaxishangpin – Wild Fungi

[Food Packaging]

The design of this packaging for wild mushrooms is inspired by nature, as the container and its protruding lid imitate the shape of a mushroom. It is designed in a classy white colour with a gold logo which accentuates the product's premium appearance. The bottom half of the container is packaged in a cardboard box featuring black-and-white illustrations. Roots drawn on the sides of the box create the impression that the container is growing out of the earth. A blue banderole is used to tie this high-impact packaging which is sure to attract the glances of consumers.

Client
Shenzhen Qansfough
Package Design Co., Ltd.
Shenzhen, China

Design
Shenzhen Qansfough
Package Design Co., Ltd.
Shenzhen, China

Project Team
Jun Li (Creative Direction)
Bo Gao (Creative Direction)

Black Truffle – Iberian Acorn-Fed Pork Rice Dumpling

[Food Packaging]

The inspiration for this design stems from the triangular shape of traditional reed leaves which are stuffed with rice and called "zongzi" in Chinese. The special feature of the design for this packaging is that it combines a box containing dumplings with the functionality of a carrier bag. The refined folding technique applied makes it quiet simple to efficiently produce those handy bags, which are also friendly to the environment and easy to carry. The packaging has a pattern depicting tender green reed leaves which suggests freshness. Additional photographs show the ingredients used.

Client
Macau Qangos Food Factory
Macau, China

Design
Shenzhen Win In Design Co., Ltd.
Shenzhen, China

Project Team
Sheng Liang (Designer)

FAMIGO

[Food Packaging]

The name of this olive oil, FAMIGO, is a combination of the words "farmer" in English and "amigo" in Spanish. It conjures up images of a farmer creating a high-quality product through diligent devotion. The oil is distilled in a brown glass bottle and the white label shows an illustration of branches of an olive tree. The restrained design aims to depict the flavour of this product. The box package, containing 12 bottles, is not only used for transport but also for storage. In addition, the upper part can be separated easily along the perforated line and be used as a display stand to sell the product.

Client
Farm Factory
Seoul, South Korea

Design
ATOB
Seoul, South Korea

Project Team
Chan Kim (Creative Direction)
Ho-Kyun Jung (Art Direction)
Oh-Seop Kwon (Artwork)

Advertising	Packaging Design	Fair Stands	Retail Design	Red Dot: Junior Award	Designer Profiles	Index
288	318	494	516	544	614	674

Skoutari Olive Oil

[Food Packaging]

The word "skoutari" means "shield" and is borrowed from the lyrics of the Greek poem "Erotokritos". In the poem, it protects the protagonist in a jousting tournament. This works as a metaphor for the way in which the olive oil protects the human body thanks to its ingredients. The jousting scene is depicted using three horses. Inspired by the ceramics of ancient Greece, linocut printing was used for the design. The bottle is coloured brown to mimic the idea of ceramics. The typography is inspired by an early Greek adaptation of the Garamond font used in the first printed version of the poem in 1723.

Client
Maria Sgourou
Lasithi, Greece

Design
Phantom
Thessaloniki, Greece

Monogram
Monovarietals Olive Oil

[Food Packaging]

Client
Monogram
Kalamata, Greece

Design
dkd
Athens, Greece

Project Team
Petros Dimopoulos (Creative Direction)
Ilektra Natsi (Graphic Design)

The packaging for the Monogram extra virgin olive oil collection has been conceived with the idea of keeping things simple, precisely because there are so many competing olive oils on the market. The product line is easily identifiable thanks to its typographic design. On the outer packaging, the product's natural shades of green or brown are enhanced by embossing, while the elegant bottle with its special label makes the product look highly decorative on the table. The finely tuned concept creates a sense of harmony, emphasising the well-balanced flavour of the product.

SAS Scandinavian Airlines Cube

[Packaging]

With the guideline of sustainability, this concept seeks to create added value for the packaging of on-board meals. The cubical box does not take up much space on an aeroplane table. The cutlery is integrated in the lid and rolled in a napkin made from recycled tissue. The FSC-certified cardboard items deliver the same technical capabilities, strength and efficiency as plastic but exude a natural warmth. In addition, the minimal print of the box facilitates composting. It also effectively communicates the message of getting back to basics.

Client
SAS Scandinavian Airlines System
Stockholm, Sweden

Design
deSter
Hoogstraten, Belgium
Bold
Stockholm, Sweden

Pinocchio and his Friends

[Retail Packaging]

This paper straw packaging uses a generous portion of irony to communicate the brand message. Lettering claims that plastic is harmless and suggests that consumers should limit their use of paper straws. All the while, the illustrations tell a different story. They centre on famous children's character Pinocchio, whose nose grows in length when he tells a lie, as well as on creatures suffering from plastic pollution. An additional level is created by the package opening: the straws become a three-dimensional extension of the illustrations, reaching out to the consumer.

Client
Test Rite Group
Shanghai, China

Design
Test Rite Group
Shanghai, China

Project Team
Wen-Hsiang Wei (Creative Direction)
Ming-Chien Chen (Art Direction)
Linlin Jiang (Concept)
Endong Guo (Artwork)
Su Juan Lin (Photography)

Preface	Red Dot: Agency of the Year	Brands	Brand Design & Identity	Corporate Design & Identity	Annual Reports
4	6	18	90	202	260

POLA APEX
[Cosmetics Packaging]

Client
POLA Inc.
Tokyo, Japan

Design
POLA Inc.
Tokyo, Japan

Project Team
Chiharu Suzuki (Creative Direction)
Yushi Watanabe (Art Direction)
Kei Ikehata (Designer)
Mai Kamiyama (Designer)

→ Clip online

Advertising	Packaging Design	Fair Stands	Retail Design	Red Dot: Junior Award	Designer Profiles	Index
288	318	494	516	544	614	674

This skincare brand offers personalised products developed using AI technologies and skin-related big data. Consumers can put together a collection of skincare items from a broad product range which matches their individual skin type. This is reflected in the packaging concept through the use of a large number of unique graphic elements which communicate this individuality as well as people's different skin types. The approach also provides users with the excitement of discovery and even creates a sensation of surprise when browsing the large array of these cosmetic products.

Preface	Red Dot: Agency of the Year	Brands	Brand Design & Identity	Corporate Design & Identity	Annual Reports
4	6	18	90	202	260

Brandfree
[Cosmetics Packaging]

Client
By-health Co., Ltd.
Guangzhou, China

Design
Grand Design Inc.
Tokyo, Japan

Project Team
Jun Fujiwara (Creative Director)
Yu Yamanoha (Art Director)
Kelvin Chen (Designer)
Huang Wei (Account Director)
Zhang Huaxia (Account Management)

→ Designer profile on page 639

Advertising	Packaging Design	Fair Stands	Retail Design	Red Dot: Junior Award	Designer Profiles	Index
288	318	494	516	544	614	674

These generic products comprise a range of everyday, eco-certified skincare products. They are aimed at middle-income earners aged between 20 and 35. The motto "The ultimate simplicity" was created to address this target group. The number "0" on the packaging indicates that the generic products are wholly natural and contain no added ingredients. The different containers are designed in a cool grey hue which is neutral and thus fits with any lifestyle. A conscious decision is made not to use a brand logo. Coloured stickers inform consumers of the content of each container.

Gaon

[Cosmetics Packaging]

"Gaon" is the Korean word for "centre". This item is a vegan skincare product focused on protecting the skin's centre. The logo contains Hangul letters in linear and circular form. The packaging design is minimalistic. The tube is green in order to highlight the product's natural ingredients and to refer to the image of a good vegan cosmetics brand. The outer packaging made from paper is ivory-coloured, emphasising the natural approach of this skincare. It is printed using environmentally friendly soya oil without any coatings or other refining processes.

Client
Coreana Cosmetics
Suwon, South Korea

Design
Coreana Cosmetics
Suwon, South Korea

Project Team
Hyang Mi Jang (Project Management)
Eun Jin Cho (Graphic Design)
Joo Yon Kim (Graphic Design)

BODY & SOUL
[Cosmetics Packaging]

The inspiration for the design of these body lotion containers was drawn from milk bottles. Their basic colour is white, with the lid and product name designed in different pastel tones. The similarity to milk bottles conveys positive associations, such as friendliness and fun, and also reflects some product features, such as moisture. The image of freshness is enhanced by the design of the lid with a wave-shaped pattern reminiscent of a drop of milk. The recyclable bottles are made using a low-carbon production method.

Client
The SAEM International Co., Ltd.
Seoul, South Korea

Design
The SAEM International Co., Ltd.
Seoul, South Korea

Preface	Red Dot: Agency of the Year	Brands	Brand Design & Identity	Corporate Design & Identity	Annual Reports
4	6	18	90	202	260

Blue Peach Antioxidant Hydrator Series

[Cosmetics Packaging]

The central design concept for these moisturisers is "At Your Will", and it is geared towards young women aged between 20 and 25. Instead of the traditional cardboard packaging, resealable vacuum bags are used. These keep the products airtight and demonstrate the anti-oxidative ability of the lotions to repair dry skin within a short period of time. The product information is printed on silver polyester stickers of various shapes, sizes and colours, attached randomly to the vacuum bags, reflecting, among other things, the gaiety of the young target group.

Client
Blue Peach Skincare
Taipei City, Taiwan

Design
Triangler Co., Ltd
Taipei City, Taiwan

Project Team
Chun-Yao Huang (Art Direction)
Chi-Yao Tang (Art Direction)
Jiang-Xin Zhang (Graphic Design)
Yun-Chien Chou (Account Management)

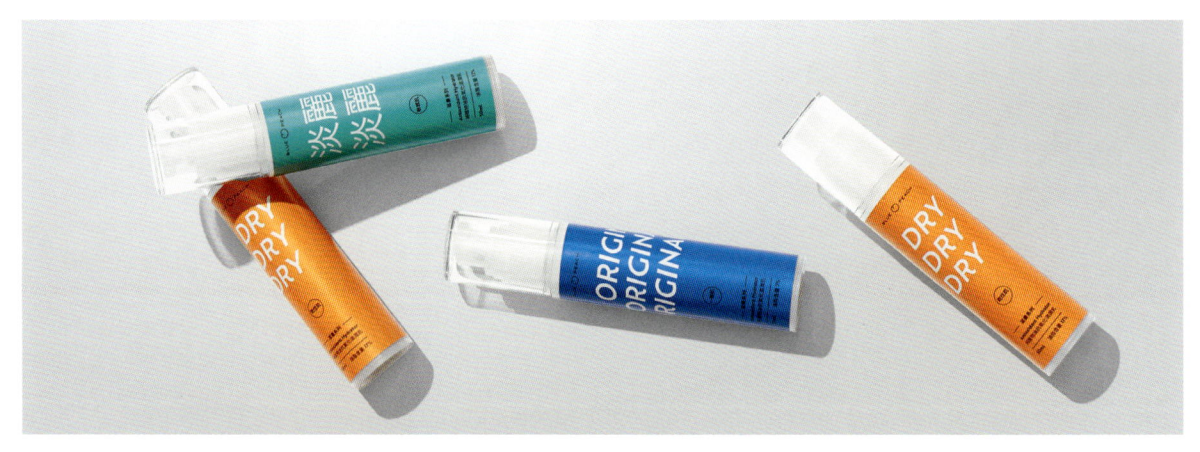

Milk Baobab
[Cosmetics Packaging]

The packaging design of these hair and body care products is, on the one hand, inspired by milk and, on the other, by the baobab tree, thus hinting at two characteristic ingredients used in all of the products. The containers are in the shape of milk cartons, with gently rounded edges to prevent injury and with subtle dots of carbon in the printing. The labels feature powerful imagery, allowing the ingredients to be intuitively recognised. In order to make sure the different products can also be distinguished easily, the containers are of different colours.

Client
Taenam Household & Healthcare Ltd.
Seoul, South Korea

Design
Taenam Household & Healthcare Ltd.
Seoul, South Korea

Project Team
Yuna Nam (Designer)
Jeongung Lee (Designer)
Hyein Kim (Designer)
Hyunji Park (Designer)
Jihyun Joo (Designer)

mä&me Latte
[Cosmetics Packaging]

These haircare products aim to provide a moment of rest for Japanese mothers under time pressure from the demands of housework, parenting and working outside the home. The custom of family bath time is interpreted as an opportunity for indulgence. Consequently, the packaging design does not feature any functional elements or child-focused images. Instead it is designed harmoniously in two complementary colours. Contrary to the norm of large bottles which stand out on drugstore shelves, these bottles are short in a bid to create a feeling of relaxation.

Client
Kracie Holdings, Ltd.
Tokyo, Japan

Design
Interbrand
Tokyo, Japan

Project Team
Yoshihiko Miyagi (Creative Director)
Sayaka Ichiki (Design Director)
Atsuko Sonoi (Designer)
Taisuke Kiyono (Designer)
Kanako Yaginuma (Designer)
Seppo Kurki (Verbal Creation)
Keiko Ueda (Verbal Creation)
Mark Garland (Verbal Creation)
Hiroyuki Yabe (Strategy Planning)
Hwasook Yanase (Strategy Planning)

Fumie Shibata (Product Designer),
Design Studio S

SK:LK–BODY CARE

[Cosmetics Packaging]

SK:LK is a series of body care products which includes a hair tonic, a shampoo and a shower gel. The aim is to achieve powerful communication through highly recognisable packaging and to convey a special skincare feeling using simple and clear language. The containers are made from a soft, matt-finish material. The numbers 0, 1 and 2, designed in organic wavy lines, are an eye-catching feature. They help the user to see, at a glance, the order in which to use the products. In addition, the design indicates that the products are safe and kind to skin.

Client
Beijing Youji Technology
Development Co., Ltd.
Shanghai, China

Design
Shanghai Version Design Group
Shanghai, China

Flamenco Shower Ball

[Retail Packaging]

The Flamenco Shower Ball packaging picks up on the product's ruffles and links these to impressions from Spain. A see-through pack displays the shower ball with a soft focus effect. In this way, the product is concealed yet on show, arousing consumers' curiosity. Since the ball completes the sketchy drawing of a flamenco dancer on the pack, it conjures up images of the dancer's twirling frills and the notion of rhythmic music. Matching the brand slogan "Passion, Sweat and Shower", the package thus emphasises the sensual aspect of body care.

Client
Gahwa
Bucheon, South Korea

Design
Kiltae Son
Bucheon, South Korea

Satisfyer

[Packaging]

The elegantly redesigned packaging for Satisfyer highlights the value proposition within every product while also creating a sense of safety and well-being. The interplay of nuances of contrasting colour in combination with the abstract single line drawings are intended to encourage the user to develop a new understanding of their sexuality as a unique way to improve the quality of their life. Each product category has its own colour code to help to streamline the purchasing process. Additional visual guidance is delivered by a dedicated set of icons which appear on both the outer and the inner packaging layers.

Client
Triple A Internetshops, Satisfyer
Bielefeld, Germany

Design
Triple A Internetshops, Satisfyer
Bielefeld, Germany

Project Team
Thomas Milewski (Chief Design Officer)
Miriam Plock (Head of Design)

ZEESEA Fireworks 16 Colors Eyeshadow

[Cosmetics Packaging]

This square eyeshadow box is a reminder of faraway places. This impression is created through the design of the lid, which is made from acrylic with a reflective finish, marrying the black background with graphic elements in bright red and blue as well as majestic gold in a striking fashion. Thanks to an innovative 3D colour printing technology, it renders the details of the graphical elements to perfection, giving the colour and the transitions a natural appearance even on concave surfaces. This eyeshadow box complements the Egyptian series created by the cosmetics manufacturer in cooperation with the British Museum.

Client
ZEESEA
Guangzhou, China

Design
Guangzhou Ai Yue Advertising Co., Ltd.
Guangzhou, China

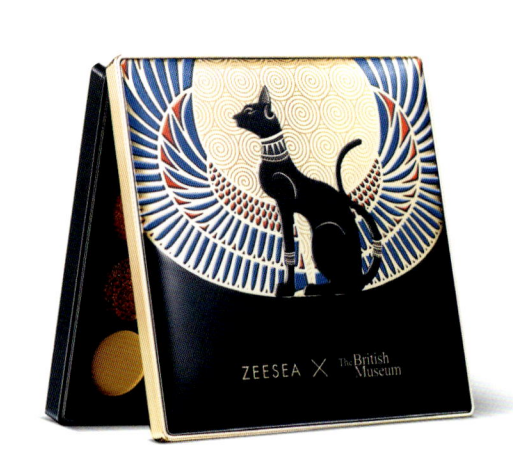

ZEESEA Refreshing Silky Powder

[Cosmetics Packaging]

The design of this compact face powder case, created jointly by cosmetics manufacturer ZEESEA and the British Museum, is inspired by the aesthetics of ancient Egyptian art. The black, high-gloss design of the lid is in sharp contrast with its gold-coloured profile decoration. It shows the goddess Hathor, who, in Egyptian mythology, symbolises prosperity, generosity and benevolence alongside beauty. The exquisite powder case with its elegant appearance has a square shape and an intentionally compact design, making it easy to carry along.

Client
ZEESEA
Guangzhou, China

Design
Guangzhou Ai Yue Advertising Co., Ltd.
Guangzhou, China

Prism Light

[Cosmetics Packaging]

The design of the pot for this cosmetic product features the shape, colour and even texture of a pebble. In line with the manufacturer's philosophy, the design is inspired by global ecology. True to the motto "The more natural, the more ergonomic", the packaging is triangular in shape with gently rounded corners. It is easy to hold, with a grip which imitates the feel of a real pebble. The pot is produced in a way that optimises recycling with biodegradable materials which are used to protect the environment.

Client
The SAEM International Co., Ltd.
Seoul, South Korea

Design
The SAEM International Co., Ltd.
Seoul, South Korea

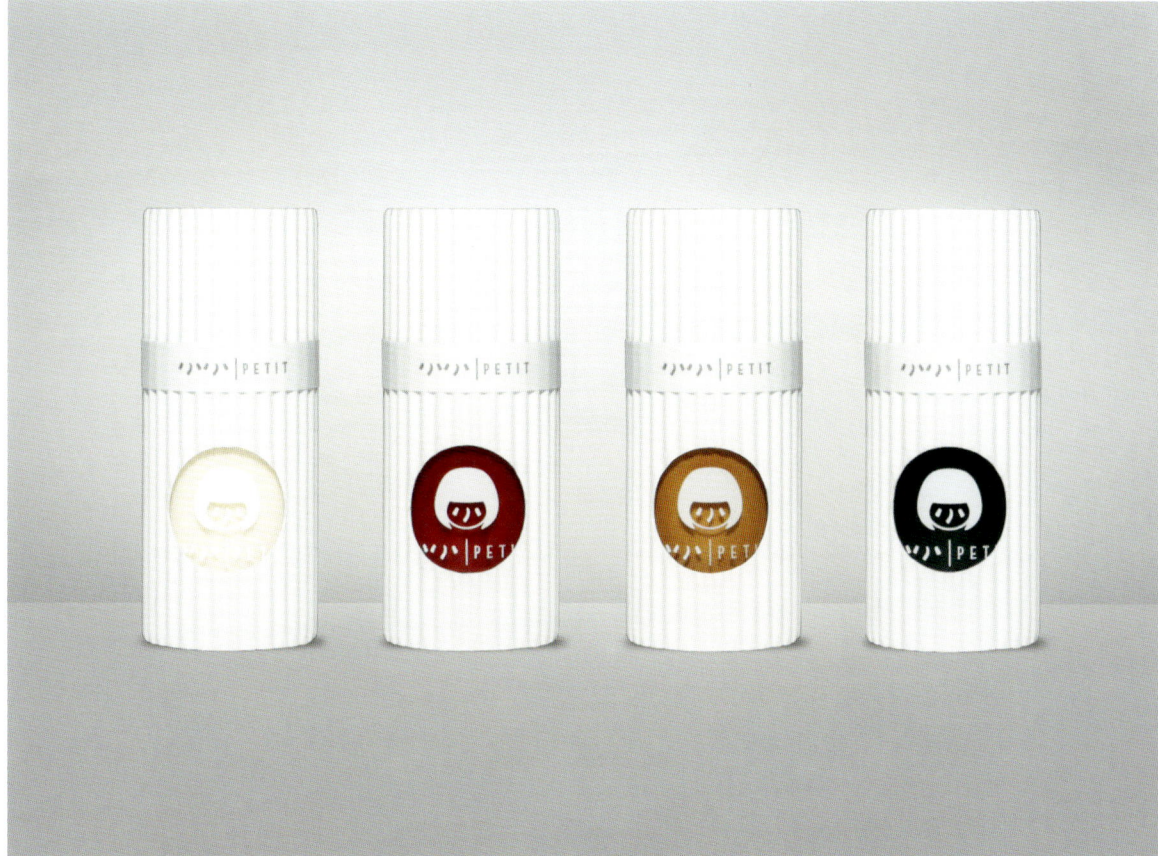

PETIT Nail Polish

[Cosmetics Packaging]

The outer packaging of the PETIT nail polish bottles is white. This restraint, along with an opening in the centre, allows the focus to shift to the colour of the respective nail polish. It also emphasises the fact that the polish is made from simple ingredients such as water and non-poisonous pigments. In order to implement the idea of sustainability in the outer packaging, it is made of paper instead of plastic. The design is supposed to remind consumers on the one hand of their responsibility to protect mother Earth, and on the other hand of the fact that even those who are not perfect can nevertheless shine brightly.

Client
PETIT RIEGO Co., Ltd.
Taipei City, Taiwan

Design
PETIT Design Center
Taipei City, Taiwan

UUcare Chunye Sanitary Napkin

[Retail Packaging]

Client
UUcare Group Singapore Pte. Ltd.
Nanjing, China

Design
Quanzhou Enjia Brand Planning Co., Ltd.
Quanzhou, China

Project Team
Zhang Jinxian (Creative Director)
Lai Baoyu (Strategic Planning)
Zhang Haiyang (Art Director)
Wu Jianlong (Graphic Designer)
Zhong Yulong (Director of Illustration)
Lu Huiling (Copywriting)
Chen Jianwei (Illustration Execution)
Wang Xinsheng (Project Management)

→ Designer profile on page 636

Advertising	**Packaging Design**	Fair Stands	Retail Design	Red Dot: Junior Award	Designer Profiles	Index
288	318	494	516	544	614	674

With the motto "Be a simple person in a complex world", this brand offers sanitary pads made from pure cotton. The core value of the brand has been translated into a clear packaging layout. By focusing on a key visual and a few graphic characters, the design visualises the idea of getting back to basics. Moreover, the packaging features a slightly nostalgic style which aims to resonate with the yearning of many young people to have a simpler life. The harmonious composition matches up to the notion of purity and ease, thus accentuating the selling points for the natural material cotton.

blbm

[Packaging]

The blbm household products are mainly bedding, such as pillows, mattresses and cushions. The brand's material technology originates from Japan and uses air fibres as a filler. The packaging makes use of on-trend calligraphy to summarise the benefits of the product, introducing a typographical key visual in front of a night-blue background. The Chinese characters represent the supported part of the body in abstract form, for example the bottom or neck, and thus reference the product's function. At the same time, the graphics reflect the texture of the filler in a memorable way.

Client
Shanghai Shangshi
Network Technology Co., Ltd.
Shanghai, China

Design
Shanghai Version Design Group
Shanghai, China

Project Team
Zhihua He (Creative Direction)
Tengxian Zou (Creative Direction)
Wenfang Ye (Designer)
Suping Wu (Designer)
Qi Tong (Designer)

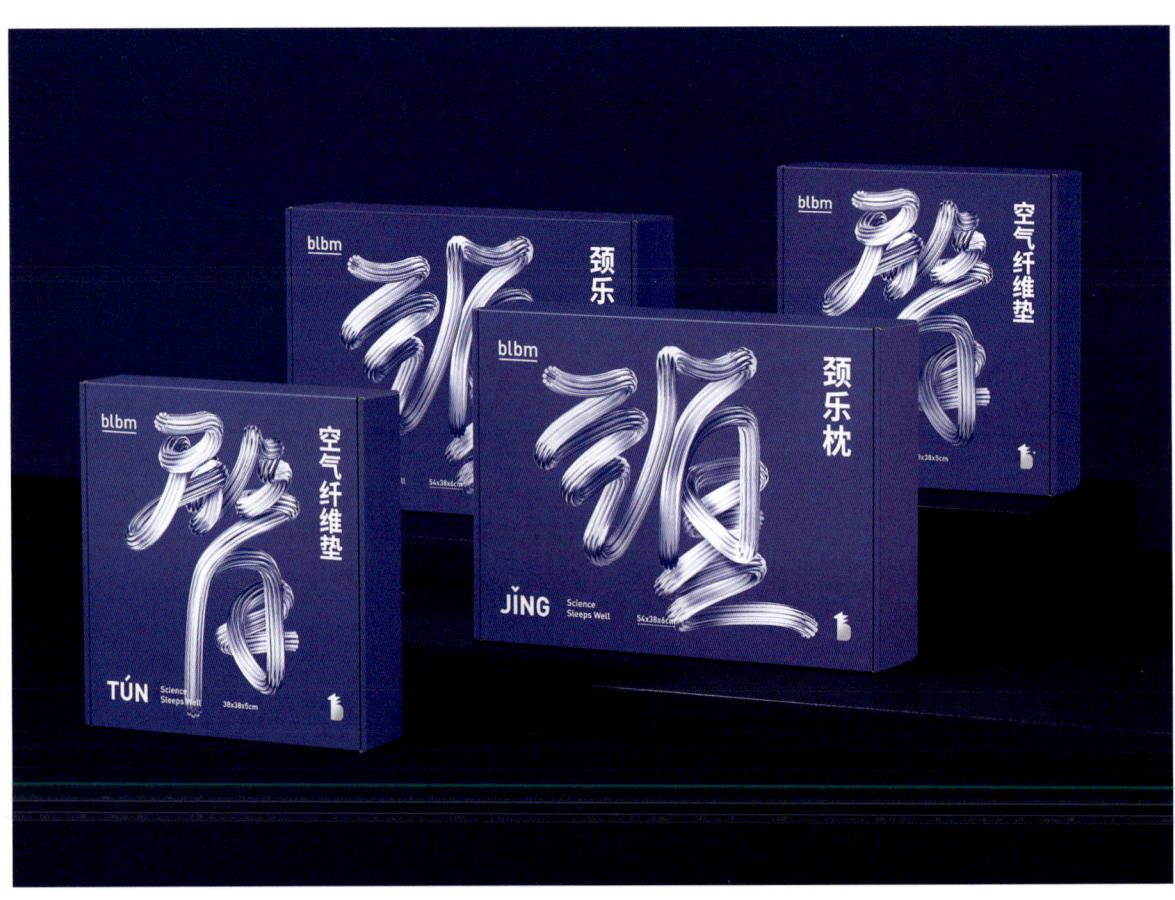

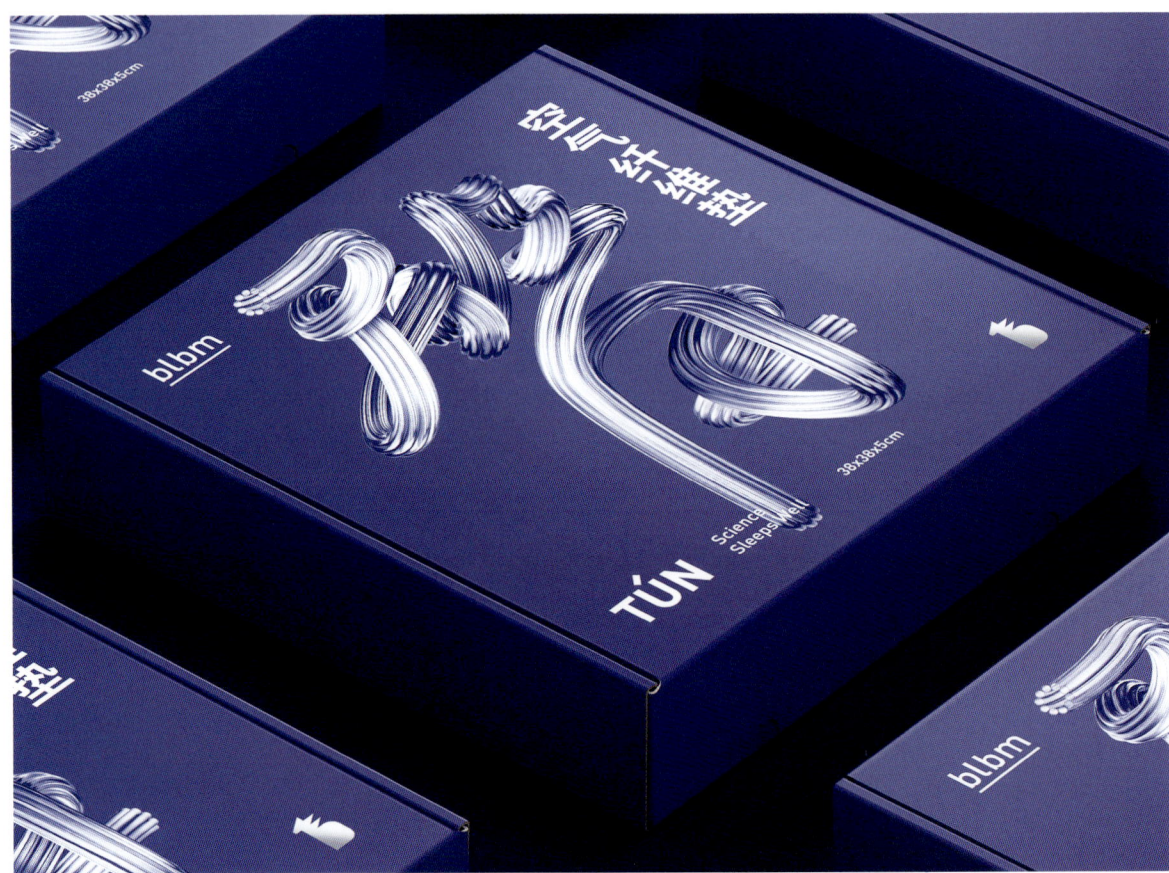

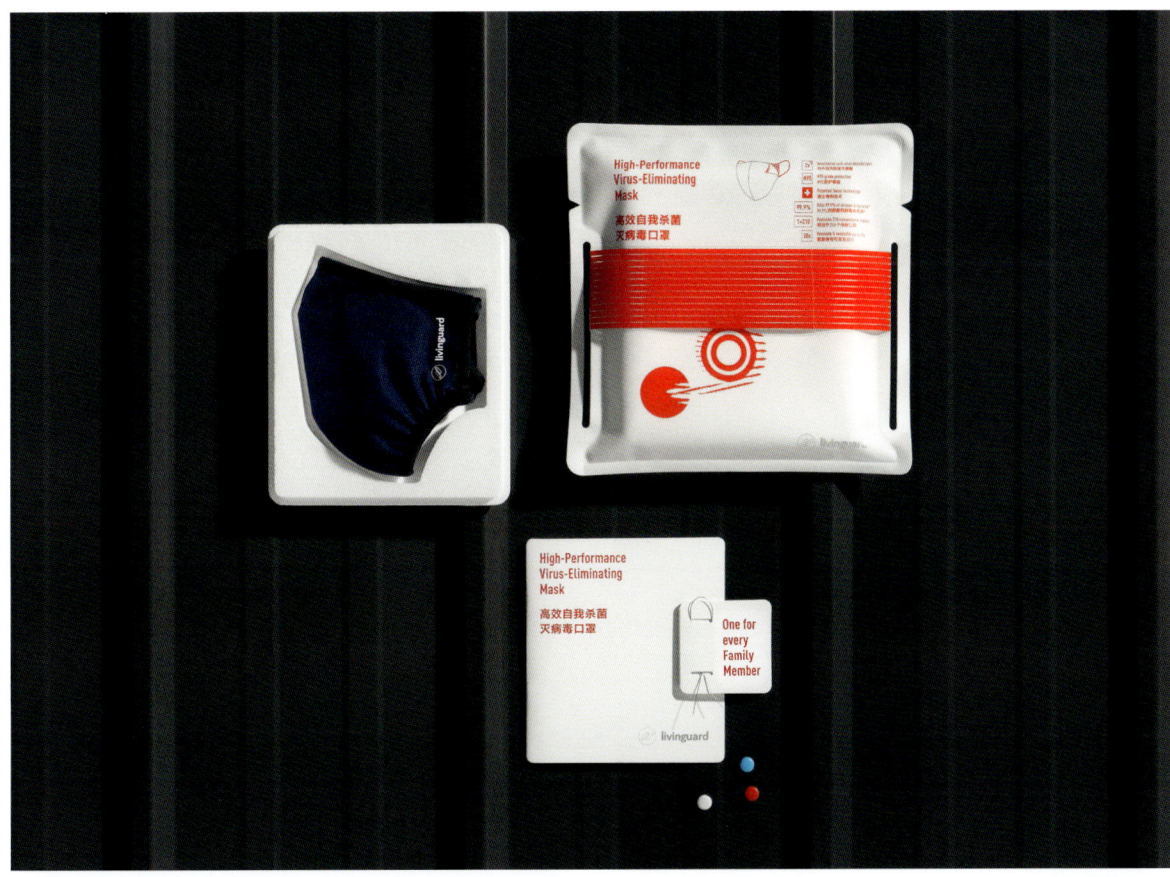

Advertising	Packaging Design	Fair Stands	Retail Design	Red Dot: Junior Award	Designer Profiles	Index
288	318	494	516	544	614	674

The Mask that Ate the Virus

[Health Product Packaging]

Swiss biotech company Livinguard developed a textile for reusable masks that deactivates bacteria, fungi and viruses (including Covid-19) upon impact. This idea is brought to life in the packaging: the mask comes in a sterile package. When an attached plastic strip is slid up and down, it animates a virus that is eaten in the process, adding some urgently needed humour in desperate days. To avoid the mix up of masks by family members and hence cross-contamination, differently coloured adjustment clips come in a separate sleeve to customise each mask.

Client
Livinguard, S.G.F. Biotechnology
Beijing, China

Design
Birger Linke Design
Beijing, China

Project Team
Chiara Ye (Photography)

→ Designer profile on page 626

Schawlow

[Jewellery Packaging]

A Chinese proverb attributed to the legendary philosopher Laozi stresses the importance of water as our most valuable asset. In the saying, a person with a noble character is compared to water, because water sustains all beings and does not compete with them. Inspired by the Eastern wisdom, this packaging design picks up on characteristics of water to stage a jewellery collection. The metal shells protecting necklaces or bracelets attract attention through their shimmering surface and organic shape. Inside, a black lining effectively sets off the silver objects.

Client
Shenzhen Schawlow Jewelry Co., Ltd.
Shenzhen, China

Design
Shenzhen Oracle Creative Design Co., Ltd.
Shenzhen, China

Project Team
Wen Liu (Creative Direction)
Chenlu Xie (Creative Direction)
Weijie Kang (Creative Direction)

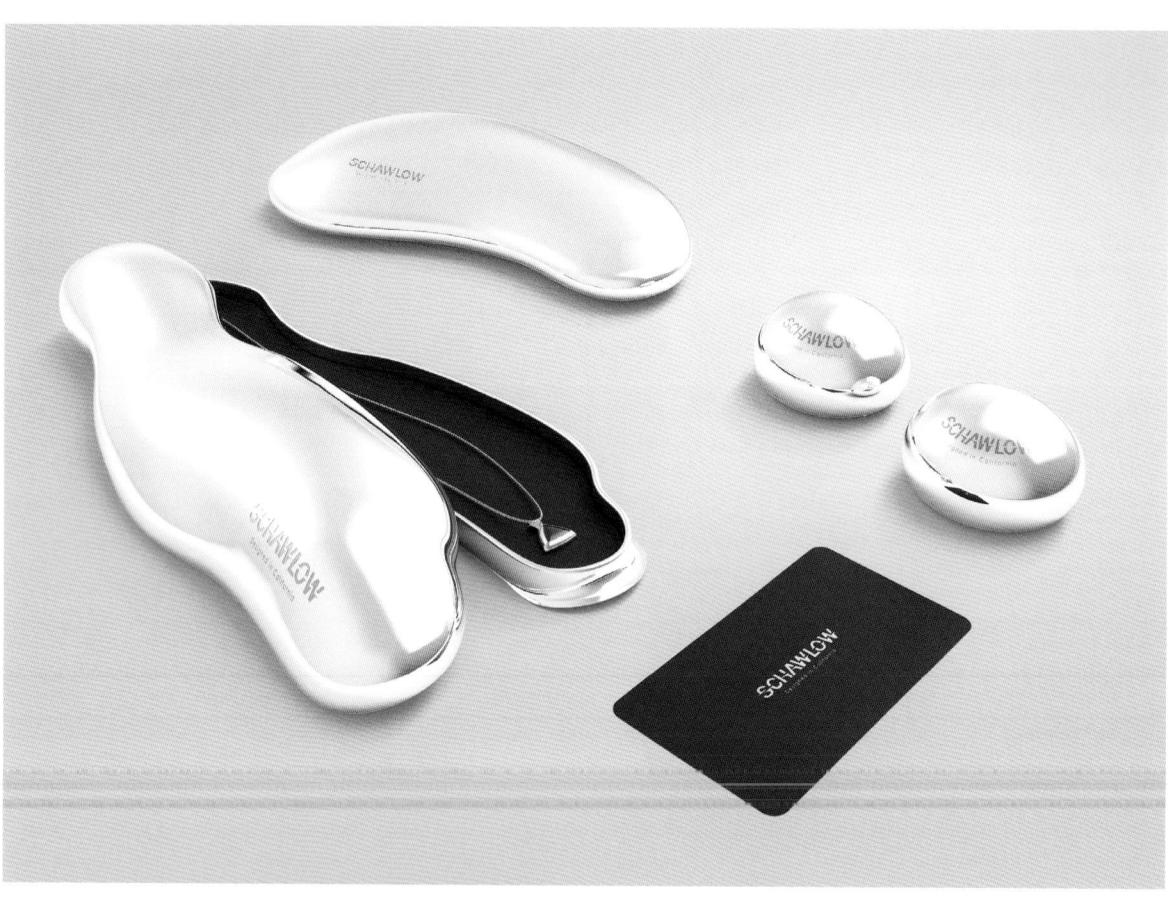

The Zen Concept Mechanical Watch
[Retail Packaging]

This packaging is inspired by Zen culture, just like the product it contains. The pattern of the outer packaging is designed to visualise three levels of awareness. Pressing marks represent the reality of the appearance of things, while the hollowed lines symbolise their inner reality and the filigree watch mechanism stands for the most essential core of things. In this way, the product is comprehensively linked to what Zen practitioners seek to perceive. The watch inside is showcased in a kind of booklet which, when opened, aesthetically unveils its finely coordinated details.

Client
Shenzhen CIGA Design Co., Ltd.
Shenzhen, China

Design
Shenzhen CIGA Design Co., Ltd.
Shenzhen, China

Project Team
Zhang Jianmin (Design Supervisor)
Jiang Xin (Senior Designer)

Preface	Red Dot: Agency of the Year	Brands	Brand Design & Identity	Corporate Design & Identity	Annual Reports
4	6	18	90	202	260

One Paper Box
[Sustainable Packaging]

One Paper Box is a design method to build packages from only one piece of paper. The concept has been developed for a series of electronic products. It dispenses with the inner structure of a paper box and works with a supporting structure that simply needs to be folded or glued at the edges. The environmentally friendly idea behind this is to reduce packaging waste by using recyclable paper instead of plastic. In addition, the fact that less manual labour, less material and less assembly work is required to produce the boxes allows cost-efficient manufacturing.

Client
Xiaomi Inc.
Beijing, China

Design
Xiaomi Inc.
Beijing, China

Project Team
Lu Chen (Creative Direction)
Zhizhuang Song
(Packaging Structure Design)

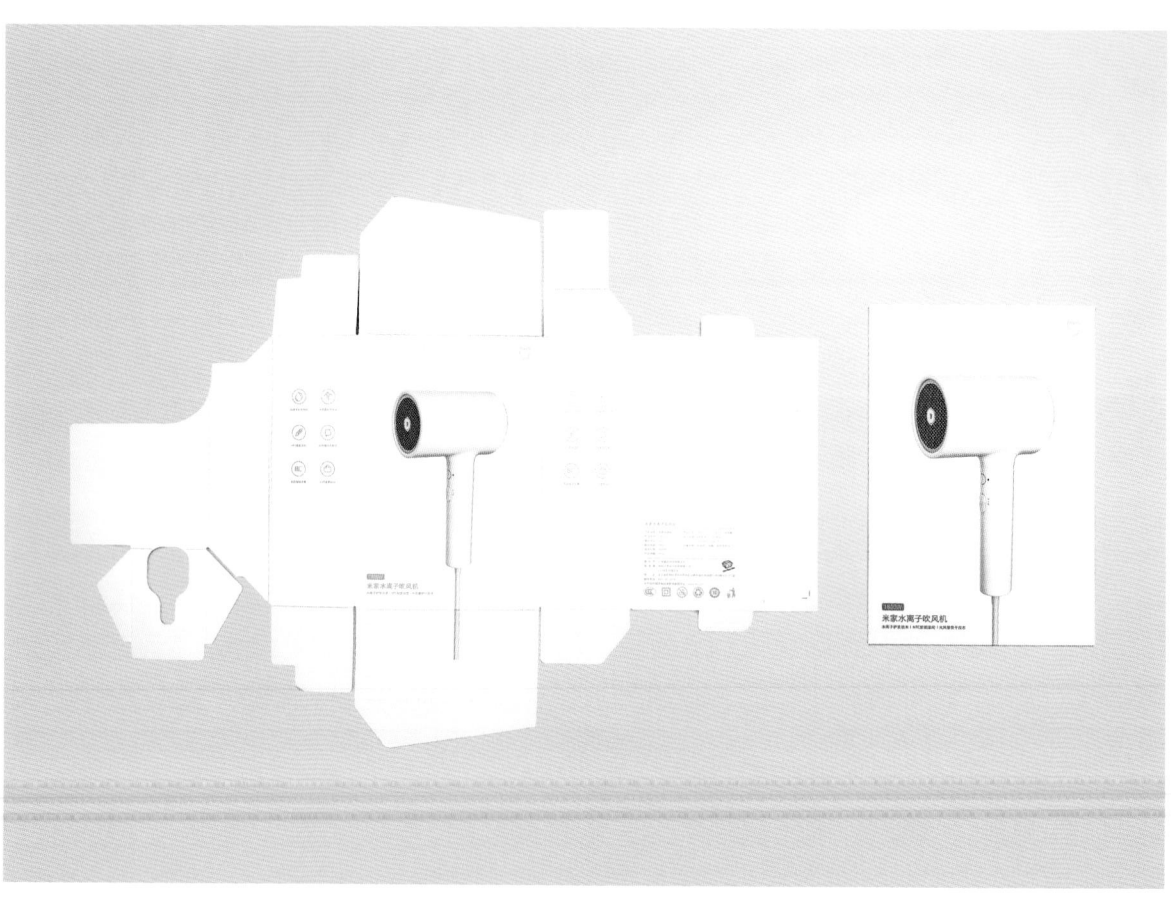

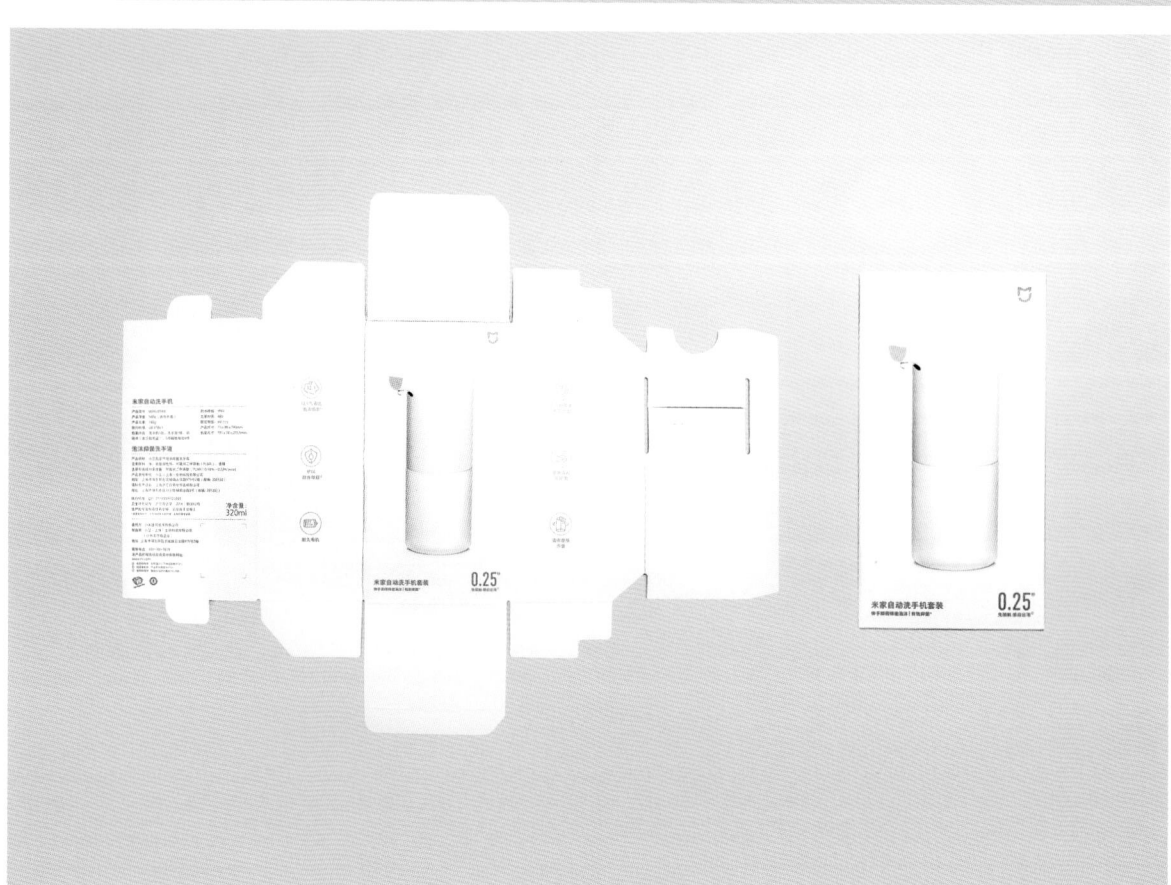

ConceptD Eco-Friendly Package

[Sustainable Packaging]

This notebook packaging applies the principles of reduction, reuse and recycling. Thanks to a fine balance between size and protection, most of the packaging components can be shared to reduce material waste. The minimalist print on the front side combines the product form with the brand logo in a striking way. The material used is completely recyclable and consists of over 90 per cent recycled cardboard. To further reduce the environmental impact, the boxes do not contain cables in plastic bags, and the computer casing is made of recycled polyester.

Client
Acer Inc.
New Taipei City, Taiwan

Design
Acer Inc.
New Taipei City, Taiwan

→ Designer profile on page 619

Preface	Red Dot: Agency of the Year	Brands	Brand Design & Identity	Corporate Design & Identity	Annual Reports
4	6	18	90	202	260

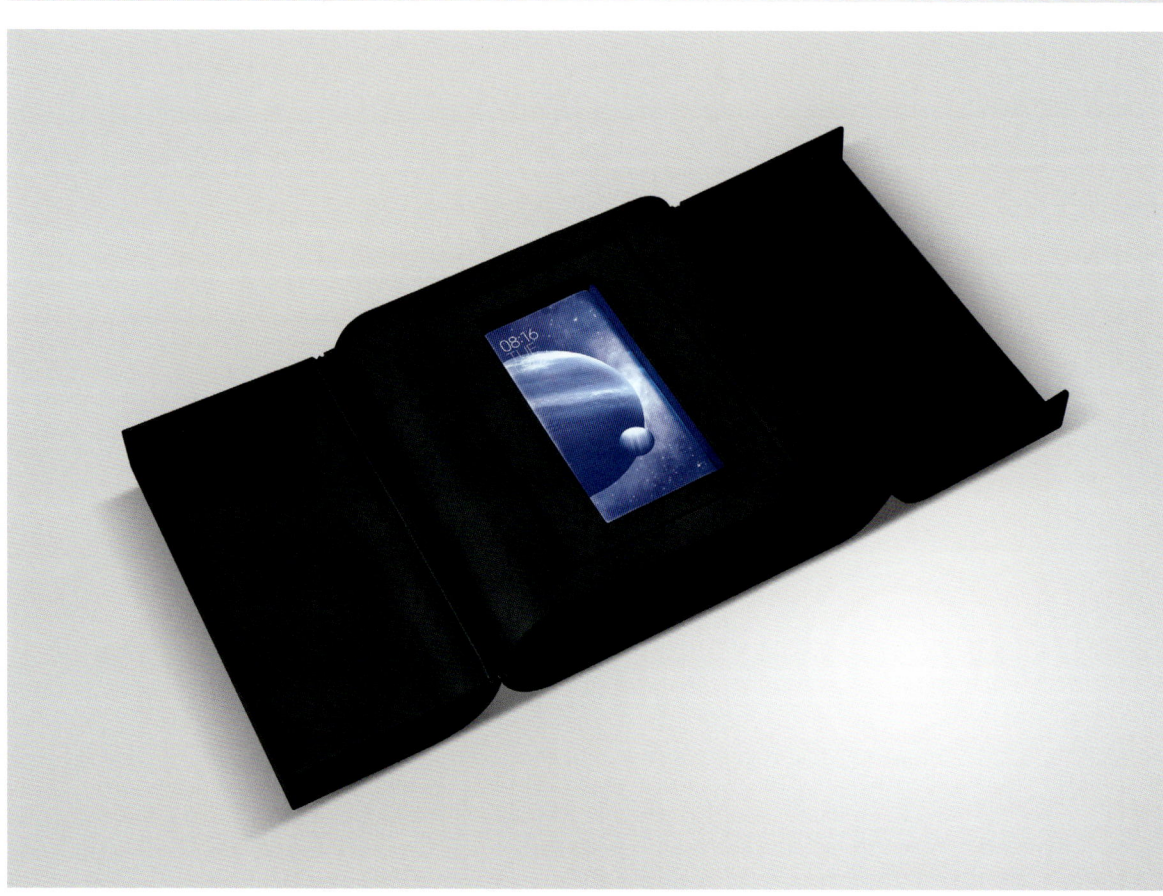

Mi MIX Alpha Box

[Retail Packaging]

The Mi MIX Alpha is a futuristic smartphone with a flexible display which almost wraps around the entire casing. The design of the packaging was inspired by the product itself. The curved edges on both sides are in perfect harmony with the phone's wraparound display. They also make the rectangular case fit comfortably into the hand. In addition, the carefully selected paperboard material is as soft to the touch as skin. In order to protect the entire display from external damage, the inside of the box is made of soft, shock-resistant plastic material, which provides excellent fixation and protection.

Client
Xiaomi Inc.
Beijing, China

Design
Xiaomi Inc.
Beijing, China

Mi Watch

[Retail Packaging]

The packaging design for the Mi Watch aims to convey the product's high level of technological innovation. The lid of the box therefore includes a hologram of the smartwatch which generates a powerful 3D effect. Embossed printing and a special print colour make the image look almost as real as the product itself. The virtual water ripples of the watch are also shown in the hologram and seem to move, depending on the incidence of light. The tray inside the box is designed in a way that the watch appears to be floating on it.

Client
Xiaomi Inc.
Beijing, China

Design
Xiaomi Inc.
Beijing, China

Project Team
Lu Chen (Creative Direction)
Jiangpeng Su (Graphic Design)
Zhizhuang Song
(Packaging Structure Design)

Mi Bluetooth Headset Basic

[Retail Packaging]

The Mi Bluetooth Headset Basic is a single earbud optimised for listening to music and making phone calls. In order to highlight its excellent wearability whilst having optimal freedom of movement, the concept of the packaging design focuses on a range of usage scenarios. The sketch-like drawings on the boxes show people in profile wearing the headset while running, cycling or driving. The simple imagery is intended to help customers to understand the product without confusing them with unnecessary details. The strong contrast of black and white not only accentuates the product itself but also makes it more visually striking.

Client
Xiaomi Inc.
Beijing, China

Design
Xiaomi Inc.
Beijing, China

Project Team
Lu Chen (Creative Direction)
Jiangpeng Su (Graphic Design)
Yan Ni (Illustration)

Mi Quad Driver In-Ear Headphone

[Retail Packaging]

The source of inspiration for the packaging design of the Mi Quad Driver In-Ear Headphone was a nautilus shell with a spiral-shaped housing amplifying sound. That is the reason why the cross section of a nautilus shell is shown on the lid of the box with an earbud at its centre in reference to the headphone's high sound quality. The use of embossing heightens the sense of realism of the nautilus shell. In order to keep visuals and aesthetics as simple as possible, the interior of the box is divided into two layers. Accessories are not visible at first glance to draw the attention to the headphone itself.

Client
Xiaomi Inc.
Beijing, China

Design
Xiaomi Inc.
Beijing, China

Project Team
Lu Chen (Creative Direction)
Weijie Jiang (Graphic Design)
Zhizhuang Song
(Packaging Structure Design)

Preface	Red Dot: Agency of the Year	Brands	Brand Design & Identity	Corporate Design & Identity	Annual Reports
4	6	18	90	202	260

BTS – Love Yourself
[Music Packaging]

"Love Yourself" is the title of a series of music albums by the South Korean band BTS. They relate the story of a young love which grows and ends. The CDs are primarily for young people, geared to console them and convey the message, that true love cannot be found by people who do not love themselves. Illustrations of flowers representing the feelings of young people are used throughout the exclusive design of the CDs and the corresponding packaging, which is aimed to strengthen the image of the brand. The graphic is flowing and designed with changing colours to reflect a shifting emotional state.

Client
Big Hit Entertainment
Seoul, South Korea

Design
HuskyFox
Seoul, South Korea

Project Team
Doohee Lee (Creative Direction)
Kiyoung Jung (Creative Direction)
Hyuncheol Ahn (Graphic Design)

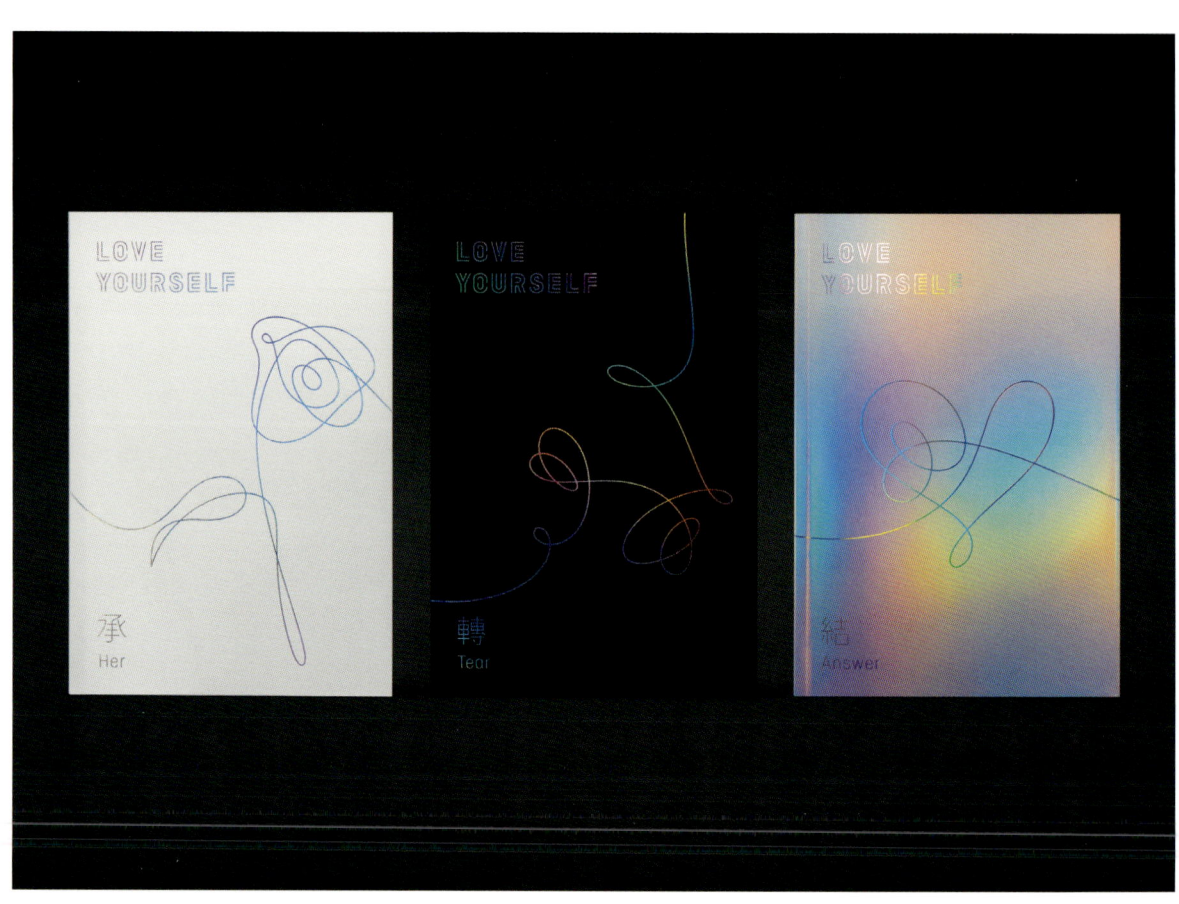

I AM ME
Hardcover Album
[Packaging]

This hardcover box, which closes magnetically, is entitled "I AM ME" and contains various material by the eponymous artist Jackie Chan. Designed to strict environmental standards, this collection combines a square and a circular shape and brings up an analogy to the strong image the actor represents. The box accommodates a film reel which is laser inscribed and contains music CDs, photos and a lyric book bound using a traditional folding technique. The packaging also includes film material with individual images which can be seen through a hole in the packaging cover.

Client
Beijing JC Family
International Media Co., Ltd.
Beijing, China

Design
Shanghai Lanzuo
Network Technology Co., Ltd.
Shanghai, China

Project Team
Yu Jingcheng (Art Director)
Synie Cheung (Designer)
Lu Lin (Designer)

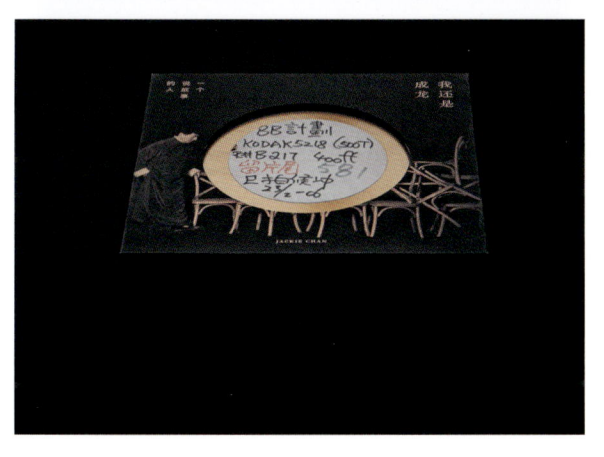

The Birds

[Music Packaging]

This LP and the accompanying brochure introduces listeners to the ancient play "The Birds" by Aristophanes in an adaptation by Nikos Karathanos. The fundamental idea informing the design is a play on light. The covers show birds in a circular arrangement. They are portrayed in a powerful illustration full of contradictions, rendering the play's characteristic final scene when the birds dance in the sunlight. The play on light is intensified through the particular printing techniques employed, such as the use of light-absorbing inks, which create an impressive glow-in-the-dark experience.

Client
Onassis Cultural Centre
Athens, Greece

Design
Beetroot Design Group
Thessaloniki, Greece

Advertising	Packaging Design	Fair Stands	Retail Design	Red Dot: Junior Award	Designer Profiles	Index
288	318	494	516	544	614	674

Hidden Elements

[Music Packaging]

These three record covers of the breakbeat music duo Hidden Elements each show a picture of a landscape taken in Ukraine. The most distinctive design element is a large block of colour which literally hides an element. The back of each cover shows objects which could have been in the original photo. Each object has its own idea selected for the respective track. For example, "A nature silently dies" is a spruce that has completely dried up. "A journey of mistakes" is visualised as a huge felled tree.

Client
Hidden Elements
Kyiv, Ukraine

Design
CREVV
Kyiv, Ukraine

Project Team
Natalia Ivanova (Designer)
Anton Ivanov (Designer)

The Swedish Film Selection

[Film Packaging]

Every year, the Swedish Institute together with the Swedish Film Institute compile a selection of the best contemporary national films. These feature-length documentaries and short films are distributed for non-profit cultural screenings around the world. The task was to redesign the packaging and bring a uniform graphic profile to this series of film box sets. The new look has bright, playful intersecting colour fields which give the design a festive feel and pay homage to classic movie premiere searchlights. The design is carried over to the discs and interactive menus.

Client
Swedish Institute
Stockholm, Sweden

Design
Kidler AB, Kidler Design Studio
Stockholm, Sweden

Project Team
Tobias Ottenfelt (Creative Direction)
Therese Laurin (Creative Direction)

→ Designer profile on page 646
→ Clip online

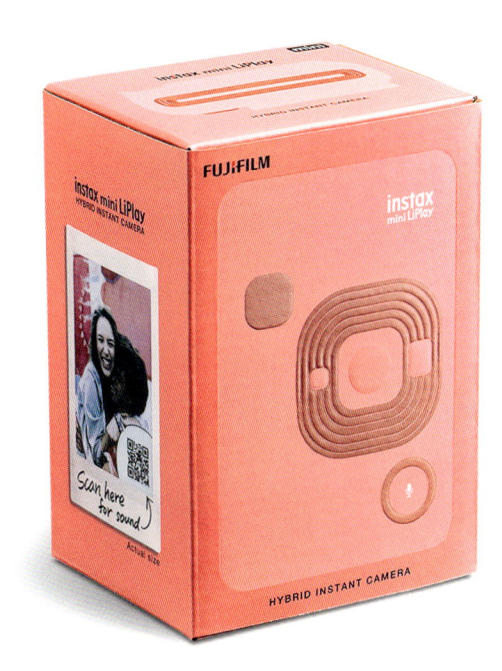

Advertising	Packaging Design	Fair Stands	Retail Design	Red Dot: Junior Award	Designer Profiles	Index
288	318	494	516	544	614	674

instax mini LiPlay – Box
[Retail Packaging]

This packaging design uses simple shapes and embossing to express the essence of a hybrid instant camera. Circles and squares are combined with different textures to create a music player-like aesthetic. This in turn references the special experiences the device offers. A corrugated cardboard box conveys the compactness of the camera, displays its colour and underlines its printing function. The camera contours are accurately recreated using paper. Certain details, such as the curved lines, are embossed and printed with metallic ink in order to highlight the texture.

Client
FUJIFILM Corporation
Tokyo, Japan

Design
FUJIFILM Corporation Design Center
Tokyo, Japan

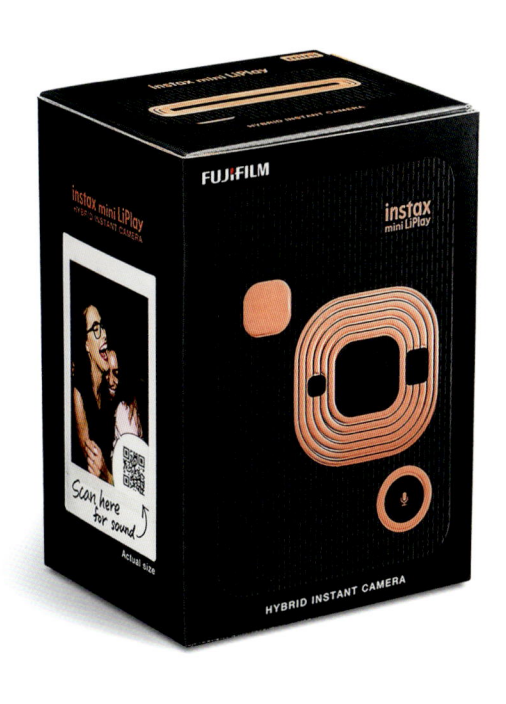

Solar Media

[Sustainable Packaging]

Solar Media is a solar-powered device for both lighting and video-playing, which is primarily produced for the African market. The packaging is designed as a practical aid for everyday life, seeking to be useful instead of wasteful. People in need can reuse the colourful boxes as drawers and fold the partition panels into coat hangers. Since the packaging includes a larger box, which holds six boxes for transport, it also provides a simple cupboard. The waterproof corrugated cardboard boxes are sturdy enough to store dishes or clothes.

Client
Shenzhen Solarrun Energy Co., Ltd.
Shenzhen, China

Design
Shenzhen Tigerpan
Packaging Design Co., Ltd.
Shenzhen, China

Project Team
Tiger Pan (Art Direction)
Yuxuan He (Graphic Design)
Yahui Wang (Graphic Design)
Yuling Zhu (Image Editing)
Zhangkun Xie (Technical Direction)
Lei Peng (Project Management)

→ Designer profile on page 671
→ Clip online

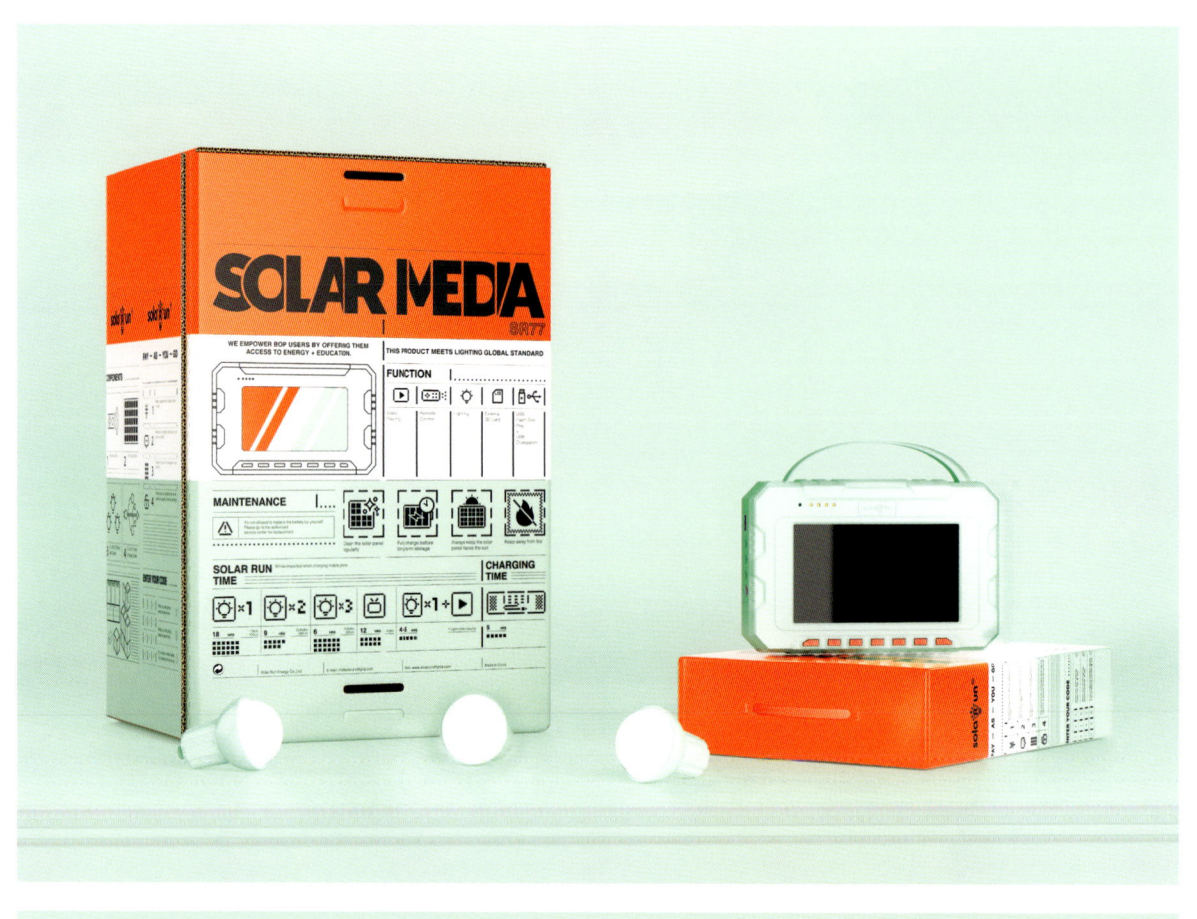

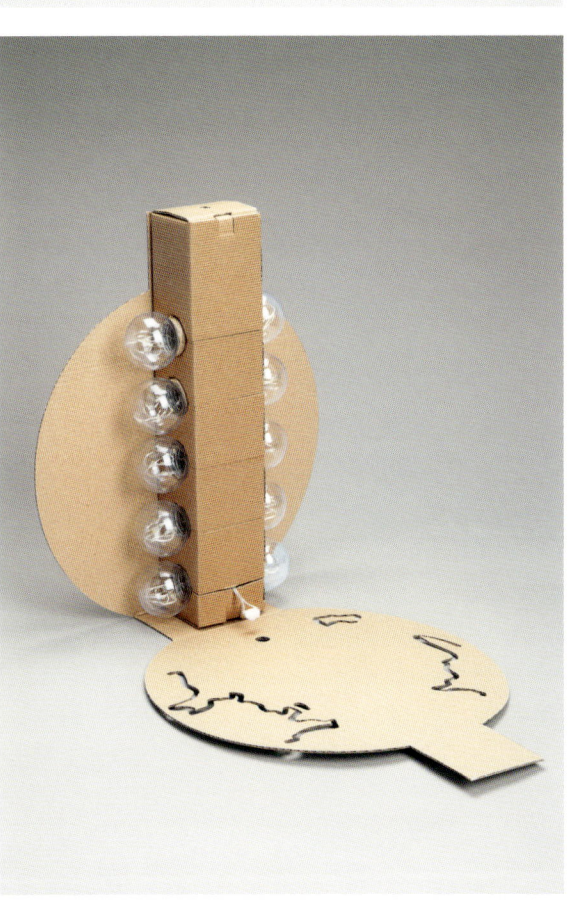

Energy Ball

[Sustainable Packaging]

To enhance a set of solar light bulbs, this packaging implements the idea of sustainability. The rustic package is composed of corrugated cardboard, with soybean ink printing only. No glue is used to affix the ten bulbs included. Shaped like a bulb itself, the package clearly references the product, while an integrated switch serves as a special incentive for consumers. Once the light is switched on, it shimmers auspiciously through the punched-out shapes. The hemp rope used to close the pack corresponds to the decoration on the bulbs.

Client
Test Rite Trading, Test Rite Business Development Corporation Co., Ltd.
Shenzhen, China

Design
Test Rite Trading, Test Rite Business Development Corporation Co., Ltd.
Shenzhen, China

Project Team
Wei Wen-Hsiang (Creative Direction)
Chen Ming-Chien (Art Direction)
Shu Liming (Concept)
Zhen Fangyi (Graphic Design)

The Book of Light

[Retail Packaging]

The Book of Light concept is geared to convenience and sustainability. The old-style packaging contains a bendable lighting tool with a magnetic head, which extends up to 582 mm. As the light is not easy to store, the user can put it back in the package after use. The compact box can be placed on a shelf like a book, and is easy to find when needed. Practical instructions and product drawings are displayed on the fold-out inner section. In order to reduce the carbon footprint, the package is made from 100 per cent recycled corrugated card.

Client
Test Rite Group
Shanghai, China

Design
Test Rite Group
Shanghai, China

Project Team
Wen Hsiang Wei (Creative Direction)
Ming-Chien Chen (Art Direction)
Endong Guo (Concept)
Chih-Sheng Yang (Concept)
Li Yang (Artwork)
Anping Wang (Artwork)
Sujuan Lin (Photography)

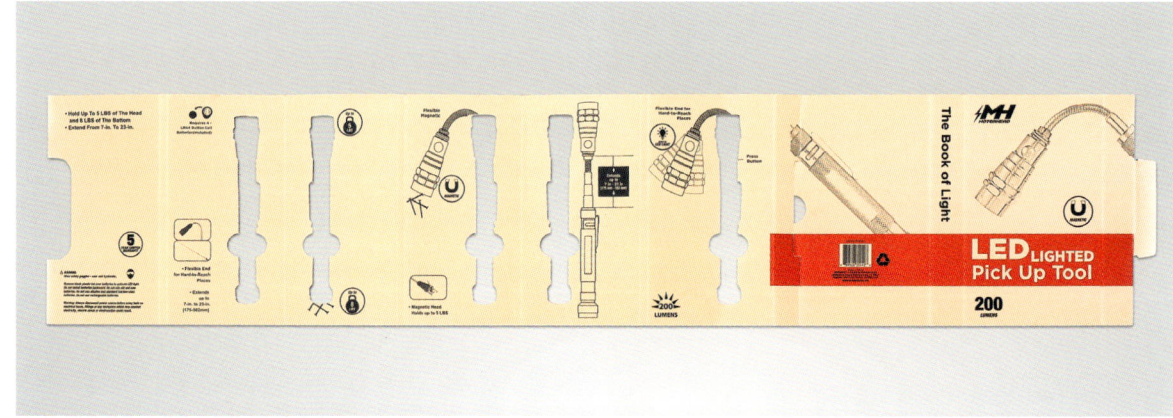

Philips SpeedPro
[Retail Packaging]

The SpeedPro packaging for a range of cordless vacuum cleaners explores the boundaries of shelf impact with an eye-catching layout. Both Instagrammable and Pinterestable, the design is customised for the millennial target group. The bright, graphic packs highlight a key characteristic of the range, namely the variety of colourways offered. Visuals are paired with descriptions in a straightforward and lively way. The product angles are clean and iconic, framing the bold typography of "Fast", which is the key product proposition, in the middle of the box.

Client
Philips
Eindhoven, Netherlands

Design
Philips Experience Design team
Amsterdam/Eindhoven, Netherlands

Fousu CC Socks

[Retail Packaging]

The Fousu CC packaging design adheres to the product concept of carbon cotton technology and is geared to the needs of young people. In order to communicate the advanced material of the socks inside, the boxes come with a futuristic look, resembling a flying saucer or a spaceship. The distinct hexagonal form reflects the typical shape of carbon structures. After removing the socks, users can reuse the packages to store various bits and pieces. This protects the environment, as does the manufacturing of the boxes from biodegradable pulp.

Client
Zhejiang Fousu
New Material Technology Co., Ltd.
Zhejiang, China

Design
Shandong Veikao
Advertising Co., Ltd.
Shandong, China

Project Team
Gaowei Xin (Creative Direction)
Cui Peng (Packaging Design)
Yuerong Liu (Packaging Design)
Yuru Wang (Packaging Design)

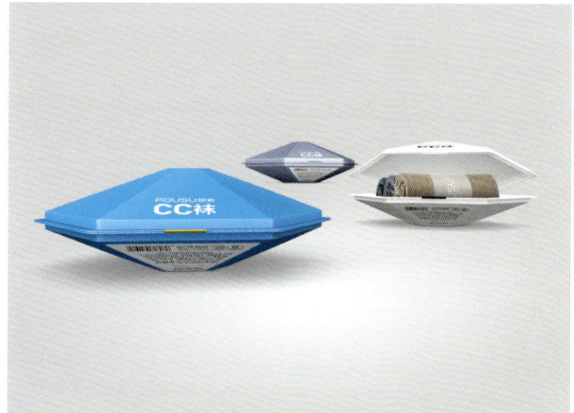

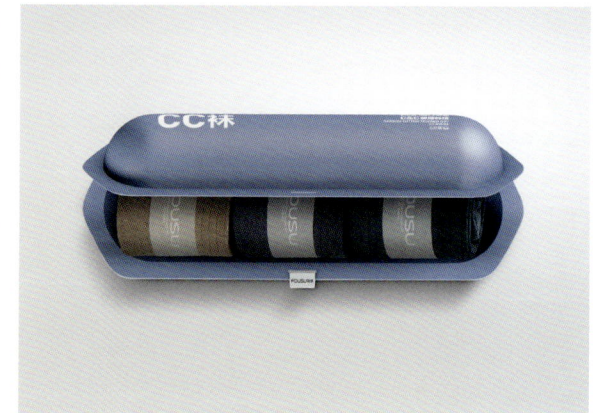

XPERIENCE BOX

[Promotional Item, Packaging]

Eberl & Kœsel is a German manufacturer of high-quality print products. The Xperience Box is the company's own marketing tool to show customers the difference between various types of packaging. The set consists of a main box and a further 14 sample boxes. The challenge was to create a concept that would not detract from the boxes' construction or be so specific that customers would be unable to envisage their own design. The subtle colour scheme and the geometric patterns together create an aesthetic overall look. The three boxes made of Gmund Gold paper in the Oro shade of gold form the visual highlights of the range.

Client
Eberl & Kœsel FinePrints
Altusried-Krugzell, Germany

Design
Clormann Design
Penzing, Germany

Project Team
Bettina Schulz (Text)

Grace of Waste

[Sustainable Packaging]

This packaging product has been developed in view of the fact that more and more plastic waste ends up in our oceans, where it collects to form large garbage patches. The design is inspired by the Japanese tradition of wrapping things in a cloth (furoshiki). This version of furoshiki, however, is made exclusively from reclaimed ocean plastic, using eco-friendly soya oil and water-based inks. To underpin the sustainable approach, the cloth's stylish pattern illustrates the location of garbage patches in the oceans. With every gift, the information is passed on to a new recipient.

Client
Peter Schmidt Group
Hamburg, Germany

Design
Peter Schmidt Group
Munich, Germany

Project Team
Norbert Möller
(Executive Creative Director)
Ulrich Aldinger (Creative Director)
Sven Rieckmann (Creative Director)

→ Designer profile on page 665

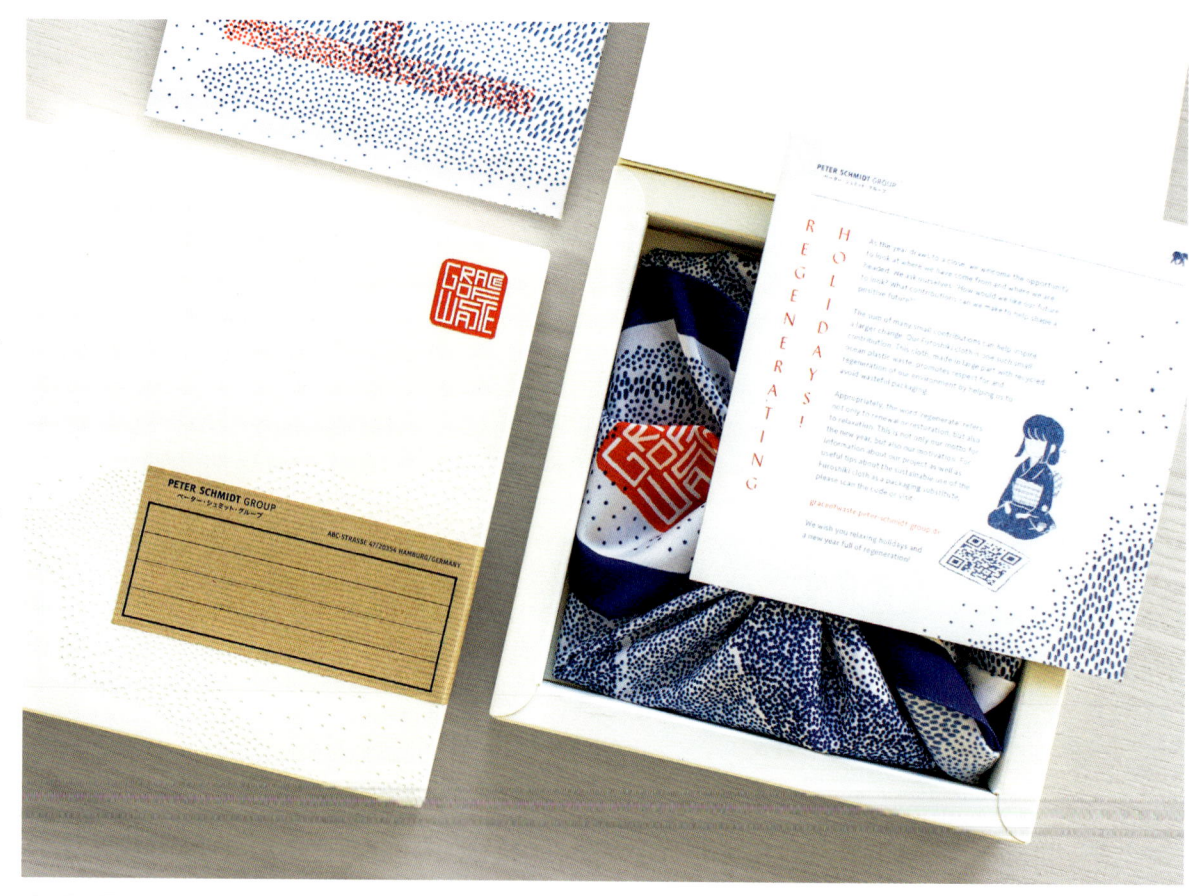

ROAZE Soothing Minky Blanket & Muslin Swaddle Gift Box
[Packaging]

The playful design of these gift packages for comfort blankets focuses on giving the consumer a warm and reassuring feeling. On the packs, childlike animal characters sum up the message that all babies need friends to keep them company. The large-scale images serve as decoration for the package, arousing the onlooker's curiosity. Each motif incorporates a see-through window, which allows to catch a glimpse of the soft muslin cloth and a part of its pretty pattern inside. A pastel colour scheme complements the harmonious overall appearance.

Client
YOHO Medical Enterprise Co., Ltd.
Changhua, Taiwan

Design
PH7 Creative Lab
Taichung, Taiwan

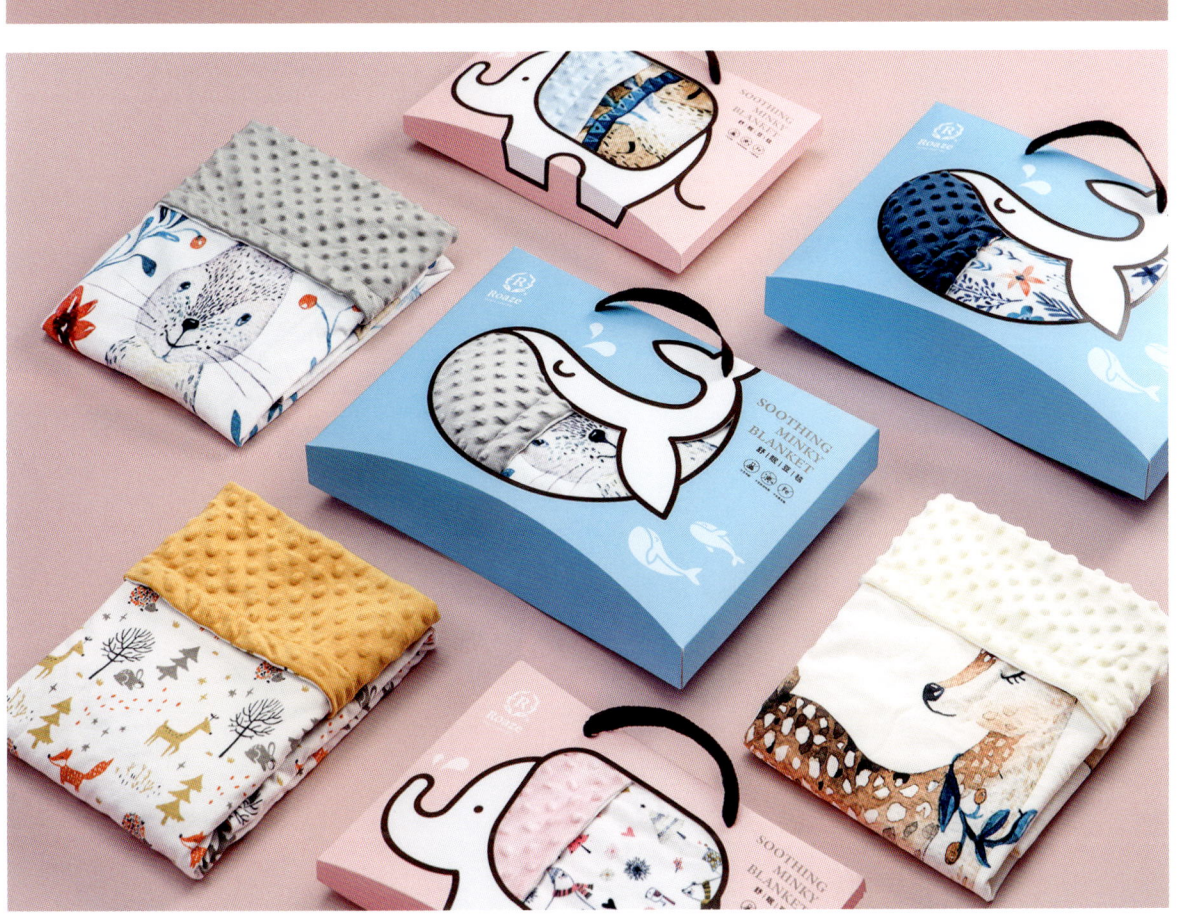

OLIVIO & CO Sunglasses
[Sustainable Packaging]

OLIVIO & CO is a lifestyle brand with a focus on eco-friendly eyewear for children. Up to the brand's high ecological standard, each pair of glasses comes in a sugarcane pulp box which is completely biodegradable. The stackable design ensures easy display and storage. The moulded clamshell container showcases the shape of the product, while touching the textured surface conveys a sense of anticipation before opening. Once opened, the bright pattern of the microfibre cloth inside provides a welcoming contrast to the natural colour of the pulp container.

Client
Olivio (Hong Kong) Limited
Hong Kong

Design
Yellowdot Design
Hong Kong

Project Team
Dilara Kan (Creative Direction)
Bodin Hon (Packaging Design)

TOYKON

[Packaging]

The TOYKON is a toy figure which can be coloured in as many ways as desired. The aim was to create a packaging design which would clearly convey the purpose of the Toykon and appeal to potential customers. Therefore a literal interpretation of the product slogan "create your own art" was pursued which resulted in a creative reproduction of the drawn figure. The artwork was carefully chosen to stimulate the user's imagination without limiting his or her own creativity. The playful use of different typographies and illustrative elements further underscores the creative nature of this product.

Client
LIME STUDIO Corp.
Seoul, South Korea

Design
astudio
Seoul, South Korea

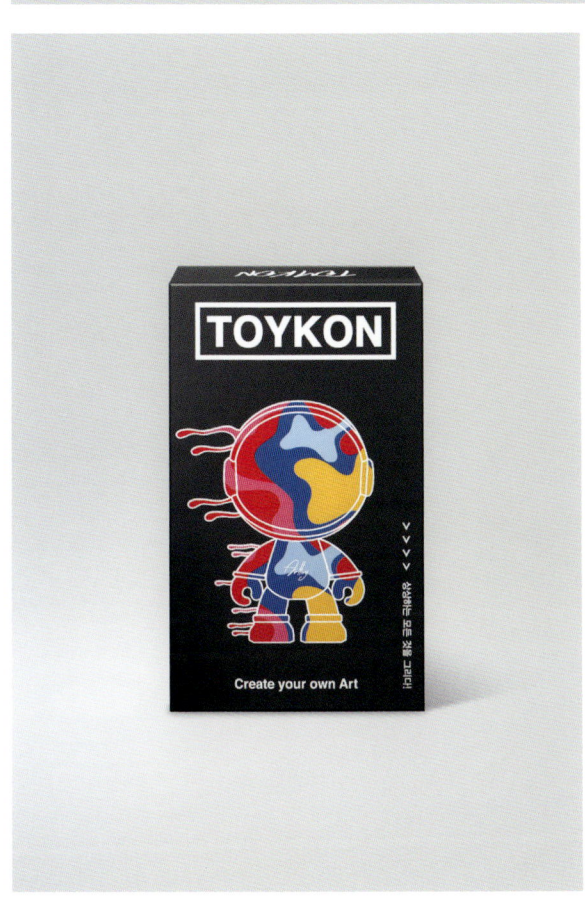

Pretend Play Toys

[Toy Packaging]

This compact packaging contains a DIY paperboard hanger. The set aims to encourage children to be creative when playing instead of using ready-made toys. Since each slipcase is reduced to the dimensions of the content, it is easy to transport. The embossed tail shape establishes a strong link with the content. Along with the product name and a dynamic font, it stimulates the imagination and arouses curiosity which animal the tail might belong to. The package is made of eco-friendly materials and thus also demonstrates a sense of responsibility for the world the kids are growing up in.

Client
Xinghan (Zhejiang)
Brand Management Co., Ltd.
Ningbo, China

Design
Xinghan (Zhejiang)
Brand Management Co., Ltd.
Ningbo, China

Project Team
PuffinKids Beijing:
Liao Jie (Creative Director)
Tianman Song (Designer)

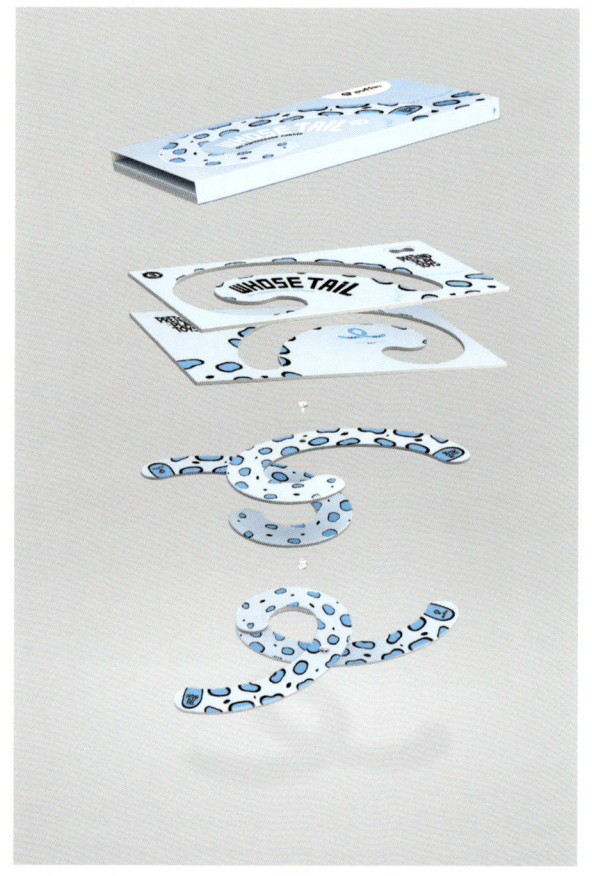

YoungYoung

[Packaging]

YoungYoung is the name of goat's milk powder products made in the Chinese province of Yunnan. Since the regulating authority requires that the packaging of newly promoted infant milk must maintain consistency of visual elements, only the colour of the package and the number indicating the target age group are allowed to differ. In a bid to inject more life into the visual appearance despite these limitations, the packaging for YoungYoung is designed in three pastel colours. The central visual element is an illustration of an adorable baby dressed in a goat onesie sitting in a colourful world of joy.

Client
Shenzhen Lingyun
Creative Packaging Design Co., Ltd.
Shenzhen, China

Design
Shenzhen Lingyun
Creative Packaging Design Co., Ltd.
Shenzhen, China

Project Team
Xiongbo Deng (Creative Direction)
Xiaoyu Li (Design)
Xing Liu (Illustration)

Minimax

[Packaging]

Client
Dong-A Pharm
Seoul, South Korea

Design
Dong-A Pharm
Seoul, South Korea

Project Team
Cha Taewoong (Head of Marketing)
Kim Hakseop (Project Manager)
Lee Kyoungmi (Brand Manager)
Kim Jungwoo (Designer)
Choi Minjun (Designer)

Minimax is a brand of nutritional supplements created for children. The products have the appearance of gummy bears and are packed in bags for portion control. In order to attract the child's attention, the logo and packaging showcase cheerful jungle characters. Befitting the brand's claim of sustainability, recycled paper fibre and eco-friendly paints have been used for the packaging. Its parts can easily be separated as recyclable waste. Moreover, the box encourages children to play, as it can be repurposed as a toy box or used as a canvas to paint on.

Goodbaby®
[Health Product Packaging]

Most children in China are given medicinal granules when they have a cold. Because many parents struggle to quickly measure out smaller doses for infants, this pharmaceutical packaging comes as user-friendly double-split bags. The packs are designed as animal figures and are matched to the brand colours. The special feature is that each pack can be creased in the middle and transformed into a cute animal puppet the children can have some fun with. Parents are thus provided with a practical aid to encourage their kids to take the medicine.

Client
China Resources Sanjiu
Medical & Pharmaceutical Co., Ltd.
Shenzhen, China

Design
JiaYi (Guangzhou) Design Co., Ltd.
Guangzhou, China
China Resources Sanjiu
Medical & Pharmaceutical Co., Ltd.
Shenzhen, China

Project Team
Cao Xue (Supervisor)
Wang Liang (Supervisor)
Duan Hongli (Art Direction)
Chen Jiayi (Art Direction)
He Ge (Graphic Design)
Xu Mengzhen (Project Manager)
Ma Lan (Consumer Analysis)
Lin Huangtao (Market Analysis)

Advertising	Packaging Design	Fair Stands	Retail Design	Red Dot: Junior Award	Designer Profiles	Index
288	318	494	516	544	614	674

Cold Medicine
[Health Product Packaging]

This pharmaceutical packaging catches the eye with the key visual of a child wiping its nose. When the user opens the box, the closing tab, which represents the tissue in the illustration, is pulled out. What remains is the image of a happy child. This surprising transformation brings the message to the point that taking the medicine leads to a quick recovery. Thanks to its expressive style, the packaging is easily identifiable. It also increases the chances of appealing to a wide target group by showing children of different sex and complexion.

Client
China Resources Sanjiu
Medical & Pharmaceutical Co., Ltd.
Shenzhen, China

Design
JiaYi (Guangzhou) Design Co., Ltd.
Guangzhou, China
China Resources Sanjiu
Medical & Pharmaceutical Co., Ltd.
Shenzhen, China

Project Team
Cao Xue (Supervisor)
Duan Hongli (Supervisor)
Chen Jiayi (Art Direction)
He Ge (Graphic Design)
Xu Mengzhen (Creative Direction)
Lin Huangtao (Communication)

Mi Kids Sonic Electric Toothbrush

[Retail Packaging]

This sonic toothbrush packaging uses cartoon elements to show children why they need to take care of their teeth. The design capitalises on interaction. As the child pulls the toothbrush out of the slipcase, different images are displayed in a cut-out on the back. The images can be read as a story, going from tooth decay to plaque and shiny teeth when the box has been fully opened. Handling the package thus increases the chances that young children get emotionally involved with the product and effectively strengthens brand loyalty.

Client
Xiaomi Inc.
Beijing, China

Design
Xiaomi Inc.
Beijing, China

Project Team
Lu Chen (Creative Direction)
Weijie Jiang (Graphic Design)
Yan Ni (Illustration)
Zhizhuang Song
(Packaging Structure Design)

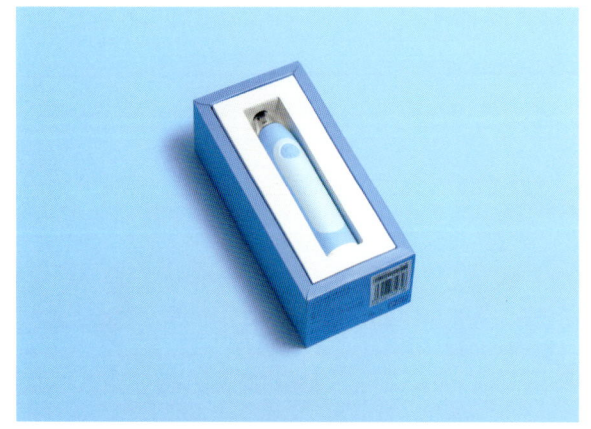

Advertising	Packaging Design	Fair Stands	Retail Design	Red Dot: Junior Award	Designer Profiles	Index
288	318	494	516	544	614	674

KUB Baby Diapers
[Retail Packaging]

In an amusing way, this concept lends added value to a Chinese nappy product. Designed for mothers, who are usually the ones to go shopping, the packages attract attention through a large bear wearing a cardboard nappy. The bear's cute look and fluffy texture is paired with a three-dimensional effect and fresh colours to enhance the product. In addition, the bear's raised arms can be used as a handle. The handling of each pack is self-explanatory: the nappy fastening can simply be torn open to remove the contents.

Client
Hangzhou KUB Baby Products Co., Ltd.
Hangzhou, China

Design
Shenzhen Tigerpan
Packaging Design Co., Ltd.
Shenzhen, China

Project Team
Tiger Pan (Art Direction)
Melissa Han (Graphic Design)
Yuling Zhu (Image Editing)
Zhangkun Xie (Technical Direction)
Krystal You (Project Management)

→ Designer profile on page 671

Childlike Mask

[Health Product Packaging]

Infection prevention has become an important issue with the rapid spread of COVID-19. Since children need protection as well as adults do, this product line features medical-grade masks for kids. Three packaging designs indicate different mask sizes. The colourful boxes with animal motifs are punched out at the front, showing some of the mask and inviting consumers to take hold of the product. Once the last mask has been used, users are rewarded with a smiling animal face inside the package. Moreover, each pack includes a motivational phrase to help children overcome their resistance to wearing a mask.

Client
inDare Design Strategy Limited
Shenzhen, China

Design
inDare Design Strategy Limited
Shenzhen, China

Project Team
Jiarong Zeng
Fengming Chen
Yujie Chen
Junlong Yang
Yanhui Yan
Mengdi Wang
Linhan Peng
Mengxuan Cai

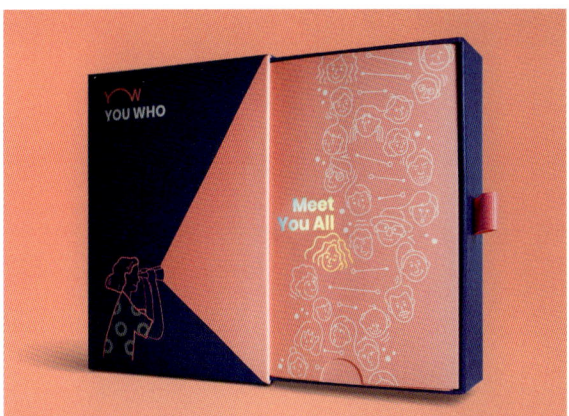

You Who – Saliva Collection Kit

[Packaging]

You Who is a genealogy set. Users can use the test included to find out how they are genetically connected to the rest of the population worldwide. To make the scientific issue more accessible for a wider audience, the design of the packaging focuses on conveying a friendly tone. The symbolic meaning of the colours is key: blue stands for trust, while pink represents unconditional love. Small holograms reflect the unknown, wondrous world of DNA. In addition, a likeable young female character is introduced who users can identify with easily.

Client
EONE DIAGNOMICS Genome Center
Incheon, South Korea

Design
B for Brand
Seoul, South Korea

Project Team
Yena Choi (Creative Direction)
Soomin Jo (Graphic Design)
Jinha Seo (Graphic Design)

→ Designer profile on page 624

The Real Treats

[Pet Food Packaging]

This dog food packaging focuses on the ingredients, which are freeze-dried and come without any additives. In order to enhance the image of the brand, a versatile yet emotionally appealing concept has been developed. Clear visuals underscored by a colour scheme with subdued and friendly shades communicate the freshness of the product. In line with the brand's nature-oriented philosophy, the resealable bags are produced with eco-friendly ink, non-adhesion and non-coating agents.

Client
Harim Petfood
Seoul, South Korea

Design
Harimholdings
Seoul, South Korea

Project Team
Jae Hyoung Yoo (Design Direction)
Ju Yeon Bae (Artwork)
Eun Ah Kim (Artwork)
Min Gi Hong (Artwork)

PET HooH

[Pet Food Packaging]

In order to offer the high-quality pet food, which is designed to be sold online at a reasonable price, the costs of advertising, packaging and distribution were aimed to be kept as low as possible. To achieve this, the design follows the motto "Only the core!". In terms of the packaging, which is also friendly to the environment, this means that the bags used to pack the food include only the necessary information, such as the brand and product name. A simple and stylised graphic shows whether the food is for a cat or a dog. Restraints have also been exercised in the design of the boxes for shipping.

Client
Glyde
Gyeonggi Province, South Korea

Design
Harimholdings
Seoul, South Korea

Project Team
Jae Hyoung Yoo (Design Direction)
Ju Yeon Bae (Artwork)
Eun Ah Kim (Artwork)
Min Gi Hong (Artwork)

Preface	Red Dot: Agency of the Year	Brands	Brand Design & Identity	Corporate Design & Identity	Annual Reports
4	6	18	90	202	260

Pet Partner

[Pet Food Packaging]

The Pet Partner packaging uses realistic images of animals as protagonists. By using a dog's or a cat's ears and face as a starting point, the entire package is strongly related to the shape of the animal. In a bid to enhance the fun factor for the user, the opening of the pouch is located at the lower rear part, creating a tongue-in-cheek reference to the claim that "good digestion" is guaranteed. The animal pictures on the front are placed against a dark background to enhance recognition. In addition, the close-ups aim to appeal to the owners' emotional bond with their pets.

Client
inDare Design Strategy Limited
Shenzhen, China

Design
inDare Design Strategy Limited
Shenzhen, China

Project Team
Jiarong Zeng
Fengming Chen
Yujie Chen
Junlong Yang
Yanhui Yan
Guoxiang Zheng
Shuyao Wang

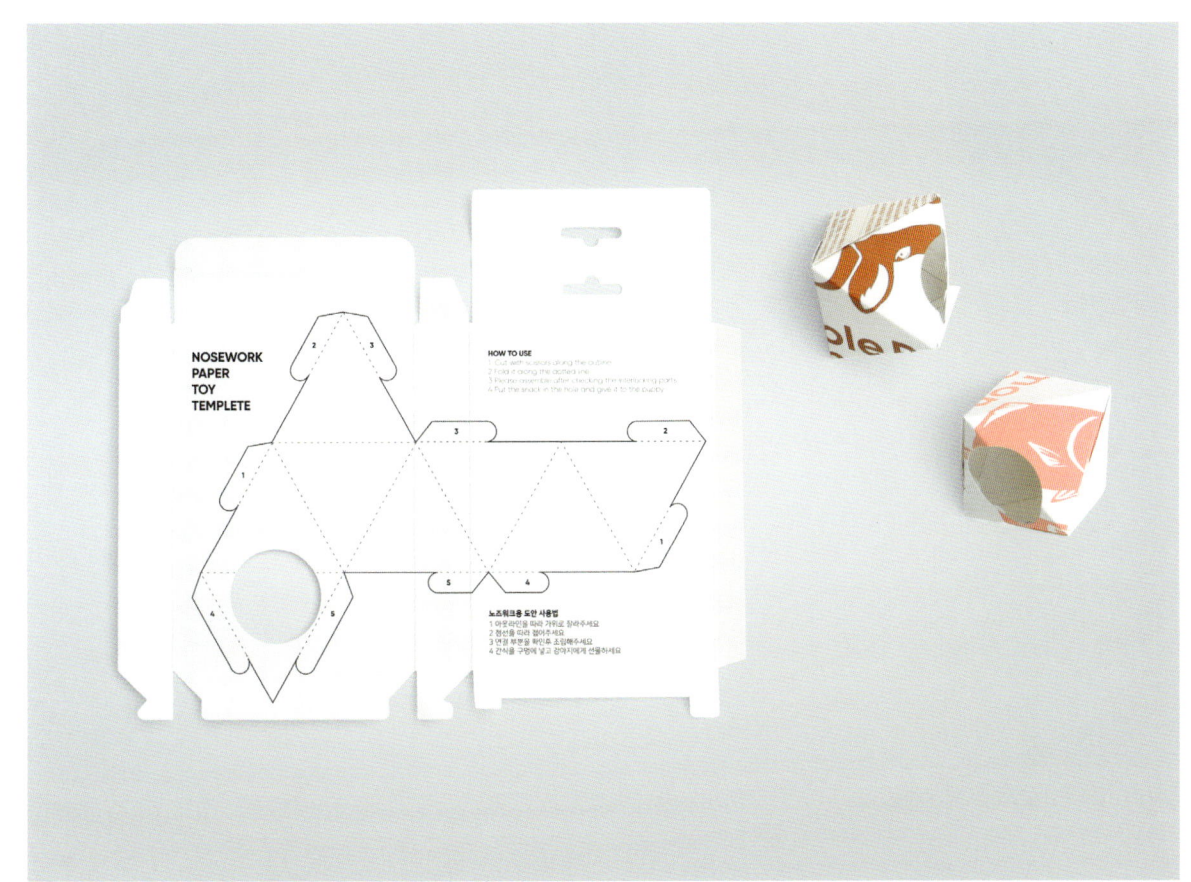

Pet Snacks

[Pet Food Packaging]

The packaging for these premium dog snacks is informative and attracts attention at the same time. A large, single-coloured illustration of the respective main ingredient is shown on the front. It allows the consumer to choose the right snack for their pet intuitively. The shiny surface of the packaging makes it stand out on the supermarket shelf. On the back of the package, there is a template which can be cut out and used as a toy. It is designed in a triangular structure which is suitable for the dog to roll along the ground and sniff at the content.

Client
BRIDGE & COMPANY
Seoul, South Korea

Design
BRIDGE & COMPANY
Seoul, South Korea

Fair Stands

Kale Fair Stand Cersaie 2019 – Bespoke Romance

Client
Kaleseramik,
Çanakkale Kalebodur Seramik San. A.S.
Istanbul, Turkey

Design
Paolo Cesaretti
Milan/Florence, Italy

Project Team
Claudia Astarita (Graphic Design)
Extrasync (Interactive Programming)
La Bottega S.r.l. (Contractor)
Ulas Vural (Project Coordinator)
Lorenzo Pennati (Photography)
Luca Rotondo (Photography)

Advertising	Packaging Design	**Fair Stands**	Retail Design	Red Dot: Junior Award	Designer Profiles	Index
288	318	494	516	544	614	674

This stand of 700 sqm represented the Kale Group at the 2019 Cersaie exhibition in Bologna, Italy. The design of the general layout and the visual identity were inspired by the symbol of infinity. Merging circles were intended to evoke the impression of perfection and durability. Sheer architectural shapes enhanced by a theatrical use of light dipped the entire setting in a metaphysical atmosphere. Also, decorative tableaux made of cut-out ceramic tiles complemented the walls and floors. The stand was built using the company's materials, thus highlighting their qualities and versatility of use in an architectural and interior design context. With the aim to disrupt the general perception of ceramic tiles as a mere solid building material at the heart of the space, an interactive installation acted as an attractor for visitors and informed about this material in a new and different way.

Gerflor Fair Stand EuroShop 2020

For the EuroShop 2020 trade fair in Düsseldorf, Germany, this fair stand created the "optical" impression that the entire exhibition stand consisted of only one floor area. A six-metre-high wall to the neighbouring stand became part of the floor via a large groove in between. A digital service for the "Creation 70" product allowed visitors to individually adapt the floor decor to their own needs and retail interiors. In order to emphasise the customisability of the product and to address each customer's visual needs, the floor covering for the exhibition stand adapted to the different furniture, fabrics and lamps.

Client
Gerflor Mipolam GmbH
Troisdorf, Germany

Design
TULP Design GmbH
Munich, Germany

INAX Exhibition Milan Design Week 2019

This exhibition, held during Milan Design Week 2019, explored Japanese water rituals to showcase the new bathroom designs by the company LIXIL. Set in a purist ambience, it presented the upcoming product lines, ranging from bathtubs and toilets to washbasins, faucets and decorative yet functional tiles. Another eye-catcher was a range of ceramics, including an elegant blue-and-white pottery toilet from the Meiji era (1868–1912) and artistic tiles.

Client
LIXIL Corporation
Tokyo, Japan

Design
LIXIL Corporation
Tokyo, Japan

Preface	Red Dot: Agency of the Year	Brands	Brand Design & Identity	Corporate Design & Identity	Annual Reports
4	6	18	90	202	260

medular
[Exhibition Design]

Client
Buchholz GmbH
Eicklingen, Germany

Design
PierraaGroup GmbH
Braunschweig, Germany

Project Team
Saskia Pierschek (CEO)
Jessica Prill (Head of Design)
Karen Heinrichs (Creative Direction)
Sandra Sosniok (Graphic Design)
Nina Mares (Graphic Design)
Lisa Kalden (Copywriting)
Julian Köchy (Animation)

→ Designer profile on page 660
→ Clip online

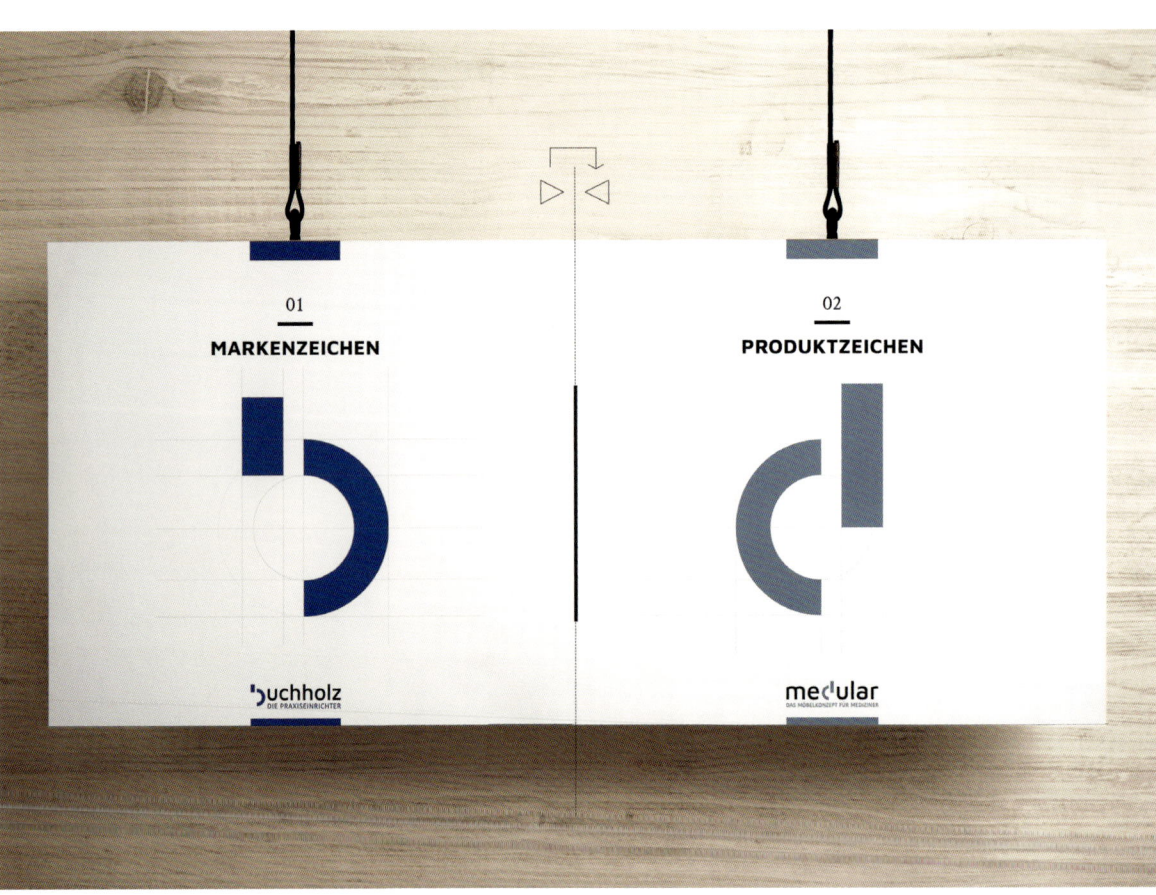

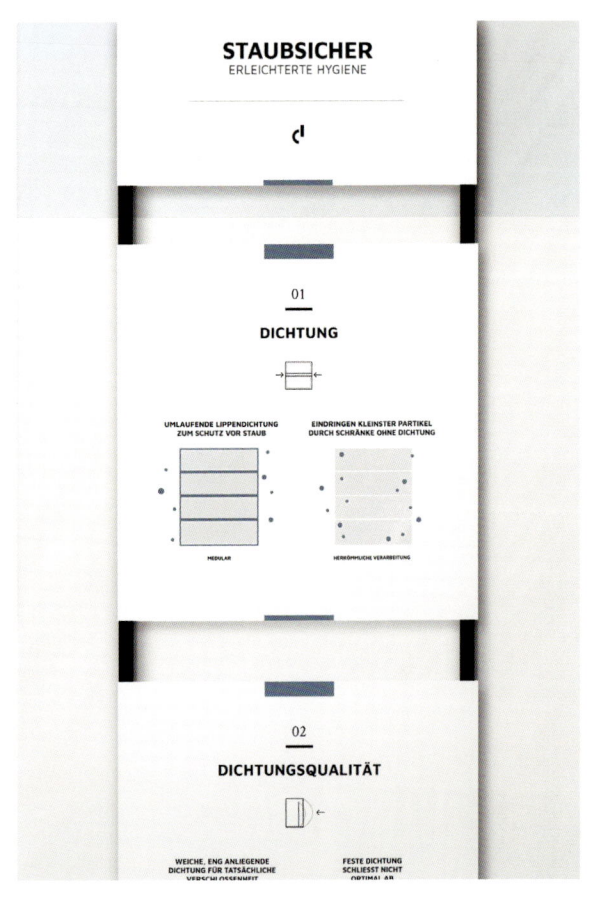

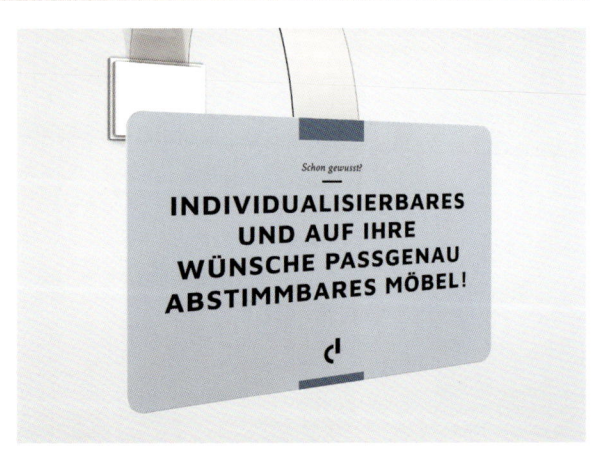

Advertising	Packaging Design	**Fair Stands**	Retail Design	Red Dot: Junior Award	Designer Profiles	Index
288	318	494	516	544	614	674

The design of this in-house exhibition for Buchholz, a furniture manufacturer for medical practices, focused on creating a customer-oriented presentation of the innovative "medular" furniture system for potential customers. In order to communicate that this furniture system can perfectly integrate into any medical practice, a hands-on experiential world was created, allowing one to discover the various special features of the system. Clear explanatory panels are connected to the individual furniture elements and explain the advantages over conventional construction methods for practice furnishings. An explanatory video, as well as the possibility of a 3D practice tour with VR glasses, visually rounds off the experience.

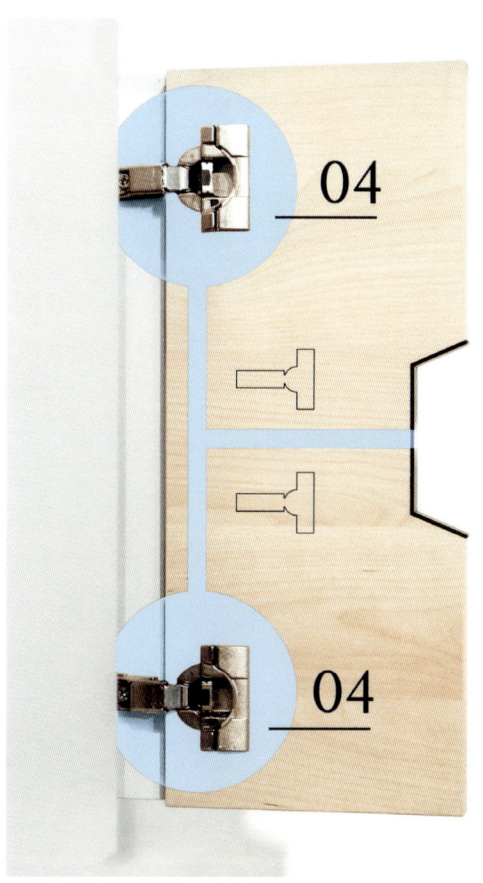

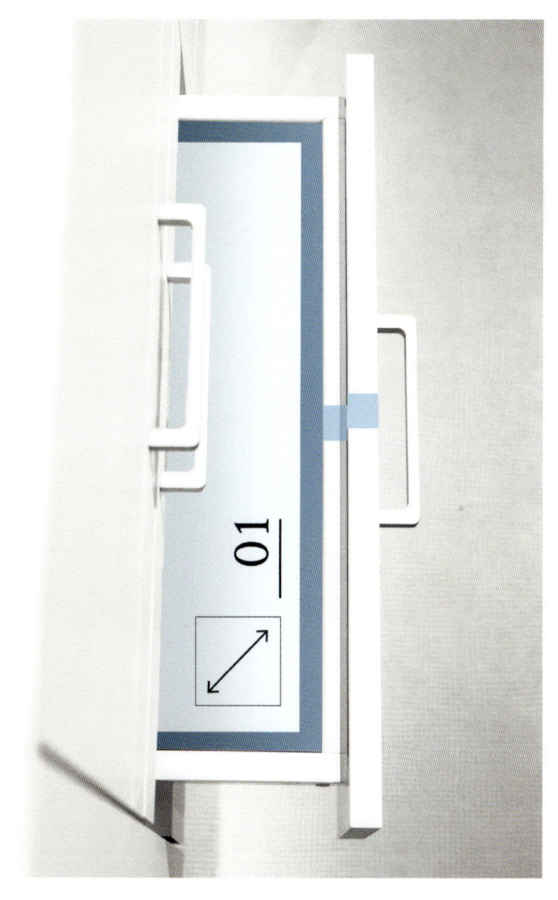

Schüco Fair Stand BAU 2019 – Experience Progress

Client
Schüco International KG
Bielefeld, Germany

Design
D'art Design Gruppe
Neuss, Germany

Project Team
Guido Mamczur (Managing Director)
Götz Schrader (Interior Design)
Olga Mocek (Interior Design)
Sadrick Schmidt (Communication Design)

→ Clip online

Advertising	Packaging Design	Fair Stands	Retail Design	Red Dot: Junior Award	Designer Profiles	Index
288	318	494	516	544	614	674

The concept of this trade fair booth for the company Schüco was centred on defining a clearly structured visitor journey through the company's experience-oriented brand environment. The focus was on holistic, large-format presentations. This yielded a clear architecture and communication concept for expressing the solution-oriented character of the brand. The design of a light installation in conjunction with mirrored ceiling panels created the abstract perception of vertical density and urbanity. A "white room" invited visitors to experience the presentation of the company's portfolio in a digital sphere. Guiding visitors through the exhibition, the "innovation walk" staged the company's key topics with animations on six LED walls.

HCOB Fair Stand Expo Real 2019

The HCOB fair stand at the Expo Real 2019 in Munich, Germany, projected a pleasant atmosphere following the idea of a well-designed hotel bar or lobby. It thus tried to address the target group of the upper middle class from the real-estate industry. The design created different zones for working and lingering, and impressed with a use of fine materials and flawless craftsmanship. Oiled American walnut, a high-quality sisal rug and an exclusive, colour-coordinated furnishing concept with elegant seating rounded off the ensemble.

Client
HCOB
Kiel, Germany

Design
holzrausch
Munich, Germany
Office Heinzelmann Ayadi
Munich, Germany

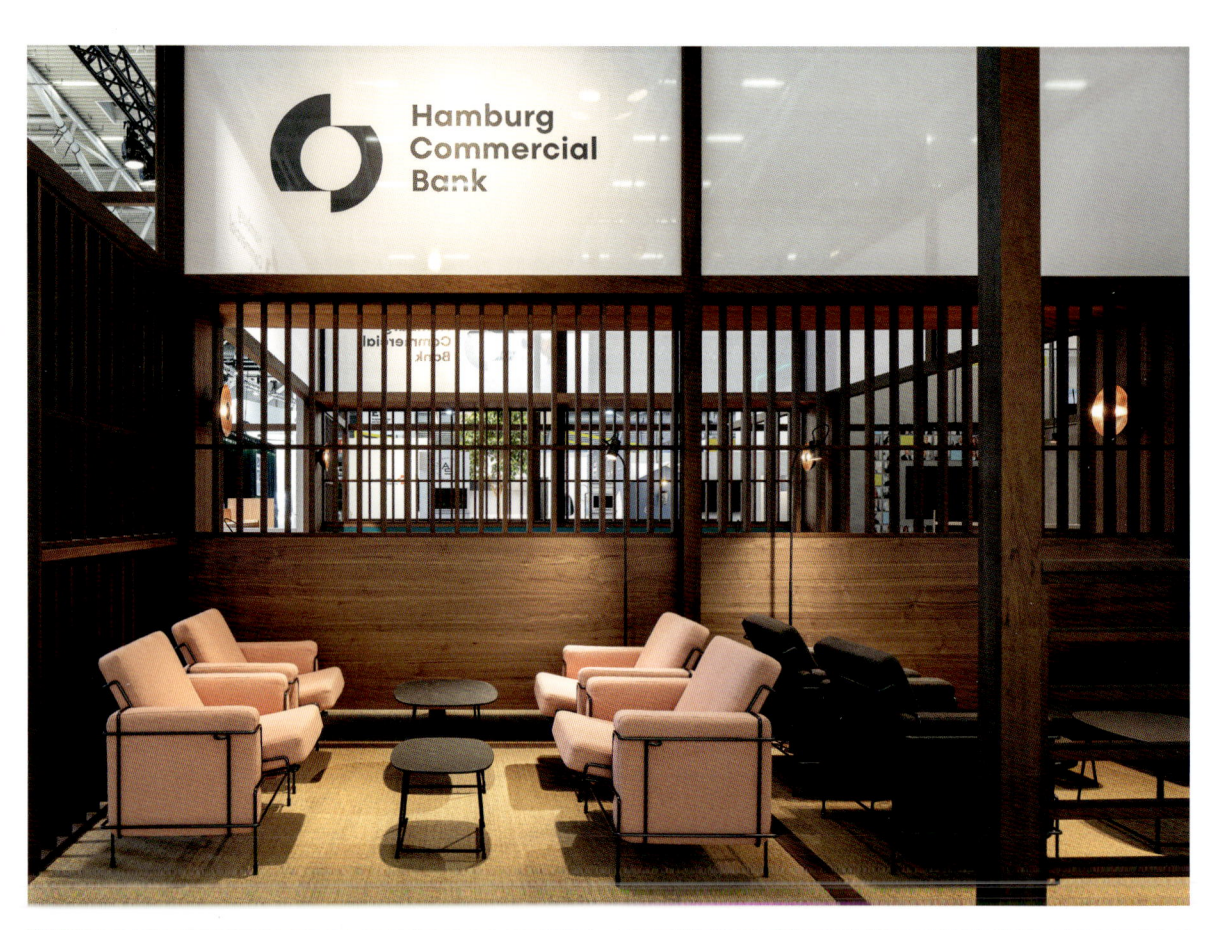

Covestro Fair Stand K 2019

The holistic concept of this brand presence for the company Covestro at the trade fair "K" in Düsseldorf, Germany, placed people and materials centre stage. The aim was to convey the brand values of curiosity, courage and diversity. In order to make these values tangible, smart digital and interactive elements were incorporated, as well as an augmented reality show on the UN's sustainable development goals, to which Covestro has committed in various projects. The core element was a large "Talk Area" focused on the presentations by experts and on the company's partners.

Client
Covestro Deutschland AG
Leverkusen, Germany

Design
Uniplan GmbH & Co. KG
Cologne, Germany

FIELD.IO Berlin GmbH & Co. KG
Berlin, Germany

NSYNK Gesellschaft für Kunst und Technik mbH
Frankfurt/Main, Germany

Walbert-Schmitz GmbH & Co. KG
Aachen, Germany

smd + partner
Aachen, Germany

LK AG
Essen, Germany

→ Clip online

The Fountain

[Exhibition Design]

This exhibition design focused on highlighting the distinctive characteristics of the LG SIGNATURE OLED R, also known as the rollable display by LG. In front of a dark water surface, a total of 20 such displays were installed to demonstrate the possibilities of this screen in redefining the capability and the value of space. Beginning with the grand appearance of a Greek sculpture, which symbolises rollable displays as a powerful innovation, immersive content storytelling took the audience on a journey created by powerful colours and motions.

Client
LG Electronics Inc.
Seoul, South Korea

Design
HS Ad
Seoul, South Korea

› Designer profile on page 643

IFA Philips Experience 2019

This concept aimed at increasing awareness of the brand for consumer audiences by showcasing a holistic 360-degree experience for Philips at the IFA 2019 in Berlin, Germany. Wrapped up in a vibrant and elegant design that expressed the human and innovative aspects of the brand, a "neighbourhood home" space was created in the consumer hall with design cues from both home and professional worlds to express unique expertise. At the entrance of the hall was the "Welcome Experience" where visitors were introduced to the brand through interactive storytelling.

Client
Philips
Eindhoven, Netherlands

Design
Philips Experience Design team
Amsterdam/Eindhoven, Netherlands

Mercedes-Benz
Fair Stand GPEC 2020

Client
Mercedes-Benz AG
Mercedes-Benz Vertrieb Deutschland
Berlin, Germany

Design
einsagentur Schäuble GmbH
Karlsruhe, Germany
Waidmann/Post GmbH
Braunschweig, Germany

→ Clip online

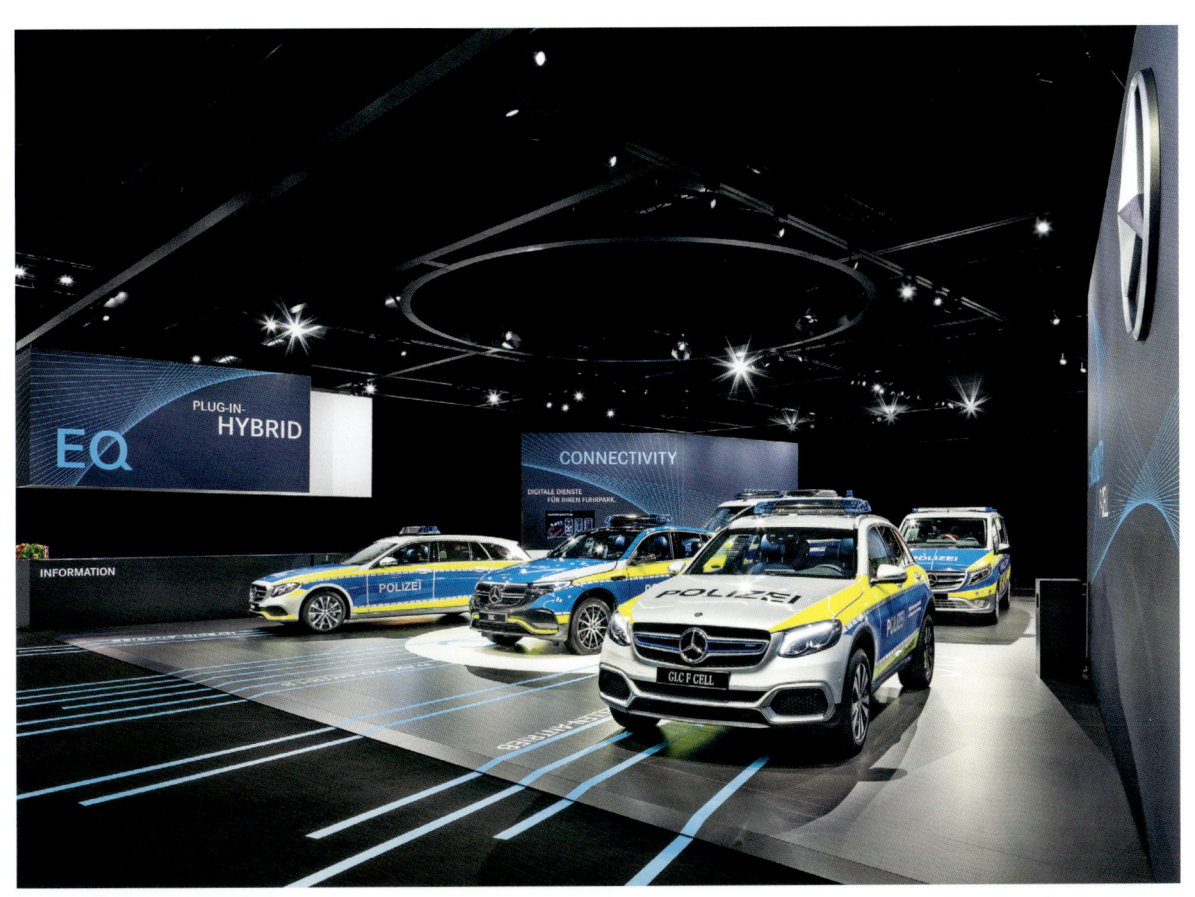

Advertising	Packaging Design	Fair Stands	Retail Design	Red Dot: Junior Award	Designer Profiles	Index
288	318	494	516	544	614	674

The design intention of this booth at the GPEC 2020 trade fair in Frankfurt am Main, Germany, was to highlight the role model function that police play in society and to outline how they may best fulfil this function by using a variety of innovative, ecologically compatible vehicles. The idea of the stand was to attract the visitors' attention directly when they step into the hall and have them enveloped in a catching sight that points out the special features of the utility vehicles. The role of the architecture and graphic design was to underline this very effect. The structural elements from the floor over the walls to the ceilings, as well as all graphic elements, were in full alignment.

VW Fair Stand IAA 2019 – Enter Vibrant Power

With the motto "Enter Vibrant Power", this trade fair booth at the IAA 2019 in Frankfurt am Main, Germany, celebrated the competence of Volkswagen in the sector of e-mobility. At the same time, it communicated the beginning of a new era of the brand. In order to turn this change into an experience, the core topics of "vibrant design" and "sustainability" were placed centre stage. The design language is based on clean, modular architecture and the bold use of light and colour. In addition, an "ID. Walk" was developed as an interactive journey for visitors to experience the features of the ID.3 model.

Client
Volkswagen AG
Wolfsburg, Germany

Design
MUTABOR Brand Experience GmbH
Hamburg, Germany

Project Team
Ben Erben (Creative Direction)
Gerd Hermes (Creative Direction)
Jan Lenze (Architectural Planning)
Charlotte Valentin-Jessen
(Project Management)

Hyundai Future Mobility Ecosystem
[Showcase]

The "Future mobility ecosystem" booth in the lobby of the Hyundai headquarters at the heart of Seoul, South Korea, aims to share the company's future mobility vision with employees and visitors. The showcase consists of a 1:8 scale model that reflects the exhibition's different thematic aspects of "Urban Air Mobility solution", "Community Hub" and "Purpose Built Vehicles". This communicates the mission statement that connecting the sky and the land provides new freedom of mobility. With its simple and minimalist design, the stand allows visitors to focus on the essence of the contents.

Client
Hyundai Motor Company
Seoul, South Korea

Design
Hyundai Motor Company
Seoul, South Korea

Project Team
Sungwon Jee (Creative Direction)
Young Jang (Creative Direction)
Seojin Kim (Creative Direction)
Jinsol Kim (Art Direction)
Sukgyu Choi (Graphic Design)
Dongchul Cho (Graphic Design)

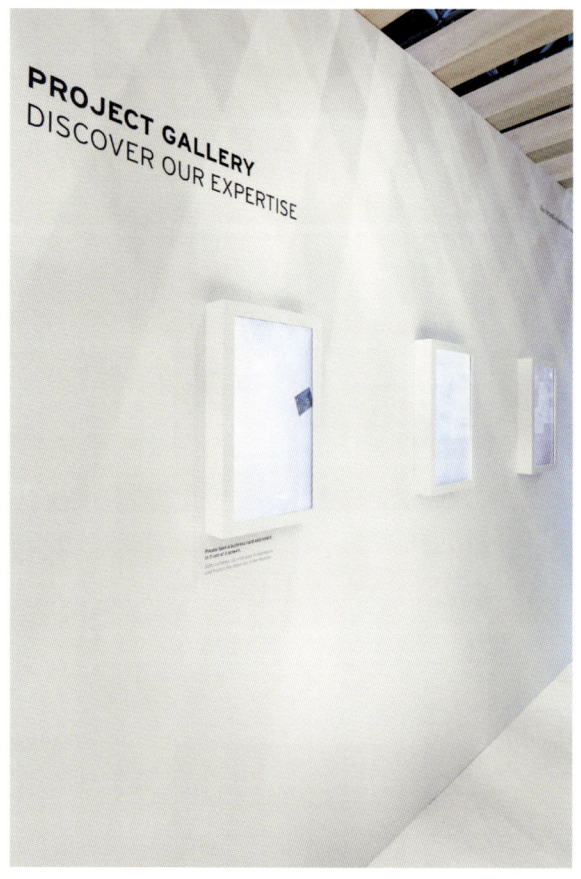

HARTMANNVONSIEBENTHAL
Fair Stand & Exhibit EuroShop 2020

This trade-fair booth combined three rooms into an immersive showcase that aimed to activate visitors and guide them step by step through the brand's world. Visitors entered the reflective reception area through an attention-grabbing portal with silver steel spheres. Transparent business cards acted as a key that brought the seemingly white screens of the gallery to life. A glance through the card revealed the company portfolio. In addition, the "Modular Individual XR" virtual showroom invited visitors to create individual prototypes.

Client
hartmannvonsiebenthal,
the brand experience company GmbH
Berlin, Germany

Design
hartmannvonsiebenthal,
the brand experience company GmbH
Berlin, Germany

Pleasure & Treasure – International Exhibition of Austrian Design

The Austrian national showcase of selected design products from Austria, presented at Milan Design Week 2019, was held in the Sala Reale, the former royal family's waiting room at the central railway station. The idea was to divide the event into two spaces, each with its own theme. The first was a dark monumental space like a treasure chamber that housed a selection of design objects majestically enthroned above a pool of golden chocolate coins. The other space was flooded with natural light and filled with white packaging material on which the exhibits seemed to float, inviting visitors to become children again by focusing on the joy evoked by the objects.

Client
Wirtschaftskammer Österreich,
AUSSENWIRTSCHAFT AUSTRIA
Vienna, Austria

Design
Vasku & Klug
Vienna, Austria

Preface	Red Dot: Agency of the Year	Brands	Brand Design & Identity	Corporate Design & Identity	Annual Reports
4	6	18	90	202	260

Snail Garden – Peak-nic

[Outdoor Amusement Facility]

The six objects of the Snail series were designed for the Snail Garden outdoor amusement facility located in Mt. Jungjeong, Busan, South Korea. With a sculptural appearance inspired by the art of origami, the objects target both children and families. Featuring different motifs, each object serves a specific playground function, such as sliding, climbing, exploring caves or sitting on a bench. The objects use Gelcoat as a finishing material for safety, lending them a pleasant feel. The park thus provides a new experience for visitors, also serving as an exciting photo zone.

Client
Daewon Plus Group
Busan, South Korea

Design
EMOTIONplanning
Busan, South Korea
Daewon Plus Group
Busan, South Korea

Project Team
EMOTIONplanning:
Heewon Kim (Creative Direction)
Hyunsu Kim (Graphic Design)
Kyunghyun Kim (Graphic Design)

Daewon Plus Group:
Hyoseob Choi (Creative Direction)
Julia Jung (Text)

Orchids to Savor
[Local Dishes Culture Exhibit]

The design of the 2019 Taiwan International Orchid Show (TIOS) with the theme "Orchids to Savor" was largely based on the surroundings of the century-old city of Tainan. This ancient city is marked by a distinctive food culture resonating through the bustling streets and laneways. Visitors could experience a floral showcase infused with the traditional charm of a city boasting 400 years of history. The show also served as a business-networking platform for collaboration possibilities and as a marketplace for promoting both orchid-related products and local agricultural produce.

Client
Tainan City Government,
Cultural Affairs Bureau
Tainan, Taiwan

Design
Jun-Liang Chen,
Freeimage Design Co., Ltd.
Taipei City, Taiwan

Yu-Ju Lin,
National Taipei University of Business
Taoyuan, Taiwan

Mo-Li Yeh, Shu-Hsuan Chang,
Ying-Shan Su, Lunghwa University of
Science and Technology
Taoyuan, Taiwan

Retail Design

Red Dot: Best of the Best

Zhao Zhao Tea Lounge
[Brand Store]

The Zhao Zhao Tea Lounge was created as a tea appreciation space where Taiwanese tea culture can extend its roots. Designed with pure, natural materials such as wood, concrete or glass, the different floors showcase an open and reduced Asian style that invites visitors to immerse in the culture and flavours of Taiwanese tea in a variety of approaches. On the first floor, the tea roasting area, guests can observe the meticulously defined steps underlying master tea-making. Next to the roasting area is a tea room where guests can rest amid the lingering smell of charcoal baking and tea and have access to the narrow backyard with planted trees. Enjoying a cup of tea there is thus intended to become a ceremony of focusing the five senses in that taste, touch, sound, smell and sight coalesce into a pleasant aesthetic experience. The tea lounge philosophy of being mindful and living in the here and now – modestly and without unnecessary decor – is expressed in a very harmonious manner.

Statement by the jury
The Zhao Zhao Tea Lounge demonstrates in a beautiful, impressive manner how an old building can be reused and transformed into a teahouse that lends new meaning to traditional culture. The architecture and minimalist design with deliberately pure and naturally processed materials imbues the rooms with a pristine sense of naturalness that consistently conveys the intended message.

Client
Zhao Zhao Tea Lounge
Taichung, Taiwan

Design
Soar Design Studio
Taichung, Taiwan

→ Designer profile on page 666
→ Clip online

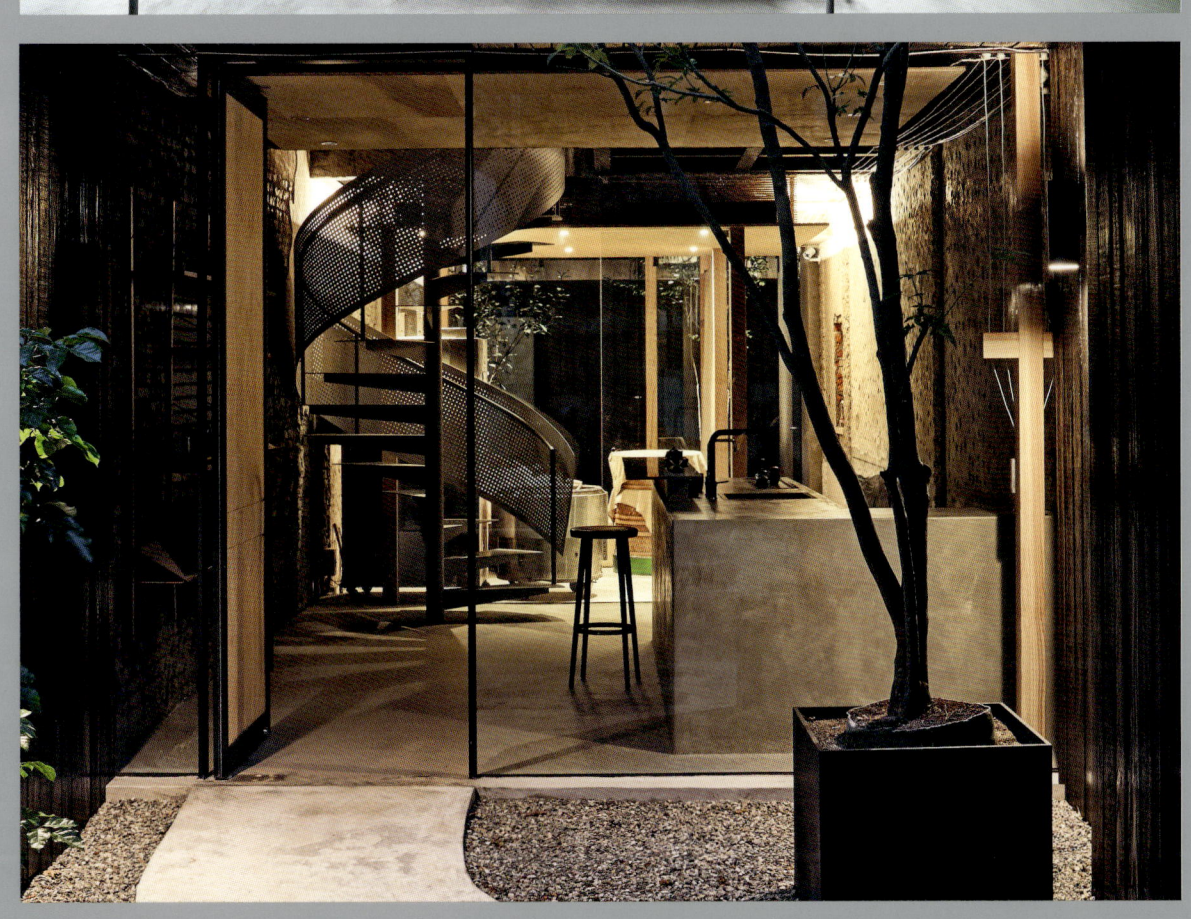

Red Dot: Best of the Best

surely. Art Space
[Art Gallery]

This art space is an abandoned old factory and now serves as a cafe and exhibition space. The design concept of the entire building is based on the idea of timelessness or time reversal, the idea of going against time or a sense of time dislocation, which creates a gap between the inside and the outside, the objects and the space. Thus, entering the space already holds a surprise, because the interior does completely without decoration in favour of retaining the former industrial character with its mottled and continuous texture of walls and floor. It is this simplicity that makes the works of art and objects on display take fully centre stage. In addition, it makes the past meet the future, because the space thus stays highly flexible and suitable for different uses in the future, such as fashion shows or product presentations. In addition, the window enlargement from the ceiling to the floor creates a higher sense of opening to the outside, allowing natural light to form lines and shadows depending on the weather and time of day and interacting in a fascinating manner with the display space.

Statement by the jury
"surely. Art Space" is an outstanding example of how a formerly purely commercial building can be successfully converted to be suitable for use in a modern lifestyle-oriented context. Contemporary creative activities thus merge with the tales told by the abandoned space and the invisible power of time to form a rare unity that presents the interplay of the various aspects in a very refined and aesthetic manner.

Advertising	Packaging Design	Fair Stands	**Retail Design**	Red Dot: Junior Award	Designer Profiles	Index
288	318	494	516	544	614	674

Client
surely. Art Space
Hangzhou, China

Design
Design Plus Design
Guangzhou, China

→ Designer profile on page 632

HEYTEA
[Tea Room]

This branch of the HEYTEA teahouse chain in Foshan, China, sets the "unity of Zen and martial arts" as the basic theme for its design. The challenge was to complement the brand image with visual references to the cultural heritage of the region. The town of Foshan is famous for Wing Chung, a traditional kung fu form. The vertical and horizontal wooden beams in the centre of the room are inspired by the wooden dummy used as a Wing Chung training tool. The images of dancing lions and vessels point to the local Lingnan culture, while the hilly cloud landscape in a glass table refers to the mountainous origin of the tea.

Client
HEYTEA
Shenzhen, China

Design
UND Design Studio
Guangzhou, China

Project Team
Yingkang Ma (Design)
Yanhao Ma (Design)
Mingtong Zhang (Design)
Shubin Huang (Design)
Runwei Wang (Design)

Greenland Mingjing Bay

[Zen Buddhism Culture Centre]

The interior design of the Greenland Mingjing Bay culture centre in Yichun, China, is based on the concept of the void, a key element of Zen Buddhist ideology. The design therefore employs large amounts of both spatially and visually empty spaces. Starting from the high ceiling, it plays with numerous symmetrical structures which, in combination with concise lines and elegant materials, specifically embody the aesthetics of Zen Buddhism. Decorative objects and art installations furthermore give the rooms a contemporary oriental touch.

Client
Greenland
Yichun, China

Design
WJID
Shanghai, China

Chongqing Hot Pot Flagship Store

[Restaurant]

The creative concept of the Chongqing Hot Pot flagship store takes its inspiration from the salt flats on the nearby coast. In order to emulate the salt fields, the tables in the dining area are divided into squares by partitions, which gives the room a clear structure. The cement-grey colour of the walls is reminiscent of the stone baths in which the salt is recovered, while the highly reflective stainless steel panels on the ceiling show a pattern which resembles waves. Orange red is used as a visual contrast in order to make central areas stand out and to create a strong identity for the entire restaurant.

Client
Chongqing Hot Pot Flagship Store
Chongqing, China

Design
Wusun Space
Quanzhou, China

Didar Cafe

With the aim of leaving the existing structure as much intact as possible, this café in Teheran was placed in the former pool of the building. Its name, Didar, which is the Persian word for visit, implies the desire to offer visitors a close encounter with nature. That is why the entire café is enclosed with glass; to connect inside and outside and make the surrounding environment part of the overall design. In order to increase the impression of being outdoors, the height of the elegant, modern furniture is level with the edge of the pool. Additionally, all surfaces harmoniously match the preserved stone tiling.

Client
Didar Cafe
Tehran, Iran

Design
Alireza Shafiei Tabar
Tehran, Iran

Project Team
Esmaeel Khaasteh (Head of Advertising)
Anahita Shariatmadari (Digital Concept)
Ahmad Mousazadeh Fahandari (Camera)
Mohammad Reza Arab Anvari
(Manufacturer), Persiadoor Part Asia Co.
Behkam Moslehi (Technical Direction)

ZooSinDang

[Bar & Restaurant]

The ZooSinDang oriental dining bar and restaurant is in the Sindang-dong district of Seoul. The design aims to create a link to the market activities and fortune teller houses of the surrounding streets. The exterior design therefore recalls an improvised market stall made of wooden slats and straw mats, while the interior offers a strong visual contrast. It is based on the idea of a mysterious forest of zodiac signs with hanging plants suspended from the ceiling adding a fascinating upside-down illusion. The leitmotif of the 12 animals of the Asian horoscope is referenced by various design elements in the bar.

Client
ZooSinDang
Seoul, South Korea

Design
Nonespace
Seoul, South Korea

→ Designer profile on page 654

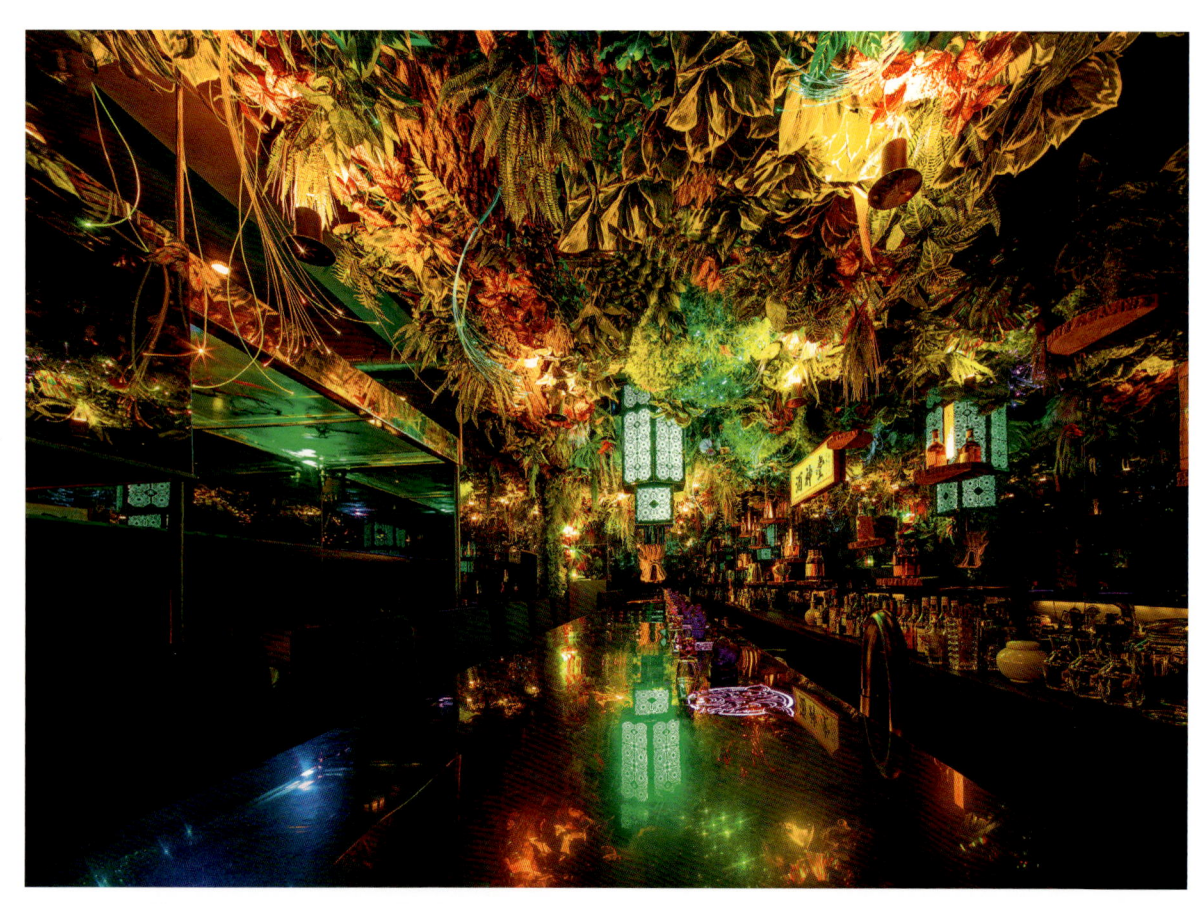

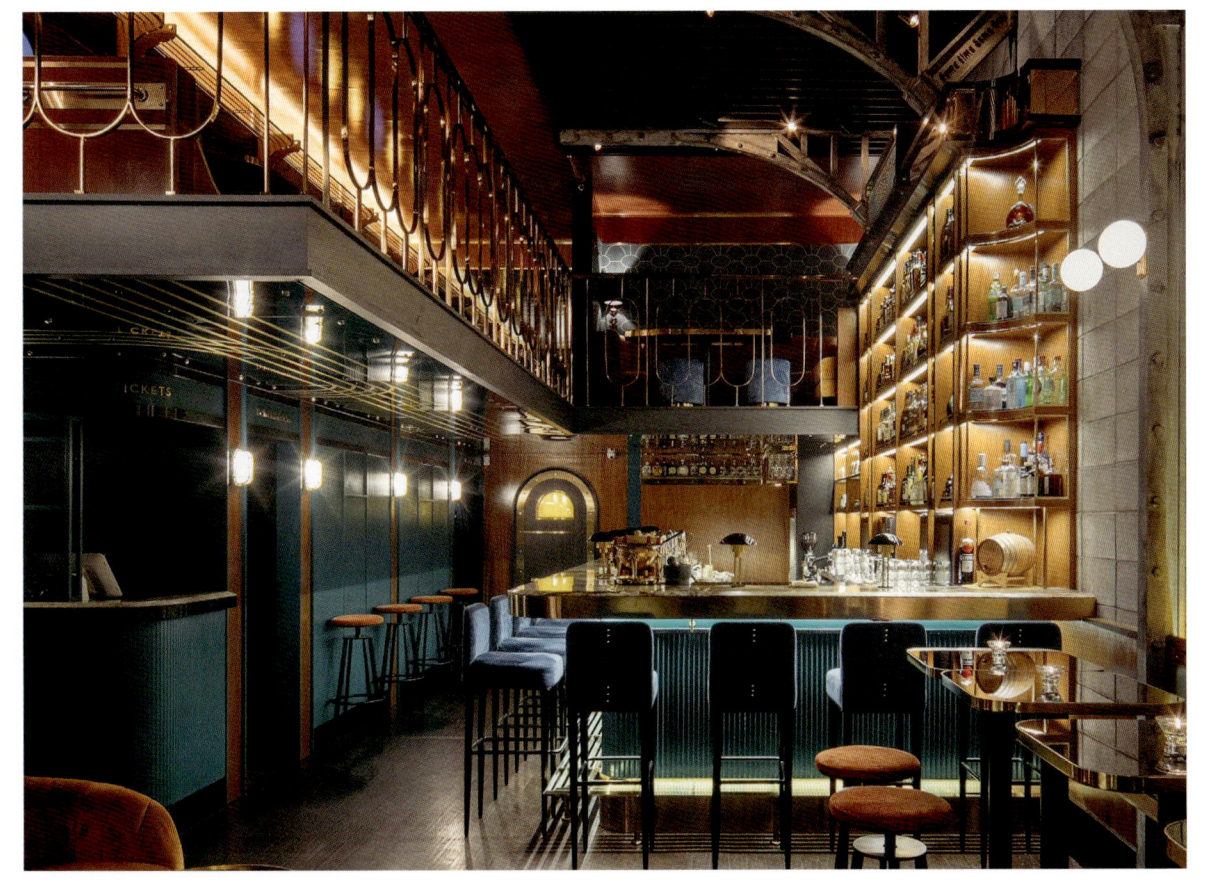

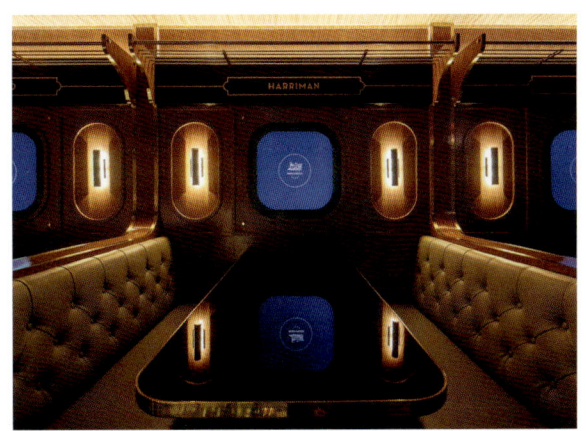

Pussyfoot Saloon
[Bar]

Pussyfoot Saloon was originally inspired by the 1920s; reviving the charm of illegal bars during Prohibition. To avoid just reproducing a bar from that period, the idea of creating a bar in a train provided the starting point for the design. The layout was based on the characteristics of classic luxury trains of the period: two signature colours, cocktail green and cocktail gold, were chosen and attuned to the materials used, such as wood and marble, and the yellowish light of the illumination. As the bar has no windows, video screens were mounted on the walls, showing video animations to reinforce the impression of a moving train.

Client
Pussyfoot Saloon
Seoul, South Korea

Design
HOHOHO Co., Ltd.
Seoul, South Korea

Project Team
Yongchae Jung (Designer)
Sunho Sin (Designer)
Dahye Oh (Designer)
Jinhye Ju (Designer)
Jeonghwan Choi (Designer)

Mosbrew
[Brand Space, Tasting Room]

Client
Moscow Brewing Company
Moscow, Russia

Design
FORM
Moscow, Russia

Project Team
Olga Treivas (Partner)
Vera Odyn (Partner)
Elena Kornilova (Architect)
Polina Nenasheva (Architect)
Fedor Katcuba (Architect)
Ilya Ivanov (Photography)

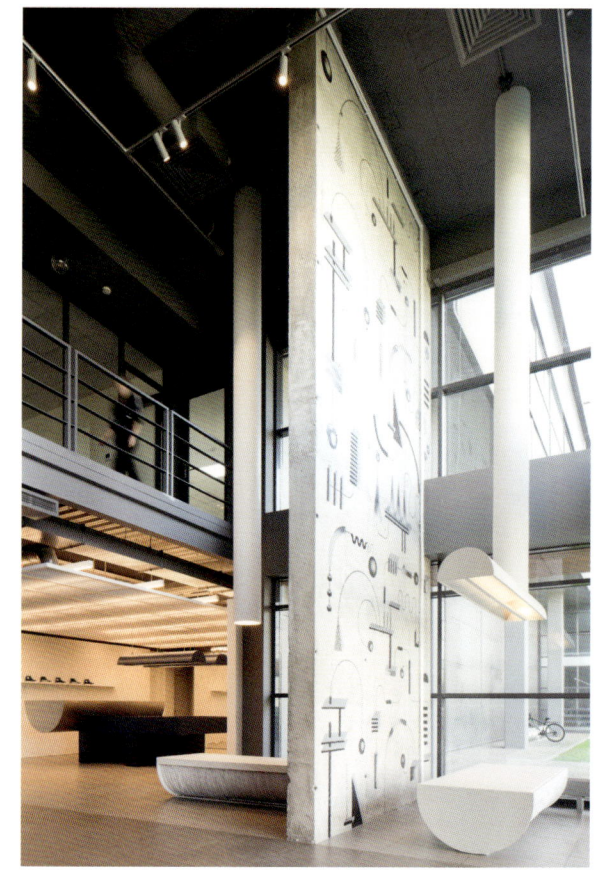

The brand space of the Moscow Brewing Company was previously used for the project "brewhouse", which provided young street artists with a platform where they could display their work. As part of the new design, fragments of the artwork were left on the walls. The entrance area is characterised by bold formal compositions which draw on the imagery and aesthetics of the corporate design. Custom interior elements, such as the steel counter and the pipe-shaped lamps, recreate the style of industrial machinery, establishing a connection to the adjacent brewery.

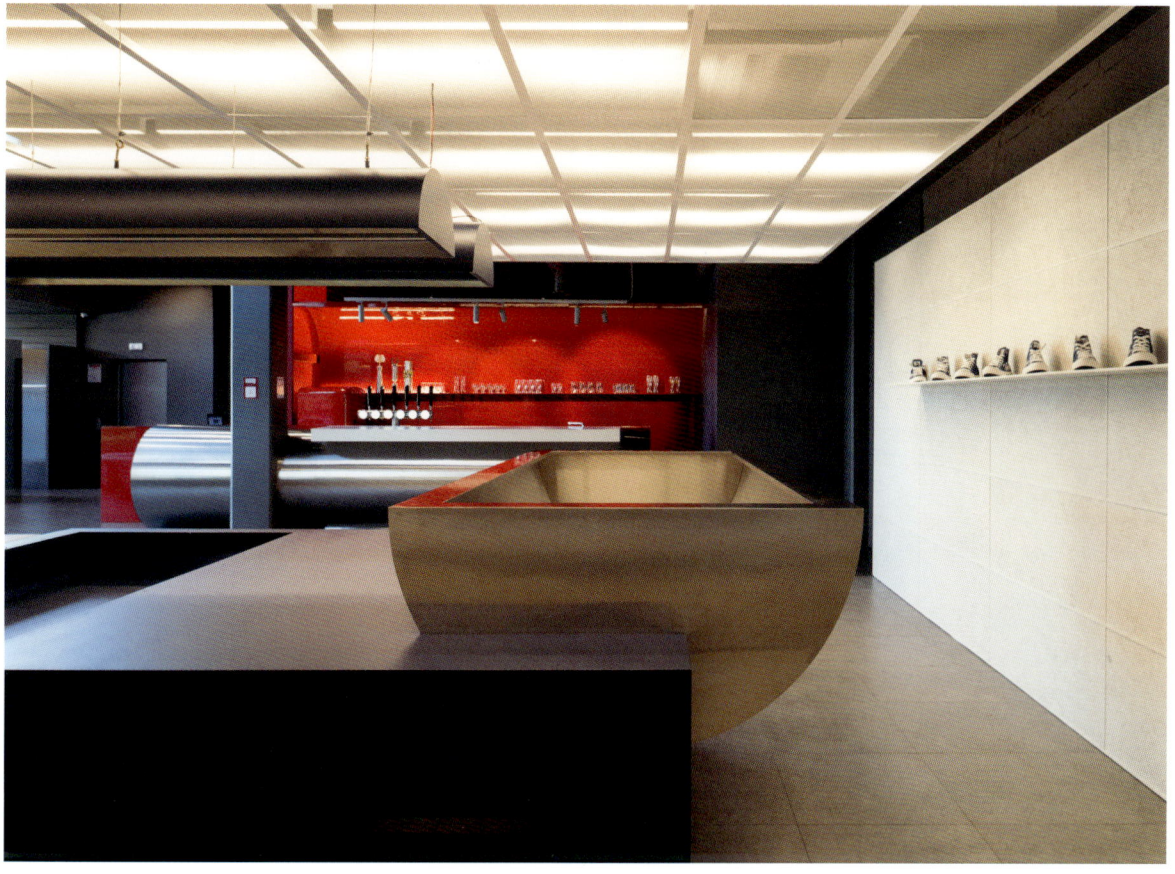

Malzers – Bäcker seit 1901

[Retail Concept]

Client
Detlef Malzers Backstube GmbH & Co. KG
Gelsenkirchen, Germany

Design
Gregor & Strozik Visual Identity GmbH
Bochum, Germany

Project Team
Thorsten Strozik (Creative Direction)
Christian Wohs (Art Direction)
Kathrin Bucholski (Project Management)

→ Designer profile on page 640

Advertising	Packaging Design	Fair Stands	**Retail Design**	Red Dot: Junior Award	Designer Profiles	Index
288	318	494	516	544	614	674

A modular concept was developed for the redesign of the German bakery chain Malzers. It had to consider functions and product groups as well as meet the expectations of the customers. Ergonomics and employee work processes were also optimised. The use of authentic materials such as wood, stone and steel is a key element of the modern, yet welcoming interior. The design of the places where the baked goods need to take centre stage, is reduced to a simple, black platform frame. Together with the high-quality furnishing of the seating area, this creates a clean, loft-like overall impression.

Kitchen Stories HQ
[Corporate Interior Design]

The newly designed headquarters of the Berlin start-up Kitchen Stories is characterised by an open-plan concept providing light and airy spaces completed by interspersed areas which offer various possibilities of use. The meeting rooms with their glass walls serve as partitions and simultaneously ensure a pleasant atmosphere, more privacy and good acoustics. In addition, carpets and seating areas create cosy, appealing islands for informal work or rest. A special feature are the five spacious kitchens with generous countertops and cooking islands where the company produces professional cooking videos.

Client
AJNS New Media GmbH/Kitchen Stories
Berlin, Germany

Design
TKEZ architecture & design
Munich, Germany

UnternehmenForm
[Showroom]

UnternehmenForm is a producer and dealer in the contract furniture sector, based in Stuttgart, Germany. The starting point for the showroom's visual concept was the managing director's love of Scandinavian design. The new premises of the company are characterised by consistent minimalism, the use of sustainable materials and a high design quality. Steel, glass, birch plywood and the natural fibres sisal and linen dominate the room. Existing concrete surfaces have been left exposed and installation pipes are visible as the authentic handling of architecture and materials is a top priority of the strict design language.

Client
UnternehmenForm GmbH & Co. KG
Stuttgart, Germany

Design
SCOPE Architekten GmbH
Stuttgart, Germany

Chasing Light

[Brand Store]

The design of this brand store follows the motto "where there is light, there are dreams". Located in a shopping mall, the lack of natural light was compensated by including a window in the wall at the far end of the room, creating a magical corridor of light. The light appears to solidify due to the effect of the yellow walls, which divide the space into different areas. The geometric shapes of the shadows are not only visually appealing but also a reflection of the passage of time. The shelves and stools are both functional pieces of furniture and part of the overall architectural staging.

Client
Bizhi Paint Decoration Co., Ltd.
Longyan, China

Design
Wusun Space
Quanzhou, China

Genesis Studio

[Showroom]

The Genesis Studio in Hanam, South Korea, was built in an effort to introduce the company's product range to the millennial generation. The design for this special exhibition, presenting the latest models, highlights the strengths of each vehicle in a playful way: a colourful light installation for the G90, a video wall installation for the Mint, and an oversized tunnel, which leads to a mirrored stage for the GV80. The result is an interactive brand experience which redefines the traditional notion of a luxury car for its target group and attracted much attention on social media.

Client
Hyundai Motor Co. (Genesis Motors)
Seoul, South Korea

Design
Suh Architects
Seoul, South Korea

→ Designer profile on page 669

Artrium

[Interactive Showcase]

This interactive showcase in the showroom of the Artrium luxury jewellery brand is part of a special exhibition, created in collaboration with the Palace Museum in Beijing. The case shows three expertly crafted royal fans with embroidered images representing royalty, longevity and prosperity. In order to learn more about the exhibits, visitors can scan the QR code next to the fans with their smartphones. Thus, the entire showcase turns into a stage on which the embroidery transforms into larger-than-life motion graphics. At the same time, an audio-visual recording relates the history of the fans.

Client
Artrium, Chow Tai Fook
Shanghai, China

Design
Noiseless Design
Hong Kong

Project Team
Christopher Lee (Creative Direction)
Chan Fly (Design)
Hung Chung (Design)
Isaac Cheung (Animation)
Yu Ng (Animation)
Meiyan Li (Illustration)
Chun Ip (Programming)
Jonathan Ho (Programming)
Wilson Hung (Project Management)
Vincent Lee (Project Management)

→ Designer profile on page 653

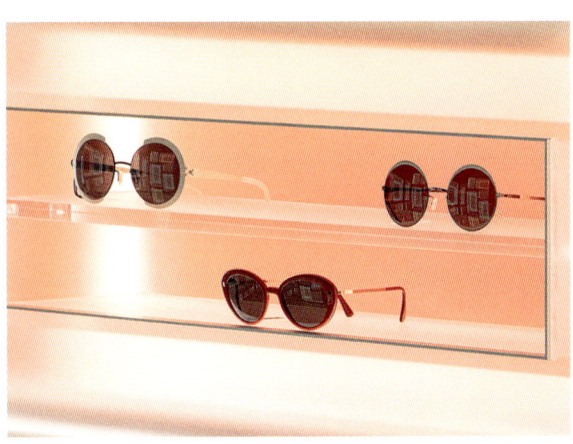

Papyrus Gwanggyo
[Brand Store]

Located in the Gwanggyo Galleria in Suwon, South Korea, this brand store for Papyrus, an optician and retailer of luxury eyewear, aims to address a predominantly female target group. Soft colours and matt acrylic surfaces were used to create an elegant and airy ambience. All functional areas – from eye examination to the assembly and storage of the glasses – are part of the store which has neither walls nor doors. The open layout is a reference to local history as it is inspired by the traditional stone-building method used for Hwaseong fortress, a Unesco World Heritage Site in the region.

Client
Papyrus
Suwon, South Korea

Design
Atelier.Archi@Mosphere
Seoul, South Korea

Project Team
Atelier.Archi@Mosphere:
Yeonju Choi (Concept)

Byung Yoon Kang (Technical Direction),
Design E-YEON
Yong Joon Choi (Photography)

Preface	Red Dot: Agency of the Year	Brands	Brand Design & Identity	Corporate Design & Identity	Annual Reports
4	6	18	90	202	260

OPPO Store – Spring 2019

[Visual Merchandising]

During the launch of the OPPO 2019 campaign for the Chinese New Year, the seasonal motto for the visual merchandising of the stores was "Red Chinese New Year". Combining traditional elements from ancient Chinese stories and a contemporary approach for the design of the installation, the layout aimed to provide customers with an intriguing shopping experience. The bright red colour is not only an inherent symbol for New Year in China but also an expression of happiness, good luck and reunion. In addition, the design features carp and copper coins to highlight the brand's key products of the season.

Client
OPPO
Shenzhen, China

Design
Leaping Creative
Guangzhou, China

Project Team
Zen Zheng (Creative Direction)
Mindong Zeng (Installation Design)
Weikang Liu (Installation Design)
Mincong Huang (Installation Design)
Mingmei Zhong (Project Management)

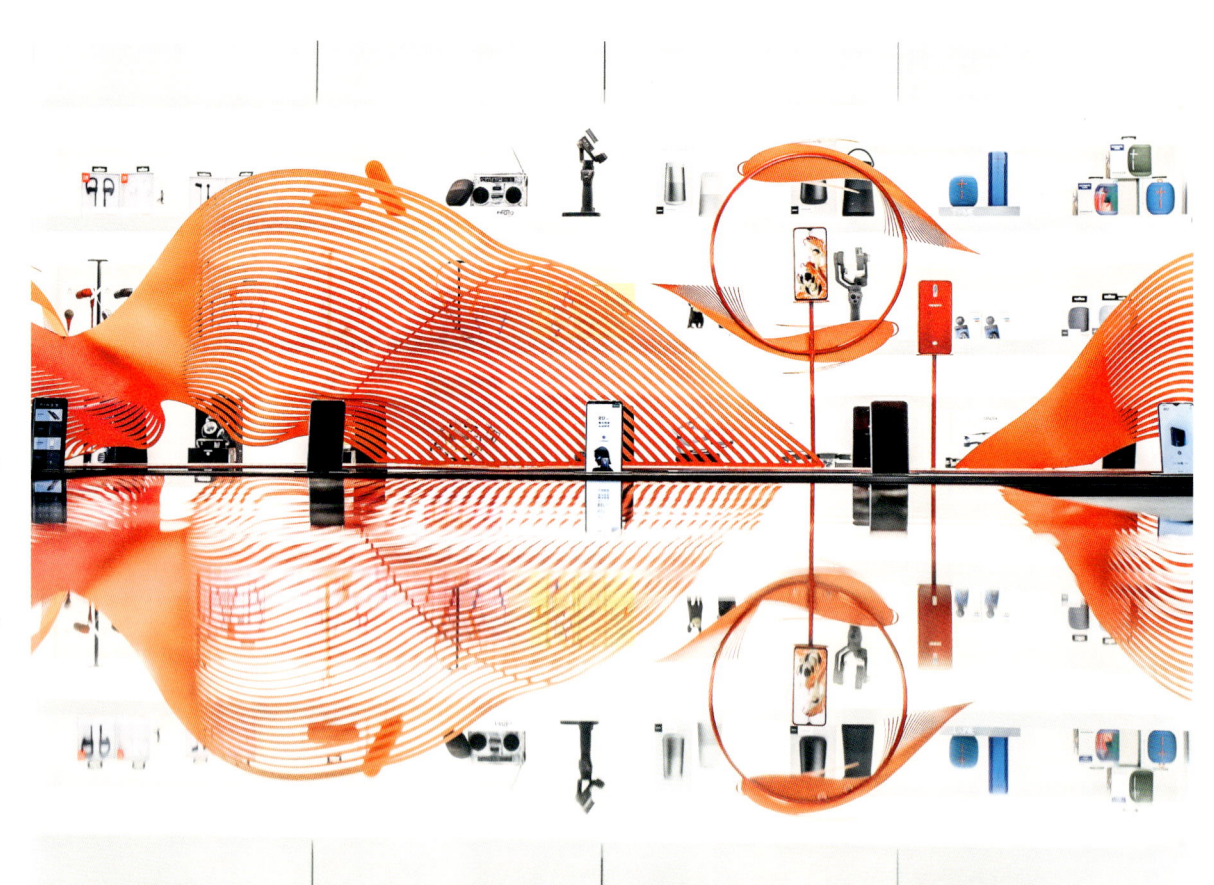

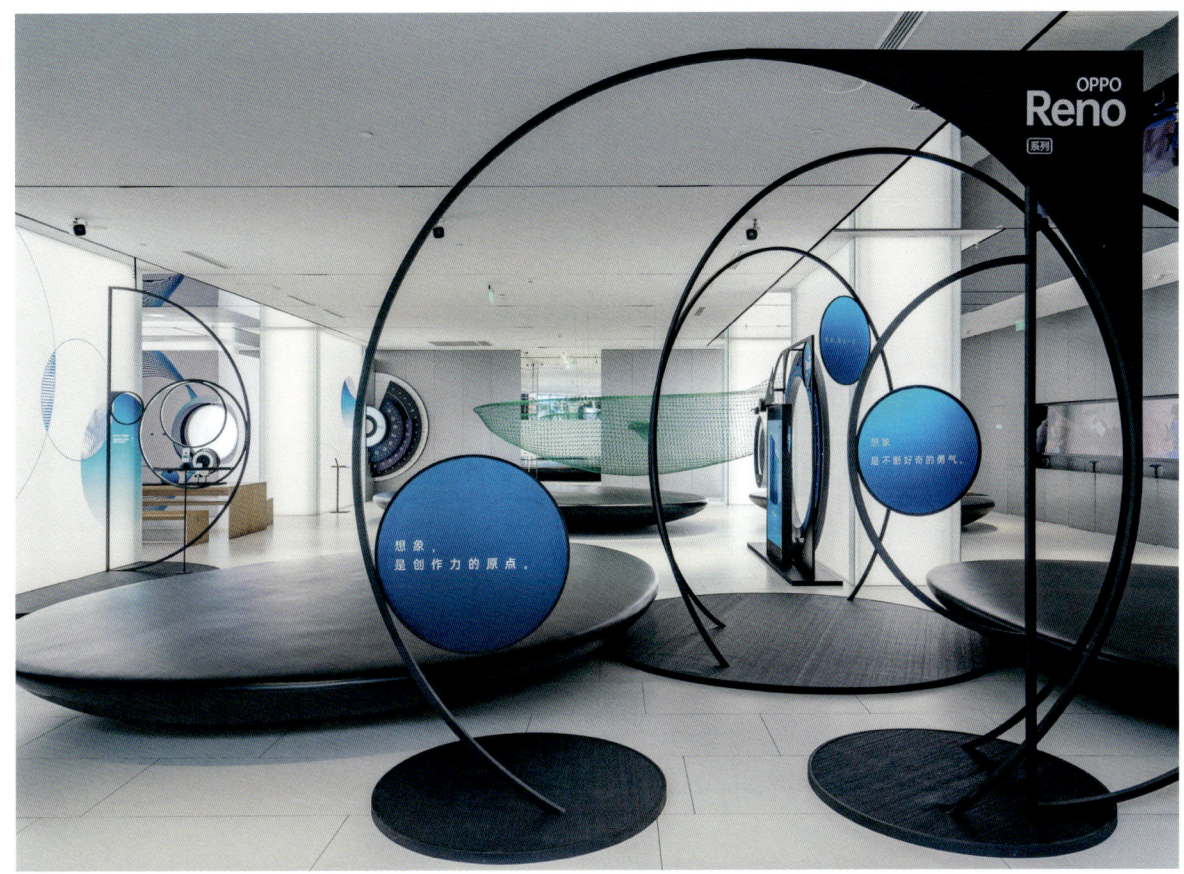

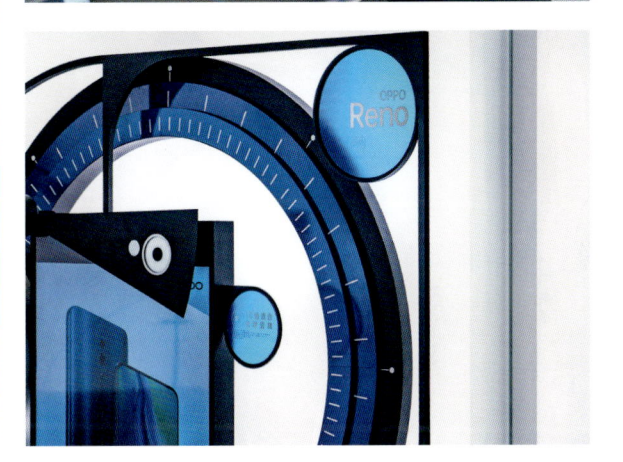

OPPO Store – Product Promotion
[Visual Merchandising]

This visual merchandising campaign combines shop windows, installations, display settings on counters and graphics in order to promote OPPO's latest smartphone and to convey its key feature: the 10× hybrid zoom camera technology. The guiding motif of the design consists of concentric circles with scale markings. They replicate the structure of the camera lens which is not normally visible to users because it is concealed inside the phone. When customers look through the circles, a vision of the universe appears at the end, which is intended as a metaphor for the product slogan "bringing you closer to the world around you".

Client
OPPO
Shenzhen, China

Design
Leaping Creative
Guangzhou, China

Project Team
Zen Zheng (Creative Direction)
Mindong Zeng (Installation Design)
Jiening Huang (Installation Design)
Leshi Gong (Installation Design)
Ying Lan (Installation Design)
Mincong Huang (Installation Design)

Samsung KX

[Brand Store]

Client
Samsung Electronics Co., Ltd.
Seoul, South Korea

Design
Cheil Worldwide
Seoul, South Korea

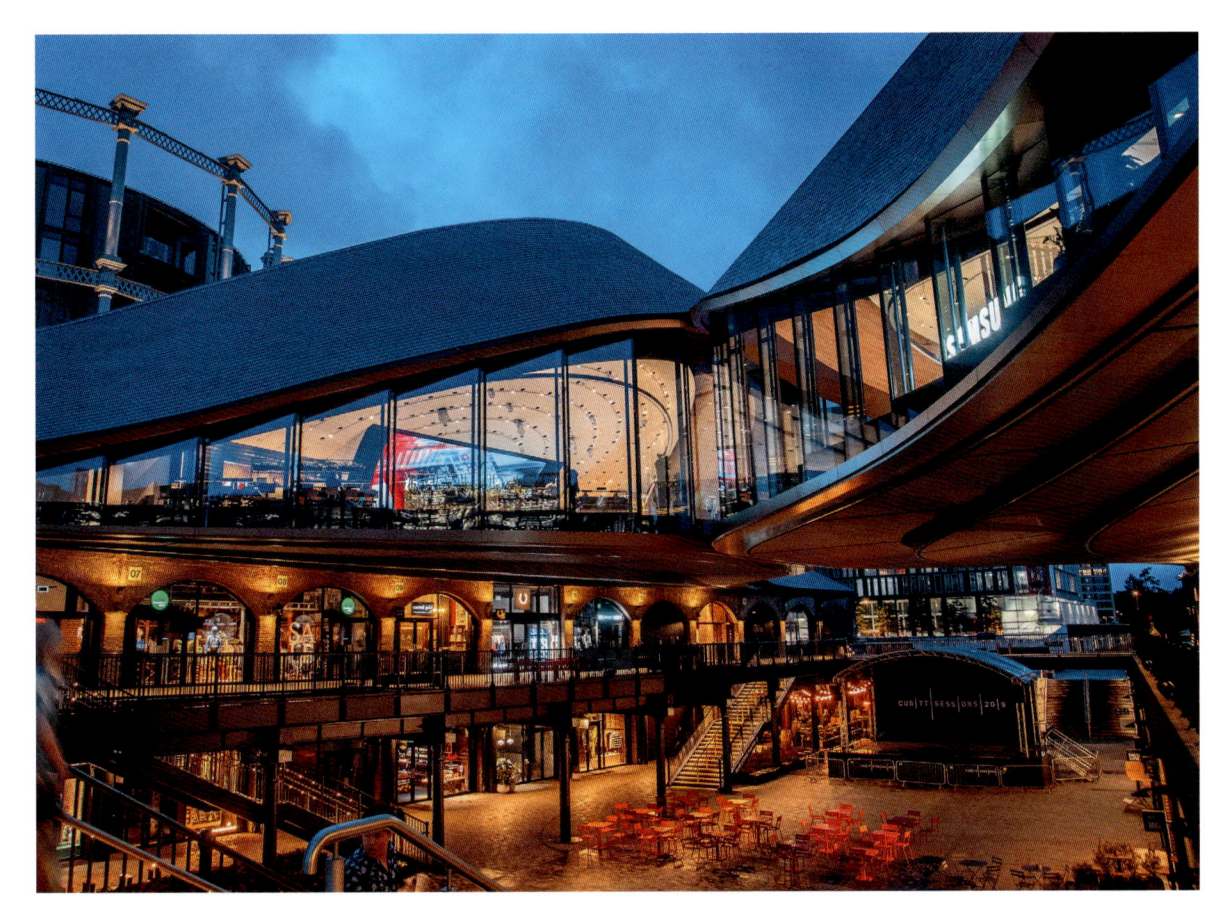

Advertising	Packaging Design	Fair Stands	**Retail Design**	Red Dot: Junior Award	Designer Profiles	Index
288	318	494	516	544	614	674

The objective was to create a unique retail experience that would fuse Samsung's high level of innovative competence with local heritage and attract both the local community and people from across the world. Located in one of London's most up-and-coming shopping districts, Coal Drop Yard at King's Cross, the Samsung KX brand store shows a design which is focused not only on sales but also on the experiential digital community. Most of the historic architecture was retained and reimagined with the modern London loft-style to create a harmonious overall impression. Stained oak, mass concrete, and reflective materials give the fixtures a premium and permanent feel.

Hyangsimjae

[Clinic]

This clinic takes a holistic approach to medical treatments, combining family medicine and dermatology. Its design aims to create an intimate atmosphere and help the doctor and the patient to establish a relationship of mutual trust. This is why the rooms are designed in such a way that only a small number of people can enter them at a time. The natural materials, colours and light conditions of the interior radiate peace and calm, and the use of glass and metal gives the building an urban appearance, while, at the same time, the rough exterior facade contrasts with the surrounding cityscape.

Client
Hyangsimjae
Daegu, South Korea

Design
100A associates
Seoul, South Korea

Project Team
Kwang-Il Ahn (Design Principal)
Sol-Ha Park (Design Principal)
Dong-Su Kim (Design Principal)
Da-Jeong Lee
Yi-Re Lee

Pilersuisoq

[Retail Concept]

Pilersuisoq is a Greenlandic retail chain with branches across the entire country. The brief consisted in positioning the grocery chain as a national brand. It was decided that the sales environment needs to reflect the culture and characteristics of each settlement in the most authentic way possible. This was achieved by including portraits of local people, local houses and symbols from the respective area. As a result, each branch looks unique and has a strong connection to its particular customer base and the Greenlandic identity.

Client
KNI
Sisimiut, Greenland

Design
Marketsquare
Copenhagen, Denmark

Red Dot: Junior Award

546 **Red Dot: Junior Prize**

550 **Red Dot: Junior Prize nominee**

552 **Red Dot: Best of the Best**

554 **Brand Design & Identity**

575 **Corporate Design & Identity**

576 **Advertising**

581 **Packaging Design**

Red Dot: Junior Prize

The Dyslexperience
[Social Campaign, Inclusive Design]

"The Dyslexperience" is an "empathy book" including an installation that has been specially designed in response to indifference to dyslexia in our society. The enhancement of digital projection mapping on a physical surface, such as here on the reduced design of a book, has facilitated creating this sensory experience that aims to communicate the emotional ordeal faced by dyslexic people every day. And for those who do not know that dyslexia is a learning disability and not a lack of vision or intelligence, it enables them to see from the lens of those affected. In this way, they see that and how the invisible diagnosis becomes visible, enabling them to vividly assess what it means to be confronted with dyslexia. The clinical symptoms slightly differ between the persons concerned. Accordingly, the letters of the text sometimes appear three-dimensional and blurred like in a hologram, sometimes they jump and change their order, or they dissolve making the text look fragmentary.

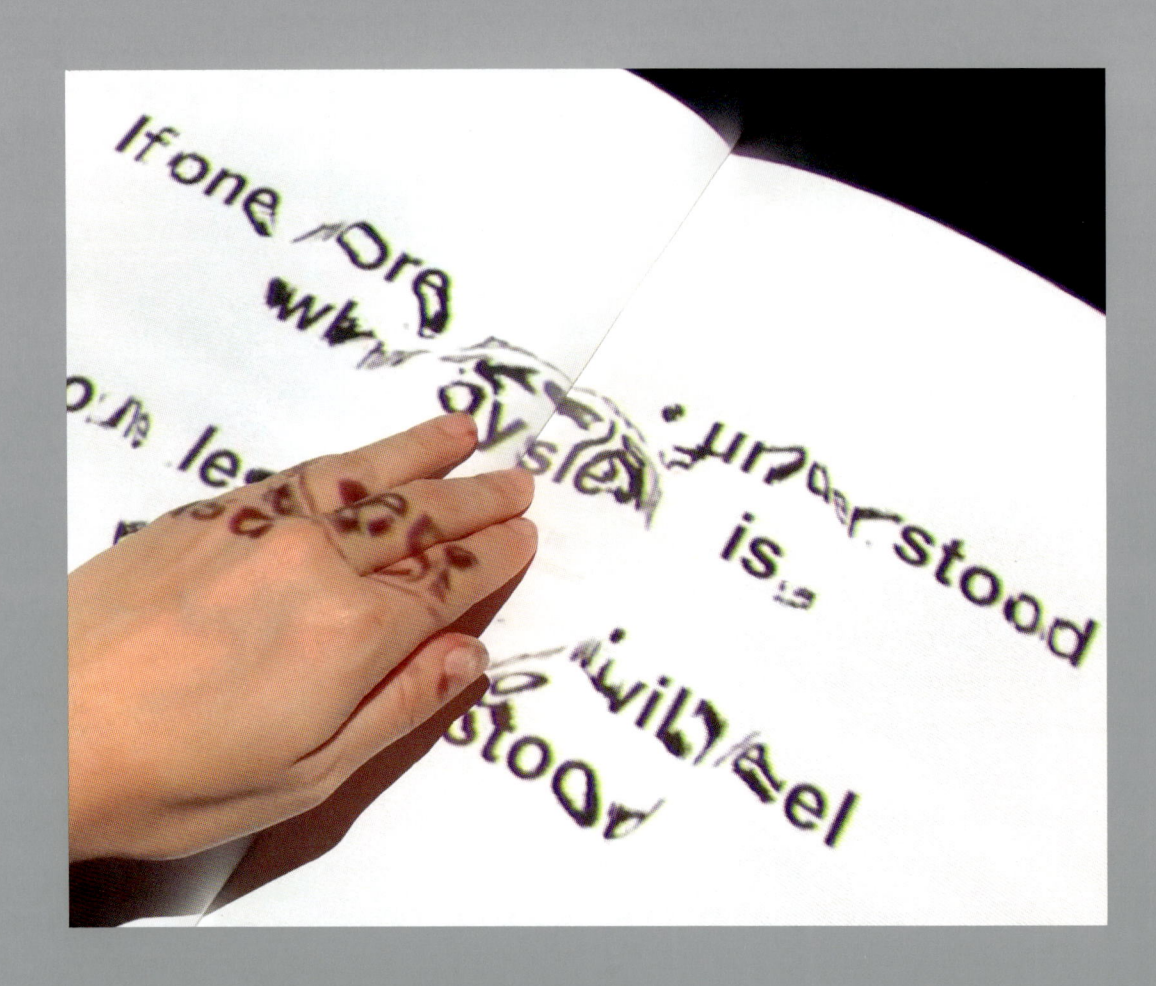

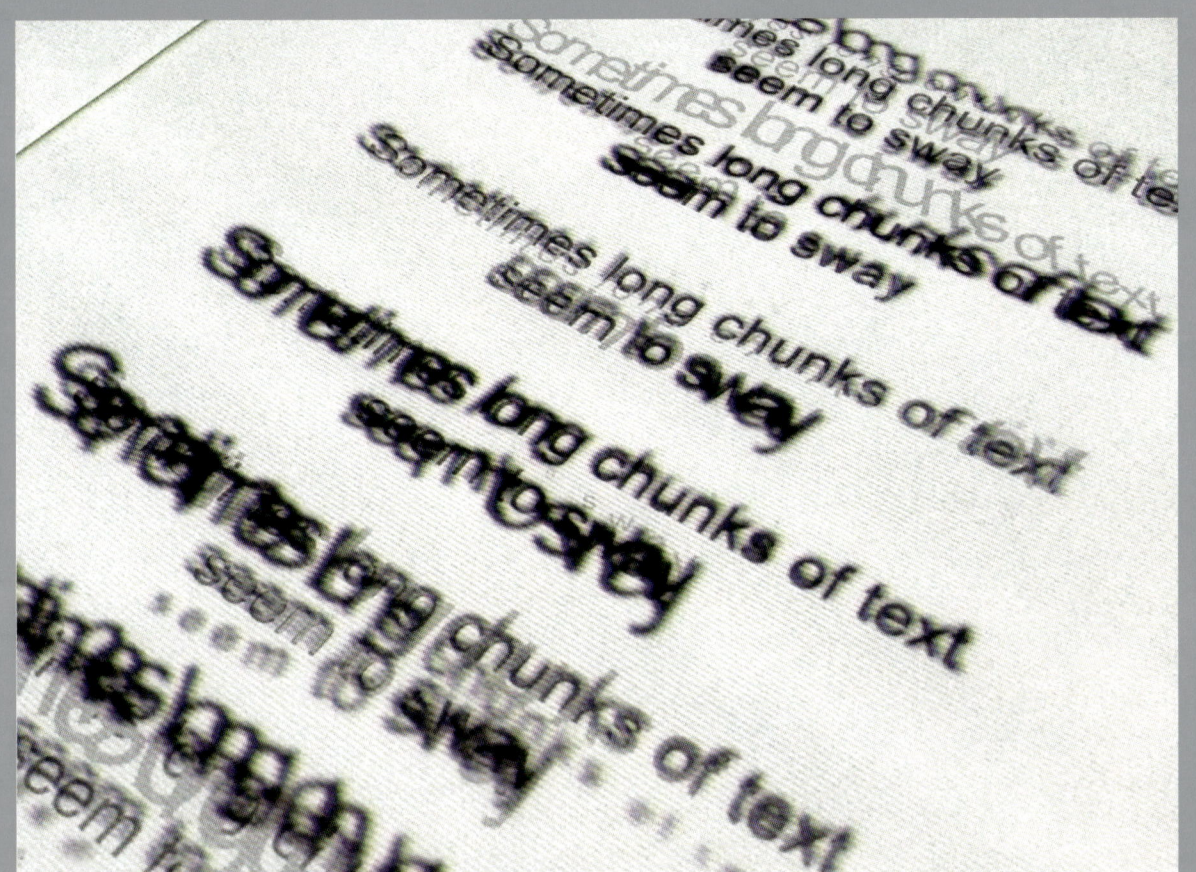

reddot winner 2020
junior prize

University
National University of Singapore

Supervising Professor
Yuta Nakayama

Design
Ai Ling Ng, Zi Fong Yong,
Division of Industrial Design,
School of Design & Environment,
National University of Singapore

→ Designer profiles on pages 652

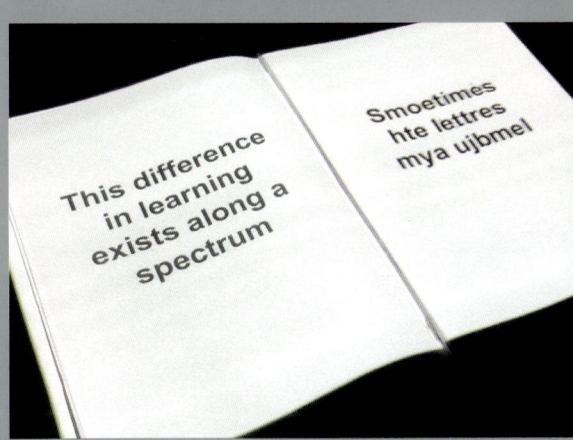

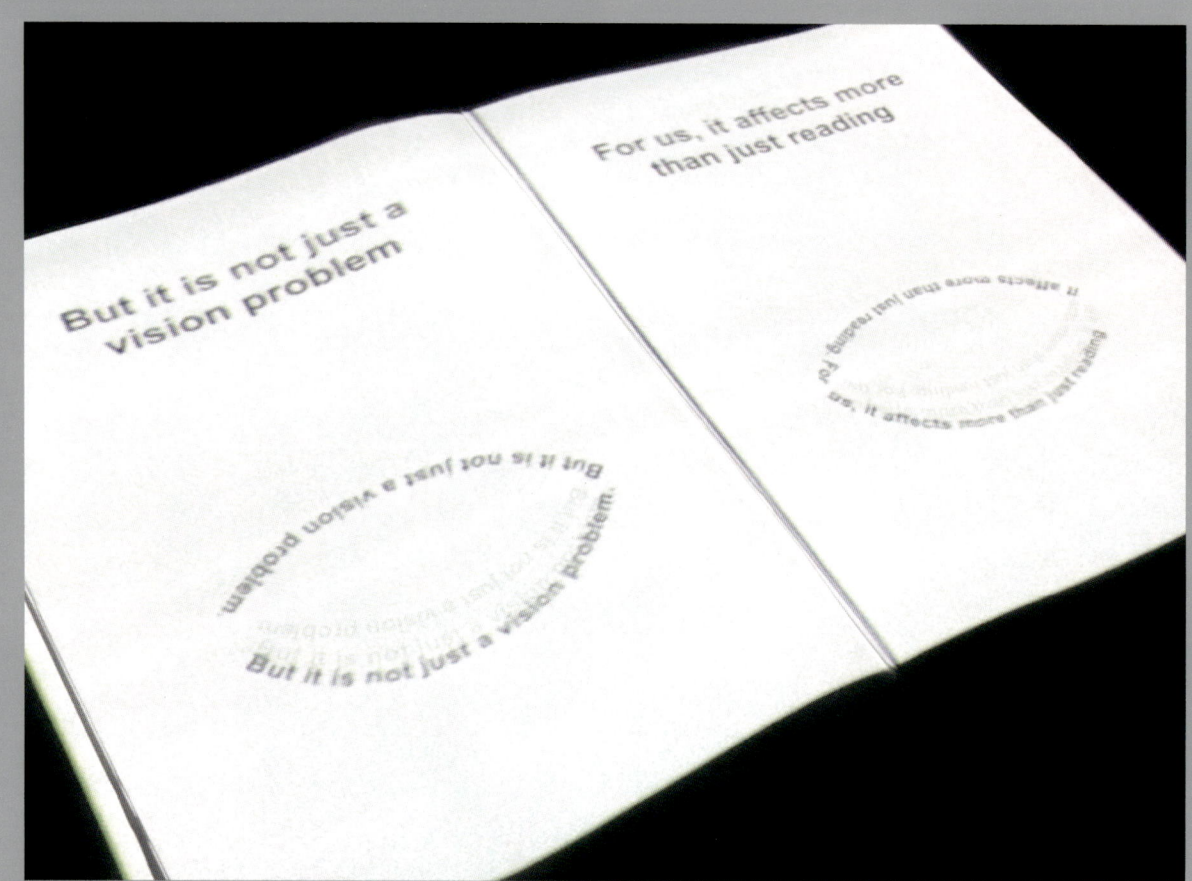

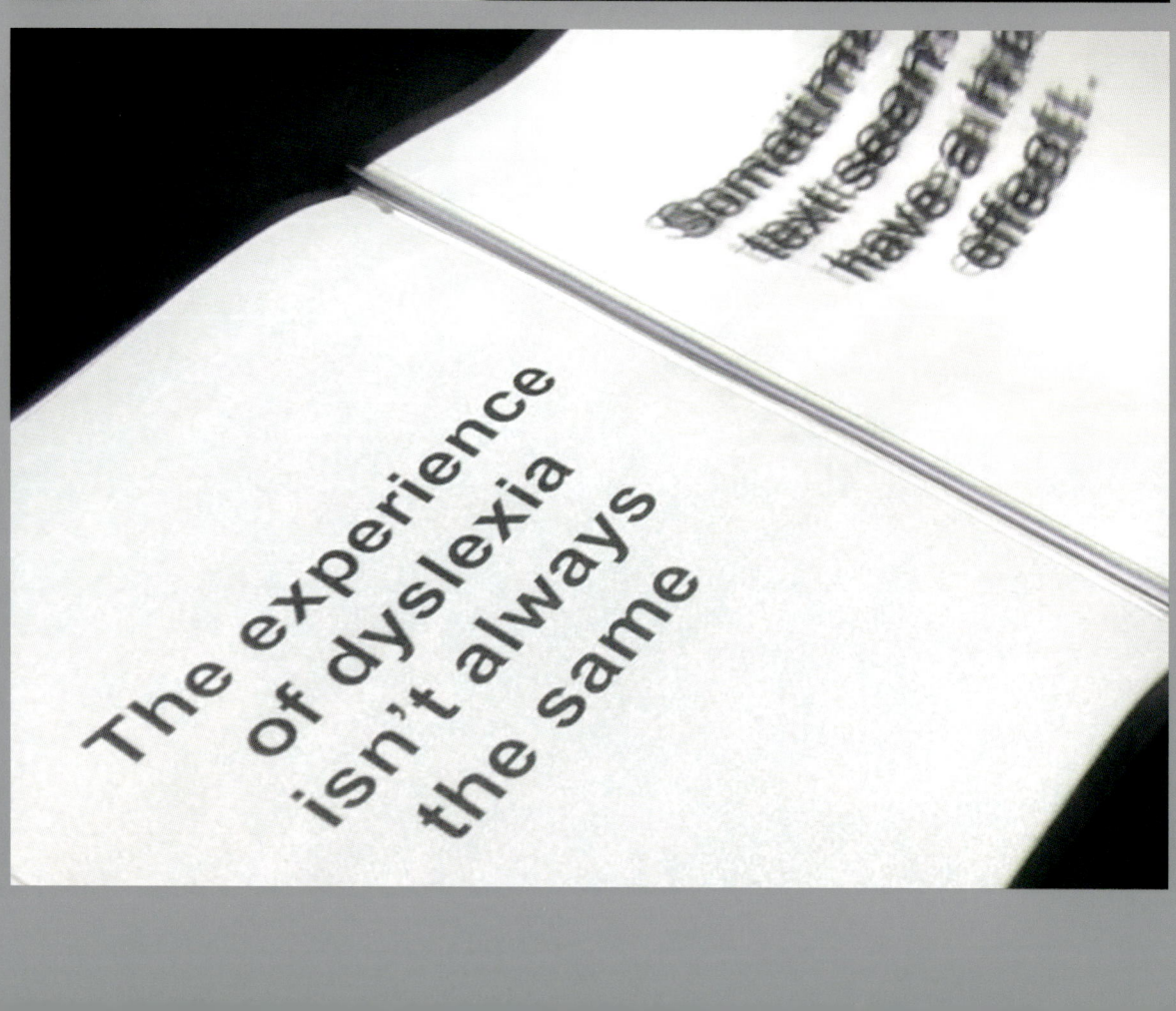

Preface	Red Dot: Agency of the Year	Brands	Brand Design & Identity	Corporate Design & Identity	Annual Reports
4	6	18	90	202	260

Red Dot: Junior Prize

Those who have never experienced it think that it doesn't exist: The Dyslexperience

[Statement by the jury]

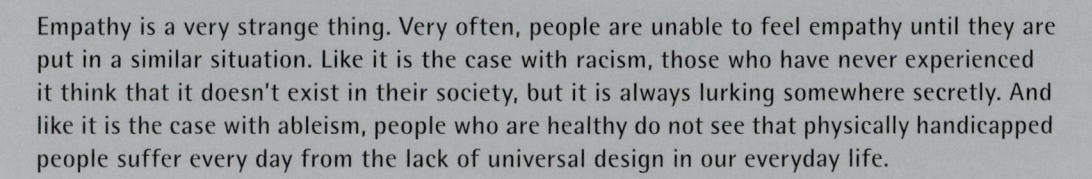

reddot winner 2020
junior prize

Empathy is a very strange thing. Very often, people are unable to feel empathy until they are put in a similar situation. Like it is the case with racism, those who have never experienced it think that it doesn't exist in their society, but it is always lurking somewhere secretly. And like it is the case with ableism, people who are healthy do not see that physically handicapped people suffer every day from the lack of universal design in our everyday life.

Dyslexia, an invisible condition, can be very frustrating for the sufferers, as reading, like walking, is a daily exercise. Those who can't read, like those who can't walk, are constantly being hampered in their life. When people see a person in a wheelchair, they feel empathy because this person's suffering is being physicalised; but with dyslexia, nobody can see a person's struggle and hence a lot of people are guilty of not being empathetic towards this person as they can't even imagine what it is like to be dyslexic. What many people do not understand too is that dyslexia is not an eyesight problem, it is a learning difficulty.

Hence, this project by Ai Ling Ng and Zi Fong Yong really moved the jury as it presented the experience of the dyslexic not only succinctly, but poetically as well. Presented as an art installation, the project employed projection mapping onto a book, demonstrating through a visual journey all the different reading hurdles that a dyslexic goes through every day – an artistic engagement that forces the audience to confront the challenges that dyslexia presents. Besides being enchanted by the curated experience that quietly and sensitively calls for empathy in the viewer, the jury is as well impressed with the technical aspects – an elegant treatment of the typography and layout in the "book" design, which is half physical, half projection.

There are many effective awareness campaigns around, but sometimes they are a little in your face. "The Dyslexperience" manages to create an advertising campaign that not only conveys the message clearly, it has won our hearts because it is at the same time artistic and poetic. To borrow the last words in the book, that summarised the message of this project befittingly: "If one more person understood what dyslexia is, one less person will feel misunderstood."

Red Dot: Best of the Best [Red Dot: Junior Prize nominee]

RED IN COMMON

[Print Campaign, Card Game]

"RED IN COMMON" is a card game which aims to eliminate racism and encourage blood donation at the same time. With the emergence of a new virus, the world can quickly be faced with several problems. First, the virus can become a catalyst for racism, as the anxiety of not knowing what is happening exactly can diminish people's judgment, while the dichotomous act of distinguishing oneself from others can easily be mistaken as a means of survival. Second, depending on the virus, the problem of sudden blood shortage can surface, making active blood donation and its promotion an important step. This game aims to recognise both of these problems and establish correct values in an easy way by making the cards of all colours necessary for winning. Ten cards each in black, white and yellow – the colours used to distinguish races – stand opposite the red cards symbolising blood and blood types, and thus what connects all people worldwide with one another. The well-thought-out game can be played for educational purposes or while waiting for a blood donation.

Statement by the jury
This print campaign masters the balancing act of linking the two socially relevant issues of racism and blood donation. Thanks to the clear design of the cards, which feature in four colours and accommodate a lot of information in a small space, this ingenious concept coherently succeeds in explaining what blood types are all about and it does so in a manner that is also playful.

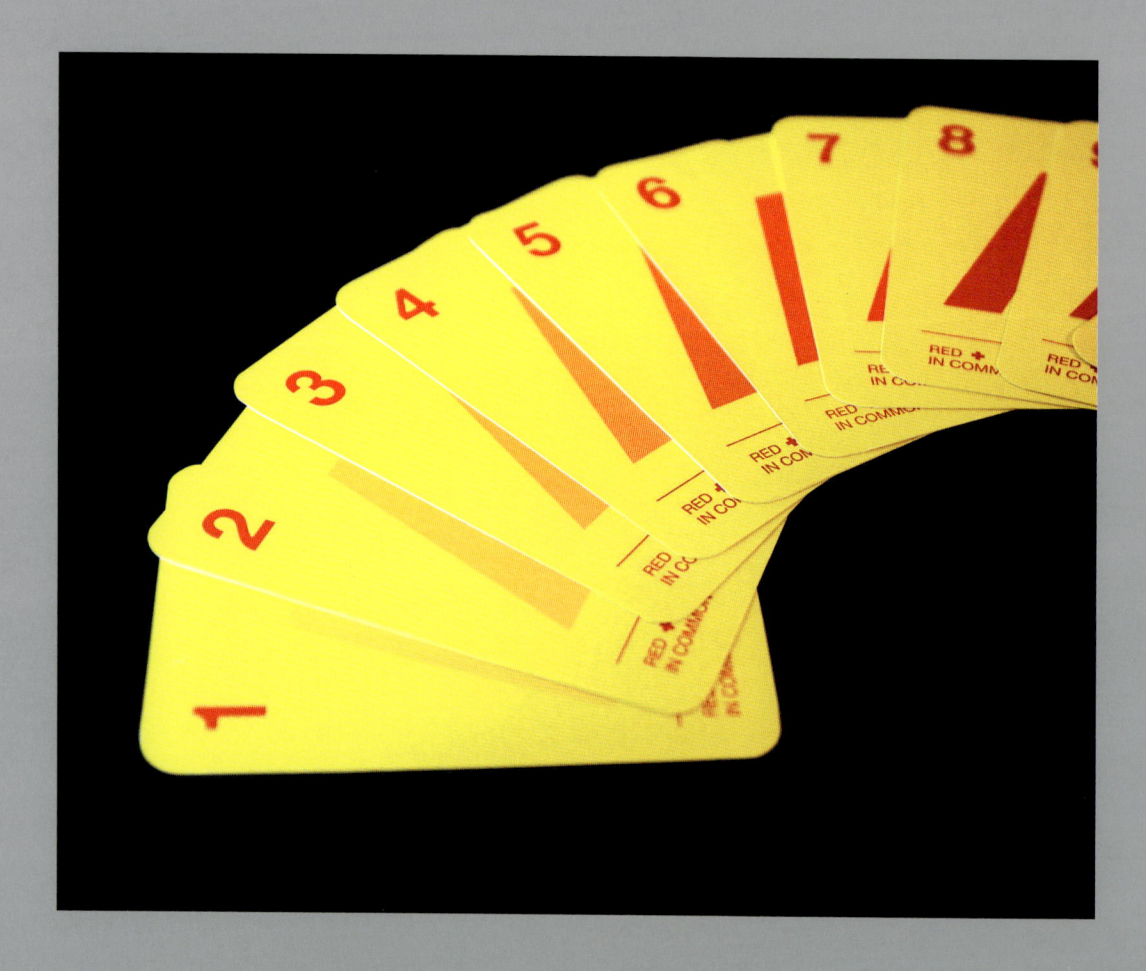

Client
Hyewon Han
Seoul, South Korea

Design
Hyewon Han
Seoul, South Korea

→ Designer profile on page 641

Red Dot: Best of the Best

Ziploc Diversity Campaign
[Integrated Campaign]

The goal in creating the "Ziploc Diversity Campaign" was that it effortlessly represented the enormous diversity of the Ziploc bags. The guiding insight in the design was that the variety of uses for Ziploc bags is actually as diverse as the people who use them. Ziploc is a universal brand that does not need any explanation – no matter what language users speak. Thus, the solution was to present Ziploc as a uniting force and to express that, despite cultural differences, all humans share certain universal truths and values. People across the world use Ziploc products to hold and store things they care about, items both big and small. As with the different people portrayed, what matters is "what's inside" – an idea that is also emphasised by the slogan, which is translated across different languages, while maintaining the same design aesthetic. Emphasising this message, the campaign also visually highlights the simplicity of the Ziploc bags with their completely unspectacular exterior.

Statement by the jury
The idea behind this campaign is outstandingly great. The simple Ziploc bag becomes interesting through the way it is being used, which in turn is as diverse as the people who use it. The analogy that inner values count is visualised in film and advertisements in a manner that is both simple and pointedly concise. The message comes across overall clear and engaging in both content and aesthetics.

University
SCAD Savannah College of Art and Design
Savannah, USA

Design
Mijin Han, Lachelle Robotham, SCAD

→ Designer profile on page 664

Preface	Red Dot: Agency of the Year	Brands	Brand Design & Identity	Corporate Design & Identity	Annual Reports
4	6	18	90	202	260

OGAIN
[Brand Design]

This final student project is dedicated to exploring the extent to which brand design can increase the willingness to donate organs. The emotionally appealing design aims to promote and explain the concept of organ donation in a cheerful manner. Thus, the design is based on the creation of likeable characters that symbolise different organs. Their shape and colour define both the logo design and the entire implementation, including stationery and a series of products. As students are the main target group, picture books convey the long-lasting significance of organ donations.

University
Fu-Hsin Trade & Arts School
New Taipei City, Taiwan

Design
Lin Yu Ting, Lin Ying Chun, Chiang Yu An,
Chen Yu Fang, Wu Pei Rong, Lin Sz To,
Yang Yi Chen, Jiang Bao Ci, Wu Fang Yu,
Yeh Li Yan, Hsiao Shi Yuan,
Fu-Hsin Trade & Arts School

Post Us, Share Freedom

[Visual Identity]

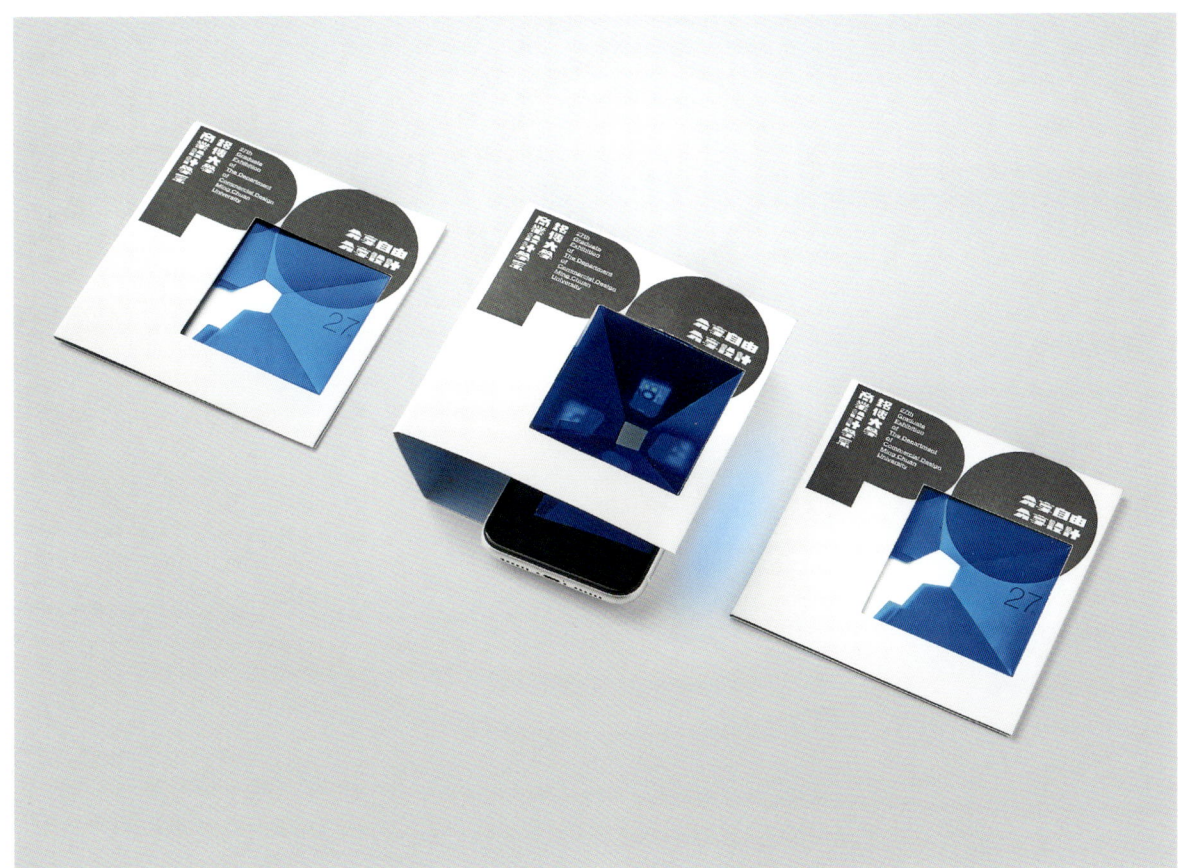

This visual identity was created to promote a graduate exhibition in Taiwan entitled "Post Us, Share Freedom". The work was inspired by the growing borderless online world, which has helped people regain their right to speak. It also attempts to express the idea that design cannot be separated from the society and politics. The young designers are confident enough to explain their position. The posters for the exhibition showcase illustrations of typical website icons. In addition, the students set up the Instagram account "a.no_27" to participate in social movements and post about issues that everyone should be concerned about.

University
Ming Chuan University
Taipei City, Taiwan

Design
Ching-Yang Lo, Yun-Wun Chen,
Man-Cheng Wang, Che-Han Yeh,
Ming Chuan University

Preface	Red Dot: Agency of the Year	Brands	Brand Design & Identity	Corporate Design & Identity	Annual Reports
4	6	18	90	202	260

Moolab

[Brand Design]

The student brand design project Moolab aims to increase people's ability to perceive subtle emotions. The project is about helping individuals learn a vocabulary that would let them better classify emotions and cope with negative ones. A branding was created to visually support this learning process. In particular the key visuals printed with ultraviolet fluorescent pigments are meant to pique people's interest and motivate them to engage with the subject matter. Moody Cruise portrays 43 sad emotions on board a cruise ship. To create a brand story, the ship represents a peaceful place where sorrows can be thrown overboard.

University
Shanghai Jiao Tong University
Shanghai, China

Supervising Professor
Tao Xi

Design
Yuanyuan Xia, Tao Xi,
Shanghai Jiao Tong University

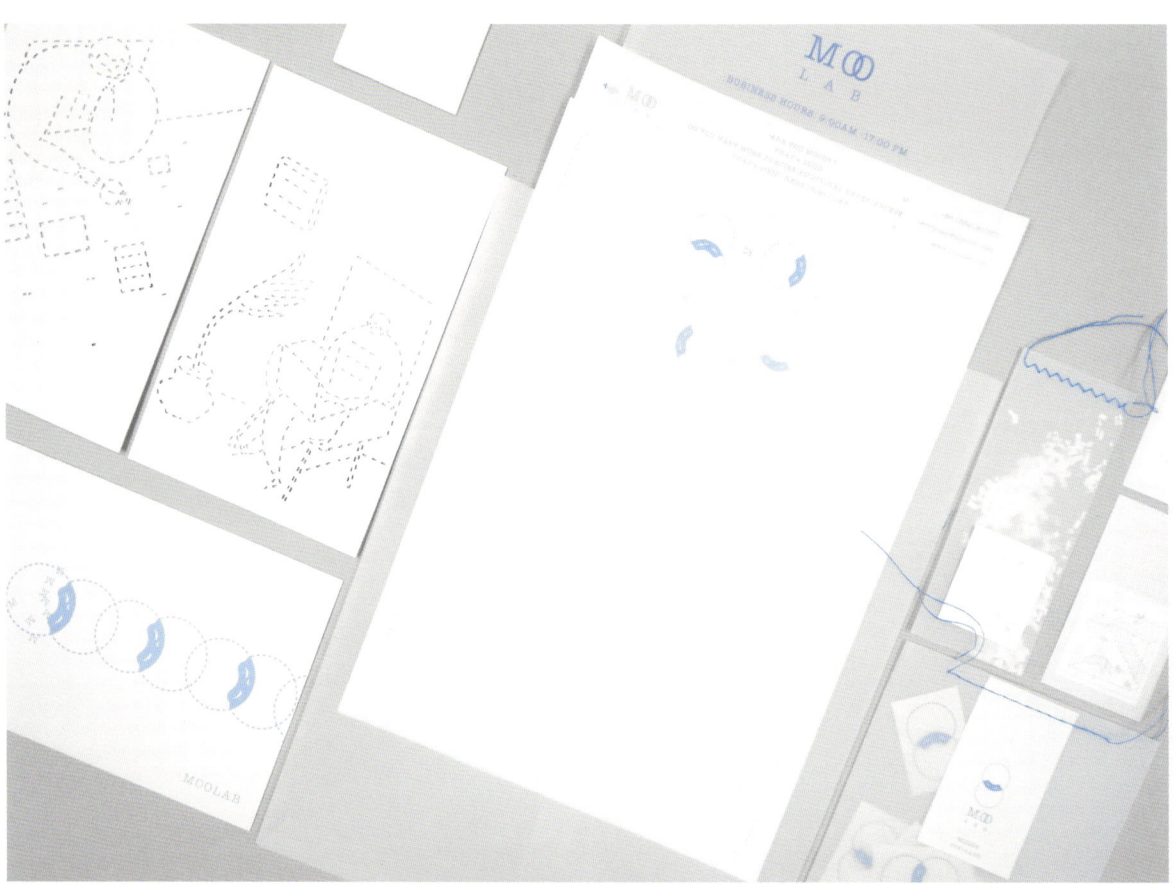

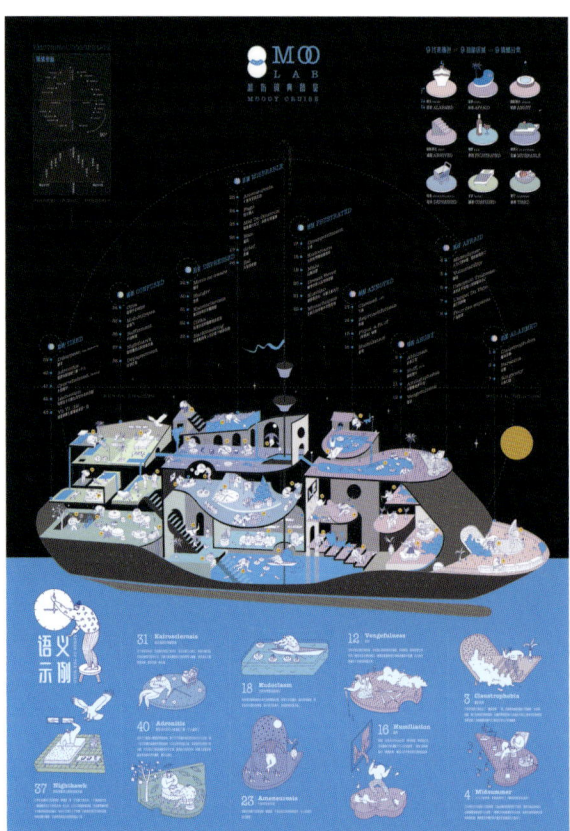

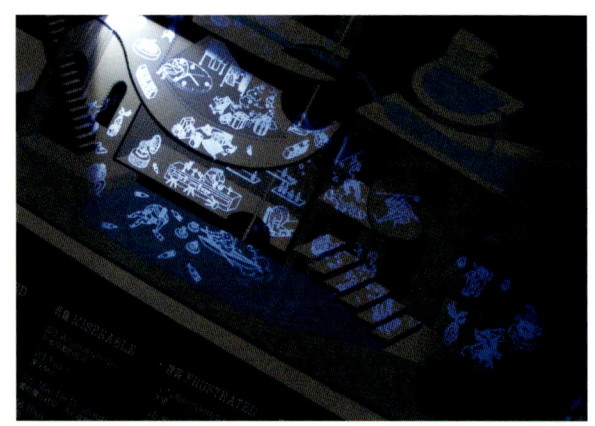

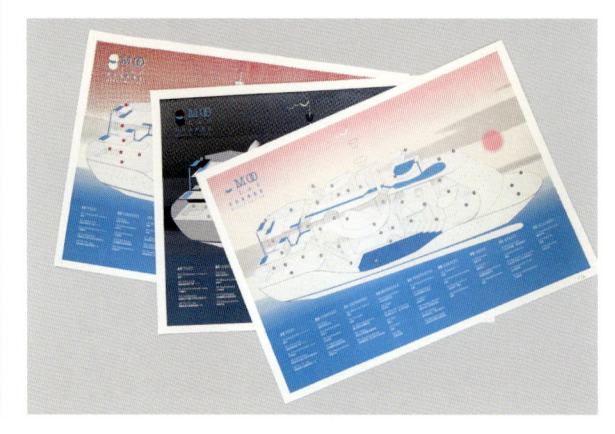

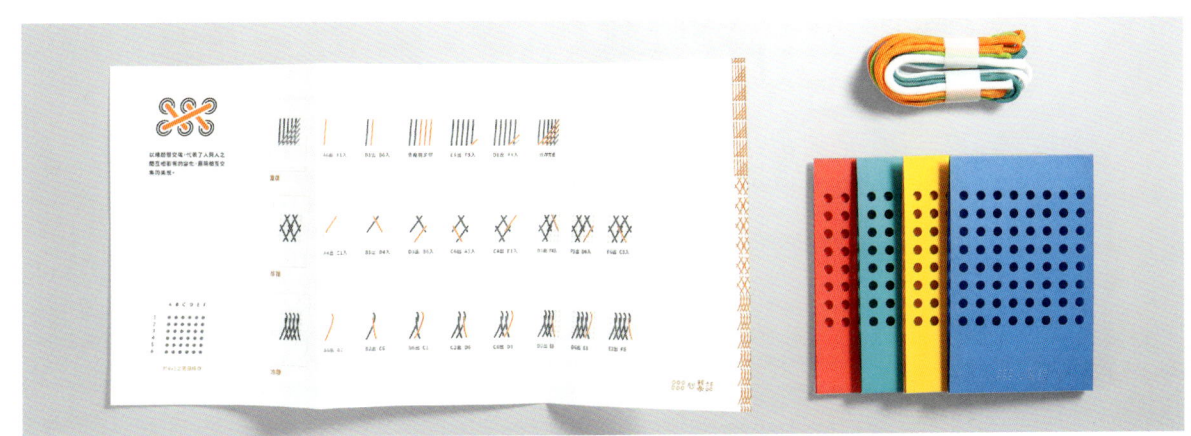

Advertising	Packaging Design	Fair Stands	Retail Design	**Red Dot: Junior Award**	Designer Profiles	Index
288	318	494	516	544	614	674

OOOOOO Studio

[Brand Design, Visual Identity]

The OOOOOO Studio aims not only to convey the beauty of spiritual connections between people, it also seeks to transmit emotions by using patterns beyond language and to create a visualisation of the essence of design through knotting art. Long before the development of written languages, knotting was an important way for people to make records and convey messages. For this brand design, each colour has a specific meaning, for instance grey represents calmness and yellow represents pleasure. Inspired by the art of knotting, holes are the main feature of the logo, using the letter O in an arrangement of six circles.

University
Ming Chuan University
Taoyuan, Taiwan

Supervising Professor
Ching-Jung Fang, Chien-Hua Lin

Design
Yi-Chieh Chen, Ting-Yu Su,
Ting-Yu Chang, Hung-Yi Lee,
Ming Chuan University

Preface	Red Dot: Agency of the Year	Brands	Brand Design & Identity	Corporate Design & Identity	Annual Reports
4	6	18	90	202	260

Ji Lai Ji Wang

[Brand Design]

Taiwanese people often use auspicious words to express their blessings during traditional annual festivals, but these terms have become old-fashioned for young people. In recent years, the rise of social networks has produced many new terms. The brand design by Ji Lai Ji Wang combines auspicious words with slang words and presents them using humorous illustrations. In terms of content, the holiday wishes were divided into the three categories of health, interpersonal and love. A variety of eye-catching merchandising products are available, including books, posters, calendars, postcards and notebooks.

University
Chaoyang University of Technology
Taichung, Taiwan

Supervising Professor
Kuo-Min Chuang

Design
Ting-Chieh Chao, Yu-Han Lin,
Chien-Kai Chiu, Shih-Jung Chiu,
Zhi-Xuan Xu,
Chaoyang University of Technology

Lazy Ant
[Visual Identity]

This group of design graduates named their graduation exhibition Lazy Ant, inspired by the behavioural patterns of ants, whereby so-called lazy ants remain inside the anthill and make themselves useful there. The design students compared themselves to these ants, working in silence on design solutions to everyday problems, but of course they are by no means lazy. The exhibition is divided into different display themes, including trophallaxis, altruistic, settlement, sniff and alert behaviours. The visual identity features upturned keyboard caps as key visuals in order to establish a connection to the working world of designers.

University
National Yunlin University of
Science and Technology
Douliu City, Yunlin County, Taiwan

Supervising Professor
Ya-Ling Huang, Fang-Suey Lin,
Tay-Jou Lin, Chih-Chung Liao

Design
Shin-Yee Lew, Tzu-Chieh Chen,
Zu-Ting Deng, Yi-Ying Chen,
Chia-Wen Lin,
National Yunlin University of
Science and Technology

Chinese Theatre Circle

[Visual Identity, Brand Design Relaunch]

This rebranding project focuses on attracting a younger generation by positioning the Chinese Theatre Circle as a cultural movement that is contemporary and progressive. The brand logo represents a character that is half hidden, half revealed behind an abstract theatre mask, an effect that is achieved by using a half circle on one side and a series of changing faces on the reverse side, which is implemented across all of their communications. The use of contrasting colours was inspired by the typical makeup and attire worn during performances and enhances the appeal of the visual identity.

University
LASALLE College of the Arts
Singapore

Design
Aileen Aurelia,
LASALLE College of the Arts

Post-Information Era
[Key Visuals]

Based on the theme of post-information era, this creative conference included a forum as well as an exhibition, which both conveyed the message that with the advent of this era, Chinese characters are experiencing an innovation in visual expressiveness. The key visuals of the event echoed this message and highlighted the role of Chinese characters in a multilingual environment. In addition, they emphasise the characteristics of information superposition and programming in a post-information era. This programmatic visual language can be adapted to different applications.

Client
Ihsoat Creative Lab
Guangzhou, China

Design
Tian Bo
Guangzhou, China

Preface	Red Dot: Agency of the Year	Brands	Brand Design & Identity	Corporate Design & Identity	Annual Reports
4	6	18	90	202	260

paart of
[Key Visual, Interaction Design]

University
Fu Jen Catholic University
New Taipei City, Taiwan

Supervising Professor
Chia-Yin Yu, Fa-Hsiang Hu

Design
Hung Yu Chen, Yao-Jhih Yang,
Yi-Xiao Zhou, Yu-Wen Chang,
Department of Applied Arts,
Fu Jen Catholic University

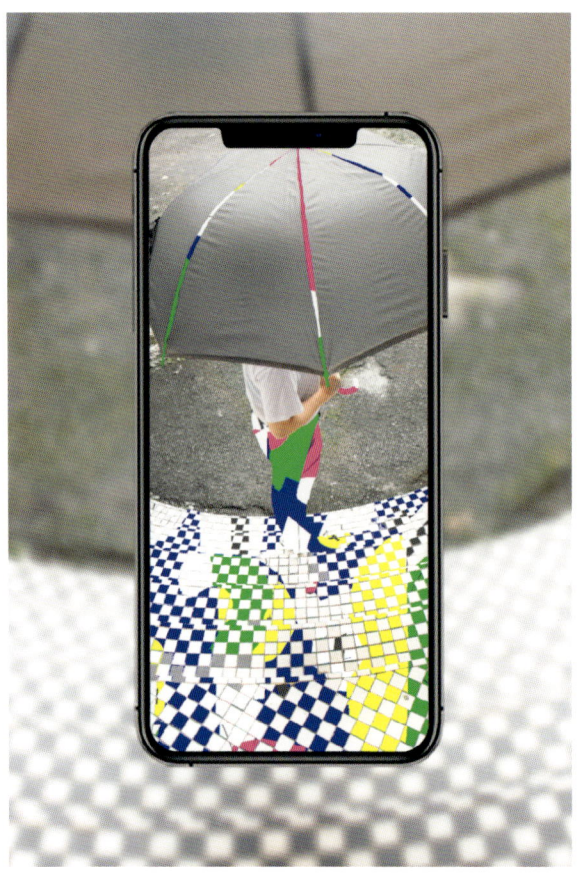

→ Clip online

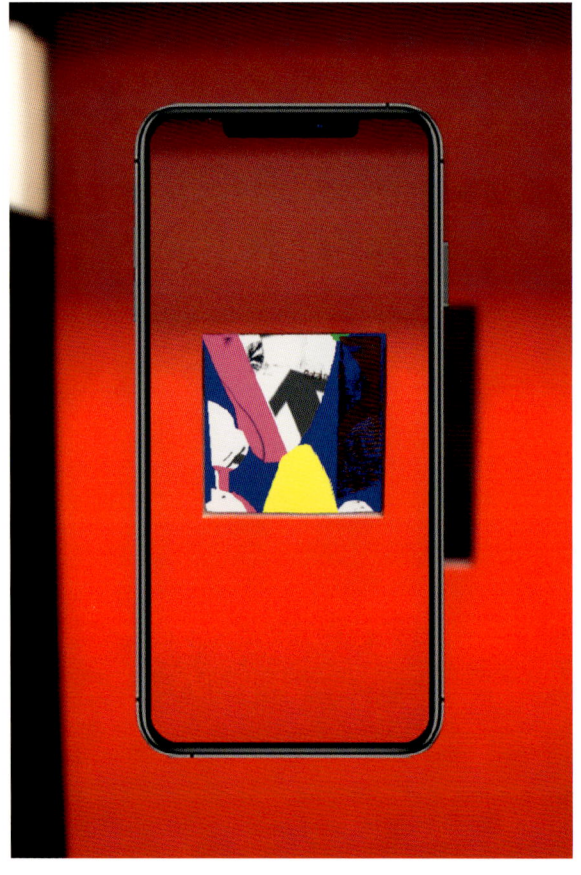

562

"paart of", the title of the final exhibition of an art academy in Taiwan, includes two components: an invitation to be part of the event, on the one hand, and an abbreviation of "applied arts" (AART), on the other. The graduates subvert the one-way visual communication by using typical social media filters to illustrate interaction as a new vision of the Department of Applied Arts. In the logo, the additional "a" is highlighted both in colour as well as graphically with a magnifying glass effect. A plus sign in a dotted circle is used as an additional graphical element, which is reminiscent of the button that users have to click before recording filters on Instagram stories.

Ceramic Panda

[Brand Illustration]

The illustration of the key visual for Ceramic Panda uses the creative technique of graffiti to connect traditional Chinese food culture with popular entertainment. The collage combines mahjong symbols, ceramics and food motifs drawn in boldly contrasting colours. This not only reflects the gourmet qualities of the hotpot shop itself, but also refers to the lifestyle of its customers. Elements of the local language and entertainment are used to add an emotional component to the brand experience and to encapsulate the closeness to the local customers.

University
Communication University of Zhejiang
Hangzhou, China
Wonkwang University
Iksan City, North Jeolla Province,
South Korea

Supervising Professor
Prof. Chao Yang,
Communication University of Zhejiang

Design
Pei Yang,
Communication University of Zhejiang
Ye Wang, Wonkwang University

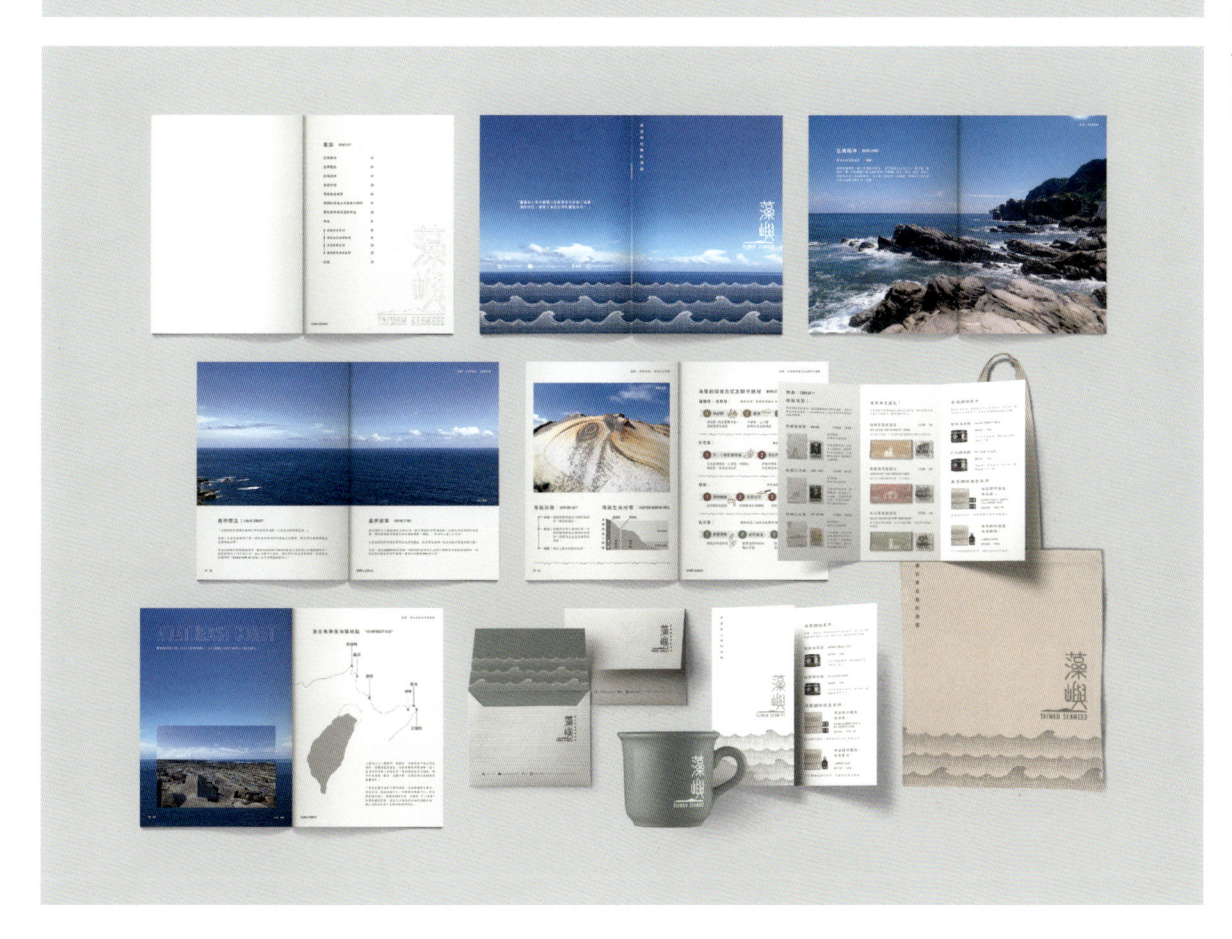

Seaweed Islet
[Brand Design Relaunch]

The seaweed industry in Taiwan has gradually declined due to changes in economic environment, an outflow of population and the rather tedious method of hand-picking algae. Since most of the seaweeds are collected and sold by local fisherwomen, there had been no uniform brand image to support this characteristic culture. The new brand design aims to reinvigorate the image of local seaweed specialities in the northeast of Taiwan. The key visual on the packaging is based on the nine most distinctive scenic spots in the region. The communication also conveys information on the local ecology, enhancing the hometown image of the brand.

University
China University of Technology
Taipei City, Taiwan

Supervising Professor
Chien-Hsun Chen, Cheng-Ta Lee

Design
Shu-Chi Hsu, Chi-Man Hsu,
Jia-Jun Lin, Sin-Yu Li,
Department of Visual Communication
Design, China University of Technology

Taiwan Street Bad Habit

[Brand Design]

This initiative has set itself the task to make the Taiwanese population more aware of the problem of street pollution. The topics discussed include the spitting of betel nut residues in public spaces as well as careless and improper waste disposal, which can sometimes even lead to traffic accidents. The brand name captures these bad habits in words. In order to raise public awareness for this initiative, a distinctive brand design was developed and implemented in a number of publications and useful giveaways. Among other things, it uses motivational illustrations that contrast good habits with bad ones.

University
Chaoyang University of Technology
Taichung, Taiwan

Supervising Professor
Hsiu-Ju Wang, Kuo-Min Chuang,
Tang-Szu Liu

Design
Cheng-Yu Cheng, Yao-Ren Zhuang,
Ching Chang, Yi-Hsiu Cheng,
Chaoyang University of Technology

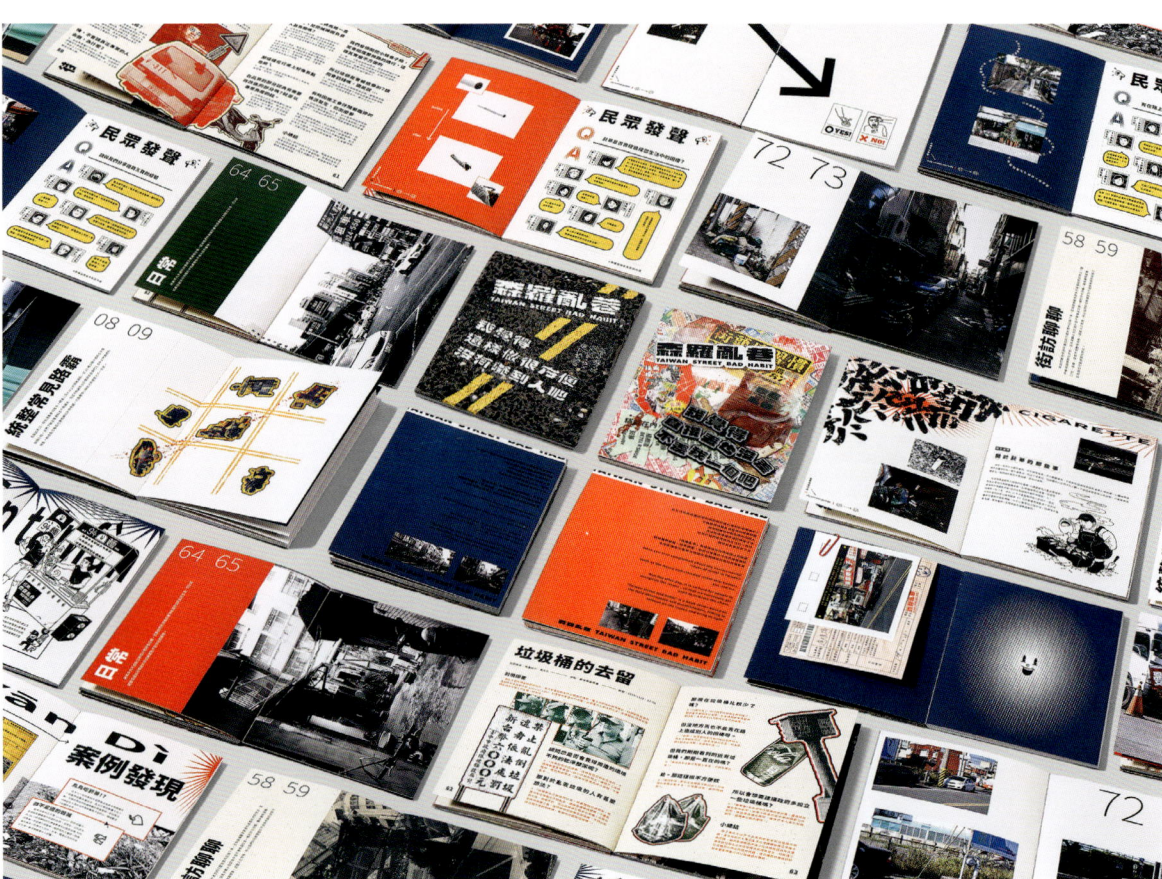

Zoonior

[Brand Design]

Zoonior, a portmanteau that combines zoo and junior, is the name of an initiative that seeks to defend animals and abolish zoos. It is aimed at teaching children the fundamental importance of animal protection and animal rights. The brand design chooses an emotionally appealing illustration style showing endangered animal species that are often kept in zoo enclosures that are too small. The brand logo is reminiscent of a smile, symbolising the joy of learning children. The sales proceeds from the appealingly branded products will be donated to animal welfare organisations.

University
Kookmin University
Seoul, South Korea

Design
Seonil Lee, Jisu Moon,
Kookmin University

→ Designer profile on page 647

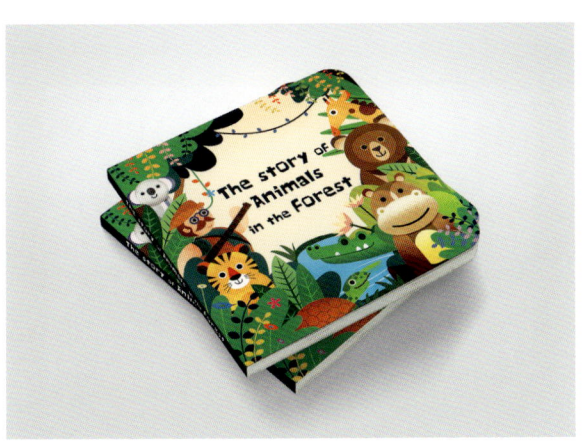

Preface	Red Dot: Agency of the Year	Brands	Brand Design & Identity	Corporate Design & Identity	Annual Reports
4	6	18	90	202	260

Protected Species in Taiwan 2020

[Visual Identity, Logo Design]

Protected Species In Taiwan 2020 (PSIT 2020) is a shoe brand whose concept focuses on creating a positive brand image. Thus, the brand design takes up the topic of animal protection, using illustrations that show species that are endangered in Taiwan. With each species, the colour palette of the design changes, which creates an appealing overall image, for instance, for the brand's stationery brand. The product range also uses the visual identity as a unique selling point by featuring the shape of animal footprints on the soles of the ten different shoe models.

University
Fu Jen Catholic University
New Taipei City, Taiwan

Supervising Professor
Fa-Hsiang Hu, Chia-Yin Yu, Pei-Ying Wu

Design
Chien-Hung Chiu, Chia-Hsing Wei,
Chia-Chun Hsu, Chia-Wei Chen,
Shih-Yu Chen, Chiao-Kang Kan,
Fu Jen Catholic University

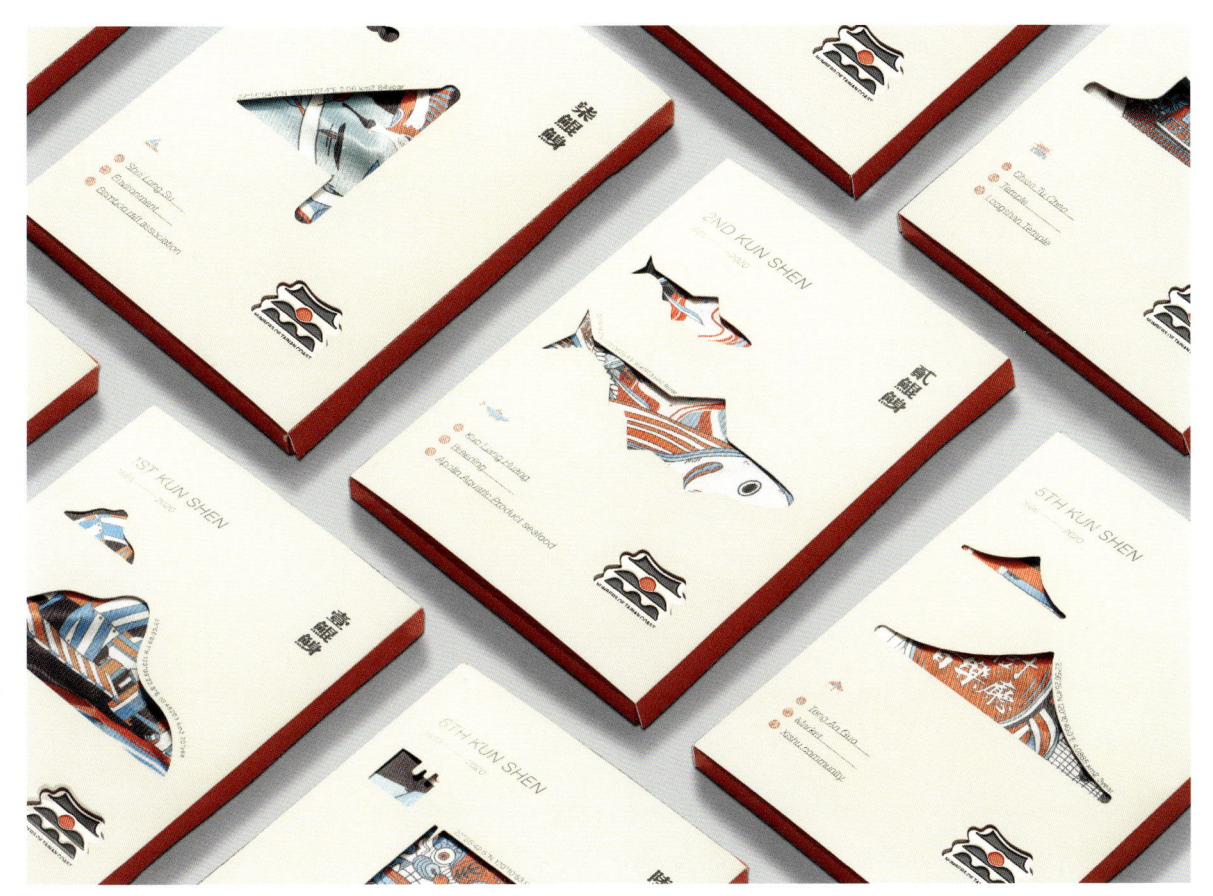

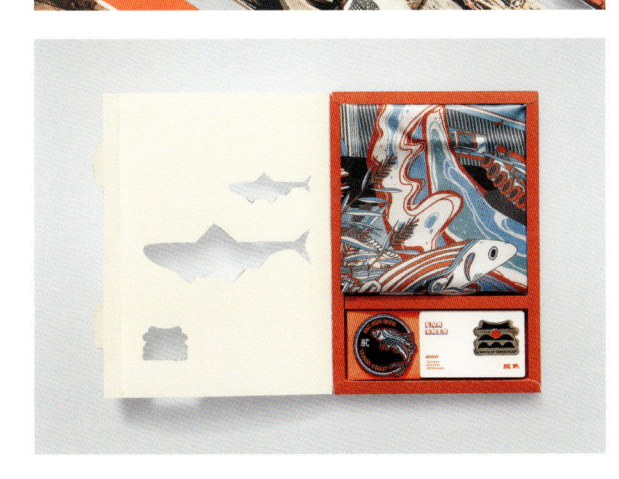

Numbers of Tainan Coast

[Brand Design]

Kun Shen is an old town on the coast of Tainan, Taiwan. In order to promote its economic development as a tourist location, a brand design was created that ties in with the former significance of the coastal city. Inspired by sandbars, the logo reflects the topography of the landscape. Furthermore, seven different motifs were created and printed on silk scarves that can be purchased as souvenirs. The design of the key visuals picks up on the colour palette of the brand and achieves an appealing overall image. In addition to the merchandising products, the new website also features the appealing brand design.

University
Ling Tung University
Taichung, Taiwan

Supervising Professor
An Hui Ching, Wei Jen Huang

Design
Chic Ying Ho, Yi Hsuan Tseng, Chi Yin Lu, Yu Cheng Lin, Xin Jie Xie, Ting Yi Huang, Ling Tung University

Eco-Friendly Growers

[Brand Design]

The Asian leopard cat was once widespread in Taiwan but is now an endangered species. To protect them in their natural habitat and hunting grounds, rice farmers who are part of this brand do not use toxic pesticides and fertilisers. The brand slogan conveys the brand philosophy that humans and leopard cats can coexist in a mutually beneficial relationship. The brand design is characterised by an artful illustration style that was appealingly implemented on both the exquisite product packaging and the information flyer. In this way, the brand experience combines environmental protection with a gourmet lifestyle.

University
Chaoyang University of Technology
Taichung, Taiwan

Supervising Professor
Kuo-Min Chuang

Design
Yu Tsen Chang, Lu Xi Jiang,
Bo Xian Chen, Cheng Han Chuang,
Chaoyang University of Technology

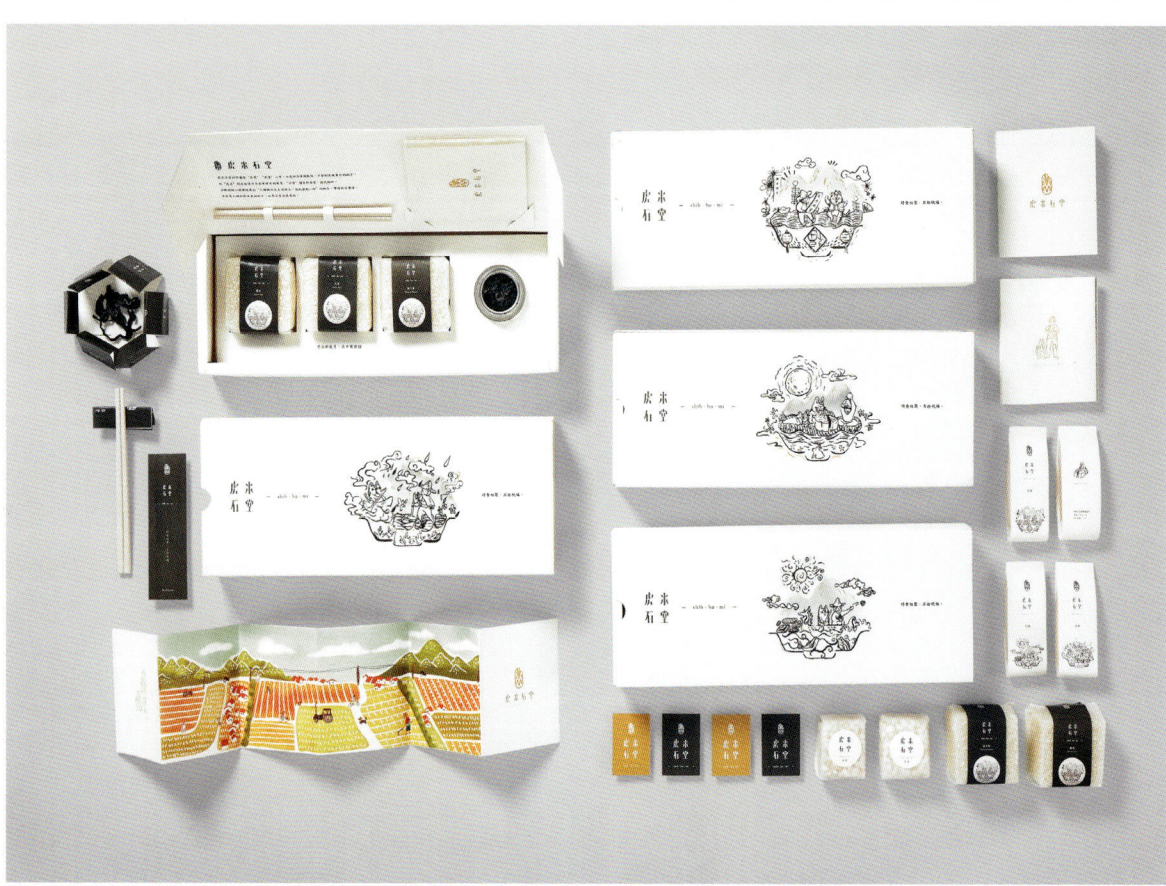

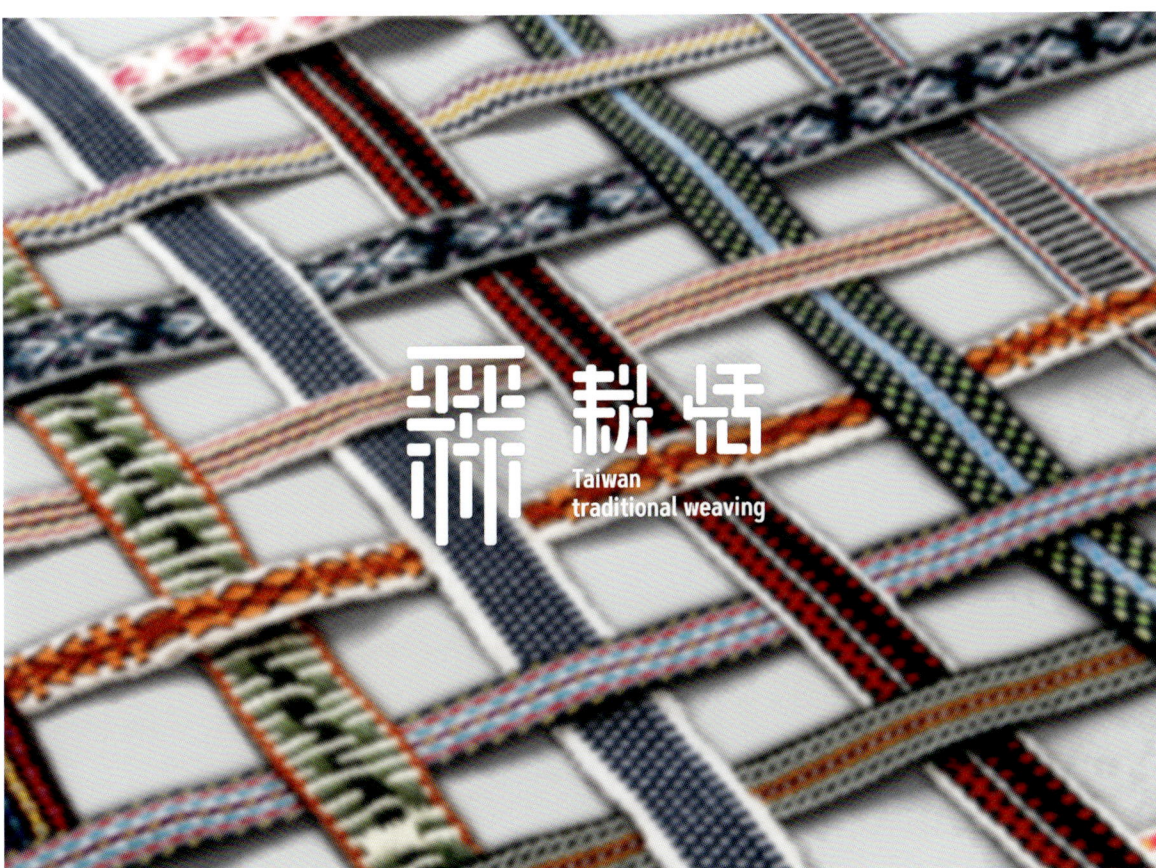

Geng Tian
[Logo Design]

Geng Tian founded this workshop with the mission to preserve the traditional Taiwanese artistry of hand weaving by teaching people how to weave on a loom. The design of the logo borrows its shape from Chinese characters and is inspired by the structure of weft and warp yarns. In order to convey the warmth of the handmade products and the weaving classes, the new brand design also aims to integrate printed patterns. The finishing on print materials imitates the feel of sewn fabrics, leaving a strong impression by appealing to the sense of touch and sight.

University
Asia University
Taichung, Taiwan

Supervising Professor
Chien-Hua Cheng

Design
Wei-Yu Huang, Asia University

Meme Together

[Brand Design]

Meme Together is a brand of fragrance diffusers that are available in four different scents: floral, citrus, oriental and wood. The brand design establishes a connection between individual fragrances and text memes, which are popular in Taiwan. Each meme is represented by various combinations of colourful symbols, creating an appealing brand image. Standing in strong contrast to the black background, luxurious gold is used as the basic colour tone to lend the brand sophistication. The versatility of the artwork supports the target group's need for a room fragrance that suits their individual character.

University
Chaoyang University of Technology
Taichung, Taiwan

Supervising Professor
Hsun-Wei Hsu

Design
Chang-Hung Hsieh, Zi-Xin Huang,
Cheng-Pang Chou, Zi-Rong Huang,
Hui-Ming Chen,
Chaoyang University of Technology

Advertising	Packaging Design	Fair Stands	Retail Design	Red Dot: Junior Award	Designer Profiles	Index
288	318	494	516	544	614	674

Blessing Lights and Soaps

[Brand Design]

The brand design for these blessing lights and soaps is an interpretation of the traditional window patterns of six famous temples in Taiwan. The six delicate ornaments, in combination with a variety of icons, serve to differentiate the products, as different candles and soaps are used or given as gifts on different occasions in Taiwan. The elegant lines are emphasised by a subtle colour palette, yielding an appealing branding that simplifies product selection and projects a harmonious overall image.

University
Cheng Shiu University
Kaohsiung, Taiwan

Supervising Professor
Chiang-Fu Chen, Chun-Hsun Wu

Design
Yu-Fang Chen, Jun-Ru Wang,
Ya-Jing Huang,
Cheng Shiu University

Mapping the Senses – Sensory Design Exhibition

[Brand Design]

"Mapping the Senses" is the title of an exhibition exploring radical innovations in the realm of multi-sensory design practices through selected projects by brands, architects, graduate students, artists and designers. The key visuals, which were especially developed for the exhibition, illustrate that multi-sensory design engages the five senses of sight, smell, taste, touch and hearing to provide a holistic experience. It accommodates the needs of a diverse audience with different physical abilities and cultural backgrounds. The implementation of the brand design includes promotional collateral, merchandise and exhibition catalogue.

University
SCAD Savannah College of Art and Design
Savannah, USA

Design
Jaspriya Sahmey, SCAD

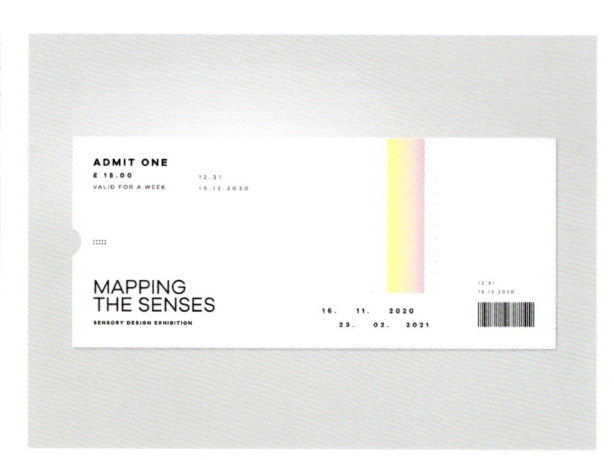

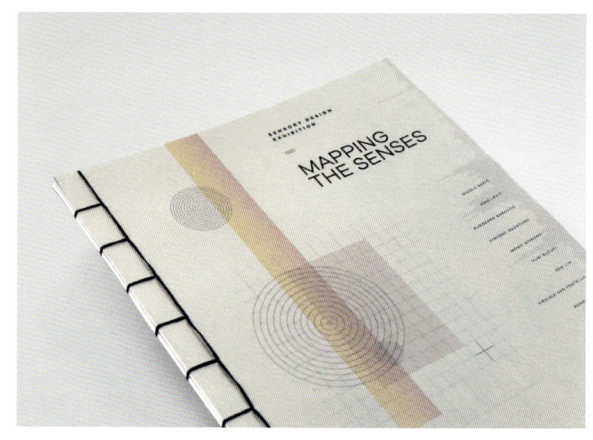

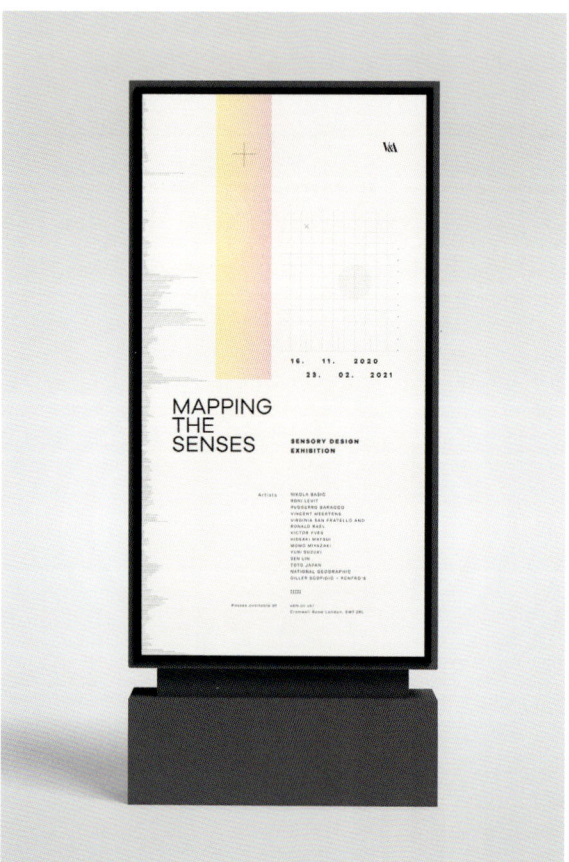

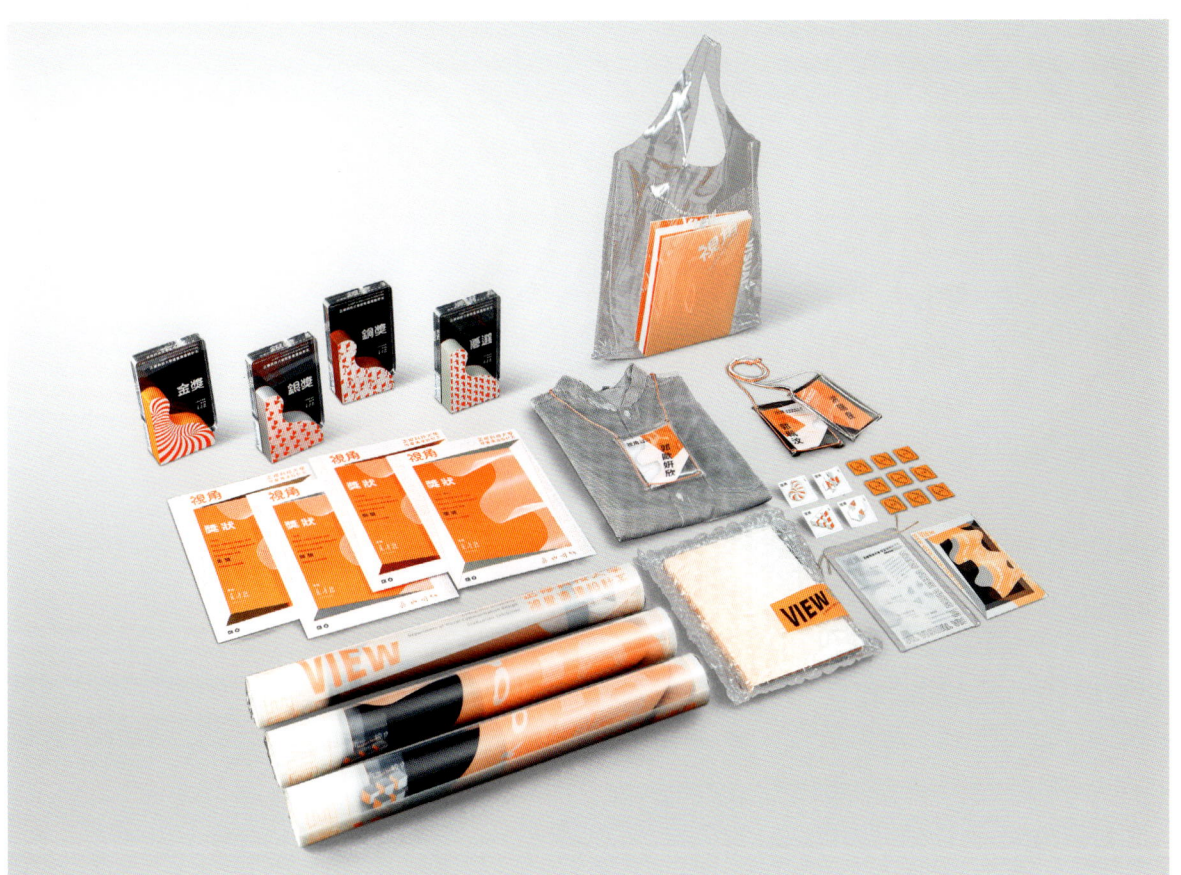

VIEW

[Visual Identity]

"VIEW" is the theme of the 2020 Graduation Exhibition by the Department of Visual Communication Design at Cheng Shiu University. It represents students seeking to push their own boundaries during the learning process and thus expanding their views and mentality. The design concept is defined by the use of lines as a basic element, creating a sense of visual depth in combination with the wavy effects of the key visuals. The dominant colours are fluorescent orange, grey and white – emphasising the students' enthusiasm to move forward. The transparent and translucent materials are used to emphasise views without boundaries.

University
Cheng Shiu University
Kaohsiung, Taiwan

Supervising Professor
Hsueh-Fen Lin, Shou-Che Wu

Design
Pei-Wen Kuo, Yi-Ling Fan,
Ou-Yen-Hsin Kuo,
Cheng Shiu University

Sharpie – With you on the fight

[Integrated Campaign]

This integrated campaign was created at the Savannah College of Art and Design. Sharpie is a brand of permanent markers and has long been a household name in the US. It is known for its bold lines and permanent strokes in vivid colours – product features that are used in this campaign. Based on the realisation that Sharpie has played an important role in creating protest signage, the posters showcase high-impact key visuals on the topics of women's liberation, justice and diversity. The claim "With you on the fight" clearly emphasises solidarity with the protest against injustice.

University
SCAD Savannah College of Art and Design
Savannah, USA

Design
Shruthi Venkatesh, Dayna Edmonds, SCAD

Advertising	Packaging Design	Fair Stands	Retail Design	Red Dot: Junior Award	Designer Profiles	Index
288	318	494	516	544	614	674

C.I.H.
[Social Campaign]

The high volume of pharmaceutical waste is creating a new kind of environmental pollution in Taiwan – a silent process that has worsened over time due to lack of awareness among many people. For this reason, this social campaign aims to inform people about the concept of drug recycling. Under the label C.I.H. (cycle, interest, habit), old habits are questioned and the conscious use of medication is promoted. A calendar is used to provide a visualisation of everyday health topics in an appealing manner, with links to websites. All illustrations are coloured in the key colour for that month.

University
Ling Tung University
Taichung, Taiwan

Supervising Professor
Izen Tu, Ching-Wei Liu

Design
Xin Yu Lu, Wei Chang Xiao, Chia Chen Wu, Yu Hsuan Chen, Pin Xuan Liu, Ying Li Yeh, Ling Tung University

Preface	Red Dot: Agency of the Year	Brands	Brand Design & Identity	Corporate Design & Identity	Annual Reports
4	6	18	90	202	260

PharmacEZ
[Image Campaign]

The student project PharmacEZ focuses on the topic of medication and the task of designing information about taking medication in an easy-to-understand and motivating manner. With the objective to make patients' attitudes as positive as possible, the design integrates simplified infotexts into an appealing image world. Bold colours accentuate the original illustration style and clearly highlight the most important information. In addition to advertising materials for use in pharmacies, the social campaign also includes a promotion on social media channels.

University
Chaoyang University of Technology
Taichung, Taiwan

Supervising Professor
Hui-Fang Lee

Design
Ching-Ting Chang, Yun-Tzu Chang, Fang-Yi Liao, Wan-Ho Pai, Jing-Ran Lin, Chaoyang University of Technology

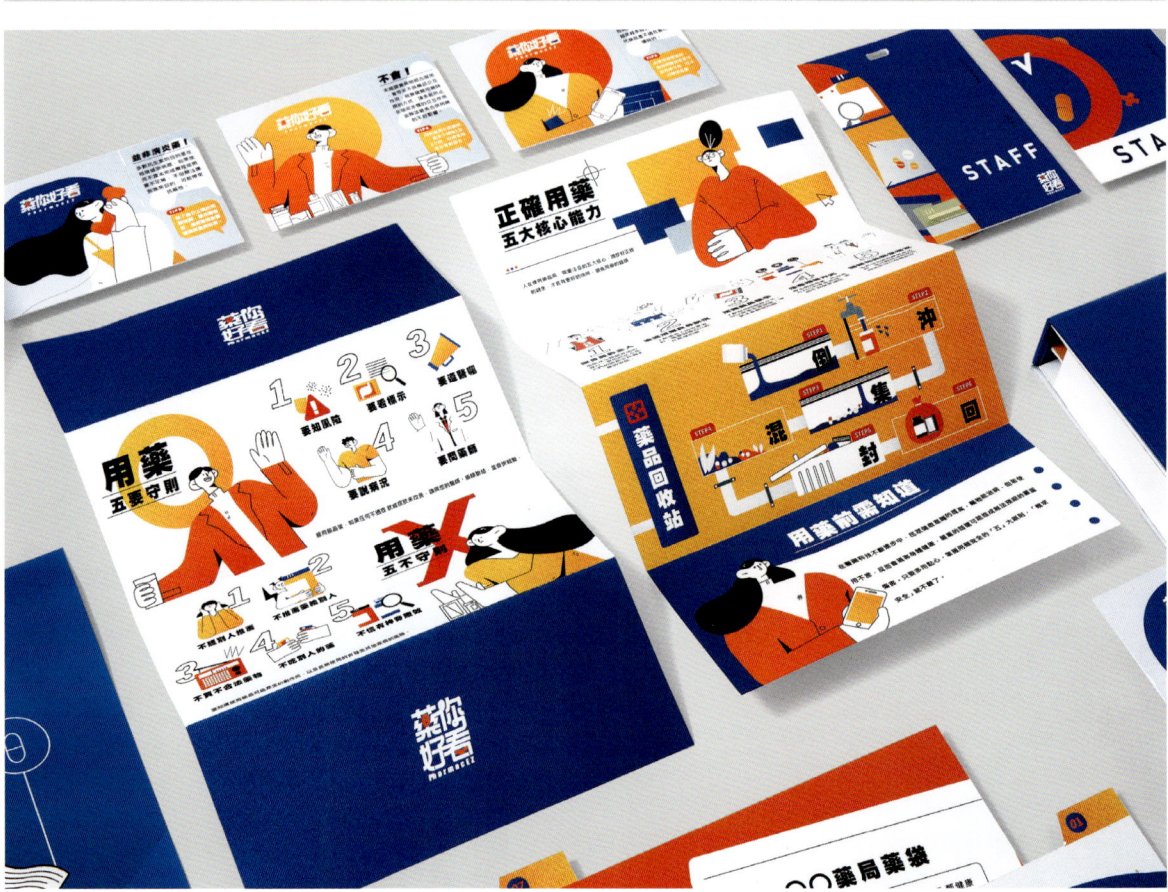

Advertising	Packaging Design	Fair Stands	Retail Design	Red Dot: Junior Award	Designer Profiles	Index
288	318	494	516	544	614	674

The New York Times – The Blank Label

[Direct Marketing]

This student assignment shows a direct marketing campaign in the form of an unusual advertising placement on product packaging. The idea is based on the observation that most people care about the quality of the food they consume, to the extent that they regularly check the nutrition fact labels. With "The Blank Label", the advertisement for The New York Times uses an advertising space that appeals to a broad target group directly in the supermarket. Nutrition fact labels could thus be used as advertising space to bring consciousness to the type of news people are consuming.

University
SCAD Savannah College of Art and Design
Savannah, USA

Design
Alberto Cuadra, Hope Thomas,
Sydney Solis, Rashed Alsubaie, Van Pham,
Remy James, Vy Phan, SCAD

Loofiber

[Promotion]

As an ecological alternative to conventional kitchen sponges, which are made from plastic fibres, Loofiber is made out of the fibres of loofah, a sponge gourd widely grown in Taiwan. The natural material enables scratch-free and thorough cleaning in the kitchen. After use, the biodegradable sponge can be used as an organic fertiliser. With the claim "Kitchen sponge from mother nature", this promotion aims to raise awareness about environmental pollution and environmentally conscious consumption. A 1.5-minute-long video clip explains both the product's use and its benefits for the environment in an easy-to-understand manner.

University
National Yunlin University of Science and Technology
Douliu City, Yunlin County, Taiwan

Supervising Professor
Kuo Shih-Mou, Hu Wen-Yuan,
Chiu Hsien-Yuan, Chiang Shyh-Bao

Design
Lim Huay Min,
National Yunlin University of Science and Technology

Rush Hanger

[Packaging]

This hanger is crafted in traditional fashion from Taiwanese bamboo and rush grass. It provides an eco-friendly alternative to disposable hangers made from plastic or wire. In line with the sustainable concept, the packaging design capitalises on a natural appeal. It also benefits from the properties of rush grass, which excellently absorbs moisture and keeps insects away with a pleasant scent. Once opened, the rolled-out parts of the woven covering can be transformed into hanging functional elements, increasing the product's versatility.

University
Ming Chi University of Technology
New Taipei City, Taiwan

Supervising Professor
Kai-Chu Li

Design
Zi-Shan Zhang, Chieh-An Chung,
Chang-Yu Lung,
Ming Chi University of Technology

Preface	Red Dot: Agency of the Year	Brands	Brand Design & Identity	Corporate Design & Identity	Annual Reports
4	6	18	90	202	260

Fragrance says
[Packaging]

The "Fragrance says" range comprises perfumed soaps and candles as well as fragrance diffusers. It is directed at young women, who can choose their personal favourites from three fragrance variations. The colourful packaging provides a helpful guide. For example, "Sweet Girl" has a vibrant and summery aroma, with packaging which features a girl holding strawberries and blueberries. "Fresh Girl" is refreshing and passionate, as symbolised by a basket of oranges and lemons. The gentle floral aroma of "Elegant Girl" is communicated by the design with a bunch of fresh flowers.

University
National Taiwan University of Science and Technology
Taipei City, Taiwan

Supervising Professor
Regina W. Y. Wang

Design
I-Ning Liu,
National Taiwan University of Science and Technology

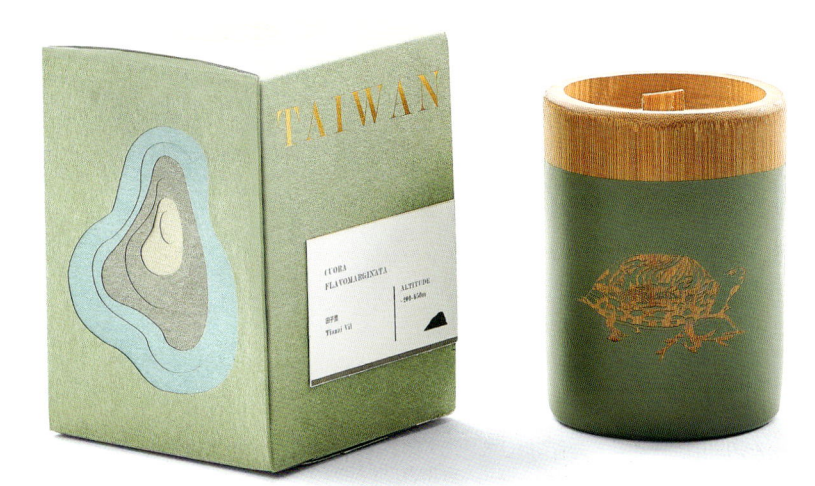

RE BOO LIFE

[Packaging]

The packaging for the candles of the RE BOO LIFE brand is made of bamboo waste materials from the Nantou Bamboo Mountain in Taiwan. The idea behind the concept is to increase awareness for ecological symbiosis and the beauty of nature. That is the reason why the packaging design for each product focuses on a different animal species which live on the mountain. It is based on a visual system incorporating various key elements such as calligraphy-like drawings of animals, topographical maps and contour lines in order to present the animals and their respective habitat.

University
Ling Tung University
Taichung, Taiwan

Supervising Professor
Yuen Hsiu Yen, Wei Jen Huang

Design
Huai Lan Chao, Tzu Mi Huang, Ju Han Yu, Fu Shun Zhang, Shu Hong Wang, Ling Tung University

Hard Rock Fragrance

[Cosmetics Packaging]

The concept of this limited-edition fragrance line follows a synaesthetic approach, as each scent is inspired by the distinctive sound of a rock song. Matching the fragrances, which are made from ethically sourced sustainable materials, the packaging is manufactured from hemp. The dynamic designs on the bottles visualise the emotional content of the songs. Easily recognisable elements like typographic artwork, atmospheric images or a logo speak to the essence of the bands. In addition, the quotation from a particular artist in each band enhances the personal feel of the packaging.

University
SCAD Savannah College of Art and Design
Savannah, USA

Design
Shruthi Venkatesh, SCAD

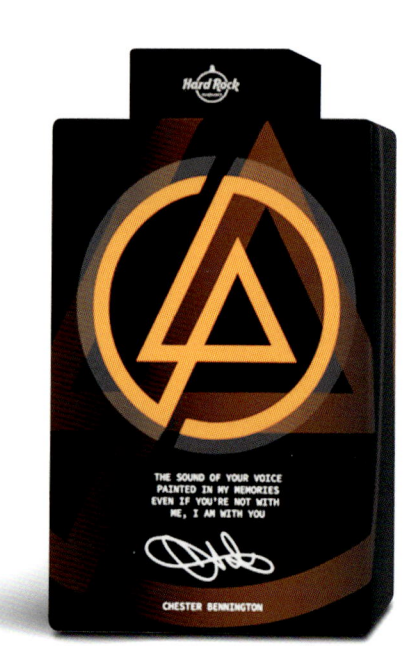

BEAU

[Cosmetics Packaging]

The design of the gift set for BEAU lipsticks in Contemporary Oriental Style constitutes a nuanced visual amalgamation of East and West. On the one hand, it uses style elements associated with Western nightclubs, such as neon lights and headphones. On the other, it reflects the classic image of an Oriental woman with a bun and a fan. This premium packaging comprises a carton with outer packaging which can be folded out to the side to create a fan. The high-quality box is held together using a banderole that looks like a pair of headphones.

University
Asia University
Taichung, Taiwan

Supervising Professor
Hsiao-Pei Hou

Design
Yu-Lin Ruan, Pei-Wen He, Asia University

Cosplay Chopsticks
[Packaging]

Using simple paper cards and plastic film, this work is a creative design of chopstick packages. The concept is based on humanising forms. In the external packaging, the chopsticks look like legs with socks, while the ring-shaped cardboard used to hang up the product is designed like raised arms. Once the cardboard has been separated from the plastic, it can be used as a chopstick holder on the table. With a large range of themes and many bright colours, the packaging communicates the originality of the brand and ensures that consumers associate the product with a lot of fun.

University
Asia University
Taichung, Taiwan

Supervising Professor
Hsiao-Pei Hou

Design
Ting-Zhen Yan, Asia University

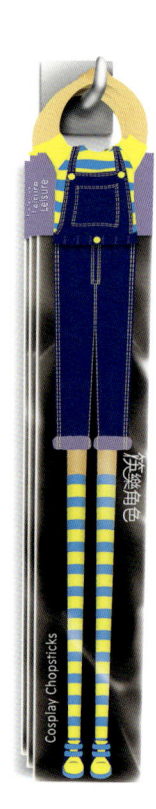

ROLL STRAW

[Packaging]

In contrast to traditional, reusable drinking straws, the ROLL STRAW is an innovative product which can be thoroughly cleaned, simply by opening it out flat. It is available in two types of packaging: a simple fold-out version and a more elaborate type, which also contains a storage box. The circular design mirrors the shape of the straw. The different colours and graphic patterns represent the various bubble teas which can be drunk with the straw. The orange packaging, for example, corresponds to the tropical fruit tea, with the dynamic pattern of dots intended as a visualisation of the bubbly freshness of the drink.

University
Ming Chi University of Technology
New Taipei City, Taiwan

Supervising Professor
Kai-Chu Li

Design
Yu-Shing Wu, Wei-Ting Wang,
Chia-Jun Hung,
Ming Chi University of Technology

Preface	Red Dot: Agency of the Year	Brands	Brand Design & Identity	Corporate Design & Identity	Annual Reports
4	6	18	90	202	260

DIDA
[Packaging]

The purpose of this work is to teach children self-discipline and, by doing so, help them to cope with life's challenges. Paper objects in the style of rides in an amusement park are provided as educational materials. The packaging communicates the product idea with a colourful layout. Catchy animals serve as key figures to attract the attention of the audience, gently introducing families to the complex content. In addition, the design is characterised by geometric shapes, with the square standing for principles and objectives, and the circle for strategy and ability.

University
National Taiwan University of Science and Technology
Taipei City, Taiwan

Supervising Professor
Yen Po-Chun

Design
Chung Ya-Hsuan, Hsu Chiau-Wei, National Taiwan University of Science and Technology

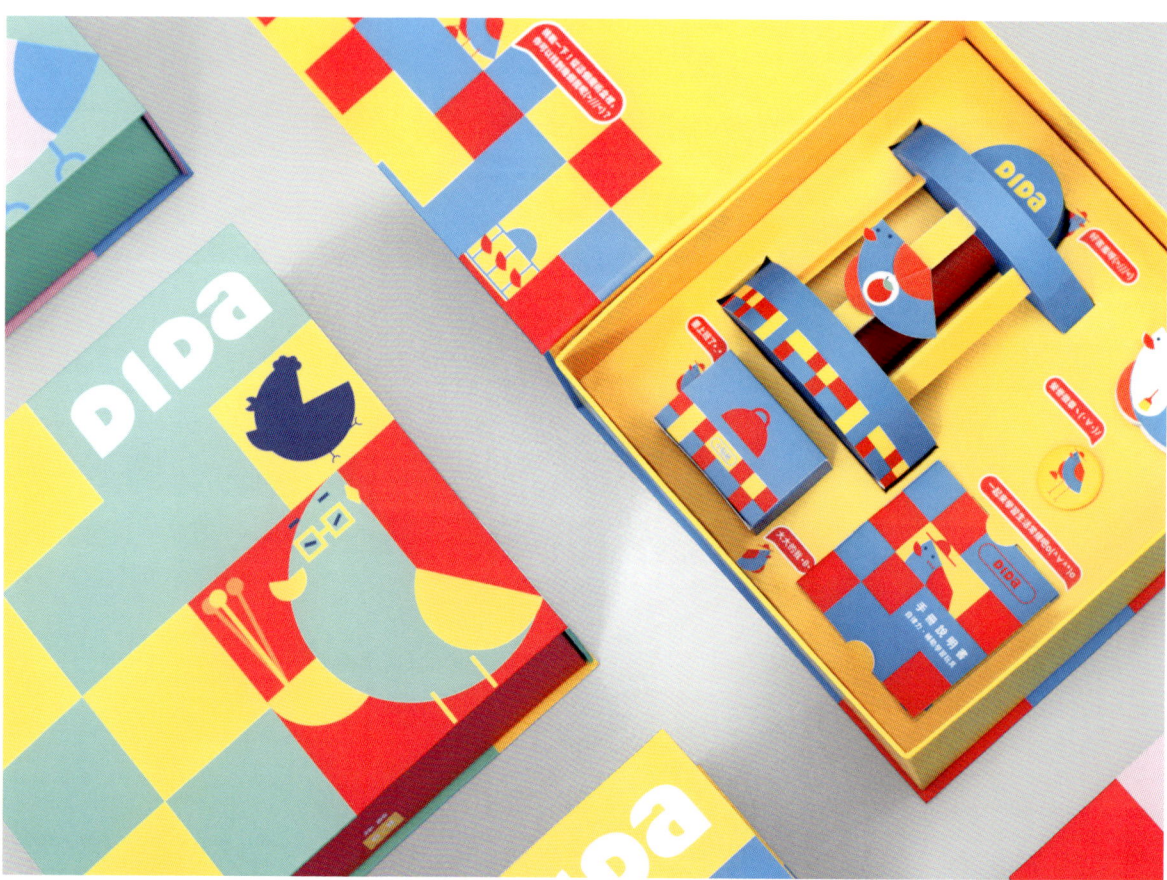

Che Pin – Taiwan Stage Truck Fleet

[Packaging]

Mobile stage trucks which provide entertainment at festivities are deeply anchored in popular Taiwanese culture. This 3D puzzle range includes six different wooden stage trucks showing how the stage-truck culture has changed over the decades. The packaging reflects the characteristic design of the various models. Each box is, for example, printed with a different, distinct tyre pattern on the bottom. Inside the cardboard boxes, a stage shows the finished model so that the packaging becomes part and parcel of the staging.

University
Asia University
Taichung, Taiwan

Supervising Professor
Hui-Ping Lu

Design
Yin-Hsuan Wang, Ding-Jyun Wang, Jyun-Fu Huang, Ruo-Shin Chou, Wan-Hsuan Cheng, Asia University

Preface	Red Dot: Agency of the Year	Brands	Brand Design & Identity	Corporate Design & Identity	Annual Reports
4	6	18	90	202	260

Headphone Home

[Retail Packaging]

This headphone package was designed to deal consciously with natural resources. The rectangle box is made up of two pieces of biodegradable corrugated paper. It can be folded out at the bottom to display the headphones on the shop counter. Customers can take the product with them by using the headband as a handle, while the sturdy material protects the headphones from damage. At home, the package can be reused as a stand. The rough texture exudes a rustic charm, while the display sides are upgraded by product illustrations on light-coloured cardboard.

University
East China Normal University
Shanghai, China

Design
Xiao-Yu Zhou, Yan-Yi Yu,
East China Normal University

→ Designer profile on page 635

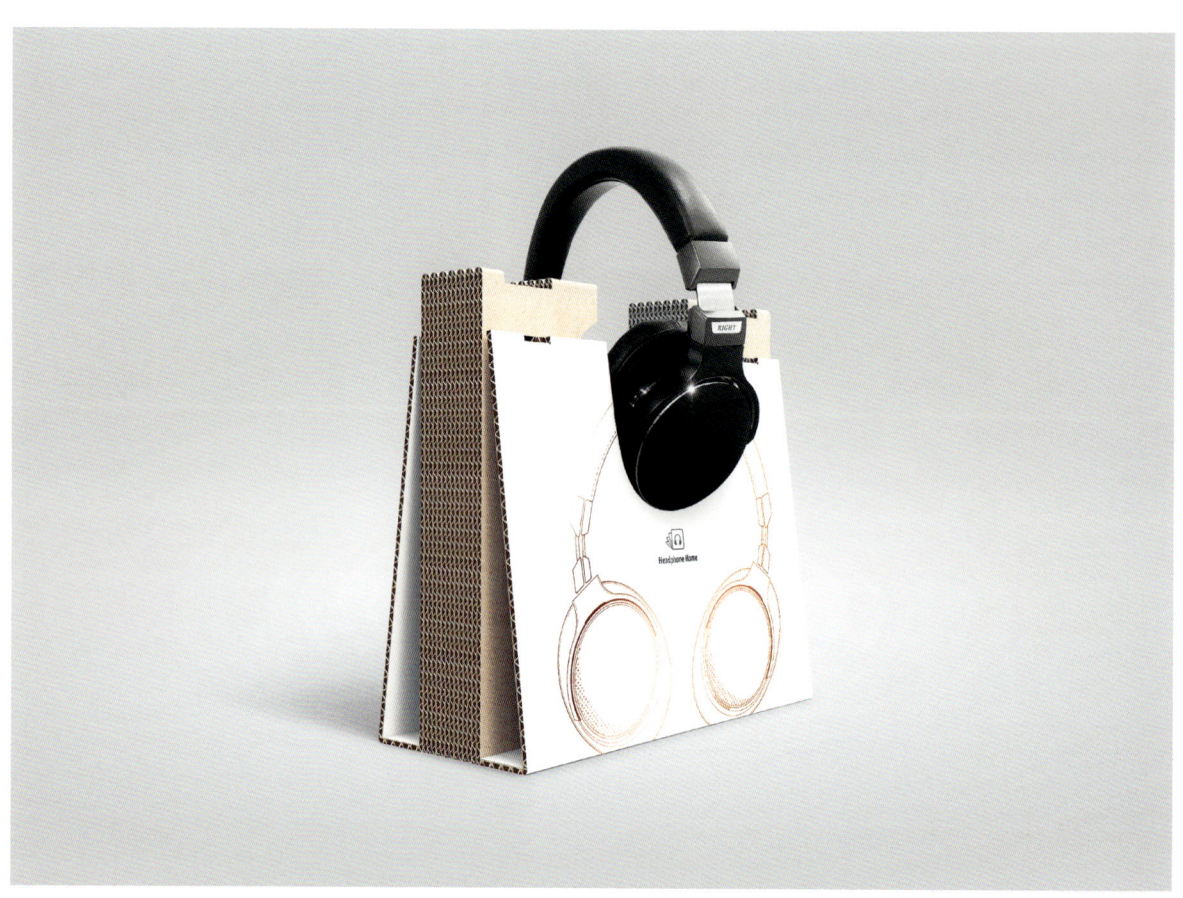

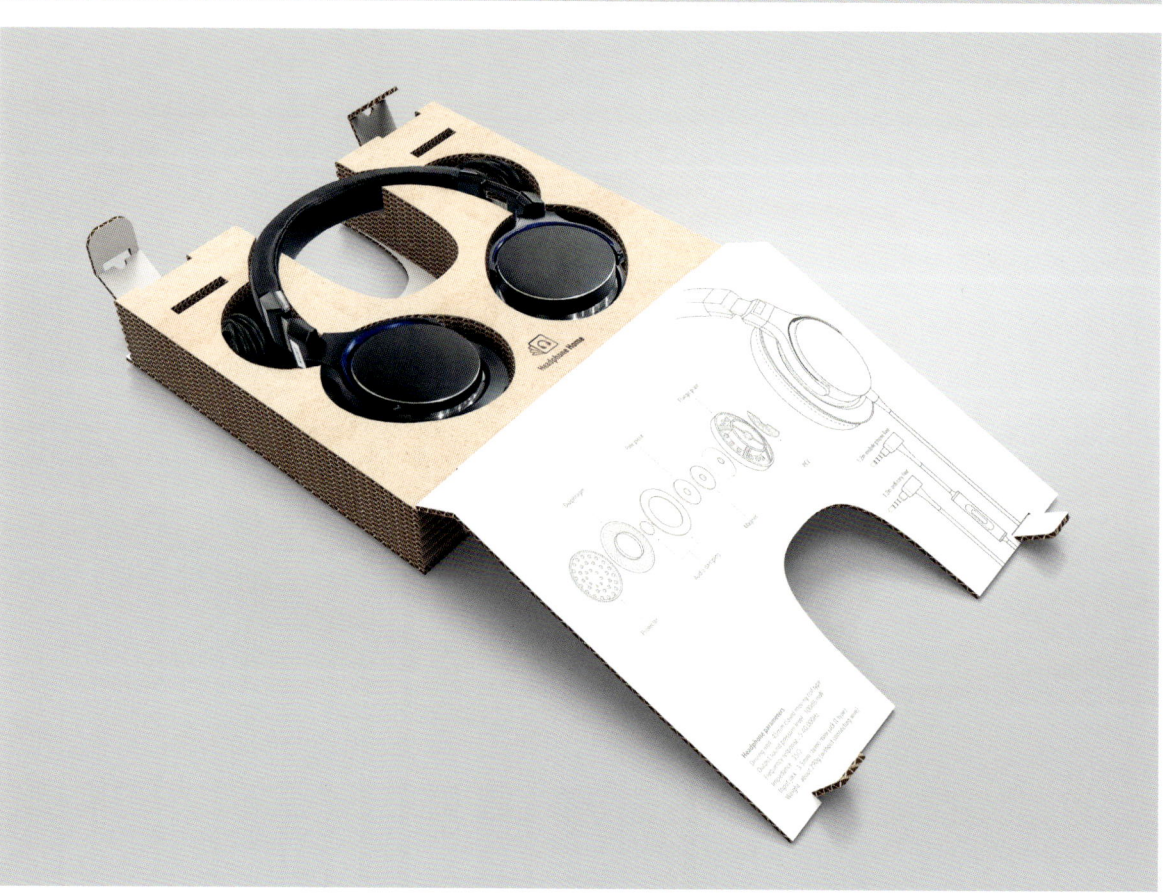

Advertising	Packaging Design	Fair Stands	Retail Design	Red Dot: Junior Award	Designer Profiles	Index
288	318	494	516	544	614	674

Sound O2

[Music Packaging]

This piece of work, comprising a book and three CDs, uses three central themes to address the decrease in seaweed volumes off the coast of Taiwan and the resulting drop in oxygen. The themes are soundtracked with a mix of music in Taiwanese style and sounds created by waves beating against seaweed-covered rocks. One of the CDs is transparent and decorated with a wave pattern which reflects both the environment in which the seaweed grows and sound waves. Seaweed manuscript paper is one of the items used for the packaging design, creating a link to nature.

University
Ling Tung University
Taichung, Taiwan

Supervising Professor
Chang-Chi Tsai, Ching-Wei Liu

Design
Tzu-Ling Liu, Xing-Ju Lu, Yi-Zhen Lai, Bin-Ru Kong, Ching-Wei Liu, Ling Tung University

Show of Love Story

[Food Packaging]

This decorative packaging comprises a combination of physical and virtual features to entertain newly-weds. The key visual on the gift box is a magpie, a traditional Chinese symbol of happiness. In addition to rice specialities and a special smartphone holder, the set also contains a small box with a see-through screen. After scanning a QR code and placing the device on a smartphone, users can watch a romantic video clip in the box. Through unpacking and discovering, the set offers a nuanced and sensual experience which can be shared with each other in a playful manner.

University
National Taichung University of Science and Technology
Taichung, Taiwan

Supervising Professor
Ming-Jen Chi, Corine Lee

Design
Hui-Ju Hsiao, Jhang-Cheng Liou,
Yi-Zhen Huang,
National Taichung University of Science and Technology

zzZen

[Packaging]

The name "zzZen" for products which help people to get to sleep indicates the ideas of sleep and of relaxing yoga. Like the darkness of the night, the main colour used in the packaging is matt black. Illustrations of a lazy cat decorate the packaging. These sleeping aids are offered in seven packs for seven days in three different sets: the Classic Limited Edition, an exquisite gift box and a large packaging series. The extravagant Classic Limited Edition comprises 3D-printed, triangular 100 ml bottles which can be nestled on top of each other and assembled into the shape of a diamond.

University
Chaoyang University of Technology
Taichung, Taiwan

Supervising Professor
Kuo-Min Chuang

Design
Lin Yu-Jyun, Kwok Ho-Shun, Li Jia-Ying,
Kwok Chi-Wang,
Chaoyang University of Technology

Preface	Red Dot: Agency of the Year	Brands	Brand Design & Identity	Corporate Design & Identity	Annual Reports
4	6	18	90	202	260

Eco-Friendly Wine Package

[Beverage Packaging]

The bag for the Kinmen Sorghum Liquor is more than a piece of outer packaging; it is a piece of art. The concept of the design is based on the easy identification of the product and the emphasises of its eco-friendly approach. The packaging is made environmentally friendly from recycled paper which also creates a simple and authentic look. Its three-dimensional design reflects precisely the distinctive, auspicious dragon pattern of the bottle. All shaping and modelling processes applied in the production of the outer packaging are based on excellent manual craftsmanship.

University
Chihlee University of Technology
New Taipei City, Taiwan

Supervising Professor
Shih-Lun Chen

Design
Xin-He Huang, Hung-Chi Huang,
Cong-Lin Chen,
Chihlee University of Technology

Frescofe

[Packaging]

Inspired by the Portuguese word "fresco" (fresh), both the name and the packaging design of the Frescofe coffee brand stand for the freshness of the product. Each carton is packed with 45 grams of coffee beans. Consumers take out portions by pulling open the carton and a box appears which contains precisely 15 grams of coffee beans. This is the amount required for a cup of coffee. Graphics of abstract clocks on the packaging represent the best time of the day to drink coffee, while the graphics on the side show the roasting degree of the coffee beans.

University
East China Normal University
Shanghai, China

Design
Jinfei Huang, Lijuan Hong,
School of Design,
East China Normal University

→ Designer profile on page 633

Herbal Master
[Packaging]

In view of the fact that liver cancer is one of the most common causes of death in Taiwan, this project combines traditional Chinese medicine and Qigong in a bid to promote good health. The carefully packaged parts of the work offer instructions for exercises, information about herbal tea culture and a special tea which is beneficial to the liver. Contrasting with the set's nostalgic external packaging, the illustrations inside are drawn like comic strips. The original mix of styles conveys the message that modern life and traditional cures can be both compatible and beneficial.

University
Cheng Shiu University
Kaohsiung, Taiwan

Supervising Professor
Yueh-Hsing Lai, Yu-Jin Lin

Design
Yun-Ru Pan, Yi-Ting Yan, Yi-Zhen Wu,
Yu-Zhen Wu, Cheng Shiu University

The Story of Shen Nong
[Packaging]

This packaging design is based on a tale about Shen Nong, in which the wise man tramps the land to taste medicinal herbs. His findings are said to be part of the "Divine Farmer's Materia Medica", an ancient Chinese book which has also inspired the design. Based on the classification in the compendium, the gift box contains packages with three kinds of herbal teas each. Lovingly drawn illustrations breathe new life into Shen Nong's journey. In addition, the outer packaging resembles a pot of traditional medicine and thus demonstrates the healing effect of the ingredients.

University
Asia University
Taichung, Taiwan

Supervising Professor
Hsiao-Pei Hou

Design
Chieh-Ying Lien, Pin-Yang Chang,
Asia University

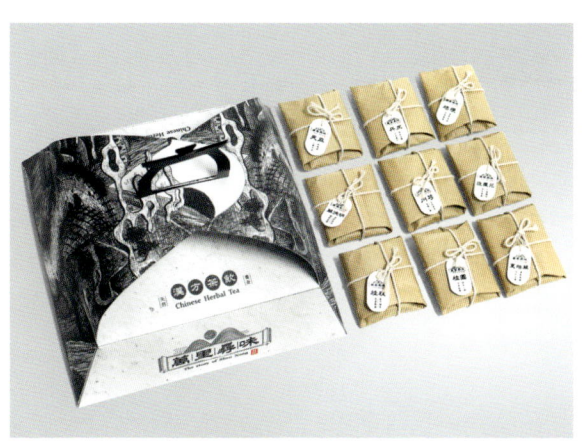

In the late summer

[Food Packaging]

The area around Sixty-Stone Mountain in Taiwan is famous for its fields of day lilies which flower in late summer. It is this landscape that serves as an inspiration for this gift set, which includes day lily tea bags and tea leaves as well as jam made from day lilies. The labels on the tea bags are designed to look like bright yellow blossoms. The hilly landscape is recreated in three-dimensional form with a paper cutting technique for the box for the jam set. The packages with tea leaves feature impressions of Sixty-Stone Mountain. When placed side by side, they show a complete image of the landscape.

University
China University of Technology
Taipei City, Taiwan

Supervising Professor
Sheng-Chuan Chang, Cheng-Ta Lee, Hsiao-Chin Wang

Design
Ya-Ting Huang, Wen-Fang Lee, Sheng-Yu Kao, Min-Zhu Zhan, Department of Visual Communication Design, China University of Technology

Advertising	Packaging Design	Fair Stands	Retail Design	**Red Dot: Junior Award**	Designer Profiles	Index
288	318	494	516	544	614	674

Taiwan Fruit Cake
[Food Packaging]

This packaging combines traditional and modern design features and contains one of four cakes made from Taiwanese fruits, each with a different flavour: custard apple, grape, strawberry and loquat. The central design element is a hand-painted illustration of the fruit used in the respective cake positioned on the front of the packaging. The colour tones are chosen to catch the eye and attract attention. Illustrations of the fruits are continued on the left and right-hand sides of the box. On the inside, the packaging is divided into three sections, making it easy to remove the cake from the box.

University
Chihlee University of Technology
New Taipei City, Taiwan

Supervising Professor
Shih-Lun Chen, Shu-Ping Chang

Design
Yu-Sheng Hung, Han-Wei Huang, Cheng-Huei Tien, Xiang-Qing Wang, Chihlee University of Technology

Dancing with Kinmen

[Food Packaging]

Kinmen Gong Candy was once used as a tribute to the Emperor of the Southern Song Dynasty. Since the Emperor's totem used to be dragon shaped, the design of the packaging for this peanut candy is based on dragon pillars just like those which can be seen in Taiwanese temples. The spiral shape folded paper boxes can be extended and hung up. They create the impression of a dragon flying in the sky. Inside the box, there is a bag containing individually packed sweets. The packaging also features illustrations which provide an insight into how the candies are made.

University
Asia University
Taichung, Taiwan

Supervising Professor
Hsiao-Pei Hou

Design
Ya-Jun Li, Wei-Ying Chen, Zhao-Xiang Chen, Asia University

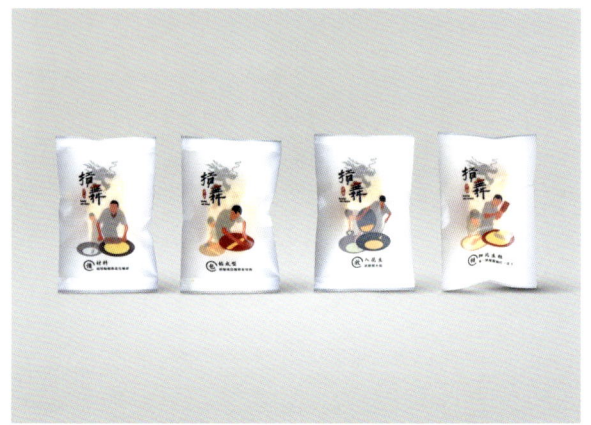

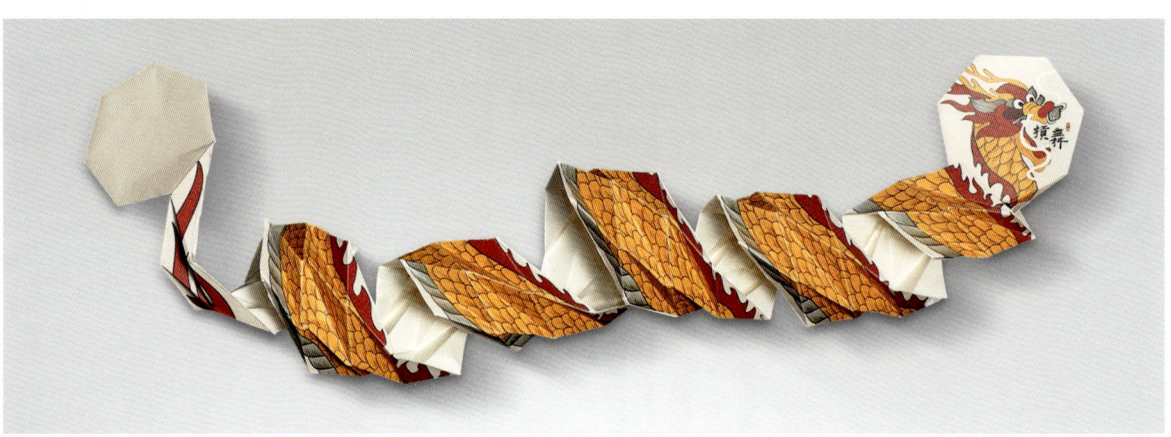

Advertising	Packaging Design	Fair Stands	Retail Design	Red Dot: Junior Award	Designer Profiles	Index
288	318	494	516	544	614	674

Seaweed Islet

[Food Packaging]

The rocky coast of Taiwan's north-east is known for its seaweed. This work aims to build a brand for this local speciality by developing the packaging design for various seaweed-based products using gentle, harmonious colours and sophisticated embossing. Nine illustrations, which depict characteristic landscapes and sight-seeing destinations along the coastal region, catch the consumer's eye. Combining the seaweed product with local culture highlights the brand's local character. Enclosed ecological information rounds off the packaging concept.

University
China University of Technology
Taipei City, Taiwan

Supervising Professor
Chien-Hsun Chen, Cheng-Ta Lee

Design
Shu-Chi Hsu, Chi-Man Hsu,
Jia-Jun Lin, Sin-Yu Li,
Department of Visual Communication
Design, China University of Technology

Preface	Red Dot: Agency of the Year	Brands	Brand Design & Identity	Corporate Design & Identity	Annual Reports
4	6	18	90	202	260

Yes!
[Food Packaging]

"Make eating betel pepper a positive habit" is the motto of this work which aims to raise the profile of this food. Eight ready meals using betel pepper as the main ingredient are marketed under the name "Yes!" and the Chinese name "ye shi", while the Chinese name is pronounced the same as the word "yes" in English. The meals are packed in boxes, with one third of the box showing the respective ingredients in colourful illustrations. This contrasts with the rest of the packaging, which is black and white with filigree illustrations of betel leaves.

University
Fu Jen Catholic University
New Taipei City, Taiwan

Design
Chen Szu-Fan, Chen Yu-Zhen,
Lee Che-Yu, Huang Yen-Yu,
Chen Ting-Ying, Hsu Chien-Ya,
Fu Jen Catholic University

Advertising	Packaging Design	Fair Stands	Retail Design	Red Dot: Junior Award	Designer Profiles	Index
288	318	494	516	544	614	674

MoReal!

[Food Packaging]

The distinctive packaging for MoReal! muesli is in the shape of the main ingredient used in the product: a mushroom, but only one half of it. When two boxes are placed side by side, they unite and become one with each other. On the front of the package, there is also a colour illustration of a mushroom against a white background. This image is complemented with a photo of flakes of cereal. The muesli is available in four different flavours. The packages are designed in the colours blue, green, pink and orange to make it easy to distinguish them. Customers can thus recognise the different varieties, even from a distance.

University
Hoseo University
Asan, South Korea

Design
Jin A Choi, Jung Mi Kong, I Ji Yoon, Yu Mi Go, Jong Hui Lee, Yu Jin Park, Hoseo University

New Grape Packaging

[Food Packaging]

New Grape Packaging is based on a design concept that is both minimalist and sustainable. Following an environmentally friendly philosophy, the package is made from recyclable corrugated cardboard. By simply folding and slotting in place, the piece of cardboard is transformed into a three-dimensional container, which can be used to transport grapes and for retail. The hexagonal design is space-saving and prevents the grapes from being handled and bruised. Instead, they are protected and held in place, while the air circulates freely through the package.

University
East China Normal University
Shanghai, China

Design
Liu Zhiyuan, East China Normal University

→ Designer profile on page 634

The Citrus Studio

[Food Packaging]

The region surrounding the Taiwanese town of Zhutong is famous for its mandarins. This packaging for the fruit and for marmalade, citrus sauce and dried fruit is designed to have a strong impact. American country-style illustrations as well as fluorescent orange as the main colour attract consumers' attention. In addition, recycled linen like the one used by farmers serves to reflect a circular economy. For example, this material lines the fruit crate put together like a jigsaw, protecting the fruit contained inside.

University
Ling Tung University
Taichung, Taiwan

Supervising Professor
Wei-Hsien Lan

Design
Ying-Chi Chi, Chia-Ying Li,
Ling Tung University

Preface	Red Dot: Agency of the Year	Brands	Brand Design & Identity	Corporate Design & Identity	Annual Reports
4	6	18	90	202	260

Dishes

[Food Packaging]

"No matter which meal you are having, we hope our lunch box can become a part of your journey." This is the core concept for a bento box brand geared especially towards those travelling by train. Typical Taiwanese meals are offered in order to familiarise tourists with the country through its dishes. The menu is designed with colour illustrations in the local language as well as in English in order to avoid any difficulties understanding the content. The meals are packed in boxes which show illustrations of various ingredients. A carrier for several boxes, designed like a shopping bag, also has a space for chopsticks.

University
Asia University
Taichung, Taiwan

Supervising Professor
Hsiao-Pei Hou

Design
Yun-Tung Heng, Chieh-Ying Lien,
Asia University

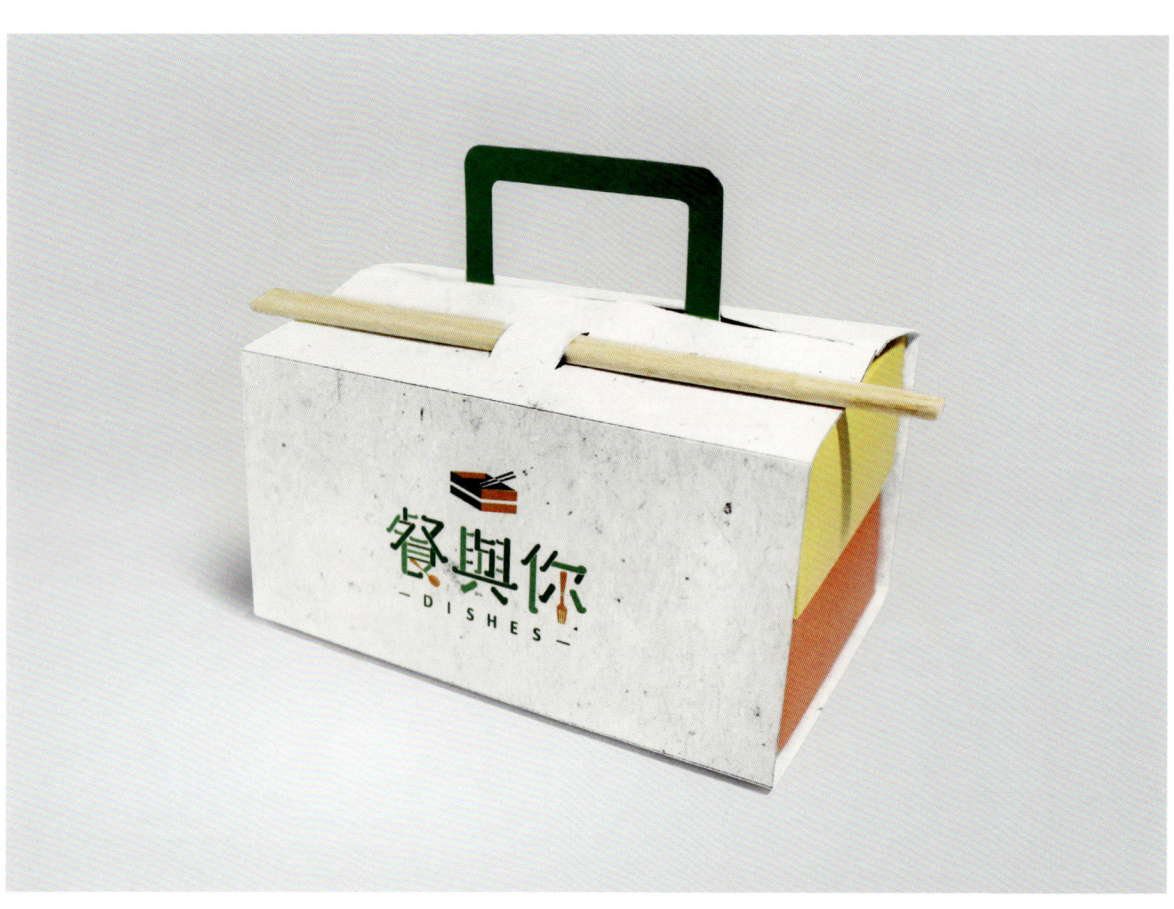

Crop Protector
[Sustainable Packaging]

The golden apple snail is a highly invasive species, which causes much damage to crops in Asia. With a special ring made from rice husk and tea seed meal, this stake protects seedlings from the hungry creatures. The roots are stabilised with a straw fibre shell. As the fibre material decomposes in the soil, it also has a fertilising effect. A functional yet attractively designed packaging reflects the product's sustainable nature. The portable box is made from biodegradable, recycled cardboard, effectively absorbs shocks during transportation and can be taken apart to serve as a tray for seedlings.

University
Ming Chi University of Technology
New Taipei City, Taiwan

Supervising Professor
Kai-Chu Li

Design
Chang-Yu Lung, Chieh-An Chung,
Zi-Shan Zhang,
Ming Chi University of Technology

SKIN SAVER

[Packaging]

The SKIN SAVER plaster is intended for people who work outdoors and are exposed to a high risk of insect bites. The product integrates the functions of wound cleaning, wound protection and cooling the affected area. In terms of packaging design, a hexagon was chosen as the core element. The geometric shape serves as a logo but is also used as a graphic motif with a dynamically flowing appeal. With simple means, the design thus echoes the edgy contours of the medical plaster and, at the same time, hints at the relief the product will bring to the user.

University
National Taipei University of Education
Taipei City, Taiwan

Supervising Professor
Kai-Chu Li

Design
Yi-Yun Li, Min-Hua Tsai, I-Jie Tsay,
Yu-Ching Chiu,
National Taipei University of Education

Wound Care Band

[Packaging]

If plasters are not changed correctly, healing can be delayed or infections can occur. Wound Care Band features a special patch which detects an infected wound by sensing a high concentration of certain biogenic amines. When this happens, the patch changes colour from mustard yellow to orange red. These bright colours and the rounded shape of the plaster also mark the packaging design, signalling the content and piquing the interest of viewers. Since the opening is placed at the bottom, the plasters can be quickly and easily removed from the box.

University
National Taipei University of Education
Taipei City, Taiwan

Supervising Professor
Kai-Chu Li

Design
I-Jie Tsay, Min-Hua Tsai, Yu-Ching Chiu, Yi-Yun Li,
National Taipei University of Education

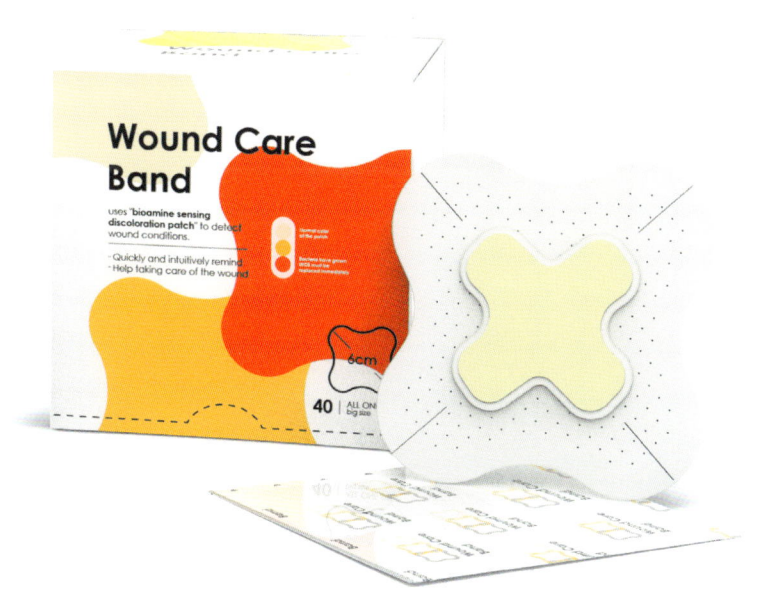

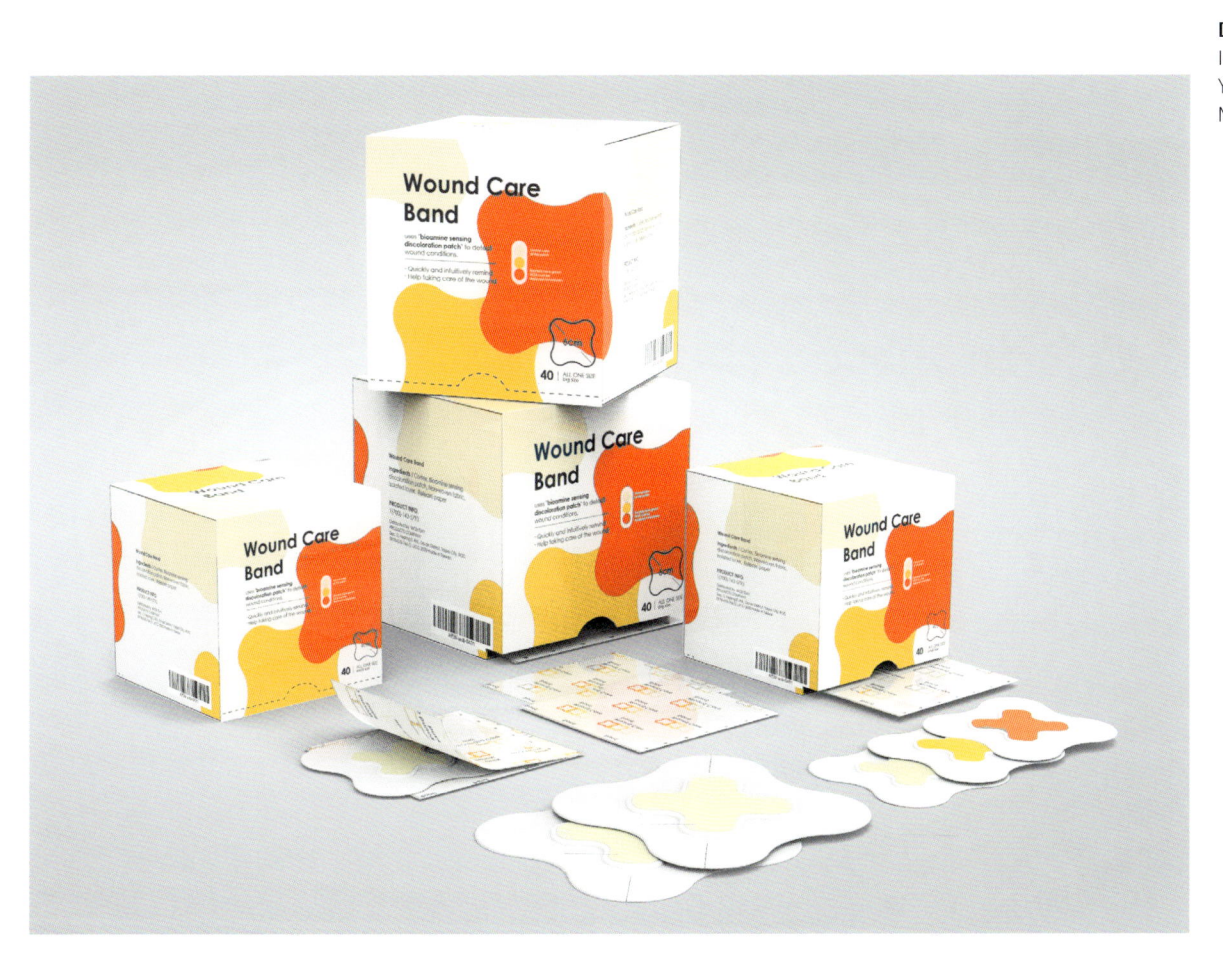

COOL DOWN

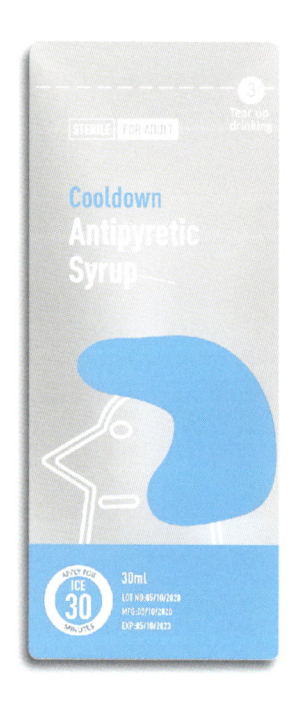

[Packaging]

This product has been developed to relieve fever in children, senior citizens or patients in areas lacking medical facilities. The set offers antipyretic syrup packs and disposable cooling patches. The medical supplies come with a compact, easy-to-use outer packaging. As a special feature, the patch package contains a temperature-sensitive hydrogel, which gives patients a quick indication whether it is necessary to take the medication. Held against the forehead, the pack changes colour in case that the body temperature exceeds 38.5 degrees Celsius, thus effectively alerting the user.

University
National Taipei University of Education
Taipei City, Taiwan

Supervising Professor
Kai-Chu Li

Design
Yi-Yun Li, I-Jie Tsay,
Yu-Ching Chiu, Min-Hua Tsai,
National Taipei University of Education

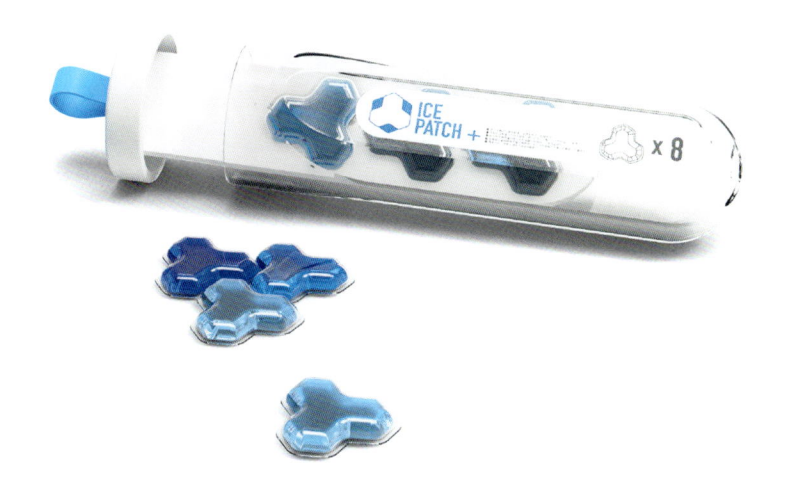

ICE PATCH +

[Packaging]

ICE PATCH + is a cooling product designed to be attached on elastic tape to avoid direct skin contact. Thermochromic microcapsules inside the pad demonstrate the change of temperature by change of colour. The package containing the pads resembles a clinical thermometer, emphasising the medical purpose of the product. It can be hung in the refrigerator using a loop to save space. The tape comes in boxes which allow the customer to have a look inside through crystal-shaped cut-outs. With this, and with a concise logo, the packaging creates a link to the special shape of the cooling pads.

University
Ming Chi University of Technology
New Taipei City, Taiwan

Supervising Professor
Kai-Chu Li

Design
Chang-Yu Lung, Zi-Shan Zhang,
Chieh-An Chung,
Ming Chi University of Technology

JUSTii

[Packaging]

JUSTii is a packaging design for condoms. Fresh, ice cream-like colours are used to make the series stand out and convey a feeling of ease. In addition, the packaging has been optimised to shorten the awkward period of unpacking. The blister pack opens with a distinctive cracking sound. Afterwards, the internal packaging can be broken open in the middle, allowing the condom to pop out of the opening in a surprising manner. Humorous illustrations, a few suggestive textual elements around the topic of sex and a QR code for further information complete the entertaining concept.

University
National Taichung University of Science and Technology
Taichung, Taiwan

Design
Hsin-Yu Shih, Huei-Jyun Yeh, Bo-Chen Chen, Yu Wang, Yung-Ni Chung, National Taichung University of Science and Technology

DISCOLORED MASK

[Packaging]

This packaging contains face masks with a double-layer design fitted with a special filter and a test strip. When the test strip changes colour, users are reminded that they need to clean the masks. For storing the masks, flat plastic containers have been developed. They are attached to a piece of string which can be used as a lanyard. The decorative packaging is reminiscent of an amulet which magically protects its wearer from harm. In a further bid to promote the concept of the masks, the folded product shimmers auspiciously through the semi-transparent case.

University
Ming Chi University of Technology
New Taipei City, Taiwan

Supervising Professor
Kai-Chu Li

Design
Chang-Yu Lung, Zi-Shan Zhang,
Chieh-An Chung,
Ming Chi University of Technology

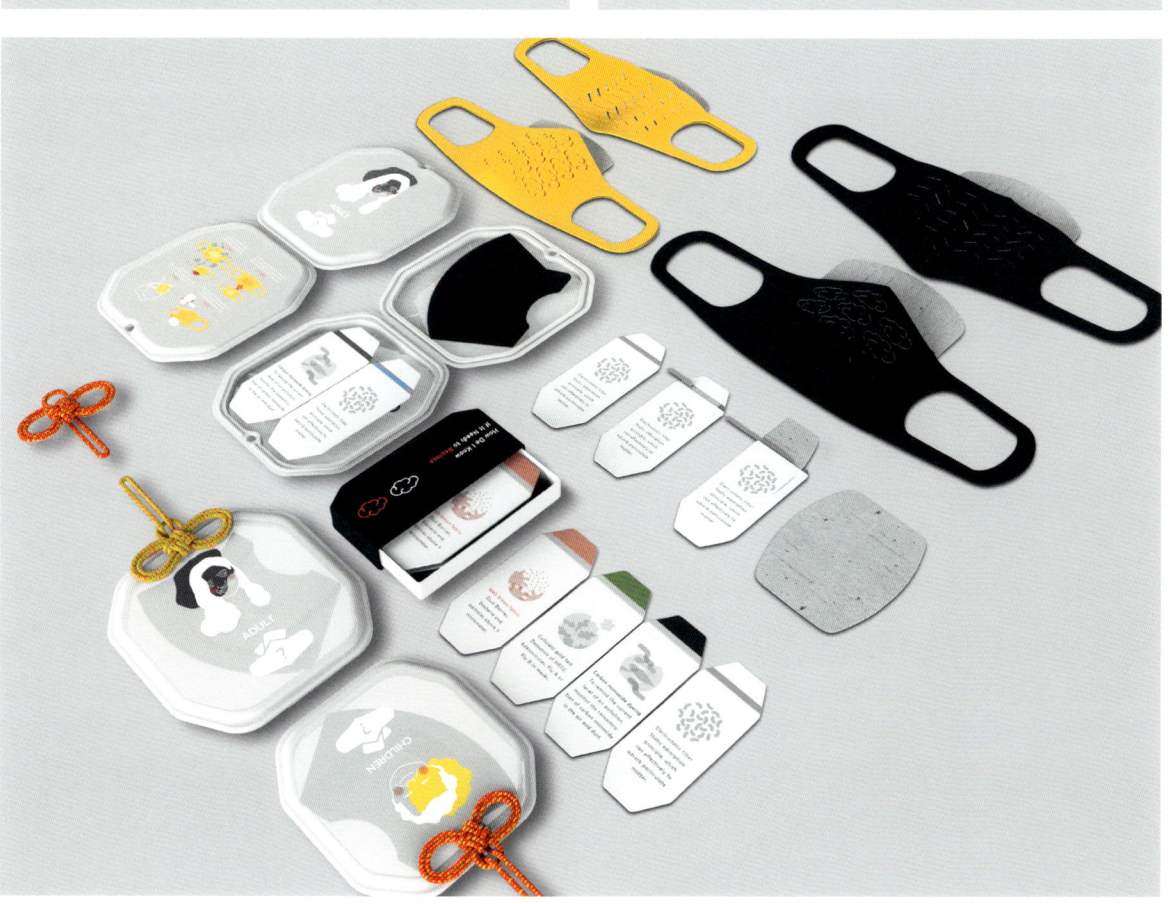

Designer Profiles

:response/SHE

Marten Deuter, Isabell Lenz, Arved Lüth, Marion Wagner, Paulina Olejniczak

— Let's redesign the economy, let's create a regenerative culture.

Red Dot
→ Annual Reports: page 282–283

:response, a consultancy based in Frankfurt, Germany, has been pioneering the exciting fields of sustainability, corporate social responsibility and regenerative economy since 2007. Working in sustainability since 1995, founder Arved Lüth met SHE's managing director Beate Scheufele in 2015. Together, they have since produced integrated and sustainability reports for multiple clients. The expertise shown in more than 1,000 consulting projects and exceptional design skills gained them multiple awards, both in sustainability and design.

What does design mean to you?
Design has an ethical mandate for sustainability. As design for sustainability is still new territory, the process is rarely smooth but includes crucial confrontations between content and layout. Sustainable design does not only convey information, but changes your perception and stimulates action. In the end, it will shape decisions and our thinking. Lastly, design happens within a process of co-creation which for many is an end in itself.

What was your intention in designing your awarded work?
To create an aesthetic context that presents the avoidance of unnecessary waste and the conscious use of plastic in a high-class setting, like a piece of art. We wanted to play with the viewer's perception – which makes you realise that you have to watch closely to understand what you actually really consume.

3st kommunikation
Thilo Breider, Alex Knaub, Marcel Teine, Florian Heine
— Curiosity goes further.

Red Dot: Grand Prix
→ Annual Reports: page 262-263

For over 20 years, 3st has stood for outstanding design, surprising content and relevant reporting. Their source of inspiration is the world and their objective to meet its complexity head on and discover new, to the point solutions among the plethora of expressive options. With around 70 specialists working in strategy, design, film, programming and editorial, the agency creates fascinating brand experience on a daily basis and pools its expertise in digital, branding and content to create a powerful unit.

What does design mean to you?
For us, design is like cooking. First, you go to the market to buy good ingredients. Then you wash and cook them. At the end, you enjoy the result together.

Why did you become a designer?
Design offers an insight into many different areas and allows one to develop many new forms of expression. Design is a limitless, dynamic profession.

What drives you to create something new?
Design thinking must always be taken a step further. It never stops and there is almost never a definitive form.

What are the biggest challenges in a creative's everyday life?
The challenge is similar to the one faced by restaurant kitchens: serving up numerous dishes of appealing quality simultaneously.

A.S. Advertising
Antonia Skaraki
— Seize the day!

Red Dot
→ Packaging Design: page 362–363
→ Packaging Design: page 408
→ Packaging Design: page 415

Antonia Skaraki studied visual communication and advertisement at Vakalo Art & Design College in Athens, Greece. She worked as head of the art department at MOTO magazine, PROTI newspaper and IDANIKO SPITI magazine. She was the creative director of the advertising company Able Communications, founded Karamella Advertising in 1993 and participated in the creation of Looking Advertising in 2007. Today, she is the founder and CEO of A.S. Advertising, leading a creative team that provides design, storytelling, communication, branding and brand mentoring, as well as transformation solutions.

To what extent do you think new technologies are changing design?
Well, designers have always worked at the intersection of cultural trends, but today these trends are being accelerated by unprecedented advances in technology. So we need to prepare for the changing nature of the industry. We need creative people who can push the limits of design, while keeping a constant focus on innovation and effective strategies.

Why did you become a designer?
I was always fascinated by the universe... The extreme fine-tuning of so many laws of nature that lead to the greatest design of all: the cosmos. You know, anything that had order and inner harmony was, for the ancient Greeks, a cosmos!

What drives you to create something new?
Curiosity and an insatiable need for harmoniously shaping everything around me.

Acer
— Breaking barriers between people and technology.

Red Dot
→ Packaging Design: page 459

Founded in 1976, Acer is today one of the leading ICT companies and has a presence in over 160 countries. Its industrial design brings together talents with backgrounds in products, user interface, graphic design, packaging design, industrial design, design research and engineering to maximise the value of a company's products and bring users the best possible experience, from concept development and prototyping through to final testing.

Where do you see future challenges in communication design?
In standing out in the infinite volume of information and being able to target the right user without interference.

Why did you become a designer?
To explore something that will improve society and the status quo.

What drives you to create something new?
We are dedicated to understanding the needs and behaviours of users and are keen to solve human problems through technology.

What are the biggest challenges in a creative's everyday life?
The biggest challenges lie in finding the balance between an ideal and reality, and in creating a win-win for both brands and consumers.

What makes your work unique?
Teamwork, communication, and understanding people's needs.

Admind Branding & Communications
Karolina Pospischil
— Find ways to build connections – between people, ideas, emotions.

Red Dot
→ Advertising: page 306–307

Karolina Pospischil graduated from the Jagiellonian University in Krakow, Poland, and was a student at the School of Brand Strategy SAR. She is co-founder of the Grube Poster Studio and runs the creative teams at Admind, guiding their strategic development and supervising creative concepts. At the Annecy International Animation Film Festival, she was recognised for her short film "The Guardian" that later won awards at the Arizona Film Festival, CIFF, River Film Festival, SPARK Animation, Animac Lleida and Mecal Barcelona. She has worked for brands such as OFFF Barcelona, the Jewish Culture Festival, the Children's Film Festival Galicja, Krakow Festival Office, Alter Publishing House, Otwarte Publishing House and Jagiellonian University.

What does design mean to you?
For me it started as a tool for self-expression. With time, I discovered all the functions it can have and that it is a great connector.

Why did you become a designer?
Representing ideas and feelings through images, illustrations, and grounding culture in image-filtered objects that evoke another wave of feelings once received, turned out to be a completely new and easy way for me to talk to people as a very shy teenager.

What are the biggest challenges in a creative's everyday life?
Not being stuck on solutions that worked before: those that have been tested, are quick, yet don't allow room for growth for brands and creatives.

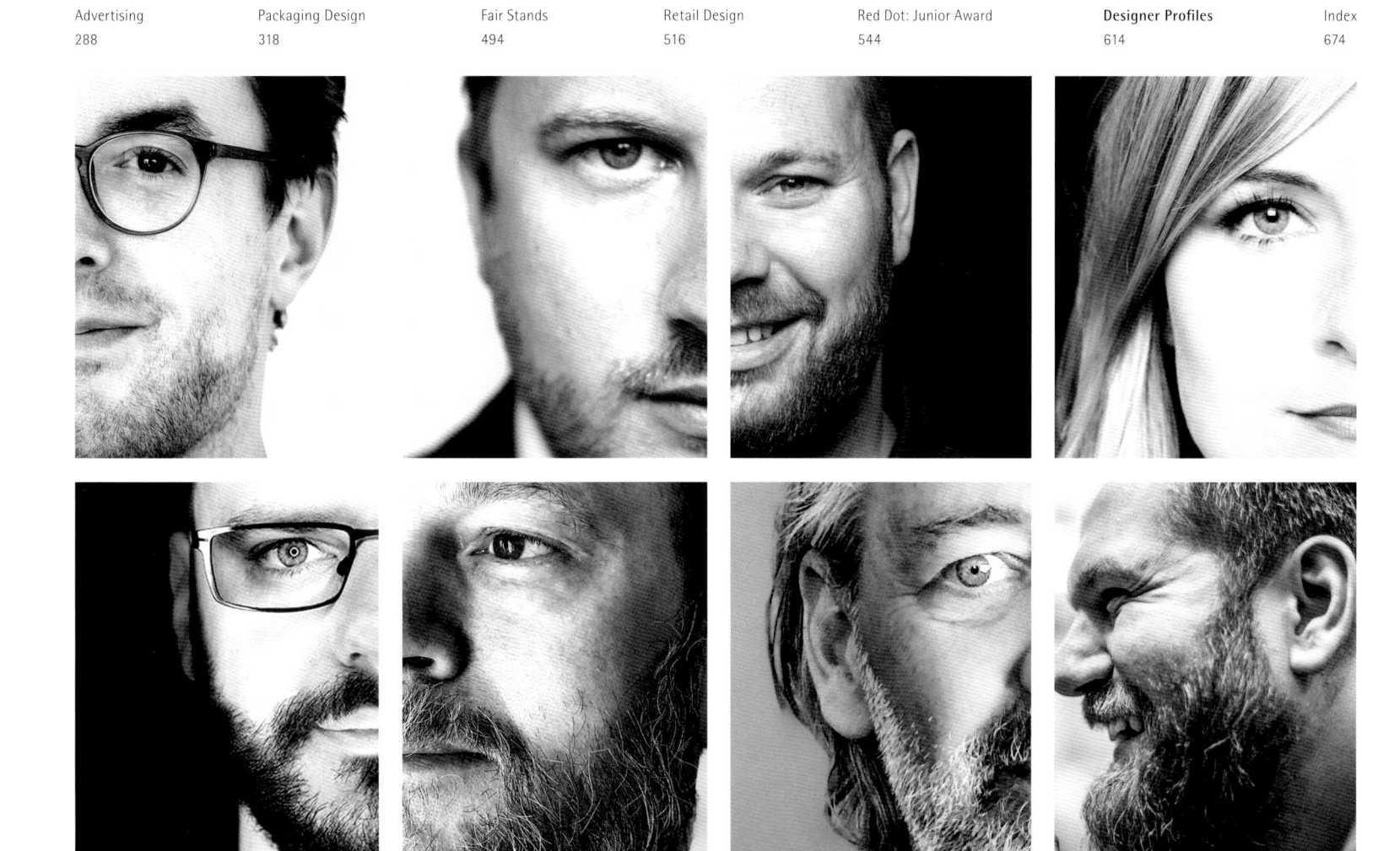

Advertising	Packaging Design	Fair Stands	Retail Design	Red Dot: Junior Award	**Designer Profiles**	Index
288	318	494	516	544	614	674

Aixsponza
— Time is of the essence.

Red Dot: Grand Prix
→ Advertising: page 290–291

Aixsponza was established in 2006 and is located in Munich, Germany, with a focus on graphic design and visual effects. Working on TV commercials, print, web, social media, retail and virtual reality, the core team of 15 people covers all kinds of media, combining cutting-edge technologies with design and creation, setting it apart from competitors. With a freelancer's network spanning the globe, it can respond to any specific task.

To what extent do you think new technologies are changing design?
New technologies have always had an immense influence on all design processes. Jacquard's programmable loom has not only had a major impact on textile design, the development of plastics and synthetic dyes has been ground-breaking in virtually all areas of life. New technologies create new possibilities and designers naturally take an interest in new possibilities. There is a strong interaction between ideas and possibilities.

What was your intention in designing your awarded work?
We were immediately impressed by the briefing. It was about sensitive perception theories, about visual enjoyment, perfect symmetries, completion, excellent mechanics, idealistic expectations, regularities. We should experiment with unexpected haptic qualities, new aesthetic forms of expression and should think in surreal and fantastic directions – always with a wink. This approach was free and courageous. It immediately made us want to start right away so that we could reach our goal of videos that are psychologically soothing and satisfying for their aesthetic value.

ARD Design Switzerland
Alexandre Guignard,
Vincent Guignard
— Everyday creative.

Red Dot
→ Packaging Design: page 391
→ Packaging Design: page 398

Back in 1987, the company founder had a clear vision that still remains to this day: "Design with consumer-centric thinking". While the agency quickly made a name for itself in the packaging field, it has now evolved to encompass every aspect of brand communication – from strategy to deployment. Founded in Vevey, on the shore of Lake Geneva, and with representation in London, the company has grown to become an international design agency, proud to count clients from a host of industries the world over as its own. Since 2012, Alexandre and Vincent Guignard have run the studio after having both studied design and worked several years all over Europe. Their most important strength lies in their team of people which combines international brand strategists and talented designers.

How do you stay innovative in such a creative industry?
We stay curious and leave our day-to-day business to discover new ways of thinking.

Please describe design quality in three words.
Emotional, singular, attractive.

How do you work out a common understanding of design with your clients?
Through trust and long-term relationships.

What is your design signature?
The signature of the brand we work for.

Autentic Consulting Sagl
Cristiano Sifari
— I design for emotions.

Red Dot
→ Corporate Design & Identity: page 238–239

After his studies at IED in Milan, Italy, and a specialisation in computer graphics, Cristiano Sifari began his career in 1997 working for a design studio as a computer animator. From 1999 to 2007, he ran his own design studio focusing on web design and corporate identity projects. Then he accepted a job as a digital marketing manager at a local bank in Lugano and, in 2011, he took a sabbatical in New York City. Back in Switzerland, Cristiano Sifari started as head of digital communication at a local communication agency. In 2015, he decided to start over again and established his brand and design agency Autentic, where he holds the role of creative director.

To what extent do you think new technologies are changing design?
We designers are facing an unprecedented period and opportunity to create something that can truly impact people's lives. And technology is, and always will be, an important part of that.

Why did you become a designer?
In the beginning, I was just fascinated by special effects in movies and wanted to recreate them. My first job was as a computer animator, but the studio where I was interning asked me to create their new logo, brochure and website. Doing some research, I found books about Swiss design, and from then on, I focused on reading books about corporate design and typography.

What makes your work unique?
A good balance between form and function. I also put a lot of effort into typography, which has a vital role in my work.

B for Brand
Soomin Jo, Yena Choi, Jinha Seo
— Small can achieve the impossible. Incredible things can be born out of nothing.

Red Dot
→ Packaging Design: page 489

B for Brand is a multiple award-winning agency founded by creative director and art director Yena Choi. She also acts as a design columnist for the leading economic newspaper in Korea, is a member of the Advisory Committee for the Korea Sport Coach Federation, a member of the Advisory Committee for Women's Human Resources Development and of the Advisory Committee for Foreign Affairs and Culture of the Southern Gyeonggi Provincial Government. Previously, she was creative designer at Grey Global Group and at Publicis Groupe Emotion. In 2007, she graduated from the Art Institute of Vancouver, Canada, in graphic design.

What does design mean to you?
Design has the unique power to transform something from being ordinary to extraordinary. It is a universal language, without any barriers. Design truly has the ability to communicate with the audience through shape, colour and layout.

Where do you see future challenges in communication design?
Design does not function in insolation. Rather, design needs to adapt to the social climate. Due to the worldwide pandemic we are currently experiencing, the new term "contactless" has surfaced. People have begun navigating contactless meetings, seminars, ceremonies and we believe design will face similar challenges. We envision growth in online design aligned with the digital era and the current climate, which consequently means appealing to online consumers without the benefit of certain offline senses such as location, scent and texture.

Berry Creative
Kaisa Berry, Timo Berry
— Design must be effective and it's great if it is also fun.

Red Dot
→ Corporate Design & Identity: page 241

Timo Berry is the founder and creative director of Berry Creative. He studied graphic design and illustration, is a member of the Association of Finnish Sculptors and works in the fields of corporate and area branding, posters, stamps, social and editorial design, environmental art and design strategy. His works have received international awards, are part of the collections of museums like the Paris and Vienna design museums and have been showcased in renowned newspapers such as The Guardian, The Washington Post, Die Welt and The Times of India, to name but a few. Kaisa Berry has degrees in architecture and set design, is a member of the Finnish Association of Landscape Architects and the Association of Finnish Sculptors. She combines architecture, landscape design and environmental art in different forms and lectures at Aalto University in the School of Arts, Design and Architecture.

What does design mean to you?
The world is full of ways to touch people and make their lives more meaningful, beautiful and functional. Design is one of them.

To what extent do you think new technologies are changing design?
New technologies are not changing the core of design. They are just new platforms and ways of doing what design should do – reaching out to people and making their lives better. Bring it on!

What drives you to create something new?
Curiosity, absolutely. The quest to understand what's behind it all in every changing situation.

Birger Linke Design
Birger Linke
— Intelligent design, beautifully brought to life.

Red Dot
→ Packaging Design: page 455

With two decades in the industry, Birger Linke is currently based in China. He previously set up TBWA\Vietnam, which, after just one year, took the country's No.1 spot in the Campaign Brief Asia Rankings. He is a partner in headphone start-up Lynxsonic while his design consultancy focuses on projects in the healthcare sector. With more than 130 national and international awards across disciplines, including Gold at Cannes and the first-ever D&AD Pencil for Vietnam, he was named most awarded direct marketing creative in Asia, "hottest" creative in Vietnam, and ranked in the Top 100 of the Hottest Creatives in Asia. His "TransMariner" campaign for the Singapore Navy was ranked 4th in the world (Won Report) and his Coke "Olympic Beat" campaign garnered 400 million views within a month on air. He also created the first WeChat ad for BMW. He is a member of D&AD, was a judge at London International Awards, New York Festivals, Adfest, Adstars and Young Guns, amongst others, and lectures across Asia.

What does design mean to you?
Finding an innovative solution to a problem.

To what extent do you think new technologies are changing design?
Advances in technology increasingly accelerate cultural trends. So, it is even more crucial to be clear about the problem at hand that the design is meant to solve – to stay relevant.

What drives you to create something new?
Putting a smile on someone's face.

Caparo
— Back in the day our motto was "Just do it". We used to have a shoe brand.

Red Dot: Best of the Best
→ Packaging Design: page 322–323

Red Dot
→ Packaging Design: page 338

Caparo was founded in 2016 by Kostas Kaparos. Based in Athens, Greece, it is a design-led creative agency. Its main services include brand identity, creative concepts, illustration, animation, motion design, packaging and copywriting with the core mission to bring out the inner values of a brand in a way that attracts attention and connects with users on an emotional level.

What does design mean to you?
Visual design in any form may be perceived as a means to an end. But for us, from a personal and creative perspective, design itself is the beginning of an exploration and imaginative journey to make something new every time and surprise yourself! It's also a passion, a culture and a way of life: looking at the world around us through the lens of design like "design heads" may be a curse, you might say!

What drives you to create something new?
A good brief.

What makes your work unique?
We are not interested in being unique but more in being impactful in what we do, which happens when your design serves the purpose and the brand in the best way possible. The reaction and the feeling that someone has every time they come across our work is the answer to your question. Despite that, it's interesting that we hear so many different opinions and comments about what makes our work great and lovable – something we prefer to being unique.

Cee Cee Creative

Red Dot
→ Corporate Design & Identity: page 242–243

Cee Cee Creative is a Berlin-based multidisciplinary agency with a focus on design, content, marketing and events. It provides continuous project support, develops contemporary concepts and creates customised solutions for its partners and customers from ideation right through to execution across all channels. In addition to working on assignments for customers, the team also pursues its own projects such as the Cee Cee newsletter which has, since 2011, attracted a distinct following and community that has been linked to customers both online and offline.

What does design mean to you?
Good design should convey a sense of rigour, either at a visual or content level, and it should create awareness. For us, design also means being passionate about developing something new and to enjoy doing so.

What makes your work unique?
We aim to understand projects holistically and to apply an interdisciplinary approach. That allows us to explore other options, create new formats and take the concept a step further. This can produce exciting results, as is apparent with Berlin Decks. As we are a multidisciplinary team, we can cover design, content, marketing, social media and events, and our large network of experts also enables us to create synergies.

CLEVER°FRANKE/
Studio Bas Koopmans

— We connect people to data and technology through design – CLEVER°FRANKE

Red Dot: Best of the Best
→ Brand Design & Identity: page 94-95

Red Dot
→ Brand Design & Identity: page 162

CLEVER°FRANKE is a renowned data design and technology consultancy that delivers data-driven digital transformation by creating innovative user and customer experiences. With offices in Utrecht, the Netherlands, Chicago, USA, and Dubai, UAE, a total of 30 people work for clients including Google, Warner Music Group, Signify, Here Technologies and Elsevier. Their work is part of the collection of the Stedelijk Museum Amsterdam. Studio Bas Koopmans in Amsterdam works for clients such as Anomaly, Cobra Museum of Modern Art, Converse, Heineken, Melkweg, Mojo/LifeNation, MTV, Red Bull Music Academy, Sandberg Instituut and the Stedelijk Museum Amsterdam.

What does design mean to you?
BK: For me design is about creating a language. Setting rules and a central narrative that the viewer can become familiar with and understand. And then to play with these self-imposed constraints, stretching these boundaries to surprise the viewer and challenge them to understand why and how the central idea is communicated.

What drives you to create something new?
C°F: We always feel the need to stay relevant. This means that we consistently try to contribute something new within the realm of design to the world around us. To do so, we often come up with new plans for tackling certain problems and making use of new opportunities.

Creative Power Unit/ lull/Dentsu

Masashi Fujita,
Daisuke Hatakeyama,
Yoshihiro Yagi
— Work like you play, play like you work.

Red Dot: Best of the Best
→ Advertising: page 294–295

In 2011, Masashi Fujita, Daisuke Hatakeyama and Yoshihiro Yagi formed a team for a reconstruction project led by JR East, following the Great East Japan Earthquake. Later, while producing long-term visual communication for mainstays of the Japanese industry like Honda, Panasonic and Japan Post, they were also involved in projects large and small, such as book bindings and company logos.

What does design mean to you?
It's a communication tool. We think that design constantly changes, just like when you talk to someone, you change your manner of speaking, tone of voice and expression according to whom you speak with.

What makes your work unique?
What we produce depends on the assignment, so there isn't a consistent distinguishing trait.

What was your intention in designing your awarded work?
This project is about the durability of the design while continuously coming up with new ideas. We began by scouting locations throughout the region to study how the scenery changed with the seasons. Natural lighting was a key factor in determining our shooting schedule, which also had to be synchronised with local train schedules to get the shots we wanted. We deliberately eschewed compositing and relied solely on our eyes and creative vision to compose each image. With this approach, we captured the emotional experience of travel with natural realism and a documentary touch.

Advertising	Packaging Design	Fair Stands	Retail Design	Red Dot: Junior Award	**Designer Profiles**	Index
288	318	494	516	544	614	674

Dentsu
Yoshihiro Yagi
— When it's tough, it's uphill.

Red Dot: Best of the Best
→ Packaging Design: page 324–325

Yoshihiro Yagi, a renowned Japanese art director, works for a diverse client base such as JR East and Honda as well as various consumer products in the fields of concept development, packaging design and advertising communications. Awarded the Collaborative Award at D&AD, his accolades document the consistent quality of his designs. He has won 19 Pencils in a single year at D&AD, six Yellow Pencils for six different pieces of work, a Grand Prix at Cannes Lions as well as Best in Design at The One Show. He also lectures at Kyoto University of the Arts.

How does a chocolate snack need to be packaged to appeal to young adults?
Pocky sticks have been Japan's top-selling chocolate snack for decades. But sales among young adults were declining. The brief was to give this target group an updated way to share and enjoy Pocky sticks. Our solution was to promote the product as a fashionable gift item for them. So, we created a stylish new packaging to be used exclusively at upscale shops and sales outlets and leveraged social media to promote the repackaged snacks as a gift item. We employed simple, iconic graphics and a carefully selected range of colours to represent the flavours offered. The result was significantly higher sales to young adults and higher brand visibility.

To what extent do you think new technologies are changing design?
I think there is no limit to the possible changes. From the invention of letters to paints, printing, digital design and then 3D printers and AI – each and every technology has expanded design.

Design Plus Design
Michael Lam
— Design is a combination of rational logic and perceptual thinking.

Red Dot: Best of the Best
→ Retail Design: page 520–521

After his master's degree in design from Hong Kong Polytechnic University, Michael Lam studied sustainable design at the Royal College of Art in the United Kingdom and became Barcelona Academy of Art's ambassador to Guangzhou. In 2012, he founded the studio Design Plus Design and went on to build a commercial beverage brand called HUNCHA.

What does design mean to you?
To me, design is like lifeblood, like the oxygen in the air. If I leave design, I am nothing. I am therefore willing to spend my lifetime struggling.

To what extent do you think new technologies are changing design?
From my point of the view, technologies only help with the expression of design. New technology or more powerful technology is only an auxiliary tool for design. What can change design is our way of thinking and sense of aesthetics, which cannot be replaced by technology and software.

What was your intention in designing your awarded work?
To express the concept of retro space in the future and therefore to give space and human behaviour a more spiritual connection, I paid special attention to the innovation of design and the effect of its combination with art in order to produce different collisions. I think innovation of design is a very important element in a project. It can make the design have different visual effects.

East China Normal University
Lijuan Hong, Jinfei Huang
— Design needs to capture every detail in life all the time.

Red Dot: Junior Award
→ Packaging Design: page 595

Lijuan Hong is a student in the master's course for product design at the School of Design of East China Normal University. She has experience in interaction design, product structure, brand visual image and brand planning, and has worked for Alibaba and DiDi China as well as other first-line internet companies. Her projects have already won awards, for example in the UXPA user experience competition. Jinfei Huang is studying for a master's degree in art and design at East China Normal University and has experience in many design fields including product design, landscape design, interactive design and packaging design. After completing various design projects and winning some awards in the student stage, he decided to pursue further studies in the field of design.

What inspires you?
Our design inspiration comes from attention to the details in our lives. Many seemingly ordinary behaviours in our life can actually become a very interesting design inspiration or a design problem to be solved.

How would you describe your style of design?
We do not have a very specific design style, which is still in the stage of trial and exploration. If there is anything that runs through our design, it is to seek a balance between practicality and experimentation, and the desire to solve traditional problems in a new way.

How do you think this award will impact your life?
This award is not only a recognition of our design ability, but also an incentive for us.

East China Normal University
Zhiyuan Liu
— If you have an idea, don't just think about it, but move to do it.

Red Dot: Junior Award
→ Packaging Design: page 604

Zhiyuan Liu is currently a graduate student at the School of Design of East China Normal University and also the design director of an educational institution in Shanghai, China. He has five years of product design experience and has taken part in numerous exhibitions. Favoured by manufacturers, he is often hired as their company's product designer.

What goals have you set for your future career?
I hope that in the future I will still be a designer who loves design. I also hope that more design works will be able to change or affect society.

Do you prefer to play it safe when designing a new project or are you keen to experiment?
I prefer to try new things, to break conventions, to continue to subvert myself and discover better innovations.

How would you describe your style of design?
As long as my design style focuses on simplicity, I try to highlight the product itself.

What was your intention in designing your awarded work?
The goal was to change the way grapes are packaged and make them more environmentally sustainable.

How do you think this award will impact your life?
It gives me encouragement and confidence to follow the career path of a designer.

East China Normal University
Xiaoyu Zhou, Yanyi Yu
– The vitality of design lies in exploration and innovation.

Red Dot: Junior Award
→ Packaging Design: page 590

Xiaoyu Zhou and Yanyi Yu are students at the School of Design of East China Normal University, majoring in product design and in environmental design, respectively. They both explore different design fields and have practical experience in dozens of design projects, such as landscape design, product design, packaging design or magazine design.

Do you prefer to play it safe when designing a new project or are you keen to experiment?
We prefer experimental design because the most important thing about good design is to be able to solve problems creatively. Especially at the beginning of a design project, we try to develop creative ideas and constantly explore problems from different perspectives. This process is not only very interesting, but also very helpful in promoting the design. Ultimately, these ideas will take us closer to the most elegant and beautiful design.

What inspires you?
In our view, "excellent design" itself constantly inspires us, whether the design is made by others or by us, because "excellent design" is born with a kind of magic.

What was your intention in designing your awarded work?
The current flashy packagings of headphones tend to be lacking in innovation and lead to a lot of waste. Therefore, our design intention was to create novel packaging with the practical function of a headphone stand. In this way, the packaging does not have to be discarded and thereby reduces waste.

Enjia Brand Planning
— Create more value for the brand.

Red Dot
→ Packaging Design: page 450–451

Enjia is an agency in Quanzhou, China, committed to brand strategy and brand creativity. It takes a professional strategic approach and offers outstanding creative solutions to help clients build brands and expand their markets. Since its establishment in 2011, Enjia has accumulated experience and professional skills in the hygienic products sector, in daily care chemicals, food, cosmetics and other FMCG industries, and has become the strategic partner of many well-known brands.

Where do you see future challenges in communication design?
Current consumer demand which is constantly changing. We believe we need to help clients cope with this change. That is a challenge, but one we regard as fun.

To what extent do you think new technologies are changing design?
New technologies have brought changes in organisational structures and behaviour. They have improved convenience and experiences, allowing us to provide our clients with a better service.

What drives you to create something new?
A sense of responsibility and mission for our clients.

What are the biggest challenges in a creative's everyday life?
To keep looking ahead, and the need to lead the team to break through established rules of thinking.

eyeteeth design/ Wallstreetdocs/Covenant
Yunyoung Lee, Dongho Kim, Naehee Kim
— Design can make people happy and guide them to a better choice.

Red Dot
→ Corporate Design & Identity: page 222
→ Corporate Design & Identity: page 237

Yunyoung Lee, Dongho Kim and Naehee Kim are a team consisting of an art director, a communication designer and a brand designer specialised in creative concepts, design and branding. Currently, they are based in London and Korea, working within the areas of marketing, branding, virtual reality and motion graphics. With excellent communication skills and extensive professional experience, they have been trying to bridge the gap between various stakeholders, more specifically production teams, directors and end clients.

What does design mean to you?
Design is a solution to a problem.

Where do you see future challenges in communication design?
In human-centred technology.

Why did you become a designer?
We like being able to help people and make them happy through our design work.

What drives you to create something new?
The desire and expectation that we can positively improve industries and people's daily lives with design.

What are the biggest challenges in a creative's everyday life?
Continuously and patiently making an effort.

FutureBrand China
Sam Yang, Feifei Jiang
— Caring about the needs of people makes the design future-proof.

Red Dot
→ Brand Design & Identity: page 131
→ Corporate Design & Identity: page 252–253

Sam Yang, the creative director of FutureBrand China, has 15 years of experience in brand design and previously worked as creative director at Alibaba and several global brand consulting firms. His clients include Alibaba, Tencent, Jingdong, AB InBev, Nestlé, McDonald's, UnionPay, China Southern Airlines, Luye and China Xiong'an Group. He used to be a university lecturer, teaching visual design and creativity at design-related schools in Taiwan. Feifei Jiang is a senior designer with seven years of industry experience and a solid foundation in brand visual design, animation and dynamic graphics. With creative visual languages and new technological expressions, she helps clients shape their brand image.

What does design mean to you?
Design is a problem-solving process.

To what extent do you think new technologies are changing design?
With the development of new technologies, each era has a different design expression. New technologies can help us improve design efficiency and articulate ideas.

What makes your work unique?
Don't fall into the trap of creating difference in order to create uniqueness. Only by truly focusing on people's needs can you make your brand design sexy and appealing.

Grand Design
— Good design is simple, essential and universal. Keep asking "Why has it never been done before?"

Red Dot
→ Advertising: page 316–317
→ Packaging Design: page 436–437

Grand Design was established by Katsunori Nishi and has been operating from its headquarters in Tokyo for 20 years, for ten years in China and five years in Hong Kong. In this time, it has developed a wealth of knowledge about how to build a bridge between Japanese and Chinese culture. The agency's work stretches from strategic planning to branding and execution for companies that are expanding their business in China. The quality of the agency's work was recognised by both domestic and international design awards, among others, from the New York ADC, Tokyo ADC and Tokyo TDC.

What does design mean to you?
The embodiment of an excellent idea.

To what extent do you think new technologies are changing design?
Changes in technology and the media will have a big impact on communication. We need to design communication in accordance with technology and media.

What are the biggest challenges in a creative's everyday life?
The development of a mechanism to continue to generate a high level of creativity in creative teams.

What makes your work unique?
The answer lies in the preparatory stage before the design process, in thinking through the question (plan) before providing the answer (design).

Gregor & Strozik Visual Identity
Thorsten Strozik
— Mottos are for advertisers ;-)

Red Dot
→ Retail Design: page 530–531

While still studying at the University of Wuppertal, Germany, Thorsten Strozik founded the agency Gregor & Strozik Visual Identity (GSVI), which specialised in branding. Along with interdisciplinary corporate design commissions, the agency also added digital projects in the new economy to its portfolio of references. Today, GSVI focuses on developing visual identities. It serves as a brand management and strategic marketing partner and also develops core elements of brand communication and corporate communication for national and international clients in the industrial, services and retail sectors.

Where do you see future challenges in communication design?
As consultants and designers, we must go where the client benefit is. Where and how to achieve this must be questioned at all times; content and the way it is communicated must be presented without any kind of self-interest. The complete overlap between all the disciplines has never been so exciting.

What drives you to create something new?
My curiosity about people and their actions. One minute, you're a specialist in the international marketing of ultrasound technology. The next minute, you're thinking about the digitalisation of municipalities, or about how to create a successful joint brand presentation for Aral (a brand of automobile fuels and petrol stations) and Rewe (a supermarket chain) at petrol stations.

Hyewon Han
— Living in the present, that'll do.

Red Dot: Junior Award
Best of the Best
→ Advertising: page 550–551

Hyewon Han is a senior student at Hongik University and experiments with various designs without being tied to genres. She has recently become interested in branding and has gained experience by leading the branding club HYPHEN.

What goals have you set for your future career?
My objective for a future career is still to be a designer, but I dream of taking many airplanes whatever my job may be. I like the first contact with land after going up and down in a plane. I would love my future career to involve travel as a designer.

What inspires you?
Inspiration is infinite and I find it in conversations, books, movies, the dawn, insomnia, showers or just lying in bed.

How do you think this award will impact your life?
This award means a little certainty to me. There are so many people who are good at design. There was a time when I doubted what I was doing. But I realised that believing in my ideas is more important than doubting them. I will also try to apply this attitude to living.

How does the design of your print campaign including the RED IN COMMON card game manage to raise awareness of the problem of racism and the need to donate blood?
We all have the same red colour blood, whatever our skin colour may be. The campaign is intended to make people realise that we are all the same inside. Racism has no role in that. Blood donation is the connection of everybody's "reds".

Heimat Wien
Simon Pointner
— Stay curious.

Red Dot: Best of the Best
→ Packaging Design: page 320–321

Simon Pointner is an award-winning art and creative director, who lives and works in Vienna, Austria. In 2012, he completed his education at Die Graphische, Vienna's school of media, and started his career in advertising as a graphic designer at the agency Zum goldenen Hirschen. In 2016, he was hired as an art director for Heimat Wien and, in November 2019, he started to work as a creative director for national and international brands. Since then, he has been head of the creative department of Heimat Wien.

Where do you see future challenges in communication design?
To turn challenges of all kind into opportunities.

Why did you become a designer?
Good design is about so much more than just making things look nice – it's a very thoughtful, challenging profession. Designers are creative problem solvers, so each brief represents a fresh challenge.

What makes your work unique?
It's smart, surprising and touching.

What was your intention in designing your awarded work?
Creating the world's first talking wine labels! Judith Beck sells unique wines that speak for themselves. We gave them a voice to make them unmistakable on the Austrian wine market by hiding barcodes in artistically illustrated labels that can be scanned with any smartphone to hear the wines talk.

HS Ad
— We seek to see the difference in brands, products, individuals and generations.

Red Dot
→ Fair Stands: page 506

HS Ad is an advertising agency and an affiliate of the LG Group. It is engaged in all advertising and creative brand communications in both online and offline platforms. Specifically, the Space Communication Team 1 creates a space that highlights a company's difference, by bringing designers, creatives, producers and clients together around the same table as they did for the award-winning project on which Bryan Youn, Sungtae Hwang, Shukjoo Sean Oh, Jungjun Lee and Deborah Kim from HS Ad worked together with Jinny (Jiyoung) Kim and Hwangyong Ahn from LG Electronics, with Sangwon Moon from the SquareGraphy design studio and with Joomyoung Song and Shinmu Lee from Habitant, also an art and design studio.

What does design mean to you?
We believe a good design is a design that can easily be seen, enjoyed and have its inspiration understood, and one that can easily be extended to the public.

What was your intention in designing your awarded work?
This artwork sat on a water surface to highlight OLED's distinctive characteristic – "Perfect Black makes Perfect Color". The top and bottom rollable display screens meet in the middle to symbolise the revolutionary beginning of a new possibility. During the three-minute screening, LG shows an impressive visual of "impossibly possible" scenes at the point where the top and bottom screens meet. These include a golden sphere fracturing the water surface to create a new form of particle, a rendezvous between day- and night-time – something we can only witness with this new paradigm of innovation.

in medias rees
Simone Rees
— BEAUTY IS FUNCTION. Combining beauty with content is my passion.

Red Dot
→ Packaging Design: page 394

After completing her studies in visual communication at HfG Schwäbisch Gmünd, Germany, Simone Rees started out as a designer at agencies including Springer & Jacoby Hamburg, GGK Frankfurt and Leonhardt & Kern Stuttgart. As creative director at H2e, she oversaw the brand presentations of Ligne Roset, Sedus Stoll, Armstrong DLW and Bauknecht. A few design awards later, she founded her own agency "in medias rees" in Stuttgart in 2002. Her intention was to develop thoughtful, holistic and unique communication concepts for SMEs. These include long-standing clients such as Martosca Speiseeismanufaktur, Domaniecki Carpetence and Gwinner Wohndesign.

Where do you see future challenges in communication design?
In the age of communication and the attendant deluge of images and information, designers have an even greater responsibility than they are perhaps aware of. Our world needs experts who understand the mechanisms of successful communication – in terms of both the visuals and the content. It's about championing quality, sustainability and relevant content.

What drives you to create something new?
I am convinced that every company, every brand is inherently special in some way. The key is to define this and render it visible, in a way that is authentic and unique. My USP is to discover the USP of my clients and to communicate it in an emotional and captivating manner. A creative concept only truly hits the mark when it is so unique to the respective brand that the concept simply wouldn't work for anyone else.

Innocean Worldwide
— Changing a situation is not a concern, but an action.

Red Dot: Best of the Best
→ Advertising: page 292–293

Kiyoung Kim underwent copywriter training at the global agency network TBWA and is now executive creative director at Innocean Worldwide, where he is, among others, responsible for Hyundai/Kia Motors. His campaigns have won awards at various advertising festivals such as the New York Festivals, Spikes Asia and London International Awards. Hyunchul Lim and Daeyoung Eum are senior copywriters, Moonhwi Lee and Daeun Lee are copywriters, Jisoo Kim, Jisoo Kim and Daehyun Kim work as art directors, and Gahee Park worked on the "Second First Steps" project as a coordinator. They are all involved in global campaigns and communication strategies for various brands and subsidiaries of Hyundai Group.

How can designers be ahead of their time?
We make an effort to improve the world by solving common, familiar problems. However, we try our best to make the world progress by discovering hidden problems before anyone else.

What do you need in order to be creative?
A team of people who have lots of interests and love human beings.

On what design concept is your brand campaign for Hyundai and its message "Technology for Humans" based?
The concept behind the design is to visualise in a lively and authentic way how mobility technology can take humanity one step further on the path to enhancing quality time.

Kidler Design Studio
Therese Laurin, Tobias Ottenfelt
— Be positive about negative space.

Red Dot
→ Packaging Design: page 468

Kidler Design Studio is an agency focusing on visual storytelling through art direction, graphic design, moving imagery, product design, exhibitions, spatial design and illustration. Based in Stockholm, Sweden, the studio is owned and run by the designers Therese Laurin and Tobias Ottenfelt, who have, for many years, worked in the field of advertising and design at a global level. Their careers have spanned three continents at some of the world's most renowned agencies. Understanding cultural diversity is imperative in cross-cultural communications. Kidler always strives to work with holistic design thinking, taking into consideration the world of commerce, art and ethics. The studio's clients are cultural institutions and companies around the globe, and its work has been exhibited in more than 40 countries.

What does design mean to you?
Everything that surrounds us is designed in some way, either by nature, by chance or by intention. Successful designs will survive, so in that sense, design is life or death.

To what extent do you think new technologies are changing design?
Significantly, but good design is always rooted in usability, and new technologies will improve usability. Conversely, usability requires good design. So, the change can only be for the better.

Why did you become a designer?
We like to tell stories and build worlds.

Kookmin University
Jisu Moon, Seonil Lee
— We always try to think, to learn something and to challenge the existing order.

Red Dot: Junior Award
→ Brand Design & Identity: page 567

Jisu Moon and Seonil Lee are students at the Graduate School of Techno Design at Kookmin University in Seoul who are involved in a lot of projects. In 2019, they were awarded at the Korean Typeface Design Competition.

Do you prefer to play it safe when designing a new project or are you keen to experiment?
We are students. Of course, we choose something that is challenging. Our student status allows us to challenge various communication methods, and society takes a more generous view of us than professional designers. But we never forget that we bear a social and moral responsibility.

What inspires you?
We are mainly inspired by people around us. Because people's perspectives are all different, listening to their story allows us to encounter various points of view and think of a wide range of designs.

What is your personal vision for the future?
We want to expand our interest in social design and would like to see how we can incorporate the function and purpose of design into the social role of designers in a more mature way. We are very eager to have a chance to work with designers from other countries after finishing our master's degree at Kookmin University. In this way, we hope to gain wider experience and a broader view of the world as a designer.

Meiré und Meiré
Mike Meiré
— Life is evolution and evolution is creation.

Red Dot: Best of the Best
→ Annual Reports: page 264–265

Meiré und Meiré is an independent design agency and creative consultancy, specialising in brand strategy, visual identity and holistic brand experiences. With a team of 70 creative experts, the agency works across all disciplines to develop and transform relevant brands – bringing them to life in analogue and digital media. Communication concepts and brand campaigns, architectures and interactive exhibits are at the core of the agency's work. Mike Meiré who founded and runs the agency together with his brother Marc Meiré is an artist, designer, art director and curator. Considered a leading protagonist of cutting-edge editorial design, he has worked for various magazines, including brand eins, Arch+, 032c, Neue Zürcher Zeitung, Interview Magazine and GQ Italia.

What does design mean to you?
Design is a state of mind.

Where do you see future challenges in communication design?
In the risk of losing the soul of design.

To what extent do you think new technologies are changing design?
Technology will democratise design.

What are the biggest challenges in a creative's everyday life?
To stay fresh.

What makes your work unique?
The way in which I decode my cultural surroundings.

Minuage Design
Chang Shi
— Simplify, then add lightness.

Red Dot
→ Packaging Design: page 406–407

Chang Shi graduated from the Royal Melbourne Institute of Technology in 2013 and established his own design company Minuage the following year. He provides strategies on branding, visual identity, product packaging, printing solutions and exhibitions for clients from different industries.

What does design mean to you?
Design has a mysterious power that can make things more aesthetic, valuable and meaningful.

Where do you see future challenges in communication design?
The development of technology results in more variable and inclusive media which turn communication design into an interdisciplinary subject. That requires the designer to have a wide range of knowledge and skill and may make the role of the designer or art director more like that of a facilitator.

Why did you become a designer?
Designers see the world from the most interesting perspective.

What are the biggest challenges in a creative's everyday life?
To retain the ability to think independently in an era of information explosion.

What was your intention in designing your awarded work?
The key objective of this work was to design an aesthetic and environmentally responsible concept that would communicate the brand image of the client.

Munchkin
Diana Barnes

Red Dot
→ Brand Design & Identity: page 114–115

Diana Barnes began her career at Munchkin in 2014 and currently serves as its chief brand officer (CBO) and creative director. She oversees global brand partnerships and manages the public relations, social media and brand design teams worldwide. Under her leadership, Munchkin's brand design team has won over 50 top international design awards in four years during which time it has developed 360 designs. A passionate advocate for trees, animals and the environment, she created and leads all Munchkin corporate social responsibility initiatives such as partnerships with the Whale Sanctuary Project, Trees for the Future and the International Fund for Animal Welfare (IFAW). Before joining Munchkin, she served as the global director of brand design for Dell. In this role, Diana Barnes led global teams in the USA, India and Asia. Prior to this, her career actually began in music and entertainment with executive creative positions at Sony, EMI and several global ad agencies. She received a Bachelor of Arts in English Literature from the University of Tennessee, Knoxville and a Bachelor of Fine Arts in Graphics/Packaging from the Art Center College of Design in Pasadena, California.

Nascent Design
Max Bosio
— Unfolding transformation.

Red Dot
→ Brand Design & Identity: page 171

Nascent Design is a brand innovation and digital creative agency with a multifaceted approach. Max Bosio, creative director at Nascent Design, holds an MA degree in architecture and design from the Polytechnic University of Milan and, most recently, was an EMBA participant at the Berlin School of Creative Leadership. With more than 20 years of experiencing in the design consultancy field, his background includes a diverse range of experiences in branding, communication and digital design.

What does design mean to you?
Always refer to that famous quote from Dieter Rams that says: good design is as little design as possible.

Where do you see future challenges in communication design?
In my opinion the password for the future will be relevance.

What drives you to create something new?
To be a good designer, you have to master the ability to see things differently and to always question the status quo of things.

What makes your work unique?
I would never describe our work as unique. I would rather describe it as effective. Uniqueness is subjective, effectiveness is not!

National University of Singapore
Ai Ling Ng, Zi Fong Yong
— If design is truly universal, no one should be left behind.

Red Dot: Junior Prize
→ Advertising: page 546–549

Ai Ling Ng and Zi Fong Yong are a design duo who graduated with a BA (Hons) degree in industrial design from the National University of Singapore. After being exposed to a wide spectrum of design in school, both of them discovered a similar passion for creating design for social good by using tech meaningfully. Their work has received the coveted Grand Prix at the Taiwan International Student Design Competition 2019, the Best Demo Award at the International Conference on Multimodal Interaction 2019 and was also a winner in the 26th Annual Interactive Competition of the Communication Arts Magazine.

What goals have you set for your future career?
Both of us are passionate about creating meaningful digital experiences that serve the public good. As millennials ourselves, technology has already become part and parcel of our lives, from the way we move to the way we communicate and live. We want to take advantage of tech's tremendous potential to empower and inspire a widespread audience.

What inspires you?
Seemingly mundane occurrences around us that somehow adapt to cope with changes in life, from the way our Asian mums make do with what little they have, altering our hand-me-downs, to seeing how the leaves of the rain trees lining our Singaporean streets fold just before sunset and before rainy weather to retain moisture. Whenever we are stuck with a design challenge or problem, these little moments inspire us that where there's a will, there's a way.

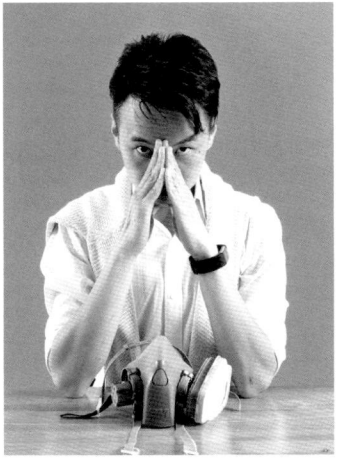

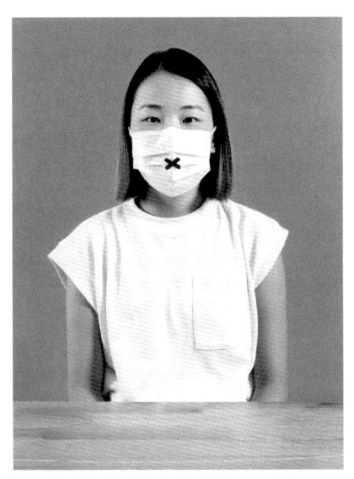

Noiseless Design / Chow Tai Fook

Vincent Lee, Christopher Lee, Hung Chung, Chanfly, Nina Qiu, Lin Lin

— Noise is distracting. The key is to be heard.

Red Dot
→ Retail Design: page 536

Chris Lee is the director and founder of Noiseless Design, Vincent Lee is a senior project manager, Chanfly is a senior designer and Hung Chung is a designer. The multidisciplinary design agency has a strong digital focus and has won multiple awards in Hong Kong, Taiwan, Korea and Germany. With a strong graphic design background, Noiseless Design fully embraces technology and new media, so that its work stretches from tactile print designs to sophisticated experience-centred master planning. Lin Lin is deputy head of the brand department and Nina Qiu is project manager of the group branding centre at Chow Tai Fook, a leading jewellery business with decades of expertise.

Where do you see future challenges in communication design?
In the ever-shorter attention span of people in the post-digital era.

What drives you to create something new?
The joy in satisfying curiosity by mixing A with B and surprising the audience in the process.

What are the biggest challenges in a creative's everyday life?
The world is noisier than ever. To find ways to rid oneself of distraction is perhaps the hardest thing to do.

What makes your work unique?
We do not pursue a specific style but focus on the elegance of design as a solution. Our project is driven by the concept, a statement that is at the basis of all our work. We protect it, no matter how many revisions we make.

Nonespace
Shin Jung Bae
— Design with purpose and significance.

Red Dot
→ Retail Design: page 526–527

Shin Jung Bae studied design at Kookmin University in Seoul, South Korea. His works have already received awards from renowned international competitions, such as the Global Architecture & Design Awards, iF Design Award and Red Dot Award.

Where do you see future challenges in communication design?
Future challenges are already here. We are in the process of focusing on the spiritual and essential values of society, literature and local narratives, beyond their decorative function.

Why did you become a designer?
Everything in our daily lives is closely connected to design. With a very slight change, design can enrich people's lives and make things fun and touching. That's what I like about design.

What drives you to create something new?
Taking common, everyday things, looking at them from a new perspective, then bringing them into harmony with the environment. I do that with brand stories and narratives, for example.

What are the biggest challenges in a creative's everyday life?
Adapting to new projects, different brand concepts, the changing market and novel technologies are the biggest challenges and also the reason why I love this job.

Jan Novák, Marek Nedelka
— Humility and clarity.

Red Dot: Best of the Best
→ Corporate Design & Identity: page 204–205

Jan Novák is a type and graphic designer who studied at the Academy of Arts, Architecture and Design in Prague, Czech Republic, and who creates typefaces, books or visual identities. During his studies, he spent one semester at ZHdK, the Zurich University of the Arts, and three months in New York as an intern at Sagmeister & Walsh. In 2020, he co-founded the type design practice AllCaps. Marek Nedelka, a Czech graphic designer and creative director, earned his master's degree in the Studio of Graphic Design and New Media at the Academy of Arts, Architecture and Design in Prague, following a bachelor's degree in architecture and urbanism from the Technical University of Liberec. He works in the fields of architecture, design and culture for clients such as mmcité+, Fránek Architects, the Technical University of Liberec, the House of Art in České Budějovice, the Jaroslav Fragner Gallery and Mjölk Architects.

To what extent do you think new technologies are changing design?
We think that in the field of visual identities, cooperation with web designers and motion designers is becoming increasingly important. Movement and dynamism have recently been part of almost every one of our projects – more powerful computers and more affordable software are making these tweaks more and more accessible. But technology is just a superstructure while the rules for good design remain the same – clarity of message, emotions and sincerity.

What are the biggest challenges in a creative's everyday life?
The biggest challenges are lack of focus and time.

Omdesign
Diogo Gama Rocha
— Omdesign: focusing on excellence since 1998.

Red Dot
→ Packaging Design: page 330–331
→ Packaging Design: page 366–367

Established in 1998, Omdesign is a 100 per cent Portuguese design and advertising agency. On a daily basis, the agency works for clients, partners and leading global companies in industries such as beverage, wine, food, mass consumption, tourism, health or transport that reward Omdesign with their patronage and loyalty. The strong relationships Omdesign has built over the years are the result of the dedication and the unique way in which they embrace each project. The agency has been recognised, nationally and internationally, with more than 300 awards for the effectiveness and excellence of its work.

What does design mean to you?
Design is everything you see, you touch, you contemplate. Today, more than ever, design is essential for humankind. It's important that all areas, decision-makers and organisations understand that it's an investment, with an immeasurable return in social development, in life quality and in communication, adding value to brands and products.

What are the biggest challenges in a creative's everyday life?
Every day is a new challenge, considering that design and advertising are constantly evolving. On a daily basis, we have to analyse each brand and come up with the best solution for it. We do not have routines or repeat our work, which is an advantage because it develops our ability to improvise and allows us also to challenge ourselves every day.

omdr
Osamu Misawa,
Mamoru Takeuchi
– Think of everything in life as time to create a design.

Red Dot
→ Packaging Design: page 414

omdr is a Tokyo-based design agency founded in 1998. Its creative director is Osamu Misawa, who had previously worked as an art director in New York for ten years. The agency's art director is Mamoru Takeuchi. Based on graphic design, the agency develops corporate identities, visual identities, advertising, sales promotions, packaging and digital communication. The agency attaches great importance to methodology and the contextualisation of communications, creating not just images, but added value through the use of narratives.

Where do you see future challenges in communication design?
We would like to try to develop a creative experience that resonates with all the five sences through digital communication.

To what extent do you think new technologies are changing design?
The evolution of online and translation systems will allow us to connect with clients around the world. That way, we can deliver our creations to people all over the world.

Why did you become a designer?
We want to let people know what is really valuable about the power of design.

What are the biggest challenges in a creative's everyday life?
It is very important to keep up with the evolution of technology. We cannot survive in the world of design in future if we do not cooperate with creators and engineers in other fields.

One More Culture Communication
Xia Jiangnan, Huang Fupeng, Mao Jian
— Believe in the power of design. Doing is better than talking.

Red Dot
→ Brand Design & Identity: page 153

One More is headquartered in Shenzhen, China, and is a council member of the Shenzhen Graphic Design Association (SGDA). Established in 2013, the founding team and core members come from front-line creative companies in Beijing, Shanghai, Guangzhou, Shenzhen and other cities. With the motto of "creating more possibilities" as the soul of the enterprise, One More gathers young talents with highly creative thinking and creativity. The company has offices in Shenzhen, Wuhan, Dongguan, Zhuhai and Macao. Since its establishment, the agency's work has won awards and been published many times at home and abroad in renowned competitions such as the Red Dot Award, Pentawards, DFA Design for Asia Awards, Japan's Good Design Award, GDC Award and Macau Design Award, among others.

What does design mean to you?
A lifelong hobby.

Where do you see future challenges in communication design?
In an age of AI and intelligent big data, design emphasises a more independent point of view and specific execution.

To what extent do you think new technologies are changing design?
To a great extent. Designers have to think about deeper values and meanings.

Why did you become a designer?
Curiosity and the pursuit of beauty.

Perfect Point Design
Wu Jie, Zheng Juanying, Li Yao
— Never doubt that a small group of thoughtful, committed citizens can change the world.

Red Dot
→ Packaging Design: page 410

Perfect Point Design has provided creative design services for fast product, film, culture, interactive and fashion industries, and is active in these fields. The company philosophy is to approach perfection through the power of art and deep insight. Wu Jie (Wu Cuixiang), also known as Jeff Wu, was born in 1980 in China and graduated in visual communication from Xi'an Academy of Fine Arts in 2004. He served as associate creative director at Ogilvy (China) and Bates141 (China) before founding Perfect Point Design in 2009, where he currently serves as chief creative director and has led the creative team to focus on brand design and packaging design. Zheng Juanying, a fashion editor and designer, is the co-founder of Perfect Point Design. Li Yao is a senior graphic designer.

What does design mean to you?
Design is part of our life. It is not separate.

Where do you see future challenges in communication design?
In the future, communication design will be more diversified. It will need to consider the mixing and matching of different elements, technologies, carriers and scenes, and it will come with higher comprehensive requirements for good designers.

What makes your work unique?
In the process of designing, we always try our best to see more, think more and produce some crossover designs. We adjust designs to tailor them to customer requirements. All creativity and ideas are generated through reflection, and communication with the customers.

PierraaGroup
Saskia Pierschek
— The design we create today, tomorrow echoes in thousands of minds.

Red Dot
→ Fair Stands: page 500–501

Saskia Pierschek has worked in the agency business for ten years, most recently as an art director, a role she held for several years. During this time, she was responsible for the digital communication and digitisation strategies of high-ranking companies and corporations. Then she ventured into self-employment and founded her own agency, Pierraa. It has since grown to become one of the leading agencies in the region, serving both corporate groups and large medium-sized businesses. The PierraaGroup is a symbiosis of management consultancy and brand management agency in the premium segment. Its four specialised units cover consulting, design, digital strategies and events, thus ensuring the highest possible quality and synergies for its customers.

What does design mean to you?
Design offers me the opportunity to unite strategy and creativity, by which I mean the brain and the heart in equal measure, within one process.

What are the biggest challenges in a creative's everyday life?
Awesome design is born by a wild mind and a disciplined hand. Keeping the perfect balance between both parts during the development process is the daily challenge.

What was your intention in designing your awarded work?
The central theme here is "symbiotic comprehensibility". Complex product details should be transported to the target group at a glance – through a variety of communication media – in a sustainable way.

Polestar/Stockholm Design Lab
— Simple, remarkable ideas.

Red Dot: Brand of the Year
→ Automotive Brands: page 20–23

Red Dot: Best of the Best
→ Corporate Design & Identity: page 206–207

Polestar is a stand-alone brand owned by Volvo Car Group/Geely that design, develop and build electrical high-performance drives. In 2016, soon after the founding of the company, Stockholm Design Lab was approached to collaborate on developing and elevating the brand to become a credible competitor in the rapidly expanding global market for electric cars. Stockholm Design Lab is an internationally recognised design agency that, ever since 1998, has worked with a wide range of clients such as Ericsson, the Nobel Prize organisation, SAS, IKEA and H&M.

What was your intention in designing your awarded work?
Polestar has no legacy, no ties to the past and is free to find the path that is right for it. In fact, it was created to break free from the conventions of the car industry. While others tend to focus on needless flair, Polestar focuses on uncompromising product performance. This is communicated through a brand that elevates technology and removes what's unnecessary. Instead, the obsession with detail characterises the brand presence down to the smallest level. We think this shows in the brand expression that is kept simple but purposeful with great attention and care.

How can sustainability and e-mobility be translated into a corporate design?
Sustainability and e-mobility are primarily about what you do as a company, rather than what you choose to express. Polestar's identity was built to highlight technological advancements and to last for a long time, with a focus on eliminating excess even in the smallest of details.

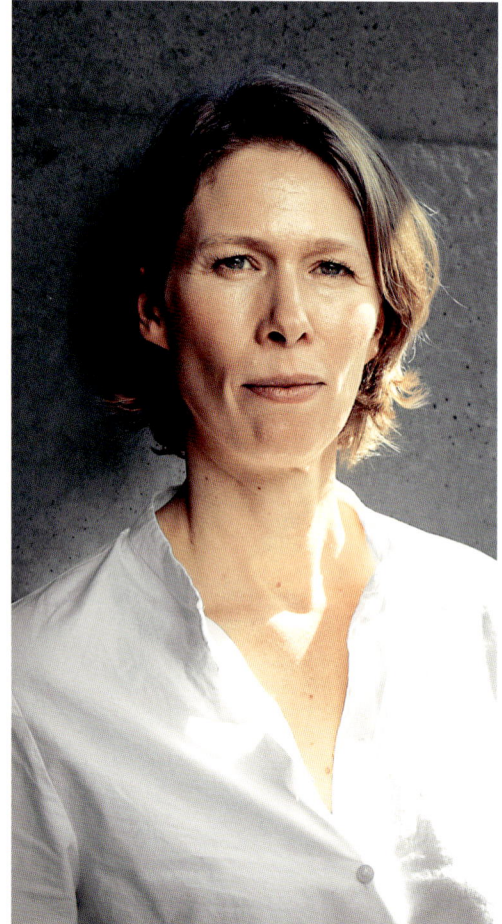

Realgestalt
Jürgen Michalski,
Anne Kohlermann,
Johannes Ritzel
— A powerful brand turns customers into ambassadors and attracts the best talents.

Red Dot: Best of the Best
→ Advertising: page 298–299

Realgestalt supports small, medium-sized and also quite large clients in managing and increasing their company value by means of a well-managed brand, an appealing design and excellent communication. The corporate design of Daimler AG and the new Berlin airport are just as challenging tasks as the various communication initiatives for the Deutsche Oper Berlin. The team of Realgestalt consists of consultants, strategists, creative and digital experts who have worked in Berlin since 1994.

What does design mean to you?
Design affects each and every part of our professional and private lives.

What drives you to create something new?
It does not have to be new. It has to be good and relevant for the audience.

What are the biggest challenges in a creative's everyday life?
The biggest challenge is to make people appreciate the great importance of design services.

What makes your work unique?
Who wants to be unique? It is about substance and relevance.

What was your intention in designing your awarded work?
To remind people of the grandiosity of opera.

rozanka GmbH
Daniel Pulina,
Julia Kanichtcheva,
Jan Rozanka, Alicja Schneider,
Przemek Bystrzynski
— GOOD DESIGN ROCKS!

Red Dot: Best of the Best
→ Brand Design & Identity: page 92–93

rozanka GmbH developed from a fashion photography studio to a full-service advertising agency headquartered in Dortmund, Germany. The agency was founded by Jan Rozanka in 2001. Alicja Schneider, his sister, joined the company in 2006. Gradually, the agency's work changed from pure photography to that of a classic advertising agency with a focus on design and communication. The agency consists of five people who make up a creative, brilliant, colourful, original and inseparable team, working for clients that are start-ups, medium-sized companies and corporations.

What does design mean to you?
The minimalism and pure beauty of shapes and lines. The interaction of light and colour to form harmonious compositions.

Where do you see future challenges in communication design?
In achieving sufficient mobile phone charge capacity.

To what extent do you think new technologies are changing design?
Unfortunately, technology changes the world of design too quickly. Sometimes this process needs to be stopped deliberately.

Why did you become a designer?
It was an inner call that couldn't be ignored.

What drives you to create something new?
The smiles of our clients!

SCAD Savannah College of Art and Design
Mijin Han, Lachelle Robotham
— Using design to enhance human experience.

Red Dot: Junior Award
Best of the Best
→ Advertising: page 552–553

Mijin Han has a BA degree in broadcasting from the Korea National University of Arts in Seoul, and, in 2016, began studying at the Savannah College of Art and Design, graduating with an MA degree in advertising and an MFA degree in film and television. She has worked for different channels and media stations, e.g. NBC or the Atlanta Film Festival, and is currently working as a content creator at Studio 91. Lachelle Robotham holds a Bachelor of Architecture from the University of Houston and an MA degree in advertising from the Savannah College of Art and Design, Atlanta, Georgia. She worked as a graphic designer at Memphis Teacher Residency and as a freelance graphic designer before becoming a visual designer at the agency Giant Spoon in May 2020.

How can communication design arouse emotions?
We believe communication design can impact emotions through a focus on human-centred principles and values. The impact of visualising an idea that speaks to the individual as well as the human race as a whole can be extremely impactful.

What was your intention in designing your awarded work?
We wanted to rebrand Ziploc by focusing on consumers rather than on the practicality of the bag itself. The head copy, "It's more than a bag, it's what's inside", can encompass so many stories from all walks of life from all over the world. Through our global campaign, we wanted to emphasise that, no matter what differentiates us, we can all find common ground if we focus less on the outside and more on what's inside.

Peter Schmidt Group
Ulrich Aldinger
— Design is question and solution at the same time.

Red Dot: Best of the Best
→ Advertising: page 296–297

Red Dot
→ Packaging Design: page 365
→ Packaging Design: page 400
→ Packaging Design: page 476

Ulrich Aldinger is creative director at the Peter Schmidt Group in Munich, a subsidiary he has run since 2016. He studied design at HfG Schwäbisch Gmünd, Germany, and began working for the Peter Schmidt Group in 2004. He has since looked after international companies including Panasonic, Coca-Cola, Carlsberg, Imperial Brands and Henkel as well as cultural institutions such as the Nezu Museum in Tokyo, the Haus der Bayerischen Geschichte (House of Bavarian History) and the Bayerische Staatsgemäldesammlungen (Bavarian State Painting Collections).

What does design mean to you?
For me, design is question and solution at the same time. A design process is also always a road to knowledge. What are the challenges – and what is their design solution?

Where do you see future challenges in communication design?
Design has to stay relevant and contribute to solutions that have a positive effect on society and the environment. In the era of the COVID-19 pandemic, we must find specific design solutions that allow us to live together sustainably in a permanent state of uncertainty.

What are the biggest challenges in a creative's everyday life?
The greatest challenge is improvisation as there are always some constraints on our work. We have to accept them and still manage to develop functional, creative solutions.

Soar Design Studio
Yu-Jui Chang
— I believe space and design are both extensions of man and nature.

Red Dot: Best of the Best
→ Retail Design: page 518–519

Yu-Jui Chang graduated from the Department of Architecture at Tunghai University with a master's thesis for which he received the Architectural Association of Excellence Thesis award from the Architectural Institute of Taiwan. Aside from focusing on architectural and urban design, he incorporates environmental concepts and ideas from the liberal arts, aspiring to present a vision and a style that are more natural and localised.

What does design mean to you?
Design is a way of redefining life, a means to connect with nature and other people. Architecture and interior design, in particular, reveal how the designer and the owner perceive nature and how they connect with it.

To what extent do you think new technologies are changing design?
New technologies may change the way we design and the tools we use to implement designs. However, new technologies do not alter the nature of design, which is the pursuit of improvements.

What drives you to create something new?
Very often, when people are trying to "use" the space, they involuntarily fall into the trap of universality and collage, cutting off their links with natural life. That's why a sense of nature and culture gradually fade. That only drives me even more to create something that is different from the market as well as from fast culture.

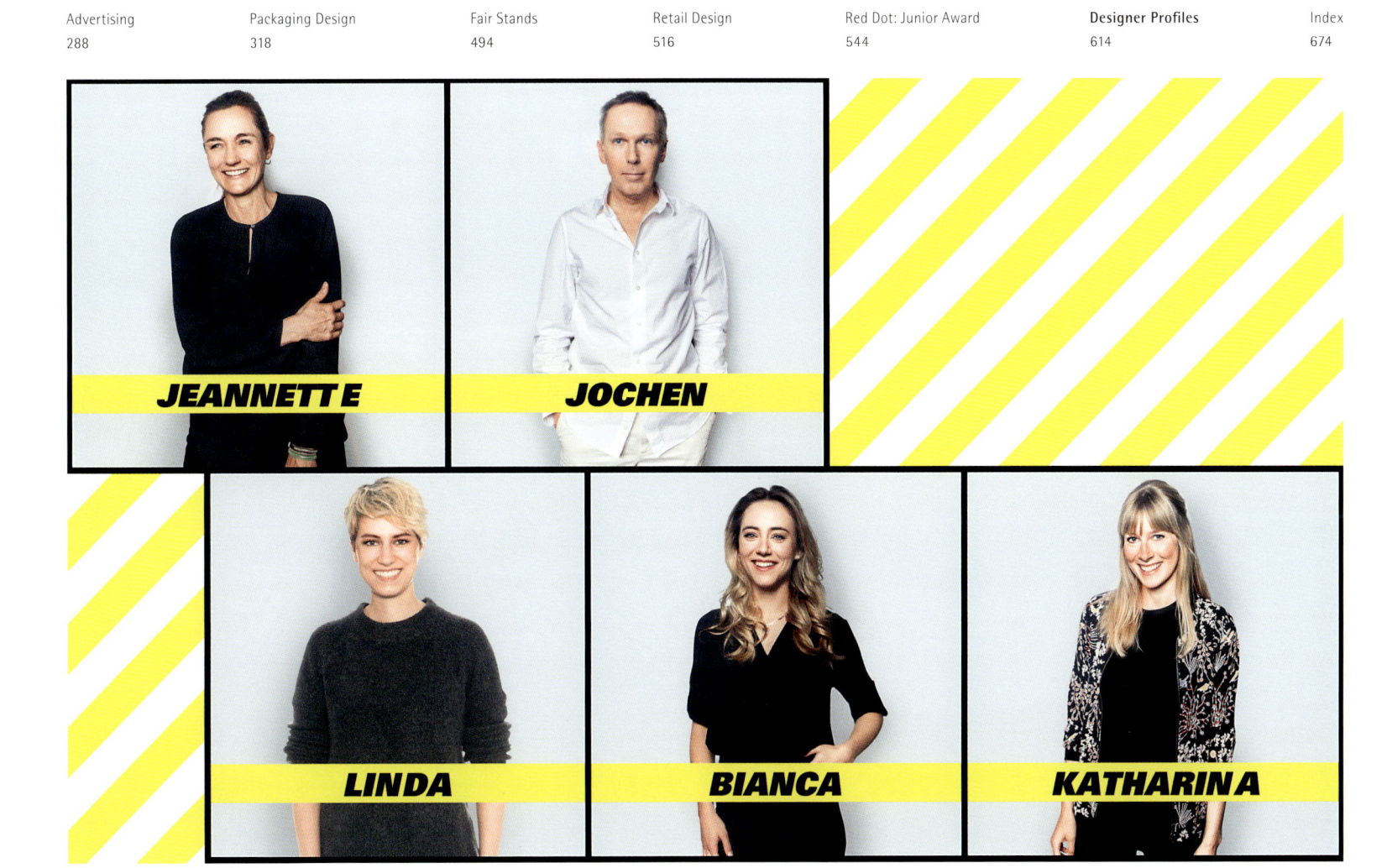

STRICHPUNKT
Jeannette Kohnle,
Jochen Theurer,
Linda Beiermeister,
Bianca Bunsas,
Katharina Bergmann
– Think outside the box!

Red Dot: Best of the Best
→ Annual Reports: page 266–267

STRICHPUNKT is a leading design agency and – from its offices in Stuttgart, Berlin and Shanghai – works for clients including Audi, Bosch, Deutsche Post DHL Group, Frankfurter Allgemeine Zeitung, Otto Group, Porsche, Schwäbisch Hall and Trumpf as well as for Asian brands such as Weltmeister and Deli. Jochen Theurer studied at the Leuphana University Lüneburg and the Merz Akademie, a university of art, design and media in Stuttgart. As creative director, he works with around 115 specialists to develop concepts and projects in the areas of brand design, experience design, culture design and business design.

What does design mean to you?
As Massimo Vignelli once so elegantly put it: "Design is not a style. It is an attitude" – that's it. Attitude.

What was your intention in designing your awarded work?
It's a passion project about the west of Stuttgart. Schwabstraße is definitely a very vibrant social microcosm that reflects our society at large: in a district where over 40 per cent of the inhabitants are migrants – from Pakistan, Brazil and, most recently, a very large number from the USA – all living peacefully – and successfully! – alongside lots of Swabians and German incomers, it is worthwhile taking a closer look and listening to people's stories (to this end, we highly recommend taking a look at the video interviews on the website wir-gesellschaft-bw.de). In any case, the report feels just like Schwabstraße, that is to say colourful and authentic with all its rough edges intact.

SUAN Conceptual Design
Susanne Hartmann,
André Konrad
— Every strong image will become reality.
(Antoine de Saint-Exupéry)

Red Dot
→ Corporate Design & Identity: page 231
→ Corporate Design & Identity: page 236

Within just five years of founding their branding agency SUAN Conceptual Design, the two founders, designers and brand experts Susanne Hartmann and André Konrad managed to position it as one of the leading creative agencies in Basel and Switzerland. With a diverse portfolio and a strong team of designers, SUAN represents visionary brands, clear messages and sophisticated design concepts. Prior to the founding of their own agency, both partners worked for several global design agencies. The subject of brand has always been a priority for them and continues to be so at SUAN.

What does design mean to you?
Design is a statement, a form of expression and at the same time something very common. Design doesn't answer to democratic structures, contrary to all the societal principles we are fond of. Whoever decides on an exceptional design has to follow a clear-cut course and enforce it.

Where do you see future challenges in communication design?
Brand design is changing from a product-based focus to more value-centred communication. Our contemporary, deeply interconnected world is being shaped by emotional narratives and stories in the context of societal change. Going forward, brands that authentically tell how they take an active part in this transition will stand out.

What makes your work unique?
Our work appeals with its strategic approach, reduced forms and high continuity in terms of design and creative quality. It is also important to us to always get to the heart of the core message.

Suh Architects
Eulho Suh, Kyungen Kim
— Passion, passion, passion.

Red Dot
→ Retail Design: page 535

Eulho Suh, born in Seoul, South Korea, graduated from the Rhode Island School of Design and later received his master's degree from the Harvard Graduate School of Design. He worked for Morphosis Architects and KPF before returning to Seoul to found Suh Architects in 2006. The company thrives in sleepless, design-loving, tech-savvy, entrepreneurial Seoul, questioning the boundaries of architecture with every material, client and collaboration. Kyungen Kim graduated from Wellesley College and received a Master of Fine Arts from the Rhode Island School of Design, before arriving at architecture via her installation work. After receiving her master's degree from the Harvard Graduate School of Design and working at CO Architects in Los Angeles, she joined Eulho Suh at Suh Architects as a partner in space-making and research.

Where do you see future challenges in communication design?
With social media and moving images replacing still ones, we only have a fraction of a second to say something, to communicate an idea. The challenge is to slow the audience down to want to see and listen.

What was your intention in designing your awarded work?
We wanted to literally frame the Genesis as a finely crafted object of desire. The Genesis Studio is a juxtaposition of raw materials and refined engineering. The telescoping linear light frame that expands the space occupied by each car has become a signature element that we see as both distinctive and timeless.

Atelier Tietchen/Brooklyn Soap Company
Tobias Tietchen, Nico Liebetanz
— Done is better than perfect.

Red Dot: Best of the Best
→ Packaging Design: page 326–327

Tobias Tietchen initially studied design communication before teaching himself the art of tattooing. After moving and travelling around Europe as a visiting tattoo artist, he opened his own tattoo studio Atelier Tietchen in 2015, renowned throughout Germany. At the same time, he has held numerous exhibitions, taken part in several design collaborations and carried out a host of creative projects in recent years. His clients include Gin Sul, Google, Hapag-Lloyd and Universal Music, to name but a few. Nico Liebetanz studied design before working as art director and creative director at various design, creative and packaging agencies in Hamburg. His clients included adidas, Audi, Beam Suntory and the Radeberger Group, and his works won several design awards. In 2019, he joined the team at Brooklyn Soap Company, where he serves as art director.

To what extent do you think new technologies are changing design?
Design is always a snapshot of the prevailing zeitgeist, technology and social mores, and therefore in constant flux. New technologies afford designers the opportunity to forge new paths. What starts out as an experiment has the potential to grow into an industry standard.

What drives you to create something new?
Making projects successful, because design plays a fundamental role in that success. Sales figures are the true measure of this success. This is a great responsibility, of course, but also incredibly exciting.

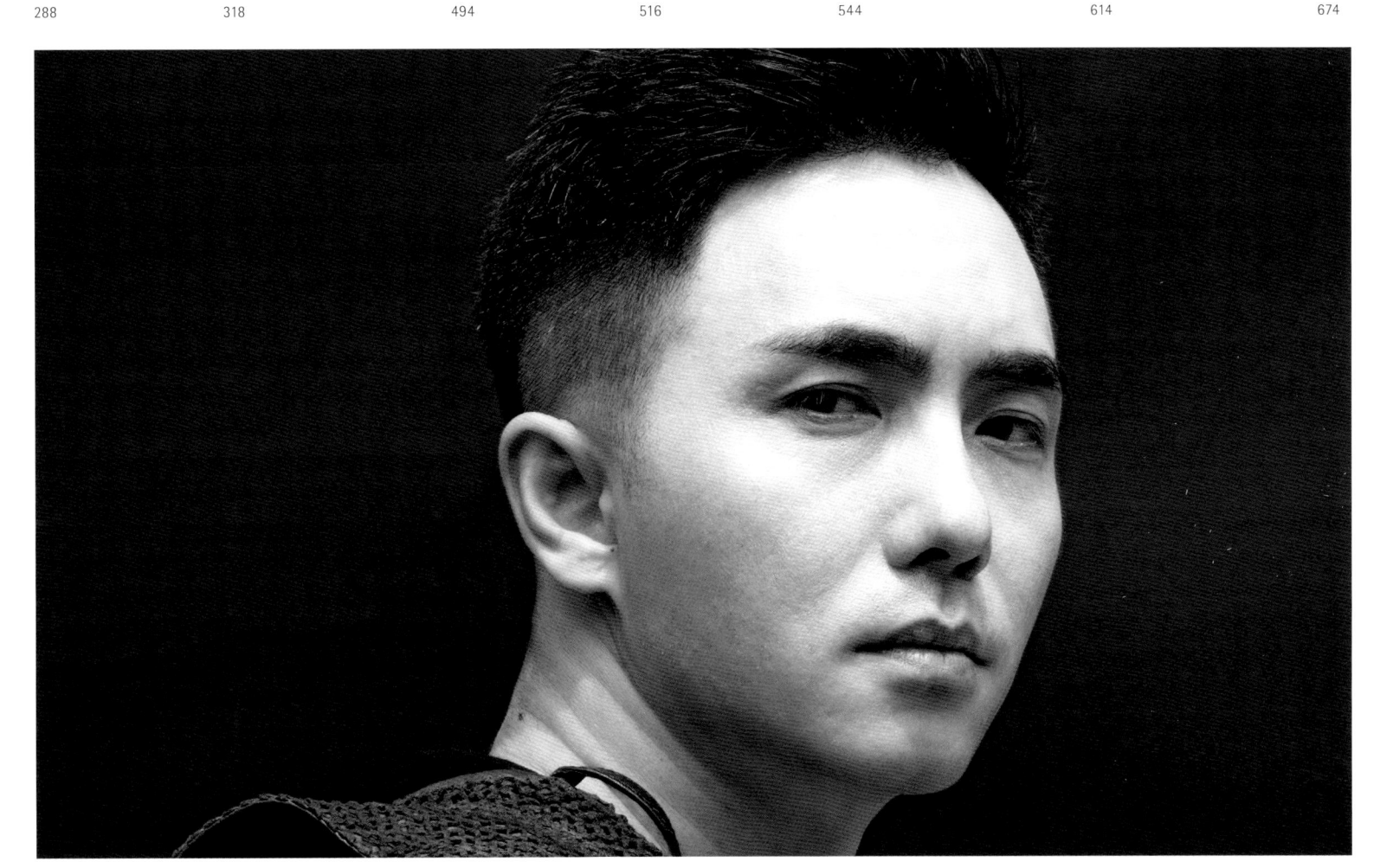

Shenzhen Tigerpan Packaging Design Co., Ltd.
Tiger Pan
— What matters most to me is creativity.

Red Dot
→ Packaging Design: page 352
→ Packaging Design: page 470
→ Packaging Design: page 487

Tiger Pan founded his own packaging design lab in 2012 and has won over 100 international professional design awards. One of the most popular packaging designers in China, he holds a bachelor's degree from the Academy of Arts and Design of Tsinghua University and an honorary master's degree from the University for the Creative Arts in the UK and is now a guest lecturer at over 15 design universities in China. He was commissioned to design the postal stamp of the Year of the Dog in 2018 for the United Nations. As vice chairman of the Shenzhen Illustration Association, he established an award for illustration.

What does design mean to you?
Design solves problems and conveys my emotions. It makes people's lives simpler and more civilised.

Where do you see future challenges in communication design?
In the time of artificial intelligence and big data, the role of communication design can partly be taken over. Designers' jobs can be replaced in a way that is very challenging for those in the industry. And, for sure, new developments, technology especially, will demand a faster reaction to trends and changes in design.

What was your intention in designing your awarded work?
There are always three goals when I design packaging. First of all, I want consumers to be attracted or moved by what I present. Secondly, I have to satisfy my client as my designs are made to solve problems. Most importantly, I can't stand poorly designed things. I have a strong drive to change what surrounds us.

Visuelle Fabrik
Roman Albertini, Linda Albertini
— Beauty is function.

Red Dot
→ Corporate Design & Identity: page 258

Visuelle Fabrik was founded by Roman Albertini in Basel, Switzerland, in 2011. Today, he runs the agency together with his wife Linda Albertini, primarily focusing on branding and corporate design. Over the years, they have gained wide-ranging experience in collaborating with a great variety of clients in a host of different sectors. Thanks to fresh challenges and current projects, the agency – assisted by a large network of specialists – constantly continues to evolve.

What does design mean to you?
Design is a craft that adheres to certain rules and principles, yet which is also, to a certain extent, a matter of subjective perception. Our aim is to use design to create beauty, in keeping with our guiding principle: beauty is function.

Where do you see future challenges in communication design?
Design must communicate ever more content, yet at the same time should also resist doing so because we live in a society drowning in information. The challenge lies in finding the optimal amount of information (function). For us, what it comes down to is perfected "Swiss Design".

What drives you to create something new?
We crave change and innovation. The status quo makes us sick and leads to chronic ennui. The only weapon to combat this is movement – no matter the direction.

WWS (Beijing) Cultural Propagation
Wang Chengfu, Chen Peng
– Good design with verve.

Red Dot
→ Brand Design & Identity: page 198–199

Wang Chengfu and Chen Peng are active in the fields of visual brand image design, urban brand design, city brand strategies, image communication, etc., integrating the identity of Chinese cultural aesthetics with a modern, international style. With 20 years of experience in guiding creative teams, they have developed thousands of outstanding creative brand and design projects for 300 international and domestic clients in various industries and fields.

What does design mean to you?
Design is part of our life.

Where do you see future challenges in communication design?
An increasingly meta-social environment, more fragmented media and faster changing science and technology will be the main future challenges for communication design.

To what extent do you think new technologies are changing design?
Design has to serve people and should use new technology to do so.

Why did you become a designer?
We love design and innovation, and love creating new things.

What makes your work unique?
The rich experience of life it offers.

Index Designers

0–9

:response
Arved Lüth
www.good-response.de
Vol. 1: 282–283, 616

100A associates
www.100a-associates.com
Vol. 1: 542

1508
www.1508.dk
Vol. 1: 251
Vol. 2: 178–179, 566

31M
Agentur für Kommunikation GmbH
www.31m.de
Vol. 1: 240, 255

3st kommunikation GmbH
www.3st.de
Vol. 1: 262–263, 617

A

A TWOSOME PLACE Design Team
www.twosome.co.kr
Vol. 1: 376–377

A.S. Advertising
www.antoniaskaraki.com
Vol. 1: 362–363, 408, 415, 618

Acer Inc.
www.acer.com
Vol. 1: 459, 619
Vol. 2: 201

Admind Branding &
Communications
www.admindagency.com
Vol. 1: 306–307, 620
Vol. 2: 406–407, 568

Guangzhou Ai Yue
Advertising Co., Ltd.
Vol. 1: 446, 447

Aixsponza GmbH
www.aixsponza.com
Vol. 1: 290–291, 621

ALINE STUDIO
www.alinecreative.com
Vol. 1: 120–121, 188–189

Amigo Invisible Studio
www.ainvisible.com
Vol. 1: 192

Amorepacific
www.apgroup.com
Vol. 1: 119
Vol. 2: 182–183, 196, 571

Atelier.Archi@Mosphere
www.archimosphere.kr
Vol. 1: 537

ARD Design Switzerland
www.ard.ch
Vol. 1: 391, 398, 622

ASCENDER BRANDING
www.ascenderbranding.com
Vol. 1: 106–107

astudio
www.behance.net/kimjina
Vol. 1: 479

ATOB
www.atob.kr
Vol. 1: 428

Aileen Aurelia
LASALLE College of the Arts
www.lasalle.edu.sg
Vol. 1: 560

Autentic Consulting Sagl
www.autentic.ch
Vol. 1: 238–239, 623

B

B for Brand
www.b-forbrand.com
Vol. 1: 489, 624

B:SCOPE STUDIO
www.bscopestudio.com
Vol. 1: 150

Beetroot Design Group
www.beetroot.gr
Vol. 1: 466

Berndt+Partner Creality GmbH
www.bp-creality.de
Vol. 1: 420–421

Berry Creative
www.berrycreative.fi
Vol. 1: 241, 625
Vol. 2: 390

Birger Linke Design
www.behance.net/birgerlinke
Vol. 1: 455, 626

Bold
www.boldscandinavia.com
Vol. 1: 432

BRIDGE & COMPANY
www.bridge-company.co.kr
Vol. 1: 493

Bronce Estudio
www.broncestudio.com
Vol. 1: 138–139
Vol. 2: 58

Brooklyn Soap Company
www.bklynsoap.com
Vol. 1: 326–327, 670

Bruketa&Zinic&Grey
www.bruketa-zinic.com
Vol. 1: 149, 339

busybuilding
www.busybuilding.com
Vol. 1: 381

Fuzhou BY-ENJOY
Brand Design Co., Ltd.
www.by-enjoy.com
Vol. 1: 112

C

C3 Creative Code and
Content GmbH
www.c3.co
Vol. 1: 268

Caparo
www.caparo.gr
Vol. 1: 322–323, 338, 627

CDR associates
www.cdr.co.kr
Vol. 1: 208–209

Cee Cee Creative
www.ceeceecreative.com
Vol. 1: 242–243, 628

Paolo Cesaretti
www.paolocesaretti.it
Vol. 1: 496–497

CFC
www.contentformcontext.com
Vol. 1: 376–377

Ching-Ting Chang, Yun-Tzu Chang,
Fang-Yi Liao, Wan-Ho Pai,
Jing-Ran Lin
Chaoyang University of
Technology
www.cyut.edu.tw
Vol. 1: 578

Shu-Hsuan Chang
Lunghwa University of Science
and Technology
www.lhu.edu.tw
Vol. 1: 515

Yu Tsen Chang, Lu Xi Jiang,
Bo Xian Chen, Cheng Han Chuang
Chaoyang University of
Technology
www.cyut.edu.tw
Vol. 1: 570

CHANNEL A B&C
www.ichannela.com
Vol. 1: 250

Huai Lan Chao, Tzu Mi Huang,
Ju Han Yu, Fu Shun Zhang,
Shu Hong Wang
Ling Tung University
www.ltu.edu.tw
Vol. 1: 583

Ting-Chieh Chao, Yu-Han Lin,
Chien-Kai Chiu, Shih-Jung Chiu,
Zhi-Xuan Xu
Chaoyang University of
Technology
www.cyut.edu.tw
Vol. 1: 558

Cheil Germany GmbH
www.cheil.de
Vol. 1: 305

Cheil Worldwide
www.cheil.com
Vol. 1: 174, 304, 540–541
Vol. 2: 32, 379, 381, 397, 399,
416–417

Hung Yu Chen, Yao-Jhih Yang,
Yi-Xiao Zhou, Yu-Wen Chang
Department of Applied Arts,
Fu Jen Catholic University
www.aart.fju.edu.tw
Vol. 1: 562–563

Jun-Liang Chen
Freeimage Design Co., Ltd.
Vol. 1: 515

Chen Szu-Fan, Chen Yu-Zhen,
Lee Che-Yu, Huang Yen-Yu,
Chen Ting-Ying, Hsu Chien-Ya
Fu Jen Catholic University
www.aart.fju.edu.tw
Vol. 1: 602

Yi-Chieh Chen, Ting-Yu Su,
Ting-Yu Chang, Hung-Yi Lee
Ming Chuan University
www.mcu.edu.tw
Vol. 1: 557

Index Designers

Yu-Fang Chen, Jun-Ru Wang,
Ya-Jing Huang
Cheng Shiu University
www.csu.edu.tw
Vol. 1: 573

Cheng-Yu Cheng, Yao-Ren Zhuang,
Ching Chang, Yi-Hsiu Cheng
Chaoyang University of
Technology
www.cyut.edu.tw
Vol. 1: 566

Ying-Chi Chi, Chia-Ying Li
Ling Tung University
www.ltu.edu.tw
Vol. 1: 605

China Resources Sanjiu
Medical & Pharmaceutical Co., Ltd.
www.999.com.cn
Vol. 1: 484, 485

Chien-Hung Chiu, Chia-Hsing Wei,
Chia-Chun Hsu, Chia-Wei Chen,
Shih-Yu Chen, Chiao-Kang Kan
Fu Jen Catholic University
www.aart.fju.edu.tw
Vol. 1: 568

Jin A Choi, Jung Mi Kong, I Ji Yoon,
Yu Mi Go, Jong Hui Lee, Yu Jin Park
Hoseo University
www.hoseo.ac.kr
Vol. 1: 603

Chung Ya-Hsuan, Hsu Chiau-Wei
National Taiwan University of
Science and Technology
www.ntust.edu.tw
Vol. 1: 588

Shanghai Chunmi
Electronic Technology Co., Ltd.
www.chunmi.com
Vol. 1: 116, 223

Shenzhen CIGA Design Co., Ltd.
www.cigadesign.com
Vol. 1: 457

Cinquesegni S.r.l.
www.cinquesegni.it
Vol. 1: 333

CJ Cheiljedang
www.cj.co.kr
Vol. 1: 424

CLEVER°FRANKE
www.cleverfranke.com
Vol. 1: 94–95, 162, 629
Vol. 2: 188, 234, 274

Clormann Design
www.clormanndesign.de
Vol. 1: 475

Coreana Cosmetics
www.coreana.com
Vol. 1: 438

Coreintive
www.coreintive.com
Vol. 1: 220–221

Covenant
www.behance.net/
gallery/86953061/UTB
Vol. 1: 222, 637

Creuna Denmark A/S
www.creuna.com
Vol. 1: 184–185, 216–217

CREVV
www.crevv.com
Vol. 1: 113, 142, 172–173, 467
Vol. 2: 75

Alberto Cuadra, Hope Thomas,
Sydney Solis, Rashed Alsubaie,
Van Pham, Remy James, Vy Phan
SCAD Savannah College of
Art and Design
www.scad.edu
Vol. 1: 579

Cueclyp
www.cueclyp.com
Vol. 1: 308–309

cyclos design GmbH
www.cyclos-design.de
Vol. 1: 247

D

D'art Design Gruppe
www.d-art-design.de
Vol. 1: 502–503

DAELIM Industrial Co., Ltd.
www.daelim.co.kr
Vol. 1: 190–191

Daewon Plus Group
www.daewonplus.co.kr
Vol. 1: 514
Vol. 2: 388

DekoRatio
Branding & Design Studio
www.dekoratio.hu
Vol. 1: 389

Dentsu Inc.
www.dentsu.com
Vol. 1: 294–295, 302, 324–325,
630, 631
Vol. 2: 235, 583

Design Plus Design
www.designplusdesign.com
Vol. 1: 520–521, 632

Hefei Designdo
Industrial Design Co., Ltd.
www.designdo.com.cn
Vol. 1: 165

deSter
www.dester.com
Vol. 1: 432

Die Goldkinder GmbH
www.diegoldkinder.at
Vol. 1: 311

die Gutgestalten GbR
www.die-gutgestalten.de
Vol. 1: 215

dkd
www.dkdstudio.net
Vol. 1: 430–431

Dong-A Pharm
www.dapharm.com
Vol. 1: 482–483

Dongdao Creative Branding Group
www.dongdao.net
Vol. 1: 122, 123, 170

DPJN
Diena Pirms Janu Nakts
www.dpjn.com
Vol. 1: 392

E

einsagentur Schäuble GmbH
www.einsagentur.de
Vol. 1: 508–509

Electric Brand Consultants
Electric Creative LLC
www.electric-consultants.com
Vol. 1: 259

EMOTIONplanning
www.emotionplanning.com
Vol. 1: 514
Vol. 2: 388

Quanzhou Enjia Brand
Planning Co., Ltd.
www.enjia.com.cn
Vol. 1: 450–451, 636

eskalade werbeagentur GmbH
www.eskalade.de
Vol. 1: 234–235

Shenzhen Excel Brand Design
Consultant Co., Ltd.
www.zhuoshang.cn
Vol. 1: 340–341

Excited
www.excited.agency
Vol. 1: 125, 244

eyeteeth design
www.behance.net/
gallery/86953061/UTB
www.dkvr.co.uk/work/fincap-law
Vol. 1: 222, 237, 637

F

FIELD.IO Berlin GmbH & Co KG
www.field.io
Vol. 1: 505

Shenzhen Fire Wolf
Graphic Design Co., Ltd.
www.fw119.com
Vol. 1: 409
Vol. 2: 422

Fjord
www.fjordnet.com
Vol. 1: 155

FORM
www.formbureau.co.uk
Vol. 1: 528–529

FUJIFILM Corporation
Design Center
http://design.fujifilm.com
Vol. 1: 469
Vol. 2: 216, 322, 323

FutureBrand China
www.futurebrand.com
Vol. 1: 131, 252–253, 638

G

G2K Creative Agency
www.g2k.nl
Vol. 1: 213

Genese Werbeagentur GmbH
www.genese-md.de
Vol. 1: 310, 312
Vol. 2: 19

Grand Design Inc.
www.grand-design-tokyo.jp
Vol. 1: 316–317, 436–437, 639

Advertising	Packaging Design	Fair Stands	Retail Design	Red Dot: Junior Award	Designer Profiles	Index
288	318	494	516	544	614	674

Index Designers

Gregor & Strozik
Visual Identity GmbH
www.gsvi.de
Vol. 1: 530–531, 640

GS Retail Co., Ltd.
www.gsretail.com
Vol. 1: 105

Harbin Guangwei
Marketing Planning Co., Ltd.
www.gw4a.com
Vol. 1: 344

H

Hyewon Han
Vol. 1: 550–551, 641

Mijin Han, Lachelle Robotham
SCAD Savannah College of
Art and Design
www.scad.edu
Vol. 1: 552–553, 664

Hanwha Life Insurance
Brand Strategy Team
www.dreamplus.asia
Vol. 1: 178–179

Happytear AB
www.happytear.com
Vol. 1: 345

Hara Design Institute
Nippon Design Center
www.ndc.co.jp
Vol. 1: 178–179

Harimholdings
www.harimholdings.co.kr
Vol. 1: 490, 491

hartmannvonsiebenthal
the brand experience
company GmbH
www.hvs.de
Vol. 1: 512

Heimat Wien
www.heimat.wien
Vol. 1: 320–321, 642

Yun-Tung Heng, Chieh-Ying Lien
Asia University
www.asia.edu.tw
Vol. 1: 606

HGB
Hamburger Geschäftsberichte
GmbH & Co. KG
www.hgb.de
Vol. 1: 279

Chic Ying Ho, Yi Hsuan Tseng,
Chi Yin Lu, Yu Cheng Lin,
Xin Jie Xie, Ting Yi Huang
Ling Tung University
www.ltu.edu.tw
Vol. 1: 569

HOHOHO Co., Ltd.
www.hohohogroup.com
Vol. 1: 527

Bureau Steffi Holz
www.steffiholz.com
Vol. 1: 229

holzrausch
www.holzrausch.de
Vol. 1: 504

Lijuan Hong, Jinfei Huang
School of Design,
East China Normal University
www.design.ecnu.edu.cn
Vol. 1: 595, 633

HS Ad
www.hsad.co.kr
Vol. 1: 506, 643

Hui-Ju Hsiao, Jhang-Cheng Liou,
Yi-Zhen Huang
National Taichung University of
Science and Technology
www.nutc.edu.tw
Vol. 1: 592

Chang-Hung Hsieh, Zi-Xin Huang,
Cheng-Pang Chou,
Zi-Rong Huang, Hui-Ming Chen
Chaoyang University of
Technology
www.cyut.edu.tw
Vol. 1: 572

Shu-Chi Hsu, Chi-Man Hsu,
Jia-Jun Lin, Sin-Yu Li
Department of Visual
Communication Design,
China University of Technology
www.cute.edu.tw
Vol. 1: 565, 601

Jinfei Huang, Lijuan Hong
School of Design,
East China Normal University
www.design.ecnu.edu.cn
Vol. 1: 595, 633

Wei-Yu Huang
Asia University
www.asia.edu.tw
Vol. 1: 571

Xin-He Huang, Hung-Chi Huang,
Cong-Lin Chen
Chihlee University of Technology
www.chihlee.edu.tw
Vol. 1: 594

Ya-Ting Huang, Wen-Fang Lee,
Sheng-Yu Kao, Min-Zhu Zhan
Department of Visual
Communication Design,
China University of Technology
www.cute.edu.tw
Vol. 1: 598

Yu-Sheng Hung, Han-Wei Huang,
Cheng-Huei Tien, Xiang-Qing Wang
Chihlee University of Technology
www.chihlee.edu.tw
Vol. 1: 599

HuskyFox
www.huskyfox.com
Vol. 1: 132, 151, 181, 254, 464

Hyundai Motor Company
Creative Works
www.creativeworks.kr
Vol. 1: 308–309, 511
Vol. 2: 331, 334, 396

I

iden.team branding agency
www.iden.team
Vol. 1: 101, 140, 402

in medias rees
www.inmediasrees.de
Vol. 1: 394, 644

Inbetween Creative Pty. Ltd.
www.inbetween-design.com
Vol. 1: 182

inDare Design Strategy Limited
www.indare.love
Vol. 1: 390, 411, 488, 492

Innocean Worldwide
www.innocean.com
Vol. 1: 292–293, 645
Vol. 2: 145

innovation.rocks consulting gmbh
www.innovation.rocks
Vol. 1: 135
Vol. 2: 329

Institut der deutschen Wirtschaft
Köln Medien GmbH
www.iwmedien.de
Vol. 1: 272–273

Interbrand Japan
www.interbrandjapan.com
Vol. 1: 6–17, 442

Interbrand Seoul
www.interbrand.com/kr
Vol. 1: 6–17, 201, 232, 378, 454

itch
www.itch.co
Vol. 1: 136

J

Japan Mountaineering & Sport
Climbing Association
www.jma-climbing.org
Vol. 1: 163
Vol. 2: 90–91

Jardin
www.jardin.co.kr
Vol. 1: 375

JiaYi (Guangzhou) Design Co., Ltd.
Vol. 1: 484, 485

Jones Knowles Ritchie
www.jkrglobal.com
Vol. 1: 354, 355

Agentur Jung GmbH
www.agentur-jung.de
Vol. 1: 334, 335

K

Seungkwan Kang
SK Telecom
www.behance.net/steve_kang
Vol. 1: 100

Yona Kang
FLAG Studio
www.designbyflag.com
Vol. 1: 100

KD1 Designagentur
www.kd1.com
Vol. 1: 284–285

Keijzer Marketing Communicatie
www.vankeijzer.nl
Vol. 1: 287

Keko GmbH
www.keko.de
Vol. 1: 135
Vol. 2: 329

Index Designers

Kidler AB
Kidler Design Studio
www.kidler.se
Vol. 1: 468, 646

KL&K Design
www.klandk.com
Vol. 1: 368–369

Studio Bas Koopmans
www.studiobaskoopmans.com
Vol. 1: 94–95, 629

Kopfkunst
Agentur für Kommunikation GmbH
www.kopfkunst.net
Vol. 1: 303
Vol. 2: 164

Chengdu Kuanzhai Food
Investment Co., Ltd.
https://kuanzhai.tmall.com
Vol. 1: 370

Pei-Wen Kuo, Yi-Ling Fan,
Ou-Yen-Hsin Kuo
Cheng Shiu University
www.csu.edu.tw
Vol. 1: 575

L

L3 Branding Experience Design
www.l3branding.com
Vol. 1: 148

Shanghai Lanzuo
Network Technology Co., Ltd.
Vol. 1: 465

LAY:D
Brand and Design Studio
www.lay-d.kr
Vol. 1: 128–129

Lazy snail Design
www.lazysnail.design
Vol. 1: 124, 144–145, 404

Leaping Creative
www.leapingcreative.com
Vol. 1: 538, 539

Art. Lebedev Studio
www.artlebedev.com
Vol. 1: 233

Ken-Tsai Lee Design Lab
Taiwan Tech
www.behance.net/kentsailee
Vol. 1: 169

Seonil Lee, Jisu Moon
Kookmin University
www.kookmin.ac.kr
Vol. 1: 567, 647

Shenzhen Left and Right
Packaging Design Co., Ltd.
www.zuoheyou.com
Vol. 1: 453

Shin-Yee Lew, Tzu-Chieh Chen,
Zu-Ting Deng, Yi-Ying Chen,
Chia-Wen Lin
National Yunlin University of
Science and Technology
www.yuntech.edu.tw
Vol. 1: 559

Ya-Jun Li, Wei-Ying Chen,
Zhao-Xiang Chen
Asia University
www.asia.edu.tw
Vol. 1: 600

Yi-Yun Li, I-Jie Tsay, Yu-Ching Chiu,
Min-Hua Tsai
National Taipei University of
Education
www.ntue.edu.tw
Vol. 1: 608, 610

Chieh-Ying Lien, Pin-Yang Chang
Asia University
www.asia.edu.tw
Vol. 1: 597

Won Lim
hebe the youth
Vol. 1: 100

Lin Yu Ting, Lin Ying Chun,
Chiang Yu An, Chen Yu Fang,
Wu Pei Rong, Lin Sz To,
Yang Yi Chen, Jiang Bao Ci,
Wu Fang Yu, Yeh Li Yan,
Hsiao Shi Yuan
Fu-Hsin Trade & Arts School
www.fhvs.ntpc.edu.tw
Vol. 1: 554

Yu-Ju Lin
National Taipei University of
Business
www.ntub.edu.tw
Vol. 1: 515

Lin Yu-Jyun, Kwok Ho-Shun,
Li Jia-Ying, Kwok Chi-Wang
Chaoyang University of
Technology
www.cyut.edu.tw
Vol. 1: 593

LINE Plus Corporation
www.linepluscorp.com
Vol. 1: 164

Shenzhen Lingyun
Creative Packaging Design Co., Ltd.
www.lingyuncy.com
Vol. 1: 348, 349, 350, 351, 481

LIQUID | Agentur für Gestaltung
www.liquid.ag
Vol. 1: 256–257

I-Ning Liu
National Taiwan University of
Science and Technology
www.ntust.edu.tw
Vol. 1: 582

Tzu-Ling Liu, Xing-Ju Lu,
Yi-Zhen Lai, Bin-Ru Kong,
Ching-Wei Liu
Ling Tung University
www.ltu.edu.tw
Vol. 1: 591

Liu Zhiyuan
East China Normal University
www.ecnu.edu.cn
Vol. 1: 604, 634

LIXIL Corporation
www.lixil.com
Vol. 1: 187, 499

LK AG
www.lk-ag.com
Vol. 1: 505

LLIWELL branding agency
www.lliwell.com
Vol. 1: 219

Ching-Yang Lo, Yun-Wun Chen,
Man-Cheng Wang, Che-Han Yeh
Ming Chuan University
www.mcu.edu.tw
Vol. 1: 555

loved GmbH
www.loved.de
Vol. 1: 137, 300, 301, 313, 314, 315
Vol. 2: 40, 49, 76, 121, 133, 159, 404

Xin Yu Lu, Wei Chang Xiao,
Chia Chen Wu, Yu Hsuan Chen,
Pin Xuan Liu, Ying Li Yeh
Ling Tung University
www.ltu.edu.tw
Vol. 1: 577

Chang-Yu Lung, Chieh-An Chung,
Zi-Shan Zhang
Ming Chi University of Technology
www.mcut.edu.tw
Vol. 1: 607, 611, 613
Vol. 2: 542

Yinan Lyu
Vol. 1: 214

M

MA'NO Branding
www.manobranding.uz
Vol. 1: 210

Madcats Agency
www.madcats.agency
Vol. 1: 103, 117, 134, 249

Made by Makers
www.madebymakers.com
Vol. 1: 269

Marketsquare
www.marketsquare.dk
Vol. 1: 543

mattweis
www.mattweis.de
Vol. 1: 270–271
Vol. 2: 143

Meiré und Meiré GmbH & Co. KG
www.meireundmeire.de
Vol. 1: 264–265, 648

Mengdom Design Lab
www.mengchih.com
Vol. 1: 212
Vol. 2: 77

Shanghai Mengji
Design Consulting Co., Ltd.
www.mengjidesign.com
Vol. 1: 379

Lim Huay Min
National Yunlin University of
Science and Technology
www.yuntech.edu.tw
Vol. 1: 580

Minuage Design
www.minuage.com
Vol. 1: 406–407, 649

mmpx
www.mmpx.kr
Vol. 1: 250

Index Designers

Jisu Moon, Seonil Lee
Kookmin University
www.kookmin.ac.kr
Vol. 1: 567, 647

Mortar Pestle Studio
www.mortarpestle.studio
Vol. 1: 224–225

Munchkin Inc.
www.munchkin.com
Vol. 1: 114–115, 650

MUTABOR Brand Experience GmbH
www.mutabor.de
Vol. 1: 510
Vol. 2: 391

MUTABOR Design GmbH
www.mutabor.de
Vol. 1: 277

MYM Co., Ltd.
www.promiz2014.com
Vol. 1: 183

MYS Group Co., Ltd.
www.szmys.com
Vol. 1: 416

N
Nascent Design
www.nascentdesign.com
Vol. 1: 171, 651

Navarra.is
www.navarra.is
Vol. 1: 118

Marek Nedelka
www.mareknedelka.com
Vol. 1: 204–205, 655

NF
www.neuronfractal.com
Vol. 1: 250

Ai Ling Ng, Zi Fong Yong
Division of Industrial Design,
School of Design & Environment,
National University of Singapore
www.sde.nus.edu.sg
Vol. 1: 546–549, 652

Toby Ng Design
www.toby-ng.com
Vol. 1: 176–177

Studio Christoph Niemann
www.christophniemann.com
Vol. 1: 298–299

Noiseless Design
www.noiseless-design.com
Vol. 1: 536, 653
Vol. 2: 324

Nonespace
www.none-space.com
Vol. 1: 526, 654

Jan Novák
www.jannovak.net
Vol. 1: 204–205, 655

NSYNK Gesellschaft für
Kunst und Technik mbH
www.nsynk.de
Vol. 1: 505

O
Office Heinzelmann Ayadi
www.oha.international
Vol. 1: 504

Omdesign
www.omdesign.pt
Vol. 1: 330–331, 366–367, 656

omdr Co., Ltd.
www.omdr.co.jp
Vol. 1: 414, 657

Omoikiri Rus
www.omoikiri.ru
Vol. 1: 168

Shenzhen One More Culture
Communication Co., Ltd.
www.onemore.com
Vol. 1: 153, 658

OPX
www.opx.studio
Vol. 1: 274–275

Shenzhen Oracle
Creative Design Co., Ltd.
www.ocdwe.com
Vol. 1: 346, 347, 353, 456

OTVETDESIGN
www.otvetdesign.ru
Vol. 1: 397, 417

P
Yun-Ru Pan, Yi-Ting Yan,
Yi-Zhen Wu, Yu-Zhen Wu
Cheng Shiu University
www.csu.edu.tw
Vol. 1: 596

PEN.Inc.
www.pen-design.jp
Vol. 1: 163
Vol. 2: 90–91

Pentagram
www.pentagram.com
Vol. 1: 98–99

PeopleFund
www.peoplefund.co.kr
Vol. 1: 280–281

PepsiCo Design & Innovation
http://design.pepsico.com
Vol. 1: 356, 357, 358, 359, 360, 361, 364, 371, 399, 401

Beijing Perfect Point Design
www.zg-ad.com.cn
Vol. 1: 410, 659

PETIT Design Center
www.petit.com.tw
Vol. 1: 449

pfeifer marketing
www.pfeifer-marketing.de
Vol. 1: 226–227

PH7 Creative Lab
www.ph7lab.com.tw
Vol. 1: 477

Phantom
www.phantom.house
Vol. 1: 429

Philips Experience Design team
www.philips.com
Vol. 1: 473, 507
Vol. 2: 247, 250, 251, 256–257

PierraaGroup GmbH
www.pierraa-group.de
Vol. 1: 500–501, 660

Pixelis
www.pixelis.com
Vol. 1: 230
Vol. 2: 420

PlusX
www.plus-ex.com
Vol. 1: 133, 143
Vol. 2: 198

POLA Inc.
www.pola.co.jp
Vol. 1: 434–435

POLARWERK GmbH
www.polarwerk.de
Vol. 1: 286

Polestar
www.polestar.com
Vol. 1: 206–207, 661
Vol. 2: 33

Kate Prior
www.kateprior.com
Vol. 1: 345

PROJECT EDDY
www.projecteddy.co.kr
Vol. 1: 156–157

Prompt Design
www.prompt-design.com
Vol. 1: 372–373, 405, 418, 419

Q
Shenzhen Qansfough
Package Design Co., Ltd.
www.china-qsf.com
Vol. 1: 413, 426

R
Ibán Ramón
Design Studio
www.ibanramon.com
Vol. 1: 195
Vol. 2: 66

Realgestalt GmbH
www.realgestalt.de
Vol. 1: 298–299, 662

Reedesign Studio
www.reedesignstudio.com
Vol. 1: 423

Lachelle Robotham, Mijin Han
SCAD Savannah College of
Art and Design
www.scad.edu
Vol. 1: 552–553, 664

rozanka GmbH
www.rozanka.de
Vol. 1: 92–93, 663

Preface	Red Dot: Agency of the Year	Brands	Brand Design & Identity	Corporate Design & Identity	Annual Reports
4	6	18	90	202	260

Index Designers

Yu-Lin Ruan, Pei-Wen He
Asia University
www.asia.edu.tw
Vol. 1: 585

Ruska, Martin, Associates GmbH
www.ruskamartin.de
Vol. 1: 328, 329

S

Jaspriya Sahmey
SCAD Savannah College of
Art and Design
www.scad.edu
Vol. 1: 574

Samsung Bioepis
www.samsungbioepis.com
Vol. 1: 201, 454

San Yang Studio
Vol. 1: 154

Changsha Saturnbird
Coffee Co., Ltd.
www.saturnbird.com
Vol. 1: 380

Peter Schmidt Group
www.peter-schmidt-group.de
Vol. 1: 296–297, 365, 400, 476, 665

Stephan Schmitz
www.stephan-schmitz.ch
Vol. 1: 278

schmitz Visuelle Kommunikation
www.hgschmitz.de
Vol. 1: 228

Susanne Schneider
www.hundertzwanzigprozent.de
Vol. 1: 422

SCOPE Architekten GmbH
www.scopeoffice.de
Vol. 1: 533

SenseTeam
www.senseteam.org
Vol. 1: 194
Vol. 2: 18

Boro Serra
www.boroserra.com
Vol. 1: 186

Alireza Shafiei Tabar
www.alirezashafiei.com
Vol. 1: 525

SHE
Kommunikationsagentur GmbH
www.she-kommunikation.de
Vol. 1: 282–283, 616

SHIFTBRAIN
www.shiftbrain.com
Vol. 1: 197

Hsin-Yu Shih, Huei-Jyun Yeh,
Bo-Chen Chen, Yu Wang,
Yung-Ni Chung
National Taichung University of
Science and Technology
www.nutc.edu.tw
www.justii9277.com
Vol. 1: 612

Shuka Design
www.shuka.design
Vol. 1: 110–111

SK Telecom
www.sktelecom.com
Vol. 1: 130

Slowalk
www.slowalk.co.kr
Vol. 1: 218

smd + partner
www.smd-partner.com
Vol. 1: 505

Charlie Smith Design
www.charliesmithdesign.com
Vol. 1: 104

Soar Design Studio
www.facebook.com/soar.design.tw
Vol. 1: 518–519, 666

Kiltae Son
Vol. 1: 444

Spazio Di Paolo S.r.l.
www.spaziodipaolo.it
Vol. 1: 332, 336–337, 342, 343

SPC Design Center
www.spc.co.kr
Vol. 1: 382–383, 386–387

SPC Samlip Design Team
www.spcsamlip.co.kr
Vol. 1: 104, 385, 388, 403

SPEN Design Agency
www.spen.co.kr
Vol. 1: 108–109

Stockholm Design Lab
www.sdl.se
Vol. 1: 206–207, 661
Vol. 2: 33

STRICHPUNKT
www.sp.design
Vol. 1: 266–267, 667

Studio H.I.M.
www.studio-him.com
Vol. 1: 245

Studio Sonda
www.sonda.hr
Vol. 1: 395
Vol. 2: 39

Ying-Shan Su
Lunghwa University of Science
and Technology
www.lhu.edu.tw
Vol. 1: 515

SUAN Conceptual Design GmbH
www.suan.ch
Vol. 1: 231, 236, 668

Suh Architects
www.suharchitects.com
Vol. 1: 535, 669
Vol. 2: 392, 393

T

Taenam Household &
Healthcare Ltd.
www.tnshop.kr
Vol. 1: 441

Test Rite Group
www.testritegroup.com
Vol. 1: 433, 472

Test Rite Trading
Test Rite Business Development
Corporation Co., Ltd.
www.testritegroup.com
Vol. 1: 471

The SAEM International Co., Ltd.
www.thesaemcosmetic.com
Vol. 1: 439, 448

think brand consultancy
www.brandbythink.com
Vol. 1: 96–97, 180

thjnk Düsseldorf
www.thjnk.de
Vol. 1: 246

ThoughtFull
www.thoughtfulldesign.com
Vol. 1: 152

Tian Bo
www.tian-design.com
Vol. 1: 561

Atelier Tietchen
www.tobiastietchen.de
Vol. 1: 326–327, 670

Shenzhen Tigerpan
Packaging Design Co., Ltd.
www.tigerpan.com
Vol. 1: 352, 470, 487, 671

TIVE
www.thetive.com
Vol. 1: 141

TKEZ architecture & design
www.tkezarchitekten.com
Vol. 1: 532

Triangler Co., Ltd.
www.triangler.com.tw
Vol. 1: 196, 374, 440

Triple A Internetshops
Satisfyer
www.satisfyer.com
Vol. 1: 445

I-Jie Tsay, Min-Hua Tsai,
Yu-Ching Chiu, Yi-Yun Li
National Taipei University of
Education
www.ntue.edu.tw
Vol. 1: 609

TU DESIGN OFFICE
www.tudesignoffice.com
Vol. 1: 102

TULP Design GmbH
www.tulp.de
Vol. 1: 498

Index Designers

U

UMP
www.ump.kr
Vol. 1: 175

UND Design Studio
Vol. 1: 522

UNGESTRICHEN Strategisches
Kommunikationsdesign
www.ungestrichen.com
Vol. 1: 248

Uniplan GmbH & Co. KG
www.uniplan.com
Vol. 1: 505

V

VANDOG agency
www.vandog.agency
Vol. 1: 159

Vasku & Klug
www.vasku-klug.com
Vol. 1: 513

Shandong Veikao
Advertising Co., Ltd.
www.veikao.com
Vol. 1: 425, 474

Shruthi Venkatesh
SCAD Savannah College of
Art and Design
www.scad.edu
Vol. 1: 584

Shruthi Venkatesh,
Dayna Edmonds
SCAD Savannah College of
Art and Design
www.scad.edu
Vol. 1: 576

Shanghai Version Design Group
www.version-sh.cn
Vol. 1: 443, 452

Visuelle Fabrik
www.visuellefabrik.ch
Vol. 1: 258, 672

Vruchtvlees
www.vruchtvlees.com
Vol. 1: 146

W

waf.berlin GmbH
www.waf.berlin
Vol. 1: 276
Vol. 2: 50

Waidmann/Post GmbH
www.waidmannpost.de
Vol. 1: 508–509

Walbert-Schmitz GmbH & Co. KG
www.walbert-schmitz.de
Vol. 1: 505

Wallstreetdocs
www.wallstreetdocs.com
Vol. 1: 222, 237, 637

Ye Wang
Wonkwang University
www.wku.ac.kr
Vol. 1: 564

Yin-Hsuan Wang, Ding-Jyun Wang,
Jyun-Fu Huang, Ruo-Shin Chou,
Wan-Hsuan Cheng
Asia University
www.asia.edu.tw
Vol. 1: 589

Steven Wilson Studio
www.stevenwilsonstudio.com
Vol. 1: 106–107

WIN CREATING IMAGES
www.win-ci.de
Vol. 1: 393, 396

Shenzhen Win In Design Co., Ltd.
Vol. 1: 427

WJID
Vol. 1: 523

Weichen Wu
Vol. 1: 166

Yu-Shing Wu, Wei-Ting Wang,
Chia-Jun Hung
Ming Chi University of Technology
www.mcut.edu.tw
Vol. 1: 587

Wusun Space
www.wusunspace.com
Vol. 1: 524, 534

WWS (Beijing) Cultural
Propagation Co., Ltd.
www.wwsz.com.cn
Vol. 1: 198–199, 673

X

Yuanyuan Xia, Tao Xi
Shanghai Jiao Tong University
www.sjtu.edu.cn
Vol. 1: 556

Xiaomi Inc.
www.mi.com
Vol. 1: 458, 460, 461, 462, 463, 486
Vol. 2: 297, 633

xiexie design
www.xiexiedesign.cn
Vol. 1: 160–161

Xinghan (Zhejiang)
Brand Management Co., Ltd.
Vol. 1: 480

XIVO Design
www.xivodesign.com
Vol. 1: 126, 127

Y

Y.STUDIO
www.yuziji.studio
Vol. 1: 384

Ting-Zhen Yan
Asia University
www.asia.edu.tw
Vol. 1: 586

Pei Yang
Communication University
of Zhejiang
www.cuz.edu.cn
Vol. 1: 564

Mo-Li Yeh
Lunghwa University of
Science and Technology
www.lhu.edu.tw
Vol. 1: 515

Yellowdot Design
www.yellowdotdesign.co
Vol. 1: 478

Yepá Estúdio
www.yepaestudio.com.br
Vol. 1: 158

YNL Design
www.ynldesign.com
Vol. 1: 193, 200

Z

Shenzhen Zdesign Co., Ltd.
Vol. 1: 147, 165

Zi-Shan Zhang, Chieh-An Chung,
Chang-Yu Lung
Ming Chi University of Technology
www.mcut.edu.tw
Vol. 1: 581

Zhejiang Gongshang University
www.zjgsu.edu.cn
Vol. 1: 167, 211, 412
Vol. 2: 102, 641

Xiao-Yu Zhou, Yan-Yi Yu
East China Normal University
www.ecnu.edu.cn
Vol. 1: 590, 635

Preface	Red Dot: Agency of the Year	Brands	Brand Design & Identity	Corporate Design & Identity	Annual Reports
4	6	18	90	202	260

Index Clients/Universities

A

A TWOSOME PLACE
www.twosome.co.kr
Vol. 1: 376–377

A-Train AB
Arlanda Express
www.arlandaexpress.com
Vol. 1: 136

A1 d.o.o.
www.a-1.hr
Vol. 1: 423

The Absolut Company
www.theabsolutcompany.com
Vol. 1: 345

ac about communication
GmbH & Co. KG
www.aboutcommunication.de
Vol. 1: 240

Acer Inc.
www.acer.com
Vol. 1: 459
Vol. 2: 201

Admind Branding &
Communications
www.admindagency.com
Vol. 1: 306–307

Aeris GmbH
www.aeris.de
Vol. 1: 224–225

AIRMATE
www.airmate-china.com
Vol. 1: 188–189

AJNS New Media GmbH
Kitchen Stories
www.kitchenstories.com
Vol. 1: 532

ALINE STUDIO
www.alinecreative.com
Vol. 1: 120–121

Fondazione Altagamma
www.altagamma.it
Vol. 1: 171

Ambulance Oost
www.ambulanceoost.nl
Vol. 1: 287

Amorepacific
www.apgroup.com
Vol. 1: 119
Vol. 2: 182–183, 196

LLC AMZ
Vol. 1: 417

Anheuser-Busch InBev China
Sales Company Limited
www.ab-inbev.com
Vol. 1: 354

Anheuser-Busch InBev Vietnam
Brewery Company Limited
www.ab-inbev.com
Vol. 1: 355

Anjuna Ice Pops
www.anjunapops.com
Vol. 1: 389

Chengde Aranya
Real Estate Development Co., Ltd.
www.aranya.cc
Vol. 1: 406–407

Arlberg Biberkopf Tourismus GmbH
www.berghotel-biberkopf.com
Vol. 1: 226–227

Artrium
Chow Tai Fook
www.ctf.com.cn
Vol. 1: 536

Arup
www.arup.com
Vol. 1: 274–275

Asia University
www.asia.edu.tw
Vol. 1: 571, 585, 586, 589, 597, 600, 606
Vol. 2: 455, 469, 489, 495, 515, 534

Associació València Capital del
Disseny
www.designvalencia.eu
Vol. 1: 195
Vol. 2: 66

AT BEER
www.atbeer.com
Vol. 1: 100

AUDI AG
www.audi.com
Vol. 1: 300
Vol. 2: 49

Avgoulakia
www.avgoulakia.gr
Vol. 1: 415

B

Backstage
www.backstage.ua
Vol. 1: 249

Baden-Württemberg
Stiftung gGmbH
www.bwstiftung.de
Vol. 1: 266–267

Baidu Online Network Technology
(Beijing) Co., Ltd.
www.baidu.com
Vol. 1: 38–39
Vol. 2: 281

Banbou Patisserie & Coffee
Vol. 1: 384

basecoffee GmbH
www.basecoffee.love
Vol. 1: 92–93

Beautiful Coffee
www.beautifulcoffee.com
Vol. 1: 378

Bechtle AG
www.bechtle.com
Vol. 1: 276
Vol. 2: 50

Judith Beck GmbH
www.weingut-beck.at
Vol. 1: 320–321

BEOS AG
www.beos.net
Vol. 1: 242–243
Vol. 2: 405

Berry Creative
www.berrycreative.fi
Vol. 1: 241

BGF ecobio
www.bgf.co.kr
Vol. 1: 156–157

Big Hit Entertainment
www.bighitcorp.com
Vol. 1: 464

Biovegan GmbH
www.biovegan.de
Vol. 1: 422

Bizhi Paint Decoration Co., Ltd.
www.beckers.cn
Vol. 1: 534

BlackYak
www.blackyak.com
Vol. 1: 143
Vol. 2: 551

Chocolats Camille Bloch S A
www.camillebloch.ch
Vol. 1: 398

Blue Peach Skincare
www.bluepeach.com.tw
Vol. 1: 440

BMW Group
www.bmw.de
Vol. 1: 290–291
Vol. 2: 160, 161

Brand Breeder S.r.l.s.
www.brandbreeder.it
Vol. 1: 332, 342, 343

BRIDGE & COMPANY
www.bridge-company.co.kr
Vol. 1: 493

Brooklyn Soap Company
www.bklynsoap.com
Vol. 1: 326–327

Buchholz GmbH
www.buchholz-praxiseinrichter.de
Vol. 1: 500–501

Bukak-Maeul
www.bukakmaeul.com
Vol. 1: 220–221

Busch-Jaeger Elektro GmbH
Mitglied der ABB-Gruppe
www.busch-jaeger.de
Vol. 1: 48–49
Vol. 2: 300

By-health Co., Ltd.
www.i-brandfree.com
Vol. 1: 436–437

C

cafe noote
www.facebook.com/cafenoote
Vol. 1: 96–97

Callaly
www.calla.ly
Vol. 1: 68–69

The Calligraphy Cut
Company GmbH
www.calligraphy-cut.com
Vol. 1: 248

Calx Station
www.calxstation.com
Vol. 1: 214

Advertising	Packaging Design	Fair Stands	Retail Design	Red Dot: Junior Award	Designer Profiles	Index
288	318	494	516	544	614	674

Index Clients / Universities

Carrot General Insurance
www.hwgeneralins.com
Vol. 1: 232

Changyu Pioneer
Wine Company Limited
www.changyu.com.cn
Vol. 1: 346

CHANNEL A
www.ichannela.com
Vol. 1: 250

Chaoyang University of
Technology
www.cyut.edu.tw
Vol. 1: 558, 566, 570, 572, 578, 593
Vol. 2: 432–433, 460, 464, 473,
478, 530, 536–537

Cheng Shiu University
www.csu.edu.tw
Vol. 1: 573, 575, 596
Vol. 2: 448, 523

Shenzhen Chengzui
Cultural Communication Co., Ltd.
Vol. 1: 353

Chihlee University of Technology
www.chihlee.edu.tw
Vol. 1: 594, 599
Vol. 2: 445, 459, 493

China Academy of Art
www.caa.edu.cn
Vol. 1: 166

China Resources Sanjiu
Medical & Pharmaceutical Co., Ltd.
www.999.com.cn
Vol. 1: 484, 485

China Shaoxing
Yellow Rice Wine Group Co., Ltd.
Vol. 1: 347

China University of Technology
www.cute.edu.tw
Vol. 1: 565, 598, 601
Vol. 2: 449, 450, 458, 461, 466,
472, 485, 487, 488, 505, 518,
524, 525

Chongqing Hot Pot Flagship Store
Vol. 1: 524

City of Chuncheon
www.chuncheon.go.kr
Vol. 1: 208–209

Shanghai Chunmi
Electronic Technology Co., Ltd.
www.chunmi.com
Vol. 1: 116, 223

Shenzhen CIGA Design Co., Ltd.
www.cigadesign.com
Vol. 1: 457

Cinquesegni S.r.l.
www.cinquesegni.it
Vol. 1: 333

City Clinical Hospital No. 40
www.gkb40dzm.ru
Vol. 1: 233

CJ Cheiljedang
www.cj.co.kr
Vol. 1: 424

CJ ENM
www.englishgem.co.kr
Vol. 1: 181

CJSC Ecotechnics
www.eko.ua
Vol. 1: 402

Clariant International AG
www.clariant.com
Vol. 1: 277

cociety
www.cociety.co.kr
Vol. 1: 175

COFCO
www.cofco.com
Vol. 1: 410

Cola Neko Japanese Learning
www.colanekojp.com.tw
Vol. 1: 180

Communication University
of Zhejiang
www.cuz.edu.cn
Vol. 1: 564

CONVALOR Projektpartner GmbH
www.convalor.de
Vol. 1: 242–243

Coreana Cosmetics
www.coreana.co.kr
Vol. 1: 438

Covestro Deutschland AG
www.covestro.com
Vol. 1: 505

Creditplus Bank AG
www.creditplus.de
Vol. 1: 279

D
D.TAILS
www.dtails.dk
Vol. 1: 124

DAELIM Industrial Co., Ltd.
www.daelim.co.kr
Vol. 1: 190–191

Daewon Plus Group
www.daewonplus.co.kr
Vol. 1: 514
Vol. 2: 388

Daming Palace
www.dmgyzq.cn
Vol. 1: 198–199

J.J.Darboven GmbH & Co. KG
www.eilles-tee.de
Vol. 1: 365

Deutsche Oper Berlin
www.deutscheoperberlin.de
Vol. 1: 298–299

Didar Cafe
www.didar.center
Vol. 1: 525

Shenzhen Do Intelligent
Technology Co., Ltd.
www.i-doo.cn
Vol. 1: 127

DOI CHAANG
Coffee Original Co., Ltd.
www.doichaangcoffee.co.th
Vol. 1: 372–373

Dong-A Pharm
www.dapharm.com
Vol. 1: 482–483

Drawbridge Health
www.drawbridgehealth.com
Vol. 1: 56–57

Dynamo Fencing Center Inc.
https://dynamo-fencing.com
Vol. 1: 140

E
East China Normal University
www.ecnu.edu.cn
Vol. 1: 590, 595, 604

East Japan Railway Company
www.jreast.co.jp
Vol. 1: 294–295

Eatrix
www.eatrix.com.ua
Vol. 1: 103

Eberl & Kœsel FinePrints
www.eberlkoesel.de
Vol. 1: 475

eigenland
www.eigenland.de
Vol. 1: 247

el origen food GmbH
www.elorigenfood.de
Vol. 1: 400

ELA Container GmbH
www.container.de
Vol. 1: 228

Emmi Management AG
www.emmi.com
Vol. 1: 396

enercity AG
www.enercity.de
Vol. 1: 268

EONE DIAGNOMICS
Genome Center
www.edgc.com
Vol. 1: 489

Public Organization
"Euro-Atlantic Course"
www.plusone.org.ua
Vol. 1: 159

Shenzhen Excel Package
Design Co., Ltd.
www.zhuoshang.cn
Vol. 1: 340–341

Excited
www.excited.agency
Vol. 1: 125, 244

Ezaki Glico Co., Ltd.
www.glico.com
Vol. 1: 324–325

F
FACT.COFFEE
www.fact.coffee
Vol. 1: 88–89

Farm Factory
www.farmfactory.co.kr
Vol. 1: 428

FIL Gallery
Vol. 1: 112

Finanz Informatik
www.f-i.de
Vol. 1: 44–45

Fincap Law
www.fincaplaw.com
Vol. 1: 237

Forum Groningen
www.forum.nl
Vol. 1: 213

Zhejiang Fousu
New Material Technology Co., Ltd.
Vol. 1: 474

FRESH BLOOD DG YOUTH
Vol. 1: 160–161

Fu Jen Catholic University
www.fju.edu.tw
Vol. 1: 562–563, 568, 602
Vol. 2: 452–453

Index Clients / Universities

Fu-Hsin Trade & Arts School
www.fhvs.ntpc.edu.tw
Vol. 1: 554

FUJIFILM Corporation
www.fujifilm.com
Vol. 1: 469
Vol. 2: 216, 322, 323

G

Gahwa
www.gahwa.co.kr
Vol. 1: 444

Gamesa Gearbox
www.gamesagearbox.com
Vol. 1: 138–139

Geberit International AG
www.geberit.com
Vol. 1: 64–65

Gelsenwasser AG
www.gelsenwasser.de
Vol. 1: 255

Gerflor Mipolam GmbH
www.gerflor.de
Vol. 1: 498

GEWOBA
Aktiengesellschaft Wohnen
und Bauen
www.gewoba.de
Vol. 1: 286

Gira
Giersiepen GmbH & Co. KG
www.gira.com
Vol. 1: 24–27

Glyde
www.pethooh.com
Vol. 1: 491

GPL
www.gpl.ua
Vol. 1: 117, 134

Greenland
www.ldjt.com.cn
Vol. 1: 523

Grundfos Holding A/S
www.grundfos.com
Vol. 1: 269

GS Retail Co., Ltd.
www.gsretail.com
Vol. 1: 105

BJ Guan Xiu
International Trade Co., Ltd.
Vol. 1: 80–81

Harbin Guangwei
Marketing Planning Co., Ltd.
www.gw4a.com
Vol. 1: 344

H

Haiyan County People's
Government
www.haiyan.gov.cn
Vol. 1: 167

Hyewon Han
Vol. 1: 550–551

Hanwha Eagles
www.hanwhaeagles.co.kr
Vol. 1: 141

Hanwha Life Insurance
www.dreamplus.asia
Vol. 1: 178–179

Happygo
Network Technology Co., Ltd.
www.happygo.com
Vol. 1: 122

Hardio
www.hardio.me
Vol. 1: 142

Harim Petfood
www.harimpetfood.com
Vol. 1: 490

hartmannvonsiebenthal
the brand experience
company GmbH
www.hartmannvonsiebenthal.de
Vol. 1: 512

HCOB
www.hcob-bank.de
Vol. 1: 504

hellonature
www.hellonature.co.kr
Vol. 1: 46–47

HEYTEA
www.heytea.com
Vol. 1: 522

Hidden Elements
www.linktr.ee/1000xxplace
Vol. 1: 467

Hoseo University
www.hoseo.ac.kr
Vol. 1: 603

Hyangsimjae
https://blog.naver.com/
hyangsimjae
Vol. 1: 542

Hyundai Motor Co.
(Genesis Motors)
www.genesis.com
Vol. 1: 535
Vol. 2: 392, 393

Hyundai Motor Company
www.hyundai.com
Vol. 1: 292–293, 308–309, 511
Vol. 2: 145, 331, 334, 396

I

IGIS Asset Management
www.igisam.com
Vol. 1: 108–109

Ihsoat Creative Lab
Vol. 1: 561

Iksundada
www.iksundada.kr
Vol. 1: 78–79

inDare Design Strategy Limited
www.indare.love
Vol. 1: 390, 411, 488, 492

Institut der deutschen
Wirtschaft e.V.
www.iwkoeln.de
Vol. 1: 272–273

International Federation of
Sport Climbing
www.ifsc-climbing.org
Vol. 1: 163
Vol. 2: 90–91

International Water &
Wellness Ltd.
www.iwandw.com
Vol. 1: 186

Into The Great Wide Open
www.intothegreatwideopen.nl
Vol. 1: 94–95

iRoman (Shenzhen) Co., Ltd.
Vol. 1: 368–369

J

Jardin
www.jardin.co.kr
Vol. 1: 375

Beijing JC Family
International Media Co., Ltd.
Vol. 1: 465

Jetlag Books
www.instagram.com/JetlagBooks
Vol. 1: 148

JICA
www.jica.go.jp
Vol. 1: 316–317

Jin Hui Organic Farm
Vol. 1: 154

Junior Chamber International Basel
Handelskammer beider Basel
www.jci-basel.ch
Vol. 1: 236

K

Kakao M
www.kakao-m.com
Vol. 1: 132

Kaleseramik
Çanakkale Kalebodur
Seramik San. A.S.
www.kale.com.tr
Vol. 1: 496–497

KASHA playing zone
www.kashaplay.com.ua
Vol. 1: 219

Kaspersky
www.kaspersky.co.uk
Vol. 1: 42–43

Katholische Kirchengemeinde
Heilige Dreifaltigkeit
www.kath-derendorf-pempelfort.de
Vol. 1: 215

Shenyang Kelagusi
Food Co., Ltd.
Vol. 1: 425

Keys Asset Management
www.keys-am.com
Vol. 1: 230

Kiriakaki Antonia SA
www.kiriakakis-foods.gr
Vol. 1: 404

Kiyotomo
www.kiyotomotea.com
Vol. 1: 374

KNI
www.kni.gl
Vol. 1: 543

Konny by Erin
www.konnybaby.com
Vol. 1: 84–85

Kookmin University
www.kookmin.ac.kr
Vol. 1: 567

Advertising	Packaging Design	Fair Stands	Retail Design	Red Dot: Junior Award	Designer Profiles	Index
288	318	494	516	544	614	674

Index Clients / Universities

Kracie Holdings, Ltd.
www.kracie.co.jp
Vol. 1: 442

KRAFTON
www.krafton.com
Vol. 1: 133

Chengdu Kuanzhai
Food Investment Co., Ltd.
https://kuanzhai.tmall.com
Vol. 1: 370

Hangzhou KUB
Baby Products Co., Ltd.
www.kubbaby.com
Vol. 1: 487

L
Lamoda Group
www.lamoda.ru
Vol. 1: 110–111

Land of Hope
www.landofhope.global
Vol. 1: 184–185, 216–217

Franz Wilhelm Langguth
Erben GmbH & Co. KG
www.langguth.wine
Vol. 1: 98–99, 334

LASALLE College of the Arts
www.lasalle.edu.sg
Vol. 1: 560
Vol. 2: 476

LEDO plus
www.ledo.hr
Vol. 1: 395

Leferi
www.leferi.co.kr
Vol. 1: 150

Weingut Lergenmüller
www.lergenmueller.com
Vol. 1: 335

LG Electronics Inc.
www.lg.com
Vol. 1: 506
Vol. 2: 103, 544

LIDL HELLAS
www.lidl-hellas.gr
Vol. 1: 322–323, 338

Life of the Children
www.lifeofthechildren.org
Vol. 1: 218

Beijing Lihe
Pharmaceutical Co., Ltd.
www.fuhegroup.com
Vol. 1: 123

LIME STUDIO Corp.
www.instagram.com/toykon_love
Vol. 1: 479

LINE Plus Corporation
www.linepluscorp.com
Vol. 1: 164

Ling Tung University
www.ltu.edu.tw
Vol. 1: 569, 577, 583, 591, 605
Vol. 2: 451, 467, 474, 479, 481, 494, 496

Shenzhen Lingyun
Creative Packaging Design Co., Ltd.
www.lingyuncy.com
Vol. 1: 348, 349, 350, 351, 481

Livet AG
www.li.vet
Vol. 1: 258

Livinguard
S.G.F. Biotechnology
www.livinguard.com.cn
Vol. 1: 455

LIXIL Corporation
www.lixil.com
Vol. 1: 66–67, 187, 499

Logothetis Farm
www.logotheisfarm.gr
Vol. 1: 408

LOTTE Duty Free
www.lottedfs.co.kr
Vol. 1: 106–107
Vol. 2: 30–31

LUXORO S.r.l.
www.luxoro.it
Vol. 1: 336–337

Luzerne Pte Ltd
www.luzerne.com
Vol. 1: 62–63

M
Madeira Wine Company
www.madeirawinecompany.com
Vol. 1: 330–331

Maistra
www.maistra.com
Vol. 1: 149

Detlef Malzers Backstube
GmbH & Co. KG
www.malzers.de
Vol. 1: 530–531

MAN Energy Solutions SE
www.man-es.com
www.pbst.eu
Vol. 1: 256–257

Martini S.p.A.
www.martinispa.com
Vol. 1: 60–61

Hubei Materia Medica
Health Wine Co., Ltd.
www.chinabencaogangmu.com
Vol. 1: 453

Max-Planck-Gesellschaft
zur Förderung der
Wissenschaften e.V.
www.mpg.de
Vol. 1: 270–271

Mercedes-Benz AG
Mercedes-Benz Vertrieb
Deutschland
www.mercedes-benz.de
Vol. 1: 508–509

Metafrax Group
www.metafraxgroup.com
Vol. 1: 259

Midor AG
www.midor.ch
Vol. 1: 391

Ming Chi University of Technology
www.mcut.edu.tw
Vol. 1: 581, 587, 607, 611, 613
Vol. 2: 446, 454, 486, 522, 542

Ming Chuan University
www.mcu.edu.tw
Vol. 1: 555, 557

Ministerium für Verkehr
Baden-Württemberg
www.vm.baden-wuerttemberg.de
Vol. 1: 34–35

Minuendo AS
www.minuendo.com
Vol. 1: 54–55

Misato Town
www.town.shimane-misato.lg.jp
Vol. 1: 197

mmcité+ a.s.
www.mmciteplus.com
Vol. 1: 204–205

Mobvista
www.mobvista.com
Vol. 1: 131, 252–253

MOKKI AS
www.mokki.no
Vol. 1: 82–83

Monogram
www.monogramoliveoil.com
Vol. 1: 430–431

MOS GmbH
www.mosconcept.de
Vol. 1: 394

Moscow Brewing Company
www.mosbrew.ru
Vol. 1: 528–529

TM Mriya
www.mia.family
Vol. 1: 101

MRPAUL & PARTNERS
www.mrpaulandpartners.com
Vol. 1: 50–51

Munchkin Inc.
www.munchkin.com
Vol. 1: 114–115

MYM Co., Ltd.
www.promiz2014.com
Vol. 1: 183

MYS Group Co., Ltd.
www.szmys.com
Vol. 1: 416

myStromer AG
www.stromerbike.com
Vol. 1: 36–37

N
Nanlian Agricultural
www.nanlian.com
Vol. 1: 153

National Taichung University of
Science and Technology
www.nutc.edu.tw
Vol. 1: 592, 612

National Taipei University of
Education
www.ntue.edu.tw
Vol. 1: 608, 609, 610

National Taiwan University of
Science and Technology
www.ntust.edu.tw
Vol. 1: 169, 582, 588

National University of Singapore
www.nus.edu.sg
Vol. 1: 546–549

National Yunlin University of
Science and Technology
www.yuntech.edu.tw
Vol. 1: 559, 580
Vol. 2: 470, 498, 532

NAVER BUSINESS PLATFORM
www.ncloud.com
Vol. 1: 40–41

Preface	Red Dot: Agency of the Year	Brands	Brand Design & Identity	Corporate Design & Identity	Annual Reports
4	6	18	90	202	260

Index Clients / Universities

neos GP GmbH
www.beos.net
Vol. 1: 242–243

Nestlé Hellas
www.nestle.gr
Vol. 1: 381

Nestlé Wagner GmbH
www.original-wagner.de
Vol. 1: 420–421

Ngai Tahu Tourism
www.ngaitahutourism.co.nz
Vol. 1: 152

Nikkei Inc.
www.nikkei.co.jp
Vol. 1: 302

Norfre Foods Co., Ltd.
www.norfre.com
Vol. 1: 414

NPO/NOS/AVROTROS
in collaboration with EBU
www.songfestival.nl
Vol. 1: 162

Nuna International BV
www.nunababy.com
Vol. 1: 86–87

Nuuday
www.nuuday.dk
Vol. 1: 251

O

OCC Assekuradeur GmbH
www.occ.eu
Vol. 1: 231

Olivio (Hong Kong) Limited
www.olivioeyewear.com
Vol. 1: 478

Omdesign
www.omdesign.pt
Vol. 1: 366–367

Omoikiri Rus
www.omoikiri.ru
Vol. 1: 168

Onassis Cultural Centre
www.sgt.gr
Vol. 1: 466

OPPO
www.oppo.com
Vol. 1: 538, 539

Oxford (Hainan)
Blockchain Research
Institute Co., Ltd.
www.dcc.global
Vol. 1: 170

P

P.I.E. Printing
www.facebook.com/
pieprintingpalau
Vol. 1: 196

Papyrus
www.papy.co.kr
Vol. 1: 537

Hangzhou Pengstars
Sport Culture Pty. Ltd.
http://pengstars.cn
Vol. 1: 182

PeopleFund
www.peoplefund.co.kr
Vol. 1: 280–281

PepsiCo
www.pepsico.com
Vol. 1: 356, 357, 358, 359, 360, 361, 364, 371, 399, 401

PETIT RIEGO Co., Ltd.
www.petit.com.tw
Vol. 1: 449

Philips
www.philips.com
Vol. 1: 473, 507
Vol. 2: 247, 250, 251, 256–257

Pinghu Farmer Cooperative
Economic Organization Union
Vol. 1: 412

Pingtung County Government
www.cultural.pthg.gov.tw
Vol. 1: 212
Vol. 2: 77

Point Rouge GmbH
www.point-rouge.de
Vol. 1: 118

POLA Inc.
www.pola.co.jp
Vol. 1: 434–435

Polestar
www.polestar.com
Vol. 1: 20–23, 206–207
Vol. 2: 33

LLC Polezzno
www.polezzno.com
Vol. 1: 397

Dr. Ing. h.c. F. Porsche AG
www.porsche.com
Vol. 1: 135, 264–265
Vol. 2: 329

Promayro Food GmbH
www.protami.de
Vol. 1: 393

Prompt Design
www.prompt-design.com
Vol. 1: 405, 418

Psiloreitis
www.psiloreitis.net
Vol. 1: 362–363

PUMA SE
www.puma.com
Vol. 1: 262–263

Pussyfoot Saloon
www.instagram.com/pf.saloon
Vol. 1: 527

Q

Macau Qangos Food Factory
Vol. 1: 427

Shenzhen Qansfough
Package Design Co., Ltd.
www.china-qsf.com
Vol. 1: 413, 426

Shanghai Qiongqi
Enterprise Management Co., Ltd.
www.qiongqi.com
Vol. 1: 379

R

Radgonske Gorice
www.radgonske-gorice.si
Vol. 1: 339

Raon Women's Clinic
www.raonclinic.co.kr
Vol. 1: 200

Red Dog Culture House
http://reddog.musign.co.kr
Vol. 1: 245

REWE Group
www.rewe-group.com
Vol. 1: 284–285

Röben Tonbaustoffe GmbH
www.roeben.com
Vol. 1: 303
Vol. 2: 164

Rotkäppchen-Mumm
Sektkellereien GmbH
www.rotkaeppchen-mumm.de
Vol. 1: 328, 329

S

Sächsisches Staatsministerium
für Energie, Klimaschutz, Umwelt
und Landwirtschaft
www.smul.sachsen.de
Vol. 1: 310

Samsung Bioepis
www.samsungbioepis.com
Vol. 1: 201, 454

Samsung Electronics Co., Ltd.
www.samsung.com
Vol. 1: 174, 304, 540–541
Vol. 2: 32, 381, 397, 399, 416–417

Samsung Electronics
Germany GmbH
www.samsung.de
Vol. 1: 305

SAS Scandinavian Airlines System
www.flysas.com
Vol. 1: 432

Changsha Saturnbird
Coffee Co., Ltd.
www.saturnbird.com
Vol. 1: 380

SCAD Savannah College of
Art and Design
www.scad.edu
Vol. 1: 552–553, 574, 576, 579, 584
Vol. 2: 434–435, 440, 497, 500, 501, 502, 503, 506, 507, 510, 511, 512, 526, 527, 528, 533, 535, 538, 540, 541, 543, 547, 548, 549, 550, 552, 555, 556, 557

Shenzhen Schawlow
Jewelry Co., Ltd.
www.schawlow.com
Vol. 1: 456

Peter Schmidt Group
www.peter-schmidt-group.de
Vol. 1: 296–297, 476

Schüco International KG
www.schueco.com
Vol. 1: 502–503

Sebrae/SC
www.sebrae.com.br
Vol. 1: 158

SenseTeam
www.senseteam.org
Vol. 1: 194

Maria Sgourou
www.skoutariooliveoil.com
Vol. 1: 429

Shanghai Jiao Tong University
www.sjtu.edu.cn
Vol. 1: 556
Vol. 2: 559

Shanghai Shangshi
Network Technology Co., Ltd.
www.tianjiajia.com
Vol. 1: 452

Shenzhen Symphony
Children's Choir
www.sso.org.cn
Vol. 1: 147

Shur Shur
www.shurshur.com
Vol. 1: 113

Index Clients / Universities

Sikinnis
www.facebook.com/sikinnis
Vol. 1: 144–145

SK Telecom
www.sktelecom.com
Vol. 1: 130, 254
Vol. 2: 370

SKVOT
www.skvot.io
Vol. 1: 172–173

Sodexo Peru
www.pe.sodexo.com
Vol. 1: 192

Shenzhen Solarrun
Energy Co., Ltd.
www.power-solution.net.cn
Vol. 1: 470

SPC Group
Paris Croissant
www.spc.co.kr
Vol. 1: 382–383, 386–387

SPC Samlip
www.spcsamlip.co.kr
Vol. 1: 104, 385, 388, 403

Srisangdow Rice Mill Co., Ltd.
Vol. 1: 419

Stadtreinigung Hamburg
Anstalt des öffentlichen Rechts
www.stadtreinigung.hamburg
Vol. 1: 282–283

myStromer AG
www.stromerbike.com
Vol. 1: 36–37

surely. Art Space
Vol. 1: 520–521

Swedish Institute
www.si.se
Vol. 1: 468

T

Taenam Household &
Healthcare Ltd.
www.tnshop.kr
Vol. 1: 441

Tainan City Government
Cultural Affairs Bureau
www.culture.tainan.gov.tw
Vol. 1: 515

TAQA Theater de Vest /
Grote Kerk Alkmaar
www.theaterdevest.nl
Vol. 1: 146

Public Council of Tashkent City
www.gorod.uz
Vol. 1: 210

Tend
www.hellotend.com
Vol. 1: 52–53

Test Rite Group
www.testritegroup.com
Vol. 1: 433, 472

Test Rite Trading
Test Rite Business Development
Corporation Co., Ltd.
www.testritegroup.com
Vol. 1: 471

The SAEM International Co., Ltd.
www.thesaemcosmetic.com
Vol. 1: 439, 448

theDesk
www.thedesk.com.hk
Vol. 1: 176–177

Tibber AB
www.tibber.com
Vol. 1: 58–59

Trerè Innovation
www.trereinnovation.it
Vol. 1: 74–75

Triple A Internetshops
Satisfyer
www.satisfyer.com
Vol. 1: 72–73, 445

Tsingtao Brewery Co., Ltd.
www.tsingtao.com.cn
Vol. 1: 352

U

ULAC Corporation
www.ulaclock.com
Vol. 1: 76–77

uncorporate.design
Institute for Project and
Discourse Design
www.uncorporate.design
Vol. 1: 234–235

Unilever
www.unilever.com
Vol. 1: 392

UnternehmenForm GmbH & Co. KG
www.unternehmenform.de
Vol. 1: 533

UTB
www.utbcoffee.com
Vol. 1: 222

UUcare Group Singapore Pte. Ltd.
www.uucare.com.cn
Vol. 1: 450–451

V

VECO Group SA
www.vecogroup.ch
Vol. 1: 238–239

VERGISSMEINNICHT
filmagentur für erinnern
www.vmn-online.de
Vol. 1: 246

Verkehrsgesellschaft
Mecklenburg-Vorpommern mbH
www.vmv-mbh.de
Vol. 1: 312

Vitesco Technologies GmbH
www.vitesco-technologies.com
Vol. 1: 137
Vol. 2: 404

VO ÜS
Vorarlberger Limo Werk GmbH
www.voüs.at
Vol. 1: 28–31

Volkswagen AG
www.volkswagen.de
Vol. 1: 32–33, 301, 510
Vol. 2: 133, 159, 391

Vöslauer Mineralwasser GmbH
www.voeslauer.com
Vol. 1: 311

VP Bank AG
www.vpbank.com
Vol. 1: 278

VTT Technical Research
Centre of Finland Ltd.
www.vttresearch.com
Vol. 1: 155

W

Wedding Book
www.wdgbook.com
Vol. 1: 151

Weimar Bauhaus University
www.uni-weimar.de
Vol. 1: 169

whowho&company
www.whowhocorp.com
Vol. 1: 128–129

Wirtschaftskammer Österreich
AUSSENWIRTSCHAFT AUSTRIA
www.wko.at/aussenwirtschaft
Vol. 1: 513

wobra
Wohnungsbaugesellschaft
der Stadt Brandenburg an der
Havel mbH
www.wobra.de
Vol. 1: 229

Wonderaum
www.wonderaum.com
Vol. 1: 193

Wonkwang University
www.wku.ac.kr
Vol. 1: 564

World Manufacturing Convention
Bureau of Expo
www.wmconvention.com
Vol. 1: 165

X

Xiaomi Inc.
www.mi.com
Vol. 1: 458, 460, 461, 462, 463, 486
Vol. 2: 297

Beijing Xin You Lingxi
Technology Co., Ltd.
Vol. 1: 126

Xinghan (Zhejiang)
Brand Management Co., Ltd.
Vol. 1: 480

Y

Shenzhen Yiyitong
Trading Co., Ltd.
Vol. 1: 409

YOHO Medical Enterprise Co., Ltd.
www.roaze.com
Vol. 1: 477

Beijing Youji
Technology Development Co., Ltd.
Vol. 1: 443

Youth against AIDS
www.youth-against-aids.org
Vol. 1: 313, 314, 315
Vol. 2: 40, 76, 121

Yu-Ho Food Co., Ltd.
www.yuho-foods.com.tw
Vol. 1: 102

Yunos GmbH
www.yunos-online.de
Vol. 1: 70–71

Z

ZEESEA
https://zeesea.tmall.com
Vol. 1: 446, 447

Zhao Zhao Tea Lounge
www.facebook.com/
ZhaoZhaoTeaLounge
Vol. 1: 518–519

Zhejiang Federation of Humanities
and Social Sciences Circles
www.zjskw.gov.cn
Vol. 1: 211

ZooSinDang
www.instagram.com/
zoosindang_official
Vol. 1: 526